AN AMERICAN TESTAMENT

AN AMERICAN
TESTAMENT

A Narrative of Rebels and Romantics

BY JOSEPH FREEMAN

OCTAGON BOOKS

A DIVISION OF FARRAR, STRAUS AND GIROUX

New York   1973

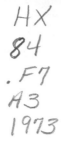

TO
CHARMION

Reprinted 1973
by special arrangement with Holt, Rinehart and Winston, Inc.

OCTAGON BOOKS
A DIVISION OF FARRAR, STRAUS & GIROUX, INC.
19 Union Square West
New York, N. Y. 10003

LIBRARY OF CONGRESS CATALOG CARD NUMBER: 72-13741

ISBN 0-374-92887-8

Printed in USA by
Thomson-Shore, Inc.
Dexter, Michigan

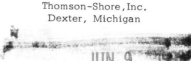

CONTENTS

CONTENTS

BOOK FIVE

PREFACE

THIS narrative is rooted in the belief that mankind is passing through a major transformation. The dissolution of capitalism compares in scope and significance with the origins of private property, the beginnings of Christianity, the ascendancy of the bourgeoisie.

It is my conviction that socialism will effect much greater and more salutary changes in the life of man than any of the great historic turning points which preceded it. I started this book, then, with a definite viewpoint, as every writer does, whether he is conscious of his bias or not. What I wanted was to explain how a man living in modern times arrives at the viewpoint known as communism.

Such an explanation may be made either abstractly or concretely. You may analyze the movement of general ideas, or recount personal experiences. For reasons which will become clear in the narrative itself, I tried to combine both methods.

I began life in a culture which can only be described as medieval. Then I had to adjust myself to twentieth-century capitalist society. Here you encountered at once the cult of profit, the ideal of democracy, the struggle for socialism, the refuge of art.

Socialism was an aspect of the American scene long before the war, and I felt its impact in my daily experience. But it was so sharp a break with the prevailing order, that you had to adjust yourself to it at every point of your existence. Whether you studied philosophy or thought of marriage, drilled in the uniform of the U. S. Army or wrote Elizabethan sonnets, wandered in Paris, worked in New York or watched events in Moscow, you were caught in the conflict between the old world and the new, and felt you had to choose between them. This narrative, therefore, deals not with politics in the narrow sense but with culture in the broad sense.

Many of us whose trade happens to be literature or art have chosen socialism because we have seen how barbarously fascism devours all that is living and sublime in the world's culture. This narrative, however, deals with the pre-fascist period; the choice was made when capitalist monstrosities assumed other forms, when socialism was in an earlier stage. Furthermore, the informed reader will understand this book better if he knows it was written in 1934-35.

The stories of those who devote their lives to the achievement of socialism are legion. They are far more significant than this narrative could possibly be. Every political prisoner, trade union worker, Communist organizer, or striker could tell a more important and dramatic story than this. If I have ventured to recount certain personal experiences, it has been on the assumption that they might be of interest to those who want to know how an American writer, starting from one set of social, moral and literary values, may arrive at another; how he may develop from romanticism toward reality.

This story deals with a period closed by the economic crisis forever. The American generation of which I am a member had neither the catastrophe of capitalist economy in this country, nor the rise of fascism in western Europe, nor the astounding successes of the Soviet Union to guide its choices. Its development was consequently confused and painful. What is obvious today was obscure yesterday; what thousands of young Americans now take for granted, and champion with joyous vigor, we had to examine, question, test, relying here upon logic, there upon emotion, and again upon accidental, dimly understood experience.

But this gives every idea poignant outline; we have not only the limitations but also the advantages of a slow-motion picture. For we were compelled to be conscious of every step when we grappled with unprecedented problems raised by the war, the October Revolution, the American class struggle, the melancholy capitals of postwar Europe, the frank and free life of Greenwich Village, the rise of the Communist party in this country, the critical relations between art and society, the transformation of love, marriage and the family.

Because this book deals with an immediate past whose meanings have been profoundly altered by the present, I must make it clear that the opinions set forth at various points of the story are not necessarily those I hold today. Many of those opinions were definitely not Marxist; they were ideas encountered on the road to Marxism. They are not, therefore, to be considered in isolation.

This is equally true of ideas ascribed to other people in this book. These, too, may have changed considerably in recent years. All I meant to say was this: such and such a man, living in this or that city, at such and such a time, held these ideas for such and such reasons, it then seemed to me. Naturally, when I cite a remark which someone might have made about me, or my own verses, I do so not in approval, but only to give the flavor of an experience.

The narrative tries to explain which ideas in my own case had to be discarded and which retained; but since the story ends where it does, it should be remembered that in a number of instances further changes in outlook took place in the tumultuous years which followed.

This book is not an autobiography in the strict sense of the word. I have tried to confine the narrative to those aspects of personal experience which seemed relevant to the central theme. Often, in order to clarify the movement of ideas, I have deliberately overemphasized certain details. Yet the book should be considered primarily as a personal narrative. It is not a history of the times, nor do I pretend that what I have described was exactly so. It simply appeared to be so. In this case appearance had a reality of its own; it helped to mold the ideas in question. But nearly always I have relied not upon memory alone; I worked with notes taken in the period described.

Furthermore, this book is not intended to present the viewpoint of the Communist party. The Party has a rich and varied literature on every aspect of life. Anyone who wants to know what it stands for can easily find out, and if he is inclined to keep abreast with what is most advanced in our epoch he will do so. But this book ends at the very moment when I became psychologically ripe for beginning to understand Marxism. What I have tried to do here has been to outline one kind of experience whereby a person brought up in the old culture moves toward the new.

In attempting to correlate the development of various individuals and of an important movement in American literature to the history of our times, I encountered special problems. Not every character in this story, for example, is a real person. Once or twice I have had to resort to the devices of fiction, creating types which are composite portraits of several people. In other instances, circumstances compelled me to give real people fictitious names. Some of them are today hounded by fascist governments. For their protection, I have had to conceal their identity. Most of the time, however, I have run the grave risk of using real names. I hope their bearers will understand the spirit in which this narrative was written, and will pardon any errors I may have unintentionally committed in regard to them.

Some of the people described in this book have altered profoundly since the year with which this story closes, or, at any rate my impression of them has altered. Hedda, for example, is at this writing the prisoner of a fascist regime; she has endured monstrous tortures with extraordinary fortitude; she is a far more heroic character than I realized a decade ago. My father, to take another example, has lost the fortune he once accumulated; in his second poverty he is far more sympathetic to the social views of his sons and daughters than he was ten years ago. Then, too, there are political figures who have lost the glamor which dazzled some of us in former years; they have sunk to the lowest abyss of counterrevolution, mad hatred, terrorist plots. There are others whose unusual gifts for leadership had no scope then, hence were unknown to us until now. Three or four writers who were in the vanguard of American revolutionary literature once, are today ineffectually hostile to it or tragically silent. Scores of other writers, once preoccupied with flight or fantasy, are today vigorous creators of a literature based on the struggle against fascism or even on the struggle for a socialist society. Yet, in describing the twenties, I have had to tell how things appeared to some of us at that time, and not how they were going to appear a decade later. This means, perhaps, that some day I ought to continue this story, recording, in one form or another, significant changes in the thirties.

There are chapters here in which I have overemphasized certain ephemeral aspects of the revolutionary movement. Every day brings a living testament to the nobility and heroism of the vast majority of men and women in that movement, whether they are fighting for liberty on the barricades of Barcelona, building socialism in the Soviet Union, distributing strike leaflets south of the Mason and Dixon line or repelling the encroachments of Japanese imperialism in China. If I have paid more attention than may appear necessary to negative people and episodes, it was in an attempt to convey a particular experience accurately.

Men and women of middle class origin are often blinded by the prejudices in which they have been nurtured; when they first come in contact with the revolutionary movement they see certain of its minor aspects out of all proportion. I wanted to describe, as precisely as I could, how one man arrived at his final viewpoint not through ignorance of the evil which naturally shadows the good everywhere, but through experiencing it and relegating it to its insignificant place in the general scheme of things.

New York
August 18, 1936.

BOOK ONE

CHAPTER I

Heaven lies about us in our infancy.
—WORDSWORTH.

§ 1

THE little Ukrainian village in which I was born toward the close of the last century lay in the province of Poltava, famous for its natural beauty and for the battle in which Peter the Great defeated the Swedes. They said it was a summer resort for the nobility and that once even the Czar himself spent several days there. Our house stood in a large courtyard behind which stretched the thickly wooded park where our landlord lived. He used to quarter Cossacks there in the summer, and during the fairs would turn his place into an inn for peasants marketing their wares.

The night I was born was extremely painful for my mother: she was only nineteen, and I was her first child. Her anguished cries awakened the peasants in the inn. They were told it was only a damned Jewess making a fuss about having a baby; nevertheless, they walked to our house, and in the night knelt in the courtyard under my mother's window, devoutly crossed themselves and prayed to heaven for the safe delivery of the child. The pious prayers of Orthodox Catholics accompanied the entrance into this world of the grandson of two rabbis; for under normal circumstances, a warm human feeling existed between the Jews and the Ukrainian peasants of our village, both oppressed by czarism.

When I was old enough, I liked to lie under the trees of the park back of the house and listen to the birds, or better still to my mother's voice. In summer the Cossacks, with deep rolls of laughter, used to toss me in the air like a ball. At night they smoked all the time, played accordions and guitars, and sang melancholy songs of the steppes. The world seemed full of music.

You entered our house through a long corridor beneath whose windows stood the water barrel. Every few days our servant Yakelina went to the village well with a long pole on her shoulders from either end of which hung a wooden pail. She came in from the street bal-

3

ancing her burden like a trained ballet dancer, and poured one pail after the other into the wooden barrel.

When it was cold we played in the corridor. Once my sister and I were alone in the house. Three gypsies came into the corridor, sat on the chilly floor and played a sad song on cello, flute and fiddle. We were frightened and started to cry. Unexpectedly my mother came home. She chased the gypsies through the big wooden gate into the street; when she returned she kissed our foreheads and tore our shirts open at the throat to ward off the Evil Eye.

You could never tell when the Evil Eye would get you, or the baba yagas, the terrible witches that prowled about at night. Yakelina told us one witch was seen hovering around the streets at dawn, and suddenly, before you could count three, poof! she changed into a black cat. I could not sleep all night thinking of the Evil Eye and the melody the gypsies played on cello, flute and fiddle. There was music beyond the gate too. Opposite our house was the church whose bells rang morning, noon and night. Did *they* have the same God as we? Mama said yes, only they treated him differently: they went in for mummery, while we were spiritual.

From our street the wooden sidewalks led to the grocery store which my mother ran. With a shawl wrapped around her head and shoulders, she stood behind the counter and sold tea, candy, sausage and tobacco to the peasants. I liked to play there because our clerk slipped me sweets when mama wasn't looking. Every time it rained, the sewer-ditch along the sidewalk was a sea on which you could sail your paper navy down the street. When the sun was out, you could go next door and look through the iron gates into the judge's yard, and watch his children play in their strange, neat, city clothes.

There was another world beyond the ghetto, a world of peasants, but I knew only what went on within the gates where Jew and gentile mixed. We were different from *them*. They talked Russian, but grandfather did not like us to talk Russian. We had to talk Yiddish and study the Holy Tongue, the language of the Bible. On Jewish holidays a wonderful peace descended on the ghetto. All the stores were closed; nobody worked; you went to the synagogue with papa and grandfather and heard the cantor singing. But *they* worked just the same; it was not their holiday. When they had holidays, we did not work, and their bells rang out across the air.

The fear of pogroms hung like a black nightmare over our village and the grownups talked about it a great deal. Once my mother—then pregnant with my third sister—sat with some friends in front of our house. Suddenly from the distance they heard the tramp of bare feet coming louder and nearer. The peasants—a pogrom! Everybody ran into the house except my mother, who was too heavy with child and too frightened. Alone she listened to the swelling thunder of bare feet, and fainted. When she regained consciousness, she looked up and saw a group of barefoot peasant girls marching and chattering gaily. They were on their way home for the Easter holidays.

Shortly afterward there actually was a pogrom in a nearby town. During the slaughter my aunt and my cousin Nachum hid in the hayloft for several days. The pogrom began with a religious procession through the Jewish quarter. At its head marched the priests with their high, black, cylindrical hats, long hair and dirty flowing beards. They carried the sacred banners and ikons of the True Faith. Church bells rang out ominously. Terrified Jews scurried into their homes like hunted animals, closed the shutters, locked the doors and crawled into the cellars. The procession continued slowly down the deserted streets. A priest turned to the well-coached "saints!"

"Brothers! A filthy Jew has insulted our Lord. The stinking little tailor Peretz spit upon a holy ikon!"

Axes battered down the doors of ghetto homes. The True Believers, frenzied with vodka, official agitation and their own curses, smashed the heads of Avram, and his wife Leah. Their son David, a year older than I, died of concussions the next day.

Less than a week later a bearded peasant came into my mother's store drunk. He asked for tobacco in a voice that frightened me, and my mother handed him a package.

"I'm not going to pay you," he said. "You filthy Jews get too much money."

"Then you can't have the tobacco."

The peasant took a clasp knife from his pocket. He opened its long blade and brandished it at my mother.

"I'll kill you," he growled. Then he walked over to me and brandished the knife over my head. "We'll have a nice little pogrom. We'll kill all the goddam Jews in this goddam town."

I was terrified and clung to my mother's skirt. She held me tightly to her and I saw the tears run down her cheeks. The door creaked. I saw it open. Our clerk came in. He seized the drunk by the collar and threw him out into the street. The man rolled head down into the sewer-ditch. A policeman came running, dragged the peasant to his feet and lugged him into a carriage. The policeman leaned back comfortably in the seat, bundled his prisoner on the floor, shoved his boots and scabbard into the peasant's back, and drove off to the station house. I felt sorry for the peasant, and felt guilty because I felt sorry. My mother took me home, set the samovar on the table, poured hot tea into two glasses, and wept softly.

"Mama, why do they hate us?"

"The peasants are good people," she said. "We might be friends with them. It's the landlords who inflame them against us."

"Why do they kill us?"

"I don't know, my son. So goes the world."

"What a terrible world!"

"No, my son, the world is good. There are bad people in it."

She stirred the sugar and lemon and tea in her glass and began singing the ballad of the Kishinev pogrom: *Mother, mother, see the moon, tonight it is red as blood.*

The baby my mother carried when she heard the tramp of bare feet was delivered by a young and pretty midwife, an *akushorka* named Shura. She and her brother had been exiled from Moscow to our village for their revolutionary activities. She frequently visited our house, where she converted my mother's brother to the cause. Shura, her brother, and my uncle Moishe, then only twenty, organized a revolutionary circle which met in secret and distributed illegal literature.

Everyone spoke of Moishe as clever, handsome, and courageous. Of my grandfather's large household, crowded with my uncles and aunts, he was my favorite. I did not know to which of the various revolutionary groups he belonged; they all appeared the same to me; there seemed to be one great movement everywhere fighting to overthrow the Czar, abolish pogroms, exterminate poverty. When I heard Moishe and his friends talking, they used over and over again a word which sounded beautiful: Gerechtigkeit: justice. They sang in low voices to a guitar the *Varshavianka,* battle song of the Polish social revolutionaries. They sang it in Yiddish: *Mir shveren, mir shveren, die hailige shvoo-sh: We swear the sacred oath.* There was also a sad song which said, *My dear friend, when I shall die, write on my tombstone I died for justice.*

My mother was not a revolutionist; yet she was affected by the spread of the new ideas among the literate young gentiles and Jews of our village. She sat at the table, darned our stockings or mended our shirts by lamplight, and sang *Chasovoi? Shto, barin, nada?* The revolutionary exile, imprisoned in Siberia, asks the guard to help him escape; the guard wants to, but is afraid; he fears not death, but torture.

The police became suspicious of Shura's circle. They searched my grandfather's house for Moishe's illegal literature. In order to uncover every possible cache, they searched our house too. There were arrests. Shura and her brother were exiled to Siberia; Moishe served a brief term in the local jail. When he came out, grandfather scolded him.

"I have nothing against your wonderful ideals, but we have enough trouble without them." Like most conservatives, grandfather believed that in joining revolutionary organizations the young Jews stimulated anti-Semitism.

§ 2

I saw my father seldom. He was away much of the time at the markets and fairs, selling boots and shoes. On the rare occasions when I saw him at home, he was a dynamo of energy and humor. He bellowed sarcastic orders and advice, and told witty anecdotes about his bitter youth. He had gone to work at twelve in a boot merchant's cellar into which the sun never came, whose dark walls stank. At fourteen he rose from messenger boy to driver; by sixteen he was a salesman who took his employer's wares to market. In the days of horse and wagon, going to market meant rising at midnight and pushing across the snow through heavy forests until dawn. The working day was twelve to fourteen hours, at the end of which, dead with fatigue, the men dropped off to sleep in the snow-covered sleds, or in their tents, acrid with the smell of new boots.

My father never let us forget that he went to work at twelve, and was now only a merchant. He had shattered his family tradition, the highest among Jews, the tradition of learning. He was the son of a rabbi, the son-in-law of another. In the ghetto's medieval code, a poor, starving scholar came first; a merchant was an inferior being, no matter how clever or successful.

My father determined that his children should not suffer as he had. They would study. Of course, they would learn the *torah,* the religious lore of the race, as must any good Jew, especially a descendant of rabbis. Still my father was hardly an old fogey. He had seen the world, at least as far as Kharkov, and knew what modern education meant. His children would go to the university. It was not easy for a Jew to get into college; restrictions were becoming harder every year. If worst came to worst, we would go only to the Gymnasium; but with God's help, even the university might be possible.

From my uncle Moishe I heard about the revolution; from grandfather about God and the destiny of the Jewish race. No two ideals could be more sharply at odds. Uncle wanted the whole of humanity to go forward; grandfather wanted his own people, a fragment of humanity, to go backward, back to the Holy Land of prophets, if possible back to their times. Grandfather did not deny that the Jews were a fragment of the human race, but they were entrusted with its most precious burden. The *goyim* were materialists; theirs was the power temporal; they were the sons of Esau. We were a spiritual people, the sons of Jacob, the sitters in tents. God was everywhere: here in grandfather's study with its musty leather-covered books, out in the sunlit street with its wooden sidewalks, across the fields, where the peasants worked, in St. Petersburg where the Czar lived and plotted massacres, in America where the cities were paved with gold.

My Hebrew teacher, Mayerke der Moroshnik, was a clown; he did not understand God. Most of the times he beat knowledge into us with his belt; your seat burned for days, and somehow the knowledge administered there by violence was to reach your mind. But now and then he tried gentler pedagogic methods. When our heads were bent over a sacred text, he would sneak behind us and drop a piece of candy on the table, right under our noses.

"An angel sent you this for being a good student," he said.

But grandfather told me the truth:

"Mayerke is a fool and a liar. Angels have more important things to do. If they bothered to drop you candy they'd give you something finer than this rotten stuff. You must be a good student for better reasons."

But there were angels, of course. I saw one at dusk flying like a white light from the dark blue sky; he disappeared behind the hill. Uncle Moishe said it was a falling star, but he could not deceive me. God loved the angels, and he loved all people, because he was *their* God too; but he loved the Jews specially. We suffered greatly and were massacred for a real reason. Grandfather told me. We had been exiled from our own Holy Land for our sins. But if there were enough good Jews, the Messiah would come some day on his white horse, and take us out of exile and bring us to Jerusalem, our own Holy City.

I would lie under a tree and look up at the sky and wonder what God was thinking. Could one get up into the sky and talk with God?

Once they took my sister and me to the circus. We slipped into the crowd, left it far behind, cut across the fields. We were alone in the world. At a little distance we could see where the earth melted into the sky red with sunset. If we could get to the top of the hill we could walk right into the sky. But Uncle Moishe spoiled everything; he found us and took us home just as we were near heaven.

In grandfather's study there hung a drawing of the Lion of Judah which he had made himself. You could not take photographs because the Bible forbade images, yet grandfather drew pictures. He taught me to copy the lion. Painfully I would follow the head and mane with my eyes and set them down on paper. I liked to draw the lion, but people were more interesting. Faces were the most wonderful things in the world. When they weren't there, when you only thought about them, you could draw them better.

God was everywhere. He was in the church across the street. Was *their* God the same as ours? Nobody could make that clear. When grandfather took you to the synagogue, you kept your hat on. When *their* funeral processions passed the store, mama said, "Take your hat off, dear." The church bells rang morning, noon and night, and the village idiot Avromtsie sat under the arches and cocked his ear to their iron music. He held a tin basin in one hand and a spoon in the other, and banged in time with the bells. He was very nice to me. He said people were cruel to him, and all he wanted in this whole world was to listen to the bells. Why were people cruel? Avromtsie was a Jew, but the Jews made fun of him too. Apanas, the village tramp, was a *goy,* but the gentiles were cruel to him. Jews and gentiles were cruel to idiots and tramps, but Apanas was very kind and walked around the town with me and told me stories, and lifted me so high in his vast arms that I could almost touch the stars.

But the nicest *goyim* were our servants. First there was Nastya, who was old and wrinkled and cackled like a hen when she laughed. She was our second mother. We saw mama only at night when she came home from the store, tired and sad; but we saw Nastya all day. In the evening, after supper, she took us up on the stove, where it was dark and warm. You could stretch out and listen as in a dream to her voice telling fairy tales—princes, princesses, baba yagas, wonderful and terrible adventures. Their heroes did not study books like grandfather; they killed monsters and bad men and married princesses with golden hair. Like Yakelina, who came to us after Nastya went back to her own village to spend her last days in peace. Yakelina was only seventeen; she was not like a servant at all, but like an older sister. Her hair was gold, her eyes blue, her skin white as snow. In the warm darkness of the stove, her voice was like music, and her stories lulled you half to sleep, and the weirdest thoughts swam through your head: *what a strange world everything mixed up they kill jews uncle moishe wants to free mankind for the sake of justice jerusalem is our holy city the angel is falling falling falling over the hill that leads to heaven grandfathers books smell like old shoes but the lion of judah shall follow the messiah on a white horse not like the cossacks horses white white like yakelinas skin mother sings about the nightingale the idiot bangs his basin under bells they kill jews mama mama see the moon of kishinev drips red blood.*

§ 3

The outbreak of the Russo-Japanese War in 1904 aroused no enthusiasm among Jews. They did not believe Czarist Russia could beat Japan. Perhaps wish was father to the thought. *Akh, Nikola, vest khapen a mapola: Oh, Nicky, you're going to take a fall,* sang the village wits.

Nor was the war popular among gentiles. The peasant, much less the worker, could not see what business he had in the Far East. The intellectuals, of course, knew all about it. Uncle Moishe shouted to my father that the Russian capitalists had timber interests in Manchuria. This was the time when Plehve said to General Kuropatkin:

"You do not understand the situation in the country; to arrest the revolutionary movement we need a little victory abroad."

The revolutionaries—gentile and Jew alike—predicted Russia's defeat. What else could be expected from the corruption which infected the whole of public life? But these people exaggerated everything.

The Czar's troops were suffering defeats in Manchuria. The empty ranks of the army were being filled from the reserves: my father would have to go to war.

Why, he argued like thousands of others, should I get killed for the Czar? While I am fighting, they may stage a pogrom and butcher my wife and children. Suppose they didn't make a pogrom? Suppose I returned alive? What future does Russia hold? This was the time to do it. Go to America, where men are free and opportunity endless.

My father was among the thousands who at this time escaped from the prison of the peoples to the land of refuge. For several months we remained in our village awaiting word that we might follow him.

Everyone now talked about America, the asylum of the oppressed of every land. I had only one thing in mind: to see my father, to enter the golden realm. In the fall of 1904 money and tickets arrived from America. It was hard to leave grandfather, Uncle Moishe, and Yakelina; it would be wonderful to see the world, to live in a big city like New York. At the last moment, mama made the parting easier by promising that she would send for Yakelina.

CHAPTER II

THE GOLDEN REALM

Thank God, I—I also—am an American!
—DANIEL WEBSTER.

§ 1

COMING to America at seven was like being born a second time. It was a shock to be lifted out of one world, to which I had painfully accustomed myself, and dropped on the threshold of another. Habits of speech, feeling and thought had formed which must be altered, bonds which must be loosened. After the village, the sea was tumultuous; after the sea, Brooklyn was insane with noise. You walked on stone; buildings were tall; there was no sky. Here was father. He had shaved off his beard. My mother wept for happiness.

"You look like another man," she said.

We soon got used to father's clean strong chin. But this new language. It was awful to hear everybody around you making sounds you could not understand. You heard voices, full of friendliness or anger. A dark wall loomed up between you and the world. You were an outsider; you did not belong; you were not like other people. Yet the older folk—your aunt and uncle, who had been in America for many years—talked Yiddish too. Two languages there were, Yiddish and English. But the iceman cursed his wife in Italian.

You must learn English. Songs were easiest. The girl next door hung out the wash from the fourth-floor fire escape and sang: *Take a car, take a car, Wherever you go, take a car.*

I had been on a streetcar, a funny long wagon drawn by a horse. A funny song too, not like Yakelina's. Learn English.

In some ways this new world was like the old one. Our poverty-stricken Williamsburg was a ghetto. Near by was the synagogue where I went Saturdays, holidays and sometimes in the middle of the week too, like grandfather did in the little village. Papa laughed. America was no place for rabbis; in America business was more important than piety. Papa felt more important now. The new country was for people like him. In the synagogue there were old men with beards. They wore skullcaps and frock coats like grandfather, and like him took pinches of snuff between brown-stained fingers.

Near by, too, was the Hebrew School where I continued to study the Bible. The rabbi was not like a rabbi at all. He had no beard and no mustache, just a young man who looked like the Irish policeman on the corner. But this was America, and you were seven. You must expect new things.

Several streets away was a church. You could hear its bells morning, noon and night. When you looked out the window you saw its spire in the sky. Our village church had been like a round fat woman; this one was like a tall thin man.

Between our window and the church passed the black "L" structure, without beginning and without end. Trains thundered. They shook the house.

"They're driving me crazy," mama said.

There was no servant here, and mama had to do everything herself—cook, wash, scrub floors, take care of the children. Fridays I helped her wash floors and windows. She had no friends, only neighbors who used to quarrel about whose turn it was to scrub the hallway. As in the village, mama sat up late at night sewing clothes for us. She made everything we wore except shoes, stockings and hats. Now, instead of a lamp there was gaslight which went out when there was no quarter for the black box under the ceiling. Mama bent over a Singer sewing machine for which an agent collected money every week.

As in the old days, I saw papa seldom. He did not go to fairs, but to "business," and he came home every night. When I got up in the morning to go to school, he had already left; when he came home very late at night, I was already asleep.

School kept you busy. From nine to three you went to public school; from four to six to Hebrew School. There was homework from each that kept you up till midnight. In public school the teacher with the golden hair and blue eyes who looked like Yakelina taught you English. What a strange language. You never could get it right. You did not say the *k* in *knife*. There was a difference between *then* and *than, men* and *man*. Your tongue was stubborn, and Blue Eyes rapped her ruler on the desk impatiently. Blue Eyes was like Yakelina in another way. She had the key to fairyland. When you finally learned to read, she gave you books about princes, princesses and witches. But the heroes were not like Yakelina's. They were not Ivan or Piotr, but Jack and Dick.

Dusty Williamsburg was in some ways closer to Poltava than to America. The old men in the skullcaps and frock coats remembered both my grandfathers.

"Ah," they said, patting me on the head, "those men were giants, *geonim,* geniuses."

They would not let me forget the village. Life itself brought the village to America: immigrants kept pouring in. Here was Liova and his sister with whom I used to play around the tailor shop near the old church; it was in their courtyard that I saw the angel fly down at dusk. And soon a girl named Dvoirah came to America: I used to play with her on the swing near the judge's house. Then came our cousins who had hidden in the hayloft during a pogrom. Nachum had grown up to be an anarchist. He walked me through Williamsburg's streets and told me about Prince Kropotkin and the free society. It was all very confusing. Here you were talking with Liova, and Dvoirah, and Nachum the anarchist, and you thought for a moment you were in the village. Then you looked up and saw you were in Williamsburg and were talking to Leon, Dora or Nathan.

I wanted to forget Russia and the Czar and the pogroms. Russia was a barbaric, cruel place. The village, of course, was different. It did not really belong to the Czar, but to Yakelina and Uncle Moishe and the tramp Apanas and the town idiot and the Cossacks. Best of all I remembered grandfather. He was now very ill, they wrote. He felt that the end was near, and he loved us so much that he broke the rule of a lifetime and sent us his photograph.

"A photograph," mama said. "Who would have thought it? The world changes."

But the world changed very slowly. Mama kept a kosher house. The milk plates were separate from the meat plates. You could not have butter with your meat, and you had to wait six hours after a meat supper before you were allowed to drink milk. She still believed in the Evil Eye. When she sewed a button on your shirt you had to hold a piece of thread in your mouth, otherwise she would sew up your wits. It was hard for all of us to become Americans, but we had the advantage of youth, and she was getting old. We quarreled and said cruel things to each other.

"Why don't you leave me alone?" I said. "I'm only ten, and you have lived your life. You are thirty already."

Mama burst out laughing and kissed me. Our quarrels were not really between her and me, but between the village and America. Mama found it difficult to change her habits. She refused to eat tomatoes and bananas. She had never heard of them.

Innovations like that meant a fight. People stick to food more stubbornly than to principles. When I convinced mama that tomatoes and bananas were kosher, she let us have them. Then I said, why not bananas with puffed rice, a real American dish? What is puffed rice, my son? I could not explain. I had never eaten puffed rice but I had seen it in a big colored advertisement in the *Saturday Evening Post*. That was no authority. Mama had never heard of the *Saturday Evening Post,* the new American bible. I had to save up five pennies over a week and buy a copy of the magazine before we had bananas and puffed rice.

Getting roller skates was much harder. You know we are poor, my son. Besides, you'll break your neck. A truck will run over you. Again I had to bring an authority, this time my new Hebrew teacher. Mr. Neuman had a beard and talked in a voice like grandfather's. But he had been in America many years and was progressive. He lectured my parents on sports. This was not the old world. In America a boy must develop his body as well as his mind. A healthy mind in a healthy body, Mr. Neuman said. He said it in Hebrew as if it were a citation from the prophets, and I got the skates.

There were limits to the compromises my parents made. Who played baseball, for instance? Bums. Our ghetto was crowded with workers, skilled and unskilled, and the street was in the hands of bums, sons of truck drivers, plumbers and carpenters. These boys were the strongest, wildest, the best athletes. They played baseball and that showed you what baseball was, a bums' game. What about the papers? Look how much they write about baseball. The national game.

I played a little on the sly, but never learned to play well. My two younger brothers, both born in America, were not going to suffer this disability. I took them into the yard and taught them to pitch, catch and bat. My parents always stressed my responsibilities as the eldest son.

From the medieval village I brought a fresh viewpoint to America. Everything seemed new, alien, terrible, beautiful. In this hostile, weird world, I had to change my whole life. Everything which the native American took for granted, which came to him simply as he grew, I had to examine, experiment with, accept or reject before I made it

my own. I had to weigh values, balance grandfather against Mr. Neuman, both against Blue Eyes. All this increased fear in my heart: fear
of the turbulent machines of America, of God who might not like the
new things I was doing, of father who was severe in his judgments, of
the gangs around the corner, of Blue Eyes who rapped my knuckles
with her ruler because I did not understand a new English phrase, of
the poverty which robbed us of milk and fruit and air and sunlight
and made us frequently ill, of life itself, so confused and so cruel.
Above all, I feared loneliness. Without English, baseball, a knowledge
of the American ghetto's customs you could not make friends easily.
The dream came: to have friends whom you love and who love you.

§ 2

Every experience—however old it may be, however many people
may have passed through it in one form or another across the centuries
—comes to us as individuals with all the clean shock of newness. This
is especially true when we are young, and do not even know that our
own unique destiny is only the cliché of a race, an age, a class. When
I grew up and went to college, I learned from books, and later from
friends, that the transition from village to city, from landscape to sky-
line, from trees to tenements, had been a turbulent episode for Western
Europe almost a century before I was born; in every land masses of
men migrated from country to city under the impact of the industrial
revolution. But when I came at seven from a little Ukrainian village to
the metropolis of America, and shuddered at the stone monsters stretching to the sky, and thought of the peace of the fields, exaggerated by
memory and longing, I had no idea that I was recapitulating a common experience, any more than I realized when I wept because some
adult was tyrannical that my difficulties as a child were more or less
universal.

Possibly this sense of uniqueness was the result not only of childish
naïveté, but of country life itself, of what has been called the "idiocy
of the village." What overwhelms the small boy, and often the adult,
is not merely being hurled from quiet to tumult, from clean to foul
air, from sunlight to shadow, from grass to asphalt. This transformation is relatively easy. The nerves, when one is young, are capable if
stubborn pupils. What is unbearably hard in adolescence is the readjustment of one's whole feeling about the world, and one's own place
in it.

In the village we feel at once more oppressed by the community and more independent of it. People are few; they know each other; the eyes of all peer into the house of each, and our innermost secrets are common gossip. We know, love or hate every individual in it, those who tenderly or maliciously meddle in our affairs. Yet, when we wander into the woods, or climb the hill and face the illimitable sky, we have the illusion of complete freedom from the rest of mankind. There is only the "I" and the universe; we are responsible only to God, who, we imagine, exists behind the vast gray billows of cloud inflamed with crimson sunset that float across the evening heavens. It was out of this life that early man built his deities and myths, which still haunt the isolated peasant, terrify the village child, and infect the romantic poet.

In the city we are relatively free of our neighbors. The streets wind out to places where we are unknown. The family next door is strange to us and we to them; we have neighbors but no community, gossip but no retribution. The moving van can take us ten blocks away to another world where we can start life anew. Yet everywhere about us there surges the crowd, anonymous and implacable. The sky is hidden behind stern towers; God is dead; we are only tiny insects crawling along the gray streets. And we are lonely in the impersonal multitude as we never were standing unaccompanied against the sky of our favorite village hill. To become part of the mass, to speak its language, to have friends in this new, strange, terrifying world becomes our driving passion. And when we cultivate with thoughtless enthusiasm every chance acquaintance in the hope that here at last is the long-sought comrade, we little know which of these acquaintances will become part of our lives, whose destiny will alter ours.

§ 3

Reconciliation to the city is only a prelude to our transformation. The conflict of cultures grows more acute as we develop new interests, and language itself becomes the symbol and index of the conflict.

At home we spoke Yiddish; in the street a form of American with a marked foreign accent, a singsong rhythm and the interpolation of Yiddish phrases; in public school we read and recited an English so pure, so lofty, so poetic that it seemed to bear no relation to the language of the street. Literature was the enemy of the street until years later, when postwar fiction and poetry gave the language of the street the dignity of art, when Joyce and Hemingway replaced Longfellow and Whittier.

The barrier of language created acute suffering. When I began to scribble English verses which seemed to tear the very soul out of me, I suddenly realized that my parents could not read them. Once or twice, perhaps, in a moment of love, when I felt this gulf most keenly, I wrote them sonnets in Yiddish, so that they might know the strange animal they had bred, disappointing all their hopes. In the street my literary English, so painfully acquired at school, was a joke.

"What'd you do, swaller a dictionary?—twenty-three skiddoo!"

In the adolescent literary groups, where most of the boys were American-born, older than I, my early efforts at writing encountered other difficulties. I was reading my first essay at the Young Zionist Club, and assumed that because *detour* was pronounced *detoor, devour* must be *devoor*. The loud ironic laughter sent me home to memorize Edmund Burke on the American colonies.

How could you become an American? There were so many kinds of Americans. Around the corner was Fox's Folly, cornerstone of a cinema fortune, where every night young gangsters met. From street-fights they had graduated to gun-fights. In a civilization where captains of industry rose to the top through force and fraud, violence was a logical instrument. My friend Jay's brother was killed by a cop in a gambling-house raid. Shortly afterward another cop tried to break up a crap game and keep the money. He beat up an Irish boy called Whitey. Whitey was seventeen and lived in my friend Robert's house around the corner. He asked Robert and me to keep a sharp lookout at the door. Then he ran upstairs and clipped his yellow curly hair. He came down with a cap pulled over his eyes and no baggage.

"So long," he said, "I just killed a cop."

We never saw him again.

The small boys of the slum had their own "gangs," which carried on continual warfare, geographic, racial and individual. We fought the gangs of the blocks surrounding ours. The chief enemy were the "Micks"—not necessarily Irish, but gentiles of any race.

Collective warfare had a special organized technique. Our instruments of defense were the corrugated tin tops of ash cans which we stole from the tenements, to the helpless indignation of the janitors. Our offensive weapons varied with the season: in summer, dry corn-cobs and watermelon rind; in winter, snowballs and chunks of ice. Shots were picked up from the gutter in the course of the running fight. Like all armies, we considered our enemies cowardly and unscrupulous. In winter they hurled coal wrapped in snow, which split one's head open. The only way to treat criminals like them was to give them a dose of their own medicine, to use the same weapons.

I say "we" in this case, following the time-honored practice of intellectuals who are part of a military machine even when they only talk for it. As the result of a delicate body and a pacifist family tradition, I did little actual fighting. Scholars were not supposed to fight. Other Jewish boys were tough scrappers, but they respected tradition. They threw the corncobs; I was a member of the general staff, plotting campaigns, addressing the troops before battle, delivering words of praise or consolation after victory or defeat.

But I could not forever escape physical injury. One night, coming home late from Hebrew School, a gang of Micks stopped me. It was a hot summer night, and they held in their hands one of the season's weapons—heavy banana stalks.

"Are you a Jew or a Mick?" they asked.

"A Jew," I said.

When I finally stumbled home and tried to take off my cap, it stuck to my head in a thick clot of blood.

§ 4

The principal of our public school was an Irishman who knew that books were by no means the best way to Americanize immigrant children. What preparation could *Stepping Stones to Literature* give us for life in a city run by Boss Murphy? Our real education was outside the classroom. We were organized into an army, a junior equivalent, you might say, of the Reserve Officers' Training Corps. The school was a barracks, and every pupil wore khaki uniform. Our commanding officer was a short, stocky Jew who kept his dignity by wearing mufti. The principal, commander in chief, had that much sense too. Every morning the bugler blew assembly, we fell into our squads amidst the boyish shouts of our sergeants and corporals, and passed in review before our commander in chief. The principal was a tall, heavy man, with large blue eyes that almost popped out of his head; his long, black mustache curled up like John L. Sullivan's in the colored pictures that came in your father's cigarette box.

Military drill was exciting. You had read someone's *Boy's Life of Napoleon* in the Bushwick Avenue library, and the dirty schoolyard, with its dilapidated black brick walls and its cheap basketball goals at the end became Austerlitz. On winter mornings, when the commander in chief came late and you were cold and miserable waiting for him, it was Moscow.

Soon our military life came to an end. The army was demobilized and we once more became civilians. Our barracks were converted into a School City, municipal equivalent of the Junior Republic of later years. The corporals became policemen, the sergeants aldermen, and the most popular boy was elected mayor. We were being inducted by the Dalton method into the mysteries of American city politics.

I became commissioner of charities. This meant spending hours after school going from house to house in the neighborhood and collecting castoff clothing and shoes for the poorest pupils. The following term I held two posts at once: I was head of the school bank and assistant police commissioner. The teacher who appointed me to both jobs explained: a bank is a private institution; the government does not control it. In the police department you are serving the government, but the bank is our own business. Actually, the bank was run by the school authorities, but the pupil could not be impressed too strongly with the rights of private property as against government.

The police commissioner was my friend Robert Smith, a shrewd lad who at twelve already gave evidence of that business acumen which was one day to net him a million dollars. He appointed me head of the detective squad. I did not like it, but Robert, native-born and precocious, undertook to give me further lessons in the politics of democracy. The commissioner and the head of the detective squad had the privilege of cutting classes for one hour every day to round up hooky-players. We played hooky in the course of our duty; other hooky-players were criminals who had violated the law. Once you started to hunt criminals, you could hardly be expected to follow a time-schedule like a train. Still, that was not very serious. If you cut classes for two hours instead of one, the authorities understood how zealous you were in the pursuit of your duties. Then again, there were material rewards. When you caught hooky-players shooting crap, you could confiscate the dice and the money. You were supposed to turn in the catch to the principal's office, but Robert said I was a fool. Government officials were entitled to something for their trouble.

One morning I was cross-examining a criminal suspected of stealing a teacher's gloves. Robert came in and started to bully the prisoner. Robert was my superior officer in the police department, but I was holding the investigation in the bank, and a bank was private property. I said to Robert, Get out. He said, I am your chief. I said, This is our bank. A jurisdictional dispute common in democratic politics, but Robert and I were both hurt and did not speak to each other for a week.

The principal decided to give us another lesson in practical civics. Personal friendship was more important than political disputes. He called us into his office and gave us a fatherly talk.

"Now, boys, I want you to shake hands and be friends."

Robert was a normal sensible boy. He was that wonderful American thing I was trying to understand, a good sport. He stuck out his hand. I refused to take it; I was not a good sport. If Robert were a true friend, would he allow our personal relations to be handled by the principal? If he felt like resuming our friendship, why didn't he come to me of his own accord, in private, and not show off his noble nature in public, in front of all those women clerks too? More important: was he right or was he wrong in butting into my work and bullying the "prisoner"? Until that question was settled, what was the use of shaking hands? I put my hands in pockets, muttered something about "principles" and walked out of the office.

Like the army, our experiment in practical civics came to an end, this time thanks to the rivalry between two teachers. Mr. Eff was a former reporter on the *World* with the nearsightedness and the aggressiveness of old Joe Pulitzer in his most energetic days. Mr. Gee was tall and thin, looked the spitting image of Sherlock Holmes as we imagined him, and was something of an aesthete who played the piano and discussed art and literature. The elections for mayor were up. Mr. Eff picked me to represent his class; Mr. Gee picked Louis Gottschalk (who was in later years to become a professor of history and an authority on the French Revolution). That was unfortunate. I liked Mr. Gee better than Mr. Eff, and would have been in his class if I had done better in my studies; and Louis was one of my best friends. Louis and I talked the matter over and decided we would both withdraw. But it turned out that candidates were not free men. This was a fight between Mr. Eff and Mr. Gee, our political "bosses," and neither would let his man withdraw. The campaign was taken out of the pupils' hands and brought into the teachers' council, and there our principal made a decision worthy of a statesman: he dissolved the School City.

Mr. Gee and I became friends. He not only let me join his debating society, but took me for walks around Manhattan. That was like traveling to a foreign country. A relative of mine, whom I had never met, was one of the engineers who had built Brooklyn Bridge, but I

had never crossed it. Our bridge was the Williamsburg, which led
from one ghetto to another. Beyond that Mr. Gee showed me the
"real" America—the homes of Carnegie, and the Vanderbilts, and
Amelia Bingham. He knew every house and its history; he knew all
about America's best people.

"When you grow up," he said to me, pointing to a palace a block
square, "you must try to own a house like that."

"But I don't want to own any houses; I want to be an artist, I
want to paint."

"Then you will end up in Greenwich Village. That's where artists
live."

I thought Greenwich Village lay outside of New York, somewhere
among hills and fields and woods, like our little village in the Ukraine.

§5

What a different world when you went from the public school to
the Hebrew School. You left behind you the city government, the bank,
the courts, the fairy tales, *Stepping Stones to Literature* and the panel
of the five New England poets. You entered the world of Isaiah, Jeremiah and Amos; the psalms of David, the song of Solomon.

Rabbi Neuman was a pioneer in the teaching of Hebrew. A devout
and passionate nationalist, he permitted no language to be spoken in
his school except the sacred tongue of the prophets. Classroom walls
carried printed signs with his slogan: *Daber Ivrith;* wherever you are,
with whomever you are, speak Hebrew. He taught the language by
surrounding his pupils with it: *Ivrith b'ivrith,* learn Hebrew by speaking it.

Mr. Neuman was a bridge between the old world and the new.
As an intense Zionist, a teacher of the youth, a figure in our ghetto, he
was like grandfather, for whom my nostalgia was still strong. As a
modern man who talked, read and wrote English and knew the American classics, Mr. Neuman spoke to me of the new world, so vast, so
puzzling, so necessary to understand. It was he who gave me the first
American novel I ever read, *The Last of the Mohicans.* It was typical
of him that he gave it to me in a Hebrew translation, so that I first
heard about the Indians and the pioneers in the original language of
that Bible which the American colonists held so dear.

But there was more than one bridge to the new world; there were
many, and one led into another. Mr. Neuman had two sons, Joshua
and Emanuel. The former became an English instructor at a univer-

sity, the latter a leader of the Zionist movement. They helped me merge into the new world by giving me my first collective life. The Young Zionist Club which they organized consisted for the most part of adolescent boys and girls from middle-class and proletarian families, equally poor.

My father, who was now selling and buying real estate in the "bourse" at Huberman's café; Daniel's father, who ran a little shoe-store; Albert's father, who was a Hebrew teacher; George's father, who was a small trader; Joe Cohen's father, who was a presser—all lived in filthy, unfurnished tenement flats, counted their pennies before buying a pair of shoes.

The Young Zionist Club discussed the higher politics—as it affected the Jews; literature—as it affected the Jews; ethics—as it affected the Jews; art—as it affected the Jews; philosophy—as it affected the Jews. Outside the club, we discussed love—as it affected the Jews; but especially ourselves.

Joshua and Emanuel Neuman edited the official organ of the Zionist youth movement of America, an English-language magazine to which I contributed stories and articles. Later I joined its editorial staff—"Ein emesser journalist," my mother said. My mother was little interested in Zionism, and my father was sarcastic about it.

"Why should I go and starve with the Arabs?" he said. "I can starve here with the Americans."

He believed that America held for the Jew the greatest opportunities of economic security and social freedom. Yet he always came to Zionist meetings when I spoke, just to make sure that I didn't "become too swell-headed." My mother sat up late nights at her Singer machine, sewing a banner for our club.

My stories for the *Young Judaean* were about the persecution of the Jews and their sole salvation—Palestine. Zionism, like other movements, had its martyrs and heroes. The martyr was Captain Dreyfus of the French army, falsely condemned to Devil's Island by the anti-Semites of Paris on the trumped-up charge of selling military secrets to Germany. Dreyfus was not a Zionist; he thought of himself as a good Frenchman. That was because he did not understand his own position in the world, the position of the Jew who was the scapegoat of the ages. We were brought up in the shadow of the Affaire Dreyfus, and always it served to stir our racial pride, our sense of isolation in the world, our desire to win back Palestine as the sole escape from the hostile world.

Our hero was the founder of the Zionist movement, Dr. Theodor Herzl. We heard his story over and over again at meetings: how he had been accepted by the gentile society of Austria, worked successfully on a leading Viennese newspaper; and could have, so far as he was personally concerned, lived a pleasant life. But the sufferings of his people would not let him rest. He abandoned his career, his privileged position, his social alliances, and gave his life to the cause of emancipating the Jew from the Diaspora. In every Zionist meeting hall you could see his portrait—the high forehead with its black hair brushed up in a thick pompadour, his dark deep eyes, his handsome regular features, his square black beard. And next to him hung the portrait of his chief lieutenant, the French journalist Max Nordau, with his white hair and beard.

I knew a lot of the Bible, in the original and by heart. The passages I liked to recite aloud were from Isaiah, Jeremiah and Amos, the resounding phrases about justice. The poetry of David and Solomon fascinated me chiefly because it was written by men of action, just as in Scott's novels it was the warrior-monk who most moved me.

Father was a man of action. He left the house early and came home late; he walked his bedroom till dawn littering the floor with half-smoked cigarettes, planning, scheming. He never read books. Grandfather was a man of thought. He never had a business. He left his study only to go to the synagogue and to visit friends. I wanted to be neither a businessman nor a scholar, but something else, something American which would combine action and thought. I longed for the good, the wise, the noble. Grandfather, Uncle Moishe, my anarchist cousin, my mother herself with her limitless love and generosity, had destroyed any practical tendencies I might have had. I wanted to be like the prophets, Dr. Herzl, my uncle's revolutionary friends. The American world presented an illusion of boundless choice. But what was good? what was wise? what was noble?

When I had read *The Last of the Mohicans* in Hebrew for the eighth time, Mr. Neuman said it was much too much, and gave me another book in Hebrew. It was the story of a young man in love with a girl. She was very beautiful and the hero wanted to marry her, but she said, You must get my father's consent. The father said, My daughter will marry only that man who proves himself truly good, truly wise, truly noble. The young man accepted these conditions. He joined his country's army, fought bravely in war, became commander in chief, returned in triumph. But the girl's father said: No, this is not true goodness, true wisdom, true nobility. The hero resigned from the army, went into trade, became the richest man in the land. But the girl's father said: No, this is not true goodness, true wisdom, true nobility. In turn, the hero tried politics, learning, charity; he even went into the wilderness and founded a new civilization; but each time he returned to claim the girl he loved in marriage, her father said: No, this is not true goodness, true wisdom, true nobility. Finally, he gave away all his wealth, and . . .

At this point the book was torn; the last page and the back cover were missing. I was denied the secret of life. Mr. Neuman was kind; he sent to Warsaw for another copy of the book, but it was out of print. For years the story haunted me. It seemed as if under everything I did was the search for the lost page.

Disappointment made me morose. I frequently lost my temper and quarreled with the other children at home. My mother reproached me: how could I be so barbaric? how could I talk about goodness and wisdom and work for the Zionist ideal, yet act like a cannibal? I said I could not help my temper; I was born that way. My mother said that was no excuse. When Moses led the Jews across the wilderness, a king of a bordering country wanted to find out what sort of man the prophet was. Court painters visited Moses and brought the king his portrait; court seers read the face. This man, they said, is godless, violent and deceitful. The king was angry. Fools, he said, you are reading the face of Moses, the holy man of God. Either the painters had brought back a false portrait or the seers could not read faces. The king decided to settle the matter by visiting the prophet himself. When he saw Moses face to face, the king realized at once that his painters had done an accurate portrait. He explained his dilemma to Moses. The prophet said: Your seers also have told the truth. By nature I am godless, violent and deceitful; but I have a mission in life; I am leading my people to freedom. This places heavy obligations on me; all the evil sides of my nature must be submerged to my task.

§ 6

We lived on the top floor of a putrid sunless tenement. In summer you sweated and lay panting on the fire escape or the roof, knocked out by the heat; in winter you froze in the icy bedrooms or huddled around the coal stove in the kitchen. At all times the street sent up its hoarse yell: the peddlers shouted their wares, the babies screamed, the neighbors quarreled, the bums punched each other in the nose or swatted baseballs into store windows; the gangsters shot craps and policemen. The street was hectic with insecure life. Today the gas went out because we had no quarter. Now the grocer said he could not give us any more credit. People spoke of a panic. Times were hard. The Kaplan boys, whose father owned the grocery store where they worked, blamed it on capitalism and Teddy Roosevelt in the White House, who was the tool of capitalism. But they were socialists, always knocking everything and everybody. Still, you could not call them loafers. They worked hard.

Here was my tenth birthday and my parents gave no party for me. It was hard to understand; they had never failed to give me a party before. My birthday came on a Jewish holiday, the last day of the Feast of Tabernacle, and the party was for both occasions. My mother said nothing about the matter, and I asked no questions. My friends surprised me; they remembered my birthday. They stopped me in the street and gave me a box of water colors because I wanted to be a painter. I thanked them and asked them to come up to the house. I was sure there was going to be a party. Even if there was none, my mother would, as usual, be glad to receive my friends and give them some of the cake she had baked, jelly of her own making, tea, nuts covered with honey. We came in and my mother lowered her eyes and said nothing. When my friends had seated themselves around the table, she called me into the kitchen. There were tears in her eyes.

"My son, my dear one, I am terribly sorry, I don't know how to tell you. We have nothing in the house, no tea, no sugar, no cake, no bread and butter."

"Not even seltzer?" I said stupidly. We always had syphons of charged water in the house even when there was no bread; my father was convinced that tenement water was bad for your health.

"Not even seltzer. The grocer won't give us any more credit. Papa isn't making a living. There is a panic."

I told my friends. There was nothing to be ashamed of; their own homes were as bare as ours. They slapped me on the back, and said it was all right. We all sat around the table, my mother with us, and we discussed the existence of God, the coming of the Messiah, and our hero Teddy, the friend of the people.

Several days after this we were evicted. Our furniture was piled up in the street on a Sunday morning and we had to move to the nearest vacant flat, across the street. We could not pay the rent; nobody was making a living these days. But that was not the real thing.

My father knew the reason for our humiliation. It was bad luck; we should never have lived in a flat whose door was marked 13. Yet life in the new flat was no better than in the old. Most of my friends were workers' sons. Their houses were as naked and miserable as ours, full of screaming kids who often went unfed. The entire neighborhood was feverish with the pursuit of bread. Day and night you heard the refrain: to make a living, to earn a little piece of bread. Often the fathers were out of work. Some of them drank heavily, the cigarettes littered the floor and sent up a sour stink. When our mothers were pregnant, we said, Christ! (We had already learned to swear by Christ like real Americans.) They can't feed six kids; how in hell will they feed seven? In some families the kids ran barefoot in the street. There was no money for shoes. In winter their legs were wrapped in rags, like Russian peasants', and they sat all day near the kitchen stove.

In our back yard the sweater factory roared all day. The sallow men and women bent over the clattering machines under the gaslight. Once Mechel, our next-door neighbor, was brought home from work, the right side of his body swathed in bandages. His arm had been cut off by the machine.

There were rich men in our neighborhood too. They owned the first automobiles, and quarreled with their wives in public over other women. All day and half the night they played cards and smoked and drank in Huberman's café. They were pillars of the synagogue. Something was wrong; evil governed the world. But there were dream worlds. Someday we would go to Palestine, which flowed with milk and honey, and was pure with sunlight and freedom for the race.

Or perhaps the three Kaplan boys in the grocery store were right? Someday, they said, the world would be socialist. There would be no more poor and no more rich; the exploitation of man by man would be abolished. That last phrase, they admitted, came out of a book, but it was the greatest book in the world, written by the greatest thinker who had ever lived, Karl Marx.

We did not read Marx. Our teachers never mentioned him, and we had to stick to our homework to get anywhere. At home the gas flickered; it was cold and dim. We leaned over the bare wooden table or stood over the ironing board of Mr. Cohen's cleaning and dyeing store, and read Edmund Burke, Daniel Webster and Percy Bysshe Shelley in loud voices with labored accents, the result of elocution courses. O wonderful world of sublime sentiments, remote from the dank sewers of slum life! We were going there someday—among the people who wrote poems, drew pictures, played the piano. We would study law and make great speeches; we would be masters of the sweet English tongue, so far from the putrid tenement, the yelling babies, the dry crusts of bread.

My friends and I were the second generation of immigrants—the "educated" people who spoke English and read books. Our fathers were tailors, grocers, storekeepers, salesmen, brokers on the pettiest scale imaginable. But they—and we—were determined that we should grow up to be neither workers nor businessmen. We would study hard, develop our minds, and through them rise to higher rungs of the American ladder whose top was lost in the clouds. We would be doctors, lawyers and teachers; some of us even dreamed of being artists and writers. Barely in our teens, we already belonged to cultural organizations—Zionist, socialist, "nonpartisan." Whatever profession we planned to enter, we all scribbled verses and stories. We wanted to know everything. Dave Abramowitz began to read through the entire Encyclopedia, but broke down at "Crustacea."

The cult of knowledge was as deep in the American ghetto as in the European. It had been transplanted and invigorated by the practical advancement which America seemed to offer to the educated. Knowledge led to economic and social heights. When the Jew achieved a higher status, the *goyim* would respect him. He would be spared the grosser forms of persecution; he could sit unmolested at the lower end of the masters' table. He might even become a Louis Marshall or a Jacob Schiff. But these economic and racial motives were suffused with the traditions of the ancient Jewish culture in which learning was essentially religious, beginning and ending with the *torah*. This was supposed to be disinterested pursuit of knowledge.

Now in America, where the businessman was the ideal, my father took revenge for the bitter humiliation of his youth. Toward scholars of all kinds he affected an ironic hostility. When we argued late at night about religion or socialism, he would crush my case by saying:

"What professor did you get that from?"

The word "professor" was his chief term of contempt, as it was H. L. Mencken's. But papa, like H. L. Mencken, his contemporary, had a secret dread of professors; he looked upon learning as the highest achievement in life. If you really wanted to insult a man you called him an ignoramus. Nothing would have pleased my father more than to see me become a professor. He never talked business to me.

CHAPTER III

To that large utterance of the early gods!
—JOHN KEATS.

§ 1

AT this time I heard socialist talk in one form or another from many people. The three Kaplan boys, sons of our grocer across the street, told me America was a plutocracy. Steel kings and coal barons oppressed the poor. The textileworker, Louis Smith, took me to street-corner meetings where the soapboxer Fitzgibbons, a retired vaudeville actor, preached the class struggle with wild humor. Classmates from the socialist citadels of Brownsville gave me party pamphlets to read. In the socialist local on Graham Avenue I came across an exciting magazine with red, blue and yellow covers which published heavy charcoal drawings of policemen clubbing pickets and ladies with mastodon breasts, and strike poetry by anonymous coal miners. Through my mind passed the words of Jackson, my history teacher, his denunciation of imperialism and his plea for Jeffersonian democracy; Frank Tannenbaum's daring speech to the court which tried him for leading hungry men into the church of St. Alphonsus; Joe Hill's pie in the sky on the lips of radical workers; these, and Teddy Roosevelt's big stick descending on the trusts with blows ostensibly socialist in their fervor. Such things stirred me deeply, but they did not touch the poetry I was beginning to write at this time. I read verses about love and beauty to my friends.

"Bull," said the Kaplan boys.

But the younger socialists liked poetry and told me to keep at it, and this flattered my vanity. But I was distressed because my father did not understand my poetry and thought socialism a mad dream.

According to the Kaplan boys, my father was a cockroach businessman. No offense, you understand, a very nice man, but from the economic viewpoint, a cockroach. Clerks, stenographers, schoolteachers were white-collar slaves. The people who counted were the plutocrats, who owned ninety-nine per cent of the country's wealth, and the proletarians, who produced it. The proletarians were coal miners, mill hands, railway workers, the men in "basic industry." We, even the Kaplan boys, belonged to the "petit bourgeoisie." We were being ground "between the upper and nether millstones." The jargon of the Kaplan boys and their long verbatim citations from Marx were confusing.

After we were evicted, I asked for explanations. Abe Kaplan—who had taken my political education in hand—made a mess of it. Weeks of talking me out of my regard for T. R. almost convinced me that the radicals were right. I said:

"If that is socialism, if it means the abolition of poverty, then I'm a socialist."

Abe became angry.

"You have no principles!" he said. "If you're a Roosevelt man, you should stick to Roosevelt."

He was one of those radicals more interested in arguing with his opponent than in converting him.

Fitzgibbons, the street-corner soapboxer, was a better pedagogue. He never used mysterious phrases. For one hour he was funny, much funnier than any vaudeville in Fox's Folly. When he described how the rich lived, the audience nearly died laughing. When he described how the poor suffered, they laughed too, because they loved the way he insulted them. He would start with a workingman getting up at dawn to go to work, his sloppy breakfast, the dingy streetcar, the filthy shop, the fat foreman, the hasty lunch, the rush to the toilet, the weary afternoon, the ride home, the hungry wife and kids, the terrible supper, the noise of the street. The poor sap drops off to sleep, and next day he goes through the same mechanical motions. Six days of it: work, eat, sleep; work, eat, sleep; work, eat, sleep. And sometimes no eat, and sometimes no work. It was all very ironical, and at the end of every sentence the audience roared with laughter.

We felt it was true. Whatever Marx may have said, Fitzgibbons knew his stuff. That was just the way my friends' fathers lived, like dogs. Then came the seventh day, and that was the funniest because it was the day of rest. The worker went to amuse himself in the filth and noise of Coney Island. We had been to Coney Island and knew Fitzgibbons was right. And when the audience was tired of laughing, he would shout:

"Fools! Jackasses! How long will you stand this slavery?"

And they would laugh some more. Then Fitz pointed at a man in the audience, any man, and said:

"I know why you're laughing. You think I mean those damned fools," indicating the audience. Everybody laughed again, the random man too.

"No, you jackass, I mean you too! I mean all of you!"

Then he would start to explain the "economics of capitalism." It seemed that not we alone were poor. Most Americans were poor; the vast majority of mankind was poor. And they need not be poor. They produced by the sweat of their brow the coal, the iron, the steel, the railways, the steamships, the cities of this world, all its magnificent wealth. They made the shoes, but went barefoot; they sewed the clothes, but went in rags; they built the houses, and lived like rats in holes. And why, you jackasses? Where does all the wealth you produce go? Who gets it? If all the wealth of America were properly distributed every man, woman and child would have security, health, happiness, a good education, decent food, good living quarters. And none of us would have to work more than four hours a day. Even the college professors admitted that. They got up statistics about it, but they know you won't read those statistics because you are idiots. When will you wake up?

The trouble was, it seemed, that the people who worked were robbed by the people who owned the machines and factories. That was what "exploitation" meant. Those who *owned* the means of production lived on the wealth produced by those who *operated* the means of production: Clear? What was the solution? Abolish this system of exploitation. Abolish the private ownership of the mines, factories, railways. Turn them over to the People, who will run them not for profit but for use.

"But, Mr. Speaker, how can we do it?"

On that point Fitzgibbons was not clear. The usual answer was vote socialist candidates into office. Gradually, after many years, the co-operative commonwealth would be ushered in.

Occasionally, distinguished candidates of the Socialist party addressed us from the soapbox. Kirkpatrick, for instance. That was extraordinary. When you wanted to hear a Republican or Democratic candidate, even if it was only for the board of aldermen, you had to go to a "rally" in a hall, and they spoke only during the election campaign. But the socialist candidates carried on their "campaign of education" all year round, and talked on street corners.

When Kirkpatrick finished speaking, boys and girls of my own age, with red bands around their arms, sold "literature." There was a pamphlet by Kirkpatrick himself called *War What For?* It explained how the capitalists, the plutocrats and exploiters, organized wars in order to get markets for their goods. And who paid the price in blood and sweat? Labor, the workers, the exploited.

William Randolph Hearst, for instance, was responsible for the Spanish-American War. That was a great surprise to me. I had thought of Hearst as a friend of the people. I remembered the indignation in our neighborhood during the 1906 elections. Even the kids were indignant; they were the "educated" ones and followed politics in their way. It was the first election I had seen. We made bonfires in the gutter, and someone projected lantern slides of the returns on a bed-sheet flapping in the November wind across the store face of the State Bank. Hearst had really been elected mayor of New York, but Tammany Hall threw the ballot boxes into the East River and put in their own man. That was because Hearst was the People's Friend. And now Kirkpatrick said he was an exploiter who instigated war.

But not all newspaper owners were as corrupt as Hearst. There was one capitalist journalist—a "prostitute of the kept press"—who saw the horrors of capitalism, gave up his job and his income and his privileges, and devoted his life to the cause of working-class emancipation. The name of this great and good man was Charles Edward Russell. Here was his book, *Why I Am a Socialist,* for only twenty-five cents or one quarter. Comrade Russell ran on every Socialist ticket. Once he spoke at a "rally" in Capitol Hall, three houses away from our tenement, and I thought he had a wonderful voice.

§ 2

Robert Smith, my friend and former chief in the School City police department, lived around the corner. His father was a clothing worker in the Amalgamated; his mother a fanatic on the Jewish religion. She encouraged our friendship in the hope that I might convert her son to Zionism. But Robert had his own propaganda. We sat on the steps of his house nights and argued about God. I feared God might not like what we were saying; but I hoped that Beatrice, sleeping at the open window above, would overhear our loud voices metaphysically wrangling through the summer air over the cobblestones of Manhattan Avenue. Beatrice was my own age and beautiful, and Robert liked her very much. He shouted at the top of his voice that there was no God; religion was the opium of the people. Who in hell made that smart crack? Again Karl Marx. But Robert had not read Karl Marx; he heard about him from his brother Louis.

Louis was almost an old man; he was twenty. He worked in a knit-goods shop. He was starting a union, and was active in the Socialist party. All the grown men in the Smith family worked in factories, but Louis was the only socialist. He had never finished grammar school, yet he read everything. He brought me books by writers of whom I had never heard: G. Bernard Shaw, for instance, who was extremely clever, and was a socialist too. Shaw was like Fitzgibbons, only better; he told you the truth about capitalism in such a way that you laughed your head off. Louis was fond of his younger brother Robert and, in consequence, adopted me too. He treated us as equals, even as superiors; we were "smart" and knew history. He was going to slave to send Robert to college, but Robert must promise to devote his knowledge and gifts to the Cause, otherwise no go. There were enough parasites and exploiters as it was.

We respected and loved Louis because he was the sincerest man we knew. He not only talked about the class struggle, he went into strikes and the cops beat him up and he went right back again. He could explain the whole business in the simplest language. He made me read too.

"If you're going to be any good to the working class at all," he said, "you'll have to know something."

He handed me pamphlets, clippings, the *Call,* leaflets, books. He also took me to workers' meetings—books weren't enough, he said. Books alone would make you nothing but a bourgeois professor. Not that there weren't professors who meant well, but the middle classes would never achieve socialism. Only the workers could do that. The Kaplan boys, Fitzgibbons and Louis talked as if the great upheaval was not far off.

"It's liable to bust any year," Abe Kaplan said. Most likely in Germany or the United States, some such industrially developed country. Big business was doing our work by creating those enormous combinations for the output and production of goods. All we'd have to do would be to take them over.

This idea was by no means confined to the small group of radicals whom I personally knew. Upton Sinclair, whose *The Jungle* I was reading, predicted in another book a socialist America by 1912, with

William Randolph Hearst as the first socialist president. This was an extreme example of the sanguine hopes which stirred American liberals at this time.

§ 3

Loud was the middle-class protest in those days. You could hear it plainly in the commercial magazines of S. S. McClure, Frank Munsey and William Randolph Hearst, building careers and fortunes by catering to popular discontent with the growth of monopoly-capitalism. Their publications, which Louis Smith constantly read aloud to Robert and myself, flourished in soil prepared by populist and socialist propaganda. Here writers of exposure and protest showed up the political and economic abuses of American capitalism, which they called Big Business. They brought out into broad daylight the sore spots—the boodling, blackmail, embezzlement, stock speculation, child slavery, adulteration of food; the fraud, graft and corruption which pervaded local and national government departments, the press, the stock exchange, indeed the whole of American economic, social and political life. The basis of the Republic was not questioned. It was pointed out, however, that there was widespread political corruption and that its cause was Big Business. The railroads, the banks, the public-service corporations on a large scale, and the saloons, the whorehouses, the gambling joints on a smaller scale, controlled politics in order to increase and protect their profits. In order to expand, they needed what the elder La Follette called "special privilege"—franchises, special legislation, protective tariffs, and interpretations of the law in their favor. They needed to, and did, control the boards of aldermen, the state assemblies, the Congress in Washington, the police, the newspapers, the courts low and high.

Privilege, according to Lincoln Steffens, was the root of all evil. Throwing "bad" men out of office and putting "good" men in their places was useless; the "good" men who came into office, just like the "bad" men whom they ousted, were under the pressure of their political party, which, in turn, was the tool of Big Business. American society as a whole set up an ideal of success whose goal was riches and power. These could be secured only through corruption; yet society, in judging the race for power and riches, punished the losers and rewarded the winners. It trampled on the "good" men and poured the material wealth of life into the laps of the "bad"; it set a premium on corruption.

The discontent expressed by Steffens, Tarbell and Baker in the magazines was echoed in the novels of Booth Tarkington, Frank Norris, David Graham Philips, Winston Churchill and Upton Sinclair. Those of us who began to read and think at this time became accustomed to the idea, first, that American capitalism was corrupt from top to bottom; second, that art and politics were closely related. Both ideas came from purely American sources. The scene involved was the United States alone; the muckrakers were native-born Americans.

Louis Smith and my other socialist friends, however, assured me that mere exposure, mere protest, mere muckraking was futile. A vice commission might be appointed and its report might be very illuminating; a pure food and drugs act might be passed; but the rot would grow deeper. There was no cure for capitalism; it had to be exterminated if humanity was to progress. The muckraking movement was dying of its own impotence. It could not even survive its name, plastered on it sarcastically by T. R. himself. In 1914 Charles Edward Russell explained the pernicious political anemia which killed muckraking. Magazines of exposure had been strangled to death by the withdrawal of advertising. The few which had survived had become purveyors of cheap fiction and open apologists for the system. But more powerful even than the advertiser, with his censorship of reading matter, was the growing indifference of the middle classes to exposure of the crimes of Big Business.

My socialist friends spoke for an American movement which had grown up alongside the muckrakers. The more alert workers had discovered the death of the Gilded Age earlier than the intellectuals did. State and federal troops and private thugs had taught them in the Coeur d'Alene, Buffalo, Pullman and Tennessee strikes that the prevailing economic system was not merely corrupt, but that it was the property of the bankers and industrialists who had no desire to "share" its blessings with the "common man," and would stop at nothing to maintain their privileges.

The first decade of the century saw the growth of two revolutionary movements rooted in America: the Socialist party and the Industrial Workers of the World. Both groups were primarily interested in the industrial worker; they advocated, supported and organized strikes; they fought for higher wages and shorter hours. But the Socialist party, as distinguished from the I.W.W., had a special appeal for the more discontented sections of the middle class. True, American socialism spoke of the powerful class of capitalists who dominated the economic and political destinies of the country, and of the large army of industrial wage earners in a precarious condition of existence; and it spoke of the clear-cut conflict between the capitalists and the wage earners. It was this gospel of the class struggle that attracted workers like Louis Smith to the Party. What attracted middle-class elements was the Party's attacks on big capital, attacks which seemed sharper and more consistent than those of the liberal reformers.

The Socialist party tried to avoid the rigidity of dogma and organizational discipline which marked Daniel de Leon's Socialist Labor party, the dominant radical group of the nineties. This led to a looseness of organization, theory and policy which opened the movement to various social classes, groups and individuals who for one reason or another were dissatisfied with contemporary society. The socialist movement contained orthodox Marxists, revisionists and Fabians, and middle-class liberals for whom the word "socialism" concealed, from themselves chiefly, the ideals of the muckrakers. It contained people who despised political action to the point of syndicalism, and people who cared more for election campaigns than for strikes. There were in it advocates of sabotage and violence, and disciples of nonresistance; ministers of the gospel and militant atheists. On the fringes of the party, as around all movements opposed to the foundations of the status quo, were faddists and cranks of all kinds with their own private schemes for rational eating, free love and the quickest way to achieve socialism.

When Eugene Debs, presidential candidate of the Socialist party in the 1904 elections, polled over 400,000 votes, radicals and reactionaries alike began to look upon the socialists as America's future Opposition party. Both sides of the barricade took the "rising tide of socialism" seriously. Around this "tide" there developed a voluminous literature, for and against. At school and in the library, my friends and I read and heard about the "menace" of socialism; on the street corners and in the meeting halls we heard about its "promise." The publications of the socialist publishing house of Charles H. Kerr Company— the red-covered pamphlets of Karl Marx and the popular brochures of American socialists—circulated by the millions. In the Middle West *The Appeal to Reason* reached an enormous mass of farmers, factory workers and railwaymen; in our own city the *Call* became familiar in every working-class neighborhood.

In Gene Debs, Mother Jones and Bill Haywood, the socialists and wobblies found remarkable leaders of native American stock and working-class origin. But just as the Russian revolutionary movement drew into its ranks at one time or another members of the middle classes and even of the nobility, so the American Socialist party stirred young men and women of the upper and middle classes to join its organizations and preach its ideas. Names like J. G. Phelps Stokes, Robert Rives La Monte and William English Walling alarmed the chief beneficiaries of the System. Such converts to socialism made it appear that the ruling caste was breaking up from within, especially since the radicals from the Social Register called loudly and immediately for a thoroughgoing revolution.

Prewar American radicalism probably reached its peak in 1912, when Debs polled nearly a million votes, and the most dramatic of the capitalist candidates ran on platforms of social righteousness and the New Freedom. It was the year when the names of Joe Ettor and Arturo Giovannitti, leaders of the Lawrence textile strike, became household words, and when Emma Goldman could pack meeting halls in any city with lectures on anarchism, free love and Shakespeare.

The flavor of 1912 was caught by Floyd Dell when he called it the Lyric Year. A new spirit had come to America, and not in politics alone. Poetry was entering upon its American renaissance with the foundation of Harriet Monroe's magazine in Chicago; the Irish Players and Maurice Brown were instigating the New American theater; Marcel Duchamps' "Nude Descending a Staircase" aroused the rebel sons and daughters of the Babbittry to the meaning of "modern" art; the emancipated sexual theories of Edward Carpenter, Havelock Ellis and Auguste Forel had emigrated to our shores and followed close on the heels of the army of men and women fighting for woman suffrage; and gay clothing, colored neckties, bobbed-haired and smoking women flaunted the victory of the younger generation of that day over the prostrate body of puritanism. For the next five years, this "new spirit" was to dominate American intellectual life.

§ 4

The day I entered Boys' High School in the spring of 1912, the opening ceremonies at the annex were presided over by Old Man Jackson, six feet tall, gray-haired, with a face as dark as an Indian's, and a voice that shook the house. He must have been sixty at this time. My class elected me to recite something on the platform, and I chose Browning's poem about the boy at Ratisbon. We were already romantics. I took all my reading in history very personally; its episodes were individual experiences. When I read about the Civil War, I was indignant with the slaveholding South and adored Lincoln; in the Revolutionary War I was on the side of Washington. But greater than all these was the brightest star of the French Revolution, the slayer of the *ancien régime* (that sounded better than the *old regime*)— Napoleon. Loyalty to a great leader in a great cause—the cause of freedom—was a beautiful thing; and Browning's poem was a beautiful poem, and in the ignorance and pride of my fifteen years I tried my best to make it sound beautiful. The auditorium started to applaud, but Old Man Jackson stood up and raised his hand.

"Stop!" he bellowed. "That recitation doesn't count! It's nothing but imperialism. Bonaparte was an enemy of mankind. That poem glorifies militarism, despotism, all that is inimical to democracy. What do you little fools know about war? I knew a man who fought at Balaklava. He told me about it. It was the most horrible, bloody affair in the world. Hardly anyone came out of it alive. And look at that bosh by that sentimental idiot Tennyson. The *Charge of the Light Brigade,* indeed! It's a lie, I tell you."

The students did not move. I started to leave the platform, dumb with embarrassment. Old Man Jackson stopped me and said gently:

"Don't forget to pronounce the *d* at the end of a word. Say kille*d*, not kil*t*. You're not an Irishman."

The students laughed and the Old Man went on:

"I don't mean to spoil your fun, boys; but you will have to make some serious decisions as you grow older. American democracy is menaced by the Man on Horseback. If you don't look out, we'll have him someday. All this militaristic poppycock from Browning to our own sword-rattlers is dangerous. You must prevent the Man on Horseback. We'll have a war someday, and that will bring him, and his name will no doubt be Theodore Roosevelt."

War seemed remote in the spring of 1912; but Teddy was all there. It was a presidential year and he was stirring up the land. But if Mr. Jackson, our history teacher, had any fear for the old principles of Jeffersonian democracy to which he clung, he must have lost it by the fall of the year. Everybody knew that Taft was done for, and that Wilson and Roosevelt were so "progressive" you could hardly distinguish them from the socialists. The "great commoner," William J. Bryan, attacked the "predatory corporations"; Woodrow Wilson, the apostle of the New Freedom, declared that the "government of the United States at present is the foster-child of the special interests"; and Roosevelt said in the platform of the Progressive party that "behind the ostensible government sits enthroned an invisible government owing no allegiance and acknowledging no responsibility to the people." Presidential candidates now sounded like the muck-raking journalists whom they had denounced. Even the Republican party had to whistle for middle-class and working-class votes. That elder statesman, Elihu Root, revealed to the betrayed public that the capital of the Empire State was not in Albany but at 49 Broadway, the office of Boss Platt.

Louis Smith and his socialist friends laughed. They said the capital of the Empire State *and* the United States was divided between 26 Broadway and 23 Wall Street. Taft, Wilson and Roosevelt were kidding the public; only the Socialist party represented the interests of the American people, of all who toiled with hand and brain. But the socialists were in a minority. The sympathies of our neighborhood were divided between Roosevelt and Wilson. We did not then understand why Roosevelt appealed so powerfully to the middle classes, although his melodramatic flourishes on behalf of Americanism, his theatrical personality as a whole, were obviously calculated to stir the "people." But, under the tutelage of socialist workers like Louis, we did understand that this *enfant terrible* was, in his consuming ambition to play first fiddle in national politics, of necessity a "tool" of big capital; for whatever a man's social origin may be, however lofty his speeches about freedom, however "sincere" his attacks on "predatory wealth," he cannot occupy a responsible role in the capitalist state without serving the interests of the capitalist class which controls that state. It was years before we discovered that Roosevelt was not especially "sincere," that he was a demagogue, pure and simple, cleverly playing the game of the Big Business he pretended to "curb." But what I have said about him above does not anticipate the story in any way; at the time I am now describing socialists denounced him as a tool of capitalism, and I heard such phrases again and again from Louis Smith.

The campaign of 1912, however, resulted in the election of another type of demagogue. Woodrow Wilson's "progressive" rhetoric sprang neither from a hatred of private property nor from a love of the masses, but from the traditions of the slaveowning Southern aristocracy; from the planter's hatred not of exploitation, but of rival exploiters who benefited by such economic arrangements as the protective tariff. Wilson's New Freedom was the slaveholder's nostalgia for the old "freedom" which he had enjoyed before the triumph of industry.

§ 5

During the presidential campaign I was partial to Roosevelt. When
T. R. was shot in Chicago, my mother hid the newspaper for a day,
fearing the shock would upset me. But to believe vaguely in socialism and to mistake Roosevelt's demagogy for it was a minor paradox
at fifteen. I had more important matters to worry about.

Who was I?

The boy who favored Roosevelt and the boy who favored socialism
were the same; both ideas appeared to him identical; both sprang
from the concept of universal justice, absorbed from relatives, teachers
and religion in childhood. But there were other selves, distinct and
seemingly unrelated, which jostled each other. I felt like a house inhabited by many strange people, unacquainted with each other, any
one of whom might at any moment become my "self."

Against some of these older "selves" I was in violent conflict. I
had begun to disbelieve in God and said so at home. The presence of
father, mother and seven children at the dinner table gave the discussions a public character. My father was no fanatic. He had grown
lax in the observance of the Law; he had himself fed me milk and
ham in restaurant, with the strict injunction to say nothing about it
to mother. But he drew the line at atheism.

"Think what you like," he shouted, "but keep your foolish ideas
to yourself! Don't spoil the other children!"

The other children were my two younger brothers whom I was
corrupting with godlessness. What the girls thought did not matter;
women were not supposed to think. But though I had ceased to believe
in God, I believed in my father. To please him, I still went to the
synagogue on the most important holidays, just as to please my grandfather he had pretended in the vanished village not to go to the
barber's.

I was also divided in my feelings about the race. I had lost
interest in the Young Zionist Club, but retained a sense of nationalism.
The stories which I continued publishing in the *Young Judaean* might
be called propaganda, but I did not know that word. I was not trying
to prove anything; that was the way I saw the world, through the
prism of the movement I had entered at ten and really earlier, when
I could first understand words of any kind, and could feel my grandfather's love for his people.

Sometimes the stories I wrote were purely imaginative, like the

one about the Maranos in Spain, those Jews, who, to escape the Inquisi-
tion, led an underground existence, posed as Christians before the
agents of the terror, but in the secret shadows of their cellars followed
the faith and rituals of their fathers. Or the one about the soldiers in
the opposing armies of the Balkan war who kill each other for "alien"
peoples although they are Jews. Other stories were attempts at realism,
with scenes of the candy store where I bought ice-cream sodas, of the
streets where our rival gangs battled with ash-can covers, banana stalks,
dry corncobs, watermelon rind picked from the gutter in the heat of
battle.

Although the sacredness and solidarity of the Jewish race was still
an appealing idea, it failed to stand up under the wear and tear of
everyday life. As Russian Jews, our parents were despised by the German Jews, the most aristocratic of the race. In turn the Russian Jews
despised the Hungarian, the Polish and, above all, the Galician Jews.

"I would rather," our mothers would say to us, "that you should—
God forbid—marry a *shikse* [a gentile girl] than a galitzianer [a
Galician Jewess]."

A common term for the Galician Jews was *die gestrofte,* the
punished ones. The defense for this prejudice was the same as for
all race prejudice; our parents said about the Galician Jews what the
German Jews said about us, and what the gentiles said about all Jews,
and what the Anglo-Saxon gentiles said about the Italian gentiles, and
what the white gentiles said about the Negroes. They were dirty, they
stank, they were low and uncivilized.

When my friends and I became acquainted with socialism, we
began to believe that these regional prejudices had an economic base.
The German Jews were the bankers, the lawyers, the judges; the Russian Jews were small businessmen; the Galicians and Poles came from
extremely poor regions; they were the "punished ones." Poverty was at
the root of the contempt to which they were exposed.

But there were divisions among the Jews which transcended even
these regional-economic differences; divisions which took no account
of German, Russian or Austrian origin, and no account even of Jew or
gentile. The myth of *kol yisroel khaverim*—all Jews are comrades—
was like the American myth that all men are born free and equal. It
exploded for us in a strike in which Louis Smith was arrested, a strike
in which Jewish bosses hired Italian gangsters to beat up and murder
Jewish workers. In the last analysis, it was obviously not race against
race, or nation against nation: it was class against class. I accepted this

idea at fifteen, yet retained the old national illusions too. My socialist friends had never given the problem of nationalities much thought. As a compromise, I began to frequent meetings of the Poalay Zionists. These were Jewish workers who were at the same time socialists and nationalists. They believed that a return to Palestine was the sole solution for the painful Jewish problem, but that in Palestine the class war between Jewish capitalist and Jewish proletarian would continue, the sole solution for which was the workers' state.

If anything was calculated to keep my Jewish feeling alive, it was the race prejudice I encountered in high school. Among teachers and students alike, the social scale began with the Nordics at the top. First and best were those of English extraction; then came the French, and below them, the Germans. Further down in the abyss of our social life, were the "inferior" races, Italians, Greeks, Russians, Poles; and lower still were the Jews. But the Jewish students were themselves divided along class lines. The boys whose fathers were bankers and lawyers belonged to fraternities from which we were excluded. The faculty did not conceal its feelings. Our French teacher, who did not permit a single Jew to join his Cercle Français, once shouted to me in class:

"What do you want to go to college for? American colleges should be for Americans! You're not even a European; you're an Oriental—a Jew!"

The school elections for officers of the general students' association reflected these race and class divisions. The gentiles had their own candidate; the rich Jewish students nominated a banker's son. The third group nominated me for president and a gentile for vice-president. This group was socialist. Its leading spirits were active in the Young People's Socialist League and wanted to break down racial barriers. Whatever we had learned about politics in the socialist locals we brought into this campaign. The gentile party had the support of the athletes, the Jewish aristocrats, the support of their fraternities. Our group, which consisted of gentiles and Jews and sought to transcend racial barriers, had the orators, writers and artists. For the first time in the school's history we organized a party called (O echoes of 1912!) the Progressive party. We made speeches at "rallies," plastered the school with posters, organized defense squads against the athletes who wanted to beat up our candidates, and were elected.

The following term we discovered that the Jews were by no means the most despised race in America. Here in the land of the free, the asylum of the oppressed, there was a race of pariahs even "lower" than we. The Negro athlete Hall was acknowledged to be one of the school's best football players; yet, when St. Paul's Academy refused to play against a Negro, our coach took him out of the game. There was a piece in the papers about it. Our players, Jew and gentile alike, were indignant, probably because they lost the game.

I organized a campaign for the restoration of Hall to the team. We called a demonstration in front of the school, gave statements to the press, and my friend Edwin Fadiman (whose brother Clifton was in later years to become a literary critic) wrote an editorial about it in the school paper which he edited. The fight was carried into the classroom where the football coach, a Southern gentleman, also taught us history after a fashion.

We were then studying the Reconstruction Period, and took advantage of the fact. Mr. Wilson, is it not true that, despite the fourteenth, fifteenth and sixteenth amendments, the Negro in the South is for all practical purposes disfranchised? Mr. Wilson, we have heard that Negroes are discriminated against in industry; is that true? Is it not true, Mr. Wilson, that even in the North, which they say fought the Civil War to free the Negro, there is the same race prejudice as in the South?

That was too much for the instructor.

"I know perfectly well," he shouted to the class, "why you're so damned excited about this nigger Hall. It's because you're Jews!"

"And you took Hall off the team," I said, "because you are a Southern gentleman."

I was a bad character. The school principal considered expelling me. He asked me whether I would not like to be transferred to another school. I refused; but felt it my duty to warn my parents that their sacrifices in getting me an education might be wasted. My mother said:

"Don't give up the fight."

The fight did not last much longer. When Mr. Wilson shouted to me in a crowded classroom, "I am not afraid of you!" I knew I was not going to be expelled.

The episode intensified my internationalism. The idea of the class struggle and the idea of freeing the oppressed nationalities became inseparable in my mind. As captain of the debating team, I had no choice of subjects, and had to accept what the faculty advisers of the competing schools selected, like the time when we debated Robert Smith's team on whether or not New York City should own and operate the local traction, gas and electric plants. But in the oratorical contests, each speaker chose his own subject, and on the night when the conservative students advocated a bigger navy, and attacked socialism, our speakers urged Philippine independence, the abolition of child labor, and improvements in the condition of the Southern Negro.

§ 6

Alongside of the self that was a fading nationalist, and the self that was a developing socialist, there was rising in me a new self, interested in something which seemed to be connected with the real world of racial persecution and class war, and yet to stretch beyond it. I still continued to draw every day, often late into the night. I showed my drawings to friends, or included them in the "magazine" (handwritten or typed) which I issued for my brothers and sisters, and to which I trained them to contribute.

But I had given up the idea of being a painter. My father was right; you cannot be everything. I was going to be either a lawyer or a journalist—I had not decided which—and drawing must remain a hobby. The acute sense of the visual world, of sound and sensation, which compelled me to draw daily had to find an outlet elsewhere. My stories in the *Young Judaean* satisfied me less and less; they began to represent ideas rather than feelings. You talked them over with the Neumans before you wrote them—and yet there were things you saw and felt which you could not talk over with anybody. One Sunday, after I had read an essay to the Young Zionist Club, I witnessed outside its doors a scene that moved me deeply.

The street lamps were low and the cobblestones dark. The gaslight shone through the opening of the saloon's half-doors across the street. Suddenly they swung open. A man was pitched into the air. He fell on the sidewalk heavily. Four men came out of the saloon and kicked the man on the sidewalk. He staggered to his feet, feebly ran a few steps, and rolled into the gutter. His hat fell off, and his high bald head glistened in the dim light. The four men came over and started to kick him again. One of them kicked the bald head and it sounded like an empty cask, hollow and loud. A red gash opened, the forehead trickled blood. I went home miserable and depressed. Men were cruel animals. I stayed up all night writing the story, for nobody in particular.

Then there were feelings which had nothing to do with events, or referred to events which happened so long ago that they no longer mattered; the details were forgotten, only the mood remained. That you could say in poetry.

Not the kind of poetry you first wrote in which you made fun of George, the Grand Inquisitor of the Young Zionist Club. George was four years older than the rest of us. He was leaving high school when we entered it, and that made him a full-grown man. He knew many things we didn't, and laughed at our ignorance.

"So you never heard of Nietzsche? And you call yourself a writer!"

He was also an expert on the greatest mystery of all.

"So you never read Schopenhauer on women? And you expect to be a man!"

We read Schopenhauer on women and became properly cynical. But George was not satisfied.

"What about masturbation? Have you read Dr. Landes on masturbation?"

George was a very educated fellow. He said "masturbation" and not slang words like the bums in the street, or like the Italian boy, Salvator, who once gave me an illustrated lecture on the subject. That part of your body was a strange thing; it could throw you into a fever and you stopped thinking altogether; you became an animal. It held your entire fate. Dr. Landes said so. You found his pamphlets lying in the streets and they said that an improper sex life could ruin your health, wreck you with the most horrible diseases, and—this was the worst of all—destroy your mind.

My friend Sam, who was the wit of the Young Zionist Club, had a collection of Landes pamphlets and knew them by heart. He was worried about himself. He thought he suffered from a mysterious disease known as General Debility. Now that he had a job in a factory and could pay his own way, three pimples on his face sent him running to doctors. He worried about his sallow complexion, and was sure he was going crazy. One day they found his body in the factory shaft crushed by an elevator. I saw it laid out in his home just before the funeral, the first dead body I had ever seen. His family lived opposite the first house we moved to when we came to America, but after Sam's death I did not go through that block for five years.

The horror of the episode made me sick of George and his discourses on Nietzsche, Schopenhauer and Landes; I circulated satirical verses about George—very unjust, no doubt.

But there was another kind of poetry. In a book by a man named

Samuel Smiles, there were stories about two very remarkable people, Byron and Shelley, which you read over and over again. You read about them, too, in a book which you found in the high-school library; it was by some woman and was called *The Vanity and Insanity of Genius*. All geniuses were vain and insane, and Byron and Shelley were geniuses. But that was a minor matter. There was something much more important. Byron and Shelley were misunderstood and persecuted, just like you. They had troubles with the people around them and with their parents, like you; and above all they loved freedom more than anything else, like you. Their poetry, which you read in Palgrave's *Golden Treasury* at school, was the most wonderful thing in the world; it was something like the prophets of the Bible. There was in their poetry a spirit which also reminded you of the stories your mother and Slavsky told you.

My mother, unlike my father, was a great if indiscriminate reader. Evenings she often read aloud to me the cheap serials in the Yiddish press, but she read better things, too. She took time to tell me patiently the details of *The Kreutzer Sonata* and *Oblomoff*. Her talk had a literary flavor. If one of the children slept late, she would say, "Get up, Oblomoff!"

Slavsky was the son of her friend who had recently come to America from the vanished village. He was then about twenty-two, but he quickly learned English and founded the *Self-Culture Club*. Here you heard lectures about socialism, anarchism, Tolstoyism, the woman question and nonresistance. Most of the members came from middle-class homes, and the girls were better looking than in the Zionist Club. Sometimes we had distinguished visitors. Once a man named Prince Hopkins lectured to us about his experimental school in California. It was like a dream. The children were free; nobody bullied or beat them; they had their own workshops in which they built furniture, their own small trains which they operated themselves and in which they went places; and they studied geography not from dull textbooks but from a huge relief map of the world built on a lake. Around this world they traveled in small boats which they learned to run, and listened to "guides" tell them about various countries. How different from our own dingy school with its army drill, its police department, its dusty classrooms, its harsh discipline, its whackings with the ruler, its wretched nights of homework. If only we had been brought up that way. That's what Prince Hopkins said: if all the children of this world were trained in the freedom of his school, if the natural instincts of the child, uncorrupted by conventional discipline, were given free play, we would have a race of men and women that could build a new, beautiful life on this earth. We thought of our younger brothers and sisters; but Mr. Hopkins explained that under present social conditions a school like his was very expensive and was unfortunately open only for the privileged few with lots of money. However, it was a *model* of what *could* be done *if*.

The main lecturer at the club, however, was Slavsky himself. He once spent two months reading us installments of a book called *Chelkash* by a writer of whom we had never heard, a man named Maxim Gorky, a Russian. It was a stirring book, unlike anything we had ever heard. It was not about princes, princesses, or knights, like *Ivanhoe;* or about traders and Indians like Fenimore Cooper; about superior people like Nietzsche and Schopenhauer; or about English gentlemen like Byron and Shelley. It was a story about a tramp, like Apanas, only better because Chelkash had begun to think for himself and was critical of conventional society.

§ 7

If I could only find out what was really good, really wise, really noble, I could feel at home in the world. Every book and magazine I read, every speaker I heard, every friend I made was for me a possible guide in my perplexity. I was so anxious to integrate myself, to reconcile the warring cultures which struggled within me for dominance, that for years I gratefully remembered every person, every phrase which influenced me. In the confused world in which I lived—whose fragments echoed Russia, America and Palestine; Theodor Herzl and Karl Marx; Byron and Shelley; Napoleon and Eugene Debs—he who helped to put the pieces together was a benefactor.

Naïvely conscious of my own efforts, I stayed up late into the night studying when I should have taken advantage of adolescence to build up my body; I read and wrote and thought as hard as I could. But I felt that the world I was trying to understand lay outside me. I could not spin it out of myself; I could only become part of it if I listened to people, watched events, pondered over books. I remembered for years who it was that first taught me to pronounce an English word correctly, who introduced me to socialism, who gave me Bernard Shaw to read. The boy felt like a house being painfully put together by many architects, bricklayers, plasterers and painters. It was there—the world. If all men would understand it properly, if all

knew what was really good, wise and noble, we would build a finer
life upon this earth.

Who would explain to me the relations of things to each other?
Our schoolteachers paid little attention to our actual lives. We had to
take exams about cross-pollinization of flowers, but no teacher would
tell us whether or not Dr. Landes was right. We knew the name of
every king of England from William the Conqueror down, but who
was this man Marx who drove wonderful people like Comrade Kirkpatrick and Comrade Russell to make speeches, and Louis Smith to
get his head cracked by the police? We had to memorize passages of
Goldsmith's *Deserted Village* for the examinations—but we memorized
Queen Mab and *Manfred* at home, for ourselves. They were not "required reading."

Under all this confusion there must be order; under the disparity,
unity. Perhaps I was only longing for the vanished village where God,
who was everywhere, explained everything by his mere existence. But
we had not yet learned to explain the present by the past, least of all
by our own psychological past. We had heard that the hand that
rocks the cradle rules the world, and did not believe it; but we had not
yet heard of Freud or the idea that the cradle contains the world.

We thought chiefly of the future, and looked for those who could
read it for us. Not everyone could do that. Only two keys could un-
lock our ears: one was moral, the other aesthetic; one password was
Justice, the other *Beauty.* Perhaps the ghosts of Uncle Moishe and
Yakelina haunted us, but were they not echoes of forces greater than
themselves? Were they not also houses painfully put together by many
architects, bricklayers, plasterers and painters? Was there not a world
outside themselves whose moods they uttered and passed on to us? IT
—the world—was there, outside.

Yet it came to us in fragments. When I talked with my mother
about Tolstoy or Goncharov, that was literature too; but you could
not talk with her about Byron and Shelley; and you certainly could
not talk with her about socialism. Louis Smith was simpler; he was a
worker with a clean will and an uncomplicated mind. He knew only
one thing: the world was divided into masters and slaves, capitalists
and workers. It was a miserable world full of poverty, ignorance, unemployment, sickness and war. That was unnecessary. Socialism would
cure it. He had no objections to Beauty, and no time for it. His whole
being was singly devoted to Justice. He smiled indulgently at my love
lyrics and took me to a meeting of his union where mistakes of the

last strike were analyzed. The socialist *Call,* too, was just without being beautiful. It could stir half our nature while leaving the other half indifferent.

One rainy afternoon, in the socialist local on Graham Avenue, the sixteen-year-old boy in search of heaven on earth found the Thing Itself. It was Just, Beautiful and American, Marx and Byron, Debs and Michelangelo, politics and poetry, the unity I was seeking. Somewhere in that mysterious Greenwich Village about which Mr. Gee had once told me, there were native Americans who had integrated the conflicting values of the world. These men did not share each other's views. But they were frank about that too. The magazine they published, the *Masses,* which lay in a neat pile on the shelves of the socialist headquarters, had no dividends to pay and nobody was trying to make money out of it. It could therefore afford to be a revolutionary and not a reform magazine; a magazine with a sense of humor and no respect for the respectable. It boasted of being frank, arrogant, impertinent, searching for the true causes; it was directed against rigidity and dogma, wherever it was found; it printed what was too naked or true for the money-making press. Its final policy—or so it said—was to do as it pleased and conciliate nobody, not even its readers. The lectures at the socialist local often bored me, but I went there every month to read this wonderful magazine.

The *Masses* editorials were written by a man named Max Eastman. He called himself a socialist, but he was different in many ways from Louis Smith. When old J. P. Morgan died in 1913, he said he could not "find any lesson in Mr. Morgan's death, will, or funeral." Morgan was not a bad man; he was about as good as the average, stronger than most, and more consistent too. He believed that his money belonged to him, and he stuck to that idea right to the end without making any deathbed restitutions. The *Masses* editor liked that. What he didn't like was the church's attitude toward the deceased. The church said Mr. Morgan had occupied himself with "the abiding" in life; but the *Masses* believed that there was only one class of people concerned in Mr. Morgan's death whom Jesus Christ would flay to the bones with sarcasm, namely, the hypocrites of the church who profess to speak his name.

Robert and I liked this editorial, but Louis furiously disagreed. No socialist, he said, ought to like anything about J. P. Morgan as a social figure. There was nothing especially attractive about his belief that his money belonged to him. Every parasite believed that; he had to kid himself as well as the public. If the *Masses* editor were a real revolutionary socialist instead of a half-ass intellectual he would not applaud Morgan's noble attitude toward his money; he would point out where that money came from—from the sweat and blood of the workers.

Louis's criticism increased our perplexity. Not only was the world divided into exploiters and exploited, masters and slaves, but the slaves themselves were divided into those who were class conscious and those who were Henry Dubbs; and class-conscious people were divided into those who were socialists like Louis Smith and those who were anarchists like my cousin Nachum-Nathan. And the socialists in turn were divided into those who were "revolutionary" and those who were "half-ass intellectuals."

But Robert and I were not to be dissuaded from the *Masses*. Its editors could write, and they were not crudely materialistic like the socialist soapboxers, like Fitzgibbons. We looked upon them as not only poets but scientists. That made their integration of conflicting values appear even stronger: politics, poetry *and* science; justice, beauty *and* knowledge. And they were revolutionary too, whatever Louis might say. For instance, they urged that in order to get a better world, the poor must be ill-content, and imprudent, and must marshal themselves against the rich. Relying on their superior numbers, the poor must take from the rich the sources of their privilege.

That was especially important for me at a moment when many of my friends who came from the poorest workers' families began to scoff at socialism. They frankly planned to use their education and their gifts to lift themselves out of the abyss to the heights of Louis Marshall and Aaron Levy, to be lawyers and judges, Republican and Democratic politicians and journalists. Socialism was only for the poor, and they were going to be rich; it was for the ignorant, and they were educated and intelligent. Yet here were people, somewhere in Greenwich Village, who were not ignorant. They had studied history and economics. You could be intelligent and educated and still be socialist.

Robert and I were extremely agitated by what we read in the *Masses*. From its pages we learned about the strike in the coal fields of West Virginia which was brutally crushed. For the first time in the history of free America, the civil courts were superseded by a military tribunal intent upon destroying the strike leaders.

There was also a silk strike in Paterson, led by the I.W.W., with Bill Haywood and Elizabeth Gurley Flynn at their head. There seemed to be some difference between the socialists and the I.W.W. Louis

Smith called the wobblies crazy; but they were all right, they fought "like steers" against the bosses. We had never seen steers fight, but we learned something about the I.W.W. from the *Masses*. John Reed described the "war in Paterson." All the violence was on one side— that of the mill owners. Their servants, the police, clubbed unresisting men and women and rode down law-abiding crowds; their paid mercenaries, the armed detectives, shot and killed innocent people; their newspapers published incendiary and crime-inciting appeals to mob violence against the strike leaders; their tool, the local judge, handed out heavy sentences to peaceful strikers whom the police arrested. The mill owners absolutely controlled the police, the press, the courts. What happened to Louis and his fellow strikers in the knit-goods shops happened elsewhere in America.

Did such things happen in Europe? We did not know. The newspapers published little European news, and what appeared we barely read. Contemporary Europe hardly existed for us. The only Europe we knew or cared about was the eighteenth century Europe of the French Revolution, the Europe of Napoleon, Byron and Shelley. We had never heard about the Russian Revolution of 1905, and when the Yiddish papers which our mothers read described the ovations in New York to Gershuni, the social revolutionary who had escaped from the Czarist police, we merely asked, Who is this man? why all the fuss?

The *Masses* taught us, among other things, the difference between liberalism and revolution. Our socialist friends who were workers felt this difference and acted upon it; but they could not explain it as lucidly as Max Eastman could. Someone wrote to the *Masses*:

"If you call yourself liberal-minded, why do you stick to socialism alone? Isn't that a dogma? Furthermore, you say you don't believe in dogmatism; then why don't you open your columns to all the other radical reform movements?"

Very important questions. You could not deny that your anarchist cousin Nachum-Nathan and Old Man Jackson, the Jeffersonian Democrat, were as sincere as Louis Smith. The *Masses* editor replied that socialism was not a movement which lay parallel to other schemes of social regeneration; it did not merely extend a little farther beyond them or move a little more impatiently. No, socialism was decidedly contradictory to them. Socialism differed from other schemes of social regeneration in its method, which was to promote the class struggle. If socialism were merely an extreme kind of reform, it would be utopian and foolish. It was not reform at all, but a revolutionary movement; it looked to the conquest of power by those who did not hold it. It advocated the conflict. Therefore, to invite into a socialist magazine those who opposed the conflict would be neither liberal nor illiberal; it would be simply foolish and untrue to principle. Liberality demanded that we be hospitable to ideas other than ours, not ideas which contradicted ours. And so, while the *Masses* believed in liberty of the mind as well as the body, it would not open its pages to those who opposed the central principle of its faith—the principle of revolution.

This sounded true; but the more you got into this socialist stuff, the more perplexing it was. America, for instance, was having some kind of trouble with Mexico. The *Masses* assured us that President Wilson did not want war. Then why was he pressing Mexico so hard? According to the *Masses* the President felt compelled to do enough in Mexico to retain the diplomatic leadership of the United States, and avert acts of aggression by European nations. He might be forced into war, much against his will. Some fifty thousand American working-men might be invited to march over the border and shoot Mexican workingmen in order to save them from being exploited by European capital. The American president, who did not want war, would be compelled to wage it in order to protect the Mexican workers against the European plutocrats.

That sounded true too. But here was Louis, kicking as usual. These *Masses* people, he repeated, were a bunch of half-ass intellectuals. They had swallowed Wilson's bunk hook, line and sinker. Wilson might hand out all the fine phrases in the world; the fact was, he did want war. And he wanted it not to save Mexican workers from exploitation by European capital, but to keep them for exploitation by American capital.

We loved and respected Louis; but he could not convince us that the *Masses* was not a revolutionary socialist publication. Perhaps they were wrong about Wilson's policy in Mexico. What did that prove? Look at the German socialists. Here was the largest and most powerful socialist party in the world, and yet when Karl Liebknecht made a sensational exposure in the Reichstag of the corruption of the French and German press by the German arms manufacturers; when he showed that these manufacturers were deliberately promoting a war-scare for the sake of business; when he also showed that the arms manufacturers were in close and corrupt relations with the German bureaucracy, *for the first time in the history of the Party, the social-*

democratic members of the Reichstag decided to make it possible for the Kaiser's government to obtain money for warlike purposes.

The *Masses* condemned this betrayal of socialism. William English Walling was heartbroken by the action of the socialist Reichstag members. A long degeneration, he called it, from the revolutionary position of the early German socialist congresses over which August Bebel presided; the majority of the socialist deputies had adopted a position on militarism less advanced than that of many nonsocialist advocates of peace. Comrade Walling felt that a socialist must oppose capitalist wars *at all costs,* and surely this attitude was revolutionary.

§ 8

Probably one reason why Louis and other socialist workers of our acquaintance could not instill in our minds a critical attitude toward the *Masses* was that it seemed to reconcile our warring selves. Palgrave was Beauty; Marx was Justice; the *Masses* was both. It not only discussed politics and economics from a revolutionary viewpoint, but published drawings and poems which themselves combined Beauty and Justice. They attacked capitalism, they called for freedom. The magazine did not separate the struggle of the working class, we thought, from the yearning for Beauty. It even published poems by workers. Here, for example, was a poem by a coal miner on strike at Paint Creek, West Virginia. The circumstances under which this poem was written were dramatic. Civil war raged in West Virginia between the Steel Trust, with its mercenary militia, and the mine workers affiliated with the American Federation of Labor. In one engagement, sixteen miners were killed with machine guns. The governor declared West Virginia to be in a state of insurrection; he promulgated martial law. The people of the United States were kept in ignorance of the armed tyranny which prevailed in that region. The representative of the Associated Press was provost marshal! Out of this bloody class conflict an anonymous worker had created this poem:

> The hills are very bare and cold and lonely;
> I wonder what the future months will bring?
> The strike is on—our strength would win, if only—
> O, Buddy, how I'm longing for the Spring!
>
> They've got us down—their martial lines enfold us;
> They've thrown us out to feel the Winter's sting;

And yet, by God, those curs could never hold us;
Nor could the dogs of hell do such a thing!

It isn't just to see the hills beside me
Grow fresh and green with every growing thing;
I only want the leaves to come and hide me,
To cover up my vengeful wandering.

I will not watch the floating clouds that hover
Above the birds that warble on the wing;
I want to use this GUN from under cover—
O, Buddy, how I'm longing for the Spring!

You see them there below, the damned scab-herders!
The puppets on the greedy Owners' String;
We'll make them pay for all their dirty murders—
We'll show them how a starving hate can sting!

They riddled us with volley after volley;
We heard their speeding bullets zip and ring;
But soon we'll make them suffer for their folly—
O, Buddy, how I'm longing for the Spring!

Was this poetry? Certainly it was not like Shelley. It sounded
more like Robert W. Service or Ella Wheeler Wilcox except for its
idea. But that was the important thing. The idea was greater poetry
than Longfellow, or Whittier, or Thomas Love Peacock. Out of the
heart of the American working class there had arisen a nameless miner
to sing a fighting proletarian ballad, a poem about a strike, a poem
calling for armed resistance against tyranny.

Louis Smith insisted that you mustn't take poetry too much to heart.
He believed in the power of the understanding and the will, synonymous for him with the proletarian revolution. Poetry was sentiment,
and sentiment about anything but Justice was likely to interfere with
the struggle for socialism.

Yet how about Beauty? One of our beloved English poets said
truth is beauty, beauty truth; that was all we needed to know. But
we wanted to know more. What was the relation of Beauty to Truth?
to Justice?

There was one *Masses* writer who seemed to be more interested in
poetry than in politics. Month after month I followed his articles
which by their charm, sincerity and directness moved me more deeply
than the cold and casuistic editorials. Floyd Dell had a disconcerting

and convincing way of connecting literature with revolution. He never beat about the bush, or hid behind ambiguous phrases. Reviewing Theodore Dreiser's *A Traveller at Forty,* Dell at once raised the question: *what has this book got to say about the socialist revolution?* Judged by this all-important criterion, Dreiser did not come off very well. The trouble with Dreiser, according to my favorite critic, was his Passive Attitude, his addiction to popular notions of Darwinism, which said that man cannot interfere with the alleged laws of evolution.

That was all wrong, Dell maintained. We had revised our biologic notions to take *revolution* into account. We could not merely look on passively while the process of life was processing; we had to *do* something about it *ourselves,* even if it was only to pull judiciously at other people's coattails. The difference between Dreiser and Dell seemed to be that Dreiser believed Life was above everything; it went on regardless of what we did. He tried to dispose of revolution not by hating or ignoring it, but by accepting it as "interesting." The revolutionist planned utopias, the artist painted, the fine lady dressed for the ball, the prostitute smiled invitations to a new man—and Life went on. Life had always been so and always would be so. A mad world but an "interesting" one. Dell, on the other hand, seemed to believe that revolution was more important than artists. The world could be changed. According to whether you lifted your hand or stayed it, the world would be different.

That was a wonderful idea. My friends and I were no longer to be houses put together by outside architects; we were to be our own architects—and architects of a new world. We had a moral choice; what the world would be like depended on what we did. But, alas, life was not so simple. Dell's essay contained a second idea which seemed to cancel the first. We are living, he said, in the twentieth century; Dreiser was still in the nineteenth. For the purposes of fiction that was all right. It was absurd to quarrel with an artist about the means by which he achieves his effects. *Sister Carrie* justified mid-nineteenth century pessimism; a book as good would justify even Swedenborgianism, or the theory that we live on the inside of the earth. It was only when Dreiser stepped out of fiction and wrote about modern Europe that he needed a modern mind.

This idea contradicted the notion of revolution as the ultimate criterion of art. The writer, it appeared, was divided into two unrelated parts. On the one hand, he was an "artist." As such you could not quarrel with him about the ideas contained in his "creative" work or the means he used to achieve his effects. On the other hand, he was also a man, subject to the judgment of other men. The writer's "artistic" self had nothing to do with his social self. In his novels he might be a nineteenth century pessimist; in his travel books, essays and articles he must be a twentieth century socialist. This was being like employers who went to church on Sundays and shot strikers on weekdays; or like myself, whose ideas were slowly and stubbornly trickling toward socialism, and whose poetry flowed secretly from the vanished village. Perhaps the integration I was seeking was not at all necessary. Perhaps you could live in several contradictory worlds at once, be a socialist on the platform and a Swedenborgian in art. Perhaps you could at one and the same time lift your hand to make the world different, and believe that we live on the inside of the earth. If you did the former as a man, no one could quarrel with you for the latter as an artist.

I lived this kind of dual life. From my verses about trees, skies and flowers one could find out little about our tenement. My poetry was Swedenborgian; it lived inside the earth; it was only my mind that tried to live in the twentieth century. That mind was the product of conflicting cultures; but the more it absorbed the culture prevailing in America, the more it was affected by its dualism—a dualism that cut deep into the socialist movement as well.

Art seemed to have no relation to life, dream to reality. When I left Russia for America, I thought I was leaving the land of tyranny, frustration and decay for the land of freedom, opportunity and progress. The America I first saw was a stinking tenement. From two such tenements we moved for lack of rent; from the third we were evicted; in the fourth we stayed until I was eighteen. The last was an old wooden box. We lived on the top floor. Feeling your way blindly, you walked up four black flights. Even when the street was sunniest, no light penetrated the tenement's hallways. The stairs were littered with paper, fruit skin and dust; the whole house gave out the acrid odor of cats. When you got up early to go to school, you could hear the machines of the knit-goods shop in the back yard rattling; when you got back at dusk from Hebrew School, they were still rattling. Our flat ran the length of the house; the kitchen faced the yard, the parlor the street. Only these two rooms had windows; between them lay three dark windowless cubicles, with a bed in each. The kitchen had a stove, a table with a torn oilcloth, several chairs. The "parlor" was bare except for an uncovered wooden table and an old couch. In the summer you could be alone in the parlor, reading or drawing, or looking out the window at the life in the street. In winter the kitchen was the only warm room, but you had to sleep in the icy cubicles.

In this tenement I read books, drew pictures, wrote stories and poems, or did homework. You learned nothing about drawing in school; the strawberry boxes and apples were not very exciting. I liked to draw people I saw and people I read about in books like *Les Misérables* and *The Three Musketeers*. The child is supposed to be an anarchist, unspoiled by conventional prejudices; his drawings are said to represent his own direct impressions of the world. I lived in a world apart perhaps even more than most children, for I was being cut off from my parents by a new language and a new culture. While they still lived in an extension of the Old World, their children were becoming Americans. Yet no child, as no adult, lives in a vacuum; we were molded not only by home, school and companions, but by magazines and newspapers. Happy Hooligan and Buster Brown marched across our imaginations with Jean Valjean and d'Artagnan.

I drew when the visual sense was strongest. There were hours when one's whole being melted into the surrounding glory of the external world, no less glorious because it was dirty. The tenement, the garbage can, the cat on the fence, the gangsters leaning against Fox's Folly seemed wonderful because they existed. If you looked long enough at anything, you became that thing; when you drew a friend and suddenly saw the mirror behind him you caught your face mimicking his.

But not all the world was visual. Things happened, and you had thoughts about those things, and you could not draw those thoughts. You could draw one episode out of the thing you wanted to tell, but the sequence of events was arrested. If you wanted to tell what happened, you had to write a story—about the Maranos in Spain, the hardships of the Jew in America, the gang fights on the block.

Not all feelings could be told in a story. Some feelings were intense and had nothing to do with any immediate episode you could remember. If the feeling came from something that just happened, or happened yesterday, it was something you didn't care to tell as an episode. Yet you had to utter the feeling; it was so strong that it overwhelmed everything else; you could not work, play, think or sleep until you expressed that feeling. First the feeling would come as a melody in your head, or as rhythm beating steadily; then words came and rhymes and you were starting to think out something which you called a poem. And you were so naïve that you took the jingles seriously.

One feeling which came often was loneliness. You were lonely in the American ghetto; you longed for some place and did not know where it was. You sat late at night in the frozen unfurnished parlor; the gaslight flickered shadows across your notebook; and you wrote verses about your secret dreams. There was a dream of love.

> The sounds that rode upon the wind,
> The dewy odors and the sea,
> Are merely mist; but this I mind:
> I dreamed of thee.

You could hear the clatter of dishes from the kitchen, the clanging of the iron stove shaking out ashes, the yelling of the kids in the hall playing cops and robbers. Oh, to get out of this filthy hellhole! That meant work; it meant going to the "roaring city." Poetry, daydreams now seemed to stand between you and the real world.

> But O! I pray a little longer,
> Let me muse upon the mountain,
> Pipe my songs to my beloved
> By the aromatic fountain.

It was a lie, a dream, a fantasy. You had no beloved; you mused in a stinking tenement; the aroma you smelt was the aroma of garbage.

§ 9

The real world was different. The workers in our neighborhood were talking not about aromatic fountains, but about wage cuts and Frank Tannenbaum. Louis Smith brought me the clippings and explained just where Tannenbaum was right and where he was wrong, where socialism and syndicalism overlapped and where they diverged. Tannenbaum was a young wobbly who that winter organized unemployed workers and led them to churches where they demanded bread and shelter. On the night of March 4, 1914, just two years after the New Freedom entered the White House, Tannenbaum made one of his usual speeches in Rutgers Square on the East Side. He told a crowd of unemployed workers what the trouble was with capitalism, why they were jobless, why the interests of capital and labor were irreconcilable; why the police, the army and the courts were the "tools" of capital.

At the end of his meeting, the young orator told the men to line up in twos and threes on the sidewalk. They would all march to a church to get food; if they failed to get it in a church, they would go to a bakery. About three hundred men under Tannenbaum's leadership marched to the church of St. Alphonsus. Suddenly two men who had been following the march from Rutgers Square came up to Tannenbaum and disclosed that they were detectives. They said the jobless men could not enter the church without the rector's permission. Leaving the three hundred men in the street, Tannenbaum, accompanied by the two detectives, went into the church to get the necessary permission. The rector refused.

"Do you call this the spirit of Christ," the young leader said, "to turn hungry and homeless men away?"

"I will not let you talk to me like this," the rector said.

When Tannenbaum and the detectives got outside the rectory, they saw the unemployed men had entered the church on their own initiative. Quietly and in perfect order the workers without work took seats near the altar. As Tannenbaum and the two detectives walked down the aisle, an assistant rector stood up in a back pew and said in a loud voice:

"All those who do not belong to this church will please leave."

Some of the workers groaned. Frank Tannenbaum stood in the doorway and said:

"Come on, boys, we're not wanted here; let's go somewhere else."

The men started to file out of the church, and about fifty managed to get into the street. Then a detective ordered Frank to close the door. He telephoned the police commissioner who presumably said, go ahead; the detective arrested Frank and all the workers who had remained in the church.

Frank Tannenbaum was tried by a jury of businessmen. We were thrilled to read of the courage he displayed at his trial. Pointing his finger at judge, jury and district attorney, he became the accuser instead of the accused. He said:

"I think now, your Honor—and I am going to say what I think—that when the first man was convicted in this court, justice flew out of the window, and never returned, and never will. You never know, and the law does not take into consideration, anything about human wants or the circumstances impelling a human being to so-called crime. . . . You don't know their life. I believe from my impressions and associations with these boys that they are more normal and more spontaneous than others, and that is why they cannot adapt themselves to this rotten society. They feel that as human beings, for the sake of a piece of bread, it is not worth while to work twelve long hours in a factory. . . . This trial for me was arranged by my friends in spite of my protest. I didn't want it. I knew what I was going to get, because I am not of your class. . . . I will never, if arrested in labor troubles, submit to a trial again. No more trials for me. The members of the jury, while they may be fair-minded, are not workmen. They don't know the life of workingmen. There is no jury—you could not get a jury of twelve workingmen, structural iron workers, for instance, to convict me; absolutely no. These gentlemen are members of your class in a way. They are capitalists. They would like to be. They would like to be rich. That's all right—but they are capitalists. . . . I consider my conviction absolutely unjust. You have tried to question the right of hungry men to get their bread. That is my crime, and I am willing to take the consequences, whatever they may be."

Frank Tannenbaum was sentenced to jail for two years, four months and fifteen days. The trial, Frank's conviction, his last speech stirred labor circles throughout the city. This heroic stand by a young worker in his early twenties, his leadership of the unemployed, his fearless defiance of the capitalist courts, his calm acceptance of the foreordained imprisonment on Blackwells Island, the heroic fight for the rights of his fellow prisoners there which landed him in solitary confinement—all this made a profound impression upon our group of sixteen- and seventeen-year-old "rebels," an impression which lasted a long time, which was still alive when we finally met Frank Tannenbaum three years later under the most unexpected circumstances.

The Tannenbaum case was only one of the striking episodes in the class war which deeply affected Robert and myself. Out in Colorado, troops acting on behalf of the Rockefeller interests destroyed the miners' tent colony at Ludlow, in their ruthless campaign of terror against the coal strikers. The tents themselves were the last refuge of the miners' families after they had been evicted from Rockefeller's company houses. The canvas booths dotting the meadow sheltered 120 women and 273 children. On April 20, 1914, the troops, without a moment's warning, swooped down on the colony, firing point-blank. Coal-oil torches were set to what remained of the bullet-riddled tents. Under the flames and rifle-fire, the women and children screamed and, crawling on their hands and knees across the fields, died in their tracks.

These strikes, demonstrations, imprisonments and shootings

seemed to increase the revolutionary ardor of the *Masses,* and from this bible my friends and I caught fire.

"Your place," Max Eastman said, "is with the working people in their fight for more life than it will benefit capital to give them; your place is in the working-class struggle; your word is Revolution."

For the circle in which I moved in adolescence, these words were not merely an expression of opinion; they were absolute truth. We remembered them for years, and cited them verbatim to convert others.

§ 10

The class struggle as such was only one of the forces in American life which the *Masses* expressed. Through its pages the winds of doctrine released by Omar Khayyám, Friedrich Nietzsche, Edward Carpenter, Walt Whitman and finally Sigmund Freud blew across America. The platonic sensualism of our elders in the radical intelligentsia came to rescue us from the crushing oppression of puritanism, from the implacable sense of guilt.

All matters connected with love and sex, the *Masses* approached in the spirit of lofty romanticism. Its ideals were supposed to be the opposite of Judeo-Christian asceticism. Like the burghers of the Renaissance and the romantics of the nineteenth century, the *Masses* fled from Moses and Jesus to Venus and Apollo. Greek paganism, dimly seen through Judeo-Christian spectacles, and draped with the pink banners of middle-class socialism, became the refuge of souls in rebellion against puritan bondage. The radicals' sense of guilt, however, was still so strong that they could reconcile their natural instincts with their inherited taboos only by surrounding their feelings with clouds of romantic-religious incense. Birth control, for example, was not only a social problem, but the mystic synthesis of truth, free speech, art, romantic love, civilization itself. Isadora Duncan was not a dancer merely; she was a sublime cult. Her language of motion foretold the time when life would be "frank and free," when it would proceed under the sky with happy fearlessness of faith in the beauty of its own nature.

A life that would be frank and free! That phrase was like a spring wind stirring our imaginations, our hearts and wills to fight against the masters of the world, against all those who hampered such a life. In this resolution, love, poetry and politics were all mixed up. But while the socialist society was far in the future, we somehow had the impression that love and poetry, at least, could be free now, if only the mind were liberated from taboos.

Already we were becoming in our own neighborhood a younger branch of the radical intelligentsia, the advance guard of the new life. We were the atheists, the poets, the socialists of our slums. Our citations from the *Masses,* our general defense of the frank and free life, and our verses written in that spirit, gave us the reputation of Don Juans. That reputation was not without irony. At this time we neither smoked, drank nor had women. Nevertheless our position as carriers of new ideas gave us a sense of both pride and isolation. We were "interesting" and "dangerous," at least to the "good" girls of our acquaintance. It was a long time before we discovered that we were anything but unique. Apart from the similarity of our adolescence in general to adolescence everywhere, we were not even alone in following the bright star of the *Masses.* Every main street in America had its choice isolated spirits who escaped through its pages from the pressure of a puritanism no less blighting than our own.

In the slums we heard about love in one of two ways. There was religion which said you must be pure. Sex outside of marriage was a sin. You must not go with "bad" women. You must not "spoil" good girls. When you were old enough and earned your own living, it was your duty to get married and have children, the more the better.

Some of the boys talked about doing "bad" or doing "it"; others talked about four letter words scrawled on sidewalks, walls, toilets. You could hear those words shouted from doorways, cellars and fire escapes.

Religion taught us a stern morality. Chastity was its central law. At ten we beat our breasts in the synagogue on Yom Kippur, the Day of Atonement. We joined our voices with those of the skullcaps and frock coats, begging God to forgive our fornication and adultery, our lusting after women, even if only in our hearts. Unlike the Catholic confessional, this prayer was public and impersonal. The adult who chanted the long list of sins together with the rest of the congregation was assured of anonymity. Even to God he did not specify his own particular sin. The child, incapable of sinning, was made to say the joint prayer presumably as an investment for the future, to obtain forgiveness for sins which he might someday commit.

At sixteen, we winked to each other behind our elders, as we tapped our breasts and mumbled the long list of sexual misdemeanors and felonies which the prayer book listed. We had begun to understand the sins which we verbally repented but secretly longed for. That longing was the source of a profound sense of guilt. It collided in our minds with the instruction of the Book of Books. Upon our hearts religion had inscribed that the commandment was the lamp, the law was light, and the reproofs of instruction were the ways of life. We must keep away from the evil woman, from the flattery of the tongue of a strange woman. We must not lust after her beauty in our hearts, nor let her take us with her eyelids. By means of the whorish woman, a man was brought to a piece of bread. The adulteress hunted for the precious life. Could a man take fire in his bosom and not be burned? Could one go upon hot coals and his feet not be burned? So with him who went in to his neighbor's wife. Whoever touched her would not be innocent. Men did not despise a thief if he stole to satisfy his soul when he was hungry; but he who committed adultery with a woman lacked understanding. Wounds and dishonor would be his, and his reproach would not be wiped away; for jealousy was the rage of man, therefore he would not spare you in the day of vengeance.

For us the Bible was, in early life, at once literature, science and law. It was God's own commandment, older than the present world, above all human custom and knowledge. Its word was sacred; what it forbade was taboo. The ancient faith of our race engendered a sense of guilt so strong that it rankled within us long after we became atheists, and had repudiated God, Bible and nationalism. It was so strong that our natural instincts, passionate and "sinful," could break through the taboos only when sanctioned by symbolism and poetry which were themselves semireligious.

Our first bridge between the old faith and the new feelings was the platonic love which Shelley celebrated. The first of his poems which I knew by heart described a love beyond mere sensual pleasure. The poet could not give what men called love, but he could offer a worship which the heart lifted above and the heavens did not reject.

> The desire of the moth for the star,
> Of the night for the morrow,
> The devotion to something afar
> From the sphere of our sorrow.

As we grew older, as our passions waxed and our religious beliefs waned, the platonic attitude failed to sustain us in the struggle between the senses and the sense of guilt. Shadowed by the ignorance and superstition of the vanished village and the synagogue, the Jewish puritanism of our parents and the American puritanism of our school-teachers, our dreams of pleasure became nightmares of pain. It was impossible to discuss our anguish and confusion with parents and teachers. Much of what they told us we discovered time and again to be untrue, and we were too inexperienced to understand that which was true.

Our cave of ignorance was haunted by the ghost of Dr. Landes, the type of quack Isidor Schneider has written about in the novel *Dr. Transit*. We still believed that if you had nocturnal emissions every two weeks you were seriously ill, and were headed for General Debility. You could save your life only by going to Dr. Landes. But when we felt the terrible symptoms of General Debility we were too terrified and too ashamed to think of going to the savior of afflicted men. Since you had no money of your own, that would mean going to your parents with the awful secret of your "illness." And how could you go to them with this burden of disgrace? Their tradition of purity was thousands of years old; their fathers and grandfathers before them had been saints whose family life was saturated with religion. For them the love of one's wife was not merely a pleasure; it was a *mitzva:* a commandment. It was an attribute of the love of God.

Nor were our older socialist friends of much help. These workers were too materialistic for us. They seemed vulgar and crude in love; they talked about sex as if it were only a biologic necessity, like food. We felt that sex ought to be a part of love; and this shameful "illness" which Dr. Landes described in such startling detail seemed to deprive us forever of love.

Our high school biology teacher restored to us a sense of health, normality and self-esteem. He told us the "facts of life"; but with them he instilled his own poison. A devout Catholic, named after one of the saints, a product of the parochial institutions, he also warned us against the perils of "sin." But he did not call it sin. He spoke of nerves, psychology, character, and the prostate gland. Priest agreed with rabbi that sex outside lawful wedlock was not only wrong but dangerous. Now religion spoke with the accents of biology. Medieval superstition was resurrected with the authority of science. When the church spoke with its own voice, we could resist; when it used the voice of science, we were helpless. And this voice thundered indiscriminate condemnation. Kissing a girl who was not your wife, and using a public toilet, might both net you syphilis.

At sixteen we were all physically and emotionally underdeveloped,

intellectually overdeveloped. At first we rationalized this mental precocity as a Jewish ailment. Even earlier, at the Young Zionist Club, the
hyperprecocious George read us essays on the subject. We believed
that Jews were the victims of pure reason. We tried to explain it on
several grounds. External pressure—the economic, political and social
disabilities forced upon the Jew by the surrounding world—had excluded him from normal pursuits, such as industry and farming. He
was locked in a ghetto where the spirit was his only refuge, and confined to occupations in which only the mind functioned. This gave
him an exaggerated regard for the taboos of the ancient faith. He
despised a body which he was forbidden to use, and worshiped the
intellect which alone opened life to him. But we imagined that the
conditions of his existence forced the intellect of the Jew into metaphysical realms. The old men studied the *torah,* their sons philosophy,
their grandsons pure science. Yet the Jews were a sensual and willful
race. Conflict arose between their sensuality and their intellect. The
old men resolved the conflict in God; they found refuge in taboos
which forbade illicit love and the taking of photographs. The modern
Jew tried to resolve his conflict in intellect. Spinoza, whom we were
studying, seemed to speak for us all when he made the emotions
synonymous with human bondage and pure reason synonymous with
human freedom.

Of course, Jews had a practical reason too. There were hardheaded
businessmen, and there were those of my friends who had little aspiration toward "pure" reason. Some of them chose early the practical
pursuits which they followed in later life. The cult of "pure" reason
affected, one might almost say afflicted, those of us who were interested
in art, literature and science. And here lay the root of this intellectualism, which was not at all racial. We were really akin in this respect
to nineteenth century romantics like the Slav Belinsky who confessed:
"I suffer from a horrid education. I reasoned at the time when one is
only supposed to feel. . . . I composed before I was able to write between the lines of a copybook; I dreamed and fancied when others
were learning their vocabularies."

Our relations with our parents and grandparents fostered precocity
and flights into the realm of "pure" reason. When they were educated
at all, our parents were educated in the Old World; we in the New.
Their knowledge and values were becoming more and more alien to
us, and ours to them. Whatever emotional contact we retained with
them, we very early became intellectually independent. Our hearts

were still tied to our mothers' apron strings; our minds already soared
into the Renaissance, the French Revolution, the Mexican War, poetry,
socialism.

Intellectual precocity, combined with emotional backwardness,
made us extremely awkward in actual relations with girls. There were
no girls at all in our high school, and "bad" girls were out of the
question. Elizabeth and Anna, for example. When I was fifteen, they
were eighteen, full-grown women ripe for marriage. Everybody said
they did "bad" with the bums, even with the gangsters around Fox's
Folly. Not for money, like the whores (we called them *whoores,* as the
Irish did) but for fun. That made it worse somehow.

Elizabeth lived on the floor below us. One day she called me
down to help her prepare for exams. She had been left back the term
before and this time was anxious to pass. I found her alone in the
house, sitting over her books in a nightgown. You could see the tops of
her breasts. She wanted my help in botany. What was this here pol-
linization? I tried to explain.

"That's just like ——, isn't it?" she said.

The ghost of Dr. Landes rose between us. I got up to go.

"What's your hurry?" she said.

"I don't like your language."

"I thought you were a smart boy."

What did she mean? And why, shortly afterward, did her friend
Anna, the other "bad" girl, take me for a long walk in the evening,
and talk to me for three hours about *Beverly of Graustark?*

It was just as dangerous to go walking with a good girl. If you
kissed her, you were practically engaged to her. That was something
you didn't dare think of until you finished college.

On some girls, however, poetry had a strange effect. Edith, for
instance, who lived in the house next to ours, and was good-looking
in a way. She had blue eyes and yellow-red hair, like the princesses in
Howard Pyle's and Alice Winter's drawings; or Yakelina, or the German grammar school teacher whom I had liked so much that I fretted
away a whole Christmas vacation, impatient to see her. Edith's "fellow" was my friend Jack. He was several years older than I, worked
in an office by day and studied law at night. Jack gave Edith some
poems, which I wrote and he signed. One day Edith stopped me in the
street:

"I like your poems."

I did not answer. Edith said:

"If you wanted to kiss a girl and she did not let you, I'd think she was an awful silly."

I did not dare kiss her. She belonged to Jack, and he was my friend. All this was very complicated. In the vanished village you knew where you stood. There were God's commandments and you obeyed or broke them; but at least you knew what was right and what was wrong. Now nobody knew. You had to make up your own right and wrong; you had to decide everything for yourself. The president of the synagogue—a rich man with a growing family—chased after the butcher's plump daughter; but the Kaplan boys, who were socialists, chased her too. You felt foolish for not kissing Elizabeth or Edith; and then you felt low for feeling foolish.

The struggle against your own inhibitions, against the voice of your grandfather, was hard enough. But there were even stronger voices to combat, living, insistent voices outside you which gave orders and enforced them. Papa dominated the household, the principal dominated the school, the policeman dominated the street. Ever since you could remember, they had whipped you—father, rabbi, teacher. Occasionally the beatings were severe, like the time when a relative tried to improve your character by knocking your head against the iron kitchen stove until you fainted. Most often the beatings were physically endurable. It was your self-esteem they hurt most. Our mentors at home and school, while never sparing the rod, did not say a beating hurt them more than it hurt us. We interpreted the painful act to mean that corporal punishment hurt our souls more than it hurt our bodies.

At one moment you were almost a man; you discussed Mexican or Japanese policy with Louis, your father, the history teacher, and they listened to you with respect, it seemed; or you came home with a gold medal for an oration against child labor. Yet here you were a baby again, being walloped in school or at home with palm, belt or ruler. It was like falling from a mountaintop into a dark abyss. The humiliation was unbearable. It was true, my father was a married man with children when grandfather slapped him in public for going to the barber's. Our rabbis and schoolteachers also had tradition behind them. But to hell with tradition. They had no right to do it. This was not Russia or seventeenth century New England. This was twentieth century America. Nobody, I said, had the right to impose authority on any other human being.

If anyone had called me an anarchist at this time, I would have resented it. Anarchists were too extreme. Look at my cousin Nathan. He refused to let anyone do anything for him. He said nobody had the right to exploit another human being. When we walked out on a Sunday afternoon and his shoes needed shining, he would sit on the high, leather-covered chair, take the brush out of the bootblack's hands, and shine his own shoes. That was going too far. Some people, like the bootblack, must shine shoes; others, like me, must write poetry. But I thought Nathan was right about authority, that is, violent authority. I could not see a father beating his son, a husband abusing his wife, drunkards kicking a bald head in the street, a policeman clubbing a striker, without wanting the whole earth to spring to pieces so that nature might start all over again with a new race of men who would build a new life. The only authority I could recognize was the authority of mind and heart. The man who could convince me, the poet who could move me, had a right to his authority.

CHAPTER IV

> World policy had come to the world explosion. The long-gath-
> ering, pent-up forces and passions . . . burst out in conflagration
> and terror more like the Apocalypse than like any real chapter of
> mortal transactions.
>
> —J. L. GARVIN.

§ 1

AT this time, two events affected me profoundly. The World War
broke out and my family moved to Pulaski Street. At first these events
seemed about equally important. The war was far away and reached
me only through the imagination, agitated by the public prints. Moving from the slums to a better neighborhood touched my daily life
at every point. But in spite of my ignorance and naïveté, the power
of history asserted itself even upon my introspective imagination. The
greater overwhelmed the lesser event. Until now I had been preoccupied primarily by the disparity in ethical standards which distinguished the New World from the Old, the proletariat from the bourgeoisie. The disillusion, the struggle to understand life, were essentially
moral. Now social disillusion was to predominate; the conflict was to
rage around political problems. It was no longer God or grandfather
who compelled you to answer inexorable questions; it was history
itself.

But even history appears to us at first in personal terms. We feel
its subjective effects long before we understand its objective laws.
By 1915 America was pouring automobiles, steel, wheat, ships and
munitions into the belligerent countries. My father's business, so remote from my intimate life, was building houses, and he shared in
the general boom. We now had meat every day. The boys slept in
pajamas and the girls in cotton nightgowns, instead of their underwear. The railroad flat of small dark rooms was abandoned for a "private" house, a one-family wooden affair on the edge of the ghetto.

The block adjoining ours was occupied on one side by a brewery,
on the other exclusively by Negroes. Nearby streets were full of wooden
tenements in which factory workers, grocers and plumbers lived. We

were within that series of three or four streets occupied by those who had begun to make a "success" in America. The "private" frame houses were the property of small businessmen, doctors, pharmacists and lawyers, the "better class of people."

Moving from the tenement to the private house was almost as great a revolution as coming from the vanished village to America. From the darkness and noise we came into sunlight and comparative quiet. The first floor had a kitchen, dining room and "parlor"; the upper floor, four bedrooms. I shared the largest of these with my two younger brothers. It was possible now to buy a secondhand office desk, to rent a typewriter and to set up a "den." In summer, the sunlight poured over your desk and books and poems; in winter it was warm. You could talk more freely to your younger brothers. Lying awake in the darkness long past midnight, you answered their interminable questions about the French Revolution, Byron and socialism.

Our new house was only ten blocks away from the old one. I went there frequently to visit my friends, especially those who were in my class at school. I also went to see Cora. When we first met in front of Kaplan's grocery store during a socialist argument four years earlier, we were only about fourteen. Now she was a woman: very beautiful, I thought, and generally conceded to be "intellectual." After quarrels in which each of us expressed unspeakable contempt for the other, we discovered that we were in love. So did her mother. But she thought I was too young for Cora. It would be five years before I would be out of college, and probably another two years after that before I could support a wife. By that time Cora ought to be married and the mother of children. Cora promised to wait for me until I finished college, but her family exiled her to relatives in Philadelphia. Cora thought the matter over. After all, five years was a long time to wait.

I could not believe that this was her own decision. We had kissed passionately without going further, but at that age and in our environment kissing was itself a profound manifestation of love. How could she forget our warm lips in the summer darkness of the Palisades? Oh, surely the decision to break was not her own. She and I were both victims of the System which was to blame for all the ills of the world. In the future socialist society, people who loved each other would not be torn apart by their families for lack of money. Perhaps, I thought, one need not even wait for the future socialist society to love freely. Across the bridge, in Greenwich Village, there were people who led a life frank and free. Money did not interfere with love; each person was his own authority and did as he pleased.

Months later I saw unattainable Cora in the street. My heart contracted but I did not stop her. I went home, set a chair against the doorknob of my "den" and wrote sonnets. Money ruled the world and made people unhappy. Poetry lifted you above these things, above money, even above the pangs of frustrated love. I did not pretend to be a real poet. The test of a real poet was whether or not the magazines published you. I had a neat pile of rejection slips in my desk. That proved I was not a real poet. The only real poet I knew was Oscar, who lived two blocks from our new house, in a wooden tenement like the one we had just left. You walked through the darkness and the smell of cats up several flights of stairs to a dank unfurnished flat. Sometimes when you sat up at night with Oscar reading poetry, the gaslight went out; there was no quarter for the meter, so we recited verses in the dark. Oscar's father did not like that, nor did Oscar's stepmother, who bossed the house. To make the quarter in the meter go further, she would turn out the light. She thought Oscar was crazy anyway with all this poetry. A sensible boy would get a job in an office, earn a living and leave the house.

Oscar went to our high school and was a member of the Scribblers' Club. But soon he quit school. I met him on a job where we solicited pupils for a business college on commission. I was trying to make some money to go to Columbia University. What proved to me that Oscar was a real poet was his hatred for everything that did not concern poetry. He hated his job, his father, his stepmother, their dark, cold flat. The only two people he liked were his younger sister and me. Some of the other "intellectuals" of the neighborhood were contemptuous of Oscar. He never read serious books; he never looked at a newspaper, he did not know what was happening in the world, he was scarcely aware of the war in Europe; he took no interest in socialism. But that proved to me he was a real poet, like Thomas Chatterton, that wonderful boy. Oscar's poems were full of trees and seas, flowers and hours. In our neighborhood there were no trees or seas, but Oscar could imagine them beautifully. His lyrics stirred you like music; they moved in another world, a more alluring world.

The ultimate proof that Oscar was a real poet was that his lyrics were published by the magazines. It was astonishing how this seventeen-year-old boy could break into any publication he tried, from the adventure magazines to the liberal weeklies. His poetry appeared in

Argosy, Scribner's, Harper's, the *Dial,* the *Nation,* the *New Republic,* the *Delineator.* His genius was universally recognized. I looked upon him with humility and reverence. When he said to me, "But you are a poet too; I am like Keats and you are like Byron," I did not believe him. He was being kind. Oscar was sheer dream, and in those troubled days, dreams like his seemed a perfect refuge from the perplexing world, from the stone streets of Williamsburg, the confusing echoes of Europe's war.

We should have been prepared for this war. Our socialist guides had instilled in us the idea that capitalism, in its struggle for markets, inevitably produced war. Old Man Jackson in high school had warned us that war would come while we were still young. We had grown up in the shadows of war, near and far. Had it not been for the Russo-Japanese clash, my family might never have come to America.

But we were not a bit prepared. News of the European war came to us with the unexpected violence of an earthquake. In this respect, we did not differ from our elders. Abstract truth was one thing, reality another. From the distance, through deliberately confusing news dispatches, we observed the battle of nations growing more fierce, spreading like wildfire from land to land, devouring more and more men. Humanity, we said, echoing our elders, was bleeding. We began to wonder whether it was not bleeding to death. We drew closer to America where peace prevailed, where the don in the White House urged us to remain neutral in our sympathies for the contending powers.

At school, the teachers of French and English origin were cool toward our German instructors. Our Irish principal found it difficult to conceal his anti-British animus, while keeping peace between the two camps in the faculty and preaching official neutrality to the students. In the slums the socialist workers denounced the Allies and the Central Powers with equal severity. This was a capitalist war, they said. Whichever side won, the workers of all countries involved would lose. Capitalists alone would coin blood into profit.

The Yiddish press, edited for the most part by Russian-born Jews, was distinctly pro-German, echoing the general mood of the pariahs who had fled the Pale. The Romanov dynasty was the greatest scourge in the world. It must be crushed. Nor was this merely a desire for vengeance. The Yiddish journalists, like our parents, hoped the fall of czarism would open the way for a democratic republic "like America."

Their relatives in the old country would know the blessings of freedom. At least there would be no pogroms.

If until now the world had been perplexing, the war exploded whatever certainty we had attained. The massacre of subject races and classes, pogroms, lynchings, Ludlow, Veracruz were terrifying enough. But here was Europe, the advance guard of civilization, slaughtering millions of its best men, wiping out fields and villages, pouring out blood and wealth. We could not accept our parents' animus against Russia. Czarism was bad. Was kaiserism better? Were the capitalists of France and England better? I felt, with Louis Smith, with the Kaplan boys, and the other socialist workers, that anyone opposed to capitalism must cry "a plague on both your houses."

Bloodshed was abhorrent to us on all counts. By temperament and training we looked upon violence as mankind's greatest curse. If it was right at all, it could be only in a "just" combat, like the American War of Independence, the French Revolution, or the Civil War between North and South.

What was the use of working, marrying, having children, studying, writing poetry, if in the end people you hated as exploiters and oppressors could send you to murder unknown young men and to be murdered by them? A life which led from tenement to battlefield did not seem worth while. There was too much hatred in the world. We recoiled from this universal hatred to such manifestations of love as we could find in personal life.

§ 2

By 1916 there was talk of America's joining the Allies; there was a nation-wide "preparedness" campaign. The capitalists wanted us to go into the war, to kill and be killed.

John Reed of the *Masses,* who had been in Paterson and Mexico, now went to the western front in Europe. He described horrors of the war; he wanted to show us what military obedience and discipline did to human beings. The curse of mankind was militarism. Now, no force stood up against it. Christianity was completely bankrupt. Philosophical anarchism and international socialism were equally futile as incentives to peace. Anarchists and socialists in Europe were all trained soldiers. America also faced the danger of militarism. At this moment they were talking about building a big standing army to fight the Japanese, the Germans, the Mexicans. John Reed, for one, refused to join. He had no illusions about the European conflict. To him, Germany was no better and no worse than Britain, France or Russia. If England had no conscript army now, it would have one soon. Its "volunteer" army was being filled by terrible means. Workers of enlistable age were fired from their jobs, their families were refused relief until the men joined the army.

John Reed's attitude seemed to my circle clearly socialist. Militarism and war were aspects of the System, and every socialist was duty-bound to oppose them. But socialism was not so simple. War had apparently blasted everyone's preconceptions. Among the spokesmen of the working class, as everywhere else, there was a babel of contradictory voices. Discord among American socialists echoed the conflict which the European war created in the ranks of socialism everywhere.

We knew the orthodox socialist position on war not only from workers like Louis Smith, but from socialist agitators who for years had cited from platform and soapbox the Stuttgart resolution, adopted by the Seventh International Socialist Congress in 1907.

This resolution declared in so many words that the struggle against militarism could not be separated from the socialist class struggle in general. Wars between capitalist states were the outcome of their competition in the world market. Wars were also caused by the race for armaments and by national prejudice, systematically cultivated in the interest of the ruling class to distract the masses from the duties of international solidarity. Wars would cease only when the capitalist system was abolished. The proletariat, which contributed most of the soldiers and made most of the material sacrifices, was a natural opponent of war. The Stuttgart resolution concluded that in case war should break out it would be the duty of the working classes and their parliamentary representatives to intervene in favor of the speedy termination of the war, and "with all their powers to utilize the economic and political crisis created by the war to rouse the masses and thereby to hasten the downfall of capitalist class rule."

The Basle resolution of 1912 reiterated these principles. It predicted that Serbia would be the pretext for the next European conflict, and indicated with remarkable accuracy the lineup of the belligerent countries. It called upon the workers of all countries to oppose the power of the proletariat's international solidarity to capitalist imperialism. It emphatically demanded peace, and reminded the governments that with the prevailing condition of Europe and the mood of the working class, they could not unleash war without danger to themselves. The proletarians considered it a crime to fire at each other for the profits of the capitalists, the ambitions of dynasties, or the greater glory of secret diplomatic treaties. The monstrosity of a world war would inevitably call forth the indignation and revolt of the working class.

For us these resolutions were no abstract political documents, but shafts of light pointing the way to thought and action; they told us definitely what attitude socialists ought to have toward war. Yet in 1913, only one year after the Basle resolution had been unanimously adopted by the socialist parties of all countries, the majority of the social democratic deputies in the Reichstag voted war credits for the Kaiser's army and navy. In 1914 they repeated this action. These votes were a betrayal of the basic principles of socialism, of the fundamental interests of the working class. What made this betrayal all the more striking was that the German social democracy was the strongest and most influential party in the Second International.

As the war went on, it became obvious that the disease of national-liberalism was not confined to Germany. Everywhere within the ranks of socialism there were leaders who had, by their economic and social position, become part of the capitalist state, or infected with capitalist ideas. Socialist leaders in France and Belgium had entered the bourgeois cabinets. In the Allied countries, those socialist leaders who supported the government tried to justify their betrayal of the workers by saying that the world had to be saved from Teutonic barbarism and Prussian militarism. Within the Central Powers, the pro-Kaiser "socialists" said they were fighting against Russian barbarism, against the savagery of the Czar, against the Slav peril.

The American Socialist party remembered the Stuttgart and Basle resolutions; in the fall of 1914 it urged the socialists of all countries to hold an international peace conference. From our socialist press we also learned that in every warring country a militant minority adhered to the Marxist position against war and militarism. Writers in the *Call* and the *Masses* attacked both sides of the European conflict, and the latter published cartoons satirizing British and German militarism alike.

Nevertheless, the "socialist" chauvinism of Europe found an echo in the United States among certain intellectuals of this period. Although these men called themselves socialists, their roots were actually in the bourgeoisie. They tended to believe in national-cultural myths. They thought not of the proletariat as against the bourgeoisie in all countries, but of the freedom-loving, cultured, poetic French as against the barbarous, militaristic Germans. Presumably, Clemenceau cared more for the arts of life than Bethmann-Hollweg did; Asquith cared more for freedom than von Bülow did; the French people were more intelligent than the German people. These national-cultural myths enabled liberal pragmatists in all countries absolutely to take sides in the conflict, to support one group of belligerents concretely while repudiating all war abstractly. Usually these radical intellectuals took the side of their own ruling class.

The *Masses,* which had previously whitewashed President Wilson's invasion of Mexico, now found that not all capitalist rulers were equally bad. Some capitalists were better than others. Let the war go on! Max Eastman exclaimed editorially in October, 1914. Not only was his heart with invaded France, reason itself dictated that the Kaiser and his military machine must be whipped back into Prussia and smashed. Let the war go on until that "sacred task" was accomplished. The *Masses* wanted the Kaiser's defeat not for the Allies, but for Germany. The German people were being held under the heel of militarism more solidly and more consentingly than any other people in Europe. Germany's feudal and absolute military oppression, linked fast with cultural and scientific-reform progress of the highest kind, was the *most* abominable monster in Europe; and it was the *only* monster that would surely be slain by the victory of its enemies. That was why the *Masses* advocated the arms of the Allies, although it had no patriotism but the love of liberty, and no faith that Russia was fighting the battle of democracy, and no delusion that England and France were the sole repositories of culture and altruism.

In the summer of 1915, Max Eastman went to Paris to give the war his personal attention. The chief impression he brought back from the front was that the war was not interesting. He had not realized to what depths of *boredom* the course of European history had sunk. This war, he said, was positively dull. He confessed that when he was in Paris he was more interested in the relics of the Napoleonic Wars and the French Revolution than in the daily reports of the final military climax of all European history which was in suspension not a hundred miles away. But though the war bored the radical editor, he wanted it to go on till Germany was defeated.

At eighteen, the contradictions within the ranks of socialism appeared more perplexing to me every day. As if it were not enough that our favorite socialist publication urged the defeat of Germany on grounds which socialist congresses had time and again condemned, it was not consistent even in this attitude. It was a "sacred" task to crush Germany, but America must not do it. The *Masses* editor did not care whether or not he was allowed to ride on a British vessel through the submarine zone. He really cared more about his right to lie down on a bench in Washington Square when he was tired, if he was looking for a right to defend. That was the way he wanted all editors to think about America's entrance into the war. He wanted them to think *personally*.

Most of America's editors did, after a fashion, think personally. They were in one way or another dependent for their livelihood and social status on the ruling class, and discussed America's entrance into the war accordingly. They realized that as a rule they would risk nothing in the war; they might gain something. The campaign for "preparedness" in the abstract became more and more identified with preparedness for the western front. The "extreme" socialists, the blind, dogmatic slaves of Marx, fought against this campaign.

The more liberal *Masses* also ridiculed the preparedness campaign. But its editor was not satisfied with mere protest. He wanted a key to permanent universal peace. Socialism taught that wars would cease only when the capitalist system was abolished. But this was a socialist "dogma," and the *Masses* was opposed to dogma wherever it was found. World peace was possible even under capitalism, the *Masses* argued. It could be established through the combined efforts of organized capital, organized labor and organized women. Incorrigible dogmatists, "socialists of the line," would no doubt object that the workers and capitalists could not have so consequential a community of interests. But after all, Eastman urged, the worker and the capitalist were both interested in having the law of gravitation maintained. Surely the continued circulation of blood through the veins of half the people of the globe was a matter of concern to both exploiter and exploited. We really did nothing more than avail ourselves of the Economic Interpretation of History if "we" availed ourselves of *both* classes in "our" efforts to build a bulwark against international war. Of course, this hope was in no sense social revolutionary; it was really only a "supremely sagacious step" to be taken by bourgeois society, completely cured of the remnants of feudalism. The reference to the "remnants of feudalism" meant that before the capitalists, workers and women got together to establish permanent world peace, Germany had to be "smashed." That was apparently the indispensable condition for the sublime hope of universal peace which the *Masses* dangled under the noses of those socialists broad-minded enough to forget the orthodox "line" a little. And the hope of universal peace through class collaboration had good chances of fulfillment. It might, the *Masses* assured me, logically come before anything like a social revolution, regardless of what Marx and Engels might have said.

But who would bell the cat? Who would take the "supremely sagacious step" of uniting capitalists, workers and women in the common effort needed for abolishing war from the earth? The messiah was there, watching the highest interests of mankind from his desk in the White House. The *Masses* appealed to the President. He could, by a great act of resolution, take the first step toward international federation and the elimination of war. The President had it in his hands to make his administration a momentous event in "planetary history," a thing not for historians but for *biologists* to tell future generations, since the elimination of war would profoundly alter the character of evolution.

For the time being, Woodrow Wilson did not assume the divine role urged upon him by *Masses* editorials. But the net effect of the contradiction within socialist ranks, which we could neither understand nor resolve, was to drive us frequently to the cynicism of despair. Probably all adolescents pass through a period of cynicism about their parents, teachers, friends, the faith of their church or the laws of their country. This period comes between the time when the youth discovers the abyss which separates theory from practice in contemporary society and the time when he becomes corrupt enough to accept the "rules of the game." Upon my generation the war imposed a heavier burden than usual. The war compelled us to question all values of the prevailing social system; and the unsocialist conduct of many socialist spokesmen during the war forced us to question socialism itself.

But if you questioned socialism, where were you? How painfully you had struggled against the superstitions of the vanished village, against the barriers of the American ghetto, to achieve a rational explanation of the world, something to guide your actions. But if the socialists whom you revered supported a capitalist war, what meaning did the world have? You could not go back to the religion of your grandfather, or to the naïve illusions about an ideal Jewish state in Palestine. You could fall back only upon sensuous experience, perhaps with poetry to relieve the chaos; but what a frightfully lonely life that was.

BOOK TWO

CHAPTER I

SAVIORS IN CAP AND GOWN

The two essentials of political progress are the judicious selection
of lawmakers and governors, and that amount of general education
which will insure that the selection be really judicious.

—DR. NICHOLAS MURRAY BUTLER.

§ 1

MY friends and I entered Columbia University early in 1916. The
more we learned there, the wider became the gap between us and the
ghetto. We were the products of an economic process whereby those
who had the means went on to the professions. We were to become
doctors, lawyers, teachers, dentists and journalists. The girls in our
neighborhood who had quit school for the stenographer's desk saw
boys they had hoped to marry climb up the social ladder beyond their
reach.

If we felt like aliens at home, we felt even more alien on the
campus. In high school, pupils came from the same district and from
families contiguous in the social scale. Columbia's ten thousand students came from every part of the United States, many of them from
well-to-do families. For the first time in their lives, students from the
slums moved in middle- and upper-class America. We had been thrown
into a gilded melting pot. Once more we had to transvalue values.

We formed an informal "fraternity" of our own, a group of students of various races and nationalities who took the same courses, had
the same social background of poverty and race discrimination, and
followed the cult of "pure" reason. Most of my college friends I knew
from the slums and from high school; among the new friends were
students from foreign countries. It was natural for Rüdiger, boycotted
by most students because he was fresh from Berlin, to seek us out.
Because we were antiwar we were not anti-German. It was natural,
too, for Mustapha from Teheran to join us; we did not despise the
minor nationalities. You could not believe propaganda about the
"barbaric" Germans after hearing Rüdiger's bitter attacks on the
Kaiser and the war; you could not have illusions about the poetic and
exotic Orientals after hearing Mustapha, who was determined to enter

Persian politics with the aid of British oil interests, ridicule all poetry. Of the old high school crowd, there were skeptical minds questioning everything: Matthew Josephson, Percy Winner, Louis Hacker, Mac Windsor, David Gould, Robert Smith, Benjamin Ginzburg, whom we called "God Ginzburg" because of his omniscience. Of the new friends we were most impressed by the studious Richard McKeon and the mercilessly analytical Kenneth Burke.

Most of us postponed the choice of a profession. We had at least two years of academic work before entering a graduate school, and for the time being decided to stick to Hamilton Hall. Professions seemed an unpleasant necessity. We had begun to develop the cult of failure. One day I overheard Matthew Josephson remonstrating with a friend:

"If you keep up this crazy, irregular life, you'll be dead by twenty-five."

The friend, who affected sideburns and a mustache which made him look like Edgar Allan Poe, taunted:

"And what will you be at twenty-five? A respectable, successful man!"

America, we had been taught, was the land of unbounded possibilities. Talent, perseverance, hard work, intelligence would get you anywhere; success was within the reach of all who deserved it, and really wanted it. If you failed, it was your own fault. The test of "success" was money. Those of us interested in "pure" art or socialism, or both, despised this "corrupt" success. Artists said it meant selling your talent to Mammon; socialists said, to capitalism. We had begun to develop an idea common to nineteenth century romantics and twentieth century bohemians, the idea that success was synonymous with philistinism. The Luddites, unable to distinguish between machinery and the capitalist use of machinery, destroyed the instruments which alone, under a higher social system, could bring the people freedom; we, unable to distinguish between success and conventional standards of success, made a cult of failure. We attacked all success in the abstract. We recognized that an artist or scientist might be successful in his work, but emphasized that he was socially a failure. He starved in a garret; he was robbed of his canvas or his invention by the propertied philistines, the acknowledged successes. Since the System put a premium on corrupt methods of achieving wealth, power and fame, we felt the artist or scientist who was a "failure" for remaining loyal to his task was superior to the mediocrities who rose in society through chance or plunder. Like Shelley, Byron and Chatterton, we were go-ing to write poetry unappreciated by the mass of people, above all by the "successes." We were to be misunderstood and persecuted, and to die young. Among ourselves, we argued: would you rather be the meretricious but successful Robert W. Chambers or the sincere but neglected Henrik Ibsen? Most of us preferred Ibsen.

Our romanticism received a rude shock at Columbia. Dr. Carl Van Doren, our English instructor, told us the poet Shelley was a ne'er-do-well who probably would have written nothing and perished unknown but for the allowance from his father. Professor John Erskine, then expounding naturalism to us, ridiculed the notion that all good poets die young. But nothing our professors said could take the romantic myth from us. They could not understand; they were "old." Already there was arising out of the European war the cult of youth. The old men had made the war, the young men were fighting it. The old men destroyed the world, the young men would remake it. We adopted new heroes for our romantic pantheon of talent destroyed in its prime— Alan Seeger, Rupert Brooke, Joyce Kilmer. The death of poets in battle seemed more terrible than that of other men. The talented, we felt, were the disinherited of life. The history of the arts, the life around us, proved this. Everything from strikes to wars convinced us that the world was dominated by men madly pursuing money, who would slaughter half of mankind to obtain it.

Our former support in these dilemmas, the hope of international socialism, seemed to have been destroyed by the war. What could one expect from a movement whose leaders in Europe supported the militarists? American socialism seemed timid and aimless. In 1916 I wrote in my notebook:

"There is not a plank in the platform of the American Socialist party that is not endorsed by the liberal bourgeoisie; the 'radical' bourgeois and the 'moderate' socialist agree."

My most intimate companions were not moderate socialists. We wanted a clean sweep of the whole System, and were ignorant of the science which pointed in that direction. We therefore became "philo-sophic anarchists above party," who hated poverty and oppression to the point where we could hate no more. But our hatred of capitalism far exceeded our understanding of it. We had only the vaguest idea of the class struggle or of our possible place in it. We hated most of all the feeling of hate, in ourselves as well as in all around us, which seemed to pervade the whole world. We felt at times that the best we could do was to quit this vile scene in romantic early death, leaving behind us songs of beauty and defiance. Feeling close to death is an adolescent experience in all periods of history, as we knew from Catullus and Keats; but the war intensified that feeling.

Perhaps this attitude was a by-product of the middle-class radicalism by which we were, without realizing it, affected at this time. This type of radicalism, especially in literary and artistic people, may be wholly negative. It may decline into a nihilism which desires the destruction of the old without wishing to build the new. An idealistic intellectual may hate the present order, which makes life for him difficult, without having either the will or the class basis to alter it.

Success in practical enterprises of any kind appeared irrelevant in those days. At times poetry—the voice of Love and Beauty—seemed more important than anything else in the world. In this we echoed one of the current American needs. The poetry "renaissance" was in full swing. You could not open a newspaper or magazine without hearing about it. Louis Untermeyer explained that with the appearance since 1912 of William Stanley Braithwaite's anthologies of magazine verse, there was ample evidence that poetry had ceased to be the diversion of the overcultured and erudite, an exercise for the parlor, an embroidery of archaic words over a pattern of archaic sentiments. Poetry, he said, had been freed from mere didacticism and decoration; it was coming nearer to the people in thought and speech; it was using the language not of the few but of the majority.

At the Commons where we ate our lunch, we read and discussed the verse of Robert Frost, Edgar Lee Masters, Vachel Lindsay, James Oppenheim, Amy Lowell, Ezra Pound, T. S. Eliot. Those of us who read the *Masses* also followed the verse of Clement Wood, Carl Sandburg, Margaret Widdemer, Witter Bynner, Lydia Gibson and Arturo Giovannitti. We did not then realize to what an extent the new poetry voiced the New Freedom, the democratic-national faith of the middle classes which Theodore Roosevelt had tried to exploit with the Progressive party and which sent Woodrow Wilson to the White House. This voice was heard even in the New York *Times,* organ of American bourbonism, which decried art for art's sake and spoke up for social poetry. The *Times* called the twentieth century the "era of social responsibility" which was sweeping away the debris of worn-out customs, formal theology and all effete things. Romanticism had vanished with the art of Swinburne in a wraith of beautiful futility, the *Times* said; now poetry was being revitalized by the genius of Walt Whitman, whose revolutionary message was expressing itself in the new freedom of our literature.

At the university we confined ourselves to the classics and wrote papers on Castiglione's *Il Cortigiano,* Sir Philip Sidney's sonnets and the chivalrous characteristics of men. From a twentieth century college we absorbed uncritically the ideas of the Renaissance. When I wrote in a college theme on "temperance as beauty" that the Platonic philosophy conceived beauty as advancing from one to all fair forms, then to fair practices, fair thoughts, and lastly to the single thought of absolute beauty, I was not merely trying to pass a course; I was seeking Truth, which, as time went on, seemed to have more and more faces. Yet under the conflicting values my romantic strain, expressed in the early love for Byron and Shelley, persisted and found new vitality in the poetry of Rupert Brooke.

§ 2

Neither my most intimate friends nor I lived in the dorms. We lived at home in or near working-class quarters, close to the original sources of our lives. Whatever we might hear during the day about Donne or Catullus, we were sure to hear at night from parents, friends, street-corner orators about the fight for bread, the struggle for existence. But we no longer needed anyone to call our attention to the economic and political news of the day. In our most cynical moments, this was a matter of prime interest for us. And neither despair over the war nor poetic daydreaming could repress the indignation aroused by the news of the Youngstown massacre. We read the dispatches with fury:

Some two hundred strikers were celebrating their Christmas holidays at the close of 1916 by parading in the streets of the steel town. Armed company guards on the bridge of the Youngstown Sheet and Tube Company's plant tried to disperse the street parade by firing over the heads of the crowd. The paraders refused to retreat. The guards, at a range of forty feet, emptied their repeating rifles into the mass of unarmed workers, leaving forty dead and dying men on the pavement. Within ten minutes every striker in East Youngstown was on the scene of the massacre. They replied to the outrage by dynamiting the buildings around the steel mill—the bank, the post office, the stores and the office buildings. Next day the steel company brought in two regiments of state militia which cleared the streets. The company achieved its aims. By killing forty workers it provoked the "riot" except for which it would have been compelled to grant the strikers' demands for higher wages. Three hundred strikers were arrested, and the wobblies and socialists among them held for criminal prosecution.

The country's attention, however, was not on the Youngstown massacre. Press, church, platform, theater and street were loud with preparedness propaganda. The National Security League and the Navy League, backed by investors in Anglo-French bonds and shippers of supplies to the Entente Powers, agitated from coast to coast for a bigger army and navy. Middle-class pacifists opposed the preparedness campaign; but the clearest opposition came from the progressive wing of labor, particularly from the socialist and syndicalist movements.

On the Columbia campus, students and faculty were sharply divided on the preparedness question and opinions were freely expressed. One of our antiwar meetings was addressed by the dapper and witty Leon Fraser, who was later to become a major in the A.E.F., and eventually head of the World Bank for International Settlements. At this time he was my instructor in politics and coach of the varsity debating team of which I was a member. In the classroom he poked fun at "Czar" Nicholas Butler and gave lurid details of how Republican and Democratic nominating conventions were packed. Now he ridiculed the war party, saying that America's entry into the war would benefit not the democracy but the snobocracy. My captain on the debating team, Edward Mead Earle, who was in later years to become a historian at Columbia, was among the leaders of the antiwar movement on the campus. He appeared before a Senate committee in Washington to testify against preparedness. But the most vigorous opposition on the campus to America's entering the war came from the School of Journalism students.

Chauvinist students had the support of many strong-arm athletes. Several of our speakers were beaten up in front of Hamilton Hall. I was among those waylaid and mauled by reactionary students in the tunnel leading from the college to the gymnasium.

Only a handful of people in the higher politics had any notion at this time that President Wilson had already decided to place America on the Allied side of the war. In the fall of 1914 the President confessed to Colonel House that the economic and political situation in the United States had got beyond him. He also made it clear to Democratic leaders and to the French and British governments that the United States might participate in the war. Yet throughout 1916 it was generally believed, even among socialist intellectuals, that Wilson genuinely desired peace and would do his utmost to keep America neutral.

The intelligentsia discussed some of the burning questions of the day in abstract terms. When the *Masses* asked a group of radicals *do you believe in patriotism?* the replies were prophetic, foreshadowing the future political development of the men and women who wrote them. Liberals like Inez Haynes Gillmore (who that year became Mrs. Will Irwin) and John Haynes Holmes said yes and no, and talked about patriotism in terms of human love. Charles Edward Russell, still a member of the Socialist party, said he most heartily believed in the patriotism that would champion and defend this country for the sake of its ideals, aspirations and history; for the sake of what it had stood for and would stand for as the last barrier against the tide of reaction and absolutism now running over Europe. By this time, certain socialist intellectuals had come to believe that reaction and absolutism were the monopoly of Germany. In this black category, Czarist Russia, militarist France and imperialist Britain were not included. Nor did the "ideals, aspirations and history" of America include Paterson, Lawrence, Paint Creek, Veracruz, Ludlow and Youngstown. The one revolutionary voice in the entire symposium was that of Elizabeth Gurley Flynn, who said:

"Do you believe in patriotism? What an odd question to ask of revolutionists! Might it not be better put: American socialists, have you the courage of your principles? Shall it be America First, or Workers of the World, Unite! Count me for LABOR FIRST. This country is not 'our' country. Then why should the toilers love it or fight for it? Why sanction the title deeds of our masters in the blood of our fellow-slaves? Let those who own the country, who are howling for and profiting by preparedness, fight to defend their property . . . The train on which I write rushes by factories where murder instruments are made for gold. I would be ashamed to be patriotic to such a country. In the black smoke belched forth from their chimneys, I see the ghostly faces of dead workers—our poor, deluded, slain brothers. I reaffirm my faith: it is better to be a traitor to your country than a traitor to your class!"

Subsequently, revolutionaries learned not to set up this arbitrary division between their class and their native land, which is theirs in a much deeper sense than it is the exploiters'. They had built it, after all. But at that time Gurley Flynn's utterance startled us not only because in the midst of liberal drivel it presented the nearest approach to the class viewpoint of the proletariat, but also because we had been led to believe that international socialism was thoroughly bankrupt. Arthur Bullard reported that the war had shot the international socialist movement to pieces. He was confident that after the war the socialist movement would be reborn. It would be a different movement, national rather than international, bitter in the extreme, fierce in its demands and its methods. But meantime socialism seemed to offer no hope for peace.

§ 3

This was the mood among certain socialist intellectuals when the presidential campaign of 1916 got under way. The general desire to keep out of the war was so strong in America that every candidate ran on a "peace" platform. Charles Evans Hughes offered to maintain "the peace of justice and right"; but radicals and pacifists were suspicious of the support he received from bankers and manufacturers with investments in the Allied armies. The Socialist party was sharply opposed to entering the war, but the socialists had "no chance of being elected." In this crisis middle-class radicals and pacifists could not afford to "waste" their votes; they could support only a candidate who would be certain to keep America out of the war. That candidate was Woodrow Wilson, whose pious peace phrases were even loftier than those of Hughes. The Democratic party exploited middle-class illusions, applauding the "splendid diplomatic victories of our great President who has preserved the vital interests of our government and kept us out of war."

When war became the central issue of the campaign, a number of socialist intellectuals abandoned their own party and openly supported Wilson. Among these were William English Walling, who had once attacked the German social democrats for voting the Kaiser war credits; Ernest Poole, whose novel *The Harbor* had marked a high point in radical fiction; Ellis O. Jones, the professional humorist; Mother Jones, labor agitator and organizer; and John Reed and Max Eastman of the *Masses*.

One possible reason for this curious alliance with the Democrats was the craft solidarity which many intellectuals of all classes felt with the professor in the White House. Many of our instructors at Columbia believed that Wilson's cap and gown at Princeton had endowed him for life with the sacred detachment of the scholar. School-teachers everywhere were thrilled to think that one of their own, a man who had taught classes and published textbooks, had risen to the highest office in the nation. On all sides we heard rapturous applause for the President's wonderful literary style. Among intellectuals, Wilson's prestige was far above that of the corporation lawyer Hughes or the professional he-man Roosevelt. When the politicians ridiculed Wilson as a "schoolteacher," that prestige was only enhanced.

But if this influenced socialist intellectuals, it was subordinate to their illusion that the President did not want war. Forgetting the class basis of politics, they surrendered completely to Wilson's hypnotic shamanism. The *Masses* of June, 1916, said editorially: the President does not want war. The illusion was further strengthened by Max Eastman's report of an interview at the White House between Wilson and a group of *Masses* editors. According to this report, the President represented "our popular sovereignty with beautiful distinction." He was a "graciously democratic aristocrat"; he handled the radical editors "beautifully"; they all liked him, and *they* all sincerely believed that *he* sincerely believed that he was an antimilitarist. Furthermore, the President sincerely hated his own preparedness policies, which he pursued under compulsion and only as a step toward the idea of world federation and the international enforcement of peace. Later, through the Woodrow Wilson Independent League, Max Eastman issued a statement which said:

"I would rather see Woodrow Wilson elected than Charles Hughes, because Wilson aggressively believes not only in keeping out of the war, but in organizing the nations of the world to prevent war."

This statement voiced the mood of the liberals in the socialist movement, and many of us mistook this mood for socialist policy. Robert Smith and I felt that the *Masses* had analyzed the situation correctly. We decided to campaign for the re-election of Wilson so that he could keep America out of the war.

Neither Robert nor I was old enough to vote, but the Democratic campaign managers did not object to "boy orators." It was useful to show that youth, the chief victim of war, supported the President who kept the country at peace. We felt uncomfortable in the camp of the enemy, but for the cause of peace one must disregard such feelings. We were sent to various parts of Brooklyn. Hardest of all was the night we spoke in the slums where we had grown up and where Robert still lived. We spoke on a street corner where as children we had heard our first socialist agitators, and opposite Capitol Hall where Charles Edward Russell had spoken. Many of the young socialists we knew in this neighborhood were now factory workers. When they heckled us from the crowd, doubts began to seep into our minds. One tall needle-trades worker, young and good-looking with his black cotton shirt open at the throat, shouted to us:

"Wilson is deceiving the people, and you are helping him!"

He read Congressional bills in a loud voice to show how the administration was preparing for war. We did not know what to reply. We were not partisans of the President. We supported him only because our socialist teachers had assured us that he did not want war.

But suppose the needle-trades worker was right? Many of our socialist friends cut us dead. Most painful of all was Louis's attitude. He said that under no circumstances might a socialist support a capitalist candidate. The treachery of Wilson's "socialist" supporters proved they were "half-ass intellectuals." The White House was the executive office of the capitalist class; the President's beautiful phrases were bait to catch votes. We should know better; we had grown up in a working-class neighborhood. With this lecture, Louis stopped talking to us.

Disturbing also was the attitude of the local Democratic bosses, from McCooey down. In our stump speeches Robert and I said we opposed capitalism, the Democratic party and the President. We favored Wilson's re-election *only* on the issue of "peace without provocation." Yet the Tammany chieftains liked our speeches. Was it possible that supporting Wilson while attacking capitalism had a special value for the Democratic machine in a proletarian neighborhood? Was it easier for someone who called himself a "socialist" to capture workers' votes for a Democrat?

We spoke only for Wilson; we refused to speak for the Democratic party or any of its other candidates. One day the district boss asked us to campaign for the Congressional candidate. He said that if we seriously wanted the President to keep us out of war, we had to give him a Congress which would back him in his pacific policy. What a calamity it would be for the country if the lofty aims of the Democratic President were wrecked by a Republican Congress!

It was true. What the socialist intellectuals had failed to explain, a Tammany boss made clear. You could not separate the President from his party. But then, could you separate that party from the capitalist class? Ashamed and humiliated, Robert and I quit the stump. Our intellectual pride was humbled. We confessed our error to Louis who restored us to his friendship and let us help him in his socialist election activities.

Middle-class liberals on the fringe of the socialist movement con-

sidered Wilson's re-election a "victory for progressivism." Amos Pin-
chot thought it meant a drift of power from Wall Street to the
People. William English Walling defended the pro-Wilson radicals on
the ground that in Europe "not even the most revolutionary socialists"
objected to co-operating with progressive bourgeois parties. Max Eastman, who continued for a long time to propagate the Wilson myth,
defended his stand in the elections by calling his socialist critics sectarians, dogmatists and cranks.

The sectarians, dogmatists and cranks replied that when the intellectuals advised us to support the Democratic party, they were giving aid and comfort to the enemy. One socialist of the "line" wrote:

"The *Masses* advertises itself as a 'revolutionary' magazine, and it
falls for the trickery of a cheap middle-class trimmer like Wilson! . . .
Revolutionists! They are but a lot of commonplace boobs who play
with great words and then swallow line, bob and sinker at the first
cast, with the mighty thin bait of a few meretricious and contemptible
reforms!"

At the moment when broad-minded "socialists" were helping to
fashion the Wilson myth, the class which the President represented
waged ruthless warfare against the American workers. In San Francisco, Tom Mooney and Warren Billings were railroaded to jail on the
false charge of bombing a preparedness parade. The New York transportation trust was crushing a streetcar workers' strike. Fake "arbitra-
tion" was smashing a railway workers' strike. In the Minnesota strike
of miners and steel workers, company gunmen murdered a number of
strikers, while Carlo Tresca and other labor leaders were arrested on
frame-up murder charges. In Everett, Washington, the employers replied to a strike of longshoremen and shingle weavers by the notorious
"bloody Sunday," when sheriffs killed five and wounded thirty out of
the two hundred wobblies who came to attend a mass meeting. In the
pitched battle that followed, two deputies were killed and fifteen
wounded, and a hundred wobblies were arrested on murder charges.
Under a President whom the *Masses* called "the most progressive since
Lincoln," the class struggle raged as never before in America.

§4

The overthrow of the Czar in February, 1917, filled us with joy.
What had been a dream for years was now a reality. The prison of the
peoples had collapsed. We sang the *Marseillaise* and the *International*

in the streets, cut classes for the day, and rushed to tell our families the great news.

Almost the entire American press, from the extreme right to the extreme left, applauded the February Revolution. The conservative newspapers correctly assumed that the abolition of Russian feudalism ushered in a bourgeois government which would pursue the war against Germany more enthusiastically than had the Romanov dynasty. Moreover, the overthrow of czarism removed the paradoxical sting from the plea that America should enter the war to defend democracy. The radicals hailed the revolution as a step toward socialism. Left intellectuals like John Reed were wisely skeptical of a revolution run by businessmen, publishers and lawyers; but they threw their hats into the air when the workers' and soldiers' councils appeared.

There was the same confusion about Russian political parties and their aims as there had been three years earlier in our attempts to understand the Mexican Revolution. Leon Trotsky's name was familiar to us. We had read about the ovations which workers' meetings gave him on his arrival in New York in 1916. Some of us had heard him speak. Now we read about his arrest in Canada, his arrival in Petrograd. Lenin was a strange name to us. We had no notion who he was. Everything was muddled by the abstract word "revolution." The radical press increased our confusion. On April 24, 1917, the *Call,* official organ of the Socialist party, published the following dispatch under a London date line:

"Petrograd reports today laid the demonstration against the American embassy in that city Saturday night at the door of the German propagandists. Nikolai Lenin, a Russian radical who returned recently from exile in Switzerland through Germany, is said to have aroused a mob to frenzy by declaring that America was the enemy of socialism and that Thomas J. Mooney, the San Francisco labor leader at present under sentence of death, has already been hanged."

The editors of the *Call* were not skeptical about a London dispatch concerning revolutionary Russia. No one we knew was in the mood to investigate what seemed to be at that moment a secondary matter. President Wilson, re-elected on a peace platform, had called us to war. It was not an army that had to be shaped and trained for war, he said, but a nation.

Early in April, Dr. Butler called students and faculty together in the gymnasium. Dr. Butler had a reputation as a pacifist prominent in various "peace" foundations. He made liberal speeches and published liberal articles. For years he had been an enthusiast for German Kultur and was proud to be the Kaiser's friend. Now, like our guides and teachers among the radical intelligentsia, he paid his respects to the political "realities." Addressing us as "gentlemen," he urged us to stand by the Republic in the hour of its peril. The fate of America depended upon its youth; we were implored to perish that democracy might live.

We sat still in the crowded gymnasium. The phrases fell like drops of heavy oil; the graying mustache quivered with calculated pathos; the deliberately heavy eyelids drooped at the Ciceronian periods as indicated in the MS. But at last, thank heaven, came Professor John Erskine, from whom we were at that time absorbing the divine sentiments of Spenser, Shakespeare and Santayana. Professor Erskine did not disappoint us. He foresaw the brutal passions which war would unleash, the prejudice and persecution which would pervade the land. He urged that we, at least, should maintain the highest standards of humanity. Let the scholar bar intolerance from the campus, keeping the sacred light of detachment and the free expression of opinion undimmed on the campus.

With growing despondency, my friends and I watched the mobilization of the country for war. We knew millions of men were being put under arms and that Congress was placing unprecedented war power in the hands of the President who had been held up to us as the champion of peace. The gracious Democrat in the White House was vested with the authority of a dictator. He could requisition supplies for the army and navy, fix the price of commodities, take over factories, mines, railways, steamships, telephone and telegraph. He monopolized the manufacture, distribution and import of all necessities of life. The government ostensibly controlled the economic machinery of the land. For war purposes it had adopted what Big Business had for years condemned as "socialism." But Big Business was safe. It dominated all the agencies formally exercising government control.

Until now the students on our campus had considered political differences irrelevant to personal relations. We could admire the private qualities of those who disagreed with us. They said to us and we said to them, what a pity a fine fellow like you is not on our side. Now we boycotted each other. From the top, too, came a spirit of harsh intolerance. Dr. Leon Fraser had arranged for our debating team to tour the country arguing against preparedness at various colleges. With the declaration of war, the tour was called off. Students could not oppose increased armaments when civilization itself was at stake. A group of Journalism students issued one or two numbers of an anti-war magazine called *Challenge,* and Morrie Ryskind got out an anti-war issue of *The Jester,* which he edited. The authorities replied to these activities by expelling from the university, on the eve of their graduation, three Journalism students—Morrie Ryskind, Charles Francis Phillips and Eleanor Parker. Professor Erskine's oration in the gymnasium was the last we heard of academic freedom.

§ 5

President Wilson was not the only savior in cap and gown who surprised our generation. Professors throughout the world abandoned their pose of scholarly detachment and became war propagandists. German savants beat bass drums for the Kaiser, hooting metaphysical epithets at the Allies. British, French and American philosophers "proved" by the strictest rules of logic that Fichte, Hegel and Nietzsche were responsible for the war. Henri Bergson, like any common jingo, painted Germany as the monster of the West. Professor John Dewey, of our own faculty, signed a declaration of "absolute and unconditional loyalty" to the government in its war against Germany, although as a pragmatist he professionally disavowed the absolute and the uncondi-tional. Thorstein Veblen, ironically inquiring into the nature of peace in general, applauded the war against Germany in particular. Professor Morris Cohen, too skeptical to fire categorical imperatives at Germany, maintained an aloof neutrality within the ivory tower of pure mathe-matics, too noble to interfere in the vulgar affairs of the day by con-demning the murder of millions.

The left intellectuals were having troubles of their own. Like the romantics of the French Revolution, these "new spirits" concentrated their fight for freedom chiefly against the prevailing sexual conven-tions. They jeered at what Europeans call philistinism, and Americans called puritanism. Hence the worship of Isadora Duncan. In radical and liberal circles she was considered at once the greatest living dancer and the symbol of the body's liberation from mid-Victorian taboos. Actually, the taboos were Judeo-Christian and even older, but the pre-war intelligentsia dated human history from Tennyson. A strange dark century, the nineteenth! Floyd Dell, for instance, refused to be consoled by the thought that across that dark age there flashed the meteors of Nietzsche, Whitman, Darwin and Marx, "prophetic of the splendor of the millenniums." Had he lived and died in the darkness of that century, he would never have seen "the beauty and terror of the human body." Grateful for the daylight of his own time, he felt that it was not enough to throw God from his pedestal and dream of supermen and the co-operative commonwealth. To die happy, one must have seen Isadora Duncan. Europe had its parallel to the Duncan cult in the Ballet Russe. On the eve of the war, the salons burned incense to the muscular legs of the Pole Nijinsky, perhaps the greatest dancer of all, whom Diaghileff, out of homosexual love and jealousy, held captive like an Albertine. But while Europe's cult of Nijinsky was the decadent intoxication of upper classes seeking to forget the abyss of war yawning wider and wider at their feet, the Duncan cult in America represented the awakening of middle-class puritans to the joys of the body, their protest against the hypocrisy of the philistines, their declaration of the Rights of Man to Woman—all of it a belated echo of the romantic movement which made Byron and Goethe symbols of a free life. Until America entered the war, the radiant Duncan myth remained intact. Now, in 1917, art joined philosophy and journalism as camp followers of the army. Isadora encouraged the war fever by patriotic dances at the Metropolitan Opera. The left intellectuals were unhappy. Floyd Dell heaped more bitter scorn upon her than upon John Dewey and Thorstein Veblen.

Duncan, Dewey, Veblen and Cohen were never socialists, however. Much more disheartening was the defection to the enemy camp of outstanding intellectuals in the Socialist party. Radicals who had supported Wilson in the "peace without provocation" elections divided into three groups. Some, like John Reed, bluntly admitted their mistake and threw themselves with all energy into the campaign against the war.

"I voted for Woodrow Wilson," John Reed said in the summer of 1917, "mainly because Wall Street was against him. But Wall Street is for him now. This is Woodrow Wilson's and Wall Street's war."

Others, like Max Eastman, opposed the war but continued to defend the President. They admitted this was no war for democracy, yet propagated the illusion that the war would advertise the idea of democracy and for that reason applauded Wilson's pharisaical utterances. Various opportunist intellectuals within the socialist movement followed Wilson from his "peace" campaign into the war. A group including W. J. Ghent, Charles Edward Russell, J. G. Phelps Stokes and William English Walling issued a "practical program for socialists," urging them to "adjust themselves to events" and advocating a large

war budget, universal military training and the conscription of men
and women. As usual, the most flamboyant and sentimental gestures
were made by Upton Sinclair. Two months before America's entry into
the war he sent a lyrical telegram to the President urging immediate
naval action against Germany in the name of freedom and democracy.
One after another, men whom we had grown up to admire as revolutionary thinkers, men whose books we had read, whose speeches
we had heard, whose loyalty to socialism was our inspiration, capitu-
lated to the capitalists without a blush. Their hysterical cries for ruthless military action against Germany made reactionaries like Elihu
Root appear sober and logical.

The conflicting forces within the socialist movement clashed
openly at the Socialist party convention which met in St. Louis in the
spring of 1917. A majority resolution, adopted by three-fourths of the
delegates, reiterated the principles of Stuttgart and Basle; it repudiated
capitalist war in general and this war in particular:

"The only struggle which would justify the workers in taking up
arms is the great struggle of the working-class of the world to free
itself from economic exploitation and political oppression. As against
the false doctrine of national patriotism, we uphold the ideal of international working-class solidarity. In support of capitalism, we will not
willingly give a single life or a single dollar; in support of the struggle
of the workers for freedom, we pledge all. . . . We brand the declaration of war by our government as a crime against the people of the
United States and against the nations of the world. The Socialist Party
emphatically rejects the proposal that in time of war the workers
should suspend their struggle for better conditions. On the contrary,
the acute situation created by war calls for an even more vigorous prosecution of the class-struggle."

About one-fourth of the delegates, led by intellectuals like John
Spargo, W. J. Ghent, Charmian London, Charles Edward Russell,
William English Walling, Upton Sinclair, George Sterling and J. G.
Phelps Stokes presented a minority report which "recognized" the war
"as a fact," and supported that "fact" in order to "minimize the suffering and misery" which it would bring our own people, to protect
"our rights and liberties against reactionary encroachments" and to
promote an early peace upon a democratic basis advantageous to the
international working class. Like the socialist opportunists of Europe,
these intellectuals supported capitalism in the name of the working
class.

My friends and I read the conflicting documents carefully, as if the fate of the world depended upon our choice. We were already beginning to be affected by the cult of youth, as expressed by Bertrand Russell. Released from an English prison where he had served a year for antiwar propaganda, that great logician now believed that humanity's ultimate hope lay in the young, especially in the young men of America. We would be performing the greatest possible service to our less fortunate contemporaries in Europe by retaining the right of the individual to judge for himself whether he would engage in destruction at the bidding of men less wise and humane than we. We alone, it seemed, were in a position to preserve man's sacred right to make choices; and we chose to abide by the majority resolution of the Socialist party. We would not willingly lift a finger to help the exploiters in their war.

On the campus, the spring air was heavy with the spirit of a military barracks. Students who enrolled in voluntary troops, hoping to get army commissions later, came to classes in uniform. Criticism of the war was now sedition, but one could still discuss questions pending before Congress. The Columbia debating team, of which I was now captain, was permitted to go to Ithaca to oppose the contemplated Espionage Act which Cornell's team defended. I argued that the act would be used primarily not against German spies but against pacifists, radicals, socialists, wobblies, dissenters of all kinds; it would exterminate the last vestiges of that democracy which the war was supposed to preserve. To my surprise, we won the debate.

The Espionage Act was passed in June and the reign of terror which we had expected was launched against dissidents of every type. It was now officially a crime to speak your mind. In the country which was defending democracy against militarism, the soldier was given a free hand against the civilian. You did not have to be a radical or a pacifist to be molested, beaten or killed. By the fall of 1917, John Reed reported that with "a hideous apathy, the country has acquiesced in a regime of judicial tyranny, bureaucratic suppression and industrial barbarism." The chief victims of the Espionage Act were radicals. Alexander Berkman and Emma Goldman were arrested and convicted under it, and neither the prosecutor nor the judge concealed that the real "crime" of these anarchists was their loyalty to internationalism. The act was also used to suppress about two score radical newspapers and magazines.

The class struggle, which some radicals thought the war would abolish, became more intense during the year. St. Louis manufacturers imported Negro workers to break the local trade unions. The result was a race riot in which the Negro quarter of St. Louis was sacked and burned, and more than thirty Negro men and women slaughtered. Under the New Freedom, battling for "democracy and civilization," several hundred striking workers were deported from the mines of Bisbee, Arizona, into the desert. They were dumped into cattle cars and shipped to Columbus, New Mexico, where "patriotic" citizens immediately shipped them back into the desert, leaving them stranded without food, water or shelter. The deportees included not only wobblies, but unaffiliated workers, and even the strikers' lawyer who was no more than a liberal. The strikers were finally picked up and fed by the local United States army corps, which talked about interning them for the duration of the war. The Phelps-Dodge corporation, which owned the struck mines and the town of Bisbee, permitted no one to enter the region without a passport. It was the president of this corporation who became head of the Red Cross and appealed for funds in the name of "mercy." In San Francisco, the frame-up against Tom Mooney was pushed vigorously despite the exposure of false witnesses. From Omaha, Carl Sandburg, then a socialist as well as a poet, reported that businessmen were importing scabs from other parts of the country and preparing to frame labor leaders as Mooney had been framed. Throughout the United States, the propertied classes, hiding behind the cloak of "patriotism," were breaking up labor organizations and persecuting labor leaders.

Yet, blind to necessary political distinctions, I was perplexed to see radical intellectuals enter the service of the government. The Bureau of Public Information, official propaganda agency, was headed by George Creel whose descriptions of industrial atrocities in Colorado we had read in the *Masses*. The bureau included among its prowar agitators other *Masses* writers, among them Arthur Bullard, the author of *Comrade Yetta,* who had called for a new socialist international, Ernest Poole, and Walter Lippmann, secretary to America's first socialist mayor.

Men and women opposed to the war now appeared like scattered ineffectual molecules. On the campus, most students looked upon the radicals with whom I associated as "traitors." At home our parents watched us with the same alarm with which, as a child, I had seen grandfather watch Uncle Moishe's activities. They were afraid our unorthodox political views would injure them and us irreparably. We were not an integral part of the American revolutionary movement, however. We were no more than remote sympathizers. Isolated on the campus, lacking that sense of comradeship which one gets in a mass organization, we were breaking from an old world without having found a new one. This bred in us the kind of social neurosis which infects the lone village atheist; we felt at once like pioneers and outcasts. There were times when we moved helplessly amidst the roar of millions cheering the boys to the front, aware that if the war continued we might be among those boys. But the feeling of isolation was not new; we had been nurtured in it. We felt our only concern was with moral values, with questions of right and wrong. In that feeling lay seeds of danger for us.

My notebook for 1917 contained comments on the course in modern European history which I took with Professor Carlton Hayes: *we have had our commercial revolution, our industrial revolution; now for our social revolution. The development of social conscience will be humanity's salvation. Always the rulers drag god into their quarrels; religion as a part of politics has been the device of all ruling classes. The bourgeoisie won a position which they are now loath to relinquish; they confiscated church property but cry out in horror at the thought of having their oil wells and railways confiscated. The lives which the Reign of Terror took helped to push humanity along the path of Progress; the lives lost in nineteenth century wars have served to fill the treasure chests of greedy financiers. Why not a social revolution? If mankind must shed its blood let it be for its own salvation!*

§ 6

I was studying history and knew the world's battles, massacres and assassinations. I knew that man had fought his way through blood from the primeval slime to his present stage, halfway on the road to civilization. I had been taught that man was war, force and fraud. Yet the war shocked me. Along with the names and dates of formal history, I had absorbed, both in the classroom and from the life around me, the illusion that mass violence was a thing of the past. I imagined that great wars belonged far back in the eras of Napoleon and Lincoln. The Spanish-American episode was a mere police raid; the Balkan conflicts were brawls among barbarians; the invasion of Mexico was the foray of the capitalist strong-arm squad in Marine uniforms. Since the sixties of the last century, the world had had a few minor colli-

sions in the backward regions; the civilized nations had passed beyond
that form of savagery.

Now this illusion was dead. My friends and I had to reorient ourselves in a world utterly different from the one we had been trained to
expect. The war became the touchstone for every idea, every moral
value; it intensified our belief that socialism alone could save mankind
from barbarism. We now looked upon Russia as the earth's most cru-
cial area. That country had taken socialism out of books, pamphlets
and meeting halls and was trying it out in real life. Russia was the
great social "laboratory"—a phrase commonly used by contemporary
liberals who forgot that a living society cannot reproduce the controlled conditions of the laboratory, and that experience is not experiment. We concentrated our hopes on the Russian Revolution in direct
proportion as American socialism became more confused.

The Soviets appealed to the citizens of the Allied countries not to
allow the voice of the Russian provisional government to remain isolated from the union of the Allied Powers, to force their governments
to proclaim resolutely a program of peace without annexations or
indemnities and the right of peoples to settle their own destinies. This
appeal inspired Scott Nearing to organize the People's Council of
America, representing all shades of radical and liberal opinion united
on the Soviet peace proposals. Socialists, wobblies, anarchists, liberals
and pacifists of every kind crowded the old Madison Square Garden
at the end of May when the People's Council was founded. I had attended political meetings since childhood, but had never seen such an
immense one. You were not alone; there were many who hated the
war as much as you did. How moving was the eloquence of Judah L.
Magnes announcing the purposes of the council: to secure an early,
democratic and general peace in harmony with the principles outlined
by New Russia, no forcible annexations, no punitive indemnities, the
free development of all nationalities; to urge international organization for the maintenance of world peace; to work for the repeal of the
conscription laws; to safeguard labor standards; to preserve and extend
democracy and liberty within the United States.

That summer Robert and I were working for an automobile tire
company in Columbus Circle. The office force was large and we considered it our duty to argue with anyone who would listen about the
war and the Russian Revolution. Executives warned us that if we did
not stop this "seditious" talk we would be fired. While we were debating the most effective way of resigning, the government suppressed the

Masses. We had become so identified in our own minds with the magazine that the suppression affected us more than our troubles at the office. Ours was only a vacation job; in the fall we were going back to Columbia. But to kill the *Masses* was to kill our real university.

The "crimes" of the *Masses* were committed in the August issue, which appealed for funds to defend Alexander Berkman and Emma Goldman, and petitioned the President to repeal conscription at once. The government considered that several editorials, some cartoons by Boardman Robinson, Art Young and H. J. Glintenkamp, and a poem by Josephine Bell hampered General Pershing in his campaign against Germany. Part of the poem ran:

> Emma Goldman and Alexander Berkman
> Are in prison tonight,
> But they have made themselves elemental forces,
> Like water that climbs down rocks,
> Like the wind in the leaves:
> Like the gentle night that holds us:
> They are working on our destinies:
> They are forging the love of nations.

For these lines Josephine Bell was arrested, together with Max Eastman, Floyd Dell and Art Young. It was rumored that President Wilson personally urged the indictment of the editors who had admired the grace and beauty of his character. The presidential ingratitude did not prevent the magazine from hailing Wilson's letter to the Pope two months later as acceding to the peace terms of the Soviets and giving grounds for "high hope" of "permanent just peace and international federation for the world." The President was now described as a man with the creed of democracy and the temper of an autocrat, a man who had altogether failed as a leader or even a defender of democratic life.

By the end of the summer of 1917 the People's Council had widened its program. Its additional demands were a concrete statement of war aims, a democratic foreign policy and referendum vote by the people on questions of war and peace; taxation of wealth to pay for the war; and the reduction of the high cost of living. The council was not a revolutionary organization; its program was strictly within the letter of the law even in wartime. But because it gathered into one nation-wide group nearly two million people unwilling to "keep their mouths shut," the patriots clamped down on it. Scott Nearing, council organizer, was barred from meeting halls in various cities and on several occasions was arrested.

On a small scale, we encountered similar difficulties in our own neighborhood. Robert and I decided to organize a branch of the council but no hallkeeper would rent us a meeting place. We telephoned New York's "liberal" police commissioner who assured us it was not illegal for the council to meet. The local police lieutenant was paternal. What did we want to get mixed up in this pro-German stuff for? The meeting was not illegal; we could meet in any hall we could rent. But no proprietor would rent us a hall. We thought of holding an open-air meeting when a young poet named Selma Robinson got another idea. She prevailed on her uncle who owned that Capitol Hall where in childhood we had heard Charles Edward Russell speak to let us meet there. Another relative of hers, wise in the ways of local politics, pointed out to us the eleven detectives in the hall. Opening the meeting, I indicated the dicks to the audience as guardians of democracy and civilization. My father, who earlier in the day had threatened to throw me out of the house for flirting with trouble, arrived in the middle of the meeting with bail in case we were arrested. The most extreme speaker of the evening was a blond young wobbly who read his speech from manuscript. At the end of the meeting, the police came to the platform and asked for the speech. It could not be found. Selma Robinson had hidden it in her blouse and lost herself in the crowd.

The meeting elected Robert and myself delegates to the People's Council which was to meet in Minneapolis. The governor of Minnesota announced that if the convention was held in his state it would be broken up by militia. We were twenty and felt solemn and important. We said good-by to our families as if we were going to war in a far-off planet. My brother, then twelve, said if the Minnesota militia killed Robert and myself, he would quit school and replace us.

On the special train which took the council delegates west, there was talk of meeting in Minnesota in spite of the governor. For me the trip had its personal exhilaration. At last I was out of New York seeing the "real" America. For the first time, too, I saw boyhood heroes face to face. On the train, and later at the convention, we met Morris Hillquit, then considered the Brains of the socialist movement; Sara Bard Field who wrote verses for the *Masses;* Robert Haberman, about whose exploits in socialist Yucatan we had read in the Sunday papers, and the socialist lawyer Jacob Panken. We also met Professor Henry Wadsworth Longfellow Dana of Columbia University with whom Robert and I had registered for a course in comparative literature for the coming fall, but whom we had never seen before.

Shaving with us in the rolling washroom of the train, Jacob Panken said:

"So you are not yet twenty? You think it's remarkable to be the youngest delegates to this convention? When I was only sixteen I was a member of a secret revolutionary organization in Russia."

Humbled I returned to my seat and began to write verses.

"What are you writing there, young man?" Sara Bard Field said. "*Love* poetry? What do you know about love at your age?"

I was grateful she did not ask me what I knew about poetry. The delegates were all friendly to Robert and me. We felt suddenly that we had found what we had been seeking, the world to which we properly belonged.

The council decided not to come to grips with the sovereign state of Minnesota but to hold its convention in Chicago. It met in a large auditorium in the West Side slums. Robert and I went to the opening meeting with two new friends, Ida Rau and Crystal Eastman. The short, olive-skinned Ida, a Jewess, was then the wife of the *Masses* editor; Crystal was his sister, a handsome Amazon, enormous and trim in her bright red shirtwaist, full of energy, practical wisdom and warm human sympathy. The two women seemed to bring us nearer by their mere presence to that magic circle of artists and writers, at once romantic and revolutionary, who were our guiding stars in the chaos of those times. The convention itself brought us still nearer. At last we saw Shelley plain. Out of the long array of speakers there emerged on the platform Max Eastman himself, tall and slim, with a pink handsome face and prematurely white hair. His voice was full of petition and persuasion. His well-ordered academic rhetoric carried to the farthest ends of the crowded hall. He seemed to embody in sensuous outline the New Spirit of the intelligentsia in rebellion against convention. He looked Beauty and spoke Justice.

The convention did not last long. On the second day, a police inspector told us to go home or we would be pinched. The socialist and liberal leaders of the council accepted this ultimatum; the wobblies sitting beside me grumbled about the "yellow socialist rats" ready to disperse without a fight. At night militia surrounded the hotel at which the delegates were staying. The executive committee of the council held one secret meeting, and the following day the delegates went home.

The resolutions adopted in Chicago echoed the appeal of the So-

viets, which now carried new connotations. We had heard little, and
all of it bad, about the "German agents" headed by Lenin. To us the
Russian Revolution at this time meant the Soviets and Kerensky. And
now Kerensky was urging the Russian soldiers back into the trenches
to defend the "revolution." Was New Russia to be destroyed by the
Kaiser's armies? Must not the revolution be saved at all costs? Many
American radicals began to echo the Menshevik phrases about "revolutionary defensism." The only way we could help Revolutionary Russia against autocratic Germany, it seemed, was through Woodrow
Wilson and "Black Jack" Pershing. Yet every day revealed more glar-
ingly the sham behind the slogan of "democracy and civilization." The
campus, which was described to us in April as the last refuge of intellectual freedom, treated us no better than did the police. When Robert
and I appeared before the bursar to complete our registration for the
coming year, we were confronted with newspaper clippings about our
People's Council meeting in Capitol Hall. The bursar came to the
point with unacademic directness:

"The next time your names appear in connection with any such
subversive activity, you will be dropped from the university. Good day,
gentlemen."

§ 7

On the campus, four streams of my life converged, thanks to the
war—literature, echoes of adolescent Zionism, American radical
thought and memories of wobbly romance.

When the fall term opened, I met Professor Dana in the classroom where he opened his course in comparative literature. Later a
student organization invited Emanuel Neuman, director of the Young
Zionist Club to which I belonged as a boy, to talk on the Jews and the
war. With campus and childhood crossing this way, I realized how
far away I had moved from nationalism. The following week, another
student group listened to Randolph Bourne, considered the most brilliant of the radical intellectuals. Himself a Columbia man, Bourne
took advantage of his lecture to settle accounts with pragmatism. He
also said that fundamental human interests were, geographically speaking, horizontal rather than vertical. They divided men not into countries, as the maps did, but into classes. German and British bankers
had more in common than either had with German or British workers.
The next day one of our literary instructors delivered a brief and
caustic sermon in class on the bad taste and ingratitude which Bourne
had exhibited in his devastating piece *The Twilight of the Gods*. At a

dinner given by liberal faculty members, I met for the first time my boyhood hero Frank Tannenbaum whom friends had enabled to enter Columbia. Tannenbaum had a dark, young, vigorous face, with the flat nose and full mouth of a young Tolstoy. He wore simple clothes and broad shoes; his manners were elaborate; and for a defiant opponent of bourgeois society his attitude toward the professors present was surprisingly respectful and diplomatic.

While the Department of Justice carried on its nation-wide snooping campaign, property holders dominating the higher institutions of learning initiated their own purges. Columbia University headed the list of patriotic academies with the expulsion of Professors J. M. Cattell and H. W. L. Dana. The former, one of the best-known psychologists in America, was guilty not only of pacifism but of poking fun at Dr. Nicholas Murray Butler. Professor Dana's crime was his activity in the People's Council.

After the expulsion, Robert and I went to Dr. Dana's room in Livingston Hall to help him pack and to say good-by. Frank Tannenbaum was there, looking more like a young Russian peasant than ever. He was packing a trunk for Dr. Dana. Randolph Bourne was there too, swinging his child's legs from the desk on which he sat. The sharp small face set in the crippled back was vivid with intellect and scorn. He talked with a grin about academic freedom. The irony of what he said was all the more acid for the quietness of his voice. For him the expulsion of Dana and Cattell was merely the dramatic symbol of an all-pervasive intellectual rot on the campus. Dr. Dana, spryly moving among his books and documents, was less disturbed by his expulsion than by the treatment he had suffered from his personal friends. Professor Erskine, so eloquent on the theme of academic freedom in April, had returned Dr. Dana's letters ostentatiously unopened. Dr. Dana was surprised and hurt.

He told us that at the faculty meeting which expelled him he was accused of teaching sedition and disloyalty on the campus. The "proof" was that he had induced Robert and myself to attend the People's Council convention in Chicago. He must take the consequences, and so must we. Dr. Dana replied truthfully that he had never seen either Robert or myself until the time of the convention. If he alone was expelled he would keep quiet, but if we were expelled he would make a scandal in the press. The authorities then decided to expel him and Professor Cattell without expelling Robert or me.

Randolph Bourne listened to this story quietly and said:

"And now that you have been expelled, Harry, will you make the scandal?"

"Certainly not," Dr. Dana said. "I've given my word as a gentleman."

"That's the trouble," Bourne replied with a wide grin. "You look upon all of this as a gentlemen's quarrel. You lack Homeric anger."

Events were later to evoke Homeric anger in the neat descendant of the Danas and Longfellows; he retained and developed the militant democratic traditions of early New England. But at this time it was another professor who precipitated a "scandal" on the campus around the expulsions.

Long before we came to Columbia we had known the name of Professor Charles A. Beard. At high school we had crammed for examinations in the history of Europe which he had written with James Harvey Robinson. His own famous work, *The Economic Interpretation of the Constitution of the United States,* was a byword among socialist agitators who liked to quote established intellectual authorities. The formula was: even So-and-so, a college professor opposed to socialism, admits this and that. The quotation was supposed to impress the prospective convert to the cause as unimpeachable evidence. Professors were assumed to have a virtual monopoly of knowledge and a desire to conceal truth in the interests of the propertied classes. When a professor admitted a socialist assertion, and out of the depths of his scholarship proved it, the assertion became doubly true. Beard's analysis of the American constitution established beyond question the socialist contention that the United States has a class society whose fundamental laws are class laws for the benefit of the bankers and manufacturers as against the workers and farmers.

In the classroom we found Dr. Beard a teacher of great intellectual vigor and integrity. He was a dramatic and concise lecturer. His thin face and aquiline nose gave him the look of a Roman philosopher. Sometimes he talked to the class with his eyes closed. His sharp voice whipped out the words lucidly; the sentences rolled over long curves like the periods of a Latin oration.

Professor Beard, like the muckrakers whose scholarly cousin he was, had no illusions about the corrupt operations of capitalism. Like them, too, he harbored the dream of a Jeffersonian democracy brought up to date—a new and better, possibly a *state,* capitalism. He described for us in minute detail the ideal administrative state based on private property, and added, one day, that in such an administrative machine every man and woman could be taught some form of civil service; with the possible exception, he added, smiling and opening his eyes, of the poets, who seem incapable of learning anything and who are not indispensable to the administration of a state.

Throughout 1916, Professor Beard urged America's entry into the war. He warned us in class that Germany was a danger to civilization. It was an illusion, he said, to think of Americans as a pacific people; they are and always have been one of the most violent peoples in history. Consider the number of wars we have waged since the establishment of our government, and the sanguinary violence of our industrial disputes. Should these disputes ever lead to civil war it would probably be the most bloody of its kind in history. One morning, when the press reported the sinking of a merchant vessel by German submarines, Dr. Beard came into the classroom pale and stern. He looked at us for a long time in silence, then closed his eyes.

"Gentlemen," he said, "the history of the world was altered today. It will now be impossible for the United States to stay out of the war. German autocracy will have to be destroyed."

He opened his eyes and they were full of tears.

Now, when Professors Dana and Cattell were expelled for views directly opposed to his, Dr. Beard protested against the expulsion by resigning from the university. The expulsion raised for him not the question of war, which Washington had settled to his satisfaction, but the question of intellectual freedom.

The radical students on the campus called a demonstration to express sympathy with Dr. Beard. It was to be held at eleven in the morning, near the gilded statue of Alma Mater on the library steps where we had recently heard René Viviani plead the cause of France. The college authorities warned us that any student cutting classes to attend the meeting would be punished. Professor Carlton Hayes, himself cynical about certain surface aspects of the prevailing society, circumvented this prohibition. On the morning of the demonstration, he came early to our class on the Causes and Origins of the Present War, then probably the largest in the college, with almost two hundred students. In a voice tense with feeling, he said:

"Gentlemen, we have lost today in this university one of the most intelligent, honest and courageous men who ever lived. There is nothing I can say to you in my course today as important as Dr. Beard's resignation. The class is dismissed."

We rushed to the library steps. Among the speakers who protested against the expulsion of Professors Dana and Cattell and approved Dr. Beard's resignation was an anarchist lecturer on philosophy named Will Durant.

To allay the turmoil aroused by Dr. Beard's resignation, the authorities offered the gymnasium for a student mass meeting to be arranged by a joint committee of radicals and conservatives. Each side was to have one speaker; each speech was to be written out in advance and approved by the joint committee; a resolution expressing regret over Dr. Beard's resignation was to be read by a "neutral," a member of the football team.

The radicals selected Frank Tannenbaum to represent them on the joint committee; I was to speak in the gymnasium. The committee agreed that no speech must refer to the expulsion of Professors Dana and Cattell or to the war; all remarks must be confined to regretting Dr. Beard's resignation. I wrote out a five-minute speech which Frank Tannenbaum and the rest of the committee approved.

Thousands of students crowded the gymnasium on the afternoon of the meeting. The conservative speaker—an editor of the literary magazine on the campus—launched into a violent attack on Dana and Cattell, and wound up with a call to arms in defense of democracy and civilization. When my turn came, I told the audience about the agreement to avoid mention of the war and the expulsions. We had not liked that agreement from the beginning and were grateful to the previous speaker for violating it. Now we could discuss the real issues involved in Dr. Beard's resignation. If we really respected Dr. Beard as much as we all said we did, there was no better way of showing our sentiments than by supporting his fight for academic freedom. Furthermore, since the conservative speaker had, in violation of his pledge, attacked Dana and Cattell as traitors, it was not out of place to say that many students shared their "seditious" views. We honored them for their integrity and courage in exposing the war for what it was—a war for capitalism.

Voices shouted:

"Traitor! He's a German spy! Throw him out!"

Other voices shouted in support of our position. There were scuffles at the back of the hall. Next day the Columbia *Spectator* ran almost the whole of the conservative speech, and cited one innocuous sentence from mine, regretting Dr. Beard's resignation.

Dr. Beard's action was an avowal of the libertarian principle of free speech. Professor Dewey also, while thoroughly in favor of war, protested against the expulsions. The Columbia dismissals initiated a reign of terror in the intellectual world. All over the country teachers were expelled from colleges and high schools for criticizing the war, and ministers were fired from churches for taking the doctrines of Christ seriously. Such expulsions were only the milder aspects of war hysteria. Patriotic fury concentrated itself on dissenters in direct proportion to their radicalism. Socialists, wobblies, members of the liberal-agrarian Non-Partisan League were whipped, tarred and feathered; mobs broke up meetings of the Friends of Irish Freedom; Rose Pastor Stokes was sentenced to ten years in prison for a talk on war profiteering; Kate Richards O'Hare was given five years for criticizing war in general. One did not have to be a radical to feel the effects of democracy and civilization. Patriotic mobs whipped German farmers to make them join the Red Cross, tortured religious pacifists of the International Bible Students Association, and threatened violence to liberals like David Starr Jordan. To combat these conditions, liberals converted the American Union Against Militarism, which had been organized in 1915 to counteract the preparedness campaign, into the National Civil Liberties Union with Roger Baldwin as director.

§ 8

Antiwar sentiment gathered around the Socialist party in the fall elections of 1917. Patriotic hysteria cost the Party many votes in the agrarian sections of the country, but in the large cities it attracted all kinds of antiwar elements. The campaign was most intense in New York City where Morris Hillquit ran for mayor. To the young socialists of my acquaintance, it appeared as if Hillquit had every chance of being elected. Radical pacifists supported him because of his stand against the war; Russian-born liberals, stirred by the overthrow of the Czar, once more saw hope in the socialist movement; and Irish Republicans expressed their hatred of the British Empire by cheering Hillquit. For the second time, Robert and I took the stump in an election campaign, this time with a clear conscience.

Soon the campaign invaded our campus. Democratic students and professors invited Hylan to address them, and partisans of the Fusion ticket arranged a meeting for Mitchel. A group of us then telephoned Hillquit and asked him to speak. Our candidate accepted but warned us to get the permission of the college authorities for his meeting. President Butler agreed to permit the meeting provided a faculty member would sponsor Hillquit. After the expulsion of Dana and

Cattell, it was asking a great deal of any professor to sponsor an anti-war candidate. Several of our liberal teachers whom we approached declined to take the risk. But Hillquit was not disturbed; his laughter over the telephone was soft and reassuring.

"It's simple," he said. "Go to my friend Professor Seligman."

Professor Edwin R. A. Seligman, head of Columbia's economics department, was an "archreactionary" whom socialists had for years attacked from soapbox and platform as the chief economic apologist of capitalism. He was charming to Robert and me when we asked him to sponsor Hillquit. He stroked his square gray beard slowly and said:

"If it's up to me, my good friend Morris can speak on this campus any time he wants to. We've spent many week-ends at my country place arguing socialism. We never convince each other and we never fail to have a good time."

Personal intimacy between the champion of our cause and the apologist for capitalism was beyond our understanding. Was it possible that the leaders of both sides did not take seriously the ideas they professed?

Hillquit's meeting at Earl Hall was crowded with students and instructors, most of them patriots curious to hear the socialist position on the war. For an hour, our candidate spoke smoothly, never raising his voice, barely making a gesture. He talked about municipal economy, and described how socialists would manage city owned and controlled power stations, streetcars, milk stations and subways. He concluded his talk without once referring to the war. From the back of the hall, a conservative student, anxious to precipitate a discussion, asked:

"Mr. Hillquit, what do you think about Liberty bonds?"

This was a direct challenge. Hillquit said:

"I cannot discuss Liberty bonds because I have not given them much thought. You see, I am not investing this year."

The audience laughed. The meeting was over. Elsewhere, however, especially at immense rallies in Madison Square Garden, Hillquit made antiwar speeches which gave him 150,000 votes in the elections, the highest any socialist candidate had ever received in New York. The Socialist party also gained seats in the State Assembly and in the Board of Aldermen.

The week which brought us these socialist victories in New York also brought us news of a socialist triumph which overshadowed them. The Bolshevik Revolution in Russia on November 7, 1917, aroused the most extraordinary enthusiasm among radicals of all shades of opinion.

Socialists, anarchists and syndicalists had despaired at the sight of their comrades in Europe slaughtering each other in the enemy's armies; they had seen their organizations crushed and their press all but destroyed. The Second International had been declared dead beyond recall, and international socialism seemed to have perished for the time being. The high hopes which the February Revolution had aroused were dimmed by Kerensky's subservience to the Allied imperialists, by his policy of "blood and iron" in forcing the disillusioned Russian troops back into the trenches. Now out of the ashes of these lost hopes flamed new expectations, brighter than the old. The Bolshevik Revolution seemed to revive and justify the most ardent socialist faith. The world's first working-class republic was established, and around it rallied all those Americans who were bitter against industrial oppression and war. The more the capitalist press lied about Lenin and Trotsky, about the bolshevik "bandits, cutthroats and charlatans," the more intense was the adherence of the radicals and liberals to the new workers' republic. Attacks by counterrevolutionary armies financed by the Allies aroused the utmost indignation here. Storms of applause greeted the mere mention of the word "Russia" at radical meetings throughout the country.

At first my friends and I had only the vaguest ideas as to what bolshevism was. The signing of the Brest-Litovsk Treaty early in 1918 seemed to us a victory of German autocracy over the workers' revolution. Many radicals now talked of volunteering in the American army to. fight the Germans. The defeat of Germany seemed essential for the defense of the workers' republic. Writing about this period years later, Floyd Dell recorded both the universal enthusiasm of the radicals for Bolshevik Russia and the bitterness against Germany which it evolved.

"This was a Socialism which meant what it said! The mind was incredulous at first—could this really be happening? Could it last? And then there was Brest-Litovsk, and Germany seemed to some of us, to me certainly, an enemy, because German militarism threatened the existence of Soviet Russia."

At a political dinner of radicals which I attended—my first visit to Greenwich Village—opinions divided sharply on this issue. I spoke in favor of "revolutionary defensism," and was attacked as an "opportunist" by a young wobbly poet named James Waldo Fawcett. That winter I was among those radical students at Columbia who joined the Reserve Officers' Training Corps which took military drill daily on the snow-covered campus.

CHAPTER II

Such men, right thinking but prey to isolation by the forces surrounding them, became themselves foreigners—in their own country.

—WILLIAM CARLOS WILLIAMS.

§ 1

ADOLESCENCE came to my generation at a time when Western culture entered upon a profound transformation which was to go on for decades. We were too young to become rigidly set in prewar attitudes, too old to benefit without anguished struggle from a younger generation's conceptual world, fashioned by Einstein, Freud and Lenin. Many an idea which was to become a commonplace a decade later came to us new, startling, incredible. The cliché of tomorrow was the revelation of our day, often contradicting the revelation of yesterday. Time and again we hung between the two horns of a dilemma, grasping both tightly for fear of slipping off into that abyss where men believe nothing. Nor were these grotesque vacillations and compromises entirely owing to our youth, or to the fact that the world at large was being refashioned amidst the roar of cannon. My friends and I were caught between two social classes—the proletariat, with which we had grown up and with which we identified ourselves, and the bourgeoisie, whose culture we were absorbing at the university. In politics the issue was clear. There seemed to be only one choice and we made it early. But the choice of socialism appeared to leave us free to make moral and intellectual choices in the opposite camp too. That camp monopolized the treasure house of art. From it we accepted what appeared to be good and true, without knowing how to fuse it with socialism.

We imagined that most of the other students were happy, integrated beings. Whether or not this was true, it was a painful fact that my own circle lived in three conflicting realms. Our home life was becoming middle-class; our political inclinations, revolutionary. Above these disparate planes was a third, a realm of literary snobbism in which my friends and I fancied ourselves intellectual aristocrats, members of a sacred caste of "thinkers" and "writers" above the vulgar realities of home and politics. Our parents sweated in offices, shops and factories, forgetting their old life in the material conquest of the new. We pursued culture. This was our flight from home, from vulgar work and crude preoccupations with money, from the oppressive memory of the slums. This, too, was our attempt to rise to what we imagined was loftiest in American life. And we continued to pursue this mirage through the world-shattering years 1917 and 1918, profoundly convinced that culture and even life itself was to be found beyond wars and revolutions.

Alas, there was no peace even in the highest of imaginary realms. The world of culture, like the world of work and money, was itself cleft by many divisions. We did not yet understand why; we noted, because we had to, only the surface manifestations of the conflict.

In American life, the culture inherited and borrowed from Greece, Rome, Jerusalem, England, France and Germany struggled for supremacy with the embryo culture of New York, Chicago and San Francisco, painfully evoked in literature out of the American scene by poetry about Spoon River, General Booth and the stockyards. This American culture was in turn divided between voices speaking for a vague national America and voices speaking for the working class of America and of the world. Both groups echoed Europe with an American accent. Ezra Pound invoked Bertrand de Born; Jack London invoked Nietzsche and Marx; and we had no clear philosophy which could explain and integrate these contradictory ideas, which could bring order and indicate purpose in the apparent chaos surrounding us.

Cloistered in the academic world, we looked upon literature not as a luxury but as a primary necessity. Literature was supposed to be a short cut to experience; reading was going to teach us the secret of living; and writing was to open for us the gates of heaven. The physical center of this highest of all human realms was the class in comparative literature. Our new professor, replacing the expelled Harry Dana, was Dr. Raymond Weaver, thirty, dapper and good-looking, with hair carefully parted in the middle, large gray eyes, and marked grace of manner. Dr. Weaver seemed remote from war and politics. Once you crossed the threshold of his classroom, you entered the world of eternal beauty, of Beowulf, the *Song of Roland,* Guido Cavalcanti, Dante, Petrarch, and Boccaccio; Ronsard, Cervantes, Goethe and Tolstoy. It was a realm of peaceful and harmonious imagination, completely severed from the fret and fever of daily life, from strikes and slums, from perplexities of right and wrong, from the puzzles of epistemology and revolution. In this free realm of art, beauty alone was truth; and each work of the imagination, regardless of the era or the society in which it was created, was good after its own fashion. Art expressed life, and life was something divorced from action. It was an end in itself. It expressed the loftiest aspects of man's nature, and man was apparently an abstract being who remained unaltered through the ages. If art had any reason outside itself for existing, if it needed to be vulgarized in terms of utility, it was described as the heightening of consciousness, the sharpening of perception. Art was experience more condensed and more lucid than the experience of daily life; it was the eternal metaphor, varying in form, unchanging in essence from age to age, from land to land. In the beginning and in the end was the Word. Of course, Goethe had said that in the beginning was the Deed. But that, too, was a Word, a metaphor on the same level as the metaphor that art exists solely for its own sake.

This literary idealism was very pleasant for young men remote from productive labor, anxious to forget a world rendered bitter by the war. But every day you took the subway from the campus to reality; you met workers, went to socialist meetings and read the *Call*. The actual world shattered your fantasies, and even laid rude hands upon the dream of pure art. Literature was one thing on the campus, another in the socialist movement; and the same book meant two different things depending on whether you heard about it from your professor in the classroom or from Floyd Dell in the pages of the *Masses*. I did not know what Dell looked like, or anything else about him; but I followed his writings regularly, and considered them a source of Wisdom, like the writings of other men personally unknown to me, Francis Bacon or Thomas Paine, who nevertheless were my teachers. He was, of all men with whose work I was then acquainted, the most persistent in trying to relate art to socialism. He appeared to bridge with his criticism that appalling abyss which my formal education left between imagination and reality. I was impressed by an acuteness of insight which did not preclude generosity of spirit. Few contemporary writers were so free of needless awe for the great or needless contempt for the unknown. Dell had the courage to damn acknowledged masters like George Moore, and to hail the early efforts of Sherwood Anderson as the work of one who wrote "like a great novelist." Most important, however, was his social approach to books. He praised *The Genius,* for example, as "tremendous"; yet reproached

Dreiser for missing the chief point about his hero who was in essence a rebel. Life at its best and most heroic, Dell said, was rebellion; Dreiser was himself a rebel; why did he not write the American novel of rebellion? In similar moods, my favorite critic lashed Anatole France and H. G. Wells for supporting the war, and praised Romain Rolland and Gilbert Cannan for opposing it. He made it clear that a writer could not escape his social responsibilities by hiding behind the skirts of art.

At other times, however, Dell gave me the impression that rebellion had implications which were personal rather than political. He described the individual in revolt against conventions from which he could escape now, before America established the socialist society. The solution for certain contemporary evils seemed to lie in the cult of vagabondage, and in the cult of love.

Vagabondage was a form of rebellion which spat indiscriminately upon all group life. To be an orphan, Dell said, a person without ties, a wanderer upon the face of the earth, a derelict, a discoverer of one's own way of life, a person responsible to no fixed and pre-existing group or institution for one's mistakes; and one to whom success, if there was any success for such a person, came in accident and surprise—that was the recipe for modernity. The Greek mythmakers, our critic said, were right. The Hero must free himself of his family entanglements at the outset if he is to be a real Hero. He must be a poet, an artist, a vagabond, a criminal—anyone who manages to escape the doom of being a mere member of a Family, anyone who shifts for himself.

The cult of the vagabond was the romantic radicals' answer to a world whose institutions cramped him; the cult of love was his reply to the Sexual Crisis which seemed to pervade Western civilization. Practically everybody, Floyd Dell said, was oppressed by the institutions, moralities, restrictions, cowardices and brutalities of the conventional sexual system. For my friends and myself, it was surprising, terrifying and comforting to discover that adult and intelligent men and women were not much better off at thirty than we were at twenty, or even than we had been at fifteen, when Dr. Landes had frightened us into insomnia.

The ideal solution for the world-wide Sexual Crisis, it seemed, was the "permanent sexual union," a phrase which sounded more advanced than the philistine term "marriage." But except for the fortunate few, Dell frankly warned us, such a union was at present only a noble and pathetic wish. Perhaps in the near future society would improve its social and economic structure to provide a wide range and unhindered freedom for serious mating. Until then, some other solution was necessary. Prostitutes were out of the question from every point of view, and Freud had demolished all illusions about the value of celibacy for either sex. There remained only the "free union" of a man and a woman living together without benefit of clergy or state. Yet even this solution had its difficulties. The people involved had a sense of dislocation from the rest of society which tended to destroy the free union; and since a union of that kind usually precluded children, it was a failure socially. Dell therefore urged a reconstruction of our customs and attitudes which would permit the sexual instinct an expression at once more free and more socially beneficent. This might come, partly conditioned by advances in the economic freedom of women from men, through the public recognition of free unions. Any increase in the number of such unions, Dell argued, would divert the passions of masculine youth from the waste of trivial and mercenary relations into a more humane and satisfying relationship. It would furnish women another escape from the cold storage of celibacy which many of them would be glad to take; and with the protection which social approval and a legal status would give them, these free unions, hitherto for the most part barren, would become fruitful with the children of love.

The members of my circle were then twenty years old, living in a world whose established values the war had smashed, and anxious to find new ones. We wanted to leave home, and so were ready to idealize the "vagabond"; we were not ready to found families of our own, and so gladly responded to the dream of the "free union." On these two points, at least, the campus and American left-wing literature agreed. Jack London had been a wanderer, as Byron had been before him; and the greatest glamour surrounding the ideal of the free union also came from the romantic poets—Byron, Shelley, Goethe. We knew the number and names of their lovers, and were familiar with the portraits, from Friederike to Charlotte, in the Weimar museum. Economically unequipped to marry, emotionally incapable of touching a woman without love, the Candides of my circle went in for free unions. They were as often miserable as happy. It was a long time before they discovered why these relationships were neither unions nor free. None of them lived in open and defiant "sin," like the unmarried lovers of Greenwich Village who tacked their individual name-plates on the door of their studio. Their affairs were painful because clandestine. In most cases, they led to marriage shortly after graduation from college; in some they were prelude to the "frank and free" life celebrated by the radical intelligentsia of our own day and the romantic poets of the nineteenth century.

Obviously, we were ourselves romantic rebels. Our daily occupation of attending classes and listening to lectures gave us every facility for living in the imagination more than in reality. Even our contacts with the socialist movement were chiefly literary. The conflict which pervaded the whole of contemporary society reflected itself in our lives primarily on the plane of ideas. The joke of it was that we considered ideas as something distinct from and superior to reality, but we did not yet know that the joke was on us. Whenever reality invaded the realm of the imagination, we translated the shock into another idea.

Our experiments with the free union, for example, convinced us that neither society nor our own mind was clear of the opiate of puritanism. Even the invisible champions of the new life, whose writings we read at a respectful distance, were not free of it. The legendary contest between heaven and hell, the soul and the flesh, Judeo-Christian asceticism and romantic aspiration had its echoes in the minds of the Liberated. Sons and daughters of the puritans, the artists and writers and utopians who flocked to Greenwich Village to find a frank and free life for the emotions and the senses, felt at their backs the icy breath of the monster they were escaping. Because they could not abandon themselves to pleasure without a sense of guilt, they exaggerated the importance of pleasure, idealized it and even sanctified it. Desire was acceptable only in the guise of love; and love endurable only if approached with awe, wonder and a sense of reverence.

The radical artists and writers who educated me through the printed page were political rebels against the bourgeois social system, and personal rebels against bourgeois sexual hypocrisy. Propaganda voiced their socialist moods; art voiced their romantic longing for pure love. Over both hovered the spirits of religion and science in mortal combat. In John Reed's lyric *Love at Sea*, the joy of kissing was bearable only as something "immense, moving and terrible," something stronger than the wind, the serene gulls, the turbines of the ship, the sea itself. The gratification of love was a heroic defiance of the taboos uttered by the resistless foam, a trembling triumph over the forbidding denials of God himself, who was not where we cried, who was shifting and balancing on the ruthless shifting planes of the sea, but who nevertheless was there.

It was this unresolved dualism which prevented left-wing literature of this period from becoming the unequivocal antithesis to the literature of the campus. The imaginary world on the fringe of the socialist movement and the imaginary world in the heart of bourgeois society had much in common. We were sure of neither the points of identity nor the real points of difference, and yet were trying, through this strange twilight, to grope our way toward reality. When you went to the left for guidance, you found that the radical intellectual was divided into the half that was socialist and the half that was romantic lover. Radical poetry spoke two utterly different languages. Edwin Justus Mayer, at this time a young socialist, could publish in the *Masses:*

> How futile is all thinking against this!
> How exquisite is the air grown, and the skies;
> The moments flutter by like butterflies:
> Bright butterflies whose passage is a kiss.

Yet in the pages of the same magazine, Arturo Giovannitti, no less romantic, could write sweeping free verse about the social struggle, as in *When the Cock Crows* which described the lynching of the labor organizer Frank Little during the Montana copper strike. Giovannitti seemed to be in the tradition of the Bible, Whitman and Victor Hugo when he concluded his poem about Frank Little with these lines:

> Arise, and against every hand jewelled with the rubies of murder,
> Against every mouth that sneers at the tears of mercy,
> Against every foul smell of the earth,
> Against every head that a footstool raises over your head,
> Against every word that was written before this was said,
> Against every happiness that never knew sorrow,
> And every glory that never knew love and sweat,
> Against silence and death and fear—
> Arise with a mighty roar!
> Arise and declare your war;
> For the wind of the dawn is blowing,
> For the eyes of the East are glowing,
> For the lark is up and the cock is crowing,
> And the Day of Judgment is here!

Such poems tended to clear your spirit. It did not seem odd that socialists should write about butterflies or poets about the class war. The revolution appeared to be concerned with everything that was good in life. Lincoln led you to Debs, and Shelley to Jack London. From the socialist meeting or magazine I often returned to the classroom on the campus with new insight. I did not dissociate Dante's poetry from his theology, or his theology from his politics. The transformation of Goethe from the rebel Götz von Berlichingen into the suave Geheimrath who amused the petty ducal court of Weimar grieved me as though the poet had been a contemporary apostate, as though he had abandoned the socialist movement to serve in George Creel's bureau of public misinformation. I wrote about Don Quixote not as a comic figure but as a rebel dashing himself against the unjust world, a Spanish Shelley with lance instead of lyre. The first poetry I had known was the moral poetry of the Bible; and now my favorite poets included Byron, Shelley, Dante, Swinburne, Hugo, Goethe, men who had deliberately used their art to propagate intellectual concepts and moral values. So long as you accepted socialism in a general way, you could have vagabondage, free love and puritanism; you could have pure art, pure propaganda and a fusion of art and propaganda. Individual writers on the fringe of the socialist movement differed from each other sharply and gloried in their differences. What bound them together was a common belief in the future classless society; and a warm, humorous tolerance toward the most contradictory values. Perhaps the actual facts were not at all as I have described them; but that is how they appeared from the distance to a group of young students trying to find clarity in a disturbed world. The professors on the campus talked about a past robbed of all specific character, about an ideal realm divorced from the society in which we lived. The radical writers whom we followed talked about our own times, about America.

§ 2

You could live in the dreamworld of art only at rare intervals. The war invaded even the campus, and whether you liked it or not you had to think about realities. The university authorities, themselves reactionary, permitted Professor Carlton Hayes to give a course in the origins of the war, possibly on the old monarchic theory that reforms had better come from above than from below. I took this course. Half of it was devoted to the industrial revolution. Required reading included the *Communist Manifesto,* Proudhon's book on the nature of property, the works of Owen, Fourier, Saint-Simon, Kropotkin and— Walter Lippmann, then emerging as a radical publicist with his *Preface to Politics*. Rich students from Riverside Drive, Flatbush, Chicago, Des Moines and points west crammed nights for exams in the agitation of Karl Marx and Friedrich Engels.

Professor Hayes was an ironic lecturer who liked to play with the Socratic method. Once he called on a student in the Reserve Officers' Training Corps who came to class in uniform.

"Lieutenant Brown, are you an anarchist?"

The class looked up, startled. Lieutenant Brown noisily lumbered to his feet, stood at attention, and said indignantly:

"No, *sir!*"

"Why not?"

"I don't believe in anarchism."

"Why don't you believe in it?"

For the moment, Lieutenant Brown could not remember what the teachings of anarchism were. He squared his shoulders and said nothing.

"Don't you believe," Professor Hayes persisted, "in the absolute freedom of the individual?"

"Yes, sir."

"Isn't that one of the basic ideas of anarchism?"

"Yes, sir."

By this method, Professor Hayes went through various anarchist doctrines, extensions of some ideals preached by the ideologues of the French and American revolutions. Finally Lieutenant Brown broke down. If that was anarchism, he said, he was probably an anarchist. Then, to Brown's immense relief, Professor Hayes assured him he was not an anarchist, and proceeded to demolish Kropotkin's doctrines.

The course was a lightning rod. While it lasted, most of the students, regardless of their social origin, professed to be anarchists, socialists or syndicalists. There were practically no apologists for capitalism. It was only a question which of three radical programs was the best. Students from the most conservative families found rational explanations of the war-shaken world in the writings of the various revolutionary schools. Some of them talked openly of renouncing the money, factory or estate which they expected to inherit.

But little came of their brief enthusiasm for the social revolution. After the war, the boys grew up to be good Republicans and Democrats. One "anarchist" became a district captain for Tammany Hall;

a "socialist" took over his uncle's shoe factory in Massachusetts; a "syndicalist" became a federal attorney. Yet in so far as their wartime discontent was general, it had some tangible by-products. There were those who remained permanently attached to some movement dedicated to social reform.

In my own socialist circle, the *Communist Manifesto* was an old guide; but now we read certain passages with renewed attention, underscoring those which bore out our increasing dislike of money culture and our growing disappointment in the prowar attitude of the bourgeois intellectuals. We drew heaving pencil lines under the section which described how the bourgeoisie had left no other bond between man and man than naked self-interest, than callous cash payment. The bourgeoisie had drowned the most heavenly ecstasies of religious fervor, chivalrous enthusiasm and philistine sentimentalism in the icy waters of egotistical calculation; it had stripped of its halo every occupation hitherto honored and looked up to with reverent awe, converting the physician, the lawyer, the priest, the poet, the man of science into its paid wage laborers.

I was becoming aware that we find in literature, past or present, that which corresponds to our own immediate memories and needs. When we read in the *Communist Manifesto* that the bourgeoisie had put an end to all feudal, patriarchal, idyllic relations, the phrase stirred all our attachments to the past, as well as our hopes for the future. Living in an academic realm seemingly removed from society as a whole, we idealized the "idyllic relations" as they appeared in feudal art and poetry. From the contemporary world, hateful for its cruelty, we fled now to the preindustrial past, as symbolized by art, now to the socialist future, as symbolized by the October Revolution. These private utopias made the present endurable so long as we confined ourselves to thought and discourse, to the "life of reason."

But we were approaching military age, and we were poor. We knew that on being graduated from the university—if we did not get killed in France—we would have to choose a profession by which to earn a living. When we marked those passages in the *Communist Manifesto* which described the servility of the intellectuals to the governing class, we not only paid homage to a general social law, but recognized its direct application to our personal lives. The war made us feel that the professional man was the serf of the propertied classes. Through 1917 and 1918 we said to each other over and over again: is it right to kill? should we kill? are we going to be killed? and if not, if we survive the war, then what?

We had lost the illusion that the professions meant social and spiritual freedom. At the university we saw scholars act like savages in order to please the campus authorities, who themselves licked the boots of the directors, who in turn crawled on their hands and knees before Big Business. This, however, was an impersonal observation. It was at home that I saw most clearly the humiliating role of the professional man. On the campus the student of architecture was something of an artist, who, like ourselves, lived imaginatively in the classic and idealized past. At home I watched the gentle, erudite and sincere architect Kaufman scraping and bowing and smiling before some of my father's business associates. These men were illiterate and selfish, I thought; but they built skyscrapers on which Kaufman could work for the support of his family.

If Professor Hayes' lectures on the campus stimulated our thinking about the industrial revolution in general, no such luxury was possible at home. Here observation was direct and subjective. I had long ago ceased to think of men as being divided into Jew and gentile, black and white, American and European. The world seemed to be divided only into those who owned and those who worked and those who created beauty—which was one and indivisible with truth and justice. Under wartime prosperity, my father and his friends were beginning to climb from the lowest rungs of the great American ladder upward and upward toward heights unknown. Money was changing them. Men whom I used to see tearful and penitent in the synagogue on the Day of Atonement, now shaved off their beards and mustaches; they wore expensive clothes, sported canes and spats, smelled of perfume, ran their own automobiles, had "private" houses with gardens, worshiped their children and bullied them, snubbed their poor friends, dined in exclusive restaurants with their bankers, mortgagees and clients. Amidst the former ghetto pariahs who now spent week-ends in Atlantic City and developed strategic sections of New York (the builders of the Chanin Building among them), the architect Kaufman sat pale and shy, talking to me about the days when, as a student in Russia, he had read the works of "your Professor Giddings in translation."

Above all, you could not get away from the war. It pervaded everything; it made all else seem trivial and unimportant, especially after Professor Hayes strengthened our belief that the war was the result of "imperialism and militarism and nationalism," the struggle for markets, colonies, spheres of influence. The world stank of death; some of the biggest men we knew were servants of death. We felt a growing contempt for the official intellectuals. To be a lawyer or a professor or a journalist meant to be like the people who urged us to kill German young men like ourselves; who, by their silence or approval, condoned the expulsion and persecution of those isolated Americans who took the Declaration of Independence to heart. We were not going to join the capitalist parade via the professions. We would not march in the Triumph of Death. We would oppose, even if it meant our own destruction, the barbarism around us.

In this mood it was natural for us to acquire a contempt for practical politics. Everybody had failed us. From the capitalists we expected nothing but oppression. But their intellectual apologists were no better; and many socialists, too, had marched in the Triumph of Death. It seemed that the moment a man entered practical politics his moral and intellectual integrity went to pieces. Power corrupted men; the greater the power, the greater the corruption.

When art and love failed to give us refuge against the uncomprehended brutalities of the world, we fell into ironic despair. In the spring of 1918, several friends and I founded the cult of futilitarianism. We argued that every path led but to the grave. Society had set us, in the end, only one goal—death. In the face of it everything else seemed ridiculous. During moments of hope we believed the most romantic dreams; during moments of despair we believed nothing. Nihilism was a compulsion. To wreck our inhibitions against killing—imperative if we went to the front—we had to break down all other inhibitions. Was killing right? Then nothing could be wrong. Western culture was based on the philosophy of utilitarianism; it had collapsed in universal war to that culture. We opposed, in our most cynical moments, the philosophy of futilitarianism. The utilitarians sought all that was useful; the young, intellectually shell-shocked cynics found everything useless. The philosophers, whom we no longer trusted because they had become military propagandists, asked of everything *why?* Our response was *why not?* If you were allowed to kill men whom you had never seen, whom you did not hate, who were "sacred individuals" like yourself, why could you not rape, plunder and lie? Our own lives were priggishly moral. Futilitarianism was a pose. It expressed not our desire for amorality but its very opposite. Cynicism was the Ideal sticking its tongue out to the obdurate world. It was the melancholy voice of our contempt and hatred for the actual conduct of the ruling caste which instigated murder, plunder, rape and false-hood everywhere. The "gospel" of futilitarianism spread among disillu-sioned students who carried it into the classroom. When the trigonom-etry instructor asked *why* such and such a proposition was true, the student would grin and say *why not?*

This was the Triumph of Death among the young men who had not yet reached the trenches but waited for the troopship daily. In one form or another, it was a universal disease among the middle classes of all countries "gone wild" under the crushing effects of the war. At all times of vehement social rupture, when old values lose their vitality and no new ones have appeared, men who are more objects of historic forces fall into the nihilism of despair. There is no God, Smerdyakov says. Then everything is permitted? And the intellectual Ivan replies, yes, *everything is permitted, even murder.* We were no longer con-cerned about God; murder was the starting point of the disintegra-tion. We may, we *must* murder; it is "heroic" and "patriotic" to mur-der; then everything is permitted, everything, everything. With the discipline of the old culture gone from us, only a new social discipline could have kept our spirits firm in the face of universal slaughter; and that new discipline was as yet lacking for us.

Contempt for practical politics was only one of our theories of flight. It gained prestige among us because the external world was be-coming more and more a riddle to which we had no key. Socialism itself, as we vaguely understood it, was no longer the simple open-sesame to history, life and art. On the one hand, there were now capital-ists who were taking their hats off to the social revolution; on the other, socialist intellectuals were licking the boots of Big Business. Here was Charles M. Schwab talking loftily about the "social renaissance" throughout the world. Call it socialism, he said, or social revolution, or bolshevism, or what you will, it was a leveling process, and meant that the workman without property who labored with his hands was going to be the man who would dominate the world. It was going to be a great hardship for the owners of property, Mr. Schwab said; but, like all revolutionary movements, it would probably work good. The sooner we realized this, the better it would be for America.

At the same time, the radical intelligentsia was swooning in ecstasy at President Wilson's feet. Upton Sinclair urged the Socialist party to call a convention which would formally declare its support of the President. Max Eastman went further: he thought the President ought to "come round and join the Socialist party." Eastman was willing "to take the risk of accepting him as a member." If Wilson would recognize Soviet Russia, he might even have, for the purposes of war and peace, "the leadership of the labor parties of the world."

From hysterical ecstasy over Woodrow Wilson to supporting the war was an easy step. By July, 1918, the *Liberator* urged that the Allied armies were fighting to prevent a German victory, and socialists—whatever they might think of Allied diplomacy in the past—*would do nothing which might retard that fight*. The alleged reasons for this change of attitude, which affected many radicals in this period, were the growing menace of a Prussian victory, the increasing power of labor and internationalist elements among the Allies, the President's peace terms, the German invasion of socialist Russia, the refraining of the Allies from such an invasion, and the Lichnowsky revelations of Germany's original war purposes.

§ 3

These were no longer abstract problems for us, like Luther's theses or Rossetti's sonnets. We now had to make decisions, to act. In the summer of 1918, the army was beginning to conscript twenty-year-olds. My friends and I discussed possible courses of action. Ought we to become conscientious objectors? Or ought we to take the advice of Louis Smith, who said that a true socialist must be wherever the masses were, in order to enlighten them about the real nature and meaning of the war? Several of us decided that the best way to avoid killing without being accused of cowardice was to enlist in the ambulance corps, which, we imagined, combined danger with mercy. But the Red Cross refused to take us. We must wait until we were drafted and assigned to a branch of the service by the army authorities. Robert and I planned to apply for the ambulance service directly through the army. We unconsciously shared the mood of people we did not know, many of whom did not know each other. At this time the ambulance corps on the European battle fronts included John Dos Passos, Ernest Hemingway, Edmund Wilson and Malcolm Cowley. Friends of ours in the School of Journalism showed us letters from the western front describing life in the ambulance corps. They were written by a student named William Slater Brown who mentioned again and again his army buddy, E. E. Cummings. These descriptions of the ambulance corps were anything but glamorous; nevertheless, that form of service seemed preferable to the fate of Abe Kaplan. My first socialist agitator had been killed in the trenches of France fighting for a cause in which he did not believe.

While we were debating possible courses of action, the government organized the Student Army Training Corps in the fall of 1918. On the advice of our dean, a liberal who later became assistant secretary of war, Robert and I joined this unit.

By October the campus was an army camp. For the first time those of us who came from the slums went to live in the dorms, now converted into military barracks under the jurisdiction of the army. Our officers had first call on us. Between drills we attended classes, some of which were taken for military purposes. Our fat, heavy-jowled major rode us hard, but we had the privilege of choosing our own squads. Mine consisted of intimate personal friends; we were assigned to the same crowded room in Livingston Hall; we drilled and ate together and, in violation of the rules, talked in whispers long after taps. Some of my older friends, including Robert Smith, were transferred to officers' training camps or regular army units.

Reveille blew at five, and we leaped into our uniforms. When the second bugle blew, we rushed down to the granite-paved quadrangle with coats and pants unbuttoned. Once the company was in order, the captain or lieutenant in charge gave us permission to button our flies. After an hour's drill in the morning cold, we were sent to the toilet en masse, then to breakfast. At night we went on guard with rifles.

Two o'clock one morning I was awakened to guard the battalion prison in the cellar under Hamilton Hall. The prisoners were kept on cots from which the mattresses had been removed; they slept on naked springs. I was ordered to guard a friend I had known for five years.

"How do you feel, Dick?"

"Like a waffle."

"What are you in for?"

"Socking a sergeant who called me a bastard."

The resentment against army discipline was general. The officers amused themselves by ragging the dreamy grinds—the intellectuals. One bright boy was compelled to go through the entire set of military exercises alone before the entire company because he had marched left when the commander said squads right. Some of us thought that was terrible, and the students got their revenge in the psychology exams. Professor Woodworth had worked out intelligence and character tests, and tried them out on us in class. Question: if you were on the battlefield, which would you miss most, books, friends or women? Question: would you rather make a speech to a crowd or talk alone with a girl? Question: do you have difficulty urinating in the presence of other men? Later several students were assigned by the Psychology Department to give the test to the battalion. The officers got the lowest ratings. The vendetta was on. Students who sneaked away from their posts on guard duty were deprived of leave for a month, put on K.P. or ordered to drill with the Awkward Squad.

It would be untrue, however, to say that we hated army life entirely. We loathed the discipline which infringed upon our "sacred human dignity," but we liked the form which relieved us of certain moral burdens. To begin with, we found the collective life of the army appealing. To act in concert with a thousand others lessened the loneliness of the individual; it expanded his ego; he felt part of an ego larger than his own. What irked us was the disagreement with the aims of that collective activity. We now appreciated more than ever William James' notions about the "moral equivalent for war," but felt that if we were part of a military machine fighting for objectives which we wholeheartedly approved, we might enjoy the experience. Yet even now army life had its attractions. We were suddenly freed of all material worries. Our food, clothing and shelter plus a dollar a day were guaranteed us. We were liberated from the need of making choices and plans, which, for young or undeveloped people, is perhaps the greatest moral burden of all. Our officers decided when we got up, went to bed, ate, studied, played, exercised and rested. It was like early childhood, in some respects, when the parents take the entire responsibility of life upon themselves, leaving the child free to follow the pleasure principle—so long as he obeys orders. It was also in some ways like the Catholic Church, where the clergy, secular and regular, takes the burden of moral choice upon itself and exercises the gift of absolution in return for unquestioning obedience. So long as you met your military, family or religious responsibilities, you were otherwise irresponsible. In all these cases—army, family, church—routine and ritual are oppressive only when there is no faith or love; when there is, form may lead to a real or false sense of freedom. If, as the philosophers say, freedom is the recognition of necessity, it is not hard to imagine why those students who recognized the "necessity" of our army life found a certain kind of freedom in its routine and ritual, as the Renaissance poet found freedom within the severely prescribed limits of the sonnet. Army life illuminated one aspect of so-called slave psychology. Many men accept slavery without resistance so long as it provides them with security; it is only when security collapses, when their masters can no longer feed and clothe obedience, that the slave revolts.

But among certain intellectuals the combination of discipline and irresponsibility led to curious results. Regimentation in the ranks led to spiritual anarchy in the barracks. Students who until now had never smoked or drunk whisky or used foul language let go with deliberate malice. A young philosopher in love with Spinoza began, for the first time in his life, to swear in four letter words apropos of nothing at all. He would lie on his back, look morosely at the ceiling and sputter as fast as he could f— f— f— f— f— f— f—. This was his ironic substitute for the dialectic, his personal comment on the war which had engulfed him. He had nothing more to say about life for the time being. He rattled his f—s so fast we called him the Machine Gun. All serious conversation was suspended. We were automatons with no right to think. We were going to kill and be killed. Old Man Jackson had been right; here we were the boys at Ratisbon without their maidenly devotion. Woodrow Wilson and his literary shamans might find a thousand good reasons for us to die—but they all sat at home basking in their little glories, leaving us to face the cannon. Some of us registered for the artillery service under the illusion that you either did not come back at all or came back whole. No crippled veterans, thank you. All back or smithereens.

A week after the battalion was organized, the Spanish flu spread through the barracks. Scores of student-soldiers were taken to the hospital. On my twenty-first birthday I woke with fever. The doctor said I had it. When I came to in the army base hospital on Gunhill Road I heard a voice in mad soliloquy.

"Philosophy—mathematics—history—all, all a terrible lie!"

The voice issued from the next cot shrouded in white curtains. Too weak to move, I asked the nurse to draw the curtains aside. It was Benny, delirious. Centuries later, half awake, I saw the doctor standing at the foot of my bed, reporting to the colonel on inspection.

"This case is hopeless. He's gone."

I sat up weakly and said:

"No, no, you're crazy. I'm not going to die."

I fell back on the pillow in a dead faint. When I woke up the enormous room was full of soldiers, invalided from the front with shell wounds, poison gas and syphilis. The place stank with gangrene. Delirium filled it with hysterical curses. The sight of the Negro with chancre, or the boy from Iowa blinded by shrapnel, made you want to do something for them, to bring them water, read magazines to them, talk with them about their homes. When you dozed, the men in the room became a vague mass insanely screaming in a deluge of blood. I wanted to know what happened out there, how you lived in the trenches, how you fought, how it felt to be hit by shrapnel. On the campus, we had been given bayonet practice. Old ladies had stood in front of the gilded Alma Mater and said aren't they sweet; and the captain had barked orders, and we had lunged forward at the imaginary foe and had pulled out the imaginary bayonet with a violent twist to the right. How did it feel to sink a real bayonet into a real man? There was no answer. The soldiers in the hospital talked about everything except the war.

§ 4

What was the use of all this abstract speculation? Life itself was so much more complicated, beautiful and painful. It was easy to analyze what other people wrote, to parade *ideas,* to talk about life. Then something happened which knocked all your fancy theories into a cocked hat; you felt foolish and helpless, only to conclude that your theories were correct after all. Take the theories of the radical writers about "free unions." How had they helped you with Joan?

To begin with, my very meeting her in the spring of 1917 was an accident. She was working in her uncle's phonograph shop, and her uncle had been my teacher in the last class in public school. I came to the shop to see him; I had no idea Joan would be there; I did not know she existed. But as soon as I saw her lucid blue eyes, her blond hair, white skin, full bosom, round naked arms, I thought I had always known her. She, too, acted as though we had been intimate from earliest infancy. Too much so, I thought. She was seventeen, but knew much more about kissing than I did. She had no theories about it; she had never heard of the *Masses* or of free unions, but had a dozen dates a week with boys much better-looking, much better-dressed than I. My little learning failed to impress her; she did not give a damn about books; she cared only for good times, riding about in automobiles, swimming, dancing. What an illiterate wench, I said to myself, trying to protect my feelings with an affected contempt, and what a beautiful one. I could not sleep nights for thinking about her. Fortunately, the summer vacation came along and I had a lot of time on my hands. Almost every day I traveled an hour and a half to her home in Flushing, and spent afternoons, evenings, nights talking with her. When we kissed the whole world seemed to melt into thoughtless joy. Happiness followed me home, where I stayed up until dawn writing poems about her. Everything was wonderful until she talked; then the world became black and hopeless. She said socialists were nuts, reading books was a waste of time; what counted was money. She wanted a lot of fine clothes and a car, and I reflected with a sinking feeling that I was penniless and had three years of schooling ahead of me.

One night we were sitting on a bench outside her house. She was lovely in her white sleeveless dress, and her eyes shone blue in the summer dusk. Out of our long silence, happy for me, at least, came her rich voice singing:

> I'm not a plumber, I'm not a plumber's son,
> But I can plug a hole as well as anyone.

I laughed to conceal how shocked I was, and she went on with the other stanzas. Her mother came out, and greeted us sweetly, and Joan stopped singing.

"Mother," she said, "I need a pair of shoes."

"But you just bought a pair yesterday."

"I need another white pair."

"Good heavens, child, how can one keep up with you? This will make the fourth pair this month. Your father is not a millionaire, you know."

Joan leaped up, her white face flushed with rage. I had never seen her so furious.

"You're a damned fool!" she yelled. Her mother lowered her eyes. "You don't understand me. What's the use of being beautiful if you can't have the clothes that go with it?" Her mother said nothing. "Answer me!" Joan yelled, stamping her foot wildly. I picked up my hat and said I had to go home. On the train I thought, where in hell could I get the money to support a wife like that? And what a temper!

But I went to see her again. Life was exciting when she was near, and she could be sweet when she wanted to. Her father now began to ask me to dinner. He said I was a nice young man, asked what business my father was in, what profession I was studying, when I would finish college. I told him I was a socialist. He laughed and said, "You'll get over that."

Once, when I came to dinner, Joan's father was in the uniform of the National Guard. He was very severe and lectured me about the war. The Germans, he said, must be annihilated; democracy must triumph. I said, echoing John Reed, this was not our war; it was not a people's war but a capitalists' war. Joan's father became very angry. He shouted that socialists were traitors and German spies, and left the room, banging the door behind him. I was upset. Good night, I said to Joan, and went out into the street. She followed me and stood in the doorway. I should have walked away fast, but I stood like a fool looking at Joan's blue eyes. They were hard and cold.

"Socialists," she said icily, "are traitors."

I went home but could not sleep. In the morning I felt terribly lonely. I knew I would never see Joan again. I wanted to talk the whole thing over with someone. My family was away in the country, and I was alone in the house. I went out into the street and began to walk around aimlessly. The hot sun poured down on my hatless head. I began to feel dizzy, and went back to the house. The phone was ringing. It was Helen. I had never thought of her as a girl before. She was only my sister's friend. I had seen her every day since we were kids of nine, but there were lots of girls who came to see my sister. Besides, Helen was not golden-haired and blue-eyed (like Yakelina, like the princesses in fairy tales or the ladies of Renaissance poetry). She had the most ordinary brown hair and black eyes. And she was too much like me, she read a lot of books and wrote poetry and believed in "advanced ideas." That was very nice of her, but not a bit exciting. Heaven knows why Joan, who was a beautiful stupid cow, was more exciting. The books and the radical magazines did not explain that.

"What is the matter with you?" I heard Helen's voice saying over the phone.

"I'm not feeling well. It's the sun. I was out in the street without a hat."

"You need someone to take care of you," she said. "I'll be over in twenty minutes."

She came in twenty minutes, and before I knew it I was talking a blue streak. I told her all about Joan, how beautiful she was and how stupid. But I forgot to mention what she had said about socialists being traitors, and pretty soon I realized I had forgotten it but I did not make good the omission. I was ashamed to admit that I had loved that kind of girl. I only repeated that Joan did not understand me, didn't sympathize with my ideas, didn't know what I was talking about.

"You have a strong sensual streak in you," Helen said, smiling. "Why are you ashamed of it?"

Indignantly I denied I had a sensual streak; I also denied that I was ashamed of it. From my grandfather's viewpoint, the sensual was sinful; from the viewpoint of the Greenwich writers and artists, the sensual was noble. I wanted to prove to Helen that I had a fine soul, after all, so I took out my verses and read them to her. Suddenly I noticed that her dark face was beautiful. How was it I hadn't noticed it before? She understood me, and the world seemed a peaceful place.

"Read that sonnet over again," she said.

I read it over and felt like a man reaching home after a long and arduous journey.

"You write better than Rupert Brooke," Helen said. My heart beat high. I took her in my arms and kissed her.

From that moment, we saw each other every day. We went to movies together, read books together, attended meetings. I wrote her sonnets and she replied with sonnets. She had a surprising gift for poetry; her talk was brilliant; her nature, affectionate. I found myself in love with her, and began to think of marriage. Instead, I talked of free unions. The idea was familiar to her. But it was not out of an idea that we first became lovers. The summer night was warm, we were alone in the house, we did not think, and were extremely happy. It was the first time for either of us.

This made the summer of 1917 seem wonderful. I threw myself into the work of the People's Council with new energy, and Helen helped me distribute leaflets, organize meetings, carry on correspondence. But the happier we were, the less poetry we wrote. We thought this was because we were so absorbed in the antimilitarist campaign.

In the early months of 1918, we had our first quarrel. That was when the young radicals on the campus were debating whether or not they should join the Reserve Officers' Training Corps. Until then we had been unconditionally against the war. But now things seemed different. The German imperialists had imposed the "robber treaty" of Brest-Litovsk upon the world's first socialist republic. German militarism threatened the existence of Soviet Russia. That made the war seem different. If we entered the army to fight Germany, it was no longer in defense of American capitalist interests, but in defense of the proletarian state. That was how we reasoned, but Helen was contemptuous of our logic.

"You are merely finding an easy way of getting out of a difficult situation," she told Robert, Louis and me. "You've been saying this is a capitalist war. Then you have no right to give it aid and comfort."

"Yes," Louis said ironically. "Keep your principles unsullied by doing nothing in a crisis. Be like the Socialist Labor party. Look how pure it is, and how utterly ineffectual in American life. No, dearie. The most important thing in the world today is the Soviet Republic. The Germans threaten to destroy it; we must do everything we can to save it, and the first thing to do is to smash the Germans who threaten it."

"Even if you have to support the American capitalists?" Helen said bitterly.

"We won't be supporting them," Louis said. "They'll be supporting us."

That week I registered with the R.O.T.C. The following morning Helen phoned me.

"Did you give in?" she asked curtly.

"What do you mean?"

"Did you join the R.O.T.C.?"

"Yes.

"Then I never want to speak to you again. A man should stick to his principles."

"I am sticking to my principles," I argued. "But you don't understand them. Socialism isn't a religion; it's the strategy of class warfare."

"Don't hand me a lecture," she said, and hung up. We did not see each other for a week, and then met by accident at a meeting. She looked reproachfully at me, and then smiled so sweetly that I took her home and we resumed our relations as if nothing had happened.

But something had happened, something neither of us had dreamed of taking into account. We had rebelled against the prevailing conventions, and had felt heroic about it, without once considering what the society we lived in might say about it. Helen's mother had been dead for many years; her father was a busy man. Since her ninth year she had been coming to our house as my sister's friend, and my parents (as if seven children were not enough) had taken her to their hearts. "You are my daughter too," mother often said to Helen. I could remember that phrase ever since I could remember Helen. For years they had said she was a wonderful girl; they held her up as an example to my sisters. And now suddenly they began to find fault with her. Everything she did was wrong. It made me unhappy to hear her criticized, and I could not understand the change in my parents' attitude.

One Sunday morning my father said he wanted to talk to me

alone. He took me into the parlor and closed the door. Then he said gravely:

"Do you love Helen?"

"With all my heart."

"What do you intend to do about it?"

"I'm going to marry her."

"When? Do you realize that it takes money to support a wife? You have three years of college ahead of you. Then another three or four years before you can earn a living. You will be twenty-seven or more before you can settle down with a family. That's all right for a man. But a woman is an old maid by that time."

"I'll marry her as soon as I get out of college."

"That's a crazy fantasy," my father said. "But I won't try to dissuade you. I only want to know how a man who loves a woman can be so unfair to her."

"What do you mean?"

"You are spoiling her." He would say nothing more. I walked out of the room overwhelmed. Was he guessing, or did he know? And what the hell was the difference? It wasn't his business, anyway. This was my affair. Yes, but how about Helen? Were you fair to her? You know damned well you can't support her for a long time to come, and meantime what? It was going to be hard on her. What a cruel clever man father was. He knew how to arouse my puritanical prejudices, my sense of guilt. I no longer felt like a romantic lover but like a criminal. Of course, you could leave home, get a job, marry Helen. I thought of that possibility seriously for a moment. Then what? Helen herself was just preparing to enter college; neither of us would want to give up our education to settle down to one of those horrible suburban family lives in Brooklyn. There was so much to do in the world. What did love have to do with marriage anyway? Money, of course—always money—always that frightful curse of bourgeois society. Even your private life wasn't your own.

I talked things over with Helen and we decided to break off physical relations. The free union might work in Greenwich Village, but it was tough in Brooklyn. We would not complicate things; we would love each other spiritually until we could get married. At first it was hard; we wrote an incredible amount of poetry, worked a great deal. Poetry was a wonderful thing; it made life endurable, even this kind of life. The summer was pleasant enough. Helen seemed happy, so did I; yet a strange uncertainty surrounded us. Once, apropos of nothing at all, she said to me: "I never realized what an ascetic streak you have."

By the fall of 1918 I was in the army. Death seemed to wait ahead. There was nothing to look forward to. You no longer planned for the future; a career, marriage, children were out of the question. You belonged to death: eat, drink and be merry. Something was dying in your heart. You stopped seeing Helen, so intent were you upon severing the bonds which made life difficult to abandon. That, at any rate, was how you rationalized it in the barracks of Livingston Hall. The army kept you busy. It seemed easy to forget. In the military hospital time stretched endlessly. You thought a great deal about her, and you knew that if you ever saw her again you would be friends. But love was over. How could you gauge the depth of the feeling, the power of remembered joy, the warning of remembered anguish? How could you know that in spite of this or that affair it would be a long time before you could really love another woman?

§ 5

When I returned to the campus from the military hospital, November had set in. I went to drill the first day, in the chill of the dawn, but felt so weak I had to be sent back to barracks. Several days later I was able to go out again, and was once more ready for France, for the trenches. Our officers told us we were going to storm Metz, about which we had read in the history textbook.

On November seventh, just a year after the Bolshevik Revolution in Russia, came the "false" armistice report. New York went wild. Sirens and whistles and crowds of people roared with joy. On the campus, we danced a snake dance in our army uniforms, insanely happy, across South Field, yelling ourselves hoarse.

The next day we heard the armistice report was not true; three days later it was true. This confirmation roused no such hysterical jubilation as had the first report. It made no difference in our feelings. The spell of the war was broken, the crazy tension was over, the war mind suddenly folded up; we awoke as from a long oppressive nightmare, completely exhausted. That is, most of us did. There were some students who were actually sorry the war was over. A Georgia boy who shared my room threw himself across his cot and wept aloud.

"I'm not going to get my commission," he sobbed.

"What of it? Aren't you glad this slaughter is over?"

"My father was a captain in the Spanish-American War. My

grandfather was a major in the Civil War. I'm the first man in my family without an army commission."

I could not understand him, and felt that he did not understand me. Most of us were glad in a dull way that the war was over. We were tired; we felt that we could feel nothing more. Now what? In December each of us received an honorable discharge from the United States army and a sixty-dollar bonus. In June we would be graduated, sent out into the world, as the phrase went, into a world altered in every respect since that brisk February morning in 1916 when we had entered Columbia University; a war-shattered world in which everything we had held dear was no longer the same.

Now all desire to study left us. After the tension of war and such army life as we had tasted, systematic scholarship seemed futile. For what? For whom? Our nerves were on edge, and we distrusted everything we studied. Why learn history? Did not the war "prove" it a pack of lies? Why waste time on philosophy which had not prepared us for the apocalypse, which had justified it, which was only another lofty lie. Reason itself was futile. The intellectuals of all countries had been as rabid in their chauvinism as the "man in the street." Worse: the man in the street at least had no pretensions to intellectual integrity. Professors and writers were the new priests who blessed the war with the same fervor, if with different incantations, as the priests of the old churches, as George Creel's propaganda bureau. Intellect was a fake; it did not make you more intelligent or more honest; it corrupted you, as money and power corrupted you. We sat through lectures in the classroom and said to ourselves: lies! lies! lies! Listen to the priests of culture: they supported the war, they called for our blood.

More and more our cardinal test for all men and women was: what was their attitude toward the war, toward the Russian Revolution? No scholarship, wit or reputation affected our judgment. He who had them was doubly damned in our eyes if he had supported the war and opposed the revolution. To whom much hath been given, from him much was expected. They who were scholars, philosophers and historians could not plead the ignorance of the man in the street. They should have known the truth, yet they betrayed it. Let us pass our exams, get our degrees and go on.

Our favorite professors had been those who were cynical about capitalism. But they were cynical about socialism too, and about themselves. The man who poked fun at the "democratic" system of politics and exposed the tricks of the ruling class, who attacked preparedness on the campus and called himself a pacifist in public, had become a major in the army, attached to its legal staff. From France he wrote ironically to friends: I am sentencing conscientious objectors to the hoosegow. He signed himself, your pacifist friend. Such somersaults were by now commonplace. The debating team captain who had testified in 1916 before a Congressional committee against war preparations, had voted in 1917 on the student governing board to fire Morrie Ryskind from the staff of the *Jester* for antiwar propaganda; and later put on a lieutenant's uniform in the army. And the professor who had exposed for us the origins of the industrial system and the imperialist causes of the war had become a major in the Intelligence Corps. But did we not ourselves join the army? Oh, that was different, we said; we had other purposes in mind. As if we could know what those other men had in mind. Then perhaps we, too, were wrong. Professors knew nothing, the radical intellectuals knew nothing, we knew nothing, nobody knew anything.

The peace intensified that moral and intellectual nihilism which the war had generated. But since we did not care for complete spiritual suicide, we fled again and again to the old panaceas, to the semireligious solace of the intelligentsia. We sought once more some semblance of stability in art, philosophy, love, friendship. At least you were sure of your own sentiments and sensations. Nobody could lie to us about such things except ourselves, and we thought we were too desperate to lie. Oh, to sit in the park on Riverside Drive; to look up at the sun in the sky; to talk with friends despairingly about the dying bourgeois world, and hopefully about the new Russia! That was heaven on earth. But that heaven would soon vanish. We would quit the campus like monks leaving the security and sanctuary of the monastery to enter the profane secular walks of men.

Actually, the matter was much simpler. We had spent sixteen years in school, living a life of leisure, completely divorced from labor and conflict. Now we would have to go to work.

I took my last semester in the School of Journalism. Professor Walter B. Pitkin was by far our most frank instructor. I am not trying, he told us, to teach you literature. I am trying to teach you stories that will sell. If a story has no market, it's no good. But in another writing course, this one in Hamilton Hall, Professor John Erskine said: I cannot, like my distinguished colleague, Professor Pitkin, promise to teach you how to write salable stories. Such stories have their value,

but I do not specialize in that line. You will get no such practical training here. Our interest is in literature.

In the long run, the market triumphed. Both men became best
sellers. But at this time, the circle of which I was a member worshiped at the sacred shrine of Art which was the highest Truth.

§ 6

Since we had no integrating philosophy which related the various
aspects of experience to each other, we continued after the Armistice,
as during the war, to pass from one realm of living to another like
travelers from land to land. We wanted to feel at home everywhere,
and felt at home nowhere. We had lived through enormous changes,
yet did not feel transformed. From moral nihilism we moved to art,
from art to the social revolution, but just how these were connected
we could not say. Yet we could not help noting the changes in the
external world, nor could we escape their influence. This was especially
the case with the revolutionary movement to which we felt emotionally
attached. But once you felt the influence of that movement you did
become aware of changes in yourself. From that source alone you
seemed to derive clarity, purpose, meaning. Where the culture of the
campus left your spirit in fragments, the revolution seemed to give
you unity. But here, too, there were differences. The socialist movement in America appeared to be chaotic; the radical intelligentsia was
divided. Such light as now came to you came from the October Revolution.

This now became the center of our life—an idea to be grasped
before action was possible. Had someone asked me at this time, *what
are you and your friends doing?* I would have answered, *nothing*. We
went to classes; we read books and newspapers and magazines; we
sat on Riverside Drive and talked. We went to meetings and talked.
We went to dances in the Rand School and talked. And always we
talked about the same thing. We knew perfectly well that within a
decade all this talk would appear silly and fruitless. The Russian Revolution would become clear to everybody; travelers would visit it; books
would be written about it; every intelligent American youngster would
be familiar with its course as we at sixteen were familiar with the
course of the French Revolution. But that would happen later. We
had to decide now, and we had to decide for ourselves, for there was
as yet no organized group and no organized literature whose business
it was to clear up the questions which perplexed us. We had to work

out those questions unaided for the time being, getting what we could out of the socialist press, out of the *Liberator*.

Some who read the following pages may say: all the long confusions of thought about the Russian Revolution are right for that time, and undoubtedly happened to the author; but the public today has a pretty fair understanding of the general situation and the author can afford to deal with it in less intellectual detail; what we want is a narrative with more emotional and pictorial detail. But that is precisely the point: our emotions at this time revolved less about the visual world which surrounded us than about a world six thousand miles away whose tumultuous course seemed to affect the most vital decisions of our life. We believed, rightly or wrongly, that upon the success or failure of the Bolshevik Revolution depended the validity of socialism, the fate of mankind, hence our own small destinies.

Under the pressure of historic events, the heroes of the radical intelligentsia were changing. The Wilson myth was not entirely dead. So-called socialists continued to adore him as a savior of mankind; but his glamour was beginning to dwindle. The image of Kerensky, too, was fading. The year before, Vachel Lindsay, a young Springfield poet, had written and recited to large audiences a poem called *This My Song Is Made for Kerensky,* the "prophet of the world-wide intolerable hope."

> Moscow and Chicago!
> Come let us praise battling Kerensky:
> Bravo! Bravo!
> Comrade Kerensky, the thunderstorm and rainbow,
> Comrade Kerensky, Bravo, Bravo!

But that was a year ago. The people of Russia had pushed forward to a dictatorship of the proletariat. Kerensky was beaten; he had fled before the victorious bolsheviks. In the autumn of 1917, John Reed had inscribed Kerensky's political epitaph; the pseudo Bonaparte did not comprehend the revolutionary movement, he had no sympathy for the people, he suffered from an absolute and utter disbelief in the revolutionary method, from nervous bitterness, wounded pride.

The fall of Kerensky raised hopes and doubts. It was reported the bolshevik government had arrested Babushka Breshkovskaya, Plekhanov, Kropotkin, revolutionary leaders whom we had loved since childhood, the grandfathers and grandmothers of the Russian Revolution. Under the spell of the French Revolution in which we had just taken exams, we asked: Is this a repetition of the Mountain and the Plain? Were we now to learn from our own revolution what we had heard from Georg Büchner, whose *Death of Danton* we had read? *The revolution devours its own children.* How could the men and women who had founded the socialist movement in Russia, had devoted their lives to it, suffered exile and prison for it, how could the teachers of Lenin and Trotsky be "counterrevolutionists"? What sort of cruel and merciless men were leading the new revolution?

To our surprise, the *Liberator,* which damned the bigots and sectarians of American socialism and applauded Wilson's diplomacy, said that Lenin was right in jailing the mensheviks. Babushka, an editorial said, *ought* to be in jail because her dream of liberty was an old dream, the political and not the industrial, the evangelical ideal and not the economic force that would make it real. Naturally, there was a risk in every temporary violation of personal liberty, but in the cause of ultimate liberty for all this risk must be taken. Louise Bryant, the wife of John Reed, returning from Soviet Russia, reported that Babushka had *not* been arrested, but the *Liberator* editorials persisted that if the Grandmother of the Russian Revolution was not careful, she would be arrested. The proletarian revolution was in the hands of a "strong, unscrupulously idealistic leadership"; it spared none who stood in the way of building a socialist society, regardless of former services to the revolution.

John Reed and Albert Rhys Williams were at this time giving us our first authentic picture of the bolsheviks. Moreover, the *Masses,* which, after its suppression during the war, appeared as the *Liberator,* was publishing Lenin's own words. These words illuminated and clarified our perplexities. Lenin was not contemptuous about our confusion; he helped us to overcome it by explaining its origin. He pointed out that mankind was passing through one of the greatest crises in its history. Everywhere around us the old order was falling apart with tumult and crash and a new order was being born in indescribable torment. It was not surprising that at the most difficult points of such a crisis some people became bewildered victims of despair, while others sought refuge behind beautiful enchanting phrases. In Russia, Lenin pointed out, circumstances compelled them to see things clearly as the people passed through the sharp and painful experience of a historical crisis which was turning the world from imperialism to communist revolution.

To read Lenin's own words was reassuring amidst the fantastic hatred and falsehood which the press was pouring out upon the October Revolution. The organs of big capital hysterically shrieked about the bandits, cutthroats and madmen in Moscow, as they had shrieked about the I.W.W. and the socialists in America. That was to be expected. More surprising to us was the blind and bitter hostility of liberal intellectuals who found their own metaphors for voicing the hatred of the bolsheviks which convulsed the middle and upper classes. Typical of this mood was the facsimile of a letter by H. G. Wells which appeared in the July, 1918, issue of Upton Sinclair's pro-war magazine. Across the upper left-hand corner of the letter Wells had written: *not for publication except in Upton Sinclair's.* The letter said in part:

"Don't write me down Bolshevik. I'm a Wilsonite. For the first time in my life, there is a man in the world that I am content to follow. Lenin, I can assure you, is a little beast like this. [Here Wells drew a crude caricature which indicated only that he could not draw.] He just wants Power & when he gets it he has no use for it. He doesn't eat well or love prettily or get children or care for beautiful things. He doesn't want order; he hates machines almost as much as he hates life. He's just a Russian Sidney Webb, a rotten little incessant egotistical intriguer. He & the Kaiser ought to be killed by some moral sanitary authority."

H. G. Wells had had the privilege of talking with Lenin; other middle-class intellectuals had not. Yet the hostility was as bitter among those who listened obediently to the *Times* as among those who returned from Moscow no wiser than when they went there. The war and the "peace" which came after it had so disillusioned us with Wilson that we had little respect for intellectuals who were "content" to follow him. Their epileptic denunciations of Lenin found no support in the reports from the revolutionary front which Rhys Williams and John Reed sent to America. Lenin's own *Letter to American Working-men,* which the *Liberator* published in January, 1919, clarified every point which the Wilsonite liberals and socialists had muddled. We clipped that letter, read it and reread it, got to know it by heart. It seemed to us that never before in history had a political leader talked so simply, honestly and wisely to the mass of mankind. Lenin evaded no problem, denied no difficulty, concealed no mistake. He faced and called attention to the "indescribable torment" in which a new social order was being born.

They were no revolutionists, Lenin said, who would have the revolution of the proletariat only on condition that it proceed smoothly and in an orderly manner, that the workers of all countries immediately go into action, that guarantees against defeat be given beforehand; that the revolution go forward along the broad, free, straight path to victory, that there shall not be here and there the heaviest sacrifices, that we shall not have to lie in wait in besieged fortresses, shall not have to climb up along the narrowest paths, the most impassable, winding, dangerous mountain roads. Such people were no revolutionists; they had not yet freed themselves from the pedantry of bourgeois intellectualism; they would fall back, again and again, into the camp of the counterrevolutionary bourgeoisie. Why did such intellectual pedants raise their hands in horror at the Russian civil war? The class struggle in revolutionary times had always inevitably taken the form of civil war, and civil war was unthinkable without the worst kind of destruction, without terror and limitations of the form of democracy in the interest of the war. Only sickly sentimentalists could not see, understand and appreciate this necessity; only they could denounce the revolution for this reason instead of throwing themselves into the fight with the whole vehemence and decision of their souls at this moment when the highest problems of humanity had to be solved by struggle and war. Lenin counted on the sympathy of "the best representatives of the American proletariat," those who retained the revolutionary tradition in the life of the American people. This tradition originated in the war of liberation against the English in the eighteenth century and the civil war in the nineteenth century. Was there an American so pedantic as to deny the revolutionary and progressive significance of the American Civil War? The bolsheviks were accused of bringing devastation upon Russia. Who made those accusations? The camp followers of the bourgeoisie—that same bourgeoisie which had "almost completely destroyed the culture of Europe," which had dragged the Continent back to barbarism, which had brought hunger and destruction to the world. This bourgeoisie now demanded that we find a different basis for our revolution than that of destruction, that we should not build it up on the ruins of war, with human beings degraded and brutalized by years of warfare. Oh, how human, how just was this bourgeoisie! Its servants accuse us of using terroristic methods. Had the English forgotten their 1649, the French their 1793? Terror was just and justified when it was employed by the bourgeoisie for its own purposes against feudal domination; but terror became criminal when workers and poverty-stricken peasants used it against the bourgeoisie. Terror was just and justified when it was used to put one exploiting minority in the place of another; terror became horrible and criminal when it was used to abolish all exploiting minorities, when it was employed in the cause of the actual majority, in the cause of the proletariat and semiproletariat, of the working class and the poor peasantry. *The bourgeoisie of international imperialism had slaughtered ten millions and crippled twenty millions in the war.* Should the war of the oppressed and the exploited against the oppressors and exploiters cost half a million or a million lives in all countries, the bourgeoisie would still maintain that the victims of the World War died for a righteous cause, and those in the revolutionary war died for a criminal cause. Yes [Lenin said], the bolshevik government was making mistakes, the Soviets were making mistakes, the workers and peasants were making mistakes. But they were not afraid of mistakes. The beginning of the revolution had not turned men into saints. The working class, which for centuries had been exploited and held down by force, want, ignorance and degradation, was bound to make mistakes in the conduct of its revolution. The dead body of the bourgeoisie could not simply be put into a coffin and buried; it was rotting in our midst; it poisoned the air we breathed; it polluted our lives; it clung to the new, the fresh, the living with a thousand threads and tendrils of old customs, of death and decay. The bourgeoisie and its sycophants heralded to the world all our mistakes. But for every hundred of these mistakes there were ten thousand great deeds of heroism, greater and more heroic because they seemed so simple and unpretentious, because they took place in the everyday life of the factory districts or secluded villages, because they were the deeds of people who were not in the habit of proclaiming their every success to the world, who had no opportunity to do so. Only through their mistakes could the workers and peasants learn to organize their new existence, to get along without the capitalist class; only thus would they be able to blaze their way through thousands of hindrances to victorious socialism.

After explaining and justifying the dictatorship of the proletariat in Russia, Lenin indicated that the European revolution was not far off. We were counting, he said, on the inevitability of the international revolution. But that did not mean that we counted upon its coming at some definite, early date. We knew that revolutions could come neither at a word of command nor according to prearranged plans. We knew that circumstances alone had pushed the proletariat of

Russia forward, that it had reached this new stage in the social life of the world not because of its superiority but because of the peculiarly reactionary character of Russia. But until the outbreak of the international revolution, revolutions in individual countries might still meet with a number of serious setbacks and overthrows. Yet Lenin was certain that we were invincible, for humanity would not emerge from this imperialistic massacre broken in spirit; it would triumph. Russia was the first country to break the chains of imperialistic warfare. It broke them with the greatest sacrifice, but they were broken. It now stood outside of imperialist duties and considerations; it had raised the banner of the fight for the complete overthrow of imperialism for the world. But the Russian proletariat was in a beleaguered fortress, so long as no other international socialist revolution came to its assistance. But the armies of the international proletariat were there; they were stronger than Russia's; they grew, they strove, they became more invincible the longer imperialism with its brutalities continued. Inevitably labor was approaching communistic, bolshevistic tactics; it was preparing for the proletarian revolution which alone was capable of preserving culture and humanity from destruction. We were invincible. The proletarian revolution was invincible, Lenin said.

The hope of world revolution ran high in radical circles during 1918. Even the cautious Morris Hillquit discreetly declared that the revolution in Russia would be of greater importance than the World War itself. The war would pass someday; it could not last forever; but the fact that one of the greatest countries in the world had broken away from the old capitalist moorings, had turned a new page in history and proclaimed the rule of the people instead of the rulers— that could not pass without the most vital effect upon the whole future of the human race.

Other American radicals were less discreet and less cautious. Socialist and wobbly circles throughout the country took over bolshevik slogans like "All power to the Soviets!" and even called themselves American "soviets." Among the radical youth, bitterly disillusioned by the war, revolutionary hopes flamed high. From the artillery fort where he was stationed, Robert Smith wrote me on November 11, the day on which the Armistice was confirmed:

"It is quite possible that the Social Democracy of Germany will triumph over the imperialism of her present enemies as the Russian Bolsheviki confounded the Potsdam gang and made possible the downfall of imperial Germany and her autocratic government. The ultimate triumph of the German revolution makes me feel optimistic over the certainty of the fact that progress cannot be stayed by the armed might and brutality of the masters; and the Allies, including the U. S. A., are not immune to the evolution of these forces. Five-sixths of Europe is in our hands. It is not too far distant when the world will be reclaimed from the pharisees, hypocrites and thick-heads who rule it now. I watch for the Day with renewed confidence. Keep yourself fit."

Toward the end of the year our hopes seemed to be justified. The socialist revolution had begun in Germany. Karl Liebknecht, liberated from prison, proclaimed that "the hour of the people has come." In Austria the people were rising, and in Bulgaria, and in Hungary.

By the spring of 1919 we were acquainted, through the socialist press, with the leaders of the German socialist revolution—the lawyer Karl Liebknecht, son of the famous Wilhelm Liebknecht who had helped to found the German social democracy; the literary critic and philosopher, Franz Mehring; the organizer and orator, Clara Zetkin; the theoretician, Rosa Luxemburg, who in her spare time painted pictures.

We were aware, too, that socialist Germany, like socialist Russia, was divided into warring groups of mensheviks and bolsheviks. The German Revolution of November, 1918, was, in the words of Karl Kautsky, "the work of the proletariat alone." The majority of the social democrats, who had voted war credits in 1914, opposed the November Revolution. When it broke out, social democratic leaders were ministers in the coalition cabinet of Prince Max. The more imminent the fall of the old regime became, the more vehemently did the social democracy appeal to the German masses against revolution. Party leaders like Scheidemann subsequently admitted that when they were compelled to demand the abdication of the Kaiser they did so in the hope of saving the monarchy. Social democratic trade unions signed a treaty of alliance with the employers as late as November, 1918.

The conflict between the social democracy and the bolshevik elements in Germany came out clearly in the manifesto signed by Clara Zetkin, Rosa Luxemburg, Karl Liebknecht and Franz Mehring which the *Liberator* published in this country. The manifesto, addressed to the workers of all countries, said that the revolution had entered Germany; but all power had not yet been lodged in the hands of the working people. The complete triumph of the proletarian revolution had not yet been attained. There still sat in the government all those socialists who in August, 1914, had abandoned our most precious possession—the International, those socialists who for four years had betrayed the German working class and the international working class.

The manifesto was the voice of a new party which called itself Spartacus and spoke for the "German proletarian himself." It appealed to the workers of all countries to "arise for action," to elect workers' and soldiers' councils everywhere, to establish peace under "the flying banner of the socialist world revolution."

By the time this manifesto appeared in the United States—March, 1919—we already knew that Karl Liebknecht and Rosa Luxemburg had been murdered by the government in which sat the social democrats who "for four years had betrayed the German working class." The intense indignation of radical America against the murders was voiced by Arturo Giovannitti in his powerful free-verse poem *The Senate of the Dead*. The shade of the murdered Karl Liebknecht enters the "vast gray meadow" where "great oaks towered in the distance unstirred," under which "in the calm of the ages that rest, and the silence of ages that wait, sat the solemn assizes of the dead." There Karl Liebknecht is embraced and saluted by revolutionary heroes of the past—Spartacus, Abraham Lincoln, Wilhelm Liebknecht, Louise Michel, Wat Tyler, Massaniello, Bruno, Marat, John Brown, Francisco Ferrer, Katoku, Tolstoy and Jesus—a strange company and a true one, for all these men, each in his time and place, had been martyred for that dream of liberty which, taking different shapes in different ages, was in our day embodied in communism. When each has spoken, Karl Liebknecht addresses his father:

"Father, O Father, I have come as you said; I have been true to your legacy, and died where you bade me remain, poor and hunted, and cursed and defeated, but not shamed.

But it was not the Monster that defeated me, Father; it was your comrades of yesterday, they who polluted the earth with the stench of their treason,

They who tore down the old ikons from their niches but held the foul temple still sacred;

They who made of Liberty an ignoble mouthing of vulgar words and of Revolution a mere exchange of seats and clothes.

But I have fought them, Father, I fought them with your words and my own bare hands, and the night is not yet, for the cannon still roared when I came."

For us the lesson was clear. The "moderate" socialists were foes of socialism. There could be no peace between the communism of Lenin and the socialism of Scheidemann. The unity of socialist leaders with the capitalists in their war for markets had split the working class throughout the world. That split came to America too. Louis Fraina was appealing to left-wing locals and sections of the Socialist party to get together on the basis of the *Manifesto of the Left*. The radicals on our campus, who had already chosen socialism as against capitalism, would now have to choose between two movements each of which claimed to speak for socialism.

The choice was not for workers alone to make; the proletarian revolution was of tremendous import to intellectuals as well. Follow us! Maxim Gorky said in the *Liberator*. All honorable and thoughtful men must see that capitalism has lost its constructive force and is a relic of the past, a hindrance to the development of world culture, that it evokes hostility between individuals, families, classes and nations. The beautiful dream of the great brotherhood of nations cannot be accomplished so long as the irreconcilable struggle between labor and capital still survives. The leader of the campaign against Russia is Woodrow Wilson; the torch of the Russian Revolution which throws its light over the entire world is firmly held by the hand of Lenin. The proletariat and the intellectuals will choose which one most nearly represents their interests, the representative of the outworn, life-destroying minority rule, or the leader and teacher of new social ideals and emotions, who is the embodiment of the beautiful ideals of the workers, of freedom of labor among all peoples.

What made Gorky's appeal all the more impressive was that it came from one who only a short time ago had opposed the bolsheviks and was still in disagreement with them on many points. His phrase "the proletariat and intellectuals" indicated for us a social unity which alone showed the way toward a new life. The old world was impossible. Its peace was no better than war. Its culture was rotting. Under its crushing greed, the worker was a slave and the intellectual a prostitute. The proletarian revolution alone could emancipate the mass of humanity from poverty and emancipate culture for the mass of humanity.

When Gorky said: *follow us to a new life, follow us in our struggle against the old order, in the work for a new form of life, for the freedom and beauty of life,* we felt that it was in his camp that we definitely, irrevocably belonged.

CHAPTER III

I am of Montaigne's country—one who eternally doubts but is eternally seeking.

—ROMAIN ROLLAND.

§ 1

UNFORTUNATELY, that feeling was not pure, nor was it an integrated attitude toward the world. Gorky was the voice of Time. Behind him we continued to hear, loud with authority, the voices of recorded history which we fancied represented Eternity. We were not active in the revolutionary movement. Graduation day was four months off; we were still in that scholastic world of passive reflection in which we had been spending a decade and a half of our lives. Every day we divided our hours between two worlds, and the internal conflict was bound to go on. No one took any special interest in our development. Our parents had long ago relinquished us, convinced that we were destined for a life about which they could tell us nothing. Our professors delivered their lectures, handed us examinations and dished out grades without any particular concern about our personal problems. We had received a mandarin education which seemed to have scarcely any connection with the real world. Now that the end of the war had left us exhausted, disillusioned and puzzled, we crept back to that mandarin education for comfort and security. Again and again, we went back to abstract considerations of art and love, philosophy and revolution, convinced (except in rare moments of lucidity) that passive reflection was more important than active participation in the work of the world.

Lying on the grass of the Riverside Drive park, looking at the slow Hudson crawling between us and the Jersey shore, we said to each other, let us enjoy this moment. The sun shines, we are happy, we can read and think and talk, living a life which the romantic poets erroneously ascribed to the active Greeks. Soon we shall be out in the "real" world. We shall perhaps never see each other again. We shall never again have this leisure and freedom, this mandarin garden of

148

philosophic discourse in which we imagine we can reconcile any number of contradictory ideas.

Each of us was a multiple personality living in a pluralist universe. We moved, often in a single day, through a series of overlapping worlds whose interrelations were obscure, whose roots lay in the middle-class home, proletarian memories, socialist dreams, the lure of an ideal art. These were by now old ideas, yet we did not think them in quite the same way. Time and the war had made a difference. Even at home the changes were deep, whether you liked it or not. Flush with wartime prosperity, our parents were fast losing the ideals of the vanished village, the awe for disinterested knowledge. Instead, they adopted the dominant ideal of America—the awe for money. They cited apocryphal scripture: *where there is no bread there is no learning;* and divided the world into the rich and the poor. They were middle people between the very rich, whom they envied and disliked, and the very poor, whom they despised and pitied. The noblest of all social classes was the middle class, to which they belonged. It was bad to be poor; that meant suffering. It was equally bad to be too rich; that meant corruption. A rich man was usually suspected of being a debauchee, but if we brought a professor or writer to the house, our parents might say:

"A fine man, but what's the good of his kind of knowledge? He's dying for a piece of bread. Shakespeare may be all right, but he has no value in the grocery store. Nobody is against culture. But who pays for it? The bourgeois. We give you an education and you call us enemies of society."

The businessman's suspicion of all knowledge which had no immediate practical value was not confined to our neighborhood. When I visited the homes of those professors who were my personal friends, I found that their business acquaintances looked upon them with that mixture of contempt, pity and respect which the medieval warrior reserved for the cloistered monk. Devotion to abstract thought and pure art was the luxury of the academics, as the worship of God was the luxury of the priests. Both were conceded to be necessary decorations for worlds built on force and fraud, but no more than decorations, and from the devotees of both the men of action expected poverty and humility, though not always chastity. Later, in the spring of 1919, when I was graduated from Columbia and was looking for a job, the head of a large publishing house asked me:

"Why do you want to be a writer? It doesn't pay. An executive in my house can earn ten times as much, and buy all the writers he wants. I earn ten times as much as I pay Montague Glass."

As befitted young wiseacres who had read a few books, my friends and I smiled tolerantly at the lawyers, builders and dentists who visited our parents and defended their position in contemporary society on moral grounds. We granted them ironically the loftiness of their motives but were skeptical of anyone's disinterestedness except our own. We harped on the fact that they, too, were cogs, and damned small cogs at that, in the "capitalist machine." They were little exploiters who would, by the laws of capitalist development, eventually be devoured by the big exploiters. Were not the trusts gobbling up the middlemen? The middle class would be ground between the upper and nether millstones of capital and labor. You as people, we said, are not the enemies of mankind, but the system of private property is. If you are interested only in the security, health and education of your children, you will be able to work peacefully in the socialist commonwealth of America as many former bourgeois are now working in the socialist commonwealth of Russia. Unfortunately, we said, such noble people are rare. Most property holders cling to their property bitterly and defend it by ruthless violence against the workers seeking to establish a new and higher society based on collective property.

Such discussions, all the more painful because of the personal affection which bound the disputants, embittered fathers and sons alike. The world of home, already remote from the ideal pursuits of the campus, was itself split for us by the struggle between that class to which we now socially belonged and that class toward which we were more and more gravitating, partly through reason, partly out of early emotional association. This growing split made us more conscious than ever of the world's divisions, the conflicts of rich and poor, Negro and white, Jew and gentile, native and alien.

But the more acutely aware we became of these divisions, the nearer we approached the day when we would have to participate actively in the social struggle, the greater became our devotion an ideal art. It has been said that the classic ethic was one of attitude, the Western ethic one of deed; and the campus, in that sense, was for us, at any rate, the sustaining and exhilarating home of attitude. There was a line, we thought whenever the problems of the external world became too pressing or too confusing, which divided mankind into two parts, regardless of class, nation or race. There was that part which loved culture and that part which did not. On the campus the average student was interested in sports, women and money. He was the philistine son of the philistine father. But there was another group, select without being exclusive, a group which anyone could enter if he deserved it, whatever his race, nation or social status, a group of Choice Spirits devoted to philosophy, science and the arts— to culture. We imagined that this culture embraced all mankind, all lands, all times. We were equally interested in Homer and Rupert Brooke, in Newton and Santayana, in Euripides and Bernard Shaw; we believed in these moods that "There is one great society alone on earth: the noble living and the noble dead."

From this all-human culture we excluded, in practice, a large section of humanity. We knew nothing and cared less about the knowledge, thought and art of Asia, or of our neighbors in Latin America. Russia, too, was outside the cultural realm in which we moved, for Russia, the myth ran, was Asiatic and barbarous. Even those of us who had read Tolstoy and Dostoevsky and Gorky repudiated everything east of the Danube as primitive. Not until the October Revolution did we become interested in Russian culture, not until Russia had ceased to be a "nation" and had become a "workers' republic." Then the people upon whom we had looked as barbarians appeared, instead, as the vanguard of the human race. We no longer thought of them as Russians, but as socialists. They were privileged to be the first of men to realize the dream of the international proletariat—a dream which had become ours through the spokesmen, the thinkers, writers and agitators, of American labor. And since a great social revolution transvalues all values, Russia's past, which until now had seemed to us one of unbroken darkness, suddenly assumed a new meaning in the light of its glorious present. Thanks to Lenin and Trotsky, we began to read for the first time Pushkin and Gogol.

We understood that in politics there were contradiction, incongruity and conflict. In art, we imagined, there were only differences of opinion capable of harmonious resolution in the imagination. As a result of this dualism, we had two sets of friends. In the city were the socialist workers with whom we discussed strike tactics, the policies of the Socialist party, the course of the Bolshevik Revolution. On the campus were the students and professors with whom we discussed Plato, Shakespeare, Edwin Arlington Robinson. The workers listened to us with amused tolerance or sober respect when we showed off our meager knowledge of the classics. The students and professors smiled loftily or argued vehemently when we asserted that the best ideas of mankind inevitably led to communism.

The two worlds were as separate as the earth and heaven of the poet's imagination. There were mundane matters, like earning a living, strikes, wars, revolutions. There was, beyond these, the celestial realm of the imagination where one talked about eternal truths with generous and gifted friends.

To resolve the contradiction between Christian tenets of love and the imperious needs of the rising bourgeoisie for profits, Martin Luther set up a false antagonism between matter and spirit, saying: let life be earth and doctrine heaven. For similar reasons, Kant later set up the analogous antagonism between pure reason and practical reason. Upon such German ideologues of Protestantism, the French Catholic apologists have blamed the woes of Europe, forgetting that the Catholic Church itself, to reconcile the conflict between ideal Christianity and the barbarities of the feudal world, set up the antagonism of the world spiritual and the world temporal, a conceptual antagonism which meant a division of temporal power between princes and prelates. Both great Christian sects, compelled by historic necessity to falsify reality in the interests of the propertied classes, drew upon the idealism of those Greeks who, for lack of scientific knowledge, identified the ideal with the real.

This heritage of dualism was a residue of our formal education. Although many of our instructors were pragmatists by profession, insisting upon the material nature of the universe and the social basis of all human activity, they were in practice dualists who lived alternately in the realm spiritual and the realm temporal, in the world of practical reason and the world of pure reason, on the earth of life and in the heaven of doctrine disguised as tentative speculation. Children of this dualism which pervaded all Western civilization, we could no more reconcile the teachings of Karl Marx than our instructors could the teachings of John Dewey with the ideal realm of poetry and art.

There was Time, and there was Eternity, my friend Irwin Edman liked to say, taking a phrase from the Irish poet AE. Let us render to Time the things that are Time's, and to Eternity the things that are Eternity's. To Time belong the economic and practical problems of the day. To Eternity belong Homer and Racine, Shelley and Goethe, Euripides and Kant, Spinoza and Morrie Ryskind. The last pair was not incongruous. In the ideal realm of the Life of Reason, there were gradations ranging from the genius who comes once in a century to the wit who comes once in a semester. No one, least of all Morrie himself, dreamed of comparing the light verse which we all contributed to F.P.A.'s ivory Conning Tower with the poetry of the Greek Anthology. We were humble citizens, pariahs, if you like, in the great and eternal Republic of Letters. Yet we lived in it, we belonged to it, it was our true home, as distinguished from the barbarians whose world began and ended with football, women and money.

Under the illusion of patriotism, the lowest slave imagines he shares the glory and even the profits of the kings, generals and merchants who send him to die for their benefit. So we humble and limited citizens of the Republic of Letters imagined that somehow the glory of Homer and Shakespeare and Goethe shone upon us, especially since, unlike the rulers of a country, the poets, instead of exploiting us, enriched us. We did not vulgarize Eternity with Time. We ceased to consider, except abstractly, the great thinkers and poets of the world as voices of specific lands and times, societies and classes, interests and parties. Above and beyond the real people we knew on the earth of life—the businessmen, workers, teachers, football players, soldiers, policemen, newspapermen, saloonkeepers, socialist agitators, good and "bad" women—there was an ideal abstract personality of which the members of the select cultural group partook as Catholics partake of the body and blood of Christ. This personality never actually existed. He was a composite of all the ideal elements of Western civilization, from God to Bakunin, from Christ to Nietzsche, from Bonaparte to Kropotkin, from Cecil Rhodes to Karl Marx, from Aristotle to Evangeline Adams. In the crucible of the unhappy imagination we sought to resolve all the contradictions of contemporary society through this ideal man of the ideal European civilization whose culture we had absorbed. We did not all do it to the same extent or in the same way. I am describing a general type rather than specific cases; yet I remember how often I came back to the dormitories on the campus from a workers' meeting, where I had spoken from the platform on American imperialism or the Russian Revolution, to stay up until dawn with Professor Raymond Weaver discussing the fine points of Catholic theology, Julian the Apostate, or Herman Melville, on whose biography my instructor was then already at work. The very room in which we talked—sometimes for twelve hours at a stretch, stopping only for food—was symbolic of our eclectic culture. The books which lined Dr. Weaver's shelves ranged from Europe's classics to Confucius. The walls were hung with his drawings, the table piled

neatly with his piano music and notebooks. The door, covered with
the Japanese print of the man crossing the delicate bamboo bridge,
failed to shut out the chatter of the students returning to their rooms,
flushed with Columbia's baseball victory. Dr. Weaver had a harmonious voice which molded perfect sentences in ordered procession as we
wandered through Eternity discussing Aeschylus, Molière and Donne
as if they belonged to our own Time. These were indeed our contemporaries, so intense was the belief that in the imagination Eternity
coexisted with Time. We were not mystics. We understood that
Eternity was a metaphor and Time was real; but the only way we
found of reconciling the two, of bridging the ideals of the Western
world with its actual monstrosities was by the Kantian subterfuge of
the pure and the practical reason.

Floating in a canoe down the waters of the Delaware, Irwin
Edman recited from memory pages of Plato; I, strophes from Swinburne. Yet neither of us could enumerate the provisions of the Treaty
of Versailles, a document less beautiful but at that moment vastly more
important. We grasped that importance; we had read the treaty and
deplored its obvious consequences, but our most vital spiritual energies
were reserved for the brighter world which existed, *sub specie æterni-
tatis,* above wars, revolutions and treaties, which preceded them and
would outlast them, as the bust outlasts the throne, the coin Tiberius—
the sublime world of the imagination. The votaries of this eternal
world, isolated from the men and women who lived in Time, sought
everywhere for others of the true faith, rejoiced when they found
them, introduced them to others of the select band, as, for example,
when Dr. Weaver in the spring of 1919 urged me many times to
meet a remarkable young man who was teaching English in Brooklyn.
I was not, however, to meet Joseph Wood Krutch until a decade later
when he was, in American letters, an outstanding defender of the true
faith, in which I had by that time ceased to believe.

But while the aesthetic cult in which postwar disillusionment
sought refuge was based on Eternity, it also extolled, by a false dialectic, the Fleeting Moment, of which Pierrot was for one of our
professors the tragic symbol. Pierrot urged that Eternity was *in* the
Fleeting Moment. He felt that all delight was a poignant sorrow, all
beauty a snare to the flesh and a thorn in the spirit, all success at best
a not ignoble failure. In the central quiet of Pierrot's mind there sat,
through pain and delight, a Spectator who judged his own actions and
those of others; but these judgments were never moral; Pierrot knew

no standard of virtue by which he dared to measure his fellow men or himself. He had neither ethical certainty nor unequivocal truth. Truth was at best an unstable equilibrium of lies; it was absurd for him to judge the good or evil consequences of any act. His sole consideration was to discover in all behavior some grace, some unobtrusive elegance, some mastery of technique. The ultimate goal of all effort was to do all things with a persuasive grace, to sanctify the meanest act by lovely enactment.

The difficulty with the golden realm of eternal values was that everything in it was supposed to be true, and its precise opposite was also supposed to be true. Only in this fantastic way could the contradictions of the real world, sublimated into the ghosts of immortal ideas, be reconciled on the plane of glamorous self-deception. If Eternity was found in a mythical Fleeting Moment, surcease from the intolerable burdens of the actual fleeting moments which compose our daily lives was to be found in an equally mythical eternity. Such, at any rate, was the impression we got from Bertrand Russell whose *Free Man's Worship* now replaced in our esteem the antiwar gospel which he had preached to us during the war. We strove to achieve those moments of insight which the English logician described with more poetry than logic, those moments when we might lose all eagerness of temporary desire, all struggling and striving for petty ends, all care for the trivial things that seemed to make up that common life of day by day. Through the eloquent aristocrat's eyes we saw all the loneliness of humanity amidst hostile forces concentrated on the individual soul, which must struggle alone, with what courage it could command, against the whole weight of a universe that cared nothing for its hopes and fears. We believed with him that victory in this undefined struggle with the powers of darkness was the true baptism into the glorious company of heroes, the true initiation into the overmastering beauty of human existence. There were whole days when we shared his conviction that from that awful encounter of the soul with the outer world wisdom and charity were born, and that with their birth a new life began. This was the metaphysics of Eternity as against Time. The free man's worship was to abandon the struggle for private happiness, to expel all eagerness of temporal desire, to burn with the passion of eternal things.

§ 2

These were not merely abstract considerations. We thought they were directly connected with our lifework, which we fondly imagined was to be "thinking" and "writing." For the professor who remained within the sanctuary of the campus, or the student about to enter his father's bank, the paradox of Time and Eternity was lightened by convention. The banker eased his conscience by patronizing the arts as he patronized the church. The savant's activity in Time was an extension of that pursuit of wisdom which was identified with Eternity. For those of us who loved the arts, yet were compelled to struggle in the world of Time in order to exist at all, a special myth was necessary to resolve the paradox. Without understanding its real significance as a symbol, we developed the cult of the Universal Man. The literary heroes we most admired combined intellect with will, imaginative with practical pursuits, art with the life of action. In the past there had been men like Sir Philip Sidney, Goethe, Dante, Cervantes and Victor Hugo. In the present we had the soldier-poets who had been killed in the war; Gabriele d'Annunzio, whom we had not yet recognized as a poseur. More important for us still were John Reed, Max Eastman, Floyd Dell, Robert Minor and Arturo Giovannitti, each of whom we supposed to be equally developed as artist, journalist and revolutionist. But since reality had an awkward and aggressive way of distorting the harmonious outlines of a myth, we went back again and again in imagination to the alleged Universal Man of Greece and the Renaissance.

Just as our myth of universal culture omitted from consideration three continents, most of Europe and nearly all of America, and concentrated on that narrow learning and art which, masked as the Hellenic spirit, glowed over the isolated circles of a few Western capitals, so the myth of the Universal Man omitted much that was manly. Few of the aspirants toward this Renaissance ideal were athletes or men of action. In practice, universality consisted of an intellectual versatility which frittered away its energies on several related fields of abstract thought or dilettante art. Abélard composed songs in the vulgar tongue and theses in Latin; so several of our academic Choice Spirits composed light verse for F.P.A. in the vernacular American, and theses on philosophy or literature for the academic journals in a Latin-English. The radical intellectuals reversed the process. We wrote theses in the "vulgar" tongue of American journalism, peppered with still more "vulgar" socialist clichés, and composed songs and sonnets in the Latin-English of the nineteenth century decadence.

Not Abélard, however, was our shining model of the Universal Man among the Renaissance scholars, but Pico della Mirandola. He had all the marks of the romantic hero. He was the prototype of Shelley and Byron and other glamorous youths in the romantic pantheon. As spokesman for a rising social class, he attempted to reconcile the moral tenets of Christianity with the aesthetic tenets of Hellenism. He wrote love songs in the vulgar tongue and philosophic theses in Latin. He had great personal beauty and was loved by many women; and he died young. We knew Sir Thomas More's English version of Marsilio Ficino's raptures over the twenty-year-old savant's appearance: of feature and shape seemly and beauteous, of stature goodly and high, of flesh tender and soft, his color white, intermingled with comely reds, his visage lovely and fair, his eyes gray and quick of look, his teeth white and even, his hair yellow and abundant. And we knew Walter Pater's languid tribute that even in outward form and appearance Pico seemed an image of that inward harmony and completeness of which he was so perfect an example.

These descriptions had for us only moral and aesthetic meaning. We knew nothing about the practice and psychology of homosexuals except what we read in Freud. Among all our acquaintances there was, so far as we know, not a single introvert. On the general principle that "everything is permitted," we were tolerant toward Oscar Wilde without having any real notion what his "sin" was. What appealed to us in the Socratic dialogues was the platonic friendship we read into them. This sublimated notion was part of the aspiration toward universal love which went with the aspiration toward universal knowledge. We fancied that we shared with the Renaissance men what Pater described as the faith of that age in all oracles, its desire to hear all voices, its generous belief that nothing which had ever interested the human mind could wholly lose its vitality. We wanted to love the true, the good and the beautiful wherever they were to be found, in men as well as women, in children as in graybeards, in art as in socialism, in the past, present and future. And since the imagination is less hampered in Eternity than in Time, we tended to identify ourselves with Pater's aesthetic critic for whom the picture, the landscape, the engaging personality in life or in a book are valuable for their virtues, as we say in speaking of a herb, a wine, a gem, for the property each has of affecting one with a special, a unique impression of pleasure. We agreed with Pater that our education became more complete in proportion as our susceptibility to these impressions increased in *depth and variety*. Not all men were privileged to receive beautiful experiences. There was a certain kind of temperament which had the power of being deeply moved in the presence of beautiful objects. Naturally, we were among the privileged few. And since beauty existed in many forms; since all periods, types and schools of taste were in themselves equal, we permitted our imaginations, when they were not absorbed by the struggles which marred Time, to wander in Eternity "over the crooked hills of delicious pleasure." The prime qualification for this privilege was sensibility, and the highest praise we could bestow on a friend was to say that he was sensitive.

Among my literary friends, this sensibility precluded an interest in the practical sciences. Psychology alone engaged our attention, and that was to literature what chemistry was to alchemy. Contemporary physicians were converting the divinations of the poets into more precise measurement. The long citations from Goethe, Nietzsche and Dostoevsky which we found in the psychoanalytic reviews confirmed our presuppositions. Freud's work in the realm of psychology was revolutionary, but like so many intellectual revolutions its effect on undeveloped people was at first chaos. We began to have alarming dreams, or perhaps, as the Freudians might say, we stopped repressing our dreams and became conscious of them. We talked psychoanalysis all day long; we analyzed each other's dreams, fantasies and slips of the tongue. In the eighteenth century intellectuals played at science, and set up little laboratories where they tinkered around with test tubes and read Newton in bed with their mistresses. Now we were all amateur psychoanalysts, tinkering about with each other's souls and our own. New fears developed. Our "sensitive" tendency to identify ourselves with people and ideas led to the conviction that we suffered from various "complexes." We concluded in turn that we were extroverts, introverts, schizophrenics, paranoiacs and victims of dementia praecox. Our literary faculties were for a time paralyzed: perhaps this beautiful poetic symbol which had just rushed through our brain was not beautiful at all; perhaps it revealed some secret forbidden wish, or a fear which was a wish in disguise.

As in the case of socialism and art, our preoccupation with psychoanalysis marked us as queer beings in the world of Time. The bourgeois pursuing profits, the organizer building trade unions, the socialist agitator fighting for the Cause, these normal people said our studies in the Unconscious rendered us cynical and even a little mad. But we argued that if mankind was to progress in a direction worthy of the pain of life, its most fundamental need was the capacity to assimilate all new knowledge.

Apart from this humanistic aspect of psychoanalysis, the new knowledge served a practical purpose. Ignorant of the moral aspects of psychoanalysis, of its gospel of sublimation, we saw it through the eyes of popularizers chiefly as an instrument against puritanism. Under the old dispensation the great sin was sex; under the new it was repression. Under the old it was said: beloved father in Christ, I have sinned, having slept with a woman; under the new it was said: beloved sister in Freud, you are a sinner, you suffer from suppressed desires. Already that postwar generation was rising which, carrying the image of Priapus before it, cried like Constantine Ἐν τούτῳ νίκα—*by this conquer!* Love was to become, in some cases, not a pleasure or an emotion, but a kind of surgical operation for removing taboos, inhibitions, repressions and complexes, a prophylactic against possible or impending neurosis. Small wonder if such operations were by themselves rarely successful.

Pico della Mirandola was no solitary figure in our Renaissance pantheon. We placed beside him the austere and passionate Michelangelo for his sculpture, painting and poetry, and even Lorenzo de' Medici for combining art with action. But of all the heroes of the Renaissance we most admired him who seemed to embody in his own person all that was greatest in that age, that *homo minister et interpres naturæ,* the truly Universal Man—Leonardo da Vinci.

Bourgeois historians, celebrating the achievements of their class, exaggerated its already great cultural role by pretending that the Renaissance sprang like lightning out of the preceding epoch which they tried to blot out with the phrase "the Dark Ages." Professors who were either Catholic apologists or real scientists took care to disabuse us of that idea. They sketched for us the cultural attainments of the Crusades, out of which came European poetry; the all-pervading influence of Christianity, fused out of Jewish and Hellenic elements, and dwelt lovingly on the thirteenth—greatest of centuries. Modern Western culture, as it came to us at the university, gave us the Christian epic intact. We were familiar with and influenced by the "ordered universe" of St. Thomas Aquinas and Dante, the concept of the life eternal, the Jewish ideal of righteousness and the Christian gospel of love which had entered into medieval culture together with the Hellenic love of wisdom, Platonic idealism and Oriental asceticism. The men of the Renaissance, the ideologues of the rising bourgeoisie, patronized by the bankers, merchants and condottieri who bossed the Italian city-states, attempted to merge what was best in this medieval culture with their own specific contribution, that humanism based on the revival of Greco-Roman culture which asserted the rights of man against institution, or, more specifically, the rights of the bourgeois man against the feudal institution. Da Vinci was the giant who in his own person combined the old and the new. He was not only painter, scholar and musician, but engineer and inventor; he represented the science of the new class, that technique of dominating external nature which was in the long run to give the bourgeoisie dominance over the world, which the businessmen expanded, transformed and advanced for several centuries before becoming deadly parasites upon its vitals.

We considered ourselves the legitimate heirs of the whole of Western culture. Those of us who happened to be Jews were brought up, as children, in the traditional feud between Hellenism and Judaism. The rabbis had kept that cultural struggle fresh in our memories after eighteen centuries, as they kept the symbol of the Sacred Temple, the *Beth Hamikdash,* in order to maintain the purity of the racial culture. The old-fashioned Hebrew teachers simply opposed Jewish monotheism to Hellenic polytheism, Jewish asceticism to Greek corruption in the Alexandrine period. The dramatic symbol of the cultural struggle was the Maccabee family: the old father Mattathias, who let himself be killed by the Greeks of Syria rather than eat pork; the young Eleazar, who plunged to death under the foe's elephants in order to stem the advance of his army; Judas Maccabeus, who led the Jewish troops to victory and cleansed the Temple of Greek desecrations. The spiritual symbols were, on the one hand, the stone idols of the Hellenes and, on the other, the invisible Jehovah of the Jews. More progressive teachers, those already steeped in Western culture yet intent upon maintaining the racial ideals, accepted Matthew Arnold's definition that "the uppermost idea with Hellenism is to see things as they really are, the uppermost idea with Hebraism is conduct and obedience." This they interpreted to mean that the Greeks were objective, the Jews subjective; the Greeks were the champions of Truth and Beauty, the Jews of Goodness and Justice.

By the time we were leaving the university we were no longer, culturally, Jews. We were Westerners initiated into and part of a culture which merged the values of Jerusalem, Egypt, Greece and ancient Rome with the Catholic culture of the Middle Ages, the humanistic culture of the Renaissance, the equalitarian ideals of the French Revolution, and the scientific concepts of the nineteenth century. To this amalgam we added socialism, which seemed to us the apex, so far, of all that was greatest in Western culture. As a matter of fact, many of our professors, while repudiating the class struggle and socialism, were themselves indebted to Karl Marx for their evolutionary and materialistic view of human history.

Their outlook, however, stopped short of the whole truth by confining itself to the framework of bourgeois thought; yet it tended to feed and support our revolutionary ideas even when it ignored or attempted to refute them. It seemed to us that if the social, materialistic, evolutionary views of the professors were carried forward, if their ideas were applied to capitalist civilization after the manner of Marx and Engels in the *Communist Manifesto,* communism would inevitably appear as the sole solution for the ills of contemporary civilization. This became all the more evident when our professors in history and politics frankly admitted many things about capitalist civilization which we were accustomed to hear from socialist agitators. They talked of social classes and of class interests; they revealed corruption in government which seemed to discredit the democratic dogma; they even used such words as "exploitation" and "imperialism." But all this was criticism of capitalism intended to improve it. The system of private property as such was questioned only in the manner of Socrates; the question contained its own answer, and the answer was that with certain abuses removed the status quo could continue for centuries improving the lot of "man."

The mirage of the Universal Man lured us out of the morass of specialization which contemporary culture imposed upon most men. From socialist doctrine, even more clearly than from our liberal professors, we knew that capitalist production was based on the division of labor. Every new mechanical improvement increased that division and chained the worker more securely to the machine whose slave he was. My own experience in the vanished village, the slums of New York, the campus, made self-evident the Marxian dictum that the first great division of labor, the separation of the city from the country, doomed the inhabitants of the rural districts to a thousand years of stupidity, and the people of the towns to be the serfs of their own handiwork. Villagers were denied the opportunity to develop their minds; city people had little chance to develop their bodies. Socialism illumined our daily lives so that we could understand why the division of labor led to the division of man, why the individual himself is subdivided. In Louis Smith's factory, I could see for myself the monotonous single operation to which the worker was doomed, the concentrated specialization which crippled him body and soul, so that his entire life was poured into a single narrow function. But the bourgeois world seemed to be equally cursed with specialization. The business men we knew neglected body and mind for profit; the lawyers were the slaves of their antiquated legal hocus-pocus which they mistook for the world; the aesthetes were helpless children who were lost everywhere except among books, pictures and concerts.

We were not going to be workingmen. We came from a social stratum which gave us a university education. Nor did we wish to be "spiritually barren bourgeois," slaves to moneygrubbing; nor lawyers dominated by "ossified notions of justice," nor refined idlers, nor even professional artists or poets. We wanted to be Universal Men, developed physically, mentally and spiritually, active in politics and creative in literature. This hope fed on regressive dreams of a romanticized world which had ceased to exist in any form, and in the form in which we idealized it had never existed at all—the mythical world of Greece and the Renaissance. It also fed on a dream of the world to come in which the separation of town and country, the gap between mind and body, would no longer exist—the world of communism.

When we looked through the eyes of the Renaissance at society about us, with its crippling division of labor, we fell into despair and nihilism. When we looked at it through the eyes of communism, our dream of the Universal Man seemed to have some roots in reality. From Marx and Engels we learned that only in so far as society obtained control over the social means of production in order to organize them socially could the existing servitude of man to his own means of production be abolished. Society could not be free without every member of it being free. But in order for society to be free, the old methods of production had to be completely revolutionized, and the old form of the division of labor eliminated. A new society would have to be created in which no single individual would be able to shift his share of productive labor to others. At the same time, productive labor, instead of enslaving men, would become an instrument toward human freedom, offering to everyone an opportunity to develop his full powers, physical and mental, in every direction, exercising them so that what had hitherto been a burden would become a pleasure. This was not a daydream. The communists demonstrated that such a world could be achieved with the present powers of production, provided society took over those forces and removed the impediment placed upon them by capitalism. Without the profit motive, modern production could supply all of society's needs with a relatively small amount of labor. The achievement of a communist society, however, was neither automatic nor exclusively dependent upon an act of will. The laws of capitalist society had to be studied, revolutionary strategy had to be mastered, the working class had to be organized, revolutionary will and intellect had to be adapted to the external movement of history.

§ 3

The classless communist society, with its Universal Men was far off. It was said that Lenin had predicted three centuries of civil strife before the world would become communist. Meantime, within our own span of life, could the artist who was also a socialist find for himself no resolution of the dilemma of Time and Eternity? Was the Universal Man to remain for us an empty dream?

Help in the solution of such problems used to come from the *Masses* group. But something had happened during the war to break the profound influence of this magazine over us. The fact that the *Masses* editors were brought to trial under the Espionage Act ceased to be a cause for wonder as the war went on. During 1918-1919 such trials were frequent, but we were no longer shocked to see the ruling class persecute spokesmen of the proletariat. We had learned to take for granted that all prevailing justice was class justice. What now surprised us was the conduct of some of the *Masses* editors on trial, as contrasted with the conduct of various revolutionaries facing similar prosecution. Eugene Debs, for instance; tried for an antiwar speech delivered at Canton, Ohio, he boldly told judge and jury that he would not retract a single word he had uttered, even if it meant going to prison for the rest of his days. His courageous loyalty to principle landed him in a federal penitentiary. From his prison cell he declared that the heart of a true socialist never beat a retreat, in jail or out; he would continue the fight without compromise until socialism triumphed and the people were free. Similarly Scott Nearing, tried in the spring of 1919 for an antiwar pamphlet, apologized for nothing, retracted nothing. Charles E. Ruthenberg, tried in Cleveland, spoke up in the courtroom with equal frankness and decision. Amidst these revolutionary voices boldly challenging the ruling class in its own courts of justice sounded the voice of our old socialist guide, Max Eastman. Taking the witness stand during the first *Masses* trial in the spring of 1918, he defended the editorials for which he had been indicted by pleading that they could not be really unpatriotic since the measures they had urged were subsequently adopted by President Wilson himself. The district attorney read from a *Masses* editorial attacking the "ritual of patriotism" and asked the defendent whether the sentiments expressed in that editorial were his sentiments today.

"No, they are not," Max Eastman replied. "My sentiments have changed a good deal. I think that when the boys begin to go over to Europe, and fight to the strains of that anthem, you feel very different about it. You noticed when it was played out there in the street the other day, I did stand up. Will you let me tell you exactly how I felt? I felt very sad; I felt very solemn, very sorrowful because I thought of those boys over there dying by the thousands, perhaps destined to die by the millions, with courage and even with laughter on their lips, because they are dying for liberty. And I thought how terrible a thing it is that while they are dying over there, while the country is gradually coming to a feeling of solemnity and seriousness of that thing, the Department of Justice should be compelling men of your distinguished ability, and others like you, all over the country, to waste their time persecuting upright American citizens, when they might be hunting up the spies of the enemy, and the profiteers and friends of Prussianism in this country, and prosecuting them."

The trial ended in a disagreement of the jury. Some of my socialist friends were shocked by what they called Eastman's "betrayal." Others said he was absolutely consistent. Had he not for years attacked the "bigots, cranks, and sectarians" of the movement on major political issues? Even after the trial he continued to propagate the Wilson myth and to support certain governmental policies. That was perhaps the real reason why John Reed resigned from the editorial staff, saying that he could not in these times bring himself "to share editorial responsibility for a magazine which exists upon the sufferance of Mr. Burleson." Reed continued to write for the paper, however, hoping for "the happy day when we can again call a spade a spade without tying bunting on it." Eastman was himself unhappy about the situation. Personally, he said, he envied Reed his power "to cast loose when not only a good deal of the dramatic beauty, but also the glamour of abstract moral principle, is gone out of the venture."

Late in 1918 the *Masses* editors were tried a second time and acquitted. John Reed, always anxious to face realities, explained the acquittal in social terms. To begin with, the four defendants in the second trial—Max Eastman, Floyd Dell, Art Young, John Reed—were native-born Americans of old American lineage; they were not Jews, Italians, Russians or Germans as was the case with so many defendants under the Espionage Act. Hence the judge gave the radical editors considerable latitude in proving their intent, and the jury was open to impressions. Furthermore, the case was tried in New York City where the war spirit was somewhat less hysterical than in certain provinces of the Middle West. Finally, the war was over, Germany was defeated, the Allies were victorious. Patriotic feeling, kept at fever pitch for more than a year, had begun to slacken. Under these circumstances, the attitude of the defendants in the second trial was in striking contrast to their conduct in the first. In the spring of the year, Germany invaded Russia; now America was invading Russia, and socialists were in a different frame of mind. The persecution of radicals had grown more bitter; it had become more and more a class issue. At the second trial, Max Eastman defended the St. Louis resolution of the Socialist party against the imperialist war, John Reed justified the class war, Floyd Dell praised the conscientious objectors, and Art Young said he disapproved of this war and all wars on economic and social grounds. The jury once more disagreed and the case was dismissed.

The second *Masses* trial did not eradicate the memory of the first. It was disheartening to recall the surrender at a critical moment. Perhaps the fantasy of the Universal Man was at fault. Men like Debs and Nearing did not pretend to be revolutionary Goethes or Lorenzos. The proletarian leader and the proletarian ideologue saw their duty clearly before them. But the radical literati who had attracted us were divided beings whose conflict, like our own, came from a dual allegiance.

When the second *Masses* trial was over, Max Eastman published a book of verse which revealed the dualism in its sharpest form. We thought he was seeking in the Colors of Life that harmony amidst chaos which we sought in the concept of Eternity. The book of verse opened with a preface:

"It is impossible for me, feeling and watching the eternal tidal currents of liberty and individual life against tyranny and the type which are clashing and rearing up their highest crimsoned waves at this hour, to publish without some word of deprecation a book of poems so personal for the most part, and reflecting my own too easy taste of freedom rather than my sense of the world's struggle towards an age and universe of it. That struggle has always occupied my

thoughts, and often my energies; and yet I have never identified myself
with it, or found my undivided being there. I have found that rather
in individual experience, and in those moments of energetic idleness
when the life of universal nature seemed to come to its bloom of realization in my consciousness. Life is older than liberty. It is greater
than revolution. It burns in both camps. And life is what I love. And
though I love life for all men and women, and so inevitably stand in
the ranks of revolution against the cruel system of these times, I love
it also for myself. And its essence—the essence of life—is variety and
specific depth. It cannot be found in monotonous consecration to a
general principle. Therefore I have feared and avoided this consecration, which earnest friends for some reason always expect me to
exemplify; and my poetry has never entered even so deeply as it might
into those tempests of social change that are coloring our thoughts
today."

Here was an Eternity opposed to Bertrand Russell's. The English
liberal logician counseled us to abandon the struggle for private happiness, to expel all eagerness of temporal desire, to burn with the passion of eternal things. The American socialist poet, like our conservative college professors, told us that eternal life was in the fleeting
moment, in temporal desire, in individual experience, in moments of
energetic idleness. This idea was not new to us. It was an echo of the
campus on which the socialist poet, like ourselves, was educated. Particularly, it was an echo of Walter Pater, whose definition of life as
depth and specific variety was repeated verbatim. What made this
restatement of the decadent credo especially significant for us was that
it came from those socialist regions where, from a distance, we had
often sought for unity between "life" and revolution. We were no
nearer to clarity than before. Individual experience was apparently
opposed to the social struggle; a thing called life was greater than
revolution; and a man like Lenin could not have life because he conse-
crated himself monotonously to a general principle.

Others voiced the conflict between poetry and politics even more
directly. Floyd Dell recorded that during the *Masses* trial he would
suddenly ask himself: *What am I doing here? Why am I not at home
writing a story? The scene became, in such moments, utterly unreal.
The fact was, I was an artist, not a politician. How in the world did I
come to be mixed up in this political cause célèbre?*

Now, after the trial, reading Eastman's preface and poems, Dell
was overcome with the same surprise. It seemed to him that Eastman

was so pre-eminently a lover of beauty and so delicately a sure-handed creator of it, that his participation even in the most vital politics appeared incongruous. *For I am not ashamed to say,* Floyd Dell added, *that to me art is more important than the destinies of nations, and the artist a more exalted figure than the prophet.* Yet the radical poets and artists of Dell's circle were in politics; the conflict could not be evaded by beautiful rhetoric, and Dell, for one, was unwilling to pretend that no such conflict existed. *It is useless,* he said, *for people to say that it is a superior type of mind which can function both in politics and in art. It is a vain compliment, which but temporarily assuages the unhappiness of the type in question. That superiority is a painful one, consisting in fact of a spiritual conflict between opposing impulses.*

Louis Smith tried to explain the conflict to me in class terms. The clash between poetry and politics, between "life" and revolution, he said, arose from the fact that the poet divided his being between two worlds. His politics proceeded from a mind groping its way toward socialism, his poetry from feelings deeply rooted in bourgeois life and culture. The bourgeois heart was at war with the socialist head. The poet suffered from the class war reflected in his own soul.

Floyd Dell essayed another explanation. His circle of artists and writers, he said, would continue to be in politics if only because the social situation of the day created "a great black void of silence and cowardice into which some brief lightning-flashes of candor must needs rip their way," and also because "it was more interesting to talk truth than to create beauty." That was the trouble with being an artist in the period of war and revolution; other things were so damnably interesting and promised to remain so. How could one be an artist when the morning newspaper might report another Bolshevik Revolution somewhere? Dell was now ironical about those artists who "patronizingly" used the events of the day as material for their art; he ascribed their "poise" to feebleness of intellect, although he confessed that he envied their singleness of purpose.

This was as far from Dell's previous appeals to Dreiser to write the American novel of rebellion as Eastman's preface was from his passionate cry of earlier years, that cry which we so vividly remembered: *Your place is in the working-class struggle; your word is Revolution.*

The dualism between poetry and politics which affected the pre-war radical intelligentsia shifted emphasis with the shifting tides of history. In peace one urged artists to write about the social revolution; in war one ran for refuge into the arms of Pater or Gautier. No wonder that I felt so direct an affinity with the men and women of the *Masses* group, not one of whom I knew in person. They were in twentieth century America the direct spiritual descendants of the nineteenth century European romantics. I believed with them, and with Wordsworth (and I believed it all the more zealously as the external world became harsh and confusing), that

> Dreams, books, are each a world; and books, we know,
> Are a substantial world, both pure and good:
> Round these, with tendrils strong as flesh and blood,
> Our pastime and our happiness will grow.

§ 4

In the summer of 1919, I was out of Columbia, with a diploma, a Phi Beta Kappa key and a lot of romantic notions. I was living in Time and longing for Eternity. The problem of earning a livelihood was related to art; your job must not engage your major energies; you must be free to create poetry. At Harper's, where I ghosted a volume in a historical series edited by Carl Snyder, I scribbled verses at lunch to break the monotony of hackwork. Later I worked on a newspaper where I made the acquaintance of the socialist poet, Sam Friedman. We drove our editors to fury by paying more attention to verse than to copy. The world of the imagination was becoming more real for me than New York City, upon which I now looked as upon a horrible prison where Time was the obdurate warden.

Like all prisoners, I dreamed continually of freedom, but freedom was as vague as God or love. My friends and I were aware of the workers' struggles; we sympathized with the steel strikers led by William Z. Foster; we wanted to help in every possible way. But we did not know how. We were groping blindly because we looked upon ourselves as literary people, and had no clear notion of how writers could be useful to the revolutionary movement. Some of my friends now wanted to struggle for "freedom" on an individual basis. Benjamin Ginzburg, for example, was contributing to a magazine issued by the Soviet bureau in New York headed by the engineer Ludwig Martens; but Benjamin despised this work as "merely" practical. He wanted something more, something he hoped to find in Europe. By the spring of 1920 he was in Paris, among the first of that postwar American caravan which sought new values and old in the capital of

Western culture. From the Sorbonne, where he was taking philosophy courses, Ben wrote me:

"I seek yet to find the light and the truth. Paris is one of the world's mountaintops where often men have communed with the gods. But alas! today there are no gods, there is no truth, there is no light. The people fight in darkness, they curse one another, they bear false witness, they make hypocritical mockery of justice. I do not clearly understand it. . . . I had a talk today with one of the professors in regard to writing a thesis on some phase of the revolutionary spirit. He remarked that I had a religious faith in certain ideas, and that like the Christians I was trying to write about things we do not know about or clearly understand. He himself is a rationalist and cannot understand that state of mind. Very well: but how can one be rational in this so irrational age, in this era of violent chaos where humanity is butchering itself to death? The war against Russia is infinitely more horrible than the war against Germany, for shut in by frontiers each belligerent nation could maintain a semblance of intellectual and spiritual order. But this new civil war without frontiers and without boundaries has devastated the spiritual domain of humanity. A discussion has been running in a number of French reviews over the question of the ivory tower. Georges Duhamel in a very learned article cites a long list of writers in ancient and modern times who did not fear to mix in the battles of their fellow men. But do Duhamel and his kind quite understand how deep is the social struggle today? One cannot live any more in an ivory tower for all the ivory towers have been shot down. But he who engages in the social struggle surrenders himself to wild currents over which he has no control. All humanity is being swept into the current to be driven past wild and desolate banks for many, many years, until thrown ashore on some Arcadian isle which no one has ever explored. I have surrendered myself to Bolshevism. The time is past to try to keep a clear and impartial head. I have adopted a cause and when one adopts a cause one is freed from a great many perplexities of the spirit. It is fascinating to observe and to think, but I have given myself over to Bolshevism and must hereafter spend most of my time writing, translating and organizing. It is painful to surrender one's time even for a worthy cause."

Again the dualism of the radical intelligentsia. There was one's own time, there was observation and thinking, the moment of energetic idleness—and somewhere outside there was the "cause" to which one gave one's self. I now felt part of that intelligentsia. The *Liberator* was publishing my verses and I was in correspondence with the editors. Floyd Dell wrote me: "We admire your work very much and regard you as quite a considerable poet indeed." The compliment was pleasing, but it was scant relief for the pessimism which engulfed me more and more. Office routine, conflicts at home over my refusal to take up the law as a profession, the general dreariness of the middle-class life surrounding me, impelled me to flight. Friends who had gone to Paris invited me to join them. France was still the traditional country of art and personal freedom. It respected the poet; it venerated love; it was the home of Voltaire, Rousseau and Hugo. And now the war had made it a part of American life. Thousands of young men of our generation had died there; thousands more remained behind to live or travel in it. The great migration had begun—and by the summer of 1920 I was ready to join it.

But this readiness was the result of something more than abstract reasoning. Psychologists have pointed out that the four major tasks of adolescence are to earn a living, to break away from the family, to find a mate, to adopt a philosophy of life. On being graduated from college, several of my friends and I proceeded to tackle the first of these tasks on the basis of two current American illusions. One illusion was that you could make a million dollars in business, retire at an early age, and then pursue your real interest—art, philosophy, science, music, yes, even socialism. The second illusion was that you could get a job which would not interfere with your real work, a job which would draw neither upon your basic energies nor upon your sense of responsibility—such jobs were newspaper reporting, ghost writing, teaching school. I tried newspaper work, ghosting and business, and found that you could not spend eight hours a day in an office without being affected by its routine and its ideas. The less responsibility there was attached to a job, the more exhausted you were physically. It was hopeless to attempt sustained writing and socialist activity after a grueling day at a job upon which you expended not only the energy of effort, but the even greater energy of hatred.

The problem of earning a living was connected with the second problem, that of breaking from the family. All about us was the money culture which judged success by your income. Our own families, riding high on the wave of postwar prosperity, were headed for financial success. Their living standards rose higher and higher, always beyond their rapidly increasing incomes. Since I no longer shared my father's ideas, it was impossible for me to enter his business. He might pile up a million dollars, but I was going to earn my own living. That was complicated by the change in our home environment. Ten years earlier, our families might have been glad to see us earn thirty dollars a week as reporters or schoolteachers; now they felt that we would be failures with less than ten thousand a year.

The third problem, that of finding a mate, was connected with the first two. The girls we knew were fine in every way—good-looking, clever, educated, warmhearted, and idealistic. Some of my friends married such girls shortly after leaving college. But those of us who wanted to see the world before we settled down encountered two difficulties: The nice middle-class girls seemed both puritanical and money-mad. Love with them meant marriage; and marriage meant money; and money meant absorption by bourgeois society. Settling down meant becoming a respectable citizen—a bourgeois.

It was, then, the fourth problem which was the key to the first three. We had repudiated the money culture of middle-class America. We wanted art and revolution, neither of which was a paying proposition. This complicated the tasks of earning a living and finding a mate, but it facilitated the task of breaking from one's family. Louis and Robert were now both married. Their wives were devoted, but a happy marriage required economic security—the last thing you could find in the revolutionary movement. Radical girls became conservative wives; they carried on an open or concealed campaign to get their husbands out of socialist activity. They fell back on the great American illusion: first make your million, then you can be more useful to socialism.

In my last month at college I walked one night with a beautiful and intelligent girl through Central Park. Her father was a wealthy manufacturer. She said:

"What will you do when you graduate?"

"I don't know yet."

"What are you interested in?"

"Poetry and revolution."

"How wonderful!" she said.

"Wonderful if you don't mind starving."

She did not mind starving. Look at Cornelia Stratton Parker, whose *An American Idyll* was the literary rage of the moment. I tried to explain that a college professor was neither a poet nor a revolutionist; he was an accepted member of conventional society, even when he did advance a few progressive notions. I would probably have a harder time. My explanation was successful. A week later the lady wrote me that she loved me very much but, life being what it was in this day and age, she had decided to marry a rich manufacturer.

In Paris, we thought, such things did not happen. There we would find Murger's *Bohemia,* a realm where rhymes were more precious than dollars, where men were more respected for creation than for acquisition. There we would be unknown. No one would burden us with great expectations. What right did our families and friends have to expect us to make a million dollars? What right had they to impose their bourgeois standards of success on us? We were the captains of our souls, the masters of our fates; if we so desired we had a "right" to fail by middle-class standards. We would rather fail pursuing the good, the true and the beautiful than succeed pursuing money. In the long run, the philistines would be the failures, anyway; they would dry up in their countinghouses; their wallets would grow fat, their souls scrawny. Then they would come to warm themselves at the breast of Art. Could one create Art in America? Nonsense! America was a wild marketplace, hysterical with the shrieks of hagglers. Here you could make money only by slaying your true self. That was why Henry James and T. S. Eliot and Ezra Pound and Amy Lowell and Robert Frost had gone to Europe, either for a while or permanently. In Europe, especially in Paris, one could find "culture." Even the European bourgeois was cultured. In Paris—friends wrote me from the cafés along the Boulevard Raspail—taxi drivers and shoe clerks quoted Racine.

Moreover, in Europe revolution seemed imminent. Here the reactionary terror was in full swing. The Palmer raids were breaking up labor and radical organizations. Provocation poisoned the air. As a student in the School of Journalism I had covered the Wall Street bomb explosion and recorded in my notebook another item in ruling-class falsehood and brutality. The *Buford* deportation and the Armistice Day massacre in Centralia were still fresh in our minds; so was the "suicide" of Andrea Salsedo and the unseating of the five socialist assemblymen in New York. The "counterrevolution" was sweeping the country. Why live in a prison? In Europe there were Berlin, Budapest and Moscow. You could go to any of these from Paris; you could join the militant proletariat in some humble capacity; you could see the old order overthrown.

I sailed for Europe in July, 1920, with Mr. and Mrs. Robert Smith, both of whom I had known since childhood. It never once occurred to any of us that we were heading for that continent from which our families had come; we felt that we were going to foreign lands, like any other Americans. Yet not like all Americans. For the upper classes, a trip to Europe was a commonplace of social life. For sailors it was part of the day's work. In our little middle-class, provincial world, going to Europe was a sensational adventure, partly heroic, partly sinful. We were the talk of the neighborhood for years, until unprecedented prosperity made travel a commonplace there too. For us, under the circumstances, it was not a trip; it was a break, a search.

CHAPTER IV

Do nothing secretly; for Time sees and hears all things, and discloses all.

—SOPHOCLES.

§ I

CITIZENS of Paris assured me that the war had robbed the capital of its glamour. The Place de la Concorde was dimly lit; cafés closed early; it was necessary to save electricity. Everywhere you saw crippled veterans, hobbling on crutches or wheeled in chairs along the boulevards. Many women wore black cotton dresses. Mourning, some said; others said, a shortage in dress goods. Over the center of European culture hovered the immediate memory of death.

Yet the city brought joy and freedom to me, an outsider, an American living on a favorable rate of exchange. I did not actually live in Paris; I lived in an American ghetto. Just as the European immigrants formed their own little Italies, Hungaries and Russias in New York, retaining their old languages, habits and customs, so the Americans had their little U. S. A. in Paris where they read American newspapers and yelled for ice-water and ham-and-eggs. The rate of exchange gave them the privilege of yelling; often nobodies at home, they lorded it over the waiters of the Café de la Rotonde.

I was surrounded by friends whom I had known since childhood —fellow students who preceded or followed me in the migrations of American intellectuals into European "exile." Robert Smith and his wife were there on a prolonged honeymoon; Benjamin Ginzburg, David Gould, Percy Winner and others worked on the two American newspapers published in the city for the growing American colony.

The Parisian bohemia was as free as we had imagined it. We became "gentlemen" with mistresses. The Sexual Crisis passed its first stage in the favorable environment of that capital which for generations has been the traditional center of the "free life" for the middle-class tourists of other countries. Perhaps the sense of freedom had nothing to do with Paris as such; perhaps it was only the result of being away from home. We were on our own, independent in every way, earning our own living, disposing of our own leisure, making fools of ourselves by our own standards rather than by the standards of the ghetto, the campus or middle-class New York. We knew young Frenchmen who dreamed of going to America; middle-class life was as intolerable for them in Paris as for us in New York. They expected our city to do for them what their city had done for us, to free them from the community in which they had been brought up, whose discipline was at the moment unbearable. Like ourselves, they talked not of going *to* a place but of getting away *from* a place.

Thanks to a letter from Carl Snyder recommending me to whom it may concern as a good journalist, I got a job on the Paris edition of the *Herald*. I worked nights writing copy by hand instead of on a typewriter. Since all my friends worked either on the *Herald* or the Chicago *Tribune* at night, we were able to lead a kind of collective bohemian life. We finished work at two A.M., talked in cafés until dawn, slept till ten, breakfasted at the Rotonde, and spent afternoons seeing the sights, reading, writing, and above all talking, talking, talking—art, sex, psychoanalysis, the social revolution. This was called a "full" life.

After a month in Paris, I saved up enough money on my job to go to Italy with Robert, his wife, and a young American pianist, Anton Rovinsky. Like most tourists, we concentrated on all that was old and outworn—the grotesquely conventional memorials in the Genoa cemetery, the wedding-cake cathedral in Milan, the Doges Palace in Venice. Renaissance Italy came alive as a marble ghost. Here in Milan was Leonardo da Vinci himself, a stone hero with square cap and long beard. It all seemed remote. The present kept impinging on the past. In Turin the streets were full of carbinieri with rifles on their shoulders; the bolshevik workers were holding the factories; we saw Premier Giolitti rush by in an open Fiat, but were not allowed to get near the factories. On churches in Genoa, Milan, Turin, Venice we saw, scrawled in chalk or charcoal: *Viva Lenin!*

Our European experience was a collective one. When we were separated on various parts of the Continent, we wrote each other long letters, exchanging impressions, analyzing our reactions. Part of our romantic heritage was the cult of friendship; we were bound by ties of sentiment which seemed stronger than those binding us to any other group. We fancied ourselves a kind of happy family growing up together, distinguished from the ordinary family by our intellectual preoccupations. We had that romantic love of comrades which we imagined bound Shelley and his circle, Goethe and his friends, the nineteenth century Russian revolutionary groups. It was a sacred dogma of our creed, as well as a habit of our practice, not to conceal anything from each other. Possibly the spread of psychoanalysis stimulated this romantic attitude to unusual extremes, although the romantics of the nineteenth century, too, believed in the necessity of always speaking the complete truth. Deception was the supreme vice; against self-deception we were presumably inoculated by the doctrines of Freud. We wrote to each other not only what we thought about Paris, London, Venice, Dresden, Warsaw; idealism versus pragmatism; art versus revolution; but also about our love affairs, our successes and defeats, our most fantastic aspirations and most desperate doubts. We believed literally that the truth would make us free, and felt that if everybody told the truth, the whole truth and nothing but the truth the world would be that much nearer to freedom.

Yet this romantic friendship had its complications. In Venice I received a letter from one of my best friends in Paris, a man with whom I had grown up through school, a passionate philosopher and now, like most of us, a devotee of the frank and free life. His letter opened with philosophic observations, decorated with a little landscape sociologically interpreted. All this was the innocent prelude to a casual piece of information of presumable interest to me:

"In regard to your lady, I tried to seduce her but was unsuccessful, owing to the fact that it was the wrong time of the month, and therefore her sexual passion was very low; I may try again in a few weeks when her sexual passion will be increased."

My friend's physiology, I knew by this time, was all wrong. But by the moral standards then in fashion among radical bohemians, his conduct was quite right. It was proper for him to try to "seduce" my "lady," and obligatory to inform me of the outcome of his efforts. On my part, the "new" mores required that I show no jealousy or resentment. The idea that women were private property was a bourgeois idea. Jealousy was a primitive and philistine passion. I recognized these moral obligations abstractly. Unfortunately my primitive feelings rebelled. I did not like the situation at all. I thought very harsh things about the "lady," my friend, myself. I condemned myself most for my inability to rise to the noble heights of the new mores. Yet my friendship with the philosopher continued for many years. I never rebuked him for his conduct; I was in style.

This was only one of the conflicts which agitated me. My whole life now seemed to be one long internal conflict. I divided my time between the real world of newspaper work and the imaginary world of idealistic poetry and philosophy. On returning from Italy I had switched jobs. I now worked on the Chicago *Tribune* from five in the afternoon until long past midnight. The newspaper had two offices. Its business headquarters were near the Place de l'Opéra, in the heart of the fashionable district of Paris. There you could hear the gigantic Floyd Gibbons bellowing orders and see Leon Stolz—who later became an editorial writer in Chicago—bend his thick glasses, mustache and ironical smile over French clippings; or you could see the poet Stephen Vincent Benét calling on the feature writer whom he later married.

The editorial office where I worked was a messy, unheated room on the Rue Lafayette, in the building of the *Petit Parisien* whose printing presses we used. Lee Wood, who later became managing editor of the *World-Telegram,* sat at the head of the desk, occasionally relieved by a redheaded Irishman named Monahan. Around the two crude wooden tables on which we typed our copy sat Percy Winner, who was later to become Associated Press correspondent in Italy and foreign editor of the *Evening Post;* Benjamin Ginzburg, whom the boys kidded as "Benny the Bolshevik" because of his loud pro-Soviet sympathies; Henry Altemus, who wrote fiction for the pulps, and John O'Brien, famous Hearst war correspondent. O'Brien was now reduced to the rewrite desk for drinking; eventually he was to die as head of the United Press bureau in Paris.

Throughout the work, the conversation flowed uninterrupted; so did the *rum chaud.* The copy boy's exclusive job was to bring up from the canteen below beer, wine, cognac and anything else the messieurs on the desk ordered. We took the copy to the printer ourselves. Percy Winner, with a full black mustache at twenty-one, rattled curses in perfect French, discoursed upon the finer points of the Higher Psychoanalysis and recited Arthur Rimbaud.

John O'Brien, drunk and sardonic, lectured me in his most fatherly manner, urging me to "quit this goddam game" before it killed me and to stick to literature. He presented me with a copy of Villiers de L'Isle-Adam's *Contes Cruels* which he advised me to translate for the good of my soul. Another time, in order to make a man of me, he invited me to see a murderer guillotined. We left the office at three A.M. and went to a café in Les Halles which remained open all night for the workers in the market. To kill time until dawn, John fed me bottles of wine and cognac. I drew caricatures on the marble tabletops which the waiter with a reproachful look patiently wiped off. The wine and cognac were too much; I got drunk, blabbed about America, for which I felt a sudden nostalgia, and fell asleep across the table. The next day I had to rewrite from the French papers the story of the guillotining I had missed: the murderer defiantly broke loose from his guards, leaped at the guillotine, and decapitated himself. This was typical of the rewrite desk. We saw France, Europe, the world through the newspapers which we read and rehashed. It was hackwork, the symbol of which was our boss Floyd Gibbons who, after years in Paris, could not read French and knew little of what was going on, even though, unlike ourselves, he had the privilege of eyewitnessing events.

Once Gibbons assigned Benjamin Ginzburg to Riga to cover the peace negotiations between the Poles and the Russians. The Soviet government had expelled Henry Clayton, the Chicago *Tribune* correspondent, for alleged distortion of news, and would accept no other correspondent from that newspaper. Gibbons assumed that Benny would be *persona grata* with the Soviet negotiators because in New York he had worked with Rustem Bek on *Soviet Russia,* the Martens bureau publication. That judgment was correct; Ben obtained an exclusive interview with Joffe, head of the Soviet delegation in Riga. He wired the interview to London which phoned it to Paris. I took the story over the phone, reading it back paragraph by paragraph. Floyd Gibbons, on his way to a party in evening clothes, top hat, white scarf and cane, walked into the office as I was repeating a sentence in which Joffe said the French had instigated the Poles in their war on Russia.

"Who the hell says the French are backing the Poles?" Gibbons asked.

"Joffe," I said.

"Kill that. We're not printing any goddam Russian propaganda."

"This is not propaganda. It's a fact. The French papers have admitted it for the past week."

"I don't give a damn who says it. It don't go in the *Tribune.*"

He took the notes from my hand and tore them up. Yet—leaving his politics aside—he was an energetic if sensational newspaperman, and for one like myself who had spent so many years in the realm of "eternity," it was lifesaving to buckle down to routine journalism which compelled me to think every day, albeit differently from Floyd Gibbons, about current events.

These events, however, never appeared in my verse. From the office of the paper I often walked home alone past the Tuileries, across the Seine, to my garret in a cheap hotel in the Rue des Saints-Pères. The room was dim and unheated; there was a coal shortage that winter, and often I had to sleep in my overcoat. Sometimes I lay awake till dawn reading—Baudelaire, *Main Street,* the *Communist Manifesto;* or scribbling verses about the Seine and its bridges; the skies, the seas, the flowers; and my own internal conflicts.

That dualism between my daily life as a newspaperman and my imaginary life as a poet was comic. But was not life older than liberty? Politics dealt with external fact, poetry with emotion; yet emotion itself could be seen as either fact or fancy. The emotions which most naturally and most frequently uttered themselves in my verses were those connected with love, a realm in which there was perhaps more ignorance and hypocrisy than in any other realm of existence.

This ignorance and hypocrisy was something of which my circle of radical friends was painfully aware from those early days when Dr. Landes haunted our nightmares. From Vienna, via the pages of the *Masses-Liberator,* had come the light and freedom which we enthusiastically attributed to psychoanalysis. But not so easily were the ancient molochs to be slain. A much more complicated pattern of reason and rationalization, made up of actual knowledge and hopeful belief, was required for those of us who, in addition to sharing the fashionable credos of art and psychology, needed also to relate these in some manner, however fantastic, to the class struggle and the socialist revolution. It was out of this need that we created for ourselves an explanation of our differences with current bourgeois standards.

For the conventional young man such explanations were superfluous. Bourgeois morality allowed men, if not women, an irresponsible form of sexual freedom which could be indulged in before, during and between marriages. A respectable youth could visit whore houses without worrying about that exploitation of woman by man which socialism attributed to the capitalist system. Nor did he frankly face the monetary basis of the average bourgeois marriage; nor did it strike him as incongruous to separate sex from love. Bourgeois tradition hallowed relationships which bourgeois morality formally condemned. Without a blush, you could look upon your sweetheart as a "mistress" and callously exploit her for surface pleasures.

For the radical intellectual this was impossible. He had to justify to himself his repudiation of bourgeois sexual standards and practices, as well as his own desire to convert "mistress" into comrade. It was out of this conflict with surrounding attitudes that we fashioned our views, combined out of fragmentary reading with thinking that was equally fragmentary. We assumed that in the twentieth century the laws of love as laid down by religion were illiterate, cruel and wholly out of date. But we also assumed that upon the falsehoods and pretenses foisted upon Western civilization by the ascetic prophets of Judeo-christianity, the bourgeoisie had erected a structure peculiar to itself.

Many of my contemporaries broke with their puritan heritage for one reason or another—the war, the decay of the family under the pressure of the capitalist metropolis, the disintegration of old values. They went in for the "pagan" life armed with various kinds of rationalization. My own circle could neither explain nor justify its conduct without taking socialism into consideration. Our most private acts could appear rational only as we related them to the most general laws of history—the ironic weakness of certain intellectuals. Starting our chain of reasoning with the French Revolution, we asserted that the bourgeois era had opened with the proclamation of the loftiest ideals. All men were declared to be free and equal by birth; in the eyes of the law, all were theoretically on a par. The feudal regime was overthrown with the battle cry *liberty, equality, fraternity*. This inspiring formula was—in theory—extended to woman.

The radiant prospect which Rousseau's *New Heloise* opened was the prospect of "free love." Above church, state, family, law, custom beat the imperious human heart whose desire was its own highest law. Love transcended class distinctions, the marriage contract, the taboos of religion. Love alone justified marriage, as it justified violation of the marriage vows. This was one aspect of the ideal society which the bourgeoisie painted in the dawn of its career when it needed the aid of other social classes in order to seize political power.

But this, we argued, was only a surface reflection of the bourgeois order, not its real essence. The bourgeoisie was incapable of giving life to the ideals it preached in its youth. There was an irreconcilable contradiction between the ideas of liberty, equality and fraternity and the economic basis of capitalism, its immanent law of commodity production, the all-absorbing goal of increasing profit. The bourgeois order could not emancipate mankind because the ideal of freedom and equality was not the real aim of the bourgeoisie, but only a means to an end. Once it was in the saddle, the bourgeois class, incapable of fulfilling its sublime preachments, was compelled to correct them in the interests of its pocketbook. To maintain its power, it was forced not only to abandon its ideals in fact, but to modify them in principle.

From the teachings of socialism we deduced that between its progressive period and its extinction, a ruling class maintains itself in power by force and fraud. As the disparity between its appearance and its reality becomes greater and greater, hypocrisy becomes its dominant characteristic. The more it oppresses the mass of people, the louder is its talk of democracy; the more frequent and sanguinary its wars, the more it talks of peace; the greater the poverty of its wage slaves, the more it prattles about universal prosperity; and the more corrupt its sex life, the more coyly it lisps about virtue. In love, hypocrisy reached such a degree of affected prudery that in Anglo-Saxon culture a term for fake puritanism is mid-Victorianism, from the name of the queen who symbolized the British bourgeoisie at the height of its power and the depths of its hypocrisy. Virtue, like religion, was meant for the enslaved masses, not for their lords. Strange tales were circulated about Victoria's son Edward, but no one considered his conduct "sinful." Sex was far too good only for the common people, as an old English joke truthfully put it.

But reality has a way of revenging itself upon appearance. The attempt of middle-class people to live up to the moral demands of bourgeois culture in its rotten ripeness led to an unprecedented spread of neuroses centering around sexual conflicts. When the spirit triumphed over the flesh, people became queer; when the flesh triumphed over the spirit, they suffered from pangs of conscience. In either case there was suffering and distortion of the personality. The novels of the late nineteenth and the early twentieth century are a record of these conflicts. Eventually wiseacres might look upon the hero of Somerset Maugham's *Of Human Bondage* as a sap; in his own day he was typical of an era in which people were brought up in utter ignorance of the physiology and psychology of sex. It was precisely the intelligent, honest and sensitive people—the Samuel Butlers, Somerset Maughams and D. H. Lawrences—those who took the ideals of bourgeois society seriously and could not reconcile them with the obdurate facts of love—who suffered from the conflict most acutely and sought a way out of it, by damning the bourgeois family, idealizing a slut, or raising sex to a religion.

The worst victims were those steeped in the literary traditions of the Western world. Ignorant of sex, they split their emotions along parallel remote planes. Sexual adventures were followed by remorse, the bitter tribute to the prevailing mores. From the arms of Venus the rebel crawled to the feet of Christ. Sex was romanticized beyond recognition; every episode was "love," endurable only after it was decorated with the trappings of romantic poetry—skies, seas, flowers, winds, perfumes. Often we did not even realize that it was sex we were writing about; we drew no conclusions from the glaring fact that we wrote love lyrics chiefly when we were not in love, or when we were unhappy in love, when we were lonely and full of desire, and seldom when we were in love and content.

While the Maughams and Dostoevskys sought refuge from the hypocritical mores of bourgeois society in the idealized prostitute, the general run of intellectuals, caught in the same dilemma, set up a more normal standard—the myth of the free woman. In love, as in politics, the first rebellions against dominant bourgeois concepts were anarchic and utopian. Against the capitalist misuse of the machine came the machine wreckers; against bourgeois morality came the amoralists. Against the oppression of the industrial towns came the utopian colonies; against the oppression of middle-class virtue came the bohemian quarters. In each case, dreamers attempted to evade the brutal present by collecting in advance on the ideal future.

Still, the ideal future was patterned on the fictitious past. People who called themselves socialists, anarchists and syndicalists set up sexual ideals dating from the *New Heloise*. The heart was its own law. General ignorance of sex psychology made it easy to err in sex physiology. No real distinction was made between the promptings of the heart and the stirrings of the genitals. Hence it was easy to fall for the utopian middle-class miasmas of H. G. Wells, the spokesman of the Anglo-Saxon petit bourgeoisie demanding the rights and privileges of the upper classes, especially the right to love freely. Ann Veronica was the free woman—until Wells and his disciples discovered jealousy.

Such was our theory, and it was important as a rational raft. Myself a product of radical petit-bourgeois culture, I shared this dream of the "free" woman—she who earned her own living, gave herself completely in love to us, made no demands upon us, granted us joy without responsibility. Among the art models and midinettes of Paris we found such "free" women. But we soon discovered that they were no more typical of France than they were of America. Hypocrisy was the middle-class badge in Paris as in New York; wherever the bourgeoisie ruled, love was the end of the equation which began with money.

§ 2

But if we lost this particular illusion about Europe, we retained others no less romantic. The group which came with me to Paris in 1920 did not feel either exiled or expatriated. At least we did not think in those terms. We were not forced from freedom into isolation; we fled from isolation to freedom. We were on a lark, traveling, drinking, loving, and—perhaps most important of all—learning to work steadily every day at the profession of journalism. We were relieved of the oppressive bonds of family love and discipline, of the puritan traditions of our permanent environment. True, we were outsiders in Europe, but that was just what we wanted to be, privileged aliens who were not responsible to the society in which we lived, Americans in Paris.

We had no intention of remaining in Europe. The immediate effect of France, England, Italy or Germany upon us was to make us self-consciously, even aggressively, American. For the first time I discovered what love of country was, as distinguished from chauvinism. I realized how attached I was to many things which at home I had pretended to despise—movies, jazz, the American language.

To see an American movie or hear an American jazz band in Paris made you homesick. You laid the slang on thick; you insisted on American shirts, hats and shoes. Patriotism was political hocus-pocus like democracy, God and the full dinner pail; love of country meant love of people, places, ways of living, thinking and feeling. Patriotism made you hate other countries and kill their citizens for the benefit of your own masters; love of country made you like other peoples and places. The longer you lived in Paris, the better you liked New York; the better you liked New York, the longer you wanted to stay in Paris. You were a visitor among people whose language, art and customs you enjoyed and who enjoyed your movies, jazz and slang. It was a curious paradox that noble all-embracing phrases like "democracy and civilization" should divide peoples, while differences in food, manners and art should unite them. But we could not help seeing that paradox. The more American we felt culturally, the more we felt at home in Europe, the more we enjoyed ourselves. It was not only romantic, it was actually agreeable to sit in cafés sipping cognac and talk-ing to strangers, to promenade along the wide Champs-Elysées or wan-der among the crooked streets of Montmartre, to glide in gondolas along the lagoons of Venice, to take cheese and ale in the public houses of London, to ponder before Leonardo da Vinci's statue in Milan.

But what probably made us feel most at home in Europe was the sense of internationalism which we had absorbed from socialist doc-trine. We felt ourselves part of a movement which knew no national boundaries. Capital and labor were alike international. The class struggle destroyed frontiers. When we read of or reported a strike, the French, British or Italian workers involved were not strangers of another land. They were ours Soviet Russia, Soviet Hungary, the red battalions of every country in Europe were ours. We did not refer to strikers or communists anywhere in the world as *they;* it was always *we*. Now *we* were having a coal strike in England; now *we* had taken over the factories of Turin, now *we* were fighting off the invasion of the Poles backed by the French, Floyd Gibbons to the contrary not-withstanding. That was our new patriotism as distinguished from our old love of country; it was loyalty to a political entity new in world history—the international working class. We found it possible to love the cafés, the Louvre, the Comédie-Française, Yvette Guilbert, the Folies-Bergères, the Luxembourg, Molière, Anatole France, Henri Barbusse, Romain Rolland, the Impressionist painters, Rodin—and at the same time dislike the French capitalists who oppressed "their" workers; just as it was possible at home to like jazz, baseball, Charlie Chaplin, Walt Whitman, the Brooklyn Bridge and to hate the class which shed the blood of American workers in Ludlow, Paterson, Lawrence, Youngstown.

Among the things which bound us to Europe was its traditional culture which we had absorbed at the university. One could hardly feel like an exile in a city with statues of Voltaire, Danton, Robes-pierre; with theaters playing Racine, Corneille and Molière; with streets named for Charles Fourier and Jean Jaurès; with cemeteries containing the bodies of Oscar Wilde and Heinrich Heine. This was our spiritual home—as was London with its monuments to Shake-speare and Byron, its grave of Karl Marx; or Venice with Titian's home intact. We felt that the poets, artists and social visionaries be-longed to us much more than to the native manufacturers, stock specu-lators and politicians whose chief concern in Europe, as in America, was an increasing rate of profit.

If, in spite of all these identifications with Europe, we were never-theless sometimes haunted by a sense of exile, loneliness and isolation, it was not because of the differences between Europe and America, but because of their similarities. Bourgeois culture was more or less the same everywhere, and we felt alien to that culture. French, Eng-lish, German, and American middle-class families differed in lan-guage, manners and mores; their basic concepts, their pattern of living, were at bottom the same. Everywhere, the bourgeois's chief standard of measuring men was money, his main interest in people was exploi-tation. The French bourgeois might read Racine while the American bourgeois read the *Saturday Evening Post;* what both loved to read most was the stock-market blackboard. When you went into the Crillon or the Ritz-Carlton, you might distinguish the American from the Frenchman, the German from the Englishman by the cut of the clothes, the curl of the mustache or beard, the tortoise-shell rims of the eyeglasses; yet essentially they dressed alike, dined in the same restaurants, talked about the same things—the stock market, race horses, women, as they did in the Waldorf-Astoria. Someone has sum-marized the Holy Trinity of the bourgeoisie as Treasure, Leisure and Pleasure.

When you went—on the other hand—into the XXth arrondisse-ment of Paris or the East End of London, it was in many respects like the slums at home. The workers had their shirts open at the throat; they were often unshaven; their shoes and pants might be patched; they ate cheap food and drank cheap beer; and when they did not talk about women they talked about jobs, unemployment, wages, the high price of everything, the straw boss, the trade union. Languages were different, but workers' meetings in the Père Lachaise district, Trafalgar Square, Turin, had much in common with those at home. Always, if the meetings were indoors, the lights were either too bright or too dim and the acoustics difficult. In winter the meeting hall was bitter cold, in summer it steamed like a Turkish bath. And always the workers sat tense, alert, leaning forward to catch every utterance of the speaker pouring out those words which you can hear in every land, in every tongue—proletariat, der Kapitalismus, exploitatsia, le combat des classes, justicia, revolution, die Revolution, la révolution.

The sense of exile, then, came from our hostility to bourgeois cul-ture in the broadest sense of that word. We no longer considered Vol-taire, Spinoza, Leonardo da Vinci, Beethoven bourgeois culture. The bourgeoisie as a class was no longer interested in philosophy, art or

music creatively, only possessively. What we as artists hated was bourgeois philistinism; as socialists, capitalist oppression. We were exiles
in Paris, London, Venice in the same way and for precisely the same
reason that we were exiles in New York. We were outside the organized bourgeoisie and not yet part of the organized working class.

"I suppose"—my sister, now married at twenty to a theatrical manager in New York, wrote me—"I suppose we might be called conventional bohemians."

That phrase was accurate. We were part of that world of declassed
people, coming from every stratum of contemporary society, who had
broken from the prevailing culture for the moment or forever. Some,
crushed by the break, sought nirvana in the anodynes of alcohol and
sex; others sought new ways of living in art, philosophy, socialism, or
all three.

§ 3

It was this search, rather than any external "adventures," which
dominated my two-year stay in Europe after the war. I was conscious
of that search long before going there. Six months prior to sailing for
Paris, I replied to Ben Ginzburg's invitations to join him that one
could escape many things but never one's self; our problems in Paris
would be much like our problems at home; the scene would be
changed, not the plot.

Nothing so emphasized this at first as the correspondence which
my friends and I carried on across the sea. But soon it was evident that
the plot was changing, thanks to time and circumstance. To begin with
that group to which I have all along been referring as "we" emerged
as separate clearly defined personalities, each with his own particular
approach to life. Just as the amoeba becomes through fissure a series
of distinct entities, so each of us was emerging from our vague social
protoplasm as a marked individual. On the campus, which we had
idealized as the golden realm of Eternity, we had pleasantly agreed
on all the misty contradictions which made up that realm. Now participation in the work of the world compelled us to make choices, to
debate, to reject, to accept, to defend. We cracked wise in conversation,
but seldom in letters. The joke of it all was that we took life seriously.
We even took ourselves and each other seriously, and to mature people
we must have appeared very funny indeed.

The old problems came up again and again in the letters which
passed between Europe and America, between Paris and Dresden, between Venice and Berlin; but they appeared on a different plane, and

so became somewhat different problems. The eternal disputes about art, life and society now took specific shape and color, not from the classical past or from the Renaissance, but from the immediate impact of the war and the October Revolution, from the compulsion to understand these turning points in human history, from the necessity of finding in relation to them our place in the world.

It was this need which made me attach such importance to Oscar's letters on the life of the pure poet, a life in which art was the whole of existence; to Bill Schack's defense of Time against my alarmed retreat to the imaginary solace of Eternity; to Horatio Winslow's defense of Freud as a cure for those neuroses without which art would be altogether unnecessary; to Irwin Edman's eloquent and unexpected paeans in praise of philosophic idealism; and finally to Louis Smith's voice, resolute and steady as always, recalling me to the meaning of the revolutionary proletariat in our age. At this time some of us still suffered from the infantile and snobbish illusion that our discussions were the unique quests of choice spirits. We little realized that after our own fashion we were embarking upon a search that was sooner or later to agitate our whole generation.

In the summer of 1920, the poet Oscar was working on a New England farm. At the *Tribune* desk in Paris I received a letter from him which said:

"I am working on a farm in Maine and I am all in, because of the HARD work. As I wrote Simeon Strunsky: 'I work like a horse, eat like a hog, sleep like a bear but do not sing like a bird.' This is the plain trite truth. Though the farmer has not quite killed the muse, yet in these federal days he has quite overtaxed the shy lady. And the few bits of verse I have written here have a starved and hungry look. Recently I have begun to doubt Harriet Monroe. She is accepting some of my mediocre poems and returning my very best. I believe that a real artist always confronts bravely any spiritual doubt. I am afraid that I am changing and very often not for the better. But perhaps this is due to the terrible strain of farm work on all my faculties. I am physically lonely and strange—not mentally; perhaps this is due to the fact that I write so very little here and that the 'singing delirium' rarely visits the primal and elementary life. Poetry, you know, is not a fulfillment; it is a haunting *desire,* a beautiful loneliness."

For Oscar, then, the problem of art and life did not exist. Everything was subordinate to his poetry. He wrote me that he hated to send me letters because these had to be written in prose, and what could be more horrible than prose? Imagine having to write *he sat down!* Since poetry was a "beautiful loneliness," the poet must stay away from society lest it mar that loneliness. For a lyric poet of that type politics, science, the social revolution presented no dilemmas; the only dilemma came from such daily routine as might fatigue the poet's body or disturb his soul.

With Bill Schack the case was different. I had known him for several years, but our real friendship began after he left Cornell and I Columbia. He had shared the faith in socialism. By profession a scientist, by taste a passionate lover of music, by inclination a speculator on the general forms of life, he was now at work on his first novel which he wrote in his off hours from a job on a technical journal. For him, as for me, the question of art versus life was an urgent one, since it disguised, in essence, the conflict of art versus the social revolution. My own ideas on this subject were now in complete confusion. I wrote to Bill in the fall of 1920, that values were both relative and absolute. When you were building a bridge, then stone, machines, shovels, pickaxes, dredges, and mathematical formulae were more desirable and more essential than harmony, counterpoint, violins, sonnets or ultramarine blue oil paint. But when you were seeking a mystical union with the universe, when you reached out for a synthesis of your senses and emotions, and tried to blend them with infinity and eternity, then the values were reversed. Apart from any direction and specific purpose, a cat was as good as a king, and a king as good as a philosopher. Why was an automobile or the law of psychoanalysis or a skyscraper emotionally more alive *in itself* than a medieval church, or a mass, or vespers, or a painting by Bellini, or a fresco by Titian? I recognized no limits of space and time. I reserved the right to become excited by the things which stirred Lorenzo the Magnificent, Attila the Hun or Jeremiah the Prophet. If any poem of mine about aged themes had no emotional value for Bill Schack, it was not because the *subject* was emotionally dead but because the *poem* was emotionally dead. Our age was beginning to look on art in a different way. Art had lost the religious significance of the Middle Ages, the moral significance of the Victorian period, the art-for-art's-sake twaddle of the decadence. We were now beginning to look at art with the eyes of psychology. We weighed it as an experience and in relation to other experiences. I did not look upon my verse as something sacred, God-ordained, inevitable, I was rather in search of intellectual and emotional synthesis, and adaptation to the world, and mighty magnificent experiences, and a number of vague indefinable things, things mystical in the real sense of the word. I realized that art was the medium through which I could find these things; at the same time poetry was for me the easiest art.

More of a realist than I, Bill gently rebuked my spineless surrender to the opiates of Eternity.

"You defy time and space; you are no longer human. That is wish-fulfillment with a vengeance. To whatever extent one can appreciate the temper of another day, to that extent one is the more enriched, but when there is so much in the world to choose from in so short a span of life, necessity literally enjoins catholicity. Besides, there are contraries. However skeptical one may be of the interpretations put on values by contemporaries, so that one may extract the more universal elements, there are nevertheless conflicts—conflicts where one side or the other must unfortunately be espoused."

These conflicts were becoming so acute that shortly after this letter from Bill came another reconsidering my semipsychological, semimystical notions about the functions of art.

"Since I last wrote you"—Bill's second letter said—"your theory of the motive for artistic creation has been borne out in my own experience much deeper than ever before. A series of small but baffling experiences made me feel like abandoning the muddy stream of experience for the lucid waters of the imagination. It struck me, too, how analogous emotional-artistic creation was to rational scientific creation, in that both seek simplification constantly. Out of an infinite number of factors determining every experiment, the scientist must vary but one or two at a time if he is to save himself. This is in part a rationalization, if we may use the term here, in that most of these factors are beyond his control anyway; which is to say, it is our great good fortune that they are of practically negligible influence in the experiment. In living it is different. Remote factors do exert an influence, factors which are even more remote than certain physical phenomena in their bearing on a particular experiment. For example, some star of the seventy-fifth magnitude certainly exerts a gravitational influence on terrestrial experiments, but it can with safety be disregarded. On the other hand, some remote personal influence cannot be disregarded with any degree of safety. The son of some banker in Wichita may run your best friend down in a machine, thereby causing all sorts of difficulties. Your sweetheart may be summoned to the funeral of a relative in whom you are not in the least interested just when you are planning a particularly pleasant day and sweet night. The subway breaks down; it rains; it doesn't rain; the mail is delayed—what not—to ruin experience or human experiment. The imagination remedies all this uncertainty, this confusion, this heartbreak. If the artist creates his own uncertainty, his own confusion, his own heartbreak, it is at least intelligibly begotten out of a number of causes over which he has control. In life the causes are hidden enough to be called chance or accident, and that is emotionally and rationally unsatisfactory. In art we can be omniscient gods on a small scale, and godliness is by all means an inducer of satisfaction if not of happiness."

This was the most poetic statement I had read anywhere of the theory of art as sublimation. But I heard that theory more directly and vehemently preached by a man whom I met by accident in a Paris restaurant. A stranger leaned across the table with a menu in his hand and asked in French is this fish? I recognized the Middle West in the accent and replied in English yes, this is fish. The man introduced himself as Horatio Winslow, former captain in the Michigan battalion which refused to fight the bolsheviks at Archangel and a former editor of the *Masses* who had brought Floyd Dell to New York from the Chicago *Daily News*. Winslow and I saw each other frequently, went to theaters and ballets together, and argued the usual subjects of the period—art, sex, social revolution. He was now lukewarm toward art and the social revolution and attributed the salutary change to the fact that he had been psychoanalyzed. He urged me to go to an analyst, to get rid of my conflicts by getting wise to my symbols.

"But it may kill my poetry," I said, feeling at that time that it was better to suffer in poetry than to be happy in prose.

"What of it?" Winslow said. "Would you refuse to be cured of opium smoking because it robbed you of your pipe dreams?"

It was evident, however, that neither Oscar, nor Bill, nor Horatio Winslow nor I was the one to talk about art. We were all people to whom art was something remote, like the government in Washington whose Capitol we could inspect externally, but whose workings we could only guess at. Oscar had to work on a farm, Bill in the chemical factory, Winslow at his French and his short stories for the *Saturday Evening Post,* I on the desk of the Chicago *Tribune*. Art was a luxury for spare time, like going to church on Sunday. That was why no painting in the Louvre could thrill us like Sinclair Lewis' *Main Street* just published, which spoke to us of our own problems. No, we had not the right to be considered true votaries of all that was best in

Europe's past. That privilege—and we recognized it in affectionate ad-miration—belonged to Irwin Edman, whom we considered fortunate because he had to make no compromises with Time, because he could remain in Eternity. There was no gap between his work and his leisure. He was an instructor of philosophy at Columbia, now on vaca-tion. Traveling among the ancient masterpieces of Europe, he was only continuing in the museums of Paris, Rome and Munich the studies which he would carry on as before in the library and classrooms of Columbia. Europe had altered Irwin's Weltanschauung as it had mine. We had exchanged roles, in a way. On the campus, he had been a disciple of John Dewey's instrumentalism, I a neo-mystic disguising his grandfather's religion in Bertrand Russell's phrases. Now daily news-paper work, contact with the world of Time, converted me to prag-matism; while the galleries of Florence and Munich tinged Irwin's thought with idealism, both changes indicating an obvious correlation between activity and thought.

"For me personally"—Irwin wrote me from Dresden in the fall of 1920—"the world these last few weeks has been almost romantically perfect. I have been moving, to quote your own phrase, through rich experiences, though not swiftly; not swiftly because the experiences have been too rich to hurry through. Munich kept me ten days crowded with superb music and color. I first really came to know Rembrandt there, though I have since learnt to know him still more completely at Berlin and here at Dresden. But I think Rembrandt for me will always mean the sheer glow of light and meaning and mystery which constitute the four pictures of the Christ story in the Alte Pinakothek at Munich. If I ever came near to losing my dogma of naturalism it happened in Chartres or at Munich. I heard Wagner, too, at Munich in the religious atmosphere of the Munich festival performance. And I came again to the conclusion that music is the clearest and most convincing of the arts, perhaps because it is so much less explicit than the others. Nuremberg was a lovely little sojourn in the twelfth cen-tury, and, as befits a modern, I got lost in its old streets of orioled windows and gabled towers. But Berlin has been the chief education here in Germany; not because it is a beautiful city, for it isn't by any means. It is a cross between Junkerdom and modern industrialism (or maybe they are the same). But the museum is incredibly rich in Dutch and German masters, and has one or two Correggios that I am not likely to see bettered in Italy. And I learnt a discouraging amount about the bitterness and hatred and *revanche* that is fomenting now in

Germany. It is a tragic irony to live here now in Germany when all that is beautiful comes from yesterday and all that is, is hunger and bitterness. For the American it is ridiculously easy to live, and live well; but for poor Germans, it must be ghastly."

Between news stories for the *Tribune,* I replied to Irwin: "It was my idealistic, religious, artistic bias which made me blind to pragmatism. As between the two, one must say—and lay himself open to the charge of compromise by dogmatic and lopsided people—that both are right. Pragmatism is true for the world of action, idealism for the world of imagination. The danger is that pragmatism is inclined to pooh-pooh the world of imagination, and idealists assume it is the world of fact. Sensible people, after having clearly established the two natures of these types of philosophy, can be counted on to synthesize the two worlds at least philosophically, even if circumstances prevent us from doing it actually. In fact, your greatest contribution to philosophy might well be such as to bring out your pragmatic heritage and idealistic acquisition: a blending of Dewey and Kant, not at all an eclecticism: something new will emerge after passing through your mind. That is what you may contribute to Western philosophy—if . . . if . . . Yes, that's the trouble. One is continually being terrified these days by people who tell us Western civilization is dying. Here Anatole France comes out with a mournful prediction of Europe's imminent death: that from an artist. Philip Gibbs responds with the antistrophe: Europe is dying, dying, dying, but America is the hope of the world: that from a journalist. Now of course it is up to a philosopher to systematize those mournful mortuary monologues, and who should do it but a German? You have probably heard of, even perhaps read, the author of *Untergang des Abendweltes,* Spengler, who is becoming a German cult. Herr Spengler flips away the idea of the whole human race moving as an entity to an eventual civilization; but insists that each civilization is an entity in itself, has its rise, its climax, its renaissance, its decay, its death. And the Occident is in its period of decay now, doomed to perish as other, perhaps greater, civilizations have perished before it. The next great civilization is coming from the EAST (not America, which, I presume, will perish along with Europe) and its initial embodiment will be Russia. This is quite astounding in view of the fact that it was written before the war, before Bolshevism made Russia even the potential advance guard of a new civilization. . . . The gloomy gestures of Anatole France, Philip Gibbs and Herr Spengler are being justified by such news as I sent you last time, and the announcement today by Lloyd George that Britain would go on experimenting with poison gases for the use of warfare until told otherwise by the League of Nations—not a likely prohibition—and his reference to 'another country which is doing the same'—the old U. S. A. as everyone knows. I watch these things with a curious detachment; I see now what you meant by 'heartless aestheticism.' This unconcern is superficial, as you know. In general I am beginning to feel that any philosopher who makes generalizations about 'the universe,' whatever generalization he may make, at once damns himself by talking through the dark quadrangle of his graduate hat. What in hell do we know about 'the universe,' or if there is any 'universe' at all? We know there are an infinite number of stars and planets, many of them so large that on a proportional astronomic diagram which I recently saw our earth looked like a pinhead. Some of these planets may be inhabited; and we haven't the slightest idea of what life on them is like. As for existence outside the solar system—itself a tiny corner of the illimitable agglomorates in space—that is almost a total mystery to us, however wise we may pretend to be. So how, in the name of Philosophy 62, can we go on making generalizations about this 'universe'? . . . Image for philosophic, poetic, musical, artistic and literary representations of the world: imagine a tremendous tower afloat in space, like the *Imperator* or the *Aquitania* afloat on unending waters. People are looking out of the windows studying the scene. It is generally the same, but the details change; as for instance, in riding from Venice to Turin you have mountains and lakes as the main theme, but there are innumerable variations; a new break in the height here, a sudden flash of blue water, fields elongating themselves, and so on. The scene shifts; the colors change; the day rushes along casting a slightly different light on the kaleidoscope; and the people in the floating tower try to make rules about this scene, to say that it is definitely so and so. Not only is it difficult to make a static law for a changing scene: the witnesses do not even see the same thing at the same time. They are all looking out of different windows, at different heights, observing the scene from different angles; and if we imagine the windows from which they are looking as being colored—some blue, some red, some green, some rose, some gray, and some like the stained-glass windows of an Italian cathedral; and if we imagine also that some of the observers, if not all, wear colored glasses like the inhabitants of Oz, only in addition to green there are all the other colors—is it any wonder that we have conflicting schools of philosophy, painting, politics, music, poetry? Is

it any wonder that we have fierce conflicts of testimony between Leib-
nitz and Spinoza, Schopenhauer and Nietzsche, Stirner and Marx,
Robert Bridges and Ezra Pound, the disciples of David and the apes
of Monet, the echoes of Mendelssohn and the mimics of Ravel?"

I was under the illusion that I had actually discovered a wholly
new idea. To this long disquisition, Irwin replied from Venice three
days later:

"Idealism is not the fruit of evolution or the industrial revolution.
It is the fruit of thinking that seems to me to have its roots almost entirely in the realm of the imagination, the same imagination that produced the woodcarving in Bavaria, the Holy Family as conceived by
Bellini or Titian, or the voluptuous other-worldliness of the Roman
Catholic Church. It is because it is the fruit of imagination that it is
astray in the realm of fact; and it is because it is the fruit of the
imagination that it is spiritually—as we both use the term—so opposite.
I am coming more and more to the conclusion that it is a cardinal
error to quarrel with the metaphysics of idealism. That is the controversy of the literal-minded, and is the business of those for whom
philosophy is a business. But understood in terms of the longings and
visions of which it is the austere metaphysical expression, idealism,
the great idealistic systems in the history of philosophy, seem to me
increasingly to be worthy of the most careful study. You seem to have
awakened as from the well-known dogmatic slumber to the meaning
of the imaginative aspiration in those unfortunately jargon-encrusted
idealisms which in my young days—Ecco!—you used to hear me condemn. . . . I am simply beginning to make explicit in my philosophical thinking thoughts that were foreign to neither of us in the summer
of nineteen-nineteen. I am, of course, much distressed by the alarming
array of evidence you suggest in regard to the new imperialistic boom.
Poor Europe! The beauty which here moves me so much is chiefly the
beauty of past achievement. Certainly the present on this side of the
Atlantic—or on the other—is a poor spectacle. And as I move and talk
with the common man, be it in Munich or Vienna, or, as far as language permits in Venice, and feel the lovely uniqueness and specific
values of each national life, I think it is pitiful what the lords and
masters of this earth are doing with it."

By January, 1921, Irwin had seen most of classic Italy. From Rome
he wrote me a long letter, full of charm and insight, describing the
effects of it all upon him.

"I feel at Venice"—he said—"as if I am reading Plato and at Flor-

ence almost as if I were reading Aristotle; for where Titian and Tinto-
retto have the glow and the life, Raphael and del Sarto have the
mastery of their craft. I have seen enough churches in Italy to know
that religion is not in them, though a harmony that is reasonable, and
a simplicity that is civilized are. I have seen enough Greek sculpture
here in Rome to feel I have found Platonic perfection on earth, and to
realize how great art can be without saying anything, unless serenity
and perfect repose are themselves the expression of an ideal. And yet
again one feels in Fra Bartolommeo or Fra Angelico that their loveliness would be thin and poor stuff if it were not bathed in such rapture
of simple belief. And I have felt after Leonardo and Michelangelo that
next to power all else in art is second rate and trifling, and that there
is no success in art save in flooding life with such strength and energy
as in the works of these. But I have given up making estimates and
appraisals. I have become an empiricist here as in the professional cave
from which I have, for the moment, emerged. . . . I wish you had
been with me yesterday in the Sistine Chapel; I think you would have
agreed with me that there never was such a furious and terrible burst
of creative power in the history of all the arts."

I brooded over Michelangelo's furious and terrible burst of creative
power and my "heartless aestheticism" reached its apex. Late at night,
I typed in the *Tribune* office:

> I have lost the key
> To good and evil;
> God and the devil
> Are one to me.
>
> I move apart
> From the coils of duty;
> Only beauty
> Can stir my heart:
>
> Skies and seas,
> A wind that passes,
> Along the grasses,
> Fragrant trees,
>
> The flight of birds,
> Imperial places,
> Music, faces,
> Perfect words . . .

§ 4

The poem appeared in *Pearson's Magazine,* then edited by Frank Harris. My radical friends in New York were alarmed. Louis Smith, now active in New York in the newly formed Communist party, wrote me disturbed and disturbing letters. It was not easy for him to write.

"I justify"—he explained—"my neglect of family, friends, and myself on the theory that my time and efforts belong to the cause of human emancipation, i.e., Communism. Every time when evening comes I either have some union activity or Party meeting, or else I am so fagged out that as soon as I come from work I have to lie down in bed."

But he had to write me this time because one of my letters to him had indicated a general cynicism about people.

"The true test of idealism"—Louis now cautioned me—"is how much ugliness one can look upon and survive. I, too, am sometimes pained by people who are stupid, or dishonest, or who have vulgar ambitions, or by people who do nothing which is not to their advantage; but I do not have a perpetual grudge. My bitterness is not against the individual, but against the scheme of things. You say you 'cannot be bothered with people whose chief concern in life is to create a good impression, or make money, or attain a cheap fame, or wield power.' For that I am glad. You recognize that we are living in a civilization whose standards of virtue are those of pirates, money-lenders, and shopkeepers; and that because of this civilization most people acquire corrupt habits of thought and living. Recognizing this you will admit that it is a rare gift that is given to one by the gods to be able to break loose the bonds of servitude to things as they are, and a still greater gift is given to one who can perceive, and one who can show the people the way out of this ugliness. But, Joe dear, to do the things we want done we must stay in contact with life. If we wish to be the torch that bears the light, we must stay in the dark—that is, among stupid people, both proletarian and middle-class."

Louis was himself acquainted with the "stupidity of mankind," but responded to it with renewed revolutionary fervor. He thought he knew the cause and cure of that "stupidity." The loss of a strike in which he had just participated led him to some important conclusions.

"I have learned"—he wrote me—"that for one who has a higher ideal in the labor movement than a temporary increase in wages or to maintain a union to co-operate with the bosses, other methods are necessary. I cannot remain an organization, man any more, in the sense that I must not give up all my time to negotiate wage contracts. It is futile. Yesterday we win, today we lose. Yesterday we organize workers; they stay organized as long as the union can get wages for them. When the union is unable to get that, they become disorganized. Our success in the past strike was very little, as the trade situation in the United States is very bad, and in the mills where the strike was most prolonged we not only lost our demands, but we lost the workers as well. They were too much cowed even to continue their membership in the union, and all because there is no idea injected into them, no understanding as to their mission, and when they get a little setback, why, they just collapse. Therefore I must fight existing practices in the unions and become a propagandist. We must organize for the revolution, or we work in vain."

Louis was a factory worker, a trade-union leader, a socialist from boyhood; it was natural for him to feel that "we work for the revolution or we work in vain." What struck me most in the letters I received from New York, however, was the spread of revolutionary ideas among young intellectuals. William Mallisoff, considered the most brilliant chemist on the campus, had repudiated the scientific career which everyone expected him to follow and was now active in the revolutionary movement. Mac Windsor, with whom I had grown up, was similarly engaged. Mac was the son of a poor tailor, a member of one of the needle-trades unions. He had, however, finished the university with high honors and was offered a post as instructor in history. He declined this; instead he went to work for the Amalgamated Clothing Workers, and was now associated with J. B. S. Hardman, editor of the union's official organ, the *Advance*. Mac was married to a girl of a well-to-do family with a house of its own in Flatbush; he drew his wife and her two sisters into labor activities and was now propagandizing me across the Atlantic by mail.

"We here"—he wrote me when I was in Italy in the fall of 1920—"are still proletarian. We are dying to know just a little more about the Red Italians and their factories, even if you have to begin learning Italian in order to be able to spread the news. I have not yet given up hope of seeing you throw your poetry overboard and raising your own red flag."

"The thing that stands out in your letters," I replied, "is Revolution. Don't think that because I have been sending you frail verses and shrill encomiums of Paris that I have been asleep in regard to the

brutal march of events. . . . We both seem anxious to serve the revolutionary movement, and if we happen to serve in different capacities,
let's not quarrel about that. Just now I am anxious to get to Russia."

I wanted to "serve the revolutionary movement"—but was there
no place in that movement for art? Did one have to throw poetry
"overboard" in order to be a communist? The problem was beginning
to engross a number of young people in or near the revolutionary
movement. Mac's sister-in-law Lillian, a young pianist now "serving
the cause" as Scott Nearing's secretary in the Rand School, wrote to
me in Paris in December, 1920:

"For weeks one is filled with a tremendous revolutionary fervor;
life is good and the struggle sweet. One's personal dreams hardly exist
as such. However, one gets bad and frequent slumps; and then one's
personal destiny becomes a matter of deep concern. In between these
acute fits of temperamental extremes, I am a good socialist, an excellent stenographer and a pretty bad musician. Mac has become a Red
to the core; the social revolution has become a matter of personal responsibility with him. We are all dreaming of the day when we can
actively dedicate ourselves to work in the movement. . . . And now
your poems in the *Liberator*. I think aesthetically they are flawless; and
yet I sometimes can't help wishing that your writing had less exquisite
finesses, more hardiness; but I guess it's my almost dogmatic prole-
tarianism that gives me such an appetite for sweaty, grimy realities."

Lillian, too, out of her own conflict between socialism and music,
had raised the problem of art and revolution; but unlike Mac she did
not urge me to throw my poetry "overboard"; all she asked for was
tougher, stronger poetry—a poetry nearer to the "sweaty, grimy realities" of proletarian life. I ignored this extremely important point in
my reply to her; my first duty, I felt, was to write, however crudely, a
defense of poesy. I said:

"A curious flaw in the attitude of many socialists—why do they
confuse communism with puritanism? Why, for instance, do you hesitate between music and throwing yourself into the movement? Can't
you conceive of serving the cause through music? Don't you think the
man or woman who plays a fine concert in the Rand School helps the
working class every bit as much as the stenographer who makes a
digest of Senator Pettigrew's speeches? It seems that most revolutionists have the curious idea that equality is to be achieved by lower-
ing the cultured classes to the standards of the uncultured masses, in-

stead of raising the masses to the finesse of the classes. This is a revolution inspired by Karl Marx not by Oliver Cromwell."

Such abstract discussions were unsatisfactory. Why try to spin out of thin air theories about art and revolution when the relationship could be studied empirically? Soviet Russia was two days' journey from Paris; it represented the future as Italy represented the past.

I wrote to Professor James Harvey Robinson at the New School for Social Research urging the formation of a committee of American scholars to study Soviet conditions, and applying for a scholarship on that committee.

"For better or for worse"—I wrote—"the Russian Revolution is the most significant event since the French Revolution, if not since the rise of Christianity. Unfortunately, most of the people who have so far given us reports about Russia have been prejudiced partisans, one way or the other; journalists who have exploited the more sensational and less significant sides of the revolution and the leaders of the revolution; emotional metaphysicians who were upset by rough contact with reality; or literary men more impressed by the drama of personalities than by those prosaic and mechanical aspects of life by which the revolution must stand or fall. Here, it seems to me, is an opportunity for the New School to make social researches in a laboratory more vast and more vital than the document room of the Forty-second Street Library. The chief defect of existing reports is that they deal almost entirely with Soviet politics and almost not at all with Soviet administration. Reading them one begins to wonder whether there are any people in Russia outside of Lenin, Trotsky, Zinoviev, Gorky and about twenty other leaders, and whether the Russians do anything outside of waging war, delivering addresses, calling congresses, posing for statues, and giving interviews to professors of higher mathematics and popular novelists."

I suggested that the New School Committee to Russia—which was to include me, in heaven knows what capacity—should concentrate on Soviet problems which at this time received practically no attention in middle-class circles. Subsequently the project which I outlined appeared to me painfully commonplace, so widespread did interest in Soviet affairs become in America; but in 1920 it was difficult to find any serious studies outside the revolutionary press of such fundamental matters as the actual administration of Soviet industry, the actual operation of Soviet politics, the actual changes which had taken place in Russian education, and the revolution in Russian arts and letters, thanks to the October Revolution. I outlined such a study in some detail and added with an anxiety that must have struck Professor Robinson as comic:

"Here is the very fabric of a gigantic experiment and we know practically nothing about it. Yet it is on this basis that the revolution must be judged, and it is on a scientific report of the facts that it must serve as an inspiration or a warning. I cannot refrain from urging again that American scholarship has a miracle of an opportunity for serving the world by working out a detailed and comprehensive report on the actual operations of the Soviet state, bearing always in mind that we are studying a transitory state functioning under adverse conditions, and supplementing a description of these conditions with an analysis of communist plans for remolding them to suit an ultimate ideal."

I had no idea what might have happened had the New School actually sent a "scholars' expedition" to Soviet Russia at that time. The country was still in a state of civil war, its economic life was disorganized, and the outlines of the Soviet system were not as clear then as they became later. Besides, at that time most Americans believed that if you went to Moscow you would either starve to death in the eternal famine which was supposed to follow bolshevism, or you would be executed by the Cheka, which was out to kill all bourgeois people; or, if you were a woman, you would be "nationalized." The prevailing hostility in America against all things Soviet, accompanied by a refusal to hear the facts, lasted for almost another decade. It was not until 1927 that a group of American scholars—including Stuart Chase, Rexford Guy Tugwell and Robert Dunn—accompanied the first American trade-union delegation to Soviet Russia and published a general survey of the Soviet state; it was not until 1930 that Louis Lozowick, Joshua Kunitz and I were able to publish the first American study of Soviet arts and letters, and not until 1932 that I was able to get out the first American analysis of Soviet labor conditions.

For the time being the plans outlined in my letter to Professor Robinson had to remain in the realm of fantasy; I was not going to Russia; I was going, instead, to England.

§ 5

Toward the end of January, 1921, I crossed the English Channel for the second time in my life. The first time, as a boy of seven, I was filled with dreams about the Golden Realm of America. This time I was going with two pictures of England in my mind. One England was an empire which oppressed its workers at home and its colonials abroad; the other was the England of the poets I most loved, those whose ideas molded my imagination and whose forms and phrases I imitated in my own verse. I was now steeped in American literary traditions which flowed directly from England. In German, French and Italian literature I knew only the giants; in English literature I could recite verses by the most obscure poetaster from Shakespeare's day to our own. I could now read French and German with a certain amount of fluency, but my language was English; and, because I knew it best, it seemed to me the richest, the most precise, the most sublime language in the world—better than all others for the rhetoric of the platform or the lyrics of the heart. In Paris I used to amuse myself reading French and German translations of Shakespeare to see how crude the best of them were compared with the original. Earlier still, at the university, my friends among the students and the faculty alike idealized English university life—an idealization which found a poetic voice in Santayana's wartime essays. And when I read and reread Rupert Brooke's lines

> If I should die, think only this of me:
> That there's some corner of a foreign field
> That is for ever England . . .

my throat contracted as if I had been banished for life from my beloved London which I knew only from books. To these literary illusions were added certain political illusions fostered by American liberals. When these protested against the government's "violations" of the free speech laws, they always pointed to Hyde Park as the world's center of free speech. England knew how to prevent "overt acts" by allowing the malcontents to blow off steam from the soapbox. England alone, we were brought up to believe, knew the real meaning of "tolerance." Going to England was, in a sense, going home.

The day I crossed the Channel was icy cold, the waters violent. All the passengers aboard became seasick. I went without food and fell into a coma for several hours. At night, when we landed on England's shores, a sailor shook me and brought me to with a glass of Scotch. On shore all the passengers were lined up before the immigration inspectors who rapidly examined their passports and sent them on to the train waiting outside the station. When my turn came, the inspector looked at my passport and said:

"Will you be good enough to wait in the other room?"

He did not return my passport. All the other passengers went on to London at once. I sat alone in a small, sparsely furnished office and listened to the locomotive whistling its way into the distance. Two men in civilian clothes came in, accompanied by a policeman in uniform, a high helmet with a strap under his chin, a wide cape falling in heavy folds down his broad shoulders, and white gloves. One of the civilians sat down at a flat desk and motioned me to a chair beside him. He was extremely neat; the dark brown suit was carefully pressed; the pale red hair parted on the side with great precision, and the white thin face as clean as a new napkin. He began to cross-examine me in an Oxford accent:

"You are employed by the Chicago *Tribune?*"

"Yes."

"Why do you come to London?"

"To work in the Chicago *Tribune* bureau there."

"Are you being sent to Ireland?"

"No."

"Is that a promise that you will not go to Ireland?"

"I do not make the paper's assignments, I can promise nothing. As far as I know, there is no intention of sending me to Ireland."

"Do you know Benjamin Ginzburg?"

I understood the meaning of that question. On his way from Riga, where he had interviewed the Soviet representative Joffe, to Paris, where he reported to Floyd Gibbons, Benjamin had stopped off in England. The immigration authorities searched him thoroughly. They ignored his protests. When the search was nearly over, Benjamin plunged his hand into his breast-pocket, pulled out a letter and quickly tore it into bits.

"What have you got there?" an inspector asked.

"A love letter."

"A love letter—from the Bolos, eh?"

Officials leaped at the scraps of paper, picked them up from the floor one by one. It took them nearly an hour to paste the letter together. The mysterious bolshevik document was a chatty note from a girl who had been at the School of Journalism with us and was now on the staff of the *Smart Set*. There was neither politics nor love in it; Benjamin had repaid the British officials for their search.

"Do you know Benjamin Ginzburg?" my examiner repeated slowly.

"Yes, he works with me on the Chicago *Tribune*."

"Where is he now?"

"I don't know."

"Are you a bolshevik?"

"I do not belong to any political organization."

The redheaded man stood up.

"I am very sorry," he said, "but we shall have to search you."

The policeman took me into the toilet and asked me to strip. He went through all my pockets, shook my pants upside down, rustled the lining of my jacket and overcoat, and turned my hat inside out. He found some papers in the breast-pocket of my jacket. These he put in his helmet and told me to dress. In the office the redheaded man examined my papers. He read my army discharge and said, as if to himself, "Hm, that's good." Then he read some personal letters, held them up to the light and turned them over. On the back of one of them was a sonnet scrawled in pencil.

"So you write verse?" the man said in a friendly tone, as one says, so you are a cousin of my Aunt Matilda's. "Are you a university man?"

"Yes."

"Ah, then you must know those magnificent lines from Catullus:

> Vivamus, mea Lesbia, atque amemus
> rumoresque senum severiorum."

The British pronounce Latin in the European manner, but I recognized the lines, and responded:

> "Omnes unius aestimemus assis.
> Soles occidere et redire possunt."

The redheaded man smiled. The lines from Catullus were like the password at the Elks' lodge. I had passed the examination; I was a gentleman. The redheaded man stood up.

"I am terribly sorry about all this," he said. "You understand it is a necessary formality. Your passport says you were born in Russia and one can't be too careful these days. Besides, the Chicago *Tribune* has not exactly been our best friend."

He called the policeman over.

"When does the next train leave for London?"

"Midnight, sir."

"That gives us twenty minutes. Will you be good enough to take this gentleman to the hotel across the street and see that he gets some tea and toast?"

"The hotel is closed for the night, sir."

"Wake them up!"

I followed the bobby down the dark street. He pounded on the hotel door, roused the owner and ordered tea and toast. Both were cold, but they tasted good; I had not eaten since seven o'clock that morning in Paris. The train pulled into the station. The policeman took my bags, found an empty compartment for me, said good night and closed the door. I promptly fell asleep. When I awoke about an hour later there was another man in the compartment. He sat directly opposite me, tall, hawkfaced, with a long gray ulster and a gray fedora pulled over his eyes, the perfect image of Sherlock Holmes. Scotland Yard is trailing me, I thought.

"I see you are an American," the man said. My suspicions increased. According to tradition, Englishmen did not speak to strangers on a train. I said nothing.

"I can see by your shoes that you are an American," the man continued cheerfully.

"I am an American," I said.

"And what do they think about the League of Nations in America?"

"Harding was elected on an anti-League platform," I said noncommittally. But Sherlock Holmes would not let me get away. He praised the League, Woodrow Wilson, Lenin, the new Russia. Obviously a provocateur.

"I don't know very much about these things," I said. "I am not interested in politics."

"What a pity," said Sherlock Holmes. "And we have such faith in the youth. You *ought* to be interested in politics. It is the only way we can put this broken world together. When you are in London, come to the Nineteen-seventeen Club and ask for me."

I had heard of the Nineteen-seventeen Club; it was an organization of liberals and radical intellectuals disillusioned by the war. Our train pulled into a suburban station.

"I am getting off here," Sherlock Holmes said.

He handed me a visiting card which I slipped into my pocket without reading.

"Be sure to see me in London."

I nodded. Holmes got off the train and waved good-by. When the train started again, I took out his card and read it. Sherlock Holmes was J. F. Horrabin, illustrator of H. G. Wells' *Outline of History* and a well-known left laborite.

§ 6

My feelings about London began with an intense hatred, doubtless because in this "my spiritual home" I felt lonely and alien. To the pianist Anton Rovinsky in Paris I complained that my job left me no time for meeting people. I started to work at about four in the afternoon, and quit about midnight. That meant that both afternoon and evening were killed. I'd simply have to wait for luck to bring me in contact with people I should have liked to meet. I was to get one night off—otherwise no theaters, no concerts, no dinners with friends, and no friends. If I could only get under way enough to do some writing in the morning, my stay in London would not be a complete waste of time. But I was drawing consolation from the fact that I was showing some practical ability at the office; I had in fact fallen so low as to be glad when Floyd Gibbons complimented me on the way I handled a big story to Chicago.

Actually, what galled me about London was not the city but my isolation from it. Paris meant bohemia; London meant the sober world of the middle classes. In general, Latin life seemed warmer, friendlier and economically cheaper than English life. Perhaps it was only that to the romantic the past was always more glamorous than the present. I complained in letters to friends that in Paris you could drop into a café on Montparnasse and your neighbors would gladly talk to you; in London you needed a formal introduction. There were no open-air cafés, only restaurants where your fellow diners looked so frigid and forbidding that you did not dare address them. London, I wrote to a friend in America, was less artistic but more powerful than Paris. In many respects it was like New York, not as vivid or dynamic, but certainly as Anglo-Saxon. Language, morals, and standards of life were much the same. Here I had to meet demands which Paris never made. I had to be more restrained.

Eventually, as I became accustomed to the city and made friends in it, I began to like London. Out of this change in attitude I tried to formulate an aesthetic theory in which art appeared primarily as a consolation for the otherwise intolerable miseries of life. As I developed this theory in long sentimental letters to Irwin Edman, I realized that here was the prose equivalent of that mood which in

Paris had impelled me, in verse, to lose the key to good and evil. It was the last frontier of hedonism, the dying gasp of a faith in art based on the pleasure motif of Eternity. Various factors were already beginning to destroy that illusion. My work on the Chicago *Tribune* brought me in contact with realities which, like hurricanes, whipped away the cobwebs of aesthetics. Instead of rewriting them on the desk, I was now covering stories directly. Events of the day were remote from the galleries of Florence and the dungeons of Venice and the "theories" they inspired; Time was stronger than Eternity, which was only antiquated Time.

I reported a British-American luncheon at which the principal speakers were Winston Churchill and Nicholas Murray Butler; present was the Prince of Wales who looked with feeble boredom into his empty water glass. In their formal speeches Churchill and Butler expressed vague sentiments of international goodwill. From an exclusive interview which I had with Dr. Butler in the cloakroom it was evident that despite America's policy of "no entangling alliances" the Harding administration proposed to assume a dominant role in European affairs backed by its strength as the world's leading creditor. Press interviews with the ruddy-faced, white-haired, adroit Lloyd George at Downing Street impressed me with the fact that neither "truth" nor "beauty" nor "goodness" played an important role in the world's affairs. Mass meetings of unemployed workers in Trafalgar Square reminded me that the class struggle was everywhere. At home I might lie awake till dawn scribbling sonnets about "beauty"; but here my daily work consisted of sending dispatches utterly different in theme, attitude, and style:

"England's unemployed are 'on the tramp' today. All over the country they are marching by the thousands to the offices of the board of guardians, demanding an 'adequate scale of relief.' More than 4,000 unemployed crossed the mountains of Wales to Tredegar, where they demanded that the board of guardians support their wives and families. The procession was a mile long, the men marching four abreast. Along the route of march housewives rushed to the procession distributing food."

The satisfaction of cabling these facts was canceled by the dissatisfaction of not being able to add other facts to clear up the economic picture of England in the postwar depression. That would have been "propaganda," and the Chicago *Tribune* did not want that. One could discuss these ignored facts only with radicals. I went down to the office of the *Communist* and introduced myself to the editors—a tall good-looking young man with rosy cheeks and the long legs of the aristocrat named Francis Meynell, and a short stocky man with glasses and a bulldog pipe named Raymond Postgate. The Triple Alliance coal and transportation strike was then dying down in defeat, and comrades Meynell and Postgate tried to make me understand the reasons. I reported to Louis Smith in New York:

"The *Communist* here has accused Thomas, Williams, and Bevin of selling out the workingmen in the coal strike; and Thomas has taken out an injunction against the paper which orders them to stop their attacks on him until the trial for damages which will take place some time in December. Francis Meynell, poet, editor and communist, tells me the Party has expelled Bob Williams. The Communist Executive Committee wrote Williams a letter asking him to explain his actions such as voting to call off the strike; failing to transmit to the Triple Alliance executive his own union's plan for food distribution in case of a Triple Alliance strike; voting to call off the week-end meetings of the locals where he knew the leaders would get hell. Williams did not reply to the communist letter and so he was expelled. However, the miners are carrying on and the rank and file of the other unions in the Triple Alliance are with them."

In the end this "near-revolution in England" fizzled out and I wrote back to friends in New York:

"I need not tell you that it seemed no little thing while it lasted; but the 'safe,' 'moderate,' 'responsible' leaders—as usual a bunch of treacherous bastards—not only prevented a general strike but set back the labor movement in England at least ten years by busting up the Triple Alliance. It's an old story—but they can't stop the revolution."

Such contacts with the British labor movement, remote as they were, revived all the feelings I had developed since boyhood about the social revolution.

By themselves, these feelings had no direct influence on my attitude toward art. Neither the labor movement nor the communist parties of England and America concerned themselves with such questions at that time. What changed my views were experiences in the world of art as such. I had begun to associate with English men of letters, but for several months my constant companion was the American poet Knox whom I had known in Professor Erskine's class in "creative writing" on the campus. Knox's style was eighteenth century English; his themes came from his two chief preoccupations—

women and the Jewish question. He had published a book of verse, run a bookshop in New York and edited a poetry magazine. This gave him something of a literary reputation. Now he was in London as a roving literary reporter for a New York newspaper which had commissioned him to interview leading British authors.

On the streets of London he was a tall, bizarre and impressive figure with his cloth cap, thick eyeglasses, J. M. Barrie mustache, fur-collared coat and heavy Malacca cane. He talked torrentially in the booming voice of a Yiddish actor of the Tomashevsky school, and his accent was a strange mixture of Oxford and Second Avenue.

I was impressed because he knew many of my literary heroes personally and despised them. His literary criticism was often curt and to the point. "Dreiser," he would say, "a *potz!* Sherwood Anderson, a *shmok*. So-and-so—why, I threw him out of my bookstore more than once."

In politics, Knox was equally cocksure but not as well informed as in literature. He knew no history or economics and spun political theories out of his lyric unconscious. This did not prevent him from having political ambitions.

"The Jews," he often explained to me, "are by nature a monarchical people, as a shrewd reading of the Bible will convince you. The Jews need a king. When they get Palestine, they will set up a king. But the Jews also adore men of letters. All our great leaders have been men of letters—Moses, David, Solomon, Herzl, Zangwill. The Jews will set up a king who is a writer, and that writer will be myself. I shall write and publish books for ten years and then my time will come."

For a time I thought Knox was suffering from delusions of grandeur, albeit in daily life he was a practical businessman of sorts. But after a while I began to wonder whether I was not underestimating a great man, for no less a Jewish leader than Israel Zangwill wrote:

"Despite his madness, Knox would make a better leader of the Jews than those who lead them now."

But perhaps Mr. Zangwill was only ironical about his rivals for Jewish leadership.

When I first met Knox by accident on the Strand, he had quite a bit of money from his newspaper. He had a room on the top floor of the Savoy overlooking the Thames for which he paid ten dollars a day. The general extravagance of his intensely lyric nature expressed itself in pitching pennies into the Thames or buying wrist watches for the chambermaids.

After his first interviews with British authors were published—dialogues between himself and them in which he always appeared the brilliant man of letters and they mere simpletons—he found it difficult to get further interviews. In reply to Knox's request for an interview, Bernard Shaw sent him one of his famous postcards on which he wrote:

"My dear Knox: I also am a professional journalist; I shall be glad to let the New York —— have my views on any subject at my usual rates."

Knox replied with a letter beginning something like this:

"My dear Shaw: If you had any idea that I wanted to interview you in order to find out *your* opinion on any subject, you are grossly mistaken. I wanted to give you an opportunity of hearing mine. You have failed to avail yourself of it; nevertheless I shall not deprive you of my wisdom."

There followed twenty closely typewritten pages setting forth Knox's ideas about Shaw, England, the Jews and the universe in general. This correspondence ended Knox's career as a newspaperman. He was broke, and moved from the Savoy to Chelsea. Through him I met a number of English writers, including charming and friendly people like Thomas Moult and John Rodker. In Chelsea, where I visited Knox frequently, I lost some of my romantic notions about the literary life. The secret of literary success sometimes lies in pretending that the ideas of other people are your own. After a conversation which would last till dawn, an author would sometimes say to me:

"Do you mind if I use that idea of yours in my next essay?" "Of course not," I would say, "go ahead." I wondered why any writer should want to borrow another's ideas.

Soon I came to realize that there were economic and social reasons for plagiarism. With the exception of people who have "independent" incomes, men like Proust or Tolstoy, or people who devote themselves selflessly to the revolutionary cause, men like Scott Nearing, most authors are compelled to live by their pen. However lofty the ethical or aesthetic aura which surrounds his writings, the average author is as dependent on ideas for his livelihood as the tailor on pants or the butcher on meat. Modern literature, in the largest sense of the word, is, like modern industry, split by the division of labor. In the offices of the Chicago *Tribune* I was, after a fashion, a literary proletarian. The plant was owned by a large company whose profits came from the gathering and dissemination of news and features. The stockholders owned the machinery; the reporters, cartoonists and feature writers produced the goods. I had no more to say about the policies of my company than a mechanic has about the policies of the Ford plant. My job was to appear at the news' factory at four P.M. every day and to remain there until after midnight. I had to tend the news ticker (machine), read all the newspapers printed by the London linotypes (machine), talk to Paris over the transchannel phone (machine); type cables and mailers (machine); and send messages by telegraph or wireless (machine).

My hours and tasks were set for me; the form of the dispatches was also set; how they finally appeared in print, and whether with or without my signature, was determined in Chicago by the *Tribune* and in New York by the *Daily News*. I had only to perform my assigned tasks. True, those tasks required the use of my mind as well as my body; I had a certain latitude in the methods of obtaining news and the form of presenting it as sensationally as possible; I was rewarded with bonuses when I beat the other newspapers on a story. But such latitude and such bonuses exist in many factories. On the whole, the reporter's intellectual operations are severely limited on his job. There is little room for "creative imagination" or "scientific thought." I had to remember Floyd Gibbons' warning in Paris—when he caught me rewriting a story for the fifth time—that I was not writing for posterity and that, in any event, a mistake is not important because the dear public never remembers anything. The World's Greatest Newspaper had its policies; reporting had its clichés, whose aim was that of all labor-saving devices—mass production and speed. For this work I got a weekly salary which was more than comfortable for an unattached young man of twenty-three, a salary equal, let us say, to that of a highly skilled worker at Vickers'. That income depended chiefly not on my intellectual but on what might be called my moral qualities, on my willingness and ability to show up on my job regularly and to carry out assignments. When I subsequently quit the paper to go back to New York, my chief, the amiable and generous John Steele, gave me a letter saying I was "a first-class newspaperman, hard-working, reliable, with a good news sense and an excellent knowledge of European affairs." Yet the fact remains that for years afterward, the World's Greatest Newspaper got along nicely without my services. A worker in a news factory is as replaceable as a worker in a cannery.

Other young men followed me in the London office, supplying the necessary skill for the job, as I followed Gilbert Seldes and Sigourney Thayer.

The poet, novelist or critic, however, is more like a handicraftsman. He not only produces the goods, so to speak, but must create his own market, obtain his own raw material. The market depends, in part, on the author's seeming originality, on his ability to present new ideas or old ideas in new dress. Upon this depends his prestige, the equivalent of that goodwill for which all business strives. From prestige or "fame" the author gets a certain psychological satisfaction—a satisfaction enhanced by his successes in society or among women. Without prestige, the market value of the author declines. Here arises a reciprocal relationship. The author's fame depends to some extent upon his success in the literary market; his success in the literary market depends to some extent on his fame. His income depends on both. Sometimes the successful author is one whose mere signature has market value, like the label of a well-known brand of canned soup or the name of a stock which has gone up fifty points on the bourse. This value exists not only for autograph hunters, who treasure it sentimentally or trade on it shrewdly, but also for publishers and editors, who know how to market it, and readers, who know that a piece of writing is good because it has the proper label.

Unlike the butcher, the baker and the candlestickmaker, the author cannot advertise the merits of his wares in the newspaper, in the magazine or on billboards, though the reader succumbs to the publishers' blurbs and advertisements. The author, like the doctor or the lawyer, must depend on word of mouth advertising and free publicity in the news columns, which in turn depend on what the literary critics say. From this arises literary politics, the extension of literary economics. There are combinations for the promotion of one's own and the restraint of others' literary trade. It does not appear so bald, however. The pontifical Mr. Fox, enjoying prestige at the moment as a critic, proclaims Mr. Cox the best American or English novelist. Mr. Cox, when the occasion arises, returns the compliment and praises Mr. Fox as the best American or English critic. The rivals of Mr. Fox and Mr. Cox call this logrolling, but Mr. Fox and Mr. Cox themselves (and their rivals, who are no different) wrap these practices in the same noble deception and self-deception as do the statesmen who carry on their economic and political maneuvers in the name of patriotism, or the church which does so in the name of God.

The less attractive qualities of men sometimes prevalent in literary circles are inevitable by-products of the law of the jungle, of competitive industry and trade in the realm of art. The writer who is spiritually barren, except for a knack of turning felicitous phrases, or a personal charm, or a university title, or a distinguished family name, keeps his ears open everywhere for raw material, for a piece of information or an idea which can be converted into cash, fame or both. Far from acknowledging his debt to other writers, he conceals it in his anxiety to advance himself in the market and salons. And since "we scorn the base degrees by which we have ascended" and treat those most unjustly to whom we owe most, there comes a day when the successful businessman calls the men whom he has exploited suckers, loafers or nincompoops, or shows off the charity of the conqueror by throwing them a few bones. The literary plagiarist treats with a similar contempt or patronage the men from whom he has borrowed the ideas which made him famous.

Perhaps it was direct contact with these aspects of the life of art in contemporary Western civilization which made me write from London to friends in New York that "to spend one's life writing poetry is not enough; to spin rhymes and do nothing else is a sterile kind of life"; or even more specifically:

"I have no intention of getting caught in the whirlpool of personal conflict, jealousy, envy, disdain, aggression and intrigue which infest literary circles. I used to believe that the world of artists, as distinguished from the world of insurance agents and cotton goods merchants, is a world of friendship, justice, peace and impersonal devotion to art. But George Moore talks about Thomas Hardy in much the same way that Lloyd George talks about Herbert Asquith. A gathering of minor poets sounds like a Tammany Hall convention. The world of art is a world of people who, whatever other qualities they may have, all have the common quality of vanity. I say all; I suppose there are exceptions: the Shakespeares, too busy making money to argue at the Mermaid Tavern as often as Jonson and Marlowe; Cervantes, bumming around as a soldier while his contemporaries, whoever they were, played the role of professional poets."

I had occasion to think over these ideas, no doubt grossly exaggerated by oversensibility and inexperience, during a long illness in the spring of 1921, an illness which revived the romantic fear of and longing for death. The repudiation of professional poetry, the concept that true art came out of deep suffering, and the belief that form and content were, in literature at least, identical were combined in a letter to Irwin who was now touring England.

"Don't call me a professional poet," I wrote him. "Specimens of that breed whom I have met have convinced me that in comparison Tammany Hall politicians are noble and dignified contributors to the progress of the human race. There are two kinds of people in the poetic world: poets and men who write poetry. The professional poet is very often the most contemptible of creatures; he is overeaten with a vanity, a pettiness, a jealousy that is equaled only among professional prostitutes. These professional poets are the fellows who leave out their personal enemies from books on Current Tendencies in Tasmanian Poetry; who, when they edit magazines, reject the works of those outside their little clique simply out of vanity and spite.

"Style is not so much a way of talking as a way of thinking. 'Shall I kill myself or shall I not kill myself' is an idea similar to the idea 'to be or not to be—that is the question.' But it is not the same idea. Shakespeare has said what my prose sentence has said; but he has said much more in addition; there is a whole hinterland of thought and emotion behind Shakespeare's phrase which the prose sentence misses. . . . I am feeling a great revulsion for the whole art for art's sake twaddle. A well-written page is a page which says something worth reading. A man who writes nonsense in a charming 'style' is like a man who talks nonsense in a charming voice."

From Paris Irwin replied:

"I thoroughly agree with you that the eighteen-ninety art for art's sake business was rubbish, said and done with the accent with which it was said and done. But I am by no means sure that content and style are not, at least for purposes of analysis and enjoyment, dissociable. Perhaps you *are* right about poetry and literature, but I am sure you aren't about any of the other arts. We're both Puritans at heart, and not in the worst sense of the word; and I feel as you do that nothing of any serious or permanent attraction in art can be empty. But the meaningless surface iridescence of a Monet, or the absolute and meaningless form of a classic Greek statue or temple seem to me to refute you. What I guessed a year ago, I feel very strongly now, that you enjoy a work of art as a work of art chiefly for its form. Where you become more interested in the content than in anything else, it seems to me you are passing out of the realm of aesthetics into that of morals; which is what any first-rate work of art, I suppose, leads one to do. There is an ideal implicit even in the meaningless perfection of form of Greek sculpture and architecture. These things seem to me so of all the arts except literature, whose materials are ideas. I am beginning to wonder whether the terms *beauty* and *aesthetics* are not more nuisances in thinking than anything else. But my feeling is that you are in danger of generalizing from the aesthetics of poetry to cover all art, and I don't think that can safely be done."

§ 7

As usual, I generalized too quickly from immediate experience in the London bureau of the World's Greatest Newspaper: I assumed that because John Steele was an honorable man, albeit a conservative journalist, newspaper work was free of what appeared to me as the spite, envy and trickery which astonished my naïveté in the literary bohemia of Chelsea. I had as yet no concrete idea of how competitive industry operates under capitalism. I did not even grasp in all its implications that the press is an industry subject to many of the basic laws which affect the manufacture of automobiles or the extraction of oil. The first story of any consequence which I covered opened my eyes in this respect. It also revised my romantic notions about the kind of personal courage which we admired during the war when we thought of Rupert Brooke, and gave me some indication of the difference between journalism and literature—a difference involving style and the type of experience which the two arts deal with.

The British captured the airship ZR-2 from the Germans during the war. Now, in the summer of 1921, they were selling it to the United States. A mixed crew of forty-nine men and officers, partly British, partly American, were preparing to fly the ship across the Atlantic to New York. The press watched preparations for the test flight which the ship would make in England before crossing the sea. O. P. Swift, a classmate from the School of Journalism, who had joined the migration to Europe, now worked beside me at the Chicago *Tribune*. We were assigned to cover the story. At the hangar in Howden we were taken through the ship—the first of its kind I had ever seen. Aviation was still a new thing in the world. We were not yet air-minded; it seemed incredible that this sausage-shaped monster, swaying gracefully from wires in the roof, should be able to glide through space. There was uncertainty as to when the ship would take off. Newspaper correspondents from every part of the world waited at the flying field at Howden for news. For days the only news was:

it depends on the weather. The rest was "color stuff," the poetry of reporting.

The center of attention at Howden was the British officer in charge of the test flight northward. In appearance and manners, Commander Maitland was the traditional English officer and gentleman. We all admired his sang-froid. Everybody knew the flight was dangerous. Several times the ship had had to be repaired. They said the cables were weak. Yet every afternoon, day after day, Commander Maitland appeared on the tennis courts near the flying field, immaculate in white flannels, aloof with self-possession. He played a brisk game and afterward calmly took tea with friends.

It was not enough to cover the news which everybody could get, or even to roll out of your typewriter pages of "color." Like the poet, the reporter must produce something "original," information which his rivals cannot get. There were plots to smuggle correspondents aboard to report the flight direct from the ship. Officers searched the ship daily. These plots were frustrated; the ship took off with no newspapermen aboard. At the *Tribune* office, O. P. and I followed the flight on the news ticker and cabled hourly to Chicago.

FLASH——ZR-2 WRECKED IN HULL . . .

It was long past midnight when the work first started. O. P. telephoned his wife, roused her out of bed, told her we were going to Hull, and asked her to make us ham and eggs. Typing a cable to the home office, I reflected how different the Americans were from the English. Major C. V., who worked with us in the same office as "political correspondent," had been friendly and fatherly to me for six months. We dined together almost every evening. He told me about his love affairs. Once he even took me to dinner at the Liberal Club where his brother, a whip in Parliament for Lloyd George, was a man of some consequence. Yet he never once took me to his home, the Englishman's castle. I knew O. P. only casually; I had never met his wife; yet here she was, out of bed at three o'clock in the morning, standing at the gas range in her dressing gown, frying ham and eggs for a stranger who happened to be her husband's colleague in an office.

At four o'clock in the morning we took the milk train to Hull. The dusty cars were crowded with British, American, French, German, Italian, Dutch and Balkan correspondents, some of them accompanied by cameramen. The benches were hard and filthy. Nobody slept; everybody drank. Tobacco smoke floated through the cars like a peasoup fog. Everybody pumped everybody else for information, and everybody lied about the dispatches he had sent to his home office. Competitive industry.

We reached Hull at seven in the morning, leaped into taxis, and made for the city's leading hotel, located on the Humber River within sight of the wrecked airship. The reporters were excited by the story, by drink, by lack of sleep. Hoping to be overheard, they commented in loud voices on the faces of the passers-by. The faces of Hull's citizens were long and sheeplike. A London reporter who affected American slang explained:

"They get that way from f—g sheep."

We all laughed. The hotel was overcrowded. The wreck meant good business for Hull. Prices soared, but we were armed with expense accounts. We viewed the wreck, questioned the cautious British and American officers in charge. I rushed a cable to the *Tribune* in Chicago which wired a copy to the *Daily News* in New York.

"The airship ZR-2, yesterday the highest achievement of man in aerial flight, tonight lies in tangles of charred metal along the river Humber within sight of Hull. Of the forty-nine men, the pick of the world's greatest balloonists, who ascended in it yesterday morning at Howden, only five are alive in Hull hospitals this midnight. Only three seem likely to live on to tell the story of one of the most spectacular and dramatic catastrophes of modern times. Of the seventeen American naval officers and men who gaily set out on this test flight, which was to precede the airship's trip across the Atlantic to its future American home, just one floated from the wreckage alive. The total dead are forty-three." And so on, and so forth. My signed story, when it appeared in the Chicago *Tribune,* took up several columns. I was not an aviation expert. I did not know for certain that the ZR-2 was the "highest achievement of man in aerial flight" or that the forty-nine men who flew it were "the pick of the world's greatest balloonists"; neither did anybody else around Hull. American reporting required stories to be inflated. The press reflected the great American lust for things which could be sold as the best, biggest and first. If you were the *first* man to sit on a flagpole for a month you rated more space on the front page than Albert Einstein and Henri Barbusse.

The home offices wired back: watch for the fishing out of the bodies. Be the *first* to cable the recovery of Americans. For the next seventy-two hours nobody slept. A ten-minute nap might rob your paper of a scoop. The hotel swarmed with reporters, army and navy officers, consular representatives. Day and night the woman who owned the hotel, a pleasant middle-aged matron whom I called Lady Hull, served us tea, but we stuck to Scotch and soda. We scoured the town for news, talking with everybody. The natives of Hull spoke English with an Elizabethan flavor.

"Where is the coroner's office?" I asked a skyscraper-policeman.

He pointed a long finger toward the cupola of a wide building: "See you yon doom?"

"You mean that dome over there?"

"Aye, 'tis yonder the coroner is."

At last Commander Maitland's body was found. It was laid out in one of the rooms of our hotel. We were not allowed to see it; day and night armed sentries guarded the door. It was rumored they had found a diary in Commander Maitland's tunic which he had kept until the ship actually began to crack up. The reporters asked a hundred questions about it and got no answers.

At night the boys played cards in the pressroom. A twenty-year-old London journalist, an ace during the war and now the author of a book of verse, drank tea to be original, and read aloud in a high nervous voice some rhymes he had just composed about the wreck. Lady Hull, who mothered the aviator-poet and myself because we were the youngest reporters there, stood in the doorway smiling applause for the rhymes. A New York correspondent walked in. Several of the American reporters leaped to their feet, seized his coat collar and punched his face. New York's nose bled; he stumbled out of the room. Another reporter explained:

"The son of a bitch tried to bribe the guard to let him see Maitland's diary."

Competitive industry.

At three o'clock in the morning Lady Hull called me aside:

"Would you like to see the commander?"

"How?"

"Follow me."

She led me through the deserted corridors to the room. There was no guard before the door. She opened it softly with a passkey and closed it behind me. She remained outside, leaving me alone in the room. The dead commander lay in uniform with his hands crossed on his breast. His face, immobile and waxen in death, was mottled with blue bruises. The diary was on the table beside him. Was it intended only for the author's eyes, or, like most diaries, was it written for posterity, mythically just but always partisan in its interpretation of the past? I picked up the diary and read it hastily. None of us had realized Commander Maitland's enormous personal courage. When he was calmly playing tennis at Howden and taking tea with friends, he knew he was going to his death. The diary showed it. Entry by entry, day by day, hour by hour, there were warnings that the ship was defective. Its wiring was bad; it would not stand the strain of a long flight; it would crack sure as fate; everybody aboard would be killed; postpone the flight until the necessary repairs could be made. The Americans were obdurate and Commander Maitland was a gentleman, a good sport. He took charge of the flight, noting in his diary every step toward death. When the sausage-shaped monster crumpled amidships, and the stern rose and the bow sagged, the young commander knew that what he had foreseen had come to pass.

But was not this courage, so impressive from the personal viewpoint, a wasteful and foolish thing socially? Had one the right, in the name of an archaic chivalrous ideal, to wreck a ship and kill forty-three men, oneself included? Had the commander vociferously resigned and protested, he might have been considered in some circles a bad sport. But might not that bad sportsmanship have been a higher kind of social heroism? Surely there must be a morality which considers the welfare of society more important than the gallant gestures of an individual, where such gestures, if socially harmful, might be considered a social crime.

There was another problem too. By sheer accident I had satisfied the demands of competitive industry; I had got a scoop for my paper. But the press was not an independent estate; it was of necessity subservient to the interests of the governing classes. There was already marked suspicion between the English and the Americans, mutual recriminations as to who was responsible for the wreck. To publish Commander Maitland's diary was to create an "international incident." Diplomacy triumphed; the diary was not published.

The same day I got a second scoop. The bodies of two Americans were found in the river and rushed to the morgue. Alert reporters hurried to view them. Brass navy tags would give the names and cities of the victims. By the time I learned the news, there was not a taxi or carriage in sight. I halted a private citizen cruising along the river front in an open roadster.

"Excuse the intrusion, sir. I am an American newspaperman who must get to the morgue."

The man smiled at my incoherence, but took in the situation at once.

"Where are you from?" he said.

"New York."

"I worked in New York for six years. A wonderful town. Hop in."

On the way we met the returning reporters.

"Don't waste your time," they shouted to me. "They won't let anybody into the morgue. An official statement will be given out later."

My benefactor kept on driving.

"Don't worry," he said. "I'll get you in. I'm an official of this city."

He did get me into the morgue. The bodies of the two privates lay still in waxen repose. They belonged to those who did the work of the world and got an obituary notice only when they were killed in a spectacular accident about which their superiors alone know in advance. From the brass navy tags attached to their wrists I copied their names and addresses. One of them was a Chicago boy: great news for the home office. The generous Hull official drove me to a telegraph station where the operator smiled and called him by his first name. She was filing the cables of the other reporters. The official took the blank which I had hastily filled in with a dispatch and said to her:

"Send this first."

For this second accidental scoop, my paper gave me a fifty dollar bonus.

Competitive industry.

§ 8

When I returned to London, I covered a slighter story which brought me face to face with one of my boyhood myths. Isadora Duncan—the symbol of beauty and freedom which so enthralled the radical intelligentsia of my home town—gave a tea at one of the London theaters. I entered a reception room jammed with artists, writers, actresses and dancers. Isadora met me at the door. It was the first time I had ever seen the idol of an older generation.

"Come in," she said, and her smile suddenly filled her face with the last rays of passing glory. "Let me introduce you to Augustus John, the man with the big beard over there. Excuse me if I sound jumbled. I'm drunk as a lord."

She took me by the arm, tried to walk, stumbled against a rug and spilled her cocktail on the floor. Isadora's body was bloated, the skin of her face loose and wrinkled, her eyes bleary and infinitely tired. Age had devoured the golden myth. Hers was the fate, I thought, of all whose radiance rested on the ephemeral—a beautiful body, a resonant voice, powerful biceps. How fortunate those who fashioned imperishable statues, canvases, poems, works of art which continued young while their creators grew old, works like the happy, happy boughs in Keats' poem which could not shed their leaves nor ever bid the spring adieu, and the happy melodist, unwearied, forever piping songs forever new, and the happy, happy love forever warm and still to be enjoyed, forever panting and forever young. . . . There was a death which overtook us before death itself, and was perhaps more terrible, the death of those faculties which made us unique and fruitful in the highest realms of human existence. The motif of Eternity returned, this time shamefaced and dubious; for I had already begun to think about the fact that the imperishable statues, canvases and poems themselves perished, if not physically, then in the estimation of men. Nobody now read Calderón; Euripides was a textbook for schoolboys, Anatole France already a joke among the rising postwar youth, reactionary and radical alike. Eternally changing fashion wiped out from the active memory of men and their admiration the marble figure, the painted landscape, the thundering rhymes which held generations spellbound. Art, too, had its mortality. Books, like men, were born, they flourished, they died; and it was as difficult to recall how or why they enthralled our predecessors as to remember how or why this bloated woman, shriveled with age and unstable with alcohol, had inflamed the imagination of America's once rebellious youth.

Was the premise which suggested these reflections a mirage? Was Isadora Duncan really as old and as broken at this time as I imagined? Was I not seeing a woman in her middle forties with the tyrannical unaccustomed eyes of a boy in his early twenties, to whom a decade's difference in age appears like a century? Perhaps.

Nevertheless, my reflections about the mortality of art appeared to be supported by other factors. I still had with me the bound volume of futurist pamphlets which I had picked up, in French translation, in a Parisian bookstall, and which the author had autographed for the man who had sold it perhaps out of the direst need: *à Otto Granoff, hommage de F. T. Marinetti.* Here was Time in revolt against Eternity, a revolt which had become general. Nearly all poets and painters, however antiquated their basic ideals, now called themselves *modern.* The present repudiated the past. Marinetti went further; he talked of the future repudiating the present as if the present were already the past. Let us, he cried, echoing Nietzsche, celebrate danger, energy, temerity. And echoing Danton, he added: the essential elements of our poetry are courage, audacity and revolt. Hitherto literature had exalted pensive immobility, ecstasy and slumber; Marinetti wished to exalt aggressive movement, feverish insomnia, the stride of the athlete, the perilous leap, the prizefighter's wallop. The world's splendor had been enriched with a new beauty: the beauty of speed. A racing auto rushing by with open cutout was more beautiful than the Winged Victory. Hence the futurists celebrated the aviator flying across the earth which hurls itself against its own orbit. The flyer replaced Nietzsche's Prussian hussars; the idea, however, assumed a reactionary meaning.

Marinetti urged the poet to create with heat, éclat and prodigality, in order to augment the enthusiastic fervor of the primordial elements. There was no longer any beauty except in battle; there were no longer masterpieces without an aggressive character. Poetry must be a violent assault upon unknown forces in order to submit them to man's will. The futurists imagined themselves standing upon the highest promontory of the centuries. They could not look behind them at that moment when they felt called upon to conquer the mysterious vantage points of the Impossible. Time and Space had died yesterday; we already lived in the absolute; we had already created eternal, omnipresent speed.

From this glorification of unscientific science, the futurists crawled back to the feet of imperialist politics:

"We glorify war, the sole hygiene of the world," Marinetti exclaimed. "We glorify militarism, patriotism, the destructive gestures of the anarchists: the beautiful ideas which kill: the contempt for women."

In art, Time crushed Eternity with one futurist puff; Marinetti called upon the artists to demolish the museums, the libraries; to combat moralism, to fight all opportunist and utilitarian sloth. Let us sing, he said, the great crowds agitated by labor, pleasure or revolt; the multicolored and polyphonic waves of revolution in the modern capitals; the nocturnal vibrations of the arsenals and dockyards under their violent electric moons; the gluttonous railway stations with their smoking serpents; the factories suspended from the clouds by strings of smoke; the bridges with their gymnastic leaps across the diabolic cutlery of the sunny rivers; the adventurous steamers flaring across the horizon; the locomotives with their great breastplates puffing along the rails, these enormous horses of steel bridled with long funnels; the gliding flight of airplanes spiraling to the roar of the propeller and the cheers of the enthusiastic crowd. . . .

Such ideas, developed on the eve of the World War, had launched literary and artistic movements in Italy and Russia. One of these was to become fascist; another was to donate gifted artists to the October Revolution. By the second decade of our century the aesthetic credos of the futurists, with their emphasis on the machine, the mass, violence and speed, were to become the clichés of groups on both sides of the barricades in the European social war, clichés which American literary circles were to echo in the third decade as if they had just discovered a new continent or set rivers on fire. The clichés were to be bottles into which each social group poured its own wine. At the opening of the twenties, when we first read them, the futurist manifestoes sounded incredibly daring and original, fatal blows to a past which was as mortal as the dancer's grace.

But upon rereading the futurists after seeing Duncan, I felt that what had aged was not the woman but the myth she had symbolized. Ideological vanguard, first of the war, later of fascism, the Italian futurists had proclaimed the contempt for woman; their painters demanded the abolition of the nude in art for a decade—this at the moment when the American radical intellectuals were discovering the glory of the human body presumably through Isadora's dance. The cult of the nude woman was now fading. Armies, navies, blackshirts and brownshirts were compelled to inflate the homosexual ideal, the manly love of comrades in arms. Moreover, through the capitals and galleries of Europe you sensed that Western culture, which had once set up the nude as a talisman against medieval asceticism, was now bored with it in life and art. It turned to the machine from which the American intellectuals fled to the nude. For New York Duncan was the beginning of a cycle whose end she symbolized in London. In the hour when both sides of Europe's barricades dressed austerely for the battle in red shirt or black, American radicals "revolted" against the tyrannies of contemporary civilization by mixed bathing parties in the nude.

§ 9

While Irwin and I were arguing by letter—and, when he came to London, in person—about the relation of art to experience, of aesthetics to morals, communist friends in New York continued, by correspondence, their campaign against art in general.

"The rebel Joe"—Mac Windsor rebuked me in the summer of 1921—"has written us very little about rebellion. Joe who went off with the ringing message that '1914 marked the end of an old era' has been sending us letters from Paris, Italy and London in which we sensed no more than the Paris of Trilby, the London of Thackeray and the Italy of the art connoisseur. In the attempt to understand man—biologically, psychologically, anthropologically—we reached back 75,000—150,000—300,000—300,000,000 years—and then reached over into the present; the struggles within the Triple Alliance in England of 1921; the dissensions in the workshops of Italy; the Communists in Paris; Radek and Lenin in Moscow. In the light of these, the puritanism of London or the medieval inscriptions of Italian cathedrals seem to lose their power to incite curiosity. In the face of the new worlds that now hover in the realm of possibility, man's present fantastic impurities and unreasoning repressions seem only part and parcel of an old age—of maleducation in a temporary, wretched, precarious system. They seem incapable now of arousing active surprise, not even violent disgust. They are taken for granted in plotting their pigmy dimensions on our vast scale. Now X and Y and a few others whom we might name seem still to be struggling with the outworn issues. They call it 'literature and art'; and the major part of your efforts in Europe seems to be directed along the same lines. A few of us here have rather drifted away into what seem to us more creative and vital experiences. Revolution looms big even on the vastest scale. I am no more excitable over brilliant verses, nor even exquisite poetry. I sometimes wish you could throw over a past that binds you to restraining activity and antiquated ideals. I see there is a new Europe coming and you seem to be too inwardly engrossed to notice this newness and to follow it. X and Y seem to be gradually losing grasp on a deeper understanding of the world situation which, though they ignore it, is influencing them most powerfully; your continued zeal for poetry writing seems to carry with it the same weakness."

Communist friends were not alone in urging that there were more important things in the contemporary world than poetry. That summer Dr. Charles A. Beard came to London accompanied by Mrs. Beard and their daughter Miriam and Spencer Miller. We all dined together, and discussed European and American politics. Suddenly Dr. Beard said:

"What are you doing outside the Chicago *Tribune?*"

"What does one do at twenty-three?" I said. "I write verses."

Dr. Beard closed his eyes as in the old days; then he opened them slowly and said with the utmost seriousness, watching closely to see if I understood his full meaning:

"When I was twenty-three, I wrote a book on the industrial revolution."

I felt it necessary once more to defend art against Mac's onslaughts. "I am still a communist," I wrote him. "It is likely, as you suggest, that we agree on communism. But I expect you to know psychology to the extent of realizing the danger of confusing your own puritan tendencies with communism, and calling everything you don't like 'bourgeois.' Even the Moscow government, which is busier with communism than you or I, is running theaters, art exhibits, concerts and printing millions of books—including books of poems. And Maxim Gorky, who again is busier with communism than you or I, is writing two novels. As I understand communism, it is a movement to distribute the good things of life among all the people, not to abolish them because only a few can enjoy them now. A comfortable house, good food, good education—these are at present bourgeois privileges—and it would be just as sensible to urge their abolition as to urge the abolition of art."

The pressure of the revolutionary current in Europe, which I followed daily in the press as a working correspondent, and letters from radical friends at home altered not only my views about art, but the nature of the verses I wrote. In a letter to Robert Smith, I announced that I intended "to leave off the kind of literature which once pleased me, expressing what you so well termed the 'fragrance' of life. True literature is the expression of what a man thinks and feels; and as I think and feel differently I shall write differently. From the poetry of beauty I shall turn to the poetry of wisdom."

The poetry of "wisdom," or, more accurately, the poetry of moral and intellectual problems and the emotions they generate, which I was now beginning to write, came from my need to orient myself toward the social revolution which I had now accepted as the central fact of my life. To produce real revolutionary literature, however, one must live with the masses of the organized workers, be part of the revolutionary movement. I was not in that position in London in the year 1921. I was then a person who fancied himself in love with art, who from earliest childhood was interested in "social justice," who now saw "social justice" embodied in communism and who was trying to clear his system of intellectual and emotional debris which stood between him and his possible usefulness to the revolutionary movement. My poetry thus became—when it was not purely subjective love poetry—the rhymed diary of a "fellow traveler" fighting his way toward bolshevism.

In the midst of these doubts, vacillations, speculations, introspections—so typical of the intellectual moving slowly toward the revolutionary movement—I received a letter from Louis—just as typical of the worker-bolshevik. This letter ignored metaphysics and art. Louis had patiently waited for me to become "useful to the cause" since I was twelve; now he thought the time had come. His letter went straight to the point:

"I believe"—Louis wrote—"that with the experience gained by your travels combined with your natural abilities you can gain a place in the American movement and in the hearts of the toiling masses. Yours can be a very valuable contribution to open the eyes of the rank and file."

Characteristic of the worker-bolshevik was that the letter ended with a practical suggestion:

"Come to work in the Party press."

BOOK THREE

CHAPTER I

A great revaluation is in progress. But it is not altogether agreeable to live in the No Man's Land between two ethical worlds. We can no longer believe in the old; and yet we shrink from the new, being still entangled in the old.

—FRITZ WITTELS.

§ 1

FROM an airplane, the city below appears neat and simple, like a diagram. Each road is well defined. The correlation of streets, squares and houses is lucid and unequivocal, small to the eye and conquerable to the mind. When you descend and walk through the city, it looms immense, strange and confusing. You are lost in the side streets. What you had grasped simply as a whole from the air becomes a complex maze to be traversed slowly and with difficulty. Similarly, living abroad gives you an illusory sense of emancipation from your own environment. Physical detachment induces emotional tranquillity and intellectual perspective. You watch the American scene from a distance, grasp it as a whole, and arrive at choices which appear purely rational. The moment you return to your own milieu, tradition and habit overwhelm you. The rational choice becomes one side of a struggle both within yourself and against your surroundings. You pass through the ordeal of making organic changes in yourself; and in close grips with reality your path is not so clear as it appeared from a distance.

I returned to New York in the fall of 1921. At the pier I was met by my father, dressed in a gray tweed topcoat, a light gray hat and gray spats. He carried a Malacca cane. To his extraordinary energy he had added the self-assurance of the successful American businessman. As I stepped into his seven-passenger green Cadillac, the blond young chauffeur at the wheel touched his cap respectfully. The car rolled smoothly over Forty-second Street. New York throbbed with a vigor which London and Paris lacked. The crowds rushed by with nervous speed, intent and purposeful. My father handed me a cigarette bearing his initials, and said:

"Are you glad to be back in America?"

"This is home," I said.

From the bridge we looked back at lower Manhattan's towers rising in tiers above the river bank. There on the other side was Brooklyn, a desert of low, square, red brick houses which might as well be five million miles from Times Square as five. When we reached the street where my family lived the respectable quiet was appalling. The house was the one I had left a year and a half earlier, but the outside had a new coat of yellow paint and neatly trimmed hedges met at the wooden gate. My mother, my younger brothers and sisters crowded the stoop, smiling and calling to me. I stepped out of the car and they kissed me exuberantly. I had never seen my mother so healthy, so handsome, so well dressed. My two younger brothers wore the golf suit now in fashion, which, in my muddled radical leanings, I looked upon as a bourgeois uniform, almost as distinctive a class garb as the cutaway. The girls had short skirts and bobbed hair and their mouths glistened with lipstick. Inside the house, there were new and more costly rugs, curtains, chairs, a piano, a new phonograph. It was all very comfortable, very pleasant.

Despite my family's prosperity, there was still no maid. My mother cooked dinner herself, and my sisters helped her serve it. As in the old days, we sang during and after the meal, and with eight of us at the table there was a loud and gay chorus. My brothers and sisters sang the latest jazz, more vigorously than I had heard it in London; I sang French songs from the Folies-Bergères and Italian songs from Venice. My mother, in a plaintive solo, sang the revolutionary ballad we had heard from her in childhood: *Chasovoi? Shto, barin, nada?*—an echo of the vanished village, which seemed now like a remote dream that someone else had dreamed and repeated to you with imperfect remembrance.

A new life was open to me, a life symbolized by my father's Sunday morning breakfasts. The cars, usually driven by chauffeurs, drew up in front of the neat hedges. The successful realtors, builders, insurance agents, architects, and bankers came into the house, sat around the large square table with the damask cloth, ate vast quantities of sturgeon, salmon, eggs, black olives, pumpernickel. They told amusing anecdotes, sang Russian sentimental ballads or Chasidic chants—and talked business. The entire universe revolved around their business, and that—heaven be praised!—was going remarkably well. They felt secure in their achievements and convinced in their faith that American capitalism was mankind's salvation. For them the great American dream had come true. They who had come here as penniless immigrants had no kick coming; if the streets of New York were not literally paved with gold, their bank accounts were mounting to unexpected heights. They attributed their good fortune partly to their own superior intelligence, partly to the virtues of the competitive system. There was nothing new in their attitude; what was new and disconcerting was the unexpected support it received from wartime prosperity.

Worse still, prosperity had canceled memories of the war. What was for my generation the central and terrible fact of contemporary life was for them an unpleasant episode which had ended happily. The younger children remembered little of the war, they had no emotions about it; to them it was a historic event, remote in time, like the Civil War or the Revolution of 1776, something they had heard about but never experienced, even imaginatively. This difference in attitude between young people of my own age and our elders, on the one hand, and our juniors, on the other, set us apart as a marked generation. Yet among us, too, there were differences. The family chauffeur, a young Irishman who had fought on the western front, talked only about the few gay hours he had spent on leave in Paris. He refused to talk about the war itself. The reticence was general among the veterans whom I met at this time. They would not or could not recall the actual fighting, a fact reflected in our literature. With the exception of John Dos Passos' *Three Soldiers,* some sketches by Edmund Wilson and two or three other things of that kind, American literature was silent about the war. Not until time had assuaged the horrors in the souls of the survivors were writers able to remember the fighting with detachment and to write the *Farewells* and *All Quiets* which, a decade after the event, converted the raw material of experience into the riches of poetry. Possibly this is true of all art and experience; perhaps we must all look down the vistas of time in order to measure experience with perspective before the event, too painful to contemplate, too immediate to gauge, returns to us shorn of its sufferings, clear in its outlines, ready for communication in artistic forms.

Such difficulties do not confront the journalist. He who can with facility conceal the truth when it is most necessary to tell it can with equal facility reveal it when it no longer aids practical decision. The press agents of the war, who earned incomes and titles by glorifying it, now added to their laurels and royalties by exposing it. We learned from the most famous war correspondents that everything which the radicals had been punished for saying during the war was true. They echoed John Reed three years too late. From them we now heard about the "hard, materialistic outlook" of champions of liberty like Balfour, Curzon and Carson; the folly of Winston Churchill; the stupidity of Poincaré, the pitiful pretensions of Clemenceau, "a poor old walrus in a traveling circus." Now it could be told—after the sanguinary show was over. Now one could with impunity strip the pretensions from the old politicians who had played the game of politics before the war, gambling with the lives of men for territories, privileged markets, oil fields, native races, coaling stations and imperial prestige, grabbed the pool which the German gamblers had lost when their last bluff was called, and quarreled over its distribution. It was now fashionable to admit that the war had been an imperialist war. The statesmen of each capitalist country insisted on their share of the booty by calling the statesmen of other countries robbers.

Who said democracy and civilization? Shortly before his election to the White House, Warren Gamaliel Harding had risen on the floor of the Senate, read the preamble to the resolution declaring war against Germany, and added simply: "Nothing there especially proclaiming democracy and humanity." It was fitting and proper that this noble man should become president, even if his nomination was put over by a few machine politicians. After Wilson's lofty and deceptive rhetoric, it was refreshing to have an inaugural address which frankly proclaimed capital's intentions to exploit the world market.

America was back to "normalcy" under the small-town smile of a chief executive in golf knickers signing bills which Wall Street ghosted. The elderly playboy in the White House, with his entourage of poker players, topers, Casanovas and oil thiefs, posed benignly for the rotogravures as the Republic relaxed from the war through a long Roman holiday on bootleg gin. Million-dollar prizefights, baseball games and horse races indicated a bigger and better Gilded Age. The public avidly followed a press which, concealing the truth about Mooney and Billings, Sacco and Vanzetti, devoted pages to beauty contests and lust murders; and the bourgeois journalists were telling the truth about the war. But as usual after the event and under compulsion; for it was the proletarian revolutions in Russia, Germany and Hungary that brought to light the secret robber treaties of the imperialist governments. The fraud, the deadly hypocrisy of the prevailing social system, which had duped millions into slaughter, stood out in all its naked horror.

In this mood it was not hard for me to understand the difference between the exposés of the war correspondents and the analysis of the communists. Lenin's *State and Revolution* had been translated into English and was available in New York; communist and left-wing socialist publications were circulating bolshevik ideas which applied the teachings of Karl Marx to the twentieth century. From these it appeared that those who said "now it can be told," did not tell the most important things of all. Neither the shot at Sarajevo nor the personalities of Poincaré, Bethmann-Hollweg, Grey and Sasonov nor the philosophy of Nietzsche nor the national characteristics of the belligerent powers were responsible for the war. The attempt to pin the "war guilt" on one nation or one statesman, the caricaturing of Carson, Curzon and Clemenceau, concealed from the mass of people the true causes of war. The communists made it clear that war was not an abnormal madness of capitalist society; it was a normal aspect of it. The "war guilt" was not Germany's or Britain's alone; the guilt lay in the capitalist system as such. This the communists stated clearly, and their thesis was supported by the facts of history and of contemporary life. That was why bourgeois society, which applauded and rewarded the muckraking journalists, continued to throw communists into jail. As in the muckraking period of the Roosevelt-Taft era, there was a sharp division between the liberals, who cried out in horror at the results of capitalism without touching its roots, and the Marxists, who pointed to basic causes and urged revolutionary measures for their removal.

§ 2

Now that I was home, would I at last "settle down"?

As my father used the phrase, it meant a bourgeois career. He was more or less reconciled to the fact that I would not follow law, but if I insisted on writing, couldn't I at least be like Arthur Brisbane? My father never read Arthur Brisbane but he knew the American middle-class heroes; he had heard that Hearst's best-known editor received fifty thousand dollars a year and fifty thousand dollars couldn't be wrong. I said, without realizing the humor of such a pompous declaration, that I would stick to "art and revolution"; and probably enjoyed being considered a crank in the circles in which my family moved.

Of all the friends with whom I had grown up, only Louis and Mac were now in the communist movement. The poet Oscar, who had never been interested in politics, had made his own adjustment to the practical world. On a train to New Orleans he had, by accident, met

Sherwood Anderson who advised him to abandon the lyric for the
novel. Oscar compromised by starting and editing a poetry magazine
for which he discovered and published Eugene Jolas. Irwin was back
from Europe in what he called his professional cave, teaching philosophy on the campus; Benjamin, the first among us to call himself a
bolshevik, was headed for the same cave; he was now in Montreal recuperating from his European experiences and planning to take his
Ph.D. in philosophy at Harvard. I visited our old campus and realized
that the ties which bound me to Irwin and one or two others on the
faculty were purely personal. The academic world as such repelled me;
it seemed to be an appendage of the commercial world; when the professor was not an out-and-out apologist for the status quo, he supported
it by his silence. Bill was in Europe, almost completely absorbed in art.
Robert was in New York, abstractly devoted to the revolution, but
drifting away from it under the pressure of his new life. His chief
preoccupation was business; when he would make a million dollars,
he said, he would be more useful to the movement. The million-
dollar dream did not seem fantastic. Wartime prosperity had enriched
people we knew; some of our own classmates had made fortunes.
Others were well-to-do, successful in their professions. Young socialists
who had refused to talk to me in 1916 because I campaigned for Woodrow Wilson now kidded me about the desire to "save the world."
They were through with saving the world. You were lucky, they said,
if in this competitive system you managed to save your own skin. The
cult of success left no room for socialism. You had your hands full
"making good" as a lawyer, doctor, dentist or college instructor. It
was hard to meet people, however much you liked them, with whom
every conversation ended in a wrangle about capitalism and communism. To break from the social class into which you were born, or into
which you were inducted by economic circumstances, was an ordeal.
It meant wrenching yourself bodily and spiritually from people you
loved, and finding new friends and new loves in the world of your
choice. This meant a second adolescence.

At first I tried to maintain old relationships on the basis of the
general "human" emotions. But the attempt was difficult. It was hard
to believe that there were feelings based on biologic sorrows and satisfactions—birth, adolescence, sexual desire, eating, walking in the country, growing old, dying—which were devoid of social elements, which
transcended the social classes whose abolition seemed indispensable for
a higher civilization. It was at the very points where the experience of

the various classes appeared identical, that class differences stood out most sharply.

In the next house to ours, for example, there lived the Benders, once poor like my family, now climbing rapidly toward a million dollars. When Mrs. Bender's babies were born in the slum, she lay in a dark, airless bedroom. The baby, delivered by an illiterate midwife, came into a world of filth, hunger and misery. No one was sure it would survive. Now Mrs. Bender was having a baby in a "private house" full of air and sunlight. A well-paid specialist was in attendance. The child, born into security, was certain of the best nutrition and care; while Louis Smith's wife, now having her second baby, faced the same uncertainties which Mrs. Bender had faced a decade earlier. The biologic factor was universal, but it never came pure to any human being in civilized society. From the moment man ceased to live as an isolated animal and entered a community, all his biologic experiences came to him modified by social factors.

So with adolescence, difficult for all of us. Could my youngest sister compare her favored youth in this prosperous household with that of her older sister who had left home, slamming the door behind her like Ibsen's Nora? As I now watched the seven children of our family, of whom I was the eldest, it seemed that there were two sets of children and two sets of parents. The four older children, born abroad, painfully acquired a new language, new customs, new habits; they had to overcome the prejudices of the vanished village. What struggles the eldest of the girls had to convince my father that acting on the stage was no "sin," or I that playing baseball did not make one a "bum"; yet here was my father, now well-to-do and Americanized, permitting my younger sister to dance in a professional ballet, and my younger brothers to run on the track team, to captain the school football squad, to appear in the rotogravure as members of the all-scholastic nine. In all the families I knew, the younger children did not have to fight for what they wanted as hard as we had, because the cultural distance between them and their parents had diminished. Wealth made the parents more generous; tragic experience with the older rebels who had stormed out of the house in the name of their "sacred principles" made them more tolerant. On the other hand, the younger children had also learned from their rebellious and romantic elders; they were more detached from the home and had acquired an adroit technique of carrying out their "principles" on the sly. Their adolescence was different from ours because time and circumstance had altered.

So, too, with sexual desire. Could one say that love had no social elements, remembering a French family that Benjamin once described in which the daughter's biologic and emotional needs were frustrated by the economic and social demands of her class? The desire, the need for love was universal but, as in the case of food, desire was modified by the possibilities and limitations of one's social status.

Now that I was at home, it struck me more forcibly than ever that in bourgeois society love was inseparable from the cult of success. The girls I knew, like their contemporaries all over America, had changed. Many of them now had jobs, their own latchkeys and sometimes even their own apartments; they smoked, drank and petted freely. The name of Freud, once known only to the advanced intelligentsia, was now used by everyone, together with lipstick, the Lucky Strike and the gin flask. The frank and free life was becoming the prerogative not of the radical writers who had preached it as the wish-dream of poverty, but of the middle classes who practiced it as the privilege of wealth. Yet love itself, which, according to the romantic tradition, transcended all barriers, seemed to be strait-jacketed within class. The bourgeois girl in love with a radical usually looked upon his political views as a mental disease, a "neurosis" which she was destined to cure. Even when she abstractly accepted those views, she believed naïvely that work in the revolutionary movement was compatible with bourgeois success. You were expected to participate in strikes, yet earn enough money to buy a house in Flatbush, a Chrysler, furs, jewels. They pointed to the socialist movement for precedents: look at Morris Hillquit who was a party leader and lived on Riverside Drive. A girl who helped me organize the People's Council during the war now said to me:

"Communism may be all very well, but we are living under capitalism. I have been poor all my life and I have no intention of remaining poor. I am going to get money, lots of it."

Eventually she got lots of it; but her frank declaration in the fall of 1921 indicated that the radical who did not wish to become a conservative could find love only among women who had broken with the bourgeois world. I felt, too, that a radical journalist could not earn a large income and remain true to the revolutionary movement. Since I had decided not to follow my family into the flourishing middle class of the Harding era, I had to earn my own living, to find a job. Despite European experience and recommendations from the Chicago *Tribune,* I could not find one for several months. Finally I landed one on a

trade paper. The first week I reported union activities from the workers' viewpoint. The pudgy little managing editor reasoned with me
paternally:

"What in hell do you want to get mixed up in this for? You
know we can't print that."

"But it's true," I said.

"O.K. It's true and you're fired. We don't want no goddam radicals
here."

Louis Smith had moved out of our old slums and was living in
an apartment house a few blocks from my parents' home. His wife,
whom he had met in the factory where he worked, had quit her job.
Every day she wheeled their baby through Tompkins Square Park and
came home toward evening to cook the dinner. Usually Louis let the
dinner grow cold. The house was a meeting place for leading members of his union. They sat up long past midnight working out organizational plans, fighting out union policies. Sometimes the discussions
became heated; the boys banged on the table, and woke the baby in
the next room.

"Please, comrades," Louis's wife would say. "You can go without sleep but a baby can't." Louis would look distressed. He had meetings every night but felt that at least two nights a week one ought to
have them at home so as to be near one's family. The attempt to mix
domestic life with trade-union activities had its difficulties.

At one of these meetings I told Louis how I had been fired. The
crowd laughed. One worker said:

"Did you expect a Congressional medal for telling the truth in a
capitalist paper?"

"Don't you know your own business?" another said. "On a capitalist rag you're supposed to write about the Dempsey-Carpentier fight,
not about the struggles of the working class."

"He's lucky at that," Louis said. "Living home, plenty of bread, a
roof over his head, a bed to sleep in. Think of the millions down in
the dust."

On Louis's bookshelves I found copies of the *Workers' Council*,
a magazine published by left-wing socialists seeking affiliation with the
Communist International through an open American Communist
party. An editorial explained the prevailing wage cuts of ten, twenty
and thirty per cent:

*"The recent industrial slump has threatened the holy profits. The
domestic consumer had grown wary and a good proportion of our*

*foreign markets have vanished while the European statesmen have
been completing the ruin of Europe. Industrial stagnation has brought
on a labor surplus here, and the masters of industry have been quick
to take advantage of it. Wages are being reduced in order that the
great god Profit may be maintained in the style to which he is
accustomed."*

America now had five million unemployed. Again, as in 1907,
there was famine amidst plenty.

"It is here again," Michael Gold wrote in the *Liberator,* "this mysterious plague of unemployment that breaks out every seven years in
the capitalist world." He added: "In less than ten years"—*that would
be sometime before 1931*—"there will be another fierce, dreadful wave
of unemployment, another American famine. I am no divinely-
informed prophet who say this; any American workingman will give
you the same information."

§ 3

A writer breaking from the middle classes does not, as a rule, go
directly to the proletariat. If he is separated from the class of his origin
by political differences, he is equally cut off from the class of his choice
by cultural differences, which is perhaps only saying that he cautiously
puts one foot into the new class while retaining the other in the old.
He associates intimately at first only with those class-conscious workers
who have absorbed something of the prevailing culture, autodidacts in
the classics. Chiefly, however, the young radical intellectual seeks out
people like himself, men and women saturated in bourgeois culture,
who are also crossing from one class to another. Bohemia is the customary residence. But I did not go to bohemia immediately. I went
first with Mac Windsor to a meeting on the East Side at which representatives of the underground communist organizations and left-wing
socialist groups discussed proposals for founding an open, legal Communist party. Considering the numerical smallness of the movement,
its isolation from the vast mass of American workers, the speakers in
the chilly, square, dimly lit hall spoke with extraordinary enthusiasm
and faith. They predicted a long, hard fight for a workers' republic in
America, but of the eventual victory no one had any doubt.

After the meeting, Mac introduced me to J. B. S. Hardman, who
was eventually elected a member of the Party's central committee.
Hardman was then editor of the *Advance,* official organ of the Amalgamated Clothing Workers. Thin, stoop-shouldered and nearsighted,

he looked the typical nineteenth century idealist, one who might have belonged to Herzen's circle. His face and voice were gentle; his mind had the subtlety, insight and softness of the man of letters grieving in the jungle of practical politics. In speech and political conduct he was cautious and elliptical; in personal relations, extremely sympathetic, especially toward young people just entering the movement. On hearing that I wrote verses, he smiled indulgently and said that in his early twenties he had, like Socrates, studied sculpture. Then he added that he also had commanded a detachment of armed workers in the Odessa uprising of 1905.

Hardman was given to penetrating paradoxes. When a young writer would say, "I don't know whether to stay at home and finish my novel, or enter practical revolutionary work," he would smile and reply, "Ah, you have a choice; then you are not free." Ironic paradox was possibly his defense against the anomalies of his own situation. He was trying to reconcile his devotion to the revolutionary movement as he understood it with his attachment to the conservative trade-union bureaucracy by which he was employed, and both with a humanistic interest in art and literature. Failing to find the necessary synthesis, he was compelled to move in all three realms as if he were dancing with bare feet on coals of fire, a living example that personal values like sweetness and liberality of spirit are seldom political virtues. In the field of education, however, they may be virtues; and it was in this field that Hardman was at his best. With workers' groups he was a patient and effective teacher. Whether what he taught was always or even fundamentally correct is another matter. He conducted classes for the needleworkers of the Amalgamated, and occasionally invited Mac to lecture to them on science or history, and myself on literature.

Often I visited Hardman and Mac, who was now his assistant, at the offices of the Amalgamated. There I met labor and radical politicians of various shades of opinion. It was when I shared their political ideas most fully that I felt the distance which separated the politician as a type from the poet as a type. It seemed that for all his orations, statements and interviews, the politician, regardless of the class he represented, could not function effectively without reticence; while the poet, reactionary or radical, however taciturn he might be in personal contact, could not function without utterance. The politician must conceal, the poet reveal. Yet from the response of the Amalgamated workers at my lectures it was evident that it made a great difference to an audience what the poet revealed. When I recited Walt Whitman,

the workers always applauded his chants to liberty; when I read aloud
Ezra Pound or T. S. Eliot, they fidgeted in their seats and looked out
the windows of the Rand School lecture hall.

"You know, comrade," a presser said to me, "this fellow Eliot is
more complicated than the Talmud. Whitman I can understand, but
this Prufrock business, if you'll excuse me, I can't make head or tail
from it. Maybe I'm dumb, just a plain presser, but then why can I
understand Whitman?"

The matter was as painful as it was simple. The creator of Apeneck Sweeney was a barrier between the workers in my class and
myself. The barrier must be destroyed. Eliot must be explained. But
the more I explained, the more the workers felt that the ideas and
feelings of the vorticists were remote from their daily struggle for
bread, their dream of a classless society. And alas, even Whitman
could make trouble. You declaimed with a full heart and a loud voice
the great American poet's declaration of faith:

> I accept reality, and dare not question it;
> Materialism first and last imbuing.
> Hurrah for positive science! long live exact demonstration!

What could be simpler? Materialism, slogans, exclamation points,
almost like a manifesto. But the comrade in back of the hall, the pale-
faced, unshaven, stooped old tailor who had fought in many strikes,
had followed De Leon and Debs and now followed Lenin, rose to his
feet dissatisfied. Imagine, he tries to heckle Whitman. Comrade, will
positive science, will exact demonstration *by itself* bring the masses of
humanity freedom? What about science in the recent war, comrade?
What about poison gas, submarines, high explosives—instruments of
death which science fashioned? And what about science in modern
industry? What about the speed-up, the conveyor, all those efficiency
tricks that convert the worker into an automaton and throw him out
of his job? O.K., comrade, long live exact demonstration, if you like,
but get down to brass tacks: would not science be more beneficial to
mankind in a socialist society?

"But, comrade," you argued, "we are discussing poetry."

"A fine thanks to you," the old tailor said ironically. "The poet
tells us the sky is blue and the grass is green. All right, we are imprisoned in the sweatshop and don't get a chance to see the living world,
so it's good to be reminded once in a while that the sky is blue and
the grass is green. But if we are lucky enough to have a poet like Whit-

man who hollers hooray for positive science, you should draw the proper conclusions from that. Whitman recognizes that poetry will progress if it understands science; and we must recognize that science will progress when it is part of socialism."

In addition to lectures on literature, Hardman assigned me to teach elementary English to a group of foreign-born workers in Brownsville. These were animated by the American dream which stirred our neighbors of the slum when we first came to this country. Bourgeois ideas molded not only the middle classes, the realtors, doctors, lawyers, dentists and professors with whom I had grown up, but the proletariat itself. The average worker wanted to get ahead under the present system. He imagined that he could individually fight his way out of his class. If he failed, his son, at least, would be a teacher, a druggist, a fiddler—anything but a worker. One old tailor in my literary classes was among the exceptions; most workers were not aware of their role in contemporary history. They were not, as we said, class conscious. They would support the system as long as it gave them something, even the smallest crust of bread. All the more important, then, the role of the working-class party, which saw the historic process as a whole, and directed the workers' struggles for immediate needs—higher wages, shorter hours, better working conditions—into fundamental channels. The communist believed there was a way out of slavery, and most of the slaves did not know it. It was the task of the communist propagandist to acquaint him with the facts. The textbook I used in this class was the *Communist Manifesto*. At first my students were interested chiefly in the externals of spelling and sentence structure. The workers stepped up to the blackboard, poised the chalk in the air for a few moments thoughtfully and scrawled:

All previous historical movements were movements of minorities, or in the interest of minorities. The proletarian movement is the self-conscious, independent movement of the immense majority, in the interest of the immense majority.

They turned to me in pride or uncertainty; they wanted to know whether they were learning to write English. But soon they became interested in the theme of their textbook. From spelling and grammar we moved to economics and politics, from the *Communist Manifesto* to discussions of their immediate problems in the shop, of the prevailing wage cuts and unemployment, of various parties and their programs.

§ 4

When Louis wrote me, "come to work in the Party press," I naturally thought of the *Liberator*. Time and experience had modified to some extent my romantic notions about the group around that literary oracle, yet even now they seemed to represent all that was best in American culture and in the revolutionary movement. For me, as for thousands of others, the magazine *was* the Party press, especially during the war when most other radical publications were suppressed. During 1920-1921 such copies as reached me in Europe revealed that the artists and writers around the *Liberator* had openly identified themselves with communism. The magazine now carried on an energetic campaign on behalf of class-war prisoners. In the issue of December, 1920, a young journalist named Art Shields outlined the salient facts of the Sacco-Vanzetti case, then at its beginning, and added prophetically: "The Department of Justice seems intent upon killing two innocent men." Editorially the magazine kept up a persistent defense of the Soviet Republic and the Communist International, at a time when these had few partisans among the war-weary radical intellectuals. The arguments about Soviet Russia, pro and con, were to be repeated by both sides for the next fifteen years essentially unaltered, although individual apologists for sovietism and capitalism were to cross over from one side of the fence to the other.

I visited the editorial offices of the *Liberator* at the invitation of Max Eastman, who had just accepted some of my verses for publication. The magazine was then located in a three-story red brick house on West Thirteenth Street, a few doors from the *Dial,* where Van Wyck Brooks, Kenneth Burke and Lewis Mumford were developing another school of American letters. The first floor was occupied by Roger Baldwin and the American Civil Liberties Union; the second by the general offices of the magazine; the third, consisting of four small rooms, by the private offices of the editors. From the windows facing the back yard you could see the dying autumn grasses; from the front windows, the quiet street and the white church on the other side.

Max Eastman appeared in loose gray tweeds, a bright-colored necktie, and a sleepy, sensuous smile. I had not seen him since the People's Council convention in 1917. He was still handsome, with his soft pink face and prematurely white hair. In our brief talk, he explained why he thought the socialist revolution in America was at least fifty years away.

Eastman invited me to dine with him, and several days later I went to his house on St. Luke's Place. There I found the charming Negro poet Claude McKay, whom Eastman had discovered and published that year. At that time, the radical editor had a warm interest in younger writers; he stimulated their work and called the public's attention to it. He did not use poetry as filler, but would devote a whole page to a single poet's verses, a policy which won him the warm affection of younger writers.

The dinner passed in trivial gossip. Soon the phone rang and Eastman answered it. His voice began to shake with agitation. He hung up the receiver, seized his coat and hurried out. For the next two hours, McKay, tropical and witty, argued that the best art had always been propaganda. Toward midnight, Eastman returned, pinker than ever. He handed us cigars, lit one himself, stretched comfortably in an easy chair and said with a persuasive whine in his voice:

"Well, poets, what are you disputing?"

We said art and propaganda. Eastman released his long legs across the carpet and expounded the ideas I had read in his *Enjoyment of Poetry,* in Walter Pater, and in Immanuel Kant, the godfather of those who, observing that aesthetic experience is characterized by enjoyment, assume erroneously that enjoyment is divorced from all other experience.

Several nights later, I was eating alone by the dim light of a dripping candle in a Village restaurant called Three Steps Down. The door opened. A man came in and sat down at a nearby table. The more I looked at his thin, translucent, sensitive face, with its large eyes and 1890 sideburns, the more familiar it seemed. I leaned over and said:

"Excuse me, aren't you Floyd Dell?"

"I am," he said cordially. "How did you know?"

"From your picture in the papers."

Something in Dell's personality broke down all barriers at once. I felt at home, convinced that there was nothing you could not say to this man. I proceeded to say what was on my mind, and he listened sympathetically. He consoled me about my internal conflicts. They were typical, he said, of the contemporary "intelligentsia."

The word "intelligentsia," European in origin and rather pretentious, did not strike me as strange; it crept into our conversation again and again, as did that other European word "literati." For want of precisely defined American terms, we resorted to these words in that period to describe writers, artists, economists and journalists who were more or less "advanced" in their ideas.

It was very soothing to discover that my troubles were characteristic of a social group which I imagined embodied the finest aspects of American culture. But what did the "intelligentsia" do about its conflicts?

"Have yourself psychoanalyzed," Dell urged. "It's the only thing to do. Everybody is being psyched these days. You will unravel your complexes and thus overcome them. You will relive your life, discover its secret pattern, and learn to direct it consciously. Confession has always been good for the soul; now we have a scientific confessional whose catharsis liberates us from the tyranny of our unconscious fears and taboos."

When he had finished his dinner, Dell invited me to his room at the Brevoort.

"I live in Croton," he explained, "but I am staying in town this week. My wife is in the hospital. She has just presented me with a son."

I congratulated him. He was obviously very happy, and under ordinary circumstances the matter would have ended there. But so utopian was the agitation of the radical intelligentsia in those days over questions of love and marriage that a blessed event was an occasion for cursed disputes. What in most cases was a private venture became, in the case of an apostle of freedom, almost a public scandal. For years Floyd Dell had promulgated the "free union" as a solution for the Sexual Crisis in our epoch; he had, so to speak, set Isadora Duncan's nude body on a pedestal beside Darwin, Marx, Nietzsche and Whitman. Then, like a bolt from the blue, he not only got married but came out in print in defense of marriage and babies. When I came to *Liberator* circles that fall, Greenwich Village was continuing in cafés, studios and, no doubt, elsewhere the debate it had heard in public between Michael Gold championing free love and Floyd Dell championing marriage.

Some of the more extreme Villagers looked upon Dell as not much better than a "renegade" to the cause of the New Freedom in sex. It was all right for him to get married. Many radicals were married; so were most of the *Liberator* editors. Even anarchists were known to submit their free unions to the blessings of City Hall, which they

damned in theory as a part of the tyrannical state. Dell's case was said
to be different; in addition to marrying in practice, he now approved
of marriage in *theory*. This was almost as if William Z. Foster had
come out openly in favor of private profit. It meant practically the
sexual counterrevolution. By the laws of dialectic, this attitude of the
extremists drove Dell, always in search of logical consistency, to a persistent apologia for the institution of marriage.

The night I met him, however, Dell did not feel a bit apologetic.
He was happy and proud over the birth of his son, and talked freely
and magnificently about that and everything else. Although he had
already begun his self-imposed exile in the suburbs, he retained a keen
intellectual interest in the revolutionary movement, and said that art,
to be vital, must reflect that movement. He believed that the artist, in
order to reach the masses of the proletariat, would someday have to
resort to the poster, the billboard, the movie and even the radio, then
beginning to roar its inanities through America's cities. He made it
clear that as a citizen he would always be interested in the political
destinies of mankind; as an artist he would find in his political hopes
a stimulus to creative effort. But as an artist he felt now a desire to
detach himself from the immediate and daily anxieties of the political
situation, to renew his contact with the ageless and timeless aspects of
nature. On the first anniversary of the Armistice, he had written a
poem saying:

> War and peace—peace and war—that is all I know:
> Shall I never see birds as I saw them long ago?

He, too, sought escape in Eternity from the relentless pressure of
Time. In his case, Eternity was the illusory remembrance of the prewar past whose naïve peace was not to return again in our age.

§ 5

A weekly bourgeois magazine paid me a good salary for the technical job of make-up man. I did not like technical work, and in my
spare time attended *Liberator* staff meetings. These meetings were
very informal, more like studio parties than business conferences. Max
Eastman, when he wasn't occupied elsewhere, usually presided with
the nonchalance of a gracious hostess pouring tea. The atmosphere
was strictly intellectual, however. Nothing was poured out for us except words. There were arguments, compromises, postponements. Mike
Gold got sore at Claude McKay, and Claude got sore at Mike, and

Bill Gropper got sore at both, but Max purred and petted like a warm-hearted mother, and the boys cooled down, and somehow the magazine came out. It was all like a family, in which the inevitable disputes were smoothed out in affection. It was probably this family atmosphere which enabled me to become part of the *Liberator* group by a kind of osmosis. There was no red tape or political machinery or simple business organization. Mike Gold brought me to staff meetings, and then I brought Robert Smith, exactly the way you invited your friends to dine with you at your parents' home. In this way I began to write verses, book reviews and features for the paper before I formally joined its staff.

Once the editors sent me to interview a group of American workers going off to Siberia to settle in the Kuzbas coal region. A decade earlier, I thought, Russian workers had come to America to seek opportunities for a better life. Now they were returning to the country from which they had fled to find it transformed by the revolution. With them went many native American workers. The Golden Realm had moved six thousand miles, to that land which had once been the prison of the peoples. Workers' eyes were turning hopefully from west to east.

On one painful point I found the *Liberator* office especially soothing. Most of the editors were native, Nordic Americans like Max Eastman, Floyd Dell, Robert Minor, Art Young, Boardman Robinson, and Lydia Gibson. Yet no racial or national distinctions ever appeared between them and the Jewish poet Michael Gold, the Negro poet Claude McKay, or the Italian poet Arturo Giovannitti. Traditional racial barriers were transcended not only in the common work of the publication and in personal friendship, but even in the more intimate relations of love and marriage. I felt that on a small scale the *Liberator* group represented that ideal society which we all wanted, that society in which no racial barriers could possibly exist.

I felt this same freedom at Floyd Dell's house in Croton, where I now began to spend frequent week-ends. Here ideas flowed without reserve, false shame, class or racial prejudice. We fancied ourselves disinterested devotees of art, revolution and psychoanalysis. All of these seemed indiscriminately to point the way to universal human freedom from external oppression and internal chaos.

At this time, Croton-on-Hudson was a kind of literary and political shrine. The sacred grove was a stretch of brown hilly earth known as Mt. Airy Road, on both sides of which, separated by an acre or two of land, stood the homes of John Reed, Boardman Robinson, Lydia Gibson, Floyd Dell and Stuart Chase. The old *Masses,* which had once influenced me as an abstract concept, was now a reality of roofs, walls, windows, chairs, bookshelves and, most important of all, living men and women.

As abstract concepts, these writers and artists had formerly molded my notions about American society. Now their suburban colony was my first real contact with the American landscape. My boyhood had been spent almost entirely in the city. In the summer my friends and I had fled from the broiling slums to the sloppy sea at Coney Island. Prospect Park had been our nearest approach to nature on this side of the Atlantic. Later, at the university, we sometimes spent a Sunday on the Jersey side of the Palisades around a bonfire over which we toasted marshmallows or roasted frankfurters—a more romantic setting, we imagined, for reading Swinburne and E. E. Cummings and T. S. Eliot than the smoke-filled rooms which we crowded at night in the metropolis. In Europe we got to know the French, English and Italian countryside, especially the landscape of the English romantic poets. Noyes' Kew in lilac time, Keats' Hampstead Heath and Rupert Brooke's Granchester moved me more than the Mississippi Valley now spreading its broad plains over American literature. This was a failing common to all romantics. At any rate it was typical of Greenwich Village romantics to whom the literary image was more actual than the reality it mirrored, who ordered their own lives into a chaotic pattern on the basis of the books they read and the poems they remembered. It was some time before I realized that Croton was only a suburb of Washington Square.

Despite my shyness at this period, despite internal conflicts and irritations, I felt at home there because of Dell's genius for friendship with younger people. In literature the poet of the moon-calf, in life he was father confessor to dozens of moon-calves to whom he opened his house, gave time and energy, literary and material help, to whom he talked with that profusion of ideas, that wealth of information, that brilliance for which he was famous in the prewar Village. There was not a problem which puzzled us, in that confused and painful transition from adolescence to manhood, from an old culture to a new one, which he did not discuss with us with boundless frankness, with a profound knowledge of men and books, and a sympathetic understanding of our troubles. And since he was one of those men who talk better than they write, we learned more from his conversation than from his books, which seemed to us to become progressively weaker as he drifted from the essay to the novel, as he prolonged his absence from the city and from the revolutionary movement.

Remembering the ghetto and the furnished rooms in which I had lived, Dell's home, simple and unpretentious, seemed like a magic little world retaining all that was best in the tradition of Greenwich Village. That tradition shone from the orange curtains at the windows, Nordfeldt's portrait of Dell as a young man, the walls lined from floor to ceiling with books. From the moment I arrived on Saturday afternoon we talked. Our conversation continued until three or four in the morning, was resumed at Sunday breakfast and went on through the day till three or four the following morning.

Long before I knew him in person, Dell had attracted me as the brightest exponent of "art and revolution." He had defended the working class, the October Revolution, Lenin, Haywood, Debs; he had explained literature from a social viewpoint; he had tried to apply the findings of psychoanalysis to our own lives. Now, week-end after week-end, he sat in his armchair, lit one Richmond Straight Cut after another—the hardest cigarette to keep alive—and his sensitive pale face, accentuated by the sideburns cultivated in his Village days, would shine with thought as he expounded these ideas to a circle of friends.

Dell was not, in the strict sense, a conversationalist. He was not fond of repartee and the short sally. Usually he sat in silence as the small talk dribbled on until the moment when gossip touched on a general problem. Then he would cross-examine a guest by the Socratic method, and finally, like Socrates, launch forth on a long monologue. Often that monologue developed ideas with which we disagreed, but it was never dull. The bohemian habit of unrestricted talk, gay and prolonged, had been transported to Floyd's living room. Outside there were probably trees and hills and skies, but we seldom saw them. For forty-eight hours we stayed within bounds, drinking dozens of black coffees, smoking innumerable cigarettes, talking. Occasionally, at the prompting of Mrs. Dell, blond, husky, genial and imperious, we would go for a brief walk down the long hill leading to the village, whose inhabitants turned to look at Floyd's black, broad-brimmed felt hat and heavy black opera cape of the nineties, relic and symbol of la vie de bohème.

At one of these Croton week-ends I met, for the first time, one of our early literary heroes, Upton Sinclair. He was short, stocky, bronzed by the Pasadena sun, and he talked endlessly with extraordinary self-assurance and energy. Stretched out on his belly along the floor, he lectured for an hour on his latest cure-all for mankind's ills, the electronic theories of Dr. Abrahams then sweeping California in a neck-and-neck race with swamis, diet cures, real estate bonanzas and mystic shrines. The guests listened to Upton as to an oracle, without criticism and without question. When he was through, only Lydia Gibson (the handsome and talented wife of Robert Minor) dared to kid Sinclair on his latest fad. After dinner, Lydia turned on the phonograph and suggested that we dance; but Dell, himself a dance enthusiast, called us aside and asked us not to dance while Sinclair was there. Lydia turned to Sinclair himself: good heavens, why? The novelist explained at great length that dancing was immoral because it was nothing more than a form of sex play. It's not true, we said; or true so remotely that it is practically unimportant. And, suppose dancing is a form of sex play, what of it? Sinclair's puritanism was obdurate; in regard to alcohol and sex his views approached those of the Methodist Church, though his rationalizations were different.

§ 6

The group around the *Liberator* was not alone in its criticism of prevailing ideas and mores. Liberals also complained. In the spring of 1922 there appeared *Civilization in the United States* written by thirty intellectuals and edited by Harold Stearns, the generalissimo of the younger sophisticates of that period. The thirty papers concentrated on one question: why did American civilization frustrate talent? The almost unanimous answer was that American life was drab, standardized, without joy or color, crippled by the worship of money and machinery. The book was a cerebral version of *Main Street*. The American intellectual was a Carol Kennicott whose artistic soul was wrecked by the overpowering mores of the Babbittry. But the intellectuals had learned the lesson of Carol Kennicott's defeat; they were not going to compromise with Main Street. There was another way out, though not in America. Only in Europe, chiefly in the Paris which my own circle had just left in disappointment, was there the culture fit for an American aesthete frustrated at home by the power of money and machinery. Harold Stearns said so not merely in print but in melodramatic gesture. On completing the manuscript of the collective indictment of American civilization, he fled from that civilization to Paris, followed by a host of younger writers from the Village. Our divergence from the "30 intellectuals" was expressed by Michael Gold, assigned to review their indictment.

"I turn over these pages carelessly," Mike wrote, "and the faint, acrid aroma of intellectual irony, cool as pine needles, breathes from them."

Mike felt he was not competent to review such a book; he was frankly "too prejudiced" against it even to read it through. But he astutely guessed its central idea; he was willing to wager "a baked apple at Childs, with cream," that fully one-half of the thirty intellectuals called for a spiritual aristocracy that would hold itself aloof from the sordid life of the nation, and create a great, free, cosmic Art and Culture, antiseptic and above the battle. That was all that American intellectuals had discovered about America, Mike concluded. He had discovered other things, he felt. There were millions of poor people in this nation who worked too hard and were slaves to the payroll. They were the vast majority here—they were the nation. They had no time to think or lead full-orbed lives. The trouble with the poor was their poverty. And the trouble with the intellectuals was that they were bourgeois, said Mike Gold.

This was the essential difference between the revolutionary writers and those who criticized the surface of bourgeois society without repudiating its basis. It was not a question of individual intelligence or character; we had personal friends among the "30 intellectuals" whom we liked and admired. It was a question of class viewpoint. We saw the world from the camp of the proletariat and could not help noticing things to which the official literary world and the rising generation of aesthetes were blind. The *Liberator* made the mistake of ignoring T. S. Eliot's *The Waste Land,* which appeared at this time but which we did not review; yet in literary circles we alone consistently devoted the pages of our publication to the Sacco-Vanzetti case, the partition of China by the imperialist powers, the oppression of Haiti by American bankers, the Garvey movement among the Negroes, the Mexican Revolution, the wage-cut campaign in this country. At the moment when liberal writers sought wisdom at the shrine of Eliot, Pound, Proust and Joyce, Michael Gold was reporting the coal strike in Pennsylvania and the clothing workers' convention in Cleveland; and Mary Heaton Vorse and John Dos Passos sent us eyewitness accounts of life in the new Russia. Later the two literary tendencies were to meet on more or less common ground under the crushing effects of a great economic crisis; but that meeting was ten years off. In the spring of 1922 we were isolated from the "main stream" of American literature, dominated by the middle classes, because of our preoccupation with the class struggle. The American tragedy, we felt, lay not in the garishness, vulgarity and drabness of Main Street. That was a by-product. The tragedy of America was the tragedy of the whole of capitalist civilization; it lay in the division of society into exploiters and exploited; and since the prevailing art ignored this central fact of contemporary civilization, we tended to despise that art as blind, trivial and stupid, and to damn it as "bourgeois."

The verses of T. S. Eliot seemed irrelevant to the strike wave that was sweeping America. There were now more workers on strike and the strikes were of longer duration than ever before in the country's history. These strikes were revolts against the organized campaign by industry and finance to destroy labor organizations. The workers were fighting to maintain groups and rights which they had painfully won through years of sanguinary struggle. The employers did not conceal their objective. The open-shop campaign was openly advertised throughout the country. It was war with all the instruments of war, soldiers and spies included.

In April, the very month in which the literati were debating the indictment of the "30 intellectuals," more than half a million coal miners left the pits in protest against the attempt of the coal operators to cut wages. A general strike followed. Again the government openly revealed itself as an integral organ of the propertied classes. It declared that if there had to be a strike, the sooner the issue was disposed of the better. Governor Sproul of Pennsylvania called a conference of sheriffs and instructed them to "suppress all revolts before they start." The state constabulary was vested with police authority. Squads of them were scattered throughout the anthracite belt, equipped with riot clubs, well-trained horses, pistols and machine guns. This was the "Americanism" of the employers, who handed over the lives of their wage slaves to armed thugs. Arms and ammunition were shipped to the National Guard of Ohio which was assigned to aid the coal operators. The West Virginia constabulary was drilled for strike duty even before a strike was called in that state; and a local federal judge issued an injunction against the United Mine Workers making it illegal to strike in West Virginia. On June 16th a detachment of 1,200 mounted police attacked 8,000 miners on parade, wounding a number of the strikers. Later Governor Sproul sent 1,100 militiamen into the bituminous district to guard scabs. This was the government's reply to the miners whose leaders had declared in 1919 that they could not "fight our government."

On the *Liberator* we voted to send Mike Gold to Pennsylvania to cover the strike. He came back with a piece of colorful and stirring reporting in the tradition of John Reed. Revolutionary reportage gave the proletarian poet a chance to exercise his creative imagination in telling the literal truth. Bourgeois reporting was often false because it concealed basic facts and distorted the essence of a story. It pretended to be impartial while actually propagating a class viewpoint. A news story was not supposed to editorialize; yet by a judicious selection of the facts, by the suppression of everything vital to the truth, it did mold the reader's opinion in the interests of the propertied classes. Revolutionary reportage like John Reed's or Michael Gold's openly avowed its class viewpoint. It wove into one living and moving story the sensuous details of the scene, things observed and heard, the appearance of the men and women involved, the economic, social and political factors in the situation. The specific and the general, the sensuous and the abstract were co-ordinated into a unified composition, and the writer frankly commented and editorialized on the events he described. He gave meaning to the facts; he interpreted the movement of events, damned the oppressors, recorded the thoughts of the workers, exhorted his reader to action.

Mike Gold's story of the Pennsylvania strike contrasted bourgeois with revolutionary reporting.

"In all the newspapers," the poet said, "this great coal strike was now being discussed. Everyone knew the academic questions involved in the situation. The miners and the bosses had an agreement that expired on April 1st, when it was provided that they meet to make another wage agreement for the following two years. The operators had refused to renew the agreement. They wanted to make local settlements in each of the separate districts. They wanted to abolish the check-off; they wanted to cut wages; they wanted other concessions. That was the faint, far-off newspaper story millions of Americans read, half-understanding, half-irritated because the miners and the operators could not iron out these tiny quarrels that after all amounted to nothing. But they amounted to everything in the world for these men in this Brownsville union headquarters. Here were the men who made the strike a reality. These miners 'knew' the facts. Big, strong men in overalls, jumpers, flannel shirts, hobnailed boots, men of ten or twelve races, Lithuanians, Poles, Italians, Austrians, Croatians, Slavs, Negroes,

Welsh, British and Americans—bold men, men who faced death every day in the hot, dripping, airless mines; men with mutilated hands, powder-marked faces; these men had formed a union to get them a living wage for their wives and children, and to protect them against the gunman, the thug and the spy. They had fought for that union, and their fathers had fought before them. The union was their self-respect; it was their children's bread; and now the bosses were making a fierce new attempt to smash it."

There was emotion in Mike Gold's reporting, but it was emotion justified by the facts. The facts were as he stated them: the great coal strike of 1922 was a struggle for the very existence of the miners' union. Toward the end of the spring, the Southern Illinois Coal Company attempted to open a strip mine in Herrin with strikebreakers imported from the Chicago slums. The idea was to break the solid front of the striking miners. Armed professional scabs were taken into the mine; others stood guard outside. On June 21st a group of unarmed strikers approached the mine; they wanted to persuade the operators and the strikebreakers to abandon the work. As they neared the mine, the superintendent and his gunmen opened fire. Two strikers were killed. Early next morning hundreds of miners from all over the county marched on the mine. This time they were armed. They surrounded the mine. The guards opened fire. In the *Liberator* we published an eyewitness account of the pitched battle that followed.

"Until dark firing was intermittent. A searchlight at the mine was turned upon the attackers. A rush was made to disconnect the power lines. A rush was made over the barbed wire and breastworks which had been erected. An airplane was fired upon by machine guns from the mine. Shortly after the airplane had flown overhead a white flag was raised by the men in the mine. A truce was arranged. The flag had been up but a short time when several of the armed men who hoisted it reopened fire. When it was seen that the flag of truce was being used as a ruse, it was decided that no quarter would be granted. The screams of the injured men in the pits could be heard above the roar of battle and a voice shouted to the men that the first man to attempt to leave the pit would be shot. At daybreak the attackers formed in column. They worked their way into the stronghold and captured those who remained alive."

Nineteen scabs and three strikers were killed in this battle. The dead on both sides were buried in the same cemetery. Wounded scabs in the Herrin hospital said they did not blame the miners for attacking them; they had been brought to the mine without being told it was a scab job. The coroner's jury brought in a verdict that "the deaths were due to the acts, direct and indirect, of the officials of the Southern Illinois Coal Company." The jury recommended that "an investigation be conducted for the purpose of fixing the blame upon the individuals responsible." The state of Illinois ignored the findings of the coroner's jury and the Chamber of Commerce collected $100,000 from its members for a campaign of revenge. The state authorities arrested 214 strikers on murder charges, and from Washington President Harding congratulated the Chamber of Commerce on its vendetta and urged it to do "justice." The President was anxious to send federal troops to break the strike. When this plan failed, he appealed to the governors of twenty-eight states to open the mines with scabs, promising them full protection. Governor Sproul of Pennsylvania sent a thousand militiamen into the strike area; Governor McCray of Indiana sent another thousand. The miners replied: "You cannot dig coal with bayonets!" The strike remained a hundred per cent effective. The two sides were deadlocked for months. Starvation depressed the miners. This was John L. Lewis' moment. As in the steel strike of 1919, he stepped forward to aid the operators and the government. The miners were striking for a single agreement to cover both bituminous and anthracite mines. Lewis signed an agreement with the bituminous owners alone. This broke the strike. Six weeks later a separate agreement was signed with the anthracite operators.

The spring of 1922 was one we never forgot. To Haymarket, Homestead, Lawrence, Ludlow, Youngstown and Pittsburgh we now added Herrin in our memory of American labor battles.

§7

That spring Max Eastman sailed for Europe. His first letter to the *Liberator*, written from the S.S. *Olympic*, revealed a hurt soul fleeing for solace to its earliest dreams.

"I sometimes feel"—he said—"as though the whole modern world, capitalism and communism and all, were rushing toward some enormous machine-made doom of the true values of life." He then added wisely: "A very counterrevolutionary feeling!"

Some of us believed that this feeling indicated that Max was emotionally prepared to be at odds with the new Russia which he was going to visit for the first time, and which was setting its face toward the machine age. Several months later, Claude McKay also prepared to leave for Moscow. His resignation left an opening on the *Liberator* staff and I was elected associate editor. This fulfillment of an old desire came in a depressing period. The Harding-Coolidge boom was under way, and with it the deflation of the labor and radical movements. The left-wing intellectuals were particularly affected. The tense romantic mood about the social revolution which had animated them from 1912 to 1921 had collapsed; the era of the Tired Radical had begun. Radicalism was to have its own lost generation. The war and the October Revolution seemed to have drained their social passions dry, and it was easy to be tired on a rising income. To some the bourgeois world appeared more horrible in 1921 than in 1911; the power of capitalism more concentrated, more ruthless; revolutionary hopes less rosy, what with the defeats in Hungary and Germany and the deflation of the labor movement in this country. To others the bourgeois world seemed to have readjusted itself; its politics might be despicable, but there was material comfort, the new art and sex. In Russia, bolshevism appeared to have passed from the "period of poetry" to the "period of prose." Left-wing poets and artists who had been excited by the drama of the ten days that shook the world could not respond to the mathematics of the New Economic Policy. No one on this side of the Atlantic had yet found the poetry for socialist construction, for machinery in the hands of workers transforming the face of the earth. Worse still, there was a faint suspicion, growing stronger day by day, in minds unaccustomed to thinking dialectically that somehow the New Economic Policy was a complete capitulation rather than a temporary retreat preceding a great advance.

This mood crept through my own generation as well as that of our elders. From Montreal, where he was recuperating after his European travels, Benjamin, who had been the first communist on the campus, wrote me:

"These last two years have made a profound difference in the case of us young men who sought to storm the walls of privilege armed with no other weapons than the trumpet of idealism. Within that time, the Russian Revolution has been slowly vanquished and its fall has sapped the faith of millions who have been thrilled by the heroic stand of the Prometheus of Moscow. Of these millions, the proletarian wage earners have remained wage earners (or, even worse, have joined the ranks of the unemployed), for they cannot but be absorbed in the problem of their daily bread. But it is the intellectuals, those for whom education and training have reserved a bit of time for the more spiritual things of life, that the disillusionment consequent upon the defeat of communism has struck the heaviest blow. . . . Who of us has learned and what have we learned from the fate of communism in Russia? . . . What about the fundamental premises of communism, that fundamental idealistic romanticism—is that still sound? . . . The experience of Russia these last two years has led some of us to question that premise—which at bottom is more akin to poetry and religion than to philosophy—and we are wondering whether the poor human will, armed with the pitiful armor of our present knowledge of social realities, can do anything else but break its neck when starting revolutions. . . . Have we enough scientific information about society to enable us to make our goodwill effective?"

"The communist revolution," I replied, "has not failed. The trouble with people like you and myself is that we sit in our studies idly speculating about problems which have only a theoretical interest for us. As soon as you get out of your study and get into actual touch with the masses, your theories will begin to look as foolish to you as to them. The fundamental premise of communism is not an idealistic romanticism; only those who approach it in an idealistic, romantic spirit become disappointed cynics and pessimists when they bump up against reality. Consider the evils of capitalism—exploitation, imperialism, militarism, the menace of a new great war which will smash what may still be left of civilization. What is an alternative solution which will be theoretically as sound as communism and have so practical a foothold? Read the *Communist* and you will see that the active revolutionaries are continually adjusting themselves to reality; that Russia is still determined to carry on the revolution; and that the American party is trying to purge itself of all dogma and romanticism."

In spite of this sententious letter, I could not conceal from myself that in the office of the *Liberator* itself the period of revolutionary "prose" was in full evidence. The old group had retired from active journalism. John Reed was buried in a hero's grave under the Kremlin wall; Max Eastman had gone abroad; Floyd Dell had withdrawn to Croton; Bob Minor had abandoned art for practical revolutionary politics; Art Young and Boardman Robinson had left the cartoons to younger men like William Gropper and Hugo Gellert. The new group did not yet have the stature of the old. Bill Gropper, now in his early twenties, was obviously a genius, but still immature, inclined to be flippant at the inopportune moment; his drawings at this early period of his development were funnier than Minor's, which were seldom touched with humor, but for that reason they were also less affirmative, powerful and moving. Mike Gold had more color and passion and identification with the proletariat than most of the men of the older crowd, but lacked their intellectual discipline and precise information. Claude McKay's warm, sensuous, affectionate heart swam in thoughtlessness; he was aggressively antirational on the principle that art comes exclusively from the emotions and that he was primarily an artist. We were all undisciplined and bohemian in those days, all a little confused, especially myself, who was five years younger than Gold and McKay, and new to the movement. There was in the magazine we ran a tepid laissez-faire atmosphere, a gay and nostalgic comradeship which placed a premium on sensibility and emotion and distrusted logic and reason.

To us Mike Gold appeared to be the outstanding "proletarian" of the group. He affected dirty shirts, a big, black, uncleaned Stetson with the brim of a sombrero; smoked stinking, twisted, Italian three-cent cigars, and spat frequently and vigorously on the floor—whether that floor was covered by an expensive carpet in a rich aesthete's studio or was the bare wooden floor of the small office where Gold's desk was littered with disorderly papers. These "proletarian" props were as much a costume as the bohemian's sideburns and opera cape. They enhanced Gold's lovable qualities; his assumed naïveté, dark animated face and deep laughter, and his ironic mode of speech won people easily.

Claude McKay had his office across the hall, in a little room facing the back yard, where he would stretch his body, lithe as a cat's, on the couch under the window, and talk or recite poetry in a low musical voice. Strange bohemians wandered unannounced among the various offices of the editors. The Baroness Elsa von Freytag-Loringhoven, loaded with cheap trinkets and heavily rouged, would invade our headquarters and boom out in a marked German accent her Dadaist verses to Claude, Mike, myself—anyone who would or would not listen—till the thin walls shook with the bizarre stanzas. Bill Gropper, blue-eyed and satirical, would bring in his sketch portfolio which he filled every day with caricatures. The magazine reflected this amiable and pointless life. Each issue was casually got together; the organized punch of the old journal was gone. Occasionally, events revived it. Once Claude McKay, invited to review Leonid Andreev's *He Who Gets Slapped,* received orchestra seats by mail. When he arrived and the theater administration saw that he was a Negro, they shunted him and Bill Gropper to the balcony.

"He who got slapped was I!" Claude exclaimed in the pages of the *Liberator*. "As always in the world-embracing Anglo-Saxon circus, the intelligence, the sensibilities of the black clown were slapped without mercy. I cry my woe to the whirling world, but not in despair. Cherish your strength, my strong black brother. Be not amazed because the struggle is hard and long, O my warm, wonderful race. The fight is longer than a span of life, the test is great. Gird your loins, sharpen your tools! Time is on our side!"

There the matter stopped. No boycott or demonstration was organized against the theater which humiliated a gifted Negro poet and through him his entire people. And who was there to organize such a boycott or demonstration? The Communist party championed the Negro, but no one at this time seriously considered organizing *writers and artists* for political action.

Shortly after this McKay went to Moscow. From there he sent us a photograph of himself surrounded by comrades in the Communist International. Out of the crowd of faces, bearded and clean-shaven, Caucasian and Oriental, I recognized three. Here was Karl Radek smoking a pipe, his wide forehead resting on old-fashioned spectacles, his clean-shaven chin surrounded by a beard that ran around his face like a handkerchief soothing a Russian peasant's toothache. Seated on the floor in front of the group was round-faced Zinoviev looking like the Yiddish actor Boris Tomashevsky. Reclining on the floor in front of him stretched Bukharin in Zinoviev's arms.

§ 8

On the *Liberator* we were at this time already convinced that the revolutionary writer had a definite role in our era and our own American environment. But abstract theories outstripped our practical sense of what was revolutionary in art. With the artists the problem was fairly simple. Most of them drew political cartoons, or at least cartoons which a caption by Mike Gold or myself could make political. Among the writers the problem was wider and more confused. We included in the general undifferentiated mass of "radical" men of letters Floyd Dell and Mike Gold of the old *Liberator* staff; Louis Weitzenkorn and William Soskin, who used to be on the socialist *Call;* liberals like Stuart Chase and Lewis Gannett; new poets like James Rorty, Maxwell Bodenheim, E. E. Cummings, Claude McKay and Lydia Gibson.

We published John Dos Passos' sketches of Soviet Russia, Carl Haessler's report of the Herrin coal strike, Anna Louise Strong's vignettes from Moscow, Stirling Bowen's verses and reports of the class struggle in Detroit; Genevieve Taggard's poems and stories; Gertrude Haessler's correspondence from Japan; Art Shields' analyses of class justice, book reviews by Karl Pretshold, correspondence from Vienna by Frederick Kuh (who was later to become ace European reporter for the United Press) and contributions by Edna St. Vincent Millay and Upton Sinclair, old friends of the magazine.

One of the main tasks which Mike Gold and I faced in 1922 was to find new talent, to develop new revolutionary artists and writers. We cultivated unknown people, younger than ourselves, with striking gifts and were often the first to publish their work. A boy named Louis Riback came in every week with a portfolio of drawings for us to choose from; another named Reginald Marsh sent us sketches of Coney Island, and a youngster named Otto Soglow gave us heavy black and white drawings of the slums, which we proudly described in an editorial note as "strong work, so full of atmosphere, poetry and sensitive observation." From Europe another unknown and extremely gifted artist, Adolph Dehn, sent us satirical drawings of postwar life in Vienna to which we put American captions. A young writer named Pierre Loving interviewed Matt Schmidt for us in San Quentin, and on returning to New York gave us book reviews regularly.

Sometimes new talent came from the most unexpected quarters. One day I received from Washington, D. C., a twenty-page letter in vibrant and lucid prose. The writer said he was partly Negro, but his coloring was so light that he had "passed." He was now employed in the civil service; but a visit to the South on a vacation had suddenly confronted him with the miseries and cruelties inflicted on the race whose blood flowed in his veins. He decided to throw off the mask, to declare openly his solidarity with the oppressed Negroes, to write about their lives. He was enclosing two sketches—*Carma* and *Becky*—one of which began:

> Wind is in the cane. Come along.
> Come leaves swaying, rusty with talk,
> Scratching choruses above the guinea's squawk.
> Wind is in the cane. Come along.

The rest was prose, a powerful and moving story about a Negro gang laborer's wife. The letter and the stories were signed Jean

Toomer, to us an unfamiliar name. I published both stories and corresponded with the author for a while. One day we heard that the police was going to raid all radical publications, the *Liberator* included; I tore up everything in my desk, Toomer's manuscripts and letters too. Later his stories appeared in a book called *Cane*. We never met. I heard of him now and then in literary groups as a very attractive and gifted person lost in the Gourdjiev movement, remote from the struggles of the Negroes who first moved him to high poetic utterance.

From Cologne my boyhood friend Bill Schack sent a piece on "art in starving Germany" in which he praises a play called *Machinenstürmer* by a man of whom we had never heard, Ernst Toller. Simon Felshin, a classmate at the School of Journalism, now flooded us with revolutionary verse. He lifted the John Reed legend from the plane of conversation to that of impassioned Biblical rhetoric:

> O John Reed—
> He had youth and beauty,
> And now he is dead.
> I shook his hand once,
> I saw him smile,
> And I heard him speak
> With the voice of a big boy.
> I introduced him once from the platform
> Calling him Jack Reed.
> And now he is dead.
>
> He brought his great heart to suffering Russia,
> He wanted to heal the wounds,
> And it was the blockade which brought a plague
> And struck down Jack Reed.
> His name is not taught in the schools,
> For he was a rebel.
> The bourgeoisie have not raised a monument for him;
> This they reserve
> For the politicians, the generals, the philanthropists.
> But in Soviet Russia
> Soldiers of the Red Army
> Stood guard over his body.
> The crowds followed his coffin,
> And a woman's heart was bleeding,
> And a woman's eyes were weeping.
> Soldiers of the Red Army—

Tall as he was tall,
Strong as he was strong,
Brave as he was brave,
Marched in his wake.
And they fired the salute over his grave
Beside the Kremlin in Moscow.
His death was a birth.

Perhaps this was not good poetry; but when we recited it at mass meetings, the workers were deeply moved; and we were moved too, despite our literary yardsticks; for the story of John Reed's life and death had already become a living link between the older and younger generations of American revolutionary writers.

§9

Summer brought a surprise. Uncle Laiba, one of my mother's numerous brothers, arrived from Europe to see what prospects there were for settling in America. All these years I had never thought of him. Now everything came back. I recalled the face with the small Russian beard, like the Czar's or Lenin's; and the nights in the vanished village when we played at his house, and my fat good-natured aunt fussed over us because they had no children of their own. She was now in Paris, waiting for news from the Golden Realm, which now seemed to Europeans even more of a paradise than it had two decades earlier. My uncle's beard was now streaked with gray; his eyes deep-sunken and tired; yet, like most of my family, he talked rapidly, with great energy, and with an enormous appetite for knowing everything.

"How time flies!" he said, kissing me. "Yesterday a little boy, and here you are a man. What are you doing with yourself?" I told him. He clapped his hands to his bald head. "No, no, God forbid! You can't be a communist. Have you any idea what monsters these people are? They captured our village. They confiscated my flour mill. I had to flee to Paris. How can you sympathize with such people?"

"How is Uncle Moishe?" I said.

"He fled too. He is in Riga. He runs a bookshop."

"Are you all against the revolution?"

"No," my uncle said bitterly. "Your uncle Mendle is a bolshevik commissar in Briansk. Grandmother lives with him. The revolution has split our family."

I talked about the American Civil War. Great social upheavals break up families. Kind and generous individuals are wrecked in the general wreckage of the old order. Uncle Laiba only shook his head.

"You can't make an omelette without breaking eggs," I said.

"Yes, but I am one of the eggs."

"And pogroms?"

"There you must give the bolsheviks credit. There are no pogroms."

"Isn't that something?" I said. But I knew I should not argue. The most ideal society could not console my uncle for his flour mill. I felt sorry for him, and even sorrier for Uncle Moishe. From a distance the revolution is seen in its finest aspects; the new world shines in contrast to the old. One does not think of the blood and fury that must precede it. When it comes, the middle-class idealist discovers that he does not want it. Why blame Uncle Moishe for running away from that which he preached as a young man? He was not a bolshevik; probably only a middle-class socialist. Look at bigger men, Kautsky and Plekhanov, for years teachers of Marxism, who paved the way for the revolution and turned against it when it came. There must be something wrong in a philosophy which does not prepare you for the hardships and cruelties necessary to alter society. Therein lay Lenin's greatness. I remembered his words: *We are accused of having brought devastation upon Russia. Who is it that makes these accusations? The train-bearers of the bourgeoisie, of that same bourgeoisie that almost completely destroyed the culture of Europe, that has dragged the whole continent back to barbarism, that has brought hunger and destruction to the world. This bourgeoisie now demands that we find a different basis for our revolution, that we shall not build it up upon the ruins of war, with human beings degraded and brutalized by years of warfare.* It will be hard, excruciatingly painful to build the new world; countless fine people would be destroyed in the process. But suppose Uncle Laiba had been killed in a pogrom? in the Russo-Japanese War? Suppose I had been killed on the western front? Bourgeois civilization made the individual's life worthless. If we must die, let us die like men for a cause which is our own. Had not my uncle who was now a commissar risked everything in fighting with the bolsheviks? The flour mill is communal property, making bread for all.

My uncle's disappointment in me received support from an unexpected quarter. One Sunday we took him for a swim at Far Rockaway. On the beach we ran into some friends with whom I had grown up. One of them, who had campaigned with us for Hillquit in 1917, was now a successful doctor.

"We thought you would be a good lawyer," he said to me loftily. "What are you doing?"

"Writing for the communist press."

"Is there dough in it?"

"No."

"Glory?"

"No."

"Then what in hell are you wasting your time for?"

My friends gave Uncle Laiba practical advice. Don't settle in New York; their parents had come here as penniless immigrants and now they had considerable money, but that was the privilege of a few fortunate ones and took years of bitter struggle. Their arguments were strengthened by the government; a ruling adopted in 1921 limited the number of aliens admitted for permanent residence to a certain percentage of their country's citizens already in the United States in 1910. The gates of the Golden Realm were guarded as jealously as the gates of heaven; it was easier for a camel to pass through the eye of a needle than for a poor man to enter America.

My uncle returned to Paris.

CHAPTER II

We were intensely alive; we inflicted blind unintentional cruelties upon those we loved; but there was no meanness and no cynicism in our hearts; and there was beauty, and trust, and candor, and
forgiveness.

—FLOYD DELL.

§ I

NOW the sensuous beauty of the landscape overwhelmed you; the
kisses of your first love haunted you at night, and the memories of
Paris midinettes could not obliterate them. Sex was easy. Scott Fitzgerald had replaced Dr. Landes; the boys and girls of the postwar generation were clever and free. But sex was not enough. To wake up
beside her whom you have wooed, caressed, melted into and find her
a total stranger, alien or even hostile to your deepest thoughts and
feelings—that was fearful, loathsome, degrading. It broke you in two,
body and mind; it threw your whole being into a civil war. No, you
wanted love; someone with whom to share the world undivided: a
friend, companion, comrade as well as female, but without conventional marriage, without the hypocritical intercession of the state,
church and society that you resented. Let her be beautiful and sensual
in body, gifted in intellect, lofty in moral aspiration. Let her be pianist,
painter or poet. Let her write the modern *Frankenstein* while you
wrote the modern *Prometheus Unbound*. Let her scorn the philistine
conventions, despise money, career, marriage, respectability; let her
be an enemy of the established tyrannical order, a socialist, anarchist
or communist. Let her love as you wished to love, out of an uncorrupted heart defying the oppressive mechanics of contemporary society.
In the future, all women would be like that. Love would come only
from the heart. It would have nothing to do with money, family or
the cult of success. At present such women were rare; they were not
to be found in bourgeois society. Church and state, bulwarks of private
property, and the middle-class woman herself, molded by church, state
and private property, broke love on the Procrustean bed of money.

From these fantastic rebellions and sentimental utopias, you turned to Greenwich Village.

In the Village, they said, things were different. For years we had heard of that happy island of "free unions"—where true feeling was unhampered by convention, greed, fear, hypocrisy, career, marriage, money or the sense of guilt. In that new Golden Realm you found the men and women whose writings and drawings you had admired for years, who had called you out of the bondage of convention to the frank and free life. These people, self-exiled to the fringe of society, had a utopian colony which mirrored the future life of men and women, equal in every respect, free to express their highest aspirations.

Yet, because bohemian life in Paris, Italy and London was richer, or perhaps because of puritan hang-overs, I did not at first like what I saw of Greenwich Village. At the beginning I looked upon it merely as the neighborhood where the *Liberator* offices were located. At the earliest opportunity I moved those offices to the Times Square district to prevent them from being the hangout of unoccupied bohemians. To a friend who wrote me from Europe asking whether he should go on to Vienna or come back and settle in the Village, I wrote:

"The Village is nothing but a sewer in which the local bourgeoisie and immigrants from the Middle West discharge their foul suppressions in speech and dance. Apartments eat up a good-sized salary, if you can locate the apartment—and have the salary. Go to Vienna, by all means!"

The high cost of living now impelled writers to go to Europe, into that exile from which they were eventually to return to dominate liberal letters in America.

My first reaction was superficial. Floyd Dell, a Village veteran, assured me that the old bohemia was dead. It had been destroyed by the barbarian invasion from uptown and the provinces. Many of the old bohemians had moved elsewhere and had settled down to support families. The new, postwar Village was full of college boys, tired businessmen, romantic stenographers and unhappy wives who came down Saturday nights to yell themselves hoarse on bootleg gin and to stalk "free love" in the badly lit, foul-smelling, loudly colored caverns with fantastic names like *Purple Pup* and *Pirates' Den*.

Around the Village, however, there still hung the aura of prewar legend. It was supposed to be the Golden Realm of genius, the happy island of art, love and friendship. We still assumed that here man was free to create beauty, and woman to order her life as she pleased. The uniform of the New Freedom included bobbed hair, cigarettes, sandals, batik blouses and Fortuni gowns. A woman could even, like the Baroness Elsa von Freytag-Loringhoven, épater the bourgeoisie by walking through Washington Square Park with an inverted market basket for a hat. This was at once the revolt of the handicrafts against the machine age, and the revolt of the sacred ego against the standardization of Main Street. The Village was a Promised Land where sensitive young men and women from all parts of the country, at odds with their environment for one reason or another, tried to live by the codes of conduct which they thought would one day prevail everywhere. At home they were the insulted and injured; in bohemia, the pioneers of a new order. Such at any rate was the story which had come down to us.

"The generation to which Waldo Frank and I belong," Floyd Dell had written in 1920, "is a peculiar and unhappy generation and I don't wonder that the older generation looks at it askance. It is a generation of individuals who throughout the long years of their youth felt themselves in solitary conflict with a hostile environment. There was a boy in Chicago, and a boy in Oshkosh, and a boy in Steubenville, Indiana, and so on—one here and there, and all very lonely and unhappy. . . . They were idealists and lovers of beauty and aspirants toward freedom; and it seemed to them that the whole world was in a gigantic conspiracy to thwart ideals and trample beauty under foot and make life merely a kind of life-imprisonment. So it was that these youths came to hate and despise the kindly and excellent people who happened to be their elders, and who were merely hard at work at the necessary task of exploiting the vast raw continent which Christopher Columbus had not very long before discovered. This generation had to make, painfully enough, two important discoveries. It has had, in the first place, to discover its own corporate existence, to merge its individual existences together, and get the confidence and courage that can come only from the sense of mass thought and mass action. But the trouble is that each one of us, in our loneliness, has become a little odd, a little peculiar, and more than a little suspicious. . . . Individualism is the very fabric of our lives, we who have brooded too long apart to become without pain a part of the social group to which we belong."

To which group did these people belong? Dell had indicated that they considered themselves a caste apart. On the surface there was an air of classlessness about bohemia. Village life was gay. Perhaps life elsewhere was just as gay, but we did not like that kind of life. It imposed upon us responsibilities which we resented. In the Village responsibility was at a minimum. The poor came to the Village to escape the burdens of poverty, the rich the burdens of boredom. The poor imitated an ideal aristocracy which never existed; they compensated for their material penury by posing as supermen of the spirit, specialists in art, above all the art of "living." The rich pretended their expensive dens in Washington Mews were simple little garrets, like Seneca writing in praise of poverty on a desk of gold. Both groups fled from the drabness of bourgeois existence to the exotic. Certain common preoccupations gave the Village the appearance of classlessness. Washington Mews and MacDougal Street, Mrs. Harry Payne Whitney and the Minna of Bodenheim's verses, Park Avenue and Second Avenue seemed one in bohemia because here everyone talked with equal enthusiasm about art, love and freedom. In so far as the devotees of art, love and freedom were at odds with conventional society they were to some extent allies. You could get only a handful of Village radicals to demand the liberation of Eugene Debs, Tom Mooney or Sacco and Vanzetti; but you could organize a one hundred per cent united front in protest against the suppression of Arthur Schnitzler's novelette about Casanova in his dotage. Debs and Mooney and the Italian martyrs symbolized the class war which interested the average Villager very little; Casanova symbolized the dream that everything is permitted, which interested the average Villager more than anything else in the world. Few bohemians knew Arturo Giovannitti's powerful verses about the lynching of Frank Little and the murder of Karl Liebknecht and his own imprisonment for leading a strike. But everybody recited the verses of Edna St. Vincent Millay, lady-Byron of America's neoromanticism, celebrating candles burning at both ends, houses built on the sand and the endless amours of the frank and free heart.

§ 2

Literary bohemia was by no means as homogeneous as I had assumed in Chelsea. It had its own group divisions and class distinctions. Some of the new friends I now made in Greenwich Village kept themselves alive by ghosting or other hackwork; in spare moments they created that "real" art which was one day to place them in the company of the elect. Others were successful professionals, who earned large incomes in the employ of popular magazines or through the nation-wide sale of their books. What these successful professionals wrote met the demand of the market; and it was on the market that they concentrated their attention rather than on vague abstractions like "truth" and "beauty."

A writer who reached this pinnacle of success became remarkably like a businessman in appearance, dress, taste, conversation and moral and intellectual standards. He talked little about "art" and a great deal about royalties. He was sensible—that is, conservative—in his politics. He had a house in the suburbs, drove an expensive car, played golf, joined clubs; in short, he did everything which he had professed to despise in his bohemian youth of painful struggle. Literature was for him a business, like real estate. His pride of achievement came not from the story truly told but from the large income earned, a fact which resulted in a warm mutual understanding between the successful businessman and the successful writer. Because of this economic standard, the successful writer was less devoured by the vanity of authorship than the impoverished beginner fighting his way from the little "art" magazines to the *Saturday Evening Post*. The Success was socially established. His neighbors did not always read his stories; but they respected his golf score, his new porch, his Packard. Hence the Success cared little about his literary standing or about fame. He often wrote under a pseudonym—his trademark. Occasionally he came back to the Village, like the Old Grad visiting alma mater on a gala occasion. At a *Liberator* ball his immaculate and sober dress suit stood out among the red, yellow and green rags of the pirates, gypsies, hoboes and cave men.

For the Failure who remained in the Village as a permanent resident there were no economic satisfactions. His pride could be assuaged only by fame. Hence the acrimonious eye with which he regarded the rivals who strove with him for the attention of his little world. He lived in a dirty, unheated, sunless room; wore old clothes; ate irregularly in the cheapest cafeterias, and made a virtue of these necessities, saying they were the essential condition of true art. When he attacked the Success, it was as the handicraftsman attacks the factory producer. The Success was glutting the market with adulterated goods which corrupted the public taste. The handmade output of the True Artist was superior to the machine-made output of the *Saturday Evening Post* —until that day when the handicraftsman of letters himself entered the process of mass production as a newspaper columnist, a popular magazine writer or the author of ten easy lessons in philosophy, science or history.

For some reason, vanity of authorship was most acute among people who already had money and could not write at all: businessmen anxious to add the spice of "culture" to their financial success; society ladies anxious to distinguish themselves from the conventional hostess; movie actresses anxious to appear as intelligent as they were beautiful; illiterate brigadier generals anxious to decorate their careers with memoirs which they could place on their library shelves beside those of Napoleon; men of the world anxious to add a book to their stock of aphrodisiacs. Such people supplied the capital and sometimes the raw material.

The Ghost Writer, prolet of the literary world, supplied the labor. Anonymous as a factory worker, the Ghost Writer sat down at his typewriter and sweated out the economic treatise, the autobiography, the volume on the immortality of the soul, the military chronicle, or the novel which the businessman, society leader, movie star, brigadier general or Lothario signed with much more alacrity than the check which they reluctantly handed the writer. The factory worker stood with his friend before the billboard advertisement flaunting the name of his absentee employer and said with bitter pride, "I made that automobile." The Ghost Writer could share only with a few intimate friends the secret that he wrote every word of the volume for which the press lauded Mrs. Vanderpip.

The Ghost Writer's economic satisfactions were those of a skilled worker; the satisfactions to his vanity could be only those of an international spy whose successes are of necessity concealed. Occasionally, Mrs. Vanderpip might drop a discreet note, secret and confidential, to the anonymous Ghost: "How proud you must have been to read the enthusiastic reviews of *our* book." At cocktail parties she always referred to *my* book, as a manufacturer refers to *my* car. By the laws of the literary market, a section of the capitalist market in general, these people were justified. The Ghost had nothing to sell but his literary skill, his labor power, with which the world is flooded, thanks to the spread of education and the monopoly of the literary market; whereas Mrs. Vanderpip or the businessman or the Lothario had, to begin with, the raw material, the confession, the gossip, the covert slander which meets the market demand; and, more important still, the trademark, the name obtained through birth, achievement or marriage which, when it appears on even the most mediocre book, opens the purses of the middle class as readily as the well-advertised labels of breakfast foods, cigarettes or automobiles.

§3

Many Villagers lived emotionally in the romantic era of the nineteenth century. An outstanding exponent of that tradition was the poet Harry Kemp. I heard that his parents had gone West in a covered wagon; they had been pioneers in settling the prairies and founding modern industry there. Kemp was born in Youngstown, scene of a historic labor battle. From his pioneering family he retained the American adoration of the man of action. He idealized deeds. But the American pioneer era was closed; there was nothing more for the trail blazer on the trails which had already been blazed. Kemp recoiled from the steel, smoke and class war of Youngstown and came to bohemia to realize another dream. Against the dirt and brutality and agony of the industrial center he set up the poised sensuous beauty of John Keats.

Tall, ruddy-faced, broad-shouldered, magnetic, Kemp threw his whole personality into "living." In the Village "living" meant an eternal youth of love, alcohol, irregular occupation; gay, boisterous, meaningless, exciting adventures in cafés and studios. Out of this Kemp dreamed of creating beautiful poetry in the romantic tradition; he was going to be the American Keats, and like him would die young. His heroes were chiefly men of the past. The idealized men of action were Sir Walter Raleigh and John Smith; the idealized poets, Keats and Shelley, images of unbounded sensuous joy and unbounded love of the heart. Here was our old dream of the campus—the dream of the "universal man," doer of deeds and maker of beauty. Like our student selves, the Village romantics lived books. Sex itself, the chief element in bohemian "living," required a literary sanction. You began making love with incantations from the romantic poets of past and present. But the illusion was reciprocal. Emotions echoed poetry which you interpreted in the light of your emotions. Shelley was a different image to different people. For Upton Sinclair, the poet meant purity of spirit, sanction for asceticism. For Harry Kemp, the poet meant unrestricted love. Disconnected from reality, the ideal led to painful complications. Mr. Fox ran away with Mr. Cox's wife in the name of the Shelleyan ideal; Mr. Cox resented the romance also in the name of the Shelleyan ideal.

Whatever individual differences the Villagers had, their common bond was a hatred for the environment from which they came. They did not want to attend the Methodist church, the synagogue, the confessional; to enter business or the professions, to settle down to marriage and babies. They were, in my generation at least, young people in their early twenties who wanted to love, to create beauty, to have friendships, to talk, all without the crushing responsibilities which they had escaped.

Free conduct in love was not the monopoly of the Village. Babbitts, too, had more than one woman, and Mrs. Babbitt had her lovers. Nor was gaiety the monopoly of the Village. Young people in their twenties were having a "good time" all over prosperous America. What distinguished the Village was not its actions, but its attitude toward those actions. On Main Street love affairs were clandestine, in the Village they were open. Over the gaiety of the young Babbitts hung the shadow of the Epworth League, the family, the priest. In the Village gaiety was intensified by irresponsibility. Theoretically, we did not hold each other responsible by the conventional code. Sex itself was not the main object, we thought. You could have that in Brooklyn, Chicago, Bronxville or Davenport. But in the provinces you could not talk to your lovers. They were "stupid" and "dull"; that is, they had different notions. They were not interested in art. They did not imagine themselves to be characters in European literature. The flappers of Fitzgerald's novels were frankly sensual; the Village girls were essentially puritanical. They needed literary and artistic sanctions for their emotions; they could love only "superior" men—poets and artists. As a result of the war, many young women now had jobs. They were able to break with their families, to be independent, to lead, as they said, their own lives; and if they were sometimes sexually promiscuous, it was less for the pleasure than for the freedom it seemed to give them. Frustrated on the social plane, the men and women of bohemia sought unhampered sway in sex. At home the father or mother dominated, on the job the boss, in society the politician, in literature the publishers, newspapers and critics. In sex alone was there freedom for those at odds with everything else. In the bedroom the bohemian was monarch of all he surveyed; and since he feared all kinds of domination, the domination of women included, he saw to it that the women he surveyed changed as often as possible. Sex was the one field where the sacred ego could function without restraint.

Occasionally individuals could not live up to the free code of bohemia. A girl promised not to take the affair seriously; but when her lover became interested in someone else she swallowed veronal and turned on the gas. A man said his sweetheart was free to love whomever she wanted, but became bitterly jealous when she loved someone other than himself. Every creed had its renegades, apostates and backsliders. But the creed remained. It was indispensable to people who could not separate real emotion from intellectual rationalization.

In his adulation of the sacred ego, the bohemian wanted above all things to be original. To be *openly* promiscuous in sex distinguished you from the Babbitt you had left behind. But the bohemian went home occasionally. Like the congressman, he reported from time to time to his constituency. Those who shared his disappointment in the life of Main Street, but did not have his courage to break away, looked upon him as a kind of hero and emulated him. Had he remained in Bronxville or Pittsburgh he would have been ostracized for his conduct; as a visitor from the Village he shone with the glamour of the pioneer. There came a moment, thanks to the war, when the stenographers, clerks and schoolteachers who remained on Main Street also had love affairs, drank gin, read forbidden books. Then, to maintain the superiority of his ego, the bohemian sometimes went to still greater excesses. Himself normal organically, he sometimes took to perversions —not because he cared about them, but because the decomposition of bourgeois society after the war set new standards for him to violate. These, however, were rare exceptions; the typical Villager was a romantic and a puritan for whom love was the Great Idea. As for the West European romantics of the French Revolution and later of the Parnassian movement, as for the Russian intelligentsia of Herzen's time and later of the Sanine period, love was for the Villager the realm to which you escaped from a world in which your creative faculties were paralyzed and your political ideals rendered cynical by the greed, drabness, hypocrisy, violence and sterility of bourgeois society.

§ 4

The *Liberator* group was breaking with that society and preparing to enter the revolutionary movement. Yet our thoughts and emotions were largely colored by the romantic tradition in which we had been reared. My notebook at this time recorded in despair: "I am, first of all, a romantic!" But to pose a problem does not by itself solve it. We were unable to find a synthesis between conflicting ideals except abstractly. Still less could we reconcile the doctrines of Marx with the teachings of Freud, both of which appeared equally true.

"Whatever liberties we may gain through political and economic changes," I wrote in the magazine, "there are certain Bastilles erected by life for all of us which only the imagination can batter down, perhaps because these prisons are themselves built out of imagination."

These words echoed the Freudian influence then prevalent in intellectual circles, especially in the Village, which was, for so many neurotics, the No Man's Land between fantasy and reality.

The *Liberator* group held aloof from most Village circles. If we could not damn as a "bourgeois," someone who disagreed with us, we damned him as a "Greenwich Villager." But since bohemia was the refuge of sensitive people seeking to escape the demands of organized bourgeois society in regard to love and money, we were of necessity part of it. The Village represented the advance guard in a struggle against traditional morality, affecting many young people throughout the country. The frank and free life of the Village was the American equivalent of a break with bourgeois ethics which marked the earlier bohemias of Europe. If, in the case of the average Villager, the struggle was waged without thought, in the case of writers and artists it was, as a matter of course, conducted under the banner of "philosophies," weird hedonisms flavored with Freudian sauces especially concocted for the purpose, grated cheese from Arthur Symons and Joris Karl Huysmans, and even alleged proletarian garnitures. Anything we did not like was dismissed as "bourgeois"—regular habits, permanent sexual attachments, steady jobs, or merely keeping one's fingernails clean.

Yet unconventional Greenwich Village had its own strict conventions, enforced by public opinion. The hue and cry raised against Floyd Dell's theoretical defense of marriage was bohemia's protest against the violations of its code. Like all codes, this one produced its own hypocrisies. In the bourgeois world a girl concealed her vices; in bohemia she concealed her virtue. The bourgeois lady, secretly deflowered, marched to the altar pretending to be a virgin; the girl poet or painter, still a virgin, pretended to be a Messalina. Bohemia demanded, whether we liked it or not, that we be Great Lovers.

In such a conflict, conscience plays a decisive role, not the mysterious voice of God or even one's grandmother, but the habits of thought, the emotional patterns implanted by the society in which we have been brought up. In nineteenth century, as well as in postwar, Europe the conflict between "freedom" and "conscience" resulted, under the stress of battle or of a brutal, shabby peace, in a return of the "sinner" to the church, to which he came crawling back on his hands and knees, recanting his former libertarian doctrines and libertine conduct. With us, Protestant self-examination, the Catholic confessional, the Jewish grappling with the "base desire" was replaced by a method which retained much of the aura of religion and art, yet appeared to bear the impersonal hallmark of science. The method was psychoanalysis. If you had not been psychoanalyzed, you were practically a barbarian.

Popular notions of psychoanalysis identified it almost exclusively with sex rather than any of the other problems investigated by the Freudian school. Popularizers of the cult encouraged the idea. A full-page advertisement which we ran on the cover of the *Liberator* announced in large green type that André Tridon's latest book contained AMAZING DISCOVERIES ABOUT LOVE—*the mightiest of all human passions!* "Do you ever dream of your 'ideal' mate? Have you ever been in love with two people at the same time? Have you ever loved a person much older than yourself? Why do certain people attract you and others repulse you? What is the chief cause of unhappiness in married life? Why does a small man fall in love with a large woman or vice versa? Why does bitter hate sometimes masquerade under the guise of love? Why do lovers kiss? How do our glands affect us? NOW SCIENCE HAS REVEALED THE CAUSE OF LOVE! In the searching light of that most curious and new method, psychoanalysis, the soul of love had been laid bare!" The new dispensation was here; and in reviewing Tridon's book for the magazine, I praised it, saying that despite its cheapness in some places and its inaccuracy in others, it made good propaganda for the cause—"the cause being the war which psychology has begun to wage against the stale and desperate morality which we have inherited from the muddled ages preceding ours." I published those words in the same issue with my editorial saying that "the documents here presented prove that the Kronstadt affair was not a revolt of Russian workers and peasants against a centralized state, but was an unsuccessful attempt on the part of Allied capitalists to destroy the fruits of the Russian revolution. . . ."

For some people psychoanalysis was a medical treatment for painful emotional disturbances connected with sex. For others, a means of obtaining the approval of science to break down the repressions imposed by conventional morality. There were some, too, who took advantage of the new psychiatric technique to transfer their pursuit of the knowledge of good and evil from the church, the classroom and the literary café to the physician's leather couch, where you could talk without interruption, saying whatever came into your head, so that out of the incessant flow of slag there might be extracted a nugget or two of self-understanding.

Psychoanalysis had a materialist base and an idealist superstructure. It sought to explain mental illness in terms of such material things as sex, money, physical deficiencies; but it atomized the human personality into such idealistic abstractions as the Unconscious, the Id, the Libido. Whatever pragmatic value such concepts might have, for want of better and more precise knowledge of therapeutics, where even superstitions like the stone at Lourdes may have effect, in the social realm it was bound to lead to falsehood, such as the theory that bolshevism was a neurotic manifestation of the Oedipus complex. Psychoanalysis did not attempt to alter society. It wanted only to "adjust" the individual rendered helpless by internal civil war to the demands of bourgeois society. Consequently, many of those who revolted against conventional morals and cracked under the burden of the sense of guilt, found themselves cured indeed, but cured chiefly of their rebellious attitudes.

Psychoanalysis was not, as the romantic rebels imagined, amoral. It was highly moral, conventional and bourgeois. Himself thoroughly steeped in middle-class attitudes, the average psychoanalyst looked upon the radical's hatred of capitalist society as a mental derangement. He saw an analogy between paranoia and the dislike of bankers, industrialists, generals and statesmen whom you had never seen. It was all right, during the war, to hate the Kaiser and sixty million Germans you had never seen; it was perfectly normal to adore Woodrow Wilson and General Pershing, whom you also had never seen. But to hate those who murdered workers in Ludlow, Youngstown, Lawrence, Pittsburgh and Herrin; to hate the men responsible for the death of ten million men in the World War; to loathe the profiteers and their political henchmen; and to respect and follow Lenin—that was queer, perverse, psychopathic, since you had never seen these men. That was only the projection of your love for your father which the sense of guilt transformed into hatred. The social struggle was reduced to a series of petty little dramas in the soul of the patient, the script for which had long ago been outlined in Vienna. It took an analyst of exceptional experience and breadth of culture, usually one with a socialist background, to dissociate nervous disorders from social disorders; to grasp that the former were a product of the latter; to differentiate between the neurotic who draws his symbols from the revolutionary movement—as others draw theirs from art, science or sport—and the completely sane and healthy revolutionary who sees the contemporary world more objectively and truly than does the "normal" philistine.

In many cases, the psychoanalysis of bohemian writers and artists opened for them a back door through which they re-entered the bourgeois society which they had repudiated in their period of romantic rebellion. It turned out in twentieth century America, as in nineteenth century Europe, that adolescent revolt against paternal authority, clothing itself in literary and political symbols, was but the repudiation of conventional mores under the pressure of a normal sensuality in conflict with an abnormal conscience. Once that conflict was resolved, once sensuality and conscience were reconciled, the road was open for the return of the prodigal to the bourgeois fold. The neurotic bohemian sought in love pleasure without responsibility. When psychoanalysis gave him a sense of responsibility, by leading him out of the realm of fantasy into the realm of reality, he could conceive of responsibility only as the complete acceptance of bourgeois society.

§ 5

The radical bohemian had his own special difficulties. He suffered from the infantile expectation that the Golden Realm of "art and revolution" should have, while capitalism still dominated the world, some of the characteristics of the classless society. There must be no money, no debtors and no creditors; we were to live in a little utopian South Sea isle of "communism" surrounded by the raging sea of capitalism; and on this happy island we were to fulfill Marx's dictum, from each according to his abilities, to each according to his needs. On those rare occasions when we had it, we gave money away to poets and artists in need; we expected others to do the same for us when we were in need, which was most of the time. We could hardly believe our ears when the *Liberator* bookkeeper told us that the former editor used to pay himself $100 dollars a week. It was probably only a legend. Lucky was that week when we got as much as ten dollars. This mode of life is possible when you are young and unattached. It does not matter if you go without food for a day or two; or sleep now and then on the floor of Sam Schwartz's restaurant on MacDougal Street. You can wear the same flannel shirt for three weeks; go with shoes unshined, suit unpressed, face unshaven. No one in the Village seemed to mind. In fact, these were not only the necessities of poverty but the insignia of "revolt." When you are very young, and a poet or artist besides, people are generous to you. They like your youth; they want to invest in the future of a "genius"; they invite you to dinners and let you live at their homes. They are good and kind and sweet, motherly and fatherly, and you can be a sort of bum glorified by the bohemian tradition. You can be grateful to your patrons who are good to you because they hate bourgeois society too; you can enjoy your youth and their friendship; you can do anything—anything except earn your keep; for bourgeois society, which monopolizes money and the printing presses will pay millions to crush strikes but not a cent for subversive articles, poems or books.

The Villager felt his poverty acutely. Sometimes extreme cases illuminate the conventional type, as the mental processes of the insane mirror in the gross the mental processes of the normal. An extreme example of the Villager of this period was the brilliant, bizarre, half-mad Baroness Elsa von Freytag-Loringhoven, art model, Dadaist poet, and living link between the bohemias of Europe and America. Her fantastic poses and actions melodramatized the concepts and mores of the Village.

In her role as Dadaist poet, the baroness reflected the Village cult of the idiot and the child, the fetish of individual self-expression regardless of what one expressed; the belief, surviving from the Middle Ages, that the mad were nearer to reality than the sane; and the creed, surviving from the nineteenth century, that every artist was a little mad. As a woman she was a grotesque survival of the Duncan cult, the cult of the human body, especially female and especially nude. Once, in the presence of several people, someone commented that the face of the baroness was less than beautiful. Her excellency shouted in her deep German accent:

"Don't look at the woman's face, idiot! Look at the body! Here!"

She ripped off her dress and stood naked, like Phryne confuting the tribunal about to condemn her for profaning the Eleusinian mysteries. Under less dramatic circumstances, and with much less provocation, other bohemian men and women displayed themselves nude at bathing or studio parties in the name of art, health or the revolution in mores. We published a defense of mixed nude bathing in the *Liberator* by a young writer who had picked up "the philosophy and practice of nakedness," he said, "at Harvard University." He explained that nude bathing was fundamentally a rapprochement between the sun and the human body.

"Once you get the feel of it, the zest of it, the freedom of it— your highest emotional outlet is physical enough to be sure—but not exactly sexual—unless it's one of those deep Freudian sexualities which take all the meaning out of the term."

We did not know that this writer, who did short stories for us now and then, had any special interest in economics. His name was Stuart Chase.

The bohemian's feelings about money, like his feelings about sex, sometimes moved in the most grandiose mist of poetry, history and philosophy. Here, too, he needed the literary sanction. He did not say simply: "The *Liberator* owes me five dollars for three poems: please remit." He wrote instead long letters on contemporary culture in which payment for his work was an obscure parenthesis. The cult of learning considered the artist too sacred to work. It relieved him of the responsibility of earning his living. Instead of wages, the artist, like a medieval monarch or a tribal chieftain, expected tribute. We felt that bourgeois culture gave lip service to art in the abstract and kept the living artist in poverty. The artist, wounded in his pride, retired to bohemia where, with inverted snobbishness, he set himself up, each in his little circle, as a vagabond king. The artist was supposed to receive tribute, not to pay it. He accepted allegiance from anyone who gave it without giving his own to anyone who demanded it. And since every social group resents defections from its code, Robert Minor, our fellow editor on the *Liberator,* was as sharply criticized in the Village for abandoning the illusory "free" life of the artist and accepting the discipline of the Communist party as Floyd Dell had been for abandoning the frank and free life of the Great Lover and accepting the discipline of marriage.

§ 6

My emotional difficulties had led me to follow Floyd Dell's suggestion to undertake a psychoanalysis. To my surprise and perhaps chagrin, my psychoanalyst kept his political ideas to himself. He appeared to be interested solely in helping me bridge the gap between fantasy and reality. Consequently, my social views were strengthened. They became more deeply rooted in the actual world, with which I was becoming better acquainted. It was clear that internal conflicts mirrored the conflicts of the world; if the pretensions of society corresponded with its actualities there would be less neurosis.

Among other things, my relations with Laura were clarified. I had met Laura in the offices of the *Liberator.* Her presence there marked her as belonging to the declassed radical intellectuals with whom I had identified myself. Her appearance, too, corresponded to a preconceived idea; her blond hair and blue eyes must have echoed

Yakelina, the golden-haired teacher of the Anglo-Saxon fairy tales, the heroines of Renaissance poetry. She was half gentile and half Jewish— neatly fitting into the conflict between my origins and my longing to transcend racial barriers. Her father was a famous British radical, her mother a Russian-Jewish anarchist, her uncle by marriage one of my bosses on the Chicago *Tribune,* her former husband an editor of the *Liberator.* She was herself a violinist of unusual gifts. That was it: she was an artist, she had a profession, she earned her own living; and she was by conviction an anarchist sympathetic to the October Revolution. In all these respects she represented old aspirations. Before I knew her as an individual, she stirred me as a type in the world toward which I was moving. Among certain men and women this is not uncommon. We sit in the theater, admire the playing of an actress, and feel we could love her before we know her; her talent, her fame, the character she has portrayed are that part of her which we see first and which first moves us. Or we ourselves write books, make speeches, publish drawings. We are identified with a literary or political movement, and women come to us with feelings aroused not by what we are but by what we represent. Around the individual glows a general idea representing a social class, a group, a clique. You are not yet in love, but you are interested. You think you have escaped class barriers, but you are moved by the requirements of your own group of declassed intellectuals. You may never love Laura and she may never love you; but she will understand you as no bourgeois girl could. Your first conversation with her, the backgrounds you both reveal, show that you are living in the same world—the first requisite for love, as distinguished from mere sex.

Later Laura and I got to know each other as individuals. We fell in love. We took an apartment in an old house on Fourteenth Street. You walked up the dark, dank stairway, so like the stairway in the Brooklyn tenement. There was one room. We had to put up the electric light ourselves. There was no bath and no washstand. You washed in the hall toilet which you shared with the Italian sculptor next door. This was not an "affair"; it was a "ménage" in the style of the old Village. There was nothing clandestine about it. Friends visited us, among them Louis Smith and my brothers, uniting my present with my past life. Writers and artists came evenings; and once there emerged from the crowd a man of whom I had heard from Irwin on the campus as William James' brightest pupil. He introduced himself as Horace Kallen.

"Three apples and three apples," he asked the crowd, "what does that make?"

"Six apples," a bright cartoonist said.

"No. One apple pie." Everybody laughed. "There you have in a nutshell, or rather in an apple pie, the theory of relativity."

Mornings I wrote editorials for the *Liberator* on an unpainted wooden table, while Laura stood at the window, facing her music stand and playing Bach. It was very beautiful and very happy and very, very painful; we sensed from the very beginning the impermanence of this relationship, which lasted for three years.

It was through Laura that I got to know the radical colony at Stelton, New Jersey, which her relatives had founded and which was noted in radical circles for its experiments in the education of the child. For us, at this time, the child was a symbol of incredible importance. In the Village the artist was supposed to be free of conventional obligations because he was a child, and the child was the bohemian's substitute for the simple and happy savage of the eighteenth century romantics, the "natural man" endowed with boundless goodness and creativeness which were corrupted by conventional society. The Villagers felt that what we needed was a new educational system which would give the child an opportunity to develop his own personality freely. A generation of children thus brought up would—as Prince Hopkins had explained to us long ago at the Self-Culture Club —transform the world into a better place. The bourgeois Villager was interested in the educational theories of Dewey and Montessori. For the radicals the cult of the child had to be connected with the revolution. This dream, too, developed its happy island cut off from the conventional world. Certain proletarians had their own kind of bohemia, on a more serious level than Greenwich Village, but as much of an isolated realm. We made pilgrimages to the school at Stelton, New Jersey, named after the Spanish anarchist martyr Francisco Ferrer. The school was conducted by a utopian colony of anarchists, socialists and communists, many of them workers in the needle trades in New York. For six months, Laura and I lived at Stelton and participated in the activities of the school directed by Mr. and Mrs. Ferm. The colony was within easy commuting distance of New York, but its utopian character made it possible to retreat into a sociologic dreamworld, if you were so inclined.

At Stelton, the child was encouraged to be "himself." There was no formal instruction. Every effort was made not to impose upon the child the notions and viewpoints of the adults, except the utopian theory of education upon which the school was based and all it involved. The child learned through play. He was expected to master hammer and nail, crayon and paper, acting and dancing through the open avenues of "self-expression." Parents and other adults were forbidden to convert their own or other children to any creed, religious, social or political. Only when the child was ready for an idea was he to hear it explained; only when he asked for books was he taught to read; only when he asked about birth was he told the "facts of life." Chiefly he was expected to find out all kinds of facts for himself. He was permitted and encouraged to follow his inclinations unhampered on the principle that the child's "natural" instincts were the safest guides to healthy development. We believed that the child got a firm grasp on life through direct physical contact with it; no one could learn from books as much about farm life as little John Clements learned by feeding his own chicks, planting vegetables, painting the walls of the house. Little John was four, the product of an education which had few do's and was based, we thought, on "creative guidance."

The children, however, did not live in a vacuum. They grew in a specific social environment and could not escape its influence. The radical views of the parents were expressed in adult collective enterprises; there were meetings, debates, feuds which the children could not help overhearing. Romantic theories of education could not prevent them from absorbing the prejudices of their parents and teachers. Some of these were valuable. The children worked in a machine shop; they cultivated gardens and mended fences and raised chickens. They learned to labor in groups. But like all utopian colonies, this one tended to isolate the child from the outside world. He was treated tenderly, respectfully, seriously; but it was forgotten that someday he would become an adult in a world utterly different from Stelton. No provision was made for a transition to that world. Stelton, like Greenwich Village, was a dreamworld from which the adolescent, when he entered the conventional high school, factory or office, awoke startled and confused. Sometimes he cursed the school forever afterwards, as we curse those who, in their fantastic love for us, surround us with myths which bind our hands in the struggle with reality. The educational ideal which animated Stelton could be valid, with essential modifications, only where the new school is an integral part of a new society. In the old society, the ideal school is as helpless, as sterile, as the ideal co-operative colony, as the utopia of Greenwich Village. It left the world unchanged, whatever it might do for some of the individuals in it. Sometimes even the individuals turned out different from what they were intended to be. George Seldes, one of the founders of the utopian colonies of New Odessa, Oregon, and Stelton, New Jersey, was the father of Gilbert and George Seldes, both of whom subsequently became well-known journalists.

Even among the adults at Stelton there was evident a drift toward the world which the colony had sought to escape. Among the workers there were those who had risen to be petty manufacturers or trade-union bureaucrats. They still called themselves anarchists, and justified reactionary policies with the noblest theories. They hated the communists at Stelton, in America, anywhere except in Russia which, thank heaven, was six thousand miles away. This enabled them to attend with straight faces parties organized by all political groups jointly whenever a colonist migrated to Soviet Russia.

At one of these parties I met an American communist who called himself simply Pete. He was just back from Moscow. Pete was small, stocky, aggressive, full of fun and friendliness. He flattered people, talked too much, pretended to know everything, and showed off a great deal. But we all agreed he was a good skate, even when we could not believe what he said. For instance, he said Max Eastman lived in his house in Moscow; Max nearly failed to get his visé to Russia because in Paris he associated with suspicious elements, with aristocrats. What aristocrats, someone asked, Ganna Walska? How should I know, Pete said; aristocrats, that's all. But now Max was O.K. Of course he was not of much use; he was, after all, only a poet. On his arrival the comrades kidded Max. They told him, write poems about the domes of Moscow! Why the domes of Moscow? someone asked. How should I know? I suppose because they are the most useless things around there! Pete echoed a notion, then common among certain American communists, that art was a nuisance which impeded revolutionary action.

At the same party I met another man who held the opposite view. He was small, with a pale face, a shock of black hair, and large, black eyes. They pointed him out to me as the director of an experimental school for children in Philadelphia and the editor of a literary magazine in that city. He was young and alternated between shyness and audacity. We talked a great deal about common problems; he was interested in art and revolution; he wanted to find a synthesis and did not know how; but the movies appealed to him as the great mass

art of the future. When we started to take leave, we remembered we
had not been introduced. He said his name was Harry Alan Potamkin.

§ 7

The "free" child of Stelton corresponded to the simple and happy
savage of the romantic credo; the "free" adult of Greenwich Village
corresponded to the free man of Rousseau's dream, whose boundless
rights and privileges the bourgeoisie proclaimed at the dawn of its
power. When the eighteenth century bourgeois proclaimed the right
of every individual to express himself unhampered, he had in mind
primarily his own right to develop free trade unhampered by feudal
restrictions. The twentieth century bohemian, hating trade of any kind,
at odds with his social environment, frustrated in his basic inclinations,
set up the ideal trinity of art, love and beauty. The gospel of art was
the bohemian's answer to the capitalist gospel of utility; the gospel of
love, the answer to capitalist hypocrisy and the marriage market; the
gospel of beauty, the answer to the unendurable ugliness of the capitalist environment. But since the Villagers were for the most part
poor and could not afford beautiful surroundings except on the simplest scale, they sought beauty in the human body. That was sacred; its
desires could not be denied. The batik blouses of the women, the
orange neckties of the men were outward signs of grace denied to the
Babbittry; they were banners in a war of paganism against puritanism.
The Babbitt worked hard, guarded his health, took laxatives to preserve his digestion, repressed his sexual desires or cheated his wife,
saved his money and lived a long sterile life. The free spirit of the
Village built his house upon the sands, burned his candle at both
ends, lived intensely, courting death in his avid pursuit of life—a life
poor in material things but rich in pleasures, adorned with art and
freedom. But, except for those associated with the revolutionary movement, art was concerned with beauty and love, with the adventurous
beginning, the confused and tumultuous course and the nostalgic conclusion of "affairs." Freedom was concerned chiefly with the holy
war against Volstead and Sumner, with the defense of people's right
to the happiness to be found in alcohol and sex.

There was something infantile in this, perhaps. The puritans
looked on the Village as a nest of vice. Yet nowhere were people more
virtuous, more cleanhearted. The bond between the Village and Stelton was the worship of childlike innocence. That innocence may have
been a myth, but under the circumstances it was probably a necessary

myth. The worker determined that his child would not go through his own agonies as a child and took him to the utopian colony; the middle-class devotee of art resented his bitter, frustrated childhood and tried to relive it in the Village. The married woman, broken by suburbia, left her husband, went to bohemia, opened the window with the bright checkered curtain, felt the wind on her cheek, looked at her sleeping lover and felt that here, for the first time, was the joy denied her ever since she could remember. She painted and danced badly— but it was in compensation for the failure of her parents to let her paint and dance at all as a child. She looked on the kids at Stelton with vicarious love and well-wishing envy. To say that the Villagers were children is not to condemn them; it is rather to condemn the civilization which dooms childhood to sterility and pain, and compels so many sensitive spirits to fight grotesquely for a second chance to live.

In so far as Greenwich Village had an adult aspect, it was a border country stretching between two worlds. It was at once a post-graduate school, a playground and a clinic for those who had broken with an old culture and had not yet found a new one, or had not yet discovered and accepted the fact that they were irrevocably committed to the old. Its character as a border country gave the Village a serious base. Its inhabitants drank, made love, wrote poems, stayed up late at gay parties, talked and wrote and drew "advanced" ideas; but all of this was significant in relation to what these people were seeking. A decade later—in the thirties—their quest was to appear trivial. The violent struggle of social classes; the breakdown of bourgeois society throughout the world; the drilling of armies for new wars; the spectacle of an entire civilization falling to pieces and another rising to take its place—these were to make the glamours and despairs of bohemia seem even more infantile than they had been. Yet the frank and free life of the Village was one aspect of the disintegration of bourgeois society.

The brooding and oddities of bohemia led to poses, theatricalism, pretense. But pretense itself requires explanation. The declassed intellectual, uprooted from his original social environment and not yet rooted in a new one, suffers from acute internal discord. Until that discord is resolved in terms of reality, he attempts to solve it by symbols. He pretends to be what he hopes to become, or at least that which will protect him from what he fears to become. In the early stages, the bohemian most fears a return to the bourgeois world from which he has just fled. That return has been the fate of most bohemians. For the Villagers of the twenties it did not entail any special hardships. The "compromise" had its agreeable side. They were no longer odd, peculiar or unhappy. The bourgeois world overtook and surpassed them. It absorbed their talents and expropriated their poses.

Bohemian pretenses were transferred from the garret to the suburban home, the Gramercy Park studio; and Village freedom of morals and dress, to Chicago, Oshkosh and Steubenville. During the boom of the twenties, the prosperous middle classes went bohemian on a bigger and better scale. The speakeasy lifted to a "higher level" the drinking, the sexual experiments and the wit of the *Pirates' Den* and the *Purple Pup*. The manners and morals of the Village became the manners and morals of the middle and even part of the upper classes. Expanding business converted the "vagabond" poets of the Village into editors, advertising writers, publicity agents, columnists and novelists; the "vagabond" artists into magazine illustrators, commercial designers, portrait painters and department store decorators. These ex-bohemians, through the medium of the press and the movies, now brought to the middle classes some of the "free" thought and "free" conduct of the Village. A balance was struck. The prosperous middle classes needed a little bohemianism to spend their money in ways not sanctioned by the puritan tradition; the bohemians needed a little puritanism to go with their newly acquired money. Indeed, bohemianism requires a certain amount of social stability. The bohemian wishes to "shock" the bourgeois. For this purpose, the bourgeois must be well entrenched, secure financially, able and willing to be shocked; and the bohemian himself must feel that the road back to the world he is "shocking" is not entirely closed. In the depths of his heart he not only fears but hopes that his eccentricities, which are part of his stock in trade, will earn him a fatted calf as the returning prodigal. It is not capitalism that he hates, as a rule, but the responsibilities which any highly developed social system imposes upon its members. The bohemian who finally accepts law and order in life as an ineluctable necessity, may, like the Russian poet Mayakovsky, graduate to communism when he realizes that it represents a higher law, a superior order, one in which the freedom of the individual has greater scope and security. The bohemian who has no fundamental objection to capitalist law and order—provided he is to some extent exempted from their burden by virtue of being a child, a wild free spirit, a divinely inspired idiot—gladly returns to the fold when the oracular visions of his studio have become the clichés of the drawing room. In the Gin Flask Era, the idealistic bohemia of Floyd Dell's days, touched with social vision, began to whither away; and those writers and artists who had no real interest in the proletarian revolution ceased to contribute to the *Liberator,* now committed to propagating the revolution above everything else.

§ 8

The more we analyzed them, the more bohemian ideas reduced themselves to the simple slogans of the French and American revolutions: liberty, equality, fraternity; life, liberty, the pursuit of happiness. Art was the medium through which all these values could be achieved. But stronger than the gospel of art was the gospel of love. That mysterious thing called "life," which was older than liberty and greater than revolution, meant in the bohemian's lexicon, boundless sex love. Like the German idealist Ludwig Feuerbach, the Villager believed that sex love was the highest activity of man. Sex love was not simple pleasure; it was a philosophy of life; it included and transcended the senses, embraced all human relationships, formed the essence of art and literature. This was the true pursuit of happiness. Against the drabness and hypocrisy of the conventional world, Village life shone gloriously; on closer contact it revealed the grime and tragedy which belonged to it as an island of the conventional mainland.

In the fall of 1921, when I first came to it, the Village was shocked by the suicide of a beautiful actress, deserted by her lover, a leading bohemian radical. As a rule, no one is really responsible for the suicide of another; but it was obvious that love was more complicated than bohemia made it appear. Unrestricted pursuit of happiness, the lust for pleasure without responsibility, may lead to the unhappiness of others; the fetish of "life" in the bohemian sense may lead to death.

Need such a tragedy compel us to revert to conventional standards? No one thought of that for a moment. Mayakovsky had not yet killed himself, and it had not yet become fashionable among former radical bohemians to repudiate a great ideal in realization because a poet could not adjust himself to the painful processes it involved. We believed that any profound readjustment in human relations was bound to have its victims. We ourselves might be those victims. It was not we who were breaking up the prevailing mores; it was the decomposition of the old order, upon whose head was the blood of ten million soldiers, the suicide of unemployed workers, the self-inflicted death of sensitive artists. We would continue to direct our personal lives as best we could between the Scylla of extravagant romantic longing and the Charybdis of prevailing social conditions.

It was now obvious, however, that as a philosophy, as a guide to social action, the Village gospel of love was futile. The emancipation of woman, like the emancipation of races, could not be achieved without the emancipation of labor, without a deep transformation of the whole of society. A few individuals might find freedom in the happy islands, thanks to their fortunate endowments of money, personal beauty or artistic gifts; outside, on the mainland, there remained the oppressed millions without whom you could not have the luxury of happy islands.

On the *Liberator* we felt that while the dreams of the Village might be valid, their basis was false. Old Engels had ridiculed the philosophy of love as developed by Feuerbach; he had called it the "old cant—love one another, fall into each other's arms regardless of distinctions of sex or estate—a universal orgy of reconciliation." Mike Gold, discussing the cult of love in its highest manifestations, attacked the "Jesus-thinkers" who cared "only for the nobility and purity of their own souls," who refused to be objective, who wanted "a fraternal world" but were unwilling to "pay the full price—which is thought and action." We were convinced that the isolated noble individual or group of individuals who tried by their own feeble efforts—none the less feeble because accompanied by great emotion—to solve the contradictions of bourgeois society were doomed to failure. Theirs was a false dawn.

Out of that conviction, we saw the Village, Stelton, all happy little islands on the fringe of society in a new light. They were not progressive; they were reactionary. The passion for "self-expression" upon which they were based made them cracked mirrors reflecting the bourgeois world which they thought they had escaped, but whose cult of rugged individualism they retained. That was why in the period of prosperity the bohemian could so easily go back to the old world. When you stripped him of his glamorous phrases, as you stripped American capitalism of its democratic shibboleths, the Village Don Juan was also a "robber baron," less heroic than the financial and industrial magnates because he operated on an infantile plane where there were no obstacles to overcome and the results were sterile.

In the happy islanders you could see the unfulfilled dreams of the bourgeois revolution of the eighteenth century carried to grotesque extremes. If the gospel of love as a social philosophy was a hang-over of religion, of "Jesus-thinking," the gospel of art as it prevailed here was a hang-over of the preindustrial era. Education at Stelton was primarily aesthetic. Hugo Gellert of the *Liberator* staff taught the children drawing; Laura taught them music; others taught them dancing, singing, dramatics, weaving. This preoccupation with arts and handicrafts had enormous value for children; but the adults themselves longed for the handicraft era. They damned the machine age, although this damnation was compensatory, since many of them worked at machines in the clothing factories of New York; their theory was a respite from their reality. It was in the Village—with its enthusiasm for Varnum Poor's handmade pottery—that the revolt against the machine was purest. Surrounded by the most mechanized and industrialized country in the world, the little island burned candles not only symbolically—at both ends—but literally. The inhabitants wore handmade batik blouses instead of factory-made dresses, sandals instead of shoes. They were, spiritually at least, machine wreckers. For many of them art was not an attempt to express contemporary civilization, but to escape from it into dreams of a nonindustrial world assumed to be full of peace, beauty and love. When they crossed the sea, they sought a Europe of the past. They did not visit the Ruhr or Manchester or the factories of France; they browsed in the art galleries, toured the countryside, frequented little suburban inns and cafés of the European bohemia which themselves were little islands of refuge from industrial civilization.

This was a general mood among the intellectuals of the West, who had been struggling against the machine for half a century. In the spring of 1923 we read Havelock Ellis' *Dance of Life,* and saw that for many intellectuals life itself was endurable only when it was an art. Capitalist civilization made the art of life impossible, and Ellis' imagination soared among the primitives of the Loyalty Islands and China a thousand years ago. Bertrand Russell transferred his "free man's worship" to modern China. Here at least verification was possible. Communism gave us a realistic picture of China; we had some notion of what imperialism and spheres of influence meant for massed millions of China, what the Boxer rebellion meant and the revolution of 1911 and the violent class conflict of our own day. The beautiful aesthetic China of which the intellectuals talked had nothing to do with the 400,000,000 miserable slaves who lived in it. It was a poetic dream woven out of their own wishes and casual contact with man-

darins and their literature. It was another form of the nostalgia for
the preindustrial era. At the moment when the factory, the bank,
the armored cruiser were spreading in China, Western intellectuals,
horrified by the results of the factory, bank and cruiser in their own
countries, invented a slow, peaceful, poised China full of wisdom,
poetry and gracious manners. And while bourgeois men of letters and
artists searched for peace and beauty in a Europe which had disappeared or an Orient which never existed, radical men of letters and
artists adored in Mexico a past which the agrarian revolution and
American imperialism were rapidly wiping out. The intellectual
suffered from a nostalgia for the past, for the golden pastoral age.

I remembered the vanished village of my childhood and with it
the defects of preindustrial life. There was peace in the fields, there
were also poverty, filth, ignorance, superstition, pogroms. My family
had moved successively from candle to kerosene lamp to gaslight to
electricity; from the stinking ditches and wooden sidewalks of the
village to the modern sewage and asphalt of New York. This looked
like progress. I was "bourgeois" in the sense that I preferred shoes to
sandals, and a suit of clothes to a smock. All the workers I knew,
radical and conservative, had the same taste. I could not romanticize
the impoverished, drab life of the preindustrial world which I knew;
instead, I romanticized the machine which was for me as much of an
abstraction as the European or Mexican village was for the tourists
from Chicago, Pittsburgh or New York. This abstraction, however,
had its value; it rendered me susceptible to the Marxist explanation
of the machine. We sympathized with the complaints of the intellectuals; the cruelties and sterilities to which they pointed were there.
But they attacked results instead of causes; what was wrong, we felt,
was not the machine but the capitalist use of the machine. While
bohemians were burning candles in New York, Lenin was calling in
Moscow for the electrification of his country. Machinery was indispensable for a higher standard of living, for universal leisure, for the
development and spread of art, for the free development of the individual; and socialism was equally indispensable. What the Western
intellectual really hated were the results of *privately owned* machinery,
the division of labor and society, the pursuit of profit and exploitation,
the crushing of the personality for the sake of the market. American
culture might be as sterile as the intellectuals said it was; but that
culture was for the majority—as Marx said of all bourgeois culture—
"a mere training to act as a machine." Not the machine was mon-

strous, but the machine in the hands of capitalists. That was the source of the mechanization of man.

Against the life of Main Street, Sinclair Lewis had set up a dream drawn from images of European culture via the campus, bohemia, the happy island of Helicon Hall. Later he was to see that culture somewhat more realistically and to repudiate it in the name of Main Street; but in the early twenties his novel remained the most striking indictment of standardized life under capitalism. The revolutionary proletariat grappled with that life *as a matter of necessity* in the interests of the future classless society; many intellectuals fled from it to the cult of love and art, the cult of the sacred ego. They even thought this made them original, daring, revolutionary. But ideas do not spring out of the void; they arise from the conflict of social realities and they stem from traditions imbedded in those realities. When a man rejects prevailing ideas because they do not correspond with the realities of his own life he must think forward to the transformation of those realities, or else dream himself away from them into the past. It was no accident that the Villagers adored Shelley and Keats, the French and German romantics and their grandsons, the symbolists. The literary credo of the Village was, curiously enough, a continuation of ideas we had heard on the campus: the artist continued to be the highest type of human being, the sanctified champion of Eternity against Time. There was already a national movement in the arts; writers were talking of rooting themselves in the America to which they belonged. But the relation of art to society echoed earlier conceptions of this subject. This may have been due to the fact that we lived in an age analogous to other ages. Like the generation which passed through the French Revolution, we, too, saw an old order crack and a new order arise. And it was something more than that. Basic ideas persisted for decades; when we now read Georg Brandes we saw the very ideas which animated people around us. The history of European literature revealed not analogies alone, but direct ancestry, the very source of the aesthetic approach to life which marked certain American intellectuals of this period. The American artist was a split personality. His roots were partly in the machine age which he damned, in the America from which he fled; and partly in the culture of that Europe to which he now exiled himself. He was seeking in France the source of his spiritual life, only to discover on the banks of the Seine the meaning of the Mississippi. But his spiritual life, molded at the university, in the library, in literary groups, had its internal history. Walt Whitman, whom he respected, was the gigantic voice of that dream of individual freedom represented by the American revolutionary war against England and the civil war against American feudalism, and justified by the free, open lands of expanding America. The European symbolists whom he adored and imitated flowed back to the romantics whose main presuppositions were now his own, whose axioms flowed from that universal upheaval of Western culture which made the French and American revolutions twins.

CHAPTER III

Party! Party! how can anyone reject it? Party, the mother of all victory! How can a poet slander such a word which bears the seed of all that is noblest? Speak out frankly like a man: are you for or against us? Is your slogan *slavery* or—*freedom?*

—GEORG HERWEGH.

§ 1

THE *Liberator* had one foot in bohemia, the other in the revolutionary movement. For us bohemia represented fantasy, the movement reality. In contact with active communists, the problems of the bohemian artist appeared trivial, especially the problem of the individual against the world, an echo of the romantic school which sprang up around the French Revolution. Numerically insignificant, compelled by historical circumstances to begin on the margin of American life, communists nevertheless did not think of themselves as peculiar or isolated individuals. Their quarrel was not with society; they spoke and acted on the conviction that the battle was between those who had nothing to sell but their labor power and those who owned the basic means of production. To this central struggle of our age, the individual of all camps was of necessity subordinated. This priority of collective purpose was called "discipline."

"If one wishes to voice his private opinions all the time," I wrote in my notebook, "if one insists on doing this even after a majority has adopted a policy, one should stay out of politics."

Although the *Liberator* was in no way officially connected with the organized communist movement, I frequently went to Party headquarters to get material for editorials, or to obtain an article from some member of the Central Committee. In this way I became acquainted with several leading communists, whom I had known only by reputation.

Of Bill Dunne we had heard a great deal as the hero of Bloody Butte. He had been active in the labor movement of the United States and Canada from his youth up, had joined the Socialist party in 1912, had been active in British Columbia as business agent of the electrical workers' union, later as vice-president of the international union. In

1916 he went to Butte where he became chief electrician for Anaconda. On June 7, 1917, a terrible catastrophe happened in one of the copper mines; 160 workers were smothered to death. This tragedy gave impetus to a strike movement already under way, a movement which had started when policemen and soldiers clubbed and bayoneted workers marching in an antiwar parade. Out of the great copper strike, in which 28,000 workers participated, there grew the *Butte Daily Bulletin,* which became the official organ of the Montana State Federation of Labor and the Central Labor Union of Silver Bow County. Dunne edited this paper, the largest labor daily in the United States at that time, and the only daily of any kind which supported the Bolshevik Revolution in Russia from the beginning.

Dunne was also chairman of the joint strike committee. The conflict was intense: company gunmen attacked the *Bulletin's* printing plant, located in an abandoned church which the union had hired as its headquarters, but the gunmen were driven off by hundreds of workers who came to the defense of their union and their paper. It was in this strike that vigilantes lynched Frank Little, about whose death Giovannitti had written such moving verses. Late in 1917, Dunne joined the Butte section of the Socialist party, became active in its left wing, and through it one of the founders of the Communist Labor party in 1919. Subsequently, when the Communist party of the United States was formed, he became one of its charter members.

Curiously enough, however, he served a term in the Montana state legislature nominally as a Democrat. This strange episode resulted from the fact that in 1918-1919, the Socialist party in Montana was controlled by the Anaconda copper trust. The Communist Labor party was illegal and ran no candidates. The Butte workers insisted upon having Dunne represent them in the legislature and wrote his name in on the Democratic ticket, adding to it such slogans as "all power to the workers and farmers." Dunne was elected by a large vote, and to this day is designated in the records of the Montana legislature as a "Democrat." For all practical purposes, however, he was labor's representative at the capital, the first legislator in the United States to introduce a resolution for the withdrawal of American troops from Siberia, and the first to introduce a resolution for the recognition of the Soviet government.

These were the tales I had heard about Bill Dunne when I began to meet him frequently in the fall of 1922, and in the following spring at Party headquarters, at John's restaurant on East Twelfth Street and at the *Liberator* office. He was short and stocky, with a tremendous barrel-chest, solid as a rock, and a dark, heavy Irish face. His close-cropped bullet head and thick neck gave him the appearance of great physical power; and his deep, husky voice, pouring out a flood of rhetoric, witty and incisive, revealed a mind that was at once brilliant and fanciful. His whole body, built like a retired prizefighter's, shook with repressed laughter when he told an anecdote. Dunne's reading was wide, ranging from Lenin to Joyce. On the platform he thundered in the style of the nineteenth century orators, and his articles in the Party press were florid, colorful and full of acid.

Dunne's chief interest was the trade-union movement.

Occasionally he dined in the Village with the *Liberator* crowd. He felt a strong affinity with writers; he had in him the traditional Irish poetry and wanted to write someday, if only an autobiography. Until then he would content himself with the next best thing—talking about literature.

Yet his contempt for the literary triflers of bohemia was boundless. Himself strongly sensuous and full of the love of life, he derided intellects dribbling away their power on the abstractly erotic. Good literature in our day, he said, could arise only out of the class war. He often used the word "intellectual" as a term of contempt, as I had heard the worker Louis Smith use it in the slums a decade earlier.

This time, however, I understood that what the communist organizer scorned was not intellect—which Lenin, for example, had to the degree of genius—but the phony arrogance of certain bohemians who fancied they had a monopoly of brains and knowledge, when they actually understood nothing of the essential struggles of our epoch.

There was this paradox, too: the intellectuals in the Party pretended to be interested only in the working class; Dunne, himself a worker, was also interested in the intellectuals, and in culture.

I first met William Z. Foster through Louis Smith, and was pleased that he who had first introduced me to communism in boyhood should now introduce me to the chieftain of the great steel strike and an outstanding Party leader. A worker by origin, the product of stockyard, streetcar, factory and ship, Foster looked more like an intellectual than most professors I had met. His thin, wiry body was surmounted by a large head which rose from a round, strong chin to a broad forehead and temples enlarged by baldness. His clear blue eyes were by turns austere and mild, his voice soft. Foster talked chiefly about the class war. His questions about my stay in Europe seldom touched on art, literature, Dada, the Rotonde, la vie de bohème. Actually, Foster was a man of wide cultural interests; his library was as full of literary as of socialist classics, and he had an unusual knowledge and appreciation of the best in music. But when he questioned me about Europe, he wanted to know about the trade unions, the growth of the communist movement, international politics.

Anything he said about himself was a parenthetical illustration of a general law of revolutionary strategy or a trade-union principle.

"That's no good," he would say about some suggestion. "I tried that in the Chicago stockyards and it doesn't work."

Then, merely to clarify his point, he would tell his experiences in organizing the stockyard workers. More personal characteristics emerged by accident. When we had dinner in a Third Avenue cafeteria, I discovered that Foster neither smoked nor drank, and that he was a vegetarian. But he had no puritanical precepts on these matters. The problems of personal conduct which agitated us in the Village did not seem to interest him. He was ascetic by a standard which determined all his actions. The class struggle was the most important thing in the world, and for that struggle he wanted to keep physically, mentally and morally fit. A touch of tuberculosis which he had cured by shipping as a sailor for several years, a bad heart which was to incapacitate him temporarily, obliged him to be especially careful.

Within the Party, Foster had an engaging modesty; in contact with the enemy class there emerged a powerful pride in which his person and his class were identical. Once the Newark police broke up a street meeting at which he spoke. The Civil Liberties Union—of which Foster was then a leading member—protested and was told that if he would appear in person before the city commission and ask for a permit he would be allowed to speak. Foster took me with him to Newark. We were ushered into a large, smoke-filled room in the City Hall with a heavy oak table in the center, wooden armchairs, and a red plush carpet studded with spittoons. The five commissioners sat around the table sullenly. They were either too fat or too thin; their faces were sallow and smirking, the typical faces of petty machine politicians. One of the commissioners, a tall, gray-haired man with tortoise-shell glasses, politely asked us to sit down. Then, very politely, he asked Foster when he wanted to speak, under whose auspices, on what street corner, on what subject, what literature was going to be distributed.

Foster answered gravely, quietly, respectfully. His views were well known, he would say what he had said at hundreds of meetings throughout the country, he would distribute the literature which the Newark police had illegally confiscated at his last meeting. Would Foster guarantee there would be no disturbances?

"Any disturbance I've ever seen at a workers' meeting," Foster said, "was created by the police or the American Legion."

This polite conversation went on for over an hour. Suddenly one of the silent commissioners, a pudgy little object, yelled:

"We're wasting time! We know what you're here for, Mr. Foster. You're here to make revolutions! We won't let you do it, understand? You can't speak in Newark."

"I am here," Foster said, "to exercise my right as an American citizen to discuss publicly economic and political questions. You said that if I applied in person for a permit you would grant it. I am applying for it now."

The commissioners laughed.

"You can't talk in Newark," the gray-haired man with the glasses said. "Not while we run this town. This conference is over."

The commissioners stood up. Foster's face turned white, then very red. He turned to me and said in a strained voice:

"Let's go."

"No hard feelings, Mr. Foster," one of the commissioners said.

Foster did not answer. We walked out of City Hall and for several blocks neither of us spoke. Then Foster broke out:

"Damn their dirty hides! They can't even keep a promise. I am the physical, mental and moral superior of any man in that room; I could wipe Newark with all five of them at once; and I've got to crawl on my hands and knees before them to beg for permission to speak. A permit to which I'm entitled—which they promised!" Then he quieted down and said gravely: "It wasn't meant for me. The working class has no rights under capitalism."

But not everyone you met around the Party was a heroic character. The man whom I shall call McGregor I met just after the Department of Justice had a communist meeting at which he had been present. Arrested and released on bail with a number of other Party members, McGregor reported at headquarters, a short, black-haired, swarthy-faced young man with a dark mustache. He breezed in energetically in a new overcoat, an elegant gray cap, and a professional

grin intended to be the warm, human smile of the "leader of men."
We were introduced.

"I hear you are a college man," he said, broadening his grin.
"I am one myself. I'm sorry I didn't remain there for a while longer.
I shouldn't have entered the Party at this early stage. I should have
studied law. I would have been more useful to the movement that
way."

McGregor had come into the Party from a middle-class background, and insulated himself at the top. He was a fluent speaker at
mass meetings, but cold, aloof, unconvincing; in caucuses, especially
when plotting intrigues, he was excellent. He had, too, a curious way of
derogating fellow communists while flattering the person to whom he
talked. This comrade was a fool, that one an idiot, the third a jackass,
the fourth a half-wit, the fifth a menshevik. When you added up all
these judgments, the obvious conclusion was that McGregor alone—
with the possible exception of Lenin—was an intelligent and loyal communist. Nor was this idle gossip; it was the higher strategy. McGregor
would tell Box that Cox had called him a moron; then he would tell
Cox that Box had called him a sap; then he would tell Fox that neither
Box nor Cox had any use for him. The result was that Box, Cox and
Fox cordially hated each other and attached themselves to their devoted
friend. Soon strategy became arrogance. McGregor got into the habit
of referring to the Party rank and file as the "rank and filth," and
called his closest adherents "my lieutenants, captains and marshals"—
phrases fit less for a communist than for an uncertain adventurer interested above everything else in personal dominion.

These impressions of the man disturbed me. Like so many intellectuals of this period, I tended to see inner-Party struggles in psychological terms, and to exaggerate their importance.

"McGregor's credo," I wrote to a friend, "amounts to this: mankind is divided into capitalists and workers; hate the capitalists and
like the workers. There are various groups speaking in the name of
the working class; hate the socialists, anarchists and wobblies, and like
only the communists. The communists are divided into Fosterites and
members of the faction of which McGregor is a member: hate the Fosterites and like only the other faction. The latter are all fools, idiots
and asses. Ergo: hate the whole world and like only McGregor. Thou
shalt have no other god before me."

Still, in the fall of 1922, McGregor was an energetic, affable lad
grooming himself with boundless push to become a Party leader.

Apropos of this ambition, a member of the Central Committee re-marked to me:

"Mac, the intriguer, as a lieutenant for a serious, responsible, de-voted leader of the Party is one thing; as a leader, it would be quite another thing, and very unfortunate for all of us. Mac is in-capable of respecting the Central Committee or the rank and file of the Party or the working class. He can only respect an individual stronger than himself."

Now and then I had conferences with the Party secretary, C. E. Ruthenberg, a blond, blue-eyed American of German stock, native of Cleveland, son of a longshoreman, accountant by profession. He had given up that profession long ago when he became an organizer for the Socialist party in his twenty-sixth year. We had heard of him for years as a leader of the revolutionary wing of the socialist movement. When the United States entered the war in 1917, he was among the most vigorous champions of the St. Louis resolution. His active propa-ganda against the war resulted in arrest; he was sentenced to a year in prison. Released on bail while his appeal was pending, he ran on the socialist ticket for mayor of Cleveland, basing his campaign on uncom-promising opposition to the war. Despite military mobilization, war hysteria, official terror and White House demagogy, Ruthenberg re-ceived more than one-fourth of the votes cast in the election. Shortly afterwards, his appeal was turned down by the higher courts and he was imprisoned in Canton for ten months. By the time he was released the war was over. Resuming his activities in the Socialist party, he organized and led the May Day demonstration in 1919 in which forty thousand Cleveland workers participated, including fifty A. F. of L. unions. Cleveland police and Ohio state troops attacked the demonstra-tion with firearms and tanks. In the street fighting which followed two policemen were killed. The police retaliated next day by wrecking the Socialist party headquarters. This demonstration led to an increase of the party's membership and of Ruthenberg's reputation as a clear-headed, courageous leader.

That was the year the Socialist party split on the question of the Bolshevik Revolution and the Communist International. Out of the Party's left wing, which Ruthenberg helped to organize, there grew two separate communist parties. The government's reply to the be-ginning of a communist movement in America was a series of raids on both parties in all sections of the country. Eventually Attorney General A. Mitchell Palmer boasted that ten thousand workers were arrested in those raids; four thousand of them were in prison at one time. Leaders of both communist organizations—among them Ruthenberg, who was now in New York—were indicted under various "criminal syndicalism" and "anarchy" laws. This mass terror against the revolutionary workers launched by the democratic and idealistic Woodrow Wilson in the interest of the propertied classes had its effect; the young communist groups were crippled. They were compelled to organize an underground movement in which Ruthenberg played a leading role. Illegal life cut the two parties off from the mass of American workers; they became sectarian and sterile; their chief activities were internal party propaganda, conflicts between the two parties, debates about abstract theoretical points. Ruthenberg was among those who favored bringing the communists into open contact with the workers. He had begun to elaborate plans in this direction when he was put on trial under his New York indictment, convicted, refused bail and imprisoned in Sing Sing. During his imprisonment, the two underground parties united and by the end of 1921 organized the open Workers' (Communist) party. Shortly afterward, Ruthenberg was released from prison and the legal party made him its secretary.

This was the abstract picture I had of Ruthenberg when I met him in the fall of 1922. I was surprised to find him a tall, suave, handsome man under forty, dressed in neat gray tweeds and a white starched collar. There was no "proletarian" pose about this proletarian revolutionary, that is, nothing bohemian. His desk, facing a window that looked out on Broadway and Eleventh Street, was orderly, as was the bookcase on which he kept the writings of Marx and Lenin. His long, narrow face with its large forehead and prominent nose was fair and pink; when he smiled his bright blue eyes became narrow slits. I never heard him raise his voice in conversation; he always spoke calmly and methodically. On several occasions he explained the Communist party to me. At my request he wrote an article on the subject which I published in the *Liberator*. In his article, Ruthenberg said:

"The Communist Party of 1919 came to life on the wave of enthusiasm inspired by the Russian Revolution. It was a spontaneous outburst in this country of the forces generated by the first proletarian revolution. . . . In the three years that have passed since the open Communist convention of 1919, the Communist movement in this country has undergone a transformation. It is no longer a spontaneous outburst of enthusiasm. It has not lost its enthusiasm, but it has learned during these three years to direct this enthusiasm into the task of creating support for Communist principles among the working masses of this country. While it again publicly announces its faith that the Soviets and the Dictatorship of the Proletariat are the instruments through which the Proletarian Revolution will achieve its ends in this country as well as elsewhere in the world, it does not expect to convert the workers to a belief in the Soviets and the Dictatorship of the Proletariat by merely holding up the example of European experience. It proposes to teach the necessity of Soviets and the Proletarian Dictatorship of the workers through their own experiences in their struggles against the capitalists; and its campaigns and programs of action are therefore based upon the actualities of the life of the workers in the United States."

The Party was seeking reality. It was a section of the international revolutionary movement operating on the national terrain out of which it sprang, in which it was rooted. Just now it was agitating the slogans of working in the trade unions, of organizing a united front of the workers, of forming a Labor party in the United States.

§ 2

Out of the war and the Bolshevik Revolution the *Liberator* group had developed to the point where it believed that the communist program was the only feasible solution to the class struggle which pervaded the world. We felt this clearly as "citizens." Had we been workers or organizers like Bill Dunne, William Z. Foster, C. E. Ruthenberg, our path would have been simpler, though our practical work would be, naturally, on a much smaller scale. But we were writers, artists, poets, critics, and we wanted to serve the revolutionary movement in our own fields. How could we do so?

On this point the Party had no policy now. It was too busy with immediate organizational tasks to pay much attention to the so-called cultural front. For the time being, we would ourselves have to answer as best we could certain questions of the utmost importance to us, questions affecting our relations *as* writers and artists to the revolutionary movement.

Here psychoanalysis loomed up no longer in the physician's study but in the realm of letters itself. Proust, Joyce and Lawrence in Europe and a dozen smaller men in America had, in their literary creations, established the "unconscious" as the ultimate source of wisdom. The prevailing, all-dominant theme of art was the subterranean life of the isolated individual, his conflicts with his parents, his frustrations and triumphs in love. The theme was old, but psychoanalysis had given it a new lease of life, opening new depths for the poet to explore.

To this there could be no objection. Experience convinced us that Freud had discovered important truths about sex, and it could not be denied that sex was a decisive human activity. We had no moralistic scruples against the Freudian thesis. It was an invaluable instrument for probing certain aspects of human conduct; it furnished rich data for the student of society. But as a system of sociology it was worthless. The world was bigger than the nursery. Quite possibly my interest at this time in Bill Dunne, William Z. Foster, C. E. Ruthenberg was conditioned by the Oedipus complex. In my early twenties, I may have been searching, as the analysts said, for a father-surrogate. If that was true, it was something I had in common with men of my age and type in all countries and all social classes. What counted now in the world of reality was not so much the origin of the search as its object. For the young people on the *Liberator,* the father-surrogate could not be in the Catholic Church, the British navy, the Viennese Medical Society. He had to be in the communist movement. This quite apart from the fact that a society which, by its hierarchical ideology, produced an enormous mass search for father-surrogates, was obviously in need of change.

Moreover, the father-surrogate had to be nearer to our pressing problems in the world of reality than a communist organizer could be. We were asking ourselves and each other: what is the relation of art to society? to the proletariat? to the working-class movement? to the Communist party? Here the aesthetic theories of psychoanalysis were inadequate. We could not consult the oracle of the "unconscious" about these matters. The analysts and their literary camp followers, so adept at probing into the individual's sex life, were as a rule illiterate in politics. To identify money with faeces, art with eros, and revolution with the Oedipus complex told us less than nothing about the Herrin massacre, the World War, the October Revolution. In any event, the "unconscious" would take care of itself. What we needed was conscious, deliberate analysis of art in the world in which we lived. And here the Party program was of little help. What it said about the class struggle, the war, the Russian Revolution, strikes, unemployment, the united front, the Labor party was for us indisputable truth. But it said nothing about art. We would have to look for our answers elsewhere.

We had before us the example of two men who had resorted to

an extreme solution of that problem. They were artists who abandoned their art to identify themselves completely with the Communist party.

I had never met John Reed in person. He had died in Moscow in the fall of 1920 and was buried with other revolutionary heroes under the Kremlin wall which faces Red Square. But his influence among us was growing with the years. His *Ten Days That Shook the World* was the classic story of the October Revolution. His life seemed to us a model for middle-class intellectuals who went over to the proletariat. When John Reed came out of Harvard he was acclaimed everywhere as a young genius; he marched straight from the campus to success. America's newspapers and magazines threw their pages open to him; they published whatever he wrote—accounts of his adventures in politics, war and love; short stories, poems and plays. Every form of success, profit and applause which the bourgeois world had in its power to bestow upon a writer was John Reed's. But during all this phenomenal success he was oppressed by the corruption first of bourgeois literature, then of bourgeois society. Max Eastman described this change shortly after Reed's death:

"There had been growing steadily in his breast a feeling of revolt against the contemporary world, against the conditions of exploitation from which our journalism, and what we call our art and literature, springs, and which it justifies, and over which it spreads a garment of superficial and false beauty."

John Reed, then, revolted against bourgeois literature because it apologized for the capitalist system of exploitation. But he went further.

"There was growing in his breast," Max Eastman explained, "a sense of the identity of his struggle toward a great poetry and literature for America, with the struggle of the working people to gain possession of America and make it human and make it free."

There could hardly be a simpler statement of the idea, developed before the Bolshevik Revolution by Americans on American soil, that great art and poetry in our age were inseparable from the struggle of the proletariat for a classless society. John Reed's first reaction to his discovery was bipolar. He continued to pursue success in the bourgeois journals and drawing rooms which paid him rich fees, and he wrote faithfully for the *Masses,* later the *Liberator,* which paid him nothing. He thus kept one foot in each camp. But the World War, and soon afterward the Russian Revolution, impelled him to make a fundamental choice between the two camps. He identified himself with the working class of America and of the world. At first he did this only as a journalist. He became a revolutionary writer. But direct contact with and participation in the ten days that shook the world roused in him the man of action. He returned to America an *organizer*. He was one of the leaders of the left wing which split off from the Socialist party and one of the founders of the Communist party of America in the fall of 1919. For the year that remained of his life he was first and foremost an active bolshevik to whom journalism, public speaking, drafting resolutions, organization were all instruments toward the same end.

Because John Reed was an American of old native stock, a Harvard boy, a lover of all joyous things, there were in this country snobs who wailed that he had "sacrificed" his life to the revolution. On the contrary, he had found his life in the revolution. As in the case of so many middle-class intellectuals, the revolution had integrated a mind divided against itself. It had cleansed John Reed of the rot he hated and sought to escape, and had given him the greatest cause of our epoch to fight for, and the strength with which to do it. His war correspondence, the fiction and the drama which the bourgeois drawing rooms so admired, were already dead and forgotten. The work of John Reed which lived on was that which he wrote in brilliant explanation and passionate defense of the Bolshevik Revolution, and that which he put into the creation of the Communist party on his native soil. If it was true of any man that in losing his life he found it, it was true of John Reed, whose measure of immortality came from the revolution for which he felt no sense of sacrifice.

In John Reed the man of action had triumphed more or less over the artist. At one of the first *Liberator* staff meetings which I attended I met another artist who was developing in that direction. Robert Minor was a Texas giant, towering over six feet, with a massive bald head and broad shoulders. Under bushy black eyebrows his dark eyes shone with a gleam of fanaticism. His deep voice uttered the simplest sentences slowly and with pontifical finality. Yet one could not help being impressed by the stubborn sincerity of everything Robert Minor said and did. The night I met him in the fall of 1921 he lectured the *Liberator* staff on the American social revolution.

"We shall probably have our nineteen-five before we have our nineteen-seventeen," he said dogmatically.

What one remembered most vitally about him were his cartoons, those vast massive black-and-white figures full of muscle, action and an internal spiritual power which marked itself indelibly on all who saw them.

Bob. Minor had made original contributions to an art which is pre-eminent in America and in which America leads the world. The newspaper, in our land of supertechnology, is a genuine mass literature; the cartoon, reproduced in millions of copies, is a mass art. In the hands of a ruling class intent upon maintaining itself in power by fraud as well as force, the cartoon is corrupt; it is either direct political falsehood, or, as in the case of the comic strips, infantile evasion. Into this field, exercising so powerful an influence over the American masses that publishers spend millions on it, Minor brought a number of innovations. The technical method of reproducing cartoons—a method employed today by the entire American press—is his contribution. He also introduced a style so vivid, so mighty in its simple masses, that it eventually produced a school. In the work of such bourgeois cartoonists as Fitzpatrick of the St. Louis *Post Dispatch* and Rollin Kirby of the Scripps-Howard syndicate, in the extremely gifted work of revolutionary cartoonists like Fred Ellis and Jacob Burck, one sees definitely and permanently the stylistic influence of Robert Minor's genius.

But Minor's significance lay not alone in his technical gifts. It lay rather in the use to which he put those gifts. A giant in the world of graphic art, a success in the capitalist newspapers by every prevailing standard, he renounced all this, all the money and all the glory which the bourgeois world offered him, to place his gifts at the service of the revolutionary working class. This, too, was in no sense a "sacrifice." Minor's gifts as an artist were an integral part of a complete revolutionary personality. They were part of his equipment, not his whole being. Art was for him only one of the instruments which he employed for the cause to which he devoted his life. When necessary he could, even in the days when he was primarily an artist, lay aside the crayon and take·up the pen or ascend the rostrum. Drawing, writing, public speaking, organizing—these were all means to a goal.

As was perhaps natural for an artist before 1917, Minor first saw this goal through the blurred prism of anarchism. After he understood the October Revolution he saw it through the archway of bolshevism. Yet at no time after he reached intellectual maturity did he sink into the morass of "pure" art. As early as 1902 he was a member of a trade union, as early as 1910 a member of the Socialist party. The diverse elements of his being, his versatile gifts were unified by the proletarian revolution. Hence there was in his cartoons something which his imitators in the bourgeois press could not take over, which only the new revolutionary cartoonists could grasp and assimilate—their revolutionary content. Minor not only had the genius for speaking powerfully with the crayon; he had something to say, something to which the class-conscious workers and radical intellectuals of all countries responded because it spoke their thoughts.

For years Minor drew for the *Masses* and its successor the *Liberator* which called itself first socialist, then communist. All that time Minor was a professed anarchist. Because of his stubborn sincerity, he came to communism slowly and painfully. His conversion was preceded by an episode which rocked the radical world of America, and raised an important question of tactics for those of us who wanted to be revolutionary writers.

In 1918 Minor visited Moscow and interviewed Lenin. When he reached Berlin he turned the interview over to Arno Dosch-Fleurot, correspondent of the New York *World,* and to Lenin's comments added his own anarchist criticisms of the bolsheviks. The *World* published the article, and editorial writers were quick to seize upon this criticism of the communists from the left. Shortly afterward, Max Eastman attacked Minor in the *Liberator* for criticizing the Soviet regime in a capitalist newspaper. The matter was eventually cleared up. Minor was able to show that what he wrote was never published; only a distorted version of his dispatch appeared in the *World.* As soon as he saw a copy of it, Minor branded this version as false. The question of publishing an interview with Lenin in the capitalist press was settled by Lenin himself. The bolshevik leader, in the presence of Boris Reinstein, had told Minor he considered it advisable to have an interview on the subject of Russia's debt payments published in a leading capitalist newspaper in America. This was considered politically necessary. Soviet Russia was at that time completely isolated. The rough draft of Minor's story was approved in Berlin by an authorized representative of the Soviet regime. In 1920 Minor voluntarily published his own sharp criticisms of the story not only as it appeared in the *World,* but as he had actually written it. He attributed its weaknesses to his own admitted uncertainty at the time; these weaknesses made easier the distortions of the *World* correspondent who cabled the story. Minor sent a copy of the original text, as drafted by him in Berlin, to Lenin in Moscow. Two and a half years later he discussed the whole matter with Lenin. For many months thereafter Minor was personally associated with Lenin in the work of the Third International, serving as the representative of the American Communist party in the Comintern presidium. During this time, Lenin's own attitude toward the *World* interview criticizing the bolsheviks was indicated by his close personal friendship with Minor.

All this came out afterward. In the spring of 1919, however, it was already clear that Minor was veering toward the Soviet regime. The *Liberator* published an excerpt from one of his letters:

"Ah, that I have lived to see such things come to pass! It is relentless and as real as a cobblestone. It is not democracy; it is plainly and frankly a dictatorship of the proletariat. . . . The whole beautiful land is even more glorious than I thought, and no one should stay away from here a minute."

On the basis of this letter, Eastman urged that no opinion be formed at present of the motives which actuated Minor's cablegrams to the American press; but he continued to harp on the principle of the thing.

"It is not a new thing," he argued, "for an honest and artistic apostle of anarchist rebellion to denounce 'the march of the iron battalions of the proletariat' as 'nationalized' and 'centralized' and all other bad names for good organization. It *is* a new thing, however, for an anarchist *to retail his criticisms of any proletarian movement to capitalist newspapers, which will use them, as he well knows, for an attack on all proletarian movements—socialist, anarchist or trade unionist.*"

Following the *World* interview, Minor moved steadily toward communism. He underwent a transformation analogous to John Reed's. Contact with the October Revolution in Russia and with large groups of American workers detached him from his art and impelled him toward active organization. If Minor shocked his pro-Soviet friends by the distorted *World* interview, he shocked his anarchist friends even more by going over completely to the communists. In doing so, however, he was no exception among anarchists and syndicalists. Bill Shatoff, well-known in American labor circles for his activities in this country, now held high office in Soviet Russia. The syndicalist Bill Foster was in the leadership of the American Communist party. Such conversion was to be expected. The bolsheviks led the first successful proletarian revolution in history; to them now came the best fighting spirits from the right, from the ranks of the social democracy;

and from the left, from the I.W.W. and the anarchists. For the latter Bob Minor spoke up in the *Liberator* in the fall of 1920. He who had roused the ire of pro-Soviet radicals for criticizing Lenin in the bourgeois press, now came forward to admit that he had "changed his mind a little." He had concluded that the Soviet republic represented the aspirations fundamental to the anarchist movement. But Minor's stubborn sincerity stopped at no half measures. If you're going to be a bolshevik, he argued, you must do it all. When we worked on the *Liberator* together in 1922 he was already active in the leadership of the open Communist party.

Many of Minor's friends—some of them sympathizers of the communist movement—were chagrined at the manner in which he chose to serve the revolutionary cause. It was pardonable for an artist to work for the proletarian revolution *as an artist;* it was silly for him to become an active fighter in the communist vanguard, to transform himself into a "politician." I heard these complaints frequently in Greenwich Village, where the word "politician" was spoken with the same contempt with which some communist organizers uttered the word "intellectual." People said Minor was selling his soul for a mess of pottage; politicians were a necessary evil; the artist should be above them. Minor, however, never did things by half; he could never be a "fellow traveler." From the day he grasped the meaning of the Communist party he gave himself to it without reserve.

At first he was compelled to face John Reed's dilemma—how to co-ordinate art and revolution. The attempt to balance two modes of energy became complicated. Minor abandoned drawing altogether and devoted himself exclusively to Party work. But the Party itself, understanding and appreciating the value of his art, again and again asked him to return to his drawing board. In 1923 Minor tried a compromise; he was active in the movement as both cartoonist and politician. I was among those pleased with this solution.

"I was delighted," I wrote to Minor in the spring of that year, "to read of your decision to go back to your drawing. When you write articles, they are always well-informed, clear, striking; but there are a number of theoreticians who can apply their Marxian formulae equally well. When you draw, you stand up like a mountain above the men and women of your generation. Politicians and statesmen and organizers are necessary; so are ditch-diggers, street-cleaners and subway-guards. None of us can do all the things which society requires; and I am happy to think that you are once more going to do the thing at which you are greatest, and which has made thousands of people the world over love you."

In subsequent years, I changed my views about politics, although I continued to believe that everyone serves the revolutionary movement best by doing that for which he is by nature and training best fitted. Minor, however, is an exceptional case. Like John Reed, his energies express themselves as vitally in political action as in art; and being a man whose temperament requires complete concentration, he abandoned art for action. The choice and the reasons for it were entirely his own; if these be an enigma, that enigma is personal. The Party's persistent efforts to induce Minor to return to his drawing have proved futile; he preferred to be exclusively an active bolshevik.

Moreover, the case of an artist renouncing his craft for action is not specifically communist. In the bourgeois world there is the classic case of Arthur Rimbaud. What distinguishes Robert Minor from Arthur Rimbaud is that Minor's action was not one of escape, of an evasive reconciliation from a distance with the bourgeois culture which he rejected in his youth. Minor carried the battle from the studio and the pressroom to the platform and the street. The story of John Reed's and Bob Minor's living example indicated to us one possible solution to our problem: *to abandon art and literature completely and to enter the Communist party as active organizers.*

§ 3

By the fall of 1922 the growing prosperity of the middle classes and the disillusionment of intellectuals with the social revolution deprived the *Liberator* of its old base. The magazine now had little middle-class support. Its old staff was scattered: John Reed dead, Max Eastman in Europe, Floyd Dell in Croton; Boardman Robinson, Art Young and Arturo Giovannitti busy elsewhere. And now Mike Gold, ill and exhausted, went off to California to work on a novel whose first draft Floyd had praised as "the Jewish Moon-Calf." Left alone with the magazine, I discovered once more Dell's generosity of spirit and extraordinary sense of duty. He was busy writing fiction and supporting a family in the suburbs, yet he remained on the staff of the magazine and traveled into the city several times a week to help me edit it. This particular arrangement was hard on Floyd, and the general situation was hard on all of us. We were working in a vacuum. We felt detached from the prosperous middle-class intelligentsia which was detaching itself from us. We needed a new and more definite base. Several courses were open to us. We could suspend the magazine entirely and thus destroy the only left-wing publication of arts and letters in America. We could compromise by converting it into a pinkish art journal, divorced from politics, like the dozens of little reviews springing up all over the country and among the American exiles in Europe for the solace of the tired radicals. Finally, we could turn over the magazine to the Communist party in whose principles we believed and which needed a monthly publication.

At a staff meeting which included Bob Minor, Floyd Dell, Bill Gropper, Hugo Gellert and myself, we voted to present the magazine to the Party. Minor and I were appointed executive editors. We moved the magazine to Party headquarters on East Eleventh Street—on the opposite side of the Village, closer to the district in which the trade-union workers lived.

I shared a back room with Louis Engdahl, one of the five socialists indicted in Chicago during the war, now editor of the *Weekly Worker,* official communist organ. Engdahl was a tall, red-faced Midwesterner with graying hair carefully brushed back and heavy glasses. He spoke in a flat monotone, and seldom laughed. In conversation, oratory and articles he was intensely earnest; and worked with the endurance and energy of ten men. No matter how early in the morning you came, or how late at night you left, Engdahl was busy at his desk. He did not leave it even for lunch, but nibbled at a dry sandwich or a piece of chocolate while typing or editing copy. He made up for lack of originality by a boundless loyalty to the cause in which his whole being was wrapped up. I worked by his side day after day for six months, and saw him frequently in subsequent years until his untimely death, and we were friends; yet it was a rare occasion when he referred to the little he had of private life. Everything revolved for him around the movement. If we went for a soda, he would ask the clerk about conditions in the drugstores; after a movie, he would lecture you about the importance of the film, how it concealed real conditions and bamboozled the masses. His greatest passion, however, was the revolutionary press; to this he gave the best of his enormous energy and loyalty; and as time went on I could not help comparing the permanent results of his devoted plodding with the ephemeral flashes of more brilliant but less disciplined journalists on the fringes of the movement.

The artists and writers who now contributed to the *Liberator* had settled the problem of art and revolution in a very general way. They thought they had broken with bourgeois culture and were ready to serve the organized struggle of the working class. But the solution of one problem often means the creation of new ones. When the Party took over the *Liberator* we felt that one period in American radical literature had closed, and another had opened. The *Masses* and *Liberator* as we had known it since 1913 had died. That publication had never been officially attached to any political group. Its contributors wrote on behalf of socialism, anarchism, syndicalism or communism as *individuals,* and the magazine printed their conflicting views. Moreover, its writers and artists were "universal" men who themselves dealt both with poetry and with politics. John Reed wrote verses and reported wars; Floyd Dell did book reviews and defended the Bolshevik Revolution; Max Eastman tried to interpret politics and composed sonnets; Bob Minor drew cartoons and commented on current events; Arturo Giovannitti led strikes, wrote heroic verse and reported trials. There was among the members of the prewar group a division of mind but no division of labor; they wrote on the assumption that nothing human was alien to them.

Under the aegis of the Party this tradition was of necessity ended. The new course was symbolized by the existence of two separate groups of "associate editors," whose names appeared in the editorial box in two separate columns with distinct headings. The "political editors" were for the most part members of the Central Committee of the Communist party—among them C. E. Ruthenberg, William Z. Foster, Ludwig Lore, James P. Cannon, Jay Lovestone, M. J. Olgin; the "art editors" were for the most part members of the old *Masses* and *Liberator* group including Floyd Dell, Arturo Giovannitti, Boardman Robinson, William Gropper, Lydia Gibson, Hugo Gellert, Claude McKay, Michael Gold. Not all of these were active, however; some were abroad, others lived out of town. The Party, quite naturally, wished to keep the direction of editorial policy in its own hands; the realm of art, presumably less serious, was left for the artists.

Bob Minor and I were the "executive editors" who co-ordinated the material which came in or was solicited. We suggested themes to contributors in both groups and planned issues of the magazine. We combined politics and poetry in one publication *mechanically* while separating them *functionally.* With one or two exceptions, the political editors had no particular interest in art, revolutionary or otherwise; with one or two exceptions, the art editors had only the most general, unspecified interest in politics. They supported the Party in its general program and participated in its special campaigns but ignored the course of political events as a whole. Some of them wanted to steer clear of "politics" altogether; they were communist sympathizers who wanted to retain their roots in literary and artistic circles. If I wanted a political article, I could get it at Party headquarters, always full of Central Committee members, trade-union organizers, Party journalists, district organizers, leaders of the Communist Youth; if I wanted a story, a poem or a drawing I would have to trace the proud isolated artist to his lair in Greenwich Village.

Here again was that dualism of politics and poetry which had preoccupied me for so many years. Working contact with Bill Dunne, William Z. Foster, C. E. Ruthenberg, Louis Engdahl and other leading communists, editing what was now an official Party organ, speaking at mass meetings of workers, attending trade-union conferences—these strengthened political interests which had been growing in me for a long time. The World War and the October Revolution continued to be the touchstones of our epoch by which I measured everything—and on that basis the Communist party alone appeared to represent the best interests of mankind. I was clarifying my own mind, as well as agitating the reader, when I wrote editorially in the *Liberator* of February, 1923:

"The clouds of war hang black and massive over the world, and they hang ominously low. . . . Five years after the 'war to end war,' Europe is again an armed camp bristling with bayonets; and again the masses of the world are facing the slaughter and disaster which are the inevitable consequences of capitalism, with its attendant imperialism, militarism and foul diplomacy. The Versailles Treaty, that insane document of pillage and revenge, is beginning to bear its poisoned fruit. . . . The Versailles Treaty was not intended to be a peace; it was intended to be, it was in fact, merely an armistice. . . . It is now clear to the whole world that no capitalist nation is interested in peace; each is interested in seizing the greatest industrial treasure for itself, and in smashing its chief economic rivals for good. This was their intent from the very beginning, which accounts for the fiasco of one 'disarmament' conference after another; it accounts for Washington and Genoa, for the sterility of the hundred and one sessions of Allied premiers; it accounts for the silence with which Russia's frank and genuine offer of disarmament was received. Capitalism cannot dispense with robbery, chicanery, brigandage and murder. . . . Unable to repair the ruins of the last catastrophe, capitalism is already preparing a new one. . . . Another world war, whether it comes now or later, means a fatal blow to capitalism. That criminal system of exploitation has already run its course in Europe. Its days are numbered, though the days of history may be a little longer than the days of man."

When the second world war would come we could not foretell; but of its coming we were certain. The governments of the capitalist countries, the bourgeois press, the liberal journalists talked piously about peace, the League of Nations, disarmament; we knew better. Lenin's *Imperialism* was now available in English—an application to the twentieth century of Marxian principles. The revolutionary Marxists had foretold the first world war, not as prophets but as social scientists; with the same method of analysis they could foretell the second. So long as capitalism existed war was inevitable—as were poverty, unemployment, ignorance for the mass of mankind. We were living in a world which was an armed camp and would continue to be one for years; for just as the war was only the first of its kind, so the Bolshevik Revolution was only the first of those social transformations which the proletariat would effect in other parts of the world. Lenin had described our era as that of imperialism, the last stage of capitalism; it was the era of the proletarian revolution. I had come to assume that viewpoint slowly, through the socialism which led to the left wing, then to the Communist party, and through art and literature which led to the *Liberator* and again to the Communist party. What restrained me from the final step was the conviction that I had no capacity for practical action. I could never be an organizer. I looked upon myself as a poet; the best I could do for the Party was journalism and public speaking; a "creative" writer was of no use to the movement. Ruthenberg demurred.

"Everyone who is with us," he said, "will find his place somewhere in the ranks. There's a lot of work to be done. Journalism is important; lecturing is important. But don't you think that novels like those of Upton Sinclair and Jack London have been useful to the movement too? Don't you think Floyd Dell's literary criticism was useful? and Giovannitti's poetry?"

From Ruthenberg's secretary I learned that he liked good prose. His letters from Sing Sing to his personal friends were extremely moving. Ruthenberg's counsel was comforting. You could serve the communist cause as Floyd Dell had served the socialist cause—in a purely literary capacity.

From other sources, too, came encouragement that the writer had his place in the revolutionary ranks. I picked up somewhere and reprinted in the *Liberator* in italics the following statement by Karl Radek:

"Jack London, in his novel The Iron Heel, *written before the war, has displayed a thousand times profounder insight into the course of the world revolution than all the theoreticians of the Second International put together. The great revolutionary novelist describes three centuries, not of peaceful evolution into the state of socialism, but of severe struggles."*

Floyd Dell, with whom I was at this time having long discussions on art and revolution, used to say: "If Percy Bysshe Shelley had lived in our era, he would have been another Jack London; and if Jack London had lived a few years longer, he would have been another Jack Reed, he would have been in the Communist party."

§ 4

One of my fellow editors on the *Liberator,* listed in the political group, was the red-cheeked, dark-eyed, buxom Clarissa Ware. Like Bill Dunne, Foster, Ruthenberg and Minor, she was an "Aryan" of native American stock, a descendant of the Pilgrim Fathers. Her family tree went back directly to both Miles Standish and John Alden. She had come from a well-to-do home and a university to work in the communist movement. In her presence the "freedom of woman," about which you heard so much in Greenwich Village, took on new meaning. She flaunted no fantastic symbols—no batik blouses, sandals or mannish clothes. She dressed conventionally; even her bobbed black hair, tousled in thick curls, was heavier than was the fashion. She was a healthy, handsome, laughing woman full of the charms called feminine, yet did not burn her candles at both ends. She had a husband and a daughter of four whom she occasionally brought to Party headquarters. The child was an energetic little devil who crawled across my desk, ruining sonnets, book reviews, and articles on trade-union policy. Once Louis Engdahl looked up at Clarissa Ware and said with his mournful humor:

"Is that steam engine a boy or a girl?"

"Ask her," Clarissa said.

"What are you, darling?"

The kid stopped tearing an editorial I had left in the typewriter. "I'm a communist," she said.

"More truth than poetry!" Engdahl roared, laughing.

At work you did not think of Clarissa Ware's patrician background, or her personal charms, or that she was a woman. In the ranks you were first, last and always a comrade. That was an old tradition of the revolutionary movement, which had set the emancipation of woman as a corollary of the emancipation of labor and of the op-pressed races. Before general equality was to be achieved in society as a whole, there was to be equality in the movement itself. We knew the heroic stories of Louise Michel of the Paris Commune, of Vera Figner, Vera Zassulich and Krupskaya in Russia, of Mother Jones and Mother Bloor in America. In the ranks there were no distinctions of race or sex. Differences in position, function or influence were individual. We cited the Marxian aphorism: from each according to his abilities, to each according to his needs. That was meant for the future communist society. Meantime you were supposed to practice it as far as possible within the movement today. The "sex war," of which you heard so much in the Village, and among the bourgeois feminists, and in the novels of D. H. Lawrence, now the rage among the intellectuals, was resolved in Party circles by the common work of men and women for a common cause which transcended sex. Yet communists were neither automatons nor angels. They loved with less fanfare and pre-tense than Villagers, with less hypocrisy than Babbitts, but they, too, loved.

Occasionally, some functionary would rationalize his male jealousy in political terms. Instead of calling his rival in love a bastard he would call him a social democrat, and with sincere self-delusion would vote against his proposals. In the long run, however, such conflicts had no effect on Party policy. Communism had no Pompadours; the welfare of the movement transcended all personal relations. As might be expected, psychoanalysts of my acquaintance explained this in their own jargon. Power, they said, dissolves love. In warfare of every kind, the libido is diverted from the love object to the leader, who, needless to say, is the father-image.

Because of her special training and education, Clarissa Ware was put in charge of the Party's research department. Her own inclinations impelled her to specialize in the problems of the American foreign-born worker. These inclinations were determined by a need for bridg-ing the gap between her patrician American background and the prole-tariat with which she identified herself. In the same way Bob Minor, nurtured in the race prejudices of Texas, overcame his "original sin" by becoming the Party's specialist on the Negro problem. My own immigrant background roused my interest in Clarissa Ware's work, and I asked her to do a piece for the *Liberator* which I entitled *Makers of America.* Here she maintained that the core of the American people was the millions of workers who had come from far lands, dug our coal, molded our steel, laid the railway tracks, ran the textile mills; who with their brawn and sweat and blood had built up the gigantic industries of America.

Shortly after this article appeared, Clarissa Ware was operated on for pancreatitis. She died suddenly, in her early thirties. Her last words were:

"I have made a good fight, haven't I?"

To make a good fight for the new society was the pride of the communist; Clarissa Ware's question uttered the attitude of many women in the ranks—the zealous and talented Rose Pastor Stokes; the gray-haired, smiling, enormously energetic Mother Bloor, who organized farmers and workers, yet took time off in Moscow to interview the Danish novelist Martin Andersen Nexö for her "boys" on the *Liberator;* the pale, hard-working, devoted organizers like Rose Wortis, precursors of a new type of woman which Party work was to develop in America.

§ 5

The labor movement in the United States had always been legal, and the political groups which grew out of the labor movement had also been legal. Until the war, both the Socialist party and the I.W.W. had been open organizations. But the Espionage Act, ostensibly passed against German spies, was actually employed to crush the labor movement. This federal law was followed by "criminal syndicalism" acts in various states. As these were interpreted and applied, it became a crime, punishable by severe prison sentences, to express any opinion not sanctioned by the reactionaries or to participate in labor activities. Under these circumstances, the I.W.W. was severely damaged; many of its leaders were arrested, and many of its members imprisoned or dispersed. The right wing of the Socialist party saved it from a similar fate by abandoning serious opposition to the status quo. The newly formed communist groups faced the most drastic persecution both from state authorities acting under the criminal syndicalism acts, and from the federal authorities directed by Attorney General A. Mitchell Palmer. This confronted the communists with a drastic but simple choice: either to disband, to commit political suicide, or to exist as best they could in secret until their right to normal political activity was restored. The underground existence of the communist movement in this country was thus owing not to any desire on the part of the communists, but to the reactionary policy of the government which deprived them of their political rights. As soon as the Palmer raids began to subside, as soon as political "normalcy" was in sight, the communists began to take steps toward the formation of an open Communist party.

In the summer of 1922, the underground Communist party held its last secret meeting in the woods around Bridgman, Michigan. A stool pigeon high in the organization's councils tipped off the Department of Justice, and the meeting was raided. William Z. Foster, C. E. Ruthenberg, Rose Pastor Stokes and others were arrested under Michigan's criminal syndicalism act. The prosecution put Foster on trial first. On that occasion, Ruthenberg wrote an article which I published in the *Liberator* of March, 1923, in which he attributed the underground existence of the Party to the Palmer raids.

"The Communists," he explained, "have no particular love for underground life or for working in secret. They have nothing to hide. They desire nothing more than to proclaim their principles openly and publicly. They had to exist underground in order to exist at all. Under similar conditions they would have no choice but to do the same. . . . The whole history of the Palmer raids . . . shows that these raids did not have as their object prosecution of crime, but persecution to destroy a movement which was feared by the capitalists who control the government of the United States."

Ruthenberg poked fun at the "bugaboo of violence which the prosecutors and the press have tried to make of the communist movement." No communist, he said, advocates the use of violence in the class struggle in the United States today.

"Communists have better sense. No Communist has been convicted of an overt act of violence in the United States. What Communists are charged with is the crime of telling historical truth. They have been bold enough to say that the slave owners of the South did not give up the special economic privileges which they enjoyed as a result of chattel slavery without resort to violence. They have told the historical truth that no privileged class has ever yielded up its right to exploit and oppress without a trial of strength outside the formal rules of the struggle laid down by law, without a resort to force and violence to protect its interests. It is a logical inference from this that the capitalist class which enjoys powers of oppression and exploitation yielding it greater wealth than any class in history has ever enjoyed, will not yield up its position without a struggle which will go beyond the formal rules governing the struggle for political power in the United States. To say this openly, the Communists contend, is not a violation even of the existing class laws. They will say it openly and in the courtroom of St. Joseph, from the public rostrum and in their press."

Eugene Debs sent me an article for the *Liberator* which indicated the meaning of "united front." He was a leading member of the Socialist party, yet he not only came to the defense of the communists on trial in Michigan, but showed the significance of those trials for the whole American working class.

"It is not the communists alone who are to be strangled," he warned, "but it is the entire labor movement, industrial and political, that is to be throttled the instant it becomes clarified and militant enough to be regarded as a menace to the Robbers' Roost in Wall Street and their subsidiaries in the several states of the union. . . . If we have intelligence enough to understand the vital issues at stake and courage enough to do our duty, we will back up our comrades on trial in Michigan to the very last."

Debs' identification with the working class enabled him to transcend his own party.

From the courtroom in St. Joseph, Bob Minor sent in an eyewitness account of the trial with biting cartoons of the judge, the prosecutor, the labor spies, the Department of Justice agents. The prosecution employed the fake testimony customary in labor cases, and was enthusiastically backed up by the Michigan press which raised lying to a fine art. But Foster, and later Ruthenberg, converted the courtroom into a public forum; the communists put capitalism on trial. Their lucid exposition of Party aims and tactics was extensively reported in the press and contributed to their eventual release.

For years I had read about "class justice" and was familiar with written accounts of the various great labor trials. This time the matter came nearer home. I knew the "criminals" personally, and understood emotionally what I had hitherto grasped intellectually. Not a man among their prosecutors could compare in disinterestedness of mind or purity of character or selfless devotion to the best interests of humanity with Foster or Ruthenberg. Yet these high-minded Americans were being hounded as criminals because they dedicated their lives to the struggle for a free society.

I got to know that hounding more directly when Bob Minor disappeared to escape an indictment for the Bridgman affair. For a while I did not see him and edited the magazine alone. In the Village you heard wisecracks from intellectuals safely barricaded behind their cocktails: Bob Minor was a romantic; he loved to mystify people; someone saw him on the street with a cap drawn over his eyes, smoked glasses and a beard like Trotsky's and he said "sh-sh" and disappeared around the corner. Contact with workers who had been picked up in the Palmer raids and with the men and women indicted in Michigan did not stimulate my respect for these intellectuals. Soon I was put in contact with Minor. It was true, he did wear a cap; but his glasses were not smoked and the beard was only a mustache. We met clandestinely in various parts of the city, in furnished rooms, sometimes in his wife's studio. It was not a bit romantic; it was a nuisance, and nobody felt that more keenly than Bob Minor, who was anxious to work in the Party openly and undisturbed. What Ruthenberg said about the Party was true of Bob; no communist liked to lead a mysterious underground life if he could help it. If he can't help it he says with the Achilles of Goethe's poem: "and now let us do that which must be done."

If I managed to get to the studio, after a lot of red tape, Bob was usually sprawled out on the floor, reading, writing or sketching. We would dummy the new issue of the *Liberator* and plan future issues. Bob always spoke in private conversation as he did on the platform, in a deep deliberate voice, slowly drawing out his words, clipping them syllable by syllable.

"Let us—see—now," he would say. "For thee next is-sue—we want—a good—deep—deescription of thee Trade Union Edu-cational League. Not from thee—viewpoint—of an—insider. A deetached—objective deescription. As though the writer—were outside—it. And thee reader—had—never heard of it. An ana-ly-sis of it—as a big—social phenomenon."

He was greatly preoccupied with the trade-union question and wanted us to publish a number of articles on it. He urged also a series of articles on American capitalism and politics "by someone other than myself"; but he warned against "empty opinionations." Bolsheviks, he said, must be serious—"only good, sound work based on research and on new knowledge, or at least new co-ordination." Nor did he forget art, but by this time he was absorbed by the problem of mass art.

"We need," he would say, "a story on POISON IN THE MOVIES or THE MOVIE MAGNATES' STRANGLE HOLD, or something like that—description of the filth factories in Hollywood which have killed every spark of life in the popular theaters of America—which have shut off the development of a great art—potentially; which have destroyed all individuality in production as well as all public freedom and choice; which have forced a whole phase of public life under the hand of a single czar—directly for money gain, and indirectly for the control of public opinion in the interests of capitalism."

Dodging the Department of Justice forced Minor into relative inactivity, and his suppressed energy now sought release in his abandoned art. Sprawling on his belly along the floor of the studio, he firmly gripped his black crayon and stroke by stroke drew "The Man on Horseback." The object of this satire was a man of whom Old Man Jackson, in his Jeffersonian dread of an American dictatorship, had not even dreamed. It was William J. Burns, labor spy, who had supplied alleged evidence against the communists on trial in Michigan. Minor drew him astride a powerful charger, trampling the prostrate bodies of men and women, and crumpled copies of the Constitution and the Declaration of Independence. The villain was wrapped in Old Glory, carried a heavy mace across his shoulder and wore a pointed German steel helmet. As Minor sprawled over the drawing paper, slowly digging his crayon into its rough white surface, his strong features grimaced each line and curve like a mime's. By turns Minor was the horse, the prostrate bodies, the helmet, the stars and stripes, the sinister sleuth. This was what the new psychologists meant by identification. The artist became his subject.

As I watched Minor draw, I was overwhelmed again by the old feeling that art was the most sublime thing in human life, and I scribbled a doggerel beginning:

> Theories formulas explanations
> clans and churches
> east India companies
> labor unions nations
> god knows we need them
> to keep our bellies full
> of bread and beer and mutton
> also we need a tailor
> to sew on a button
> but the whole damned show

wouldnt be worth a cuspidor
without a michelangelo.

For my generation the problem of art and revolution was to remain a thorny one. Even on the level on which we worked, to break
trails meant to struggle with the most elementary questions. This
struggle led me to literary criticism, which I have always liked to
read and never liked to write. Now there was no longer a choice.
When you are deeply rooted in one world, you can create poems and
stories out of emotion, out of unquestioned presupposition. When you
are in the No Man's Land between two worlds, you must analyze,
weigh, compare, question, test, hypothesize. The quest of the intellect
transforms the assumption of the emotions. This has its advantages too;
it gives you an opportunity for grappling with fundamentals.

The critic, I soon discovered, is as autobiographical as the poet,
only he speaks more impersonally and abstractly. In a review of
Genevieve Taggard's first book of poems, published in the *Liberator*
of May, 1923, I tried to state a new attitude which I thought our poets
were expressing. But this attitude was now my own, as it was that of
the young communists whom I met at Party headquarters.

Genevieve Taggard's verse, I thought, expressed the mood of the
postwar radicals.

"This mood is a reaction to the chaos and tumult which has filled
the world these last ten years. It is the desire for building new things
which comes after destroying old ones. The reaction to the repressions
of puritan America was a poetry which broke all bonds, plunged reck-
lessly into all sorts of experiences and experiments. It was the poetry
of a generation repudiating its fathers, throwing out its passions and
energies with a beautiful and terrible extravagance; a generation defiantly living in shining palaces built upon the sand and singing by the
flame of candles burning at both ends. But the new mood, separated
from the old by these brief years of defiance and destruction, is of a
more intellectual fiber. The new youth seeks self-discipline; it wants to
understand all limitations in order to overcome them, and to prefigure
all possibilities in order to achieve them. It seeks to master its own intellect and emotions in order to control machines. This is evident in every
field. Foster's amalgamation replaces aimless vituperation; T. S. Eliot's
considered criticism replaces Anatole France's personal impressionism;
a historic materialism replaces a mystical and noncommittal bergson-
ism; in art mere energy gives way to definite form; and in personal

conduct the passion of excitement gives way to self-reorganization."

I did not know Genevieve Taggard at this time. When she wrote me that of all the reviews of her book, mine had come nearest to her thought, I felt that I had not spoken for myself only. Yet it was incorrect to assume that the mood described was typical of the entire post-war generation. For the middle classes, the jazz age had begun, and the new American literature was loud with it. This isolated the revolutionary writers from official literary circles. But I continued to lecture on literature for workers' clubs. At one such meeting, a pale hunchbacked young worker rose to ask one of those questions which become a thirty-minute speech.

"That was a very nice exposition of social factors in American literature," he said ironically, "but where is Karl Marx? You haven't mentioned him once!"

The speaker emphasized for me the gap between revolutionary politics and revolutionary literature which existed in our thinking during this period. Among the workers the meaning of the class struggle was lucid and forceful. The qualms which agitated the intellectuals did not exist. You were either a communist or you were not; if you were, your place was in the ranks. The problem of art and revolution would be worked out in the course of time. Meantime there were plenty of other things to do. I thought I understood and accepted the theories and tactics of communism. These laid great stress on a disciplined, centralized Party, described as the vanguard of the proletariat. To join the Party seemed to me normal and logical, even for one who imagined himself a poet.

CHAPTER IV

IDEALISTS

The silent bleed of a world decaying,
The moan of multitudes in woe,
These were the things we wished would go;
But they were staying.
                              —THOMAS HARDY.

§ 1

THE bourgeois press was closed to left-wing writers. Our own publications confined themselves to the political and economic aspects of the class struggle. Confronted by the task of building a mass working-class movement in the United States, the *Worker* gave nearly all its space to politics; the *Liberator,* now in the hands of the Central Committee of the Party, was developing in the same direction. This placed radical writers and artists in a paradoxical position. Among aesthetes we defended revolutionary politics; among Party comrades we argued for art. In the spring of 1923, for example, Mike Gold was running a column for Fremont Older's paper in California, and I was editing the *Liberator* in New York. Deprived of a specifically literary magazine, we wrote each other long letters, half solemn, half ironical, about "art and revolution." Gold urged me not to let myself be "swamped by the new regime" and not to "give up trying for the literary people and the artists in the matter of contributions." Fight for fiction, poetry, pictures, he wrote. But while preaching art to me to counteract what he considered the too political atmosphere of New York, Gold urged politics upon the bohemian aesthetes of San Francisco. The Western radicals, he complained to me, needed to learn about Russia now more than ever; they needed to be able to hope about the new Russia; everyone seemed tired and discouraged in America anyway.

My own complaints were in another direction: I was going through all the growing pains of the neophyte. Still enmeshed in the illusory world in which I had spent so many years, I found all reality harsh. I was shocked and puzzled to find that certain communists called each other comrades when they were fierce rivals for power. I wrote to Mike Gold bitterly about "the incompetents who seek to fulfill among the workers the petit bourgeois ambitions which they could not attain among the capitalists." Why could not every comrade be as unselfish as Foster, Ruthenberg or Minor? Older than I, more experienced, Gold corrected my dark thoughts about the "power drive" which seemed to animate some communists. The myth of unselfishness, he explained, was one of the silliest of all myths. Men fighting in groups for something were almost like any other men in groups opposing them. The only intelligible thing about the whole affair was the flags under which men fought, the opposing philosophies. We both agreed that a historic crisis would bring the best communists to the fore. As for himself, Mike Gold said, he had never wanted to be a politician and was not going to become one; he was happier trying to write.

Neither of us was aware to what an extent our moods, undisciplined by Marxist analysis, fluid and contradictory in the bohemian tradition which cried anathema on will and worshiped sensibility, were the result of the historic period in which we were living. Postwar prosperity surrounded us with the fragrance of vast, steaming fleshpots; it was easy, as Mike said, to "get by." The Comintern now talked of the temporary and relative stabilization of capitalism, and some American radicals stretched the relative toward the absolute, and the temporary toward infinity. The NEP, then in full swing in Soviet Russia, strengthened this illusion. The "romantic" period of the world revolution was, for the time being, over, and our "poetic" sensibilities recoiled from the hard, undramatic, indispensable day-to-day labors required of communists by the necessities of this period. If we were not to fall back into the morass of aestheticism, it was imperative for radical writers to face those necessities, to work with them.

Again we had to rely upon literary criticism in order to resolve, if only by a tour de force of the mind, the dualism which hampered us. The younger *Liberator* group was now completely cut off by political differences from the official literary world. On questions of literature, as on those of politics, we addressed ourselves to working-class groups, clarifying our own ideas while sharing them with our proletarian readers. In the spring of 1923 I published an article in the *Worker* which seemed to me an obvious corollary of Marxism, and a continuation of the socialist literary tradition both here and abroad. All books, this article said, were "the expression of desires, fears and prejudices which are colored by the culture of the *class* from which the writer springs. This point is particularly important." This article also discussed the illusion that there was a mysterious and fundamental difference between literature and propaganda. If there was a difference, it could be stated thus: literature was propaganda in favor of accepted ideas; propaganda was literature in favor of new ideas. All the important books that had ever been written had some message; they were based upon some definite philosophy of life, some distinct conception of good and evil, right and wrong, justice and injustice.

Strictly speaking, my article was not literary criticism, but pedagogy. Party life at this time tended to make us skeptical of "literature." We read *Proletcult* by Eden and Cedar Paul, and felt that the first duty of the radical "man of letters" was to participate in all the educational activities of the Party. Nor was our press to be the only avenue for circulating communist ideas among the workers. An equally important medium was to be the Workers' School, which the Party founded toward the close of 1923. I was chairman of the organizing meeting, and subsequently taught classes in literature and journalism at the school. By the spring of 1924, teaching became my chief activity in the movement. The *Liberator* offices were moved to Chicago where the magazine became more of a political organ than ever. I was unable to leave New York, and resigned from the magazine. The left-wing literary group was now dispersed, though as individuals we continued to contribute to the magazine. We wrote verse and fiction in isolation and rarely; and when the *Liberator* disappeared altogether by the end of 1924 we felt acutely the need for a new magazine of arts and letters expressing the revolutionary viewpoint.

Nevertheless, the dissatisfaction which Mike Gold, I and others felt with the *Liberator* was caused less by the Party's policy than by our own shortcomings. Our approach to the revolutionary movement was still aesthetic and moral rather than scientific and political, and our own writings suffered accordingly. Those radical writers and artists who had not retired into the cozy bosom of postwar prosperity came to the Party with bohemian hang-overs. In their poetry and fiction the revolutionary worker found little which corresponded to the realities of the economic struggle in America as he experienced it from day to day. The aesthetic world from which we came still influenced us more than we were willing to admit. I fell into an error common among "intellectuals" of petit bourgeois origin, soaked in what Engels called "aesthetic-sentimental philanthropy." Because I had found that capitalists were less than angels, I expected communists to be more than saints. Saturated with psychoanalytic guesses, I saw chiefly the strivings of personal ambition in what was essentially a struggle over important Party policy. The ambition was undoubtedly there, but it was inseparable from the policy. The important thing was whether or not we should fight for a Labor party or form separate unions or base ourselves on shop nuclei. Always personal ambition was the subjective individual stimulus to action; but the action was group political action.

Moreover, we had exaggerated the absence of art and literature in the pages of the *Liberator*. During 1923-1924 politics and economics had occupied a large part of each issue, but if we considered those subjects dry and dull it was owing to our own political immaturity, our immersion in the aesthetic cult. Actually those articles were prophetic in their incisive analysis of the American scene. But in addition to important pieces on politics and economics we had published drawings, poetry, fiction and literary criticism some of which had considerable influence in the development of left-wing American letters.

If in the face of this rich material we nevertheless complained, it was partly because we were still attached to the aesthetic ideas which we combated, and partly because we felt the limitations of radical art and literature, the need for growth and development in our own specific craft. Furthermore, the maturest art comes from complete emotional assurance. Where a tradition is strong and forms an integral part of the artist's unconscious, he creates freely and prolifically. With us the communist movement was new. We approved it intellectually; we still had to absorb it emotionally. The spiritual presuppositions out of which we had previously poured out stories, poems and articles were now shadowed in a doubt intensified by our divorce from our literary contemporaries. One thing, however, was clear: the Party was grappling with objective reality; it was we who had to make ourselves over if we were to be of any use to the working class. To achieve emotional assurance, I felt it necessary to work less in the realm of the imagination and more in the external world.

§2

With the *Liberator* in Chicago, I was free to seek other work. At the beginning of 1924, I joined the staff of the American Civil Liberties Union as publicity man. The labor movement at that time did not have its own defense organization and was represented on the executive committee of the Union by William Z. Foster. The Union was then a united front of liberals, pacifists and radicals of all shades of opinion banded together to defend the civil rights "guaranteed" by the Constitution of the United States. Foster was interested primarily in defending free speech, press and assembly for the working class; men and women like Oswald Garrison Villard, Jane Addams, Frank P. Walsh, Frederick C. Howe and John Haynes Holmes believed in the abstract liberties promulgated by the Fathers of the Republic and violated by their successors in the manner intended. The motto of the American Civil Liberties Union was one attributed to Voltaire: I disagree completely with what you say, but I shall defend to the death your right to say it. The protests which we sent to police chiefs, mayors, governors and legislators all over the country, wherever a labor meeting was broken up or an agitator arrested, bristled with quotations from the constitution, the Declaration of Independence, Thomas Jefferson, Abraham Lincoln and Woodrow Wilson. It seemed that American law was committed to freedom of expression, but that the administrators of the law withheld that freedom from all opponents of the capitalist system. American prisons were full of wobblies, socialists and communists whose sole crime was their criticism of exploitation and oppression. Since it was radicals of this stamp who were the chief victims of government persecution, liberals who accepted the foundations of the present society defended men and women who wished to alter them.

The Civil Liberties Union conducted an intensive campaign on behalf of Mooney and Billings, Sacco and Vanzetti, the victims of the Centralia frame-up, and thousands of others clubbed, arrested, jailed or deported for exercising their "rights" of free speech. This campaign, however, was legalistic in spirit, aim and technique. The average civil libertarian was more interested in protecting the chastity of the existing law than in forwarding any new social ideal. He championed the arrested labor organizer not as spokesman for the progressive historic class, but as a dot in the graph indicating the rise and fall of constitutional "freedom." To communists the persecution of labor organizers was not a violation but an *application* of capitalist law; it was *class* justice in normal operation; it was the organic functioning of the law which was an instrument in the hands of the exploiters against the exploited. The Civil Liberties Union, however, evaded the political and economic implications of the cases it handled; it ignored the class basis of repression. It protested against the violation of constitutional "guarantees" as if the constitution did not first, last and always guarantee the "sacred" rights of private profit. In restricting free speech fights and frame-up cases to the legalistic side alone, the Union tended to obscure the political factors involved and to encourage democratic illusions.

The director of the Civil Liberties Union and its moving spirit was Roger Baldwin. I had known of him earlier as a conscientious objector who had served a year in prison for his opposition to the war. Now, in personal contact, I found him a thin, sharp-eyed New England puritan of extraordinary energy and efficiency, abstemious in his personal life, a demon for work. Of all the offices in and around the labor movement, his was one of the best organized and most productive. Although he lived in Greenwich Village, he was outside its traditions. He painted a little, tinkled on the piano, wrote verses now and then, some of which we had published in the *Liberator;* but there was nothing bohemian about him. These hobbies were the avocations of a Harvard man whose ruling passion was a social idealism that went back to the moral fervor of the Puritans, and the political doctrines of the French Revolution. Even his major hobbies distinguished Baldwin from the average socialist, communist or bohemian intellectual, who was, as a rule, a metropolitan animal, a creature of the gin-filled studio or the smoke-filled meeting hall. Baldwin spent every moment he could spare in his cabin in the Jersey flats, on the Hackensack River. Here he cooked his own meals, economically and well, paddled a canoe down the stream, swam naked, and studied the trees and birds of the neighborhood. Like Sir Edward Grey, he could identify any bird by its song and, like Tolstoy, he was opposed to hunting the bird or any other living creature. Love of animals extended pacificism to nature.

The spirit of Thoreau was strong in Baldwin; he was happiest prowling through the forest with a friend, working with his hands, and reading Shakespeare's sonnets aloud. He once complained to me that Norman Thomas, whom we both knew at this time as a Socialist propagandist rather than as the political leader of his party, actually talked politics in the *woods.* Baldwin felt that my own soul might eventually be saved because I gladly joined him one evening when he knelt in the grass at dusk and held his breath reverently as the woodcock, uttering its pure notes, rose high into the air, circled the heavens and glided back into the grass. But my soul was not saved; I was a metropolitan, more interested in the man than in the bird; the latter was for me only an object that stirred the man. Although I spent seven impressionable years in a little twelfth century village, life in New York and other capitals had eradicated in me all feeling for the countryside, and I was not to regain it until a decade later. At this time I looked upon Baldwin's love of nature as a romantic accompaniment of his political ideas which stemmed from the preindustrial era.

His energy, however, was restless; partly, perhaps, because he mistook its essential direction and struggled to divert it. He never admitted to himself that his chief interest lay in political power, rather than in the arts, in nature or in abstract social justice. His was a "faustian" nature wearing a "magian" mask, a John Adams who imagined himself a Prince Kropotkin. From the day that he met Emma Goldman in St. Louis, he fancied himself an anarchist of the philosophic kind, devoted to the ideal man in the ideal society, contemptuous of practical politics; a libertarian above the battle, impartially appealing to labor, capital and the government to exercise justice and forbearance toward each other. In spite of this image of himself, he poured out his indefatigable energy in a hundred committees and organizations, busy morning, noon and night playing the very politics he despised, from which he always longed to escape and to which he always returned. His need for affecting his environment directly and externally was so acute that nothing was too great or too small for him to meddle with. He took as much pride in preventing shrub fires in his Jersey village, or compelling the local railway to regulate locomotive whistles so that the villagers could sleep in peace, as in securing the release of political prisoners condemned under the criminal syndicalism laws.

Despite our political differences, we were very fond of each other. He kidded the communists, and I kidded the liberals, though Baldwin denied he was a typical liberal. I owed a great deal to the discipline of his office which forced me to organize my faculties around the "objective" work I was trying to master; he was amused by my verses, even when they were at the expense of his political philosophy. When I said that in spite of his quarrels with the communists he would probably wind up in the Soviet government of America, he laughed and said:

"No doubt, and probably as a police commissar."

At this time Baldwin was opposed "in principle" to the dictatorship of the proletariat. For him it was "no better than" the dictatorship of the bourgeoisie. The classless society, after the state had "withered away," was very fine. But the transition period with its "force and violence," its absence of civil rights, its punishment of people who had committed no "overt act," was, so far as he was concerned, no better in Soviet Russia than in capitalist America. He was ready to fight both social systems on that specific issue. Freedom—*for everyone—every-*

where—now was his imagined aim, though he was ready enough to admit that without the economic and social reorganization of the world freedom was a dream.

Sometimes his doctrines led him into curious situations. In the midst of our protests to officials against the persecution of wobblies, socialists and communists, we read in the newspapers that Mayor Curley had forbidden the Ku-Klux Klan to parade in Boston. The same gentleman had on previous occasions broken up radical meetings. It was clear that, in interfering with the Klan, the mayor was acting not as a Democrat but as a Catholic. The Civil Liberties Union, opposed to everything the Klan stood for, was bound on principle to protect the "right" of the Klansmen to parade, a right "guaranteed" by the constitution. To spare my communist "prejudices" in this matter, Baldwin himself wrote Mayor Curley in the usual manner: we are opposed to the Klan but every American citizen is entitled to the right of assemblage. As Jefferson said . . . as Lincoln said . . . as Theodore Roosevelt said . . . as Woodrow Wilson said.

The Boston mayor replied briefly: my dear sir, I know perfectly well what these great statesmen said, but I also know what they *did*.

The Klan did not march. Baldwin's sense of humor enabled him to enjoy the joke.

Experience in the Civil Liberties Union strengthened my conviction that under capitalism democracy was an illusion. The rights of free speech, press and assembly were ours only so long as we did not exercise them against the propertied classes. The moment a worker became conscious and articulate about the antagonism between his interests and those of his exploiters, he became a criminal under laws written and administered by the exploiters. A Catholic like Mayor Curley might curb the Klan, but on the whole that reactionary organization was permitted to flourish. The gunmen and bootleggers who dominated the prohibition era were unmolested. All antilabor groups, however "lawless" and violent, were given a free hand. The "criminals" in the gay twenties, as before the war and later in the great depression, were those workers and middle-class idealists who exposed the horrors of capitalism. This policy was carried so far that Upton Sinclair and a group of friends, representing the Civil Liberties Union, were arrested for reading the Declaration of Independence in an effort to secure free speech for the harbor workers on strike in San Pedro.

I could not help noticing that the administrators of the law made distinctions between the middle-class idealist and the worker. The former was arrested and released, the latter jailed or deported. There was not a single middle-class reformer or liberal in the prisons of America; these were filled with men and women, regardless of their social origin, who espoused the cause of the socialist revolution.

The average free speech case which we handled at this time had the following pattern: The police of Ameba, New Jersey, let us say, broke up a strike meeting held outdoors and beat up the speakers. Thereupon the Civil Liberties Union sent a stinging communication (Form No. 1) to the Ameba police chief protesting against his abridgment of the constitutionally guaranteed rights of free speech and assembly. It also advised the strikers to hold a "test" meeting on the very spot where the first meeting was "unlawfully" dispersed, and to confine their utterances, for "test" purposes, to reading the Declaration of Independence. The strikers followed this excellent advice, but the police of Ameba was unimpressed. It interrupted the reading of our great declaration of the rights of man, clubbed the strikers and broke up the meeting.

This called for drastic action. The Civil Liberties Union arranged for a "test" meeting of its own. This time the speakers were not strikers and labor organizers, but a prominent lawyer, a famous bishop, a celebrated senator, two well-known editors of respectable journals and a wealthy lady of liberal views. These distinguished people defended the constitution, and explained at great length that they were not one whit concerned with the issues of the strike or the "industrial philosophy" of the strike leaders, but *solely* with the legal right of American citizens to express opinion short of committing an "overt" act. The Ameba police listened with profound respect to these good people who were well dressed and spoke in modulated tones, long words and cultured accents. It was obvious that they had no desire to interfere with profits, to increase wages, to lower hours. If they wished to deliver lofty lectures on the Philosophy of the Law, that was O.K. with the Ameba police. The meeting ended peaceably. From the Civil Liberties Union offices we sent out releases to the newspapers announcing that free speech had scored a victory in New Jersey.

The lawyers, bishops, editors, senators, and rich liberal ladies could have lectured on the constitution in the first place without police interference. The "test" meeting tested and proved what needed no test and no proof. Middle-class reformers were not considered dangerous by big business. The real "test" came after such "victories," when the police, acting on behalf of the employers, continue to beat up and arrest strikers, to break up labor meetings, to crush workers' efforts for better living conditions.

At the same time common sense told me that, for all its defects, an organization like the Civil Liberties Union was useful, especially when the workers at the same time had their own defense organization which stressed the social-economic factors ignored by the liberals.

Historic necessity compelled the civil-libertarians to aid the proletariat in spite of themselves: for while they believed in abstract freedom for everybody under all circumstances which did not involve "overt acts," the ruling class saw to it that the vast majority of those arrested for exercising free speech were radical champions of labor. I often wondered what would happen if a Klansman or fascist, denied his "constitutional rights," were to appeal to the Union for the same kind of assistance that it gave to wobblies, socialists and communists. But since the reaction lumped the civil-libertarians with bolsheviks, anarchists and socialists in the same general category of "Reds," no such case ever arose. In practice the Union helped every group, individual and publication in the labor movement persecuted by the police and the courts of the propertied classes. Its records of class justice, meticulously kept by Baldwin, were a startling, because factual, indictment of capitalist law and order as employed against the American working class.

It was, perhaps, his preoccupation with civil liberties cases involving thousands of radical labor agitators, journalists and organizers that eventually propelled Baldwin ahead of the average liberal, who wanted to redress social grievances in order to secure the continued existence of bourgeois society. Outside his duties as director of the Civil Liberties Union, Baldwin was interested in political and social problems from a radical viewpoint, although he was always energetically careful not to commit himself to any specific political group. He was also interested in personalities, and once asked me to draw up a list of those members of my generation, a decade younger than his own, who might one day "amount to something" on the liberal or radical side of the social struggle. I listed, among others, Michael Gold, Edwin Seaver, Matthew Josephson, Genevieve Taggard, Malcolm Cowley, Kenneth Burke, Benjamin Ginzburg and Benjamin Stolberg.

§ 3

Through the Civil Liberties Union I got to know Scott Nearing, whom we had learned to respect during the war for his anti-imperialist stand. Unlike the radical poets, literary critics and champions of civil rights, he was a trained economist whose work in the labor movement was concerned to a large extent with wages, hours, production, living costs. I had also published in the *Liberator* some articles by him on general political questions.

Nearing was a popular lecturer whose clear blue eyes, ruddy windburned complexion, resonant voice and simple method of presenting complicated facts stirred audiences to enthusiasm. In personal life he was ascetic. He wore flannel or denim shirts, coarse trousers, and farmer's shoes. He liked physical labor on his Jersey farm, and often prepared his own meals, consisting chiefly of raw fruits and vegetables. When he dined at other people's houses, he insisted on washing the dishes afterward. He was a vegetarian, neither smoked nor drank, and never told or listened to dirty stories. Often his puritanism was disguised as hygiene; when he chose to sleep on the floor of his farmhouse or on the grass outside, it was presumably for the sake of good health.

The flannel shirt he wore on his body was a symbol of the hair shirt he wore on his soul. Behind many of his political beliefs was the anterior conviction that wealth, luxury, riches, surplus destroyed a man's initiative. Naturally, a man must not go hungry, but if he had more than enough to maintain efficiency and social usefulness it tended to destroy his efficiency. Nearing approached the revolutionary movement from the moral presupposition that the psychology of many possessions was bad. It was as disastrous, he said, to live among many good things as it would be to spend all your time in the Metropolitan Museum of Art, where your attention would be constantly diverted by the variety of things about you. If a room had too much furniture, it was hard to concentrate on any one thing. That was why the younger generation of the wealthy were often scatterbrained; they dispersed their energies. They were not necessarily vicious, but they tended to be useless because their life consisted of a vast number of choices.

From this individual asceticism, Nearing developed a social morality which held that it was difficult for a man to sit down in a starving group of people and eat to satiety without offering them a share. Yet one-sixteenth of the people of the world were living in the United States with a tremendously high standard of living, and among the other fifteen-sixteenths, hundreds of millions were living in misery. One group of people could not expect to monopolize wealth and keep hold of it; one group in the community could not expect to live in luxury and let others go hungry; an increase in the individual's wealth meant an increase in his own unhappiness, as well as the unhappiness of the community.

This Tolstoyan philosophy was essentially an appeal to the Christian "conscience" of the well-to-do; it was akin to the self-abnegation of the "penitent nobleman" whose "revolutionary" morality stressed surrender by the idealistic bourgeois rather than acquisition by the realistic proletarian. But, unlike most penitent noblemen, Nearing lived his creed literally, renouncing all personal comfort, and preaching the gospel of the new world with the intensity of a Savonarola. For this reason he was considered the "purest" of American communists in those liberal-bourgeois circles who suspect the sincerity of all radicals who do not wear sackcloth and ashes. But even in communist circles, which judged a man by his revolutionary actions rather than by his personal "purity," Nearing's selfless labors won universal respect. Though he was a dramatically extreme type, he nevertheless embodied characteristics prevalent among leading figures in American revolutionary politics and literature. Like Debs, Haywood, Foster, Ruthenberg, Browder, Minor, Reed, Dell and others who influenced my generation, he was a native American, a hard and able worker, and essentially a puritan. As time went on, I could only marvel at the persistent bourgeois myth—bandied about by "aristocratic" journalists like H. L. Mencken—that communism was confined to aliens, rakes and incompetents.

Nearing's political ideas were a mixture of eighteenth century libertarianism, nineteenth century socialism and twentieth century communism. He believed simultaneously in the materialistic conception of history and in a personal God. Not the Old Man with whiskers, to be sure, but some being who bore the same relation to man that man bore to the monkey. He believed both in the Tolstoyan gospel of doing everything with your own hands and in Lenin's idea of a great, organized, planned industrial society administered collectively by its members. He was opposed to shedding the blood of cows and chickens and so ate raw lettuce, carrots and apples; but he wanted socialism, and so cheered the victories of the Red army over the White Guards and approved the dictatorship of the proletariat. Those of us who were Freudians liked to tell him that since his grandfather, the dominant figure in his life, was a Pennsylvania coal operator and an atheist, it was natural for the grandson to be a socialist and a deist;

but Nearing's political paradoxes had more obvious and immediate roots in his tutelage under the liberal economist Simon Patten and his training in the Socialist party in its reformist period.

It was typical of his sincerity, a sincerity so profound that it moved people even when they least agreed with him, that he never attempted to deceive either himself or anyone else about his political contradictions. He was aware of them and struggled to overcome them, but until he did overcome them, he neither ignored nor concealed them. He lacked the gift of a certain type of practical politician of appearing consistent when he was not. Hence the chief impression he created in personal contact was not one of assurance but of search. On the platform, however, the impression was the precise opposite; his sentences came crisp and authoritative, like gospel truth; and his habit of organizing his utterances into simple points—one, two, three—increased the air of absolute certainty which he imparted to his audiences.

Nearing's uncertainty involved specific political programs rather than the general faith in the proletarian revolution. Here his belief was so deeply emotional, albeit supported by rational data, that it took the form of daily, usually individual action. While the radical aesthetes confined themselves to the literary world, spent their time with other radical aesthetes, lectured before literary groups or ladies' clubs, and kept within the confines, first of Greenwich Village, later of suburban family life, Nearing moved constantly among workers and students, preaching the gospel of the revolution as he understood it, writing pamphlets, publishing them at his own expense, selling them at cost price at his meetings, and taking the smallest possible fees for his lectures, just enough to live on within his own extremely modest scale.

Nearing was a methodical worker; he budgeted his time for each day, and planned his work ahead for years to come. Once he took me through the cellar of his Jersey home and showed me rows and rows of files, boxes of steel and wood, card catalogues and folders and notebooks of all kinds in which he kept his material as he gathered it. Here every book and article that interested him was outlined, and plans were plotted for books to be written in the future. In 1924 I saw plans for books and pamphlets which Nearing wanted to write in the next ten years; by 1934 these were actually written and published. This inflexible literary will inspired among the literati who gravitated toward Nearing a mixture of awe, envy and ridicule, but little emulation.

A book which Nearing wanted to do at this time was one dealing with American imperialism, a theme he had already treated in a pam-

phlet called *The American Empire*. He generously asked me to col-
laborate with him. We worked on the manuscript during the latter
part of 1924 and the early part of 1925, mostly in our spare time.
Nearing was busy teaching and lecturing; my working day was
divided between the Civil Liberties Union and the Workers Health
Bureau. Despite these handicaps, we determined to do a solid piece
of research. Our anti-imperialist bias was known; it was therefore
necessary to avoid all bombast and agitation, to present only carefully
documented facts. Our preface explained that the book had two chief
purposes: first, to indicate how far the United States was following
an imperial policy; second, to suggest some of the outstanding characteristics of United States foreign policy. To this narrow theme we
stuck as closely as we could. We did not write a history of American
imperialism, but "a description of certain type cases in which United
States economic and diplomatic interests have come into collision with
the economic and political interests of certain 'undeveloped' countries.
These cases were picked, first, because they represented distinct phases
in imperial development; and second, because sufficient firsthand
material was available to make possible a reasonably competent study.
The History of American Imperialism is still to be written."

Our documents were for the most part official state papers, published, as always, long after the event had ceased to be of immediate
interest. Neither of us, however, was free of the naïve belief that state
papers were *prima facie* evidence; we did not sufficiently understand
that official documents could distort facts as thoroughly as can deliberate newspaper propaganda.

The title of the book—*Dollar Diplomacy*—was taken from the
anti-imperialist literature of the liberals who at the opening of the
century opposed the purchase of the Philippines. The book itself did
no more than "expose." We deliberately avoided carrying the facts to
their logical revolutionary conclusion; we knew that such a conclusion
would automatically blind the educated classes to the facts. We were
anxious, to begin with, to have those facts known, the indisputable,
officially admitted facts attested by the State Department, facts which
revealed the oppression, exploitation and robbery of colonial and semicolonial countries by American capital; but we confined ourselves to
presenting these facts on a national rather than on a class basis. Ours
was essentially a liberal, not a Marxist, analysis; we did not illuminate
the class characteristics either of the imperialist or of the colonial
countries, or show the relation between the two in the light of the

general development of capitalism. We refrained from indicating the revolutionary way out of imperialism, though we were familiar with Lenin's classic and with numerous Party documents on that subject. The book's limitations arose chiefly from the fact that no publishing house at that time was willing to bring out a volume presenting the communist viewpoint on contemporary political problems. Even the mild piece of scholarly research which we wrote encountered one obstacle after another.

"The authors do not claim originality either for the ideas or for the material collected in this volume," we said in our preface, "but so far as they are aware, these data have not been assembled elsewhere in this form, and with this general purpose in mind."

That was seemingly the case, for subsequently sections of *Dollar Diplomacy* were cited in various university textbooks. But the obvious conclusions indicated by our material caused several publishers to reject the book, always, of course, with the irrefutable excuse that such a volume had no market. A committee of twelve well-known liberal professors promised, on the basis of our outline, to endorse the book by having their names appear on the title-page; they declined to do so on seeing the completed manuscript, although most of them were kind enough to read the manuscript privately and to make valuable suggestions.

Finally, B. W. Huebsch, former publisher of the *Freeman,* and now with the Viking Press, brought out the book without suggesting political changes in it. It was published in the fall of 1925, and within the next few years translations of it appeared in Germany, Spain, Mexico and Russia.

The book was well received by the press; it was pleasant to read the praises of critics like Rexford Guy Tugwell and Paul Douglas, and to be assured by the theoretical organ of the French Communist party that our study would "find its place in all the Leninist schools." Nevertheless, we had a sense of void; we felt that we had made only a crude step toward a revolutionary study of American imperialism.

Almost daily contact with Nearing stimulated my interest in economics. The writing of *Dollar Diplomacy* was, in the eyes of Party comrades, serious work, as distinguished from the trivialities of art. They had never read Clausewitz, whom Lenin liked to quote, but they instinctively followed his advice that a commander in charge of a battle must pay no attention to the sensuous beauty of the landscape. Inclined too much toward the sensuous beauty of the landscape, I now took delight in statistics. Against the introspection of postwar poetry, you barricaded yourself behind the immanent laws of capitalist development, those vast, luminous abstractions which explained the course of human events. Imperialism molded your life whether you were poet or machinist, philosopher or clerk. But the sensuous beauty of the landscape was ineluctable; and the conflict between politics and poetry was by no means confined to Party circles. In connection with the campaign which the Civil Liberties Union conducted on behalf of the Virgin Islands, I met Eric Walrond, a young, tall, good-looking Negro from the West Indies who was writing short stories. Walrond was active in various Negro emancipation movements, but complained to me:

"They are draining my energy; I want to see the Negro liberated. But why pick on me? There are hundreds of others who can do better practical work, and who will do it gladly. I want to write; I must write; everything else is secondary."

Walrond wrote well, and eventually published a brilliant book of short stories on Negro life in the Caribbean.

To my surprise, Nearing was also interested in art; but his aesthetic views, like his politics, were a blend of puritanism and socialism. He wrote me a tirade against an art show he had seen: how could painters waste time and effort on flowers and richly gowned ladies in the face of the "titanic struggle for existence that is gripping the masses"? The criticism was just, but the solution, I felt, lay not in the destruction of art.

"Your paragraph about the art show says a mouthful," I replied. "Somehow there will have to be developed in this country an art to tell powerfully and memorably about the 'titanic struggle for existence that is gripping the masses.' We already have an economics, a sociology, even a journalism that tells the story; but there has yet to be an art form as adequate to the new world as the art forms you saw are adequate to the flowers, the landscape, the richly attired women. It will take a lot of energy and sweat and thought to hew that art form, but hewn it will be."

I felt myself unequipped for writing the kind of literature which our epoch seemed to require, but I was anxious to help in stimulating it. For this purpose a new magazine of revolutionary arts and letters was necessary. Such a magazine would not only publish "creative" art—drawings, poems and stories—but would furnish that critical soil without which no creative art could develop in modern times.

Although I still suffered from "poetic" prejudices against criticism, conditions now made that form of writing primary. I said to myself that the average "creative" writer felt about criticism the way the sentimentalist felt about astronomy: knowledge destroyed the beauty of the stars. The "artist," who looked upon his meanest mood or fantasy as sacred and inviolable, cried out against the profanations of reason, as the priest cried out against the profanations of science. But it was clear that the sacred and inviolable imagination of the artist was no divinely inspired oracle. The poetic image was effective but not necessarily true; the poet was a man who intensely and obliquely dramatized the credo of his class. Often the spontaneous, emotional, "creative" outpourings of the artist were only the elegant condensation of blind philistine assumptions; the rhetoric of *The Hairy Ape,* as Floyd Dell had shown, was the cry of the petit-bourgeois soul in distress between heaven and earth. In the long run, analysis revealed the worship of the primitive, the unconscious, the childish, the "natural" to be nothing more than the shibboleths of the educated classes lost in the No Man's Land between the embattled major forces of modern society. That was why reactionary poets resented analysis, as bourgeois politicians resented Marxian interpretation of events, an interpretation which always started out as *critique.* There were, to be sure, bad critics; there were also, for that matter, bad poets. One might as well abolish medicine because there were quacks as abolish criticism because there were pedants. Or why not abolish the human race because many men were evil? It was an academic question anyway: most "creative" writers of our day published criticism, as better men had done before them, Goethe, Shelley, Swinburne, Tolstoy, Poe among them. True criticism made the unconscious conscious, and stripped the mask from the intoxicated mummer; it was a bridge between the symbol and the reality, the touchstone which revealed the reality behind the symbol, the emotion behind the dream, all the more important for us who, saturated in bourgeois falsifications of the world, had to decipher the sonorous incantations of the priests of art.

Now Mike Gold came back from the coast, and we wandered about the streets of New York discussing once more the possibility of founding a *New Masses.* We were convinced that apart from the older writers and artists formerly connected with the *Liberator,* we could now count on the new generation of liberal and radical talents which had grown up since the war. The chief problem was financial, but here, fortunately, we could count on Scott Nearing and Roger Baldwin. Both were influential in the American Fund for Public Service, to which Charles Garland, a Yankee philosophical anarchist, had turned over his million-dollar inheritance. Nearing and Baldwin assured me that if we organized an effective group of writers and artists—and a reliable business department—the Garland Fund would subsidize the magazine for three years.

I discussed the proposed magazine with Malcolm Cowley and Allen Tate and learned that writers of my generation who had grown up in the liberal as well as the socialist tradition felt, as we did, the need for a new kind of American literature, one which would touch on politics as well as poetry, philosophy as well as fiction. These conversations convinced me that the new magazine could be wide in scope. A tentative list of contributors which I outlined for the Garland Fund included Kenneth Burke, Malcolm Cowley, Matthew Josephson, Slater Brown, Edmund Wilson, E. E. Cummings, Hart Crane, Isidor Schneider, John Dos Passos, Jean Toomer, Michael Gold, Genevieve Taggard, Edwin Seaver, and Louis Hacker. In a letter to Scott Nearing, I added:

"I feel satisfied that a splendid literary section could be turned out. Our real difficulties will come in the political section of the magazine. The old *Masses* had a wide appeal because it expressed the vague rebellious impulses current in this country before the Russian Revolution. It published articles by dogmatic Marxians, I.W.W. sympathizers, sentimental socialists, pagan individualists, anarchists. The Russian Revolution has tightened certain trends of thought, dissipated others. Nevertheless, there still exists an ideological chaos. On the political side of the magazine we must begin where the revolutionary journals of ten years ago left off."

This plan for a "broad united front" of liberal and radical writers around a new magazine was approved by Scott Nearing, Roger Baldwin, Michael Gold, William Gropper, Hugo Gellert and others who considered the matter. For various reasons we were unable to launch the magazine until the spring of 1926, but the broad policy on which we agreed remained in force. It flowed from the general political situation in the United States at that time, and from the consequent relations of the various liberal and radical groups to each other.

CHAPTER V

Do not be startled, comrade,
I grasp naked realities . . .
—ERNST TOLLER.

§ 1

THE decade following the war was recorded in official mythology as the Golden Age of American economic life. Shekels rolled so fast into the pockets of the propertied classes, big and small, that only a handful of liberals and radicals were stirred by the stench of Teapot Dome, the strike in Passaic, the murder of Sacco and Vanzetti. The seven years of plenty, unparalleled in the history of this or any other country, began while the Good Guy from Marion, Ohio, was still alive, playing poker and letting his pals fleece the people. Oh, everybody was in the dough, making and spending plenty of sugar, doubling and trebling the sales of rayon, cigarettes, electric ice-boxes, cosmetics, telephones, movies and chewing gum. The war had made Europe poor and America rich. Our great and glorious republic had lots of raw materials at home and in its Latin-American "spheres of influence." Its domestic market seemed to be inexhaustible; its human energy and efficiency, the marvel and envy of the world. Europe grew lyrical over America, "the land of unbounded possibilities."

Yet even when the Golden Age was most golden, a lot of "dirty Reds" were "disgruntled." Everywhere workers' wages lagged behind profits. The mass of Americans, workers and farmers, were not invited to the prosperity party at all. But the middle classes were. Small businessmen felt the pressure of the trusts and the chain stores, but there was plenty of gravy to go around. Lawyers, doctors, engineers, accountants, salesmen, advertising men, journalists, editors, big shots in the theater, the film and literature found large incomes rolling into their laps, and big, juicy bones were thrown to labor leaders willing to play the game. Since the middle classes were the most articulate, since their sons and daughters were the literary spokesmen of the land, the world got from American books, newspapers and magazines a picture of 120,000,000 men, women and children riding in autos, tuning in on

Amos 'n' Andy, drinking bootleg gin, attending million-dollar prize-fights, dancing to Negro jazz bands and enjoying the delights of Flaming Youth. These illusions were shared by the labor aristocracy, favored by the best jobs on the working side of industry and with the best wages.

Overwhelmed by the voice of the crooner issuing from the radio in a worker's home, some communists rushed into print with theoretical articles about the well-fed backwardness of American labor. But most communists had a different picture of America. The period of 1920-1923 had been one of great and bitter industrial conflict. The workers fought with unusual endurance and solidarity against the offensive of the exploiting class, but the net result was unfavorable. In many industries the unions were almost entirely destroyed, in others they were so weakened that they were unable to protect the most elementary interests of the workers.

These facts roused the political consciousness of many workers who remembered the police clubs, army bayonets and court injunctions of the postwar strikes. The Democrats had gone and the Republicans had come back, and the status of the workers remained the same. Both capitalist parties faithfully and effectively defended the interests of the bankers and manufacturers who exploited the workers in the cities and the farmers on the land. Sections of the rural population lost faith in the capitalist parties, and in the trade unions many were becoming dissatisfied with the traditional "neutrality" of the A. F. of L. which, by rewarding labor's "friends," helped to keep the capitalist politicians in office. In response to pressure from the rank and file in the direction of independent political action by the workers and farmers, there were a number of conferences for the formation of a labor party. The Communist party offered all labor organizations and political groups a united front on this all-important question. Socialists, communists, trade-union leaders and rank-and-filers participated in such conferences, but these came to nothing when the reactionary labor leaders time and again broke the pledges which committed them to a labor party and finally came out in support of La Follette in the 1924 presidential campaign. In the face of this situation the Communist party nominated its own candidates for president and vice-president; but Ruthenberg explained that in doing so the Party was not abandoning the united front. In an article which he gave me for the *Liberator,* he explained that the Party would continue to agitate for the united front and for a genuine mass farmer-labor party.

The conferences at which the fight for a labor party was carried on brought the Communists into national prominence as a serious party, rather than a mysterious sect. Its united front policy had a profound effect upon intellectual circles, which had drifted away from the fringes of the revolutionary movement. Tired radical writers underwent a change of mood, and young writers just climbing over the literary horizon began to relax their fear and suspicion of the organized working class.

There was no conscious program in left-wing arts and letters; there was merely the conscious, semiconscious and unconscious reaction to an atmosphere. On the one hand, the political agitation for a united front made the radical writers feel that they could and should co-operate with all writers and artists who were opposed to capitalism, however far they were from understanding or supporting communism. On the other hand, the emergence of the Party from its secret, underground, illegal life into the open arena of national politics, its energetic participation in mass movements which attracted the attention of the country as a whole, its emphasis on mass political action uniting all anticapitalist elements, drew many liberal writers out of the ivory towers into which they had retired after the Versailles Treaty or after the NEP. The barriers which had arisen between the liberal and radical writers during the sectarian period now seemed to melt away. Besides, we all felt that somehow the creative arts touched on essences beyond economics and politics. We were thus able to plan for a *New Masses* based on various shades of opinion so long as they proceeded from what appeared to be an anticapitalist bias.

§ 2

After wrestling with his soul, Nearing applied for membership in the Party. Earl Browder, then acting secretary, wrote him from Chicago that it was the practice of the Party to scrutinize carefully all applicants for membership who were nonproletarian and who were prominent in public life. The reason for this special care was obvious, Browder explained. In the case of nonproletarian elements, especially those who were active in public life, the Party had to make doubly sure that it was acquiring the membership of conscious communists in complete agreement with the Party and the Communist International. For this reason, the Central Executive Committee requested Nearing to answer the following questions. What was his estimate of the present situation in the United States and of the immediate tasks of the Party? What was his position on the proletarian dictatorship and on the historic role of the Communist party? What were his views on imperialism, war, pacifism and social revolution? Moreover, Browder pointed out, the matter of discipline in the Party and in the Comintern was of paramount importance. What, then, were Nearing's views on national and international discipline? Was he ready to sever all connections with all the educational and political institutions of the Socialist party in which he had been active? Was he willing to accept Party control over his writings and educational activities?

When he showed me Browder's letter, Nearing was well aware that the Party's attitude toward intellectuals of bourgeois origin dated from the very foundations of the revolutionary movement of the proletariat. Forty-five years earlier, Engels had said it was "an inevitable phenomenon, rooted in the course of development that people from what have hitherto been the ruling classes should also join the militant proletariat and contribute cultural elements to it." This idea had been clearly stated in the *Communist Manifesto*. But in this connection, Engels had stressed two points. First, in order to be of use to the proletarian movement, these people must bring real cultural elements to it. Nor must they try to trim revolutionary science to fit their old viewpoints "which they had brought with them from the university or elsewhere." The party of the proletariat needed clarity, not confusion, and "cultural elements whose first principle is to teach what they have not learnt can very well be dispensed with by the Party." Secondly, if people of this kind from other social classes join the proletarian movement, the first condition is that they "should not bring any remnants of bourgeois, petit-bourgeois, etc., prejudices with them, but wholeheartedly adopt the proletarian point of view. But as a rule, such people were "stuffed and crammed with bourgeois and petit-bourgeois ideas." In a petit-bourgeois country, such ideas had their own justification, but only *outside* the proletarian party. If such people formed a petit-bourgeois social democratic party, one could negotiate with them, form a bloc according to circumstances; but in a workers' party "they are an adulterating element."

It was in this spirit that Earl Browder had asked questions of Scott Nearing which a worker would have been exempted from answering; and Nearing replied in the same spirit:

"You ask whether I am willing to accept Party control over my writings and educational activities. I understand this question to mean that the discipline of the Party extends to the writings and utterances of its members who are held accountable for the expression of opinion on public questions. I believe that this is a *sound policy and would accept and support it.*"

The other questions Nearing answered in a thirty-page document which was a remarkably concise expression of the radical intellectual's credo of this period, revealing the radical's differences with the liberal, on the one hand, and with the bolshevik, on the other. At a time when the bourgeois intelligentsia was going into ecstasies over the vast prosperity, Nearing opened his "credo" with the Leninist axiom that capitalism had entered on its final stage—imperialism. Country by country, Nearing analyzed capitalist economy and concluded (in 1925!) that "a large part of the industrial machinery of Europe and of the United States must remain idle, since no one is willing or able to buy the entire output." The postwar economic situation, he said, had intensified the pressure, in the form of unemployment and wage cuts, on the home industrial populations, and at the same time given subjugated peoples an incentive to revolt. Capitalism was thus attacked from without and from within.

Faced with economic disaster at home and with bitter economic and military struggle for world supremacy imposed by capitalism, Nearing argued, the workers of the imperialist countries could try pacifism or class collaboration or the proletarian dictatorship. ·

He defined the proletarian dictatorship as a "transition stage from capitalism to socialism," as the sole alternative to the fascist dictatorship. If the state is a tool in the hands of a dominant economic group, Nearing argued, the workers, if they are to control their own destiny, must take possession of the economic machinery at the same time that they take possession of the state. "At this stage of social development, there seems to be no other way in which the transition from capitalism to communism can be achieved," he said. After considering fascism in Italy, class collaboration in Britain and the proletarian dictatorship in Russia, he concluded that the Russian workers seemed to have got the best bargain.

But the prospects of the proletarian revolution seemed to Nearing less bright in America than in Europe. The United States, he said, had emerged from the last decade of strife and chaos triumphant, immensely rich and with a large portion of the world in her debt. The American ruling class occupied a very strong position; it had no organized opposition; no other class was prepared to oppose or even seriously question it. Furthermore, the American workers occupied a favored position in the capitalist world. Their standards of living were relatively high. They were carefully graded and ranked. The office or white-collar worker felt far above the artisans; the skilled workers in the building and printing trades, the railway operating crews, the skilled steel workers were organized, reasonably well paid, extremely craft conscious and generally indifferent to the economic fate of other crafts, even in the same industry. The American worker hoped to climb out of the working class, and bent his energy to that end.

There were of course, Nearing admitted, class-conscious elements; but on the whole the American workers were not yet prepared for any class action. If this analysis was correct, Nearing concluded, the tasks of the Workers (Communist) party in America were "obvious enough." The communist movement in the United States, for some time to come at least, *would not be a mass movement but a propaganda movement,* sowing its ideas particularly, of course, among the industrial workers. This phase of activity would of necessity continue until some issue, such as another war or a period of hard times, created mass sentiment that could be converted into class sentiment. There was some question in Nearing's mind as to whether the severe economic depression would come in 1926 or whether it might not be delayed until 1927.

The work of the Party during this interval, Nearing maintained, should therefore be devoted, first toward the organization of the unorganized, and toward the most active usefulness within the existing unions; and toward maintaining an effective propaganda organization of which the three chief parts would be: literature, including papers, magazines, pamphlets and books which would present the fundamentals as well as the day-to-day events of the class struggle; schools for training Party members as well as general classes for nonparty students; and forums, mass meetings and other demonstrations "calculated to bring to the masses of the workers a knowledge of the principles and purposes" of communism. What interested Nearing most were the purposes. He felt that it was a waste of effort to discuss methods of reaching a goal when people did not believe in the goal itself; hence the "discussion of tactics should, for the present, be subordinated, so far as possible" to the paramount task of convincing the American workers of the aim.

It was typical of Nearing, too, that in his political credo he included a statement of his high moral concepts of personal conduct. He urged that each section of the Communist International should hold its members "strictly accountable for all their actions that bear

directly or indirectly on the class struggle and the new social order";
he felt that "we are laying the foundations of a new social order,
which, as it spreads over the world, will mean a new way of life for
the entire human race." But to him this was no logical abstraction; he
believed that one of the most important aspects of the new life would
be "the decenter relations that are established between human beings
—the sounder comradeship that it makes possible." But the new social
order was a long way off; to a slight degree, but none the less appreci-
ably, the "new life" may be lived *now* within the ranks of the revolutionary movement." Every effort should be made by the Communist
party "to cultivate the highest standards of personal integrity—sound
health, clean living; trained, vigorous and courageous thinking; honest,
straightforward dealing." And, as part of the same policy, the Party
membership should be trained and accustomed to specific tasks, so
that, "as far as possible, each comrade will be an efficient specialist
in some form of activity that will be of immediate or of ultimate use
in the social revolution." The Party, Nearing urged, should "maintain
in its internal life a standard of generosity and mutual aid that will
make the Party, on a small scale, the kind of co-operative fellowship
that we are seeking to establish upon a world scale."

Before mailing his credo in to the Central Committee, Nearing
showed it to me. I thought it was a fine statement of the communist
viewpoint. There was nothing new in it; the basic ideas were imagined,
those of revolutionary socialism; but I liked Nearing's lofty method of
presentation—and was especially pleased with the section about "the
highest standards of personal integrity."

To my surprise, although not to Nearing's, his application for
membership in the Party was rejected. A letter from Secretary C. E.
Ruthenberg explained that Nearing's views on the social revolution
and the proletarian dictatorship, and particularly on the situation in
the United States and the immediate tasks of the Communist party,
were not in accordance with the views of the Communist International
and the Central Executive Committee of our Party.

"Your conception of the Communist Party is that of a propaganda
society," Ruthenberg wrote. "The difference between a Communist
propaganda society and a Communist Party . . . is the difference between a party such as you outline in your statement on the immediate
work of the Party and a Party which *enters into the immediate struggles of the workers, endeavors to become the leader of the struggle,
develops the struggle, and in the process builds its influence and its*

organization. . . . While all the work which you describe in your statement is necessary for the upbuilding of the Communist Party in the United States, it is not sufficient. We would never be able to build a mass movement of the workers against capitalism if we restricted our efforts to the proposals which you outline. No organization was ever built through these methods. The mass party of the workers can only come into existence in the heat and conflict of the present-day struggle of the workers. It is only in so far as we play a part in the struggle today, take leadership in the struggle, and maneuver before the workers that we will draw the most militant workers into our Party and build it into a real fighting organization against capitalism. Our task today is to mobilize the workers for struggle against the capitalists on every issue that arises out of their present-day experience. We must fight wage cuts, unemployment, the open shop, imperialism, and every form of oppression and exploitation, not merely through propaganda speeches against these things, but through actual efforts to draw the masses of workers into a struggle against these things today. . . . On this point of Communist tactics you seem to be in disagreement with our Party and the Communist International."

First, last and always the teacher, Nearing had thought of the communist's work primarily as that of instruction, enlightenment, conversion to the ultimate goal. Strongly social in his views, he was a rugged individualist by temperament, and did not consider the requirements of politics, which was foreign to his nature. But when these were called to his attention, he acknowledged the correctness of the Party's stand. Subsequently he became a member of the Party, in which he functioned exclusively as a teacher, lecturer, writer-propagandist. But his political career had a curious denouement. In his credo he accepted the principle of Party discipline. Yet when he wrote a book on imperialism at variance with Party views, he insisted on publishing it. It was on this issue that he was expelled. He later worked as an active sympathizer of the Party outside its ranks.

But I am getting ahead of my story. In 1925 the Nearing episode impressed me with the sharp differences on immediate tasks and tactics which existed among radicals. The gulf between liberals and communists was emphasized by an incident in which my friend Roger Baldwin played a conspicuous role.

§ 3

Baldwin was asked to act as chairman of a meeting to protest against the imprisonment of politicals in the Soviet Union and elsewhere. The request came on the letterhead of *Der Wecker,* an anti-Soviet weekly published by the socialist and trade-union bureaucrats in control of the Jewish *Daily Forward,* and was signed by Mrs. Simeon Strunsky, well known for her anti-Soviet views. Material on political prisoners in the U.S.S.R. came to Baldwin by mail from Berlin, some of it from his old friend Alexander Berkman, the anarchist who had once served a long term in an American prison for the attempted assassination of Frick.

It was obvious that the proposed meeting was called by socialist leaders anxious to discredit the Soviet Union. Communists were suspicious of the "humanitarian" impulses of people who had remained silent about the murder of German workers at the order of Noske, Scheidemann and other social democratic leaders. The proposed meeting was political and partisan in the extreme, but it was not hard to see why the antibolshevik agitators needed the presence of a non-party libertarian like Baldwin.

I called these facts to Baldwin's attention. This only gave him an idea for "improving" the meeting. Instead of making it primarily an appeal for political prisoners in the U.S.S.R., as was originally decided, he now planned to turn it into a meeting on behalf of politicals in all countries. To assure an atmosphere of "impartiality," he invited communist speakers to participate. The Party declined to join the symposium on the grounds that the Soviet Union imprisoned political offenders only for counterrevolutionary activity. Regardless of Baldwin's intentions, the capitalist press would use the symposium as an occasion for an attack on the U.S.S.R. and on communism.

Baldwin then tried to get the Civil Liberties Union to participate in the international political prisoners campaign. The executive committee of the Union took up the matter at a special meeting. Dr. Harry F. Ward, then chairman, opposed participation.

"The Civil Liberties Union," he argued, "is an American organization. It would weaken its activities in this country if it got mixed up in this international campaign. Besides, you will do more harm than good. A campaign on behalf of 'all political prisoners in all countries' will be interpreted by anti-Soviet elements as an attack on Russia. The press will neglect everything you may say about

Poland, Hungary, Italy and other countries, and will play up every-thing you say about prisoners in Russia—without giving any explana-tion as to why these people are in prison. Whatever your intentions may be, this campaign will turn out to be a campaign against the Soviet Union. Furthermore, most of the politicals in Russia have been arrested for *overt counterrevolutionary acts,* and not merely for expres-sions of opinion; and even in this country the Civil Liberties Union does not defend *overt acts* against the government. We must also re-member that in civil war the expression of opinion may be equivalent to the firing of a gun. The Civil Liberties Union as such must keep out of this business."

Dr. Ward's speech created an impression with which the socialist leaders had to deal. Dark, curly-haired Charney Vladeck, known in his youth as "the Lassalle of Poland," but now business manager of the *Forward,* said quietly:

"We want this campaign to be effective. For that purpose it must have an impartial character. People like myself should be kept off the international political prisoners committee which we have formed. We are too well known as opponents of the Soviet regime. This com-mittee should consist of friends of Soviet Russia who are opposed to the imprisonment of people for the expression of political opinions."

Someone interrupted: "You mean the committee should consist of Russia's enemies who are not generally known as such!"

The question was put to a vote. The executive committee of the Civil Liberties Union decided that the Union as such should not par-ticipate in the campaign. But any member of the Union was at liberty to participate as an individual. Tall, white-haired Norman Thomas, spokesman for the Socialist party, stood up and said gravely:

"I am going to avail myself of that liberty."

The International Political Prisoners Committee went ahead with arrangements for the Carnegie Hall meeting. It announced Charney Vladeck as one of the speakers; his theme was to be the Soviet Union. Feeling between the communists and socialists was at this time ex-tremely strained. The Party sent a delegation to Roger Baldwin, headed by Ludwig Lore, then a member of the Central Executive Committee. We all met in Baldwin's office. The conversation was friendly. Baldwin and Lore cracked jokes, but the Party position was firmly stated.

"Whether you mean it or not," Lore said, "you are organizing a direct attack on the Soviet Union. The idea of Vladeck discussing political prisoners in Russia impartially is ridiculous. Many of them are in jail for carrying out in action Vladeck's own views—the views of the menshevik opposition to the Soviet regime. There will be many workers in your audience. I do not see how anyone can prevent them from expressing their disapproval of out-and-out counterrevolution-aries."

Later Baldwin called Vladeck to his office and told him what had happened. Vladeck was a seasoned politician.

"I withdraw," he said. "I will not speak at this meeting."

"You must speak," Baldwin said. "Free speech must be vindicated at all costs."

The night of the meeting, Carnegie Hall was jammed with work-ers, communists, socialists, liberals. Norman Hapgood opened the meeting as chairman. He made the usual remarks about abstract free speech. Carleton Beals spoke on political prisoners in Latin America; Emil Lengyel on Hungary. There were several speakers in foreign languages. The meeting dragged on. Then the chairman introduced Charney Vladeck as the speaker on Russia. The Lassalle of Poland stepped to the edge of the platform. A handful of people in the front rows applauded. He looked about him, coughed a little, and said:

"Friends . . ."

"Boo!" someone in the audience yelled.

Suddenly there was a loud commotion overhead. The entire gal-lery lumbered to its feet.

"Sit down!" Chairman Hapgood shouted. Other voices in the or-chestra took up the cry: "sit down! sit down!" No one knew what to expect. From the gallery came two or three wavering, uncertain voices:

> Arise, ye prisoners of starvation,
> Arise, ye wretched of the earth. . . .

In a moment the entire gallery swelled into the *International*. Half the audience in the orchestra stood up and joined the anthem, grow-ing louder as the individuals became a mass. On the platform there was pandemonium. Hapgood rushed up and down among the speakers and committeemen seated there. Vladeck alone was calm, always the seasoned agitator. You could see his lips moving. He continued speak-ing, but no one heard him. The *International* grew louder and louder. From the audience, Charlie Ervin, gray-haired socialist editor, once with the *Call,* leaped to the platform. His eyeglasses and paunch shook violently. Seizing a chair, he raised it above his head and shouted:

"If there are six huskies in this crowd to help me, I'll clean up that bunch of dirty communists in the gallery!"

Several young men jumped to the platform, shouting to the gallery:

"Shut up, you fools! Get off there! This isn't Moscow!"

The speakers on the platform blushed but did not move. The hall roared. Norman Hapgood raised his hands to the gallery in mute appeal. The singing went on. Finally he motioned Vladeck to sit down, and himself rushed down the platform steps, across the hall into the lobby. He came back with several policemen. The crowd broke into laughter, in which even many socialists joined.

"How about some free speech here?" someone shouted.

Baldwin came down to where I sat at the press table under the platform and shook his head.

"Poor Hapgood," he said. "He doesn't know that you can't call the police to settle arguments in the labor movement."

Next to me at the press table, Ludwig Lore, representing the communist papers, smiled into his black mustache, curling upward at the edges like an Italian barber's. Baldwin went up to Hapgood, whispered in his ear, and the chairman announced that the meeting was over. The speech against the Soviet Union was not made.

The next day I ran into a communist organizer.

"You look down in the dumps," he said. "Is it last night's meeting?"

"Yes."

"Don't you think these counterrevolutionaries needed a lesson from the workers?"

"I suppose so. But does it make you happy to see the labor movement split up like this? What a good time the bourgeois press had this morning over the sight of socialists and communists fighting each other."

"It's too bad," he said. "But whose fault is it? They split the labor movement when they supported the war, when they threw the left wing out of the Socialist party. They're splitting it now by kicking us out of the unions, by attacking the Soviet Union. We are with the socialist workers, and if they have anything against us it's because of the lies they are told by their misleaders."

"I suppose so," I said. "But why not let Vladeck speak, and have one of our people answer him?"

"Do you think this kind of debating with bitter and unscrupulous enemies will get us anywhere? We'll answer them in our own press. They don't care about the truth. Mensheviks are in prison for helping the counterrevolution. Then what about Karl Liebknecht and Rosa Luxemburg? What about the workers shot down in Hamburg by a socialist government?"

"It's all cruel," I said.

"And you are too soft. Have you read Lenin on Kautsky the Renegade? or Trotsky on Dictatorship versus Democracy? The revolutionary movement grows by splitting off from its corrupted elements. It's not pleasant, but neither is the class struggle pleasant. You don't do what is pleasant, but what is necessary. These people don't give a damn for the justice they gab about. They don't know the facts about political prisoners in Russia. It's only an excuse for the anti-Soviet campaign which they carry on day in and day out. The capitalists imprison thousands of workers; the jails of this country are full of people whose only crime is opposition to the system. And the dictatorship of the proletariat imprisons the active and dangerous enemies of the working class. Sure it's unpleasant, but you know, I hope"—the organizer's face lit up with an ironic grin—"that this is the class war and not a Greenwich Village party."

The International Political Prisoners Committee published a book on Russian politicals. Some of the material was furnished by a venomous journalist, professionally anti-Soviet, named Isaac Don Levine. Baldwin wrote the preface. The bourgeois press played it up, making all the political capital it could out of the book. Editorials used it as a springboard for general anticommunist propaganda. Obviously, noble intentions did not count much in politics. Baldwin, for instance, said he hadn't the slightest intention of helping the anti-Soviet campaign; but there was the book and there were the editorials.

"Look," I said. "When the Civil Liberties Union handles a free speech case in this country it always, without exception, communicates first with the police, the mayor, the governor. I've been working here for a year, and I don't remember one instance in which you took action without first ascertaining the official side of the case. Your action is based on all the available facts. Then how is it that your so-called international committee gets up a meeting and rushes out a book with only one side of the story? I notice, you did not write to the Soviet government asking for its side of the story. Is the Soviet Union worse than a New Jersey police chief, or a West Virginia sheriff, or Mayor Curley?"

"Of course, good heavens, you are right," Baldwin said. Several days later the International Political Prisoners Committee announced that it had sent an appeal to Moscow. But by that time the Carnegie Hall meeting was history, the book was off the press and in circulation, the anti-Soviet editorials based on it had sunk into readers' heads, the damage was done.

§ 4

What was the truth about political prisoners in Russia? What was happening in that country in general? If one could only go there and see with one's own eyes! The living test of our faith in the socialist revolution was six thousand miles away, and I did not have the money to go over. I could only read the reports, favorable and unfavorable, and try to guess the truth. But I was now skeptical of public men. Everyone seemed to have an ax to grind, whatever side he was on. We had been fooled about the war. What guarantee was there that the Soviet leaders were any more honest than Woodrow Wilson? I wanted to hear from people who had no axes to grind; from those who had no posts, no privileges, no power; from the rank and file.

On a Saturday afternoon, Roger Baldwin said to me:

"I've got to go out to my Jersey camp. Anton is coming in today. Will you take care of him?"

I said O.K.

"Here is thirty dollars," Baldwin continued. "Tell him it's a gift from a group of liberals—for clothes, food and a room. But he gets it on one condition: he must go back to Russia. The Civil Liberties Union promised the government that Anton will go back—and we must keep that promise."

I knew Anton's case. For about a year I had written press releases about it. Anton was a young Russian who had joined the American army in 1917. His regiment was sent to Siberia. There he deserted to the bolsheviks. On one occasion he fired on American troops. When the civil war was over and he was demobilized, the American army in Vladivostok arrested Anton for desertion, court-martialed him and sentenced him to death. New York liberals took up his case and appealed to President Harding. They argued that an unnaturalized Russian could not be compelled to fight against his own countrymen. They also emphasized Anton's youth; he was only twenty-one when all this happened. The President commuted the death sentence to twenty years' imprisonment in a federal penitentiary. Anton had served five years when the Civil Liberties Union took up the case again. The federal authorities decided to release the boy provided he returned to Russia immediately. The Union guaranteed his return, and now Anton was expected at our offices.

Late that afternoon he arrived, a pale, freckle-faced, sandy-haired Slav peasant with watery blue eyes, remarkably thin and small for his age. We shook hands.

"Well, it's sure good to get out in the world," he said in a shy, low voice, tinged with prison huskiness. "And now right away I want a nice suit of clothes, new shoes, a new hat, shirt, tie, socks, everything." He spoke English fluently, with a Russian accent. "I can't wear these prison suit where I'm going." He pointed to the faded blue serge suit that hung on his skinny little frame like a sack.

"Where are you going?" I asked.

"Before I went to prison, I knew a schoolteacher in Philadelphia. For five years she wrote me every day to jail. She sent me books, and flowers and candy and cake. But most important—letters. Five years is a long, long time. And every day I get letter from Philadelphia. So tonight I am going to Philadelphia and I want to look like sport."

I took him to a haberdasher and he picked the gayest clothing in the place: a light gray suit, an almost white fedora, a pink shirt, green socks and a bright red tie. On the street corner, he bought two red roses, stuck one in my lapel and one in his own.

"I will now take train for Philadelphia," he said. "I will see you Monday. Meantime, ask Baldwin what's chances of my staying in U. S. A."

"You can't stay in the U. S. A. We have promised the government that you will go back to the Soviet Union. We must keep that promise. You must keep it."

"I don't want to go," he said. "What will I do there? I am now an American. I know English. Better I stay here."

"It's impossible. Besides, you will have finer opportunities there."

"No," he said, "I will be a plain worker there. If I stay here, I study engineering. Then I go to Russia. An engineer is better off in Russia than plain worker."

"Perhaps you can come back here and study engineering later. Now the promise must be kept. If you stay, you will only be sent back to prison."

We had arrived at the boardinghouse where I had rented a room for him. He drew up two chairs, and said:

"Sit down. I will tell you my life. You are a writer; you will understand."

From childhood I had been familiar with the Russian habit of telling your life story to strangers. But here something else was involved. The writer was popularly supposed to understand life better than other people; he had more insight and more sympathy; he understood and forgave; he did not judge men but loved them. I had already moved in literary circles and should have known better. Such a writer comes once in a blue moon. Yet I shared Anton's illusion that every man who scribbled stories, poems or plays, however bad, was a priest to whom people could pour out their hearts and receive the absolution of understanding. Perhaps our illusion was an echo of the Middle Ages when scribe and monk were identical.

I was born in a little Russian village—Anton said—on a farm. The work was terrible hard. My father was always drunk and he beat me. I heard that America was free. Everyone had a chance to become rich. So at fourteen, I run away from home and went to America. I could not speak English so I went among Russians, and that was how I came to Pennsylvania coal mines. I dug coal ten hours a day. Damn little money, too. Eighty men slept in one room, in beds, like an army barracks. Forty men slept at night, forty by day. Two shifts in the mine, two in the beds. The sheets were black with coal dust. Bedbugs eat your flesh. All week you work, Sunday you get drunk.

I was happy when America went into the war. Better to die in the trenches like a man than to break your guts with pick and shovel. In the army, the food was good, the beds clean, you had your own cot. I was a good soldier. They transferred me to San Francisco to drill recruits. I was made a corporal.

One day the captain said:

"We are sending troops to Siberia. We are going to fight the bolsheviki. Are there any volunteers for this job?"

I hated the bolsheviki. I heard they were cutthroats, bandits, German agents, enemies of Russia. I wanted to travel, to see the world, to fight. So I volunteered. We got to Vladivostok. I was the only one in my company who knew Russian, so they made me post-office censor. Soon in Vladivostok cafés I met bolsheviks. They argued with me, gave me books and pamphlets. I realized it was a lie that bolsheviki were bad people. They gave the land to the peasants; they were fighting to make Russia free. I became a sympathizer of them. At the post office,

I let their messages and pamphlets pass. My officers became suspicious. They court-martialed me, but they could not prove anything. They removed me from censor job, and demoted me from corporal to private.

Now don't tell this to Baldwin. He does not know about this. If he knows, he will get sore and maybe drop my case. He does not understand that when you believe in something good you must do everything in your power to help it.

Now I was a private in U. S. army and under suspicion. What was the use of staying? I took off my uniform, put on civvies and gave them the slip one night. I came to the bolsheviks and said:

"I am with you."

They said: "O.K. We appoint you Red commander of partisan troops."

"But where is my army?"

"Go and get yourself an army," they said.

"Now where in hell I am going to get an army!"

"Go to such and such a village," they said, "recruit the peasants and organize an army."

So I went all alone to this village. I did not know a soul there. I got up in the main street and began to make a speech. A big crowd came. I told them the bolsheviki are fighting for bread, land and peace. I handed out pamphlets to those who could read. I called for volunteers for a partisan army. Many young fellows joined. They went to other villages and soon we had about five hundred men.

We had guns but no horses. I ordered all the kulaks in that country to give up their horses. Some did, some did not. So I wrote out a sign and I hung it up on a tree. I said: In three days everyone must bring his horses. If not, I will hang three kulaks.

You think it is terrible to hang kulaks. But I will explain. If we do not get horses, the Whites and the Japanese will kill us. They will wipe out whole villages. Isn't it better to hang three kulaks than to let the counterrevolutionaries kill hundreds of our people? Yes, this is much less cruel.

The kulaks were stubborn. They did not bring their horses. They thought I was bluffing. So I hung three of them, and soon every one of our men had a horse. Now we began our fight against Kolchak. At first, I was very democratic, and anyway I was only twenty-one, and I had great respect for peasants with beards. So before every battle I held a mass meeting of my five hundred men, and we talked over our plans. But a couple of times, the Kolchak people attacked our mass meeting. Before we could grab our guns and jump on our horses they butchered some of our fellows. So I made a new rule. No more democracy, no more meetings. I am the boss. What I say goes.

One day the Kolchak crowd drove us to a place near Vladivostok. It was a hell of a fix and we had no more ammunition. I remembered that near by was my old company in the U. S. army—Company A. They had plenty ammunition against us, why not some for us? At night I took a detachment with me. We crawled on our hands and knees to the American munition train and detached a car. The guard fired on us, soldiers came on the run, and we were in for it. Five of my men were killed. I shot one of the U. S. men.

Anyway, we had munitions, and drove the Kolchakists back. Then came the Japanese. They gave us a tough time. We had to retreat into the mountains, about a hundred miles. We passed through one village which the Japanese had destroyed. Every house was burned, every man, woman and child in it was killed. I got sore as hell. We jumped into our saddles and went after the Japs. Several miles away we caught up with a detail—about thirty of them. There was a sharp fight, very short. They gave up. I ordered them to take their clothes off, and there they stood as naked as they were born. This was winter too, and in Siberia. The cold ate into your guts and froze your blood. They were absolutely naked, and without food, and this way we marched them into the snow and ice of the forest to die of cold and starvation. Very, very cruel. All war is cruel. They were cruel to us and we to them.

Finally, the civil war was over. The Soviet government was in Siberia, master of all. Our army, as you might call it, just peasant guerilla fighters, was disbanded. I didn't know what I was going to do. One day I was walking in civvies down the main street of Vladivostok. An American M.P. stopped me.

"You are Anton?" he said.

"Sure thing."

"You are under arrest for deserting from the U. S. army," he said.

They took me to the Philippines and court-martialed me. One of the judges in the military tribunal was my old lieutenant in Company A. There was a scar on his face; I gave it to him the night we fought over the munition car. I got the death sentence. Some New York people appealed to Harding and when he pardoned a lot of politicals, my sentence was commuted to twenty years.

Well, there I sat in my cell in prison. My girl in Philadelphia sent me books. She was a schoolteacher, not a foreigner, a real one hundred per cent American. There were books on mathematics, and pretty soon I got to like that subject. You get plenty of time to think in jail. I was a Red general, so to say, at twenty-one; but if I knew then what I know now, I don't think I would have done what I did. I am not a communist; I am an anarchist. I am twenty-eight. I want to be an American engineer, get married and settle down. If I go back to Russia now, I will have to take up my old trade: I will be a coal miner. Now you see why I want to double-cross Baldwin and the Department of Justice and stay right here.

"You are going to Philadelphia," I said. "Why don't you ask your girl if she'll go with you to Russia?"

"That's an idea," Anton said. "Maybe that's the whole point."

He came back Monday jubilant.

"Everything is O.K.," he said. "I am going back to Russia and she will come with me. Tell Baldwin he can sleep easy."

Several days before Anton was to sail, the progressives of the Russian colony arranged a farewell meeting for him under the auspices of the liberal newspaper *Russky Golos*. The hall on East Fourth Street was jammed, everybody was sweating, and the bar in the back was doing a heavy business in 2.5 beer. Anton was happy. His usually pale face was flushed above his wilted collar, and he drank beer incessantly. His girl, plump and sunburned in her yellow summer dress, was even happier.

"Think of it," she said when we were introduced. "I am actually going to Russia! Don't you think it's wonderful of Anton to take me?"

Anton smiled proudly. From the platform, his name was boomed out by the orators of the evening, who extolled this young peasant as a revolutionary hero. He had fought for his own class, had faced death for it, had suffered in prison for it. When Anton rose to speak, the audience stood up and broke into song. The applause was prolonged and deafening at the end of each sentence. Then a balalaika orchestra played. Anton took me to the bar and bought me a beer.

"I am not taking Anna to Russia," he said.

"Why not?"

"I made up my mind tonight. After all, I am a hero. She is only a plain schoolteacher. In Russia I will be an important man. I am sure I will find a better woman, more my equal."

"Anton, you're a damned fool. This meeting has turned your head.

You will not be an important man in Russia. You will find a million heroes there like you—and better ones. Suppose you do become an important man? You will never find another girl like Anna."

In the lobby I found Anna crying.

"It's terrible to be let down like this," she said. "But that's not the worst. I can't bear to see him spoiled."

§5

Anton sailed for Russia alone. At first his letters were cheerful and enthusiastic. He lectured in various cities on his jail experiences, and on political prisoners in the United States. Then the holiday was over. Anton had to go to work. From the Kuznetsk coal region he wrote me in the fall of the year:

"I am in Kuzbas already more than a month—the last place I wanted to come. Circumstances, as well as the whole disappointing situation in Russia, compelled me to come here. I am working at my old trade, building community hall, and am getting one ruble a day. The greater number of communists in Russia suffer from Holy Roller phobia. Holy Rollers tell you nothing shall save you but the blood of Jesus. Communists tell you nothing shall save the world but the whiskers of Marx. Actually, workers under their rule must live on tea and bread, and the higher officials enjoy the luxuries. Before coming here, I took a trip through Central Russia with an American journalist. We visited a group of political prisoners, members of the anarchist, syndicalist and Zionist underground parties. They said they had been exiled administratively, without public hearing, to the coldest parts of Russia, after being kept for months in solitary confinement. We found them on a hunger strike in protest against abuses by the guards. The sight of the political prisoners and their surroundings made me sick. I did not fight for this! I did not sacrifice seven years of my life to give new tyrants an opportunity to torture people. As long as there are Russian workers in jail, I will consider the bolsheviks enemies."

Anton's letter disturbed me much more than had the Carnegie Hall meeting at which Vladeck had been prevented from speaking. Anton was no public figure; he had no ax to grind; he was a simple, honest boy who had spent his life on the farm, in the coal mine, on the battlefield, in prison. He saw life in the Soviet Union not from the "luxurious" heights of the commissars, but from below, from the coal shaft.

But as I read and reread Anton's complaints, certain facts which he had stated in his sincerity impressed me. Was it not significant that the Soviet censorship, painted in such black colors here, had let his letter pass uncut? Was it not equally significant that the American journalist, for whom Anton had acted as interpreter, had been permitted to visit political prisoners, to see their conditions in prison, to hear their protests? I could understand Anton's identification with the prisoners, he who had just been released from prison himself. But apart from the bitter memories which the sight of them aroused in him, was there not something else to be considered? When Anton justified his sending the thirty Japanese naked into the frozen forest, he said all war is cruel, everyone in it is compelled to be cruel. The cruelest of all wars is civil war. Fighting the enemies of the revolution, Anton was capable of incredible harshness; returning unwillingly to a land where he was no longer a military hero but a coal miner, he looked with a disappointed eye upon everything. I had read a Soviet short story in *Azure Cities* describing the bitter disillusion of many civil war heroes: the thrill, the excitement, the sublime tension were over; they could not adjust themselves to the routine of daily anonymous labor; some blew out their brains. Was not Anton, perhaps, such a disillusioned hero, resenting his demotion from the glory of a "general" to the labor of a miner? And if so, what value did his testimony have, except in so far as it threw light upon his own psychology? Moreover, was Kuzbas typical of the Soviet Union? Later, that region was to become a great industrial center; but we did not know that; we only knew it was a far-off place in the Urals founded by American wobblies. Could one generalize about a country of 160,000,000 people, about so vast a thing as a social revolution, from one's limited, immediate personal experience, however harsh, however truthfully described?

"I have been glad to receive your letters," I replied to Anton, "especially since you have been so honest about your reactions. Frankly, these reactions have puzzled me. I cannot help feeling that the picture you have drawn of present-day Russia is one-sided. There are many evils resulting from the civil war, from Russia's backward industries, from the general world situation. Also, in times of great upheaval, and with the general slowness of human development, injustices are bound to continue for a long time to come.

"What appeals to me is: (1) the revolution has improved the life of Russia since the Czar's time to such an extent that if that were its only accomplishment, all the horrors of the war and civil war, of famine and suffering, were worth while; (2) the bolsheviks are honest about their problems, face them, talk about them; (3) they look on the difficulties of present-day Russia as things to be *overcome;* they are there, they cannot be helped, no one wished them to exist; what we can wish is to abolish them. This is the great task of the new Russian generation which will be assisted by the working class of the world; (4) Russia is the only country in the world whose government and social organizations look on life as something to be directed, to be 'molded nearer to the heart's desire.' Not profits, not exploitation is the chief aim of the Russian leaders, but the betterment of industry for all, the advancement of the people's culture.

"Despite the marvelous accomplishments of the last eight years and the great aims of the Communist Party, is there injustice and stupidity in Russia? No one denies it. Trotsky says somewhere: 'A new class, a new life, new vices and new stupidity.' But he points out that two attitudes are possible toward these evils. One can say: 'See what we have been brought to; let us go back to the nice old nobleman's nest.' That is a backward attitude. But one can say: 'We are building a new life now, and yet *how much piggishness, vulgarity and knavery of the old and the new are about us. Let us make a clean sweep of them.'* That, it seems to me, is the right attitude. I have thought these things as I read your letters. Do not think I fail to realize your personal difficulties, or the difficulties of thousands of others. But ought one to generalize about Russia from one's own personal difficulties? Ought one to revile and slander the greatest social experiment in history as an easy way of relieving our personal chagrin and anger at problems which should be faced for what they are—personal problems?

"Carl Branin came to see me. Think of it: he is the American journalist whom you accompanied through Central Russia as interpreter; he saw the very same things you did, and talked with the very same political prisoners. And Carl Branin tells me a different story than yours. Dr. Harry Ward, chairman of the Civil Liberties Union, has come back from Russia and he, too, tells a different story. There are people in jail—but they took part in counterrevolutionary activities. Perhaps the Soviet government is blundering in keeping them in jail now. Is that a reason for repudiating everything, the entire achievement of the October Revolution, the abolition of capitalism and landlordism, the giving of the land to the peasants, the tremendous increase in literacy, the establishment of a society based on working-class power? After all, one must retain some sense of reality and balance in judging these things. It is not the facts I am quarreling about, but the interpretation of the facts—and above all the *attitude* toward the facts."

By a strange coincidence, a new roommate was assigned to Anton in Kuzbas. I had met Powers Hapgood on a mountaintop near Woodstock, where Roger Baldwin once took a group of friends to discuss politics. Powers was a nephew of Norman Hapgood, the journalist, and of Hutchins Hapgood, who had written a moving book on the ghetto. Young Hapgood bore a striking resemblance to Baldwin both physically and intellectually. He was tall and dark, with the austere, willful, thoughtful face of the New England puritan. From Harvard he had gone neither to Greenwich Village nor into the liberal research groups, but into the coal fields as a miner. While he was mastering the trade, he entered the United Mine Workers and became a popular union organizer. During 1925—the year with which I am now dealing —he went abroad and worked in the coal mines of England, Germany, France, Belgium and Italy.

It was therefore not as a mere observer that he now wrote me from Kuzbas, but as a man who knew mining and miners at first hand, with a real basis for comparison at his command. Moreover, he was not a communist, but a socialist by no means inclined to accept official bolshevik interpretations of conditions and events. Yet how differently this Harvard coal miner viewed life in Kuzbas from the peasant-soldier Anton. It seemed as if class origin was in itself no golden key to the truth. Another Harvard boy, John Reed, had died for the working class and lay under the Kremlin wall; the cigarmaker Samuel Gompers was a faithful aide-de-camp of Big Business. From the Kuzbas colony at Kemerovo, Powers Hapgood wrote me:

"I have been living in the U.S.S.R. for two and a half months now, and am enjoying life here very much. For the last seven weeks I have been here in Kemerovo, working as a miner in the Central Shaft Mine, and rooming in the Community House with Anton. I like Anton very much and we get along well, but we have many arguments, as I see things differently than he does.

"Conditions here are far better than I expected to find them in view of the difficulties which have had to be overcome. There is much that is disappointing, to be sure, in the personalities of some of the members of the Communist Party in high positions here who seem to be thoroughly bourgeois in their grasping for the comforts of life; but then one cannot expect any organization to keep its membership perfect. There are many excellent conditions here—a six-hour day from bank to bank—for miners; a six-hour day for office workers whose work is done in an unhealthy atmosphere; an eight-hour day for outside workers; one month's vacation a year with full pay for miners, and at least two weeks for all workers; sickness and accident compensation at the rate of forty per cent of wages for single men and women, and seventy-five per cent for married workers; free hospital and doctor service with a change of climate when necessary; and many other good conditions which do not prevail in capitalist lands. The standard of living, however, is low. Miners average about 35 rubles a month, and the cost of living is high in terms of these wages. Fortunately, free rent and fuel are given in addition to wages, and things are continually getting better. Each year sees an improvement over the preceding one. Right now we are getting a twenty-five per cent wage increase. In other countries where I've worked—America, England, Germany, France—things are going from bad to worse; unemployment, a sinking standard of living, strikes, lockouts, general depression and gloom are the order of the day. Here, on the other hand, things are going ahead and there is hope."

It was amazing how differently two men could view the same experience. Hapgood wrote me that he was "enjoying life very much" in Russia. Anton, living with him in the same room, working on the same job, said that *both* of them were having "an awful time in every respect." One of the "awful" things from which Anton suffered was arguing with his roommate and with the Kuzbas communists. Two years as a "Red general" with absolute power over his men and five years in a prison cell had made this already sensitive boy oversensitive to contradiction. He told me that in Kuzbas he made it his "general policy" to get "under the skins" of the communists, and when he left he was sure "many members of the Party in Kemerovo were glad to get rid" of him.

The manner of his leaving was significant. Despite his continual attacks on the Party members, several of them recommended him for an office job in the war docks of Vladivostok at fairly good pay. That streak of ingratitude which made him ditch Anna on the eve of his sailing from America led him to write me that he still believed ninety-five per cent of the Party members "ought to be hung by the neck until they are dead"; but the longing for distinction which had made him a "general" now aroused his interest in the new job.

"Who knows," he wrote me, "perhaps I will be manager yet of this enterprise!"

In general Vladivostok changed Anton's mood about the Soviet Union. He was now back at the scene of his early youth, his military glory, his arrest by the American troops; he was also in a large city instead of the Kuzbas wilds.

"Vladivostok in comparison with Kemerovo is as far as Heaven from Hell," he wrote me. "Here in Vladivostok I have found practically all members of the Party are trying to do something, quite sincere, it seems to me, and energetic. Perhaps it is because the Soviet government is not quite three years old in Vladivostok; and also perhaps it is because Vladivostok is the outpost of the Far East and the best workers are sent here. Anyway, this is the first place in Russia where I could not find so much fault with the members of the Communist Party."

Also perhaps it was because Anton hoped to become the manager of the enterprise, for he soon wrote me: "No doubt you will be glad to hear I have made up my mind to join the Communist Party here. Owing to my past revolutionary record I can perhaps succeed in getting through without formalities." The scene of his arrest must have reminded him of his prison life, for he added: "I want to do something for the comrades I left behind me in the filthy jails of America. I feel cowardly that I haven't done a thing for them yet because of my 'reaction.' I begin to think that I cannot be of use to all the world at once. So it is better to try to do something good for a little corner of this world and for a few people, instead of crying for all and doing good for none."

CHAPTER VI

THE NEW MASSES

Performances, assortments, résumés.
—HART CRANE.

§ 1

DIFFERENCES of viewpoint made my position at the Civil Liberties Union difficult. I therefore quit that organization and took a job with a news agency. As in Paris, but this time more intensively, the daily routine of journalism compelled me to grapple with external reality. On the one hand, the newsroom was a kind of ivory tower, remote from action, dedicated to thought and language and the interpretation of action; on the other hand, newspaper routine immersed you in the social-political-economic events of the day, in the flow of American life. Again a reorientation of attitude became compulsory, a crossing over to a new plane of experience. But my thought was becoming more integrated. The America which I described in my news stories was the America I saw in my private thoughts. To Scott Nearing, then in Europe, I wrote:

"It's the same U. S. A. you left. Gitlow has had to go back to jail; the Supreme Court has upheld the conviction of Charlotte Anita Whitney under the California Criminal Syndicalism Act; Ford, released from a California jail where he had served twelve years for alleged participation in the hop strike riot of 1913, has been rearrested on a murder charge growing out of the same strike. In the New York municipal campaign, Gitlow has been barred from running for mayor on the communist ticket because of his jail sentences. The coal strike is dragging on, with no definitive action in sight. Loans keep flowing out of the country—to German towns, South American towns, to European governments. The State Department has told Mexico where to get off in regard to the pending amendment to Article 27, defining under what conditions foreigners may own property in Mexico. The New York landlords are attempting to prevent an extension of the rent laws. American industrialists have called for intensified competition with Europe. Production in basic industries has been rising; employment has increased about nine per cent, and wages are about what

365

they were when you left. Instead of the 'monkey' trial, the Rhine-lander trial engages the attention of the masses.

"You know the story? It's a perfect picture of American social life and morals: A young millionaire marries a girl with Negro blood. They get along until his family steps in. The Rhinelanders own millions, are in the Social Register, descend from the Huguenots. The boy is induced to sue for annulment on the grounds that he was deceived. The girl, he claims, told him she was Spanish. Sensation! Scare-heads! The tabloids publish pictures of the girl—full face, profile, bust, full length, in fur coat, in apron. The Rhinelander scion appears in the press all over the country in all sorts of poses. Lawyers, judges, relatives, everybody has his picture taken. The trial is given four and five columns. It brings out the degraded social position forced on the Negro. Think of the girl's crime: she has a good deal of white blood but she has Negro blood too. Unpardonable! The boy's lawyer thrills the courtroom by reading the boy's love letters—full of tenderness and obscenity. The letters are published in full by the press. The boy is forced to admit—who would believe it!—that he actually had sexual relations with his wife before they were married. The girl's lawyer, the jury, the spectators, all of whom, no doubt, came to the marriage altar unspotted virgins, are shocked and delighted. Detailed descriptions of two weeks in a New York hotel before marriage. When you slept with Alice in a hotel didn't you see she was colored? No. The question is asked time and again; time and again the millionaire says no.

"Finally the climax: let the jury see for itself that the girl could not possibly have deceived her husband as to her color. Jury, judge, lawyers and girl file into the judge's chambers. The girl strips. Clad only in a single garment covering her hips and waist, she exhibits her body to twelve good men and true—and white. Let them see she belongs to the race so despised and rejected. When the boy is defeated, his lawyers petition the court to change the charge: the girl is guilty now of *negative* fraud; she had failed to tell him—what he could have seen for himself—that she had Negro blood. Such is the American comedy. . . ."

My outlook was crystallizing so that I scarcely remembered the past. The vanished village, the Brooklyn ghetto; Shelley and romantic socialism; Woodrow Wilson and the war; Greenwich Village and romantic love—all these now appeared to be someone else's experience. But this was an illusion born of a violent attempt to remold myself.

Soon I met an extraordinary poet who made it clear that in no existence, whether of an individual or of a society, is the present entirely
divorced from the past or from the future.

§ 2

The bourgeois press paid little attention to Vladimir Mayakovsky
when he came to New York in 1925. At this time it was generally
believed that famine, murder and robbery were the essence of the
October Revolution, and that the bolsheviks had killed all art. Only in
radical circles did you run across Mayakovsky; only there did you
hear about his remarkable talent, his great reputation at home as
Soviet Russia's leading poet.

Everything about Mayakovsky distinguished him from most of
the writers we had been accustomed to meet in Greenwich Village.
He was big, with the broad shoulders, thin torso and long legs of a
Dempsey. It was summer, and in accordance with the Russian custom, Mayakovsky had shaved his head, so that he looked like a hard-
boiled officer. Yet there was extraordinary sensitivity in his typically
Russian face, clean-shaven, sensuous and strong. In the East Fourth
Street hall where Anton had been hailed as a hero, we heard Mayakovsky recite his verses in a big, booming voice. The crowd went wild.
The handful of American writers present—Mike Gold, Genevieve Taggard, myself among others—had to rely on extemporaneous translations; yet even from these we got a sense of power which came from
the poet's mastery of his craft, his gigantic feeling and his new
theme—the October Revolution.

Later, the group which was organizing the *New Masses* gave
Mayakovsky a party at a private house. It was typical of the gay
Twenties—jazz records, bathtub gin, dancing in shirt sleeves. Mayakovsky danced with the strength and awkwardness of a bear, and
liked it. So did the girls. Then the poet was urged to read his verses.
He took a little notebook out of his pocket and read his latest. We
all drank too much. Mayakovsky, twice my size, lifted me to the ceiling to show his strength. I made fun of his booming voice by reciting
the first two lines of his poem in mangled form without knowing
their meaning.

"Take the potatoes out of your mouth," he said.

"The revolution doesn't need a megaphone voice," I said. "Look at
Lenin."

"Lenin's voice did not matter. He talked with cannon. I have no cannon, but I have my voice."

Mike Gold recited *A Strange Funeral at Braddock*, broke into tears, and made an eloquent speech about the proletarian revolution. The gin was bad; my head ached; my conscience bothered me; revolutionary writers shouldn't drink.

"Don't get foolish," Mike Gold said. "Mayakovsky drinks three times as much as we do."

Mayakovsky admitted it.

"Yes, I am a bohemian," he added. "That is my great problem: to burn out all my bohemian past; to rise to the heights of the revolution."

Despite our typically bohemian argument, Mayakovsky and I became friends, and he asked me to translate some of his poems for the magazines. Freda Kirchwey of the *Nation* offered to publish them. I knew no Russian at that time; the little I had known as a boy had been completely obliterated by the years. Leon Talmy of the *Freiheit* staff helped me: he translated the verses literally, and read them over and over again until I heard their rhythm in my sleep. I believe that the two poems we published in the *Nation* were the first translations of Mayakovsky ever to appear in this country. One of them, *Decree to the Army of Art,* had special significance for those of us who had wrestled with the problem of art and revolution:

> They brag, the old men's brigades,
> Of the same old wearisome goals:
> Comrades,
> To the barricades!
> Barricades of hearts and souls.
> He alone is a Communist true
> Who burns the bridge for retreat;
> Stop marching slowly, Futurists,
> Into the future—leap!
> Engines are easy to build,
> Wind the wheels and they go—
> But hurl your song like a bomb,
> There's a railway depot to blow!
> Pile up sound on sound,
> March on
> With whistle and song;
> Loud-ringing letters abound
> To roll
> Under

Your tongue.
Pants creased like a feather's edge—
That's the easy officer's way;
All the soviets won't budge the troops
Unless the musicians play.
Drag pianos into the street,
Let drums rend the air asunder,
Whether drums or pianos beat,
Let tumult be,
Let thunder!
What good to slave in a shop,
To soil your face and growl,
Why stare at the joy
Of others,
Flapping your eyes like owl?
Enough of pennywise talk—
Sweep the old from the heart who dares!
The streets shall be our brushes,
Our palettes shall be the squares!
The thousand-paged Book of Time
Revolution's song shall know;
Into the streets, Futurists,
Drummers and poets, go!

There was nothing specifically Russian in this identification of art and revolution. It was a high point in an old socialist literary tradition. While Mayakovsky was still in New York, Upton Sinclair published *Mammonart*. For all its errors, confusions and sentimentalism, this book had a profound effect on us because of its central theme, illustrated with a wealth of detail. Sinclair's books on religion, journalism and education, powerful pamphlets in the muckraking tradition, had dealt specifically with the American scene; *Mammonart* took the whole of world literature for its field. It was less an exposé of facts than an exposition of opinion, a passionate polemic against the theory of art for art's sake, a frank defense of "propaganda" art. This idea was not new in the history of literature. Brandes and Taine had done similar work in Western literature, and all the great Russian critics defended social art against "pure" art.

What was significant was that Sinclair had developed similar views out of his American background and experience. He was not a communist, and his book bore no traces of the influence of Soviet literature. From the beginning of his literary career, Sinclair, interested in social justice, anxious to portray the industrial and social conflicts of the day, came up against the stone wall of bourgeois literary criticism which maintained that art was a sacred realm above the vulgar conflicts of society, a refuge from the materialism of everyday life, a beautiful, exquisite, fragile spirit concerned not with time but with eternity. Literature which dealt with the realities of industrial America— *The Jungle,* let us say, or *The Iron Heel*—was dismissed as "propaganda." When Sinclair tried to arouse sympathy for the struggling poet, as in *The Journal of Arthur Stirling,* that was art; when he tried to arouse sympathy for the struggling proletariat, as in *King Coal,* that was propaganda.

Now, in looking back over the history of the world's literature, he saw that it was full of "propaganda." Time, the remoteness of our own day from the struggles of earlier epochs, the innocuousness or acceptance of old disputed ideas, had converted propaganda into art. Aristophanes satirized the democracy of Athens; Virgil celebrated the founding of Rome; Juvenal exposed the corruption of high Roman society in the true spirit of the muckraker; Shakespeare made fun of the "mob" in revolt; John Milton demanded that God avenge the massacre of the Protestants in Piedmont. Was not all this propaganda as well as art? Is not all art, Sinclair asked, of necessity an expression of some view of life? Is not all literature in one sense the propagation of ideas?

Sinclair surveyed world literature and found that mediocre poets like Southey were called artists in their time because they said all the conventional things, while great poets like Shelley were damned because they wanted to change the world. The snobs of the *Quarterly* told Keats to go back to his pills because he was radical and a friend of the rebel journalist Leigh Hunt. Obviously, aesthetic criticism was not as objective as it pretended to be; it was bound up with the prejudices of the ruling class.

I was seeing a great deal of Floyd Dell at this time, and he supported Upton Sinclair's viewpoint.

"Those who praise the existing scheme of things," he said, "will find their artistic virtues readily enough acclaimed. The rash young revolutionist who turns his coat and comes out for law and order will likely enough be made poet laurcate. Morals, too, are involved. The writer who is a rebel in politics will have his moral frailties emblazoned before a shocked world, and will be regarded as a monster. The writer whose opinions are correct may, if he is careful, enjoy his adulteries and perversities and remain the darling of respectable society. And when one looks over the world's literature, how many first-rate writers are there who have not been social rebels? How many writers have written anything worth while after they ceased to be rebels? And of those writers who were notoriously hostile or indifferent to the great social rebellions of their time, how much has their art lost by their blindness to what was going on?"

I have taken these sentences from Floyd Dell's book on Upton Sinclair in order to give his ideas exactly; but it was the substance of many of his talks with me, especially during 1925, when we discussed the Sinclair biography. Floyd felt that he was a link in the socialist literary tradition between Upton Sinclair and my generation. My own age group felt that we were links between the generation of Dell, Reed and Minor and our juniors. Already at this time we were drawing younger people into the revolutionary movement, some of whom, like Sender Garlin, A. B. Magil and others were to become effective left-wing writers. Apart from the personal satisfactions we got out of such activities, there was the great, impersonal Cause. It came before us, was bigger than any of us, would go on after us. You worked not for yourself but for the masses, for the social revolution. Sinclair's literary beliefs, as developed in *Mammonart,* emphasized not *self*-expression but the propagation of social ideals. Agreeing with him, Floyd Dell called for "social revolutionary criticism," a phrase he used a great many times in our talks at this time.

"The artist," Floyd was fond of explaining, "is an interpreter of life, and judges the truth and value of his interpretation by the test of how fully he shows himself aware of what is going on in the world, with special reference to social change, and whether he helps his audience to understand and sympathize with such changes. He is recognized as a discriminator of spiritual values, in some sense a creator of them, and he is judged by the spiritual values he helps to create in a world that struggles toward something greater and finer than its past. He is not asked to be consciously attempting to create such values, and least of all is he asked to believe in this or that specific program of change—he is judged as an artist and not as a politician. Social revolutionary criticism is *frankly partisan criticism, but represents the genuine aesthetic response of those who feel themselves to be living in a changing world lighted by the hope of revolutionary improvement.*"

Mayakovsky, in the poem which I put into crude English verse, went further and urged the artist to destroy and create values, to fight on the barricades of hearts and souls, to hurl the song like a bomb, to budge the troops with revolutionary music, to be, as Heine had said of himself, a drummer of the revolution.

§ 3

In his booming voice Mayakovsky said to the girl who was translating our conversation:

"How is it that these so-called revolutionary writers of America have no organization of their own?"

"We are starting a new magazine," I said.

"That is not enough. You should have an association of proletarian writers. We have several of them in our country, the German comrades have them, other countries have them too."

"Why form a special group?" I argued. "If a writer believes in communism, let him join the Party."

"But not every writer who believes in communism wants to join the Party, or is fit for the Party," Mayakovsky replied. "Besides, many writers are against capitalism without understanding communism. Don't you think they ought to get together in an organization?"

"I'm afraid it wouldn't go. American writers are not accustomed to work in groups and organizations. They are lonely individuals, each working in the isolation of his study."

"It will go, it will go even here," Mayakovsky said. "As soon as the writers learn that they are not really free individuals, that they are dependent on the publishing houses and the magazines, that the workers will open new paths for culture—they will organize then."

Mike Gold was not surprised when I mentioned the idea to him. He had recently returned from the Soviet Union and felt that writers sympathetic to the working class ought to organize. He had, in fact, already participated in the organization of the Workers Drama League together with Paul Peters, Hugo Gellert, Arturo Giovannitti, William Gropper, Louis Lozowick, Florence Rau, and Bertram D. Wolfe. This group produced a revolutionary play translated from the German of Karl Wittfogel. Sparks of the revolutionary idea were visible even on Broadway, where John Howard Lawson's *Processional* was running.

We tried to start an organization of left-wing artists and writers, but nothing came of it. Early in 1926 we tried again. Subsequently, in Moscow the group known as the Proletarian Artists and Writers League, issued a form letter to various well-known American writers asking them to join its National Executive Committee. The letter sent out by my younger brother Harry was signed among others by John Dos Passos, John Howard Lawson, Mary Heaton Vorse, Genevieve Taggard, Michael Gold, William Gropper, Joseph Freeman, Robert Wolf, Harry Freeman, Louis Lozowick, Simon Felshin and Hugo Gellert.

This group, ignorant of or forgetting the history of *Clarté,* repeated the errors of Barbusse's literary organization. Knowing too little, it attempted too much. Itself uncertain, it sought to organize uncertain elements. It proposed to "tackle such jobs as the organization of newspapermen, the translation of foreign radical literature, the co-ordination of workers' colleges and cultural groups, and perhaps the publication of a small monthly magazine devoted solely to the problems of the proletarian writer and artist."

The invitation which the league sent out elicited surprising responses which indicated the mood of the American intelligentsia of that period toward the working-class movement.

Van Wyck Brooks wrote in, saying: "I thoroughly sympathize with what I take to be the objects of the League, and am much complimented to be asked to join it in this way."

From the University of Wisconsin, William Ellery Leonard wrote that he sympathized with the organization and "would be glad to see my name on the list of the National Executive Committee."

Waldo Frank, too, was glad to let the committee use his name; so was Langston Hughes, then editor of *Fire,* a magazine issued by young Negro artists and writers. Lola Ridge, who was "happy to serve as a member of the National Executive Committee," described the league as "the most significant and important social movement" she had heard of in a long while. Babette Deutsch did not see how she could "lay claim to the status of proletarian writer," yet she was "glad of an opportunity to register" herself on "the side of those who are working for a just social order" and for that reason was glad to serve.

William F. Dunne accepted without reservation, and added the characteristically communist phrase that he was "awaiting further instructions" from us. Even the liberal philosopher Horace M. Kallen wrote an emphatic O.K. across the invitation. Eric Walrond, the Negro writer; Sam Ornitz, author of *Haunch, Paunch and Jowl;* Maurice Becker, *Masses* artist; Louis Engdahl, *Daily Worker* editor; M. H. Hedges, author of the labor novel *Dan Minturn;* Miriam Allen De Ford, Floyd Dell, and E. Haldeman-Julius also accepted. So did Upton Sinclair.

Lewis Gannett declined because it appeared to him that the purposes of the league were mixed. He favored organizing newspapermen, but did not want to "bid for the designing and decoration of the workers' co-operative apartment houses"—a fantastic plank which some of the artists had inserted into the league's program. Nor did he think that another magazine was necessary for revolutionary writers and artists when the *New Masses* was already there.

Sinclair Lewis declined because he was going abroad, and would be so absorbed in his new book that he would have time for nothing else. Roger Baldwin declined because he was "not a proletarian anything" but "just a parasitic agitator," like most of his "friends among the proletarian intellectuals."

William Allen White, the Sage of Emporia, also declined, but for other reasons. He said he read the *New Masses* and enjoyed it hugely, but he was not in New York enough to take active part in the league's work as a directing executive and he disliked "tremendously to be a dummy executive on a matter so vital as that." However, he added, "you have my good will, and if you ever need it sometime you may have my good money."

There was a good deal of confusion as to just what proletarian art was. Was it fiction, poetry and drama written by people of working-class origin? Then what about D. H. Lawrence who fled from the coal mines to the passionate pursuit of abstract sex? Was it writing about workers? Then how about the "confession" stories which some of my friends were writing for the Macfadden magazines—stories frankly rewritten from the classics in which Anna Karenina became Milly Jones and Richard Feverel emerged as Dick Brown? Obviously proletarian art was one created from the viewpoint of the class-conscious, organized, revolutionary advance guard of the working class. Nevertheless, it seemed incongruous for a university graduate whose father had risen into the million-dollar class to call himself a "proletarian" writer even when he had broken from the class of his origin and thrown in his lot with that of the proletariat. Then how account for the fact that in 1925 John Dos Passos, John Howard Lawson, Mary Heaton Vorse, Van Wyck Brooks, William Ellery Leonard, Waldo Frank, Horace Kallen, and William Allen White expressed their willingness to serve on the executive committee of a proletarian writers' league? A decade later the middle-class intelligentsia was to thunder from coast to coast that such a literature was impossible, that it was an importation from Russia, a mechanical fantasy contrived by dogmatic dialectical materialists in the pay of the Kremlin. Yet here in 1925, the phrase "proletarian writers" appeared normal to most of these people, some of whom offered not only their goodwill but their money to the league.

This was partly owing to the fact that in 1925 the word "proletarian" was taken to be synonymous with "labor." No one thought it odd for a member of the educated classes to engage in labor activities. The socialist professor, journalist, preacher, surgeon, lawyer, was as common in America as in Europe. Every major trade union in the world had its staff of economists, editors and teachers, drawn to a large extent from the middle-class intelligentsia. In literature men like Shaw, Wells, Sinclair, Zola, Barbusse had spoken loudly and vigorously for labor. No one thought it incongruous for Floyd Dell to write in defense of the Bolshevik Revolution, for John Reed to give his life to it, for Powers Hapgood to go from the Harvard campus to the coal mines.

There was a long period in American history—the first quarter of our century—in which the progressive intelligentsia felt sympathetic toward labor. To assist labor in one way or another, to give your talents and energies and money to it was considered rather noble. The middle classes, pressed hard by the expanding trusts, often allied themselves with labor; their intellectuals often entered the Socialist party, some even the I.W.W. Thus a "proletarian" writers' and artists' league meant for the intelligentsia a league of writers and artists sympathetic to labor, and willing to help it through the medium of art and literature—as Upton Sinclair, Jack London, John Reed, Floyd Dell, Art Young, Robert Minor and Boardman Robinson had already done.

The foundation of the league was for us an act symbolizing the need for a division of labor in the revolutionary movement. It separated us functionally from the bohemian intelligentsia, on the one hand, and from the practical politicians of the Party, on the other.

"Politics concerns the life of the entire world," I wrote at this time to Laura, with whom my intimate relations had ended, but who was still a good friend. "Yet people who would be ashamed to admit that they had never heard Rachmaninoff are not a bit ashamed to admit that they had never read Lenin. The workers must learn certain elementary principles in order to live. It is the liberals and bohemians and 'intellectuals' (self-styled) who live half their lives on the meager political diet of the other half; a few general notions, vague and without roots, about 'freedom,' the 'full life,' justice, whatnot, suffice them; and when they have exhausted their store of smutty stories, gossip and threadbare reactions to a few books and psychoanalysis, and do turn to political and social questions, they dispose of these with a few 'elementary principles' they picked up in their youth. A living political party, on the contrary, is forced to face concrete problems every day, problems which cannot be solved by the mere repetition of general principles, but only by their *application.* Marx left no specific instructions for the proper tactics to be followed in the Passaic strike now going on; and more real thinking has to go into finding the right tactics than I have observed in most of the remarks about Bach, Joyce or sex among the people who are free of the 'monomania' of wishing to prevent the destruction of human culture by capitalism and the creation of a socialist commonwealth. I say this obvious stuff because it's true, not because it's new. *It's probable that I shall be happier as a writer than as a politician, but bourgeois writers are so flat and blind precisely because they do not try to understand social and political forces.* More and more I see the world from the revolutionary viewpoint. Most of the poets, artists, intellectuals, musicians and other people I meet make me realize that the middle classes are spiritually bankrupt. That's a stale phrase, but the fact is still here. Everybody seeks sanctuary in mystery. Some go to the Gourdjiev school; some write mystical plays like *Nirvana* and the *Great God Brown;* some rave about *The Dybbuk* or the *Goat Song;* some shut themselves up in their little souls and turn out little songs about their little troubles; some go from party to party and wash their lives out in gin and jazz; some drool away their week-ends talking the same damned gossip about the same damned friends; some call themselves proletarians, radicals and revolutionaries and make fun of the bourgeois intellectuals and aesthetes, and all the time they are the slaves of ignorance, prejudice, terror; some live in their tiny little worlds which they wrap up in big names and shut their eyes, learn nothing, see nothing, do nothing. The people I admire are people like the 25-year-old leader of the Passaic strike who has harnessed his brains and feelings to the revolutionary movement, who is living in the real world; who knows what is going on three feet away from his 'heart' and testicles; who is doing something with all his might; who doesn't squat down and worship his belly button in the face of impending wars, prevailing slavery, the possible collapse of civilization. I admire all artists, scientists, writers, journalists, workers who are honestly trying to understand themselves and their times, who do not think of themselves as isolated from the world but as part of it, as sharing in its responsibilities and its destiny. *We live once; let us not live like rats burrowing in some little hole, but like wise and courageous men and women who conquer some part of nature in their own generation."*

§ 4

The Passaic strike to which I referred in my letter had broken out early in 1926, and I was now covering it as a newspaperman. This strike was attracting world-wide attention because it was the first important one in American history under communist leadership. It had its origin in a ten per cent wage cut, which the owners of the Passaic textile factories had announced in the fall of 1925. Even before that the workers had been receiving as low as $10 a week. These wages had forced mothers of large families, as well as their children, to go into the factories to supplement the family income. The wage cut so reduced their already miserable living standards that by January, 1926, a thousand workers in the Botany mill joined the textile union which the United Front Committee had been organizing under communist direction. A committee of workers visited the owners of the Botany mill and requested them to restore the wages which had prevailed prior to the ten per cent cut. The mill owners replied by discharging all the members of the committee from the mill.

Immediately all the Botany workers, 6000 strong, went on strike. Within a week they were joined by 3000 workers from the Garfield mill and the Passaic Spinning Company. Other factories went on strike. Soon about 16,000 workers were out. The entire textile industry of Passaic was at a standstill.

Under the leadership of the United Front Committee the strikers now altered their demands. Instead of a restoration of the old pay, they now demanded a ten per cent increase over the old wage scale; the restoration of money taken in the wage cut; time and a half for overtime; a forty-hour week; decent sanitary conditions; no discrimination against union workers; and recognition of the union. The aim of the new union was to organize the unorganized, to join the main stream of the labor movement in this country by joining the American Federation of Labor through the United Textile Workers, to fight for the amalgamation of all existing organizations in the textile industry, to win the demands of the workers. The slogan of the strike was: *The united front of the workers against the united front of the bosses.*

I went down to Passaic several times a week, and reported the mass demonstrations, thousands of men, women and children marching through the streets of the city, picketing the factories with songs of class solidarity on their lips. Police brutality was boundless: I saw firemen turn the hose on strikers; cops threw gas bombs and clubbed men, women and children. Professional thugs, organized in a "Citizens Committee," terrorized the city, slugging strikers on the picket line. These outrages moved liberal circles throughout the country to indignation. As so often happens, a dramatic labor struggle impelled certain intellectuals to the left.

It was under these circumstances that the first issue of the *New Masses,* which we had been organizing for a year, went to press. Our editorial board might have taken its title from the Passaic strike committee. We, too, had a united front; we were anxious to join the main stream of American literature without modifying our basic principles, as the strikers wanted to join the A. F. of L. We were consciously influenced by the Passaic strike; it gave us our first issue to fight for.

The five editors who got out the magazine were Egmont Arens, Joseph Freeman, Hugo Gellert, Michael Gold, James Rorty and John Sloan. The executive board included these five and, in addition, Maurice Becker, Helen Black, John Dos Passos, Robert Dunn, William Gropper, Paxton Hibben, Freda Kirchwey, Robert Leslie, Louis Lozowick and Rex Stout—who was our business manager. Our list of contributing editors was a roster of the most progressive American writers and artists of the period—Sherwood Anderson, Cornelia Barnes, Van Wyck Brooks, Howard Brubaker, Stuart Chase, Glenn Coleman, Miguel Covarrubias, Stuart Davis, Adolph Dehn, Floyd Dell, Max Eastman, Waldo Frank, Al Frueh, Arturo Giovannitti, Susan Glaspell, H. J. Glintenkamp, John Howard Lawson, Claude McKay, Lewis Mumford, Eugene O'Neill, Elmer Rice, Lola Ridge, Boardman Robinson, Rita Romilly, Carl Ruggles, Carl Sandburg, Upton Sinclair, Genevieve Taggard, Jean Toomer, Louis Untermeyer, Mary Heaton Vorse, Eric Walrond, Walter White, Edmund Wilson, Robert Wolf, Charles W. Wood and Art Young.

I have given this catalogue of men and women—as poets once gave catalogues of ships—to indicate not only the rich intellectual and artistic resources of the new magazine, but the wide range of opinion it represented. This range was bound to lead to differences.

Among the fifty-six writers and artists grouped around the *New Masses* only two were members of the Communist party, less than a dozen were sympathetic to it. Full editorial meetings were marked by sharp debate, reflecting in literary terms the general social conflicts of the period. The liberals and radicals were sharply at odds. Between them were people undecided, ready to listen to both sides before committing themselves. What sort of magazine ought we to get out? What was the role of the writer in our epoch?

"First a restriction about proletarian literature," John Dos Passos said. "It seems to me that people are formed by their trades and occupations much more than by their opinions. . . . The word-slinging organism is substantially the same whether it sucks its blood from Park Avenue or from Flatbush. . . . Writers are insulated like everyone else by the enforced pigeonholing of specialized industry. As mechanical power grows in America, general ideals tend to restrict themselves more and more to Karl Marx, the first chapter of Genesis, and the hazy scientific mysticism of the Sunday supplements. I don't think it's any time for any group of spellbinders to lay down the law on any subject whatsoever. Particularly I don't think there should be any more phrases, badges, opinions, banners, imported from Russia or anywhere else. Ever since Columbus, imported systems have been the curse of this country. Why not develop our own brand? What we need is a highly flexible receiving station that will find out what's in the air in the country anyhow. . . . Why shouldn't the *New Masses* be setting out on a prospecting trip, drilling in unexpected places, following unsuspected veins, bringing home specimens as yet unclassified? . . . The terrible danger to explorers is that they always find what they are looking for. . . . I want an expedition that will find what it's not looking for. . . . The tendency of the masses has always been to be more disciplined in thought than in action. I'd like to see that state of things reversed for once. I'd like to see a magazine full of introspection and doubt that would be like a piece of litmus paper to test things by. . . . But Mike Gold says that skepticism is merely the flower of decay, the green mold on the intellect of the rotten bourgeoisie. He may be right. Anyway I don't think it is skepticism to say that November, nineteen-seventeen, is in the past."

"I am an internationalist," Mike Gold replied, "but I stand with John Dos Passos in his declaration that American writers in general and the *New Masses* writers in particular ought to set sail for a new discovery of America. Yes, let us explore this continent. . . . And what is the plan we shall follow? . . . I will not deny that Soviet Russia and its revolutionary culture form the spiritual core around which thousands of the younger writers in every land are building their creative lives. . . . What I deny is that I, or anyone else, demands of young American writers that they take their 'spiritual' commands from Moscow. No one demands that, for it is not necessary. . . . Moscow could not have created John Reed, Upton Sinclair, Jack London, Max Eastman, or Horace Traubel. American life created them. It will create others like them and better. Let us forget Moscow in this discussion. Let us think of America. . . . America today, I believe, offers the honest young writer only one choice—Revolt! No humane and sensitive artist can assent to this vast Roman orgy of commercialism, this wholesale prostitution of the mind, this vast empire of cheapness and shallowness and hypocrisy that forms the current America. We are not satisfied. We are not part of this American empire. We repudiate it, if only in the name of art. . . . Shall we revolt blindly, however, or with full, bold, hard consciousness? John Dos Passos says blindly. And he and John Howard Lawson and others formulate a vague aesthetic creed of impressionism—of sensationalism —of empiricism. They try to shut their eyes to the main drifts of American life. . . . They hug chaos to their bosoms, and all the heroes of their fiction wind up in chaos and failure. Other writers choose the same paths of 'introspection and doubt.' Eugene O'Neill has definitely strayed into a queer mystic universe of his own. Waldo Frank is discovering tragic 'beauty' in the bullfight and in parlor Zionism. Sherwood Anderson is still mumbling prayers before the ancient phallic gods. Carl Sandburg has suddenly become a sentimental American nationalist. Floyd Dell is busy turning out bedroom romances for the adolescent. H. L. Mencken is still hypnotizing poor driven little press agents or advertising slaves into the delusion that they are 'free' aristocrats and supermen. Robinson Jeffers offers serious epics on the solitary theme of incest. Carl Van Vechten prattles upper-class nonsense for the amusement of our nouveaux riches. James Branch Cabell plagiarizes from a thousand healthy folk fantasies and weaves the results into flashy patterns for the same nouveaux riches. One can go on indefinitely with the tale. A hundred younger writers express their revolt in the same blind futile way."

It was all right to say harsh things about a common oppressor like J. P. Morgan—but to attack the literary gods of the hour was lese majesty, blasphemy and, even worse, bad taste. But left-wing writers of this period never worried about taste.

"Is this exploring America?" Mike Gold asked. "Is this revival of the dead horses of Bible mysticism, Greek fatalism, Roman decadence, and British snobbery what you mean by a fresh start, dear John Dos Passos? Is pessimism, defeatism, despair, the fundamental chaos in your own brilliant and gifted work, the path you say leads to a new world? I beg to differ dogmatically, if you say it does, John. And I beg very humbly and diffidently to submit that perhaps some of our younger writers have stumbled into the real path. Let us call our discovery the world of revolutionary labor. It exists in America as in Russia. It has its schools, its unions, its tragedies, its defeats, its philosophy, ethics and science. It has written plays and produced them. It has poetry. It has painters and singers. It has an aesthetic. It has great men and women to write about. It has giant new themes. It has a hopeful, unsentimental spirit. It inspires one with faith and courage. . . . It makes great and even cruel demands on its writers. But when they understand it, and live in it fully, burning all bridges behind them, it can make them great in turn."

The dispute went on sharply at editorial board meetings, in print. Younger writers listened, swayed now to this side, now to the other. Some came out clear and determined.

"The time for lyrical radicalism is past," Edwin Seaver wrote me. "We want a literature and art that meets today on its own ground, a hard, fast, plumb-line literature and art, disdainful of lyrical escapes and that particular mysticism that is more like a mental chess game than anything more practical. I think you know that I have always been and always will be radical in my work and my outlook. And by radical I mean not one who is merely different, but one who seeks the roots of things. And as such a radical, as one who is conscious of the terrific struggle going on today, who sees wars and rumors of wars all about him, and the ever-widening chasm of the class struggle and revolution that is constantly evolving and is not a pistol shot or a page in a history book, as such a radical I am with you and Mike Gold."

The war generation of literary radicals was beginning to find its direction.

§ 5

Nevertheless, the editorial board of the *New Masses* consisted overwhelmingly of liberals. It was decided that the magazine would not be one "of communism or Moscow, but a magazine of American experiment." It would be for the working class, but not for any particular party speaking in the name of the working class. I soon discovered what this formula meant. In the course of my daily work as a newspaperman, I made the acquaintance of a high executive in a leading American news agency. One day he said to me:

"I hear you are connected with the *New Masses*. How would you like to publish a swell speech by Trotsky on the world situation and Soviet foreign policy? Our Moscow correspondent has just sent us this speech. It's good reading and good news."

"Then why don't you send it out to your papers?"

"They wouldn't print it," the executive said. "They would consider it propaganda."

"I should imagine any editor would be glad to print the views of an official speaking for a hundred sixty million people, for a country as big and important as Russia."

"Three years ago they might have. Three years from now they may. But not now. You can have the speech."

I said, thanks, this will be a break for the *New Masses,* a great piece for the first issue. But the majority of our staff thought otherwise.

"Trotsky's name," they said, "will damn us at once as a propaganda sheet. We don't want to be marked as a communist magazine."

The staff overwhelmingly voted not to publish the article. Later, however, there was a compromise. Unwilling to publish a Soviet spokesman on politics, the majority of the editors finally agreed to publish him on poetry. The Russian poet Sergei Yessenin had killed himself. Ignorant of Soviet literature as a whole at a time when the Russians were translating and publishing contemporary American writers from Sinclair Lewis to Genevieve Taggard, the American intelligentsia knew Yessenin chiefly as the husband of Isadora Duncan, once goddess of the cult of the free life. The handsome, wild, blond genius had been in New York, drunk excessively as always, beat up la Duncan, to her great delight, staged scenes at private houses, insulted the Jews at a studio party and was thrown down the stairs by several Yiddish poets who had come to pay their respects to the peasant genius. This was generally known; Yessenin's poetry was unknown. For passionate partisans, however, facts are of little importance. Despite Yessenin's notorious alcoholism, neurosis and sadism, the conservative press here, as well as in Europe, attributed the poet's suicide to the horrors of the Soviet regime. We published Trotsky's article *On the Death of a Poet* as a reply to these fantastic accusations. It was a beautiful piece of writing, poignant with sympathy and understanding for the poet's gifts, his problems, his tragic end.

"The peasant background, purified and refracted through his creative art, is very strong in Yessenin," Trotsky explained. "But the strength of this peasant background constitutes the real weakness of Yessenin's personality: he was uprooted from the old without striking root in the new. . . . The poet perished because he was not akin to the Revolution. But for the sake of the future the Revolution will adopt him forever. . . . Yessenin aspired to death from the very first years of his creativeness, realizing his inner lack of defense. . . . To whom did Yessenin write in his last hour with blood? Perhaps he was only crying out to the friend who has not yet been born, to the man of the approaching future, for whom some prepare through battle, and for whom Yessenin was preparing through song."

Clear enough: the poet did not die by his own hand because bolshevism hounded art, but because of the disparity between his temperament and the revolution: "Yessenin is intimate, tender and lyrical; the Revolution is public, epic and catastrophic." Yessenin could have gone on creating to the end "only in a society alive with song, harmonious and happy, in which not struggle but friendship, love and tenderness rule." Trotsky predicted that such a day would come—that "approaching future" which some prepare for through battle and some through song.

When we published Trotsky's essay, we did not dream that long before the day of "friendship, love and tenderness" some of his American partisans would take up the cry of the reaction and blame the Soviet regime for Mayakovsky's suicide, or that they would drag out Yessenin's corpse to lay it at the gates of the Kremlin in pathetic accusation, or that they would deny Trotsky's thesis that the poet who is not alien to the revolution prepares for the man of the approaching future through song as the worker-warrior does through battle. All these ideas were one day to be lost in a storm of partisan and personal abuse. At this time the discussions were on a different level. Commenting on Trotsky's *Literature and Revolution,* a translation of which appeared in the United States in the fall of 1926, Michael Gold wrote:

"Trotsky's book on literature is an amazing performance. This man is almost as universal as Leonardo da Vinci . . . Trotsky in every line of his book shows that he loves literature with a deep and permanent passion. . . . Trotsky comes to literature as to other social phenomena with the scientific tools of the Marxian methodology. He gives us, what no American critic has yet fully given us, a sense of the social changes which precede each new school of art, and which determine the individual psychology of the artist, however 'free' he thinks he is. . . . It is a masterly summary of Russian literary history of the past ten years. There have always been great writers in Russia, and each of them has some prototype in America. It is strange and amusing to meet all the familiar slogans and evasions of American literary specialists in Trotsky's pages. They are priests of the aesthetic god, they are servants of a divine classless mystery, and then suddenly the worker confronts them, a giant problem against the sky, and they flock to the White army, where their real roots had always been. This happened in England, also, during the general strike. It will happen here."

The unbounded admiration for Trotsky was not confined to Mike Gold; it marked all the extreme radicals of this country, who followed Russian events at a distance in both space and time. We were always three or four years behind events, and operated with vague rumors, assumptions, hopes, in the light of which we interpreted all the partially interpreted actions of the October Revolution from phase to phase. Next to Lenin, Trotsky was the best-known Soviet leader here, thanks not only to his remarkable gifts, his lofty position, and his genius for dramatizing himself, but also to the tendency of the American press to interpret historical events through personalities.

Those of us who fancied ourselves communists passionately asserted that the individual's role in history was negligible. The times were ripe: had it not been George Washington, Abraham Lincoln, Napoleon Bonaparte, Nikolai Lenin, it was bound to be another who would have carried out the same historic tasks. Of course, individuals did play an important part; will, character, intelligence, genius were part of the "dialectic process"; but one must not exaggerate heroes, and one must avoid hero worship. Lenin sustained this notion by direct utterance, and even more so by his extraordinary modesty. When he died and his embalmed body was laid in state in the mausoleum of Red Square, we were a little shocked and greatly puzzled. Such an action was meet for a "petit-bourgeois ideologue" like Carlyle, but certainly not for the collective man. A comrade who had seen the mausoleum came back from a trip to Moscow with internal conflict.

"I was puzzled by it," he said. "Was this hero worship? Was it a substitute for the ikon? But I watched the long queues of workers and peasants and was reassured. They learn that the body is embalmed, question religious dogma, show an interest in science, transfer their love of Lenin to the ideas he propagated."

Despite theories about the relation between the individual leader and the mass, we identified one with the other. With Lenin's death, there loomed upon the revolutionary horizon Trotsky, Radek, Stalin, Bukharin, Tomsky. These men, so recently obscure, oppressed, persecuted, imprisoned, branded and hounded as criminals against civilization, marched into the consciousness of the world as immortal historic figures, the peers of Danton, Robespierre, Marat, Bonaparte; the superiors of Gladstone, Disraeli, Clay and Webster. What a strange, extraordinary thing power was; how it transformed men and the opinion which mankind had of them. The flamboyant Bronx journalist whom Frank Harris had once described as a cross between a natural captain of men and Sidney Webb, was hailed by Mike Gold and his like as a combination of Leonardo da Vinci, Danton, Voltaire, Shelley, Blake, Walt Whitman and John Brown. Nevertheless, Michael Gold, lyrically applauding Trotsky's book on literature, added these significant words:

"Trotsky goes into a profound discussion of proletarian art, advancing the thesis that the term is a misnomer. He argues that the proletariat is but a transitory class in history, and that its object is not to perpetuate itself as a class, as was the object of the bourgeoisie, but to wipe out all classes. The bourgeoisie had a long period in which to create its art, some two hundred years. But the proletarian dictatorship will be necessary for only a few decades, when it will establish the classless society, and therefore the classless human art of the future.

"I do not agree with this," Michael Gold said. *"Even if for only fifty years the proletariat remains in subjection to capitalist society, will there not be some art growing out of this mass of intense, tragic, active human beings? Will they not sing, and need cartoons, plays, novels, like other human beings? Are they not studying, groping, reaching out hungrily for culture? It is not a matter of theory; it is a fact that a proletarian style is emerging in art. It will be as transitory as other styles; but it will have its day."*

We knew little at this time of the conflict within the Russian party. Trotsky was for us still a symbol of the October Revolution. It was possible, however, to admire him extravagantly and to disagree with him about proletarian literature, on literary rather than political grounds, as one disagreed with John Dos Passos.

But the literary disputes which were to assume such bitter significance a decade later meant little to us in the second year of the second

Coolidge reign. The things that bound us loomed bigger than those which separated us. Three hundred New York intellectuals—"agitators," Dos Passos called them—went down to Passaic to support the textile strikers. Some of them were arrested; others were beaten up by the police. All of them learned something about the kind of justice which the American ruling class handed out to its rebellious slaves.

The second issue of the *New Masses* saluted these public-spirited "agitators"; it saluted Rabbi Stephen Wise, Elizabeth Gurley Flynn, Clarina Michaelson, Freda Kirchwey, Forrest Bailey, Justine Wise, Mary Heaton Vorse and others who had "thrown themselves gallantly into the fight." The editors of the new magazine considered the Passaic strike the most heartening event in years; it seemed to have dispelled the cloud of pessimism and defeatism which had hung over the radical movement since the vast calamity of the war. It united the different sections of the movement on a vital issue. It proved that "cynicism and Menckenism have not conquered all the free minds in America—justice still has friends in this country."

Once more, as on the eve of America's entrance into the war, progressive American intellectuals allied themselves with the militant proletariat. Yale graduate Robert Dunn was thrown into a Passaic jail for his strike activities. John Dos Passos participated in a demonstration of intellectuals which the Passaic bulls broke up. Grace Lumpkin, who was later to write a fine strike novel, saw a law of 1864 "enforced by great blue arms swinging clubs against human, quivering flesh—God save the state and to hell with human beings." Arthur Garfield Hays, observing the "organized tyranny and disregard of law that exists in Passaic," was optimist enough to believe that "when the people realize this there will be a great wave of indignation." Esther Lowell, fresh from the west coast, described the poverty-stricken homes of the textile workers. And Norman Thomas cried, *Here's to the strike and the ultimate victory.* All spoke in the pages of the *New Masses,* uniting around a great labor struggle.

The Passaic strike was under communist leadership; its outstanding figure was Albert Weisbord, pale, intense, spectacled Harvard law graduate who had entered the labor movement. A passionate and eloquent speaker, vibrant, somewhat hysterical, Weisbord was a popular leader. Strike strategy was decided by the United Front Committee; the young student contributed the gifts of the spellbinder. He was at once morbidly ambitious and morbidly shy. On the rostrum he was Lassalle; in private Chatterton.

CHAPTER VII

GRETA

Untamed, radiant, proud and high.
—ROBERT WOLF.

§ 1

ONE evening I went alone into a Japanese restaurant on Eighth Street. From the crowded room a voice called me. I looked up and recognized Bishop, of the Party's educational department. He was a tall, lanky, exceedingly skinny young man with a mustache and a bulging Adam's apple that made him look like Andy Gump. His wife was with him, a little vivacious dark ball of energy who reached only to her husband's elbow. With them was a stranger, a blond girl I had never seen before. I waved a greeting.

"Come and eat at our table," Bishop said.

I pulled up a chair. The friendly Japanese waiter came and took my order. Bishop began a long political discourse. I looked at the blond girl and she looked at me, but no one introduced us.

She opened her pocketbook, searched in it for a long time, closed it. She began playing with her knife. Her blond hair was cut close, boyish bob; it was parted on one side and the longer end fell down her right temple. Her eyes were bright blue; her face round, white, handsome, intelligent, sensual.

Suddenly she leaned across the table and said to me in a quiet voice with a marked German accent:

"Would you like to save my life?"

"Are you dying?"

"For a cigarette."

I handed her one, struck a match and held the light for her.

"I'm terribly sorry," Mrs. Bishop gurgled. "This is Greta, a German comrade."

Greta and I shook hands. We talked about Germany for several minutes. I looked at my watch.

"I must go," I said. "I've got a meeting at eight-thirty."

I forgot about Greta. The following week she came to my literary class at the Workers School. I passed out a sheet of paper, and said:

387

"If there are new comrades in this class, let them please register."

I lectured on Sherwood Anderson as a prophet of the revolt against the machine and against American puritanism. Greta stood up. The crowded classroom stirred, heads turned back to look at her neat, stocky figure moving down the room. She walked to the front row and sat down directly in front of me. I went on with Sherwood Anderson.

"No, no, that's quite wrong!" Greta's voice startled the class.

"I must request the comrades not to interrupt in a disorderly manner," I said. "We shall have an organized discussion later."

"Why be so formal?" Greta's German accent went on inexorably. "Is this a parliament or a class in the revolutionary interpretation of American literature? You were off on a wrong line." The class roared with laughter. "What you should tell us about is not the puritan soul of America but Anderson's social-political outlook."

"All right," I said. "You tell us."

"I will," Greta said, grinning. I noticed that her face was at once hard and sweet. "The world of Sherwood Anderson is the world of the small producer crushed by the big cartels—what you call trusts. Their little tragedies come from this central tragedy."

The class voted to discuss Anderson from that standpoint. At the end of the session, Greta came to me and said:

"You think I am fresh, no?"

"That's one way of putting it. Why on earth did you come here? You are not interested in American literature."

"I am interested in you."

"Thanks."

"Don't hurry to thank me." She laughed. "I will give you lots of trouble yet. I'm a terrible person."

"It's very kind of you to warn me like this. Good night."

"Wait a minute. I have a message for you. Bishop says you are to attend a meeting of some organizers tonight. It will be held in the next room twenty minutes from now."

I went out alone for a sandwich. In the restaurant one of my students, an organizer, joined me.

"Don't mind Greta," he said. "She has a queer sense of irony and can be fresh as hell. But she's all right. She is probably upset because she is breaking up with her husband, one of the cleverest leaders of the German party. You'll find her amusing, well informed and a hard worker."

When we entered the organizers' meeting, the room was jammed with people. All the chairs were taken and many comrades sat on the floor. I sat down on the floor, too, leaning back against the wall. Through the clouds of cigarette smoke, Bishop was talking, his Adam's apple moving in rhythm with his rhetoric:

"We must face the fact, comrades, that American capitalism is advancing in this period of relative and temporary stabilization. The past year, the year of 1925, was one of tremendous production. The output of coal was 517 million tons as against 408 million in 1924. The output of steel was 44½ million tons as against 37½ millions in the previous year. . . ."

Someone was pressing against my knees. I saw first a round back in a white waist, then Greta's blond, bobbed hair with a big brown comb in it. She turned her head and smiled. I looked at Bishop who was saying:

"The political situation in the United States today is characterized by the increased domination of the government by monopoly capital and by the intensification of the imperialist spirit in politics."

Greta slipped a note into my hand.

"You should drink lots of milk," it said. "Get a little fatter. Your knees are like nails—very, very uncomfortable, I assure you."

I turned the note over and scribbled on the back:

"And you shouldn't wear a big comb with a boyish bob. It makes you look even funnier than you naturally are."

"The American trade unions," Bishop said, "are more than ever following a policy of class collaboration with the employers, with the exploiting groups. Why is this so, comrades? It is so precisely because of the increase in the imperialist trend. American imperialism, in its aggressive striving for world domination, faces two necessities. First, it must decrease production costs. Second, it must have the goodwill of part of the working class. How can it obtain this goodwill, comrades? The superprofits of imperialist exploitation have enormously enriched American capitalists. Out of these superprofits obtained from the colonial and semicolonial peoples, imperialism is able to bribe a section of the trade-union bureaucracy and of the labor aristocracy."

Greta was shaking my knee, trying to get my attention. On my lap was her comb, wrapped in a piece of paper which said:

"Add this comb to your museum."

After the meeting, when the crowd was breaking up, Greta said to me:

"You will now take me for coffee."

"Why should I?"

"Because you like me."

We went to Childs on Fourteenth Street, then I took her home to the Bronx, and saw a great deal of her from that time on. From her own lips and from mutual friends I learned something about her. At seventeen, she had been, to use her own phrase, "an ordinary petit-bourgeois dope" with an excellent job. She was a secretary in the foreign ministry of Bavaria. When the workers of Munich revolted in 1918, she handed the keys of the ministry to the leaders of the revolution. Then she threw herself into the fight. She fought on the barricades, rifle in hand; was jailed in the same cell with a group of prostitutes; thought a great deal in prison and read pamphlets by Lenin and Liebknecht. After her release, she became a friend of the playwright Ernst Toller, whose *Man and the Masses* we had seen in New York. In succession she became the sweetheart of various revolutionary leaders in Munich; Greta always went to the man who headed the victorious faction of the moment, and there was a proverb among the comrades: Who takes Munich takes Greta.

Her roots were primarily in Munich's bohemia; they were strengthened when she married a painter of local fame. But behind bohemia there lay half slumbering in the memory a devout Catholic home, a romantic mother, a stern father who disciplined his children with a whip, the nuns of the convent where Greta got her education. Then came the awakening of spring: high-dreaming love, the cafés and the relentless pursuit of pleasure and power, mixed strangely with social idealism. Germany's postwar breakdown and the crazy inflation which followed so battered down the middle classes that thousands of intellectuals, artists, professionals, bohemians flocked to the Communist party along with hundreds of thousands of workers, schooled in social democracy, the trade unions, the monstrous nightmare of the war. Greta absorbed these political trends through love; she joined the Party through love—when she was only eighteen. Political understanding came later, altering her love pattern. She divorced her artist husband and married a leading member of the Party's central committee—a young man in his early twenties, but already internationally known as a brilliant speaker, writer and "theoretician." A new life opened for her: she went to Moscow, traveled through the Soviet Union, had held a job there. Her husband (let us call him Kurt) knew most of the important leaders, and Greta moved in the highest political circles. Yet she never ceased to be a bohemian, remarkably like certain types of women one met in Greenwich Village. She was a devotee of the frank and free life; but now at twenty-seven she was no longer governed by the pleasure principle; she granted what used to be called favors in return for favors, exchanging pleasure for power. She specialized in politicians, but did not hesitate to give her favors to a sailor on the ship which brought her to this country because he came each day into the third-class cabin with first-class food. Nor did she romanticize this act; she did not pretend that the sailor was the "proletariat." Her excuse was frank:

"He was good to me, why shouldn't I be good to him?"

§ 2

In our circles Greta enjoyed extraordinary prestige, partly because of her own wit and charm and force of will, but more so, I think, because she had "seen Shelley plain"—had fought in the German Revolution, lived and worked in the Soviet Union, been the real thing, a militant bolshevik, albeit corrupted by a bohemian background. There were girls in the Village equally "free" but politically illiterate; there were women in the Party immensely Greta's superiors in character and political talent, but inclined to be extremely serious and puritanical. Greta combined the joy of life with militant politics. Once in a fit of jealousy she upbraided me for attending a party given by a girl who was by turns her best friend and her bitterest enemy.

"You are entirely mistaken about this business," I said. "But even if your fantastic suspicions were true, don't you think it funny that you should become so virtuous in your standards?"

Greta broke into tears. She was the last person in the world you would expect to see cry—she who had fought on the barricades, sat in prison, and organized workers; who now made a cult of being "hard" and "realistic." She wiped her eyes with her sleeves like a street urchin and said:

"I know you think I'm rotten. I *am* rotten. But don't take me as an example of what a communist girl should be. I am a very bad communist. Someday when you go to Moscow you will find out what they think about people like me. I don't belong to the new world; I belong to the old. I have been corrupted by the decay of postwar Germany—anyway, the decay of the petit bourgeoisie from which I come, the bohemia of Munich and Berlin. My whole generation is rotten. The disease of the past is in my bones; I can't wash it out. I am fighting to create a world in which there won't be women like myself."

This contrition was exceptional. For the most part she was an incorrigible flirt with an astonishing collection of rough anecdotes and expressions in four languages.

"O my little saint," she would say to me, "go on, keep your soul pure; you will go to heaven when you die and St. Peter will put a garland of lilies around your brow, and they will let you play a harp, and you can recite your lousy sonnets to the good Lord. He will appreciate them even if nobody else does, for the good Lord loves everyone and everything, even the sparrows and the naïve intellectuals like you."

She liked to sing Munich street songs, took a great fancy to American jazz, learned to dance the fox-trot, and used to play *I'm Sitting on Top of the World* on her phonograph for hours at a time. But this was only one side of her. She could be very serious. At meetings of the German groups to which she took me I noticed the workers treated her with great respect. They knew her only as a devoted organizer who made stirring speeches, wrote leaflets, and explained the "world situation" so that it meant something. This was what she liked most in life, and she was always blaming herself for political shortcomings.

"Here I am one year already in America," she would say, "and outside of improving my English, what have I learned? Damned little. I will go back to Europe, and the comrades will ask me about the movement here, about national politics, the economic situation, the trade unions—and I will only know a few catch phrases. Don't be like me; get this dirty bohemianism out of your soul. Study, read, be active among the workers. Art is O.K., but the kind of art I see around here can ruin anybody."

She had that contempt for art which was typical at this time of the communist organizer in New York. She knew Toller and Piscator and Johannes Becher and Georg Grosz and Mayakovsky; she liked them; they were her friends; but art was pretty small potatoes in a world of colossal struggle. Yet she proudly kept a volume of verse which a German poet had written out for her in his own hand. I found myself writing verses to her, too:

> here where the Hudson's glass back breaks in March
> where the subway shoots from darkness into light
> let us observe the sunlight on the stone yard
> five floors below:
>
> we kiss with Lenin smiling from the wall
> a red cotton flower hanging from the frame:

under Ilytch's picture the desk stands
like an altar without candles:

soft hands have lit
in twenty centuries
candles under the Virgin's image,
praying for love, blessing lovers:

red lips have kissed with profane beauty
under the crucifixion of a Jew
(forgive them, father—they know not what they do)

there are no candles here, no prayers—
tracts stand orderly like German theses
Was ist die Bolschewisierung?
here's my polemic to my mistress' eyebrow.

she has a library of books
written exclusively by her lovers
she has a library of 2000 volumes:

here then is another trophy—
schlaue Bauern aus Bayern
rotes Mündchen aus dem roten München

I was now finding it difficult to write verse. Emotions kept recurring out of my old life which seemed irrelevant to the class struggle. In addition, there was the pressure from one or two Party pundits who scorned art of all kind, or pretended to do so, since they went to the movies, the theater and concerts when they wanted relaxation. These Savonarolas were rather grotesque compared with vigorous and creative personalities like William Z. Foster and C. E. Ruthenberg, or the direct, hard-working rank and file which, without fanfare or self-adulation, carried on the arduous tasks of the Party from day to day. Ruthenberg had understood the importance of revolutionary art, and had encouraged us to develop it; the rank and file, after a day's tense work, crowded lecture halls in which art and literature were discussed. The sectarians considered art a waste of time.

"You must fight for political leadership," Bishop urged me.

"I am not a politician," I said. "I want to be a revolutionary writer."

"He who does not obtain political leadership fails to carry out his ideas. The wrong people will control the Party; they will initiate wrong policies."

"We must have revolutionary leaders, but we must also have revolutionary poets."

"Poetry is self-indulgence," Bishop said. He was a college graduate, anxious to conceal the fact. In his anxiety to pose as a real proletarian, he ridiculed rank-and-file intellectuals on the principle that the best form of defense is attack. As a result, Sender Garlin, A. B. Magil, Whittaker Chambers and other young people who were just coming into the movement occasionally collided with people like Bishop who sneered at them as intellectuals. Yet the movement as a whole counteracted the influence of isolated individuals like Bishop, and even his extreme attitude helped develop a writer like Garlin or poets like Chambers and Magil from the pages of Walter Pater to the realities of the class struggle. In the spring of 1926, the few pundits who tended to hamper revolutionary art and literature were able to do so chiefly because the writers themselves were not very clear about their own problems and tasks.

From these pundits, Greta was a relief. Her past record and present activities set her above political reproach. In spite of her own occasional digs at art, she read widely and with pleasure everything from Goethe to *Gentlemen Prefer Blondes*. In her serious moments she would say:

"Pay no attention to bureaucrats like Bishop. Go to Russia. You will see how bolshevism creates a wonderful art. See Eisenstein's movies and talk with him. But for heaven's sake, don't make art the beginning and end of the world. It is only part of life. Know all of life. The world is split into two camps; there is a great battle going on, and everything is related to everything else. When you will really understand communism, you will understand art."

Greta was more mature than I, more experienced. I was in love. Her words impressed me profoundly, especially after I saw her in action at a German workers' club in Yorkville. The club met above a restaurant. When we arrived, only a few workers were present.

"Franz," Greta said to one of them, "where are the others?" Her white face was stern and beautiful with impersonal preoccupation, her voice quiet and determined.

"Downstairs," Franz said. "Eating sauerkraut and drinking beer."

"Get them up at once," she said. "We are not social democrats. Let the Bonzes eat sauerkraut and drink beer and play pinochle. We have work to do." Then she returned to me and said, not without irony: "Go with Franz. Maybe they will mistake you for a member of the Central Committee and will come up quicker."

When the hall was at last full, Greta took the chair, laid her notes in order on the speaker's table and began in a quiet voice:

"Comrades, I will commence with a few remarks about Germany's position in the world capitalist system today. We can draw the necessary lessons for our own life and work here from the experience of our European comrades in the advanced capitalist countries. The German bourgeoisie has signed the so-called guarantee pact, and is ready to enter the League of Nations. The first year of the Dawes Plan is over, and with it is concluded the first phase of capitalist stabilization. But despite the relatively good crops of the past six years, the living standard of the German masses has by no means been improved."

Was this the bohemian Greta I knew? The workers listened with rapt attention. Afterward they asked scores of questions and Greta answered them with earnestness and understanding. At the close of the meeting, we all went down to the restaurant, and here Greta changed again. She laughed and joked and drank beer with us, and told risqué stories. And she also asked seriously about the life of every individual worker. Her face became tense when Franz said he had been out of work for four months, and his four-year-old kid was sick, and he hadn't a cent.

The meeting had started at seven and ended at half past nine. There was time for a movie and Greta and I went to see *La Bohème* on Fourteenth Street. On the screen Mimi was dying in her garret, and in the darkness I heard Greta weeping softly.

"Don't mind me," she whispered. "I'm awful sentimental."

As we came out of the movie, Greta stopped in at a delicatessen store. She bought a huge package of assorted foods, and handed it to me.

"Here is Franz's address," she said. "Be sure to mail this to him early tomorrow; he will need it."

That week Greta and I went down to Passaic together, marched in the picket line, surrounded by thousands of workers and their families singing:

> Solidarity forever,
> Solidarity forever,
> Solidarity forever—
> For the union makes us strong!

The strikers were unarmed, peaceful. The women smiled, some of them holding children in their arms. Suddenly the police swung around the corner. Clubs crashed down on workers' heads. Greta was cool:

"Keep your heads, comrades!" she shouted. "Don't break the ranks! Keep marching!"

Motorcycles with hard-jawed men in blue uniform plowed the line. Strikers were thrown into a big black wagon and taken off to jail. Later there was a meeting in a nearby hall. Albert Weisbord spoke; Norman Thomas spoke; I was induced to say a few words on behalf of the *New Masses*—to express "the solidarity of the intellectuals with the strikers." Greta pulled at my sleeve as I sat down:

"Look at these people," she said, pointing to the strikers. There were not enough seats in the hall; most of the workers were standing —men and women of all races and nationalities, poorly dressed, but washed and combed as on a holiday, with shining, determined, militant faces. "You talk about man, you write about man—there is man," Greta said. "The mass of humanity are toilers. Until now science has neglected them, politics has neglected them, art has neglected them. But their era has come. Stop dreaming. You've been wanting to go to Russia. Why don't you go? You will see the realities of the revolution: they are not always sweet: they are often harsh, cruel, merciless, like all birthpangs. But if you have eyes you will see a wonderful great world coming out of the pain and harshness. I am sailing in two weeks. I hope to see you in Moscow this summer."

§ 3

For the moment I wanted to stay in America. The "battle of Passaic" overshadowed everything. No American strike of this size had ever had such parades or such picket lines. Two by two the workers marched out of the three strike halls, singing and shouting and waving flags. Men, women and children, mothers and grandmothers, shouted in unison:

> One, two, three, four
> Who are we for?
> The Union!
> Two, four, six, eight
> Who do we appreciate?
> Weisbord!

The cops broke into the line. One of them grabbed Nancy Sandowsky, young textile worker.

"If you don't stop that yelling I'll pull you in!"

"I don't care."

"You'll go to jail, you bitch."

"I don't care."

Five times the cop threatened arrest, five times Nancy said, I don't care. They took her to court. The judge was furious. What? She dared to shout, One, two, three, four, who are we for? Ten days! Strikers and their friends, crowding the courtroom, smiled. They dared not laugh; that would be contempt of court.

The picketing went on. Picketing became the most exciting part of Passaic's life. Children played at it, picketing their schools and homes. They went from the classroom to the picket line, joined their fathers and mothers on strike, sang and shouted the songs and slogans of the workers.

Police Chief Richard O. Zober, company henchman in uniform, heads a squad of police facing the strikers. The criminals! They dare to demand bread for their children, some of whom never drank milk until the strike relief committee gave it to them. The cops let the strikers pass two by two between the horses. Suddenly, the gap is closed. The line halts. It cracks and overflows the sidewalk. In the tense silence, strikers and cops face each other.

Chief Zober sticks his paw into his pocket and fishes out a round object; nobody can make out what it is. The strikers watch him curiously, quietly. Like an awkward pitcher ten years out of practice, Zober hurls the round object into the broken picket line. There is a mild explosion. The air is filled with smoke. Eyes and lungs fill with gas; the strikers cough and wipe their tears and stand where they are.

The chief gallops off and rings a general alarm for the fire department. Listen to the engines clanging down the street!

> Solidarity forever,
> Solidarity forever,
> Solidarity forever,
> The Union makes us strong!

The firemen pull up their horses, unwind the hose, attach it to a pump. Violent streams of water smack the strikers. Women and children run yelling down the street, drenched to the skin, their hair wet and wild, their clothes pasted to their bodies.

Across the way, the newspaper cameramen are clicking their machines. Next morning America reads its newspapers over ham and eggs. The world knows that workers, their wives, their children have been clubbed, drenched, gassed for demanding bread, milk, shoes, coal for winter, the merest necessities of life.

The strikers are not afraid of clubs, water and gas. They come back to the picket line the next day. They stream into the strike halls where they listen to Albert Weisbord and Elizabeth Gurley Flynn—she who had fought in the Paterson strike a decade before, stirring the heart of young John Reed.

From the strike hall, we march out two by two along the sidewalk. The cops follow us in the gutter. The cameramen are across the street, ready to snap the next engagement. Many of us carry newspapers with photos of the previous day's police attack. Some of the strikers laugh to the cops, waving their papers.

Suddenly Chief Zober and his officers lunge to the other side of the street. They beat up the newspapermen, smash their cameras, chase the reporters down the gutter. The strikers watch the fleeing journalists, the pursuing cops.

"Hooray for free press!" a striker shouts.

"Now they know for a change what we're up against," a woman near me says.

The cops return. They rush at our line, throw tear-gas bombs, club heads, break up the line.

The next day, the war veterans among the strikers got out their wartime gas masks and helmets. Six thousand workers marched that day, the men in the front lines wearing masks and helmets as in battle. At the head of the parade was little Barbara Miscolocsy, wheeled in a baby carriage by her grandmother. Everyone was singing and shouting and waving, full of cheer and courage and the will to win. The newspapermen now followed us in armored cars and airplanes; they barricaded themselves on the roofs like snipers.

From the picket lines some of us went to strikers' homes. See a worker's home and you understand a strike.

Here is the tenement in which I lived my first ten years in America, a little worse in Passaic than in Brooklyn. The hall is a black tunnel that stinks with foul air, garbage, cats. The door opens into a black kitchen with one small window! In the rear is a still blacker bedroom with no window at all.

The whole family lives in these two rooms, father, mother, children, grandmother. Do you remember that black Brooklyn hole in which you slept, four kids in one bed?

These textile slaves all work, all, all, father, mother and children, half the family by day, the other half by night. The women know no rest. Every hour of their lives groans with relentless burdens. Five nights a week they sweat in the textile mill, ten hours a night, up to the threshold of midnight.

You stand in this dark, stinking cave, the habitation of human beings, and a world rises before you. This is not Passaic alone. It is not only my tenement whose unhappy memories still haunt my mind, and not only Mike Gold's tenement whose bedbugs he still feels crawling over him. It is millions of poverty-stricken, wretched, dirty holes all over America, where hunger and illness and ignorance and the dread of tomorrow and the shadow of death dominate the day and the night.

It is the living grave of the coal miners, and the meat packers, and the copper smelters, and the steel workers, and the clothiers, and the furriers, and the oil drillers, and the farm laborers, and the auto workers, and the dock hands, and the longshoremen and the stevedores and the cotton pickers and the hat makers—all who create the goods of the world—some better off, some worse—but each and every one, Negro and white, native and foreign born, a slave chained with the chains of necessity to the profit system, a beast of burden sweated and driven and exploited day after day, beaten and gassed and jailed when he dares to ask for a few more pennies of the wealth he creates, for a little respite in the long dreary grind. To hell with such a world: it hasn't the slightest excuse for existence.

Margaret Larkin, publicity director for the strike committee, took us to the courts and the prisons. A few months before she had arrived in New York from her native New Mexico, where her mother was a member of the state legislature. She came, young and good to look upon, with a big felt sombrero and a guitar and a collection of cowboy songs and delicate poems of her own. Now the strike has altered her life. Like another American from the West before her, like John Reed, she felt the tremendous impact of the class struggle. She had put aside the sonnet for the pamphlet.

She took us to the Passaic jail to see Jack Rubinstein, picket captain, arrested for the fifth time. The police did not like Jack. His tactics on the picket line outwitted them many times. He was refused a lawyer and hustled off to jail under heavy bond. Translated into simple

English, the legal hocus-pocus in the indictment against him said Jack was a good picket captain. That was his crime.

Later, new crimes were manufactured against him. Jack tried to settle a dispute among the prisoners in the bull pen. Voices became angry and loud. The cops rushed in, and caught Jack red-handed: he was leaning quietly against the door of his cell.

"What's the trouble here?" a cop yelled. He didn't wait for the answer. There was that goddam picket captain. He smacked Jack in the jaw, kicked his shins. Then Jack was hauled into court. Charge: assaulting an officer of the law.

The strike spread. It tied up the dyeworks in Lodi and East Paterson. A committee of Paterson strikers went to Washington, accompanied by their lawyer, Frank P. Walsh, chairman of that Industrial Relations Commission whose report had stirred us so deeply a decade earlier. They went to the White House to ask for another federal investigation of industrial conditions.

President Coolidge refused to see them. The President was too busy to see workers. He had other things to do: he was protecting Business, the cornerstone of our civilization. He spoke to the American people from a great height, telling them they needed learning and virtue, the Bible, moral power, thrift, industry, evolution instead of revolution. He told us that large profits meant large payrolls, that we needed less government and more culture, that democracy meant building up. Oh, the pearl of wisdom of our great silent President who talked as much as Bryan and wrote as much as Brisbane! He had time for everything, for fishing, for dressing up like an Indian, for rocking himself on the electric horse; but he had no time to see American workers who wanted to explain their misery to him, who naïvely asked that a capitalist government shall "investigate" capitalist industry.

§ 4

Sometimes Scott Nearing would come to Rex Stout's Fifth Avenue penthouse. He stayed there overnight when it was too late to return to his Jersey farm. By the time he arrived from his lecture room or mass meeting, Rex Stout's party was over and the night was quiet above the city. Rex would smile, above his Henry VIII beard, and badger Nearing:

"How do you think you'll ever have communism in this country?" Rex said. "Prosperity is everywhere; people are rolling in money, getting drunk every night, raping each other's wives. They're having too much fun to want any change. Of course, the great silent idiot in the White House gives us all a pain in the neck—but he's not enough to start a revolution. What America needs is not Lenin but Casanova."

Nearing replied with a long, serious discourse on the social-economic-political situation, but this only made Rex laugh. Still, he admired Nearing personally, and without him the *New Masses* would have had no business department. The quarrel between the bohemian intelligentsia and the radical intelligentsia went on everywhere. In a Village speakeasy—Sam Schwartz's—I watched Elizabeth Gurley Flynn, heroine of a dozen strikes, argue with E. E. Cummings. The poet was playing with two tall glasses, pouring ginger ale from one into the other with the skill of a veteran soda jerker juggling a bromo seltzer.

"Flynn," he said, "what in hell makes you a radical?"

"The world is a lousy place. It's full of poverty, misery, ignorance, war. The mass of people live like hell. We could have a decent world for everybody. Is there anything better than to fight for that?"

"Flynn, you're a savior, a rabble rouser, a pulpit thumper. You're kidding yourself. Men don't want to be saved. They want to have a good time."

"There are various ways of having a good time. Mine is as good as yours—and more useful."

"Men want love and liquor."

"Men need security, freedom, creative labor."

"Bah! Have a Scotch on me."

The next time I went to Croton I repeated this conversation to Floyd Dell. Why was the American intelligentsia so cynical? Floyd said it was the result of the Russian Revolution; we were passing through a Byronic period like the one that came after the French Revolution, or the Saninism which followed the failure of 1905.

"After a brief enthusiasm," he said, "the intelligentsia has for the most part become indifferent to the new order in Russia—an indifference which masks a secret antipathy. The reason for this antipathy lies in the fact that the bolsheviks are actually imposing order upon chaos —an order much resembling, in its governmental and industrial paraphernalia, and in its rigorous concepts of duty, that order against which the intelligentsia is still in hopeless rebellion at home. The introduction of machinery into Russia, and eventually throughout Asia, is not the sort of change to warm our hearts. Far from it. The American intelligentsia has a deep sentimental attachment to barbarism and savagery, preferably of a nomadic sort. The only possible effect which the Russian Revolution could have upon the American intelligentsia would be in the nature of a final disillusionment concerning its fundamental belief, the one which has remained when everything else was shattered —the vagabond's belief in his 'freedom.' The Russian experience would show up that 'freedom.' It would set up in place of 'freedom' certain definite and realizable goods of a not unfamiliar sort, and it would teach us that these are to be achieved by organized social activities involving all of the customary personal virtues, including such dull matters as honesty, sobriety, responsibility, and even a sense of duty. On the other hand, it would offer us the possibility, in the nature at present of a religious hope, of shaping the whole world nearer to the heart's desire. It is obvious that these chastened and sober notions of revolution can make no real appeal to a typical member of the present-day intelligentsia. If he had to make himself over into what is to almost all intents and purposes a good American businessman, he would prefer to enjoy the American businessman's rewards."

Floyd Dell's analysis had a good deal of truth in it; the former rebels and romantics were becoming "sober" in their politics while getting drunk on their gin; they were becoming, in a way, good American businessmen, and on a small scale were getting the businessman's rewards. In this atmosphere of easy well-being, the two main interests were body and soul—sex and psychoanalysis. Even the extreme radicals were not free of the prevailing cult. The first issue of the *New Masses* contained Babette Deutsch's philosophical dialogue between the shades of Lenin and Anatole France, Robert Dunn's exposé of labor spies, Michael Gold's attack on police brutality against workers, Bishop Brown's criticism of religion, Mary Heaton Vorse's report on the Passaic strike, Norman Studer's analysis of radicalism among university students, Scott Nearing's study of the American economic scene. It also contained sexual references which led to the suppression of the issue by the postal authorities.

On April 30th the *New Masses* received word from the New York postmaster that our first issue had been declared unmailable. A member of our staff who went to Washington was told by the Post Office Department that the May issue was unmailable under the law which bars "lewd and obscene matter." What was obscene? A single brief poem, the general tone of a story by William Carlos Williams called *The Five Dollar Guy,* and passages in several other articles and stories. This was an echo of the old days when the *Masses* got into similar difficulties over a poem about the birth of Christ. But how America had changed since then! Every twenty-year-old who played with literature knew Mrs. Bloom's soliloquy by heart; Hemingway had introduced four-letter words into the best society; D. H. Lawrence was comme il faut—and the newsstands were full of cheap, salacious magazines. The post-office officials were polite, and it was clear that if we had not attacked the status quo *politically* the sexual passages would have been overlooked. Eventually we got our second-class mailing privileges— but it was obvious that if we had been a little more serious politically, if we were not ourselves caught up in the great pseudo-Freudian dance of the period, we would have avoided our difficulties in the first place.

That dance was everywhere—in the Village, in Harlem, in Flatbush, in Iowa, in Los Angeles. Everywhere the saxophones whined, feet shuffled to hot jazz, the cocktail shakers shivered in millions of hands, and Rudolph Valentino was the national saint. Puritanism was suspect.

Floyd Dell was interested in the younger generation; it seemed to him to live the principles for which he had fought. Janet March was the courageous protagonist of the postwar youth; she dared to do what her mother only dared to think. I took Greta up to Croton; she was the new, free woman. The guests talked, as was then the custom, about love.

"Why is Upton Sinclair such a puritan?" someone asked.

"It's his neuroses," another guest ventured.

"No, you're wrong. He is not exceptional in America, he is typical. What is a neurosis anyway? The puritan heritage of America sets up a conscience for us. This conscience disturbs us when we try to indulge our natural instincts."

"The myth about the puritanical American is bunk," Floyd said. "Aside from neurotics, I have met few Americans who have any qualms or fears about sex. American puritanism is a legend so far as personal conduct is concerned. Puritanism is a public, not a private standard. Its chief commandment is *thou shalt not get caught*. I come from the Middle West; I know the native Americans; I'm one of them. You will find very few Americans who go through the internal torments, the shame, the self-reproach typical of certain intellectuals."

"In this morning's *Daily Worker*," I said, "Comrade P., who poses as something of a philosopher, claims that the universal preoccupation with the sexual problem which has swept the country like a disease is confined to the upper and middle classes. Sex is bourgeois. The workers do not waste time on it."

"Comrade P. probably just graduated from your college," Greta laughed. "Does he think workers are made of wood?"

"When you get to Russia," Floyd said, "I hope you will write me about their new sexual conventions in great detail."

"Oh, are you going to Russia?" a lady-writer exclaimed.

She said that as one might have said to Stanley: are you really going to Africa? In the spring of 1926 Russia was generally looked upon as a dark continent. The Red cannibals were sure to eat you because of the famine which, in the average mind, had been Russia's chronic state since the October Revolution. People urged you to write them the truth about *everything*. By everything they meant the most commonplace trifles of daily life. They thought the revolution had converted Russian human beings into something else—no one could say just what. The abolition of private property, an amazing, even a monstrous fact, gave rise to fantastic corollaries: women had been nationalized; all members of the former bourgeoisie had been slaughtered; all thought had been suppressed; personal life no longer existed. Was it possible that the bolsheviks really walked on two legs, loved their wives and children, enjoyed Chaplin films?

What prevailed was the fantastic picture of unrelieved misery and oppression invented by journalists in New York offices who had never seen Soviet Russia, or by returning travelers who had seen Moscow through the dark spectacles of middle-class prejudice. The occasional traveler—businessman, professional, writer—usually went from his comfortable home in a large, efficient American city; he went first or second class on a modern steamer. From these privileged surroundings he plunged without transition into the life of workers and peasants harassed by the ruins of civil war, fighting to transform a backward agrarian into an advanced industrial country, to leap from feudalism to socialism. This bourgeois visitor was ignorant of the life of American workers. He imagined that the whole of the United States was covered with cozy suburban bungalows. Often the first factory he ever saw in his life was a Soviet factory. The image of himself working in any factory was too horrible to bear. He rushed back to America with tales of woe about the building of socialism. He who had ignored the American proletariat all his life now shed bitter tears over the fate of the Russian proletariat. He was unable to compare the life of the workers under the Soviet regime with their life under czarism, like M. J.

Olgin could, or with the life of workers in the capitalist countries, like Powers Hapgood. He knew only the life of the successful, middle-class American—and there was no doubt that Soviet life was not quite like it.

There were confusion and stagnation in New York. Casanova and Freud could not solve everything. The older members of the radical intelligentsia had lost the tension of the war days and the days immediately following October. My own life was a mass of disconnected fragments, contradictory actions and beliefs. Peace and prosperity had disintegrated the radical intellectuals as a group; each man moved in his own solitary orbit. The Party was rent by a bitter factional fight which repelled me because I did not grasp its full implications. I hoped Russia would illuminate the chaos, that contact with revolutionary reality would integrate the fragments.

§5

Just before Greta sailed for Europe, we quarreled. It was ostensibly about the other man, about Fred. He was only a few years older than myself yet had already managed to climb into the Party leadership. Fred was ambitious, clever, unscrupulous; he always made me wonder why he had become a communist instead of a successful Tammany politician, a career for which he had every aptitude. In private life, Fred posed as an anchorite so devoted to the cause that he had no time for a personal life. He said he was still virgin. It was a shrewd political mask. From Greta I knew he was not telling the truth; and I was jealous of Fred.

It is not uncommon for lovers to be jealous. But my feelings were in conflict with our "principles." We were not supposed to be jealous. Such primitive feelings were "bourgeois prejudices."

In general, anything you didn't like was "bourgeois." If a man was a puritan and you were a frank and free person, you criticized that man for his "bourgeois prejudices." If *you* were a puritan and he was liberal in personal conduct, you also damned him as a bourgeois. Rake equals bohemian, bohemian equals declassed bourgeois, ergo, Q.E.D. The argument was more complicated, but the results were the same. Jealousy arose from the competition which was the basis of bourgeois society, and from the bourgeois treatment of woman as private property. To be jealous of Fred was painful enough; to admit you were jealous meant that you had not cleansed yourself of bourgeois prejudices. First you tried to deny to yourself that you were jealous.

You put the whole matter on a political level. But you could not kid
yourself very long. You saw the same thing in others and you realized
what it was. When someone else was jealous, it was all clear enough.
In your own case you kept on rationalizing: See, Greta can play politics
through men, she can influence someone as politically important as
Fred; he can win her because he is a big guy. I am only a rank-and-
filer suffering from jealousy and from a sense of guilt because jealousy
is bourgeois.

My feelings on this subject were intensified by Greta's slip of the
tongue when I phoned her one night. She would have been more cautious if it had not been so late, but our unit had met till long after midnight, and I knew Greta was in bed by that time. As the phone bell
rang, I could hear the click of the receiver being lifted, then her
yawning voice:

"Fred?"

"No."

"Oh, it's you. Forgive me, darling. I was expecting a call from
Fred. Come over."

I was furious when I got there, and could hardly talk. She
laughed and said:

"You are jealous? Don't worry. Fred was going to call me on
business. He is going to London and I think he will take me with
him."

I put on my hat and started to go.

"Are you crazy?" she said.

"Not at all. If you are going to London with Fred, what do you
need me for?"

"I am going with him only to save fare. I love travel."

"Then you are no better than a bourgeois gold digger, and he's no
better than a butter-and-egg man."

"You think you are very advanced," Greta said bitterly, "but you
are through and through petit bourgeois. You will always be faithful
to your friends; I will always betray them."

"A fine bolshevik boast."

"I've told you a hundred times: that side of me is not bolshevik.
That's the bohemian in me, the adventuress."

"You're not just anybody. People like the Bishops adore you, and
you adore Fred because he is important."

"I'm not in love with Fred any more," Greta said. "I need him
now only for political reasons."

"That's the whole point. You don't know what love means. You understand only power—and you are supposed to be fighting for a better world!"

Greta switched the subject.

"Jealousy is a bourgeois prejudice," she said. "I am not your private property, you know. I'm free to do what I like."

"Of course you are. So am I. You are free to go with Fred; I am free to break with you. And don't hand me any bunk about bourgeois prejudices. I know we are supposed to be free of jealousy, but I haven't forgotten how furious you were because I went to your friend's party."

"That's different. I'm spoiled forever. If you ever go to Germany you will see what I mean."

"Isn't it pleasant to think that our movement has its Lola Montez. It's a great improvement over bourgeois society."

"You want everyone to be a saint like Scott Nearing?"

"No, no. Let's have some variety. But I'd like to keep out of the kind of messes people like you make."

"All right," she said. "This is the end. I will never see you again. You have no regard for my feelings."

"For whose feelings have you any regard? You have no soul."

"Soul! Ha-ha-ha-ha! The last straw! A philistine with a soul! Listen, idiót, we don't need souls; we need brains."

I walked out of the house. She followed me to the subway. Neither said a word. We rode down to Times Square in silence; there we got out and stood in the station awkwardly. Her eyes filled with tears. She took my hand and said:

"If I could apologize, I would, but I never apologize."

"It's not necessary."

"Good-by. Probably we shall never see each other again."

"Probably not."

"I hope I made you a little happy." She wiped her eyes with her sleeve.

"A lot."

"I hope you learned something from me too."

"Yes—even the revolutionary movement has its Pompadours."

"Foolish boy! I am not the revolutionary movement."

From the ship Greta sent me a photograph of herself and bubbling little Mrs. Bishop. Both had their arms full of flowers and were laughing. Greta sailed alone; I said to myself I would never see her again; I felt miserable and lonely.

§ 6

Newspaper work now took up most of my time; but the impulse to go to Soviet Russia, insistent since those Paris days when I had urged a committee of American intellectuals to study the proletarian republic, was becoming stronger than ever. I was convinced at this time that Greta's departure from Moscow could have no influence upon my own going there. This may have been a rationalization. If so, objective facts helped my self-deception. Various friends who had returned from the Soviet republic urged me to go there, among them Michael Gold, Scott Nearing and Ruth Stout, the novelist's sister, then secretary of the *New Masses* editorial staff.

I resigned from my job, and borrowed six hundred dollars from a generous friend. Then I signed up as supercargo with a small freighter bound for Batum. It was the first ship flying the American flag which went to Russia after the October Revolution. It carried no passengers, only a crew of twenty-eight men.

Batum would give me a chance to enter Soviet Russia through the back door, so to speak. I would see large sections of the country before I reached the official atmosphere of Moscow. And for thirty days I would live with American workers on their job at sea. I would come to proletarian Russia not from bohemian America but from proletarian America. The freighter would be my bridge from radical bohemia to Bolshevik Russia, from romance and rebellion to revolutionary reality —a reality which had hitherto come to me only through reports as various as Anton's and Hapgood's, Nearing's and Mayakovsky's, Eastman's and Mike Gold's.

I went to say good-by to my family. They now lived in a three-story, seventeen-room house in an exclusive section of Flatbush. Its previous owner was a nationally known manufacturer high in American society.

As always, my father told me nothing about his business. From friends I heard he had made somewhere between a million and two million dollars during the building boom.

In front of the house stood his big green Cadillac. The Negro chauffeur waved his hand and grinned.

"Hello, Joe, where in hell have you been keeping yourself? What have you been doing?"

"Chasing rainbows. And you, Roy?"

"Chasing women! Ha-ha-ha-ha!"

I went through the vast, glass-enclosed porch with its grass rug and wicker chairs, the vestibule, the dining room with its heavy oak furniture and expensive cut glass. The kitchen door swung open; my mother came out in a neat print apron. She embraced me, kissed my cheek and said in Yiddish:

"Ach, my dear one! It's years since we've seen you. Where do you keep yourself? We were terrible worried—maybe you are sick or something."

"I've been busy," I replied in Yiddish. "How are you, darling?"

"You must excuse my appearance. I've been working in the kitchen. These cooks are all right, but they can't make *gefillte fish* properly."

"You look fine, mother. Here are some flowers for you. Where is dad?"

"Upstairs, reading the paper in the Rose Room. Go and talk to him, my son. I'll call you for supper. The children will be here soon."

The Rose Room was on the second floor. It was an immense oblong which ran the length of the house. On three sides it was enclosed by a series of windows, thirty of them, through which the bright afternoon light poured munificently. It got its name from the rose-colored carpet and plush furniture which my father had taken over with the house.

The radio was playing Russian music. My father sat in a big rose-colored plush armchair with a newspaper in his hand, his feet on a rose-colored footstool. He looked up through his reading glasses. I noticed he was getting bald, but his clean-shaven face was still young, fresh and powerful. He was dressed in a silk shirt, a bright new tie, an expensive gray suit. His ankles were covered by dark gray spats.

"Aw, *borukh habo!*" he said. As he spoke it, the ancient Hebrew greeting sounded half tender, half ironical. Then he added in English: "I thought you were dead, honest. I've been reading about this Passaic strike of yours, and I said to myself, maybe the police broke his neck. It will do him good, teach him a lesson not to stick his nose in where he doesn't belong. But I see you are alive. Well, some people have more luck than brains."

He went to a small closet, took out a bottle of Scotch and filled two glasses.

"Here," he said, pushing one of the glasses toward me. "But wait a minute, maybe I'll get you in trouble. Does your Radek allow you to drink?"

"He's not interested in my private habits."

"Thank heaven for small favors," my father said. "And now tell me, to what do we owe the honor of this visit?"

"I've come to say good-by. I'm going to Russia."

"Crazier and crazier, day by day." He filled my empty glass. "Do you have to go ten thousand miles to starve to death? I thought you were starving to death in New York quite successfully."

I should never have told him that story: Last year I looked for a job; I was broke and walked from my rented room to the Pulitzer Building. It was a hot summer day, but I had to walk back. As I passed Brooklyn Bridge, I saw my father's green limousine swing into Manhattan. I was too proud to hail him, and walked home. He had kidded me about it ever since I had told him.

"I haven't starved in New York," I said, "and I won't starve in Russia."

"The papers say it's a terrible country."

"What papers? Do you have to believe their propaganda? You can afford to travel. Why don't you go and see your home town? Maybe you'll change your mind about the bolsheviks."

"No, siree!" my father said emphatically. "I don't want to travel. I don't care about France or England or Russia. America is plenty good enough for me—even Brooklyn. I wouldn't live in Europe for anything, especially Russia."

"Tastes differ," I said. "I like America, but it's not your America. And I'd like to see Russia too. At least the people there are interested in something else than making money." I could not understand why I was talking like a book, why I wasn't saying what I really felt.

"Listen, my son," father said tenderly, putting his hand on my knee. "Why don't you give up this foolishness? Why do you worry about mankind? Does mankind worry about you? Does mankind care whether or not you have a pair of shoes or a suit of clothes or a roof over your head? Worry about yourself a little. Believe me, if you should be dying of hunger, the bolsheviks wouldn't care."

"I don't expect them to."

"Why don't you settle down? If you had sense, you would have studied law. But at least do something practical now. You have wonderful opportunities. America is the richest country in the world. Look at me. We came from a little Russian village, poor and persecuted. We lived in a dirty hole in the ghetto here. We didn't have a piece of bread. Now, thank heaven, we have everything."

I said nothing. I could see his point of view, but he could not see mine. I thought I understood the gratitude and triumph he felt in succeeding by the prevailing standards, but I could not explain my own attitude in personal terms without sounding like a prig, even to myself.

"Look at your friend Robert Smith," my father went on. "He was a lunatic like you once. Another one of those crazy socialists—wanted to save the world. Now he is married, has children, a house of his own, servants, a good car. They say he made half a million in real estate—may God grant the same to you. I have a good business; I'm getting on in years and I have no one to succeed me. Why don't you use some of that brain you think you have?"

"I'm not interested in business."

"All right: if you want to scribble, at least be like Elmer Rice. Write a Broadway hit like *On Trial*. Be a success."

"It's too late to change now, dad. I couldn't write a Broadway hit if I wanted to, and I don't want to." Noble youth. I felt more like a prig every minute.

"Look at Louis Smith," my father went on inexorably. "A labor organizer, a socialist. Why, he made you a socialist—your teacher! And now he's in business too. Doing nicely in insurance. Your friend Max W. studies to be a doctor; Max G. edits a Wall Street paper. Edman, what's his name, is a professor. All your friends have settled down. They are making money, a name, a position. And you? Going around with people that get put in prison! Why am I cursed that my children should be different from other people's?"

His voice broke a little. Our family had indeed undergone extraordinary changes. Starting as a conventional, religious Jewish family in a little Ukrainian village, it had broken up under the impact of American life. The energy and egoism we had inherited from our father, the love which our mother had lavished on us, the conflicting values of the new American world had hurled us out of our original groove. My father had long since abandoned the ideals of the vanished village. He was a successful American businessman. I was in the radical movement. The sister next to me had gone into the theater and—worse still, from my father's viewpoint—had married a gentile. My younger brother, just out of Cornell, hesitated for a brief moment between my father's ideals and my own, and was now working with Scott Nearing and the *New Masses*. The feudal past, the capitalist present and the socialist future were colliding in our home, tearing it apart, straining hearts passionately devoted to one another.

"Don't you think I have your own good in mind?" my father continued. "Where will this communism lead you? You'll be an outcast from decent society."

"I don't care about decent society. Ninety per cent of humanity is an outcast from decent society—which it supports. It's that ninety per cent I care about, not the ten per cent that oppresses and exploits it."

"Then I'm an oppressor and exploiter too!" my father cried ironically. "I'm a capitalist. I own property. I employ labor. That's what you are saying: you are calling your own father an oppressor and exploiter. But ask anyone downtown: I pay my workers the highest wages; I've never had a strike on my hands."

"Please, dad, don't make this a personal quarrel. I like you. Our quarrel is not with individuals but with a social system." What could I say? My father talked out of his life; I talked out of books, repeating abstractions as if I did not realize what America meant to him, as if I were unaware of his long and bitter struggle for the security, comfort, respect and authority which he now enjoyed.

"I know you like me," he said, "but if you had a bolshevik revolution in this country you would confiscate my property just the same!"

"We can't make any exceptions. But don't worry, your property will be confiscated before that."

"How do you mean?"

"You're not a big capitalist. You're not a Morgan, Rockefeller or Schwab. You are a middleman. Don't be deceived by this prosperity. There's going to be a crisis worse than nineteen-seven. Then we'll have what Germany has had—inflation, unemployment, and the expropriation of the middle classes." That was the line of the Comintern.

"You mean we will lose the money for which we worked all these years?" my father asked.

"I'm sorry to tell you this, but it's a fact. Not this year, not next, or the one after the next. But sometime soon Wall Street will confiscate your property. The middle classes will be robbed along with the working classes. That's the kind of system in which we live."

My father leaned back and laughed.

"Ah, my son, my son, these bolsheviks have really made you crazy. You're all as crazy as bedbugs. We know these prophecies of yours. Where is Lenin's world revolution?"

"We are not stock market speculators," I said bitterly. "We don't operate with minutes. History takes years. The world revolution will come—maybe not this decade or the next, but it will come."

"Yes, I know, everything is in the future—the collapse of capitalism, the world revolution—it will come some fine day. So will the Messiah on a white horse. And by that time you'll be so dead that you won't be able to stand up on Resurrection Day. So why waste your time on it?"

"I don't expect to get anything out of it for myself."

"An idealist!" my father said ironically.

"No, not really. It gives me much more than I give it."

"Surely, with a home like this to come back to, with your opportunities, you're not doing this work for the couple of lousy dollars you make. I know you've never understood the value of money and never will, but at least get some glory, something sensible."

"You don't understand, dad. Look at Scott Nearing. He was doing very nicely at a big university. No one compelled him to attack the exploitation of children in industry, to lose his job, except his own sense of what is right. He works for the Cause without money or glory; his own comrades sometimes make life miserable for him, yet I am sure he would not change places with J. P. Morgan."

"Neither would I," my father said. "A man should not have too much money. He should have just enough to live securely."

"You say that because you are a middleman. You fear poverty and despise your economic superiors—but you will be compelled to go chasing dollars. The appetite for money feeds on itself. You get ten thousand and want twenty—you get twenty and want fifty. Look at all your friends hysterically piling up their dunghills of gold. That's Business for you. Then when you get to the top, like the Morgans and Rockefellers, and own the country, you go abroad and pile up more in colonies—and fight for the money of the world. You make wars and kill millions of people for your profit."

"The bolsheviks are angels? They killed plenty people too."

"It's a pity man hasn't got beyond force," I said. "But there it is, for the time being, an inexorable necessity. But it makes a difference who kills whom and for what. If the Whites and the imperialists had let Russia alone, the bolsheviks would have been glad enough to avoid blood. You cannot blame them for defending the most important thing in the world today—the first workers' socialist republic. Besides, less people have been killed in the Russian Revolution than in the

French Revolution or in the American Civil War. History will forgive the wrath of the revolution; it will applaud its enormous advances. It will appreciate the pioneers of our own generation who give their lives for the future classless society."

"So you are working for future glory"—my father laughed—"like the pious Jew who gives up joys on this earth so that he may enjoy the glory of the World to Come? Your Nearings and Baldwins and Hapgoods and the rest of them are investing in the applause of posterity? Then you are all even crazier than I thought."

"No, they are not. None of them will be remembered, and they know it. Their satisfaction is an immediate one; it's the satisfaction of being right, of being on the side of progress."

"But why should you people worry about it? I can understand a worker being a radical. What has he got to lose? I can even understand a Lenin. It must be nice to leap from obscurity to fame, to be in history together with Napoleon and Washington. But you people —you will never be Napoleons or Lenins. What gnaws, what drives you to this silly agitation?"

"I think I can tell you about the workers. They are the ones who have nothing to lose. That is why they are the ones who make the revolution. But we are bound to help them. We have had the misfortune to take our education seriously, to acquire a historic sense. When you don't see what is right and true, you are free to follow your little egotistical interests. You can chase after money and women and glory. But when you do see the right thing, you must either fight for it or go to pieces. If you don't see the truth, you are merely blind. But if you see it and do not support it, you become corrupt."

"Ah, my dear philosopher," my father said gently, "a great help you must be to the communist movement. They need practical people too, and you are nothing but a dreamer."

"There you are right, dad. I'm not good in practical enterprises. But Trotsky says the revolution will conquer for everyone not only the right to bread, but also the right to poetry. Those who have the talent for it fight for bread. I'll stick to the poetry."

"Sonny, the bolsheviks are not half as foolish as you. Bread I can understand, but who needs poetry?"

"Man lives not by bread alone. A Jew said that—Jesus."

"You can't eat ideals."

"You can't live without them. You have ideals too. The family is your ideal. You have given every ounce of your energy and love and hope to it. But it's an old ideal. It's based on the individual, and we need a new civilization based on co-operative effort."

"Don't be a child," my father said. "You think Radek and them other fellows don't believe in the individual?"

"Sure. But they don't mean one individual out of a million, the way the businessman does. They mean every individual."

"Nonsense, my boy. Every man looks out for Number One. I read in the papers that Trotsky is having a fight with his pals, who should play first fiddle in Russia. What's the difference between that and Morgan?"

"The aim. The bolsheviks don't fill their pockets with the people's money. Their fight for leadership is a fight for principles, for policy. The personal ambition is secondary."

"I read in the papers that your friend Max Eastman claims the Soviet government has fallen into the hands of crooks. You see, human nature doesn't change. When people get power, they lose their ideals." My father put his finger on the sorest spot of all. I was bitter that he should be able to cite a man reputed to be a communist to prove the degeneration of the Soviet system.

"Trotsky says Eastman lies," I said.

"How do you know he lies?"

"Even if what he says is true, it makes little difference. The revolution is bigger than any man. The leaders of the French Revolution guillotined each other—but that revolution was later called by everybody the most progressive historic event since the rise of Christianity. The Russian Revolution is an even greater event—and the Russian leaders will not guillotine each other. The quarrels are part of the vast growing pains of a vast social transformation. What is our alternative? Capitalism, war, unemployment, poverty for the mass of people. We live in an inferno. Think what life has meant for most people in our times. The bolsheviks may be hard, they may make mistakes—but they are building a better world."

"All right, son. Go ahead with these noble fantasies. You're old enough to know what you're doing. Everyone in America is making money and living a normal life—and you are wasting your life on a wild-goose chase."

"Is everyone making money? I've just come from Passaic."

"Of course there are poor people. But the smart ones don't have to be poor."

"Most human beings are poor and wretched. They slave, they starve, they are sent on the breadline and to the trenches, and their bosses grow fat on the wealth these millions of slaves produce. To hell with that kind of world. It's unnecessary. We have the machines, the knowledge, the science to make a decent world for all. All we need· is the proper social organization for it. The bolsheviks have found that. I'd rather work for such a new world than for anything else. Nothing else means anything to me."

My mother's voice came up the stairs.

"Come on, boys, the supper is getting cold."

Below the children were gathered around the table, the youngest now twelve. How much cleverer they were. They never argued with my parents. My father did not even know that my younger brother was engaged in the same work as myself, just as my youngest sister went about quietly doing those very things for which my older sister had to leave home. I often thought then and afterward that such is the relation between all pioneers and epigoni, in the family as in society at large. The pioneers make the noise, fight the authorities, wear themselves out battling for something new, then that new thing becomes the old, the taken-for-granted; the epigoni do normally and naturally what we preached and suffered for in anger and pain. No wonder some of the older Russian bolsheviks could not understand the new Soviet generation which had not known czarism, which grew up in a socialist-minded world as if it had existed from the first hour of creation. But I had not forgotten my classics: the epigoni, or "descendants," were the sons of the seven heroes who fought against Thebes. Ten years later, to avenge their fathers, the epigoni undertook a second expedition which was completely successful.

The Friday evening candles glowed above the white tablecloth. My father mumbled the prayer over the wine—the *kiddush*—in a very perfunctory way, without rising. He had long since ceased to take the ritual seriously, and now ate ham and drank milk with his meat. The servant brought in the bright yellow soup with noodles, and the children broke into chorus—it was Greta's favorite:

> I'm sitting on top of the world
> Just rolling along, just rolling along

BOOK FOUR

CHAPTER I

EXPEDITION

I want an expedition that will find what it's not looking for.
——JOHN DOS PASSOS.

§ 1

IN the sunlight flooding the bay our ship looked very small. Stevedores were stuffing her holds with beds, toilet seats and collapsible bungalows for the workers in the Harriman manganese concession at Chiatouri. Hatches were jammed with Ford tractors and tin Lizzies for the agricultural exposition in Tiflis, trucks and tractors for Odessa.

A dark, square man leaned over the railing next to me watching the stevedores. His blue dungarees were stiff with oil and dirt. Apropos of nothing at all, he said he was Paul, the third assistant engineer, a Greek from Constantinople and an American citizen. We shook hands politely.

"During the war," he said, "I was in the U. S. navy. But before that, in nineteen-thirteen, I sailed on a freighter to Batum. Lots of things have happened since then. I am very curious; I want to see what it's like under the bolsheviks. Some say it's better, some worse. I must see with my own eyes. If the bolsheviks are O.K."—his dark face crinkled with silent laughter—"why, maybe I will be a bolshevik myself."

On the deck below a sailor was marking cases with red paint. He tipped the pot and a lagoon of red sprawled over several boxes. Everybody laughed.

"Just the right color for the bolsheviks," a voice said.

Later I looked up the steward amidships—a short, redheaded Englishman with thick glasses, false teeth and a lisp.

"You are supercargo," he said. "You will take the second mate's cabin." He called the mess boy over, and introduced us.

"This is Heinz," the redheaded steward said. "He's all right, except he's Dutch—Allemagne. Look at him, the only bloody German in a crew of twenty-eight real men."

Heinz was young, tall, blond, blue-eyed, with the perpetual smile of a man a little afraid of everybody, and trying to please the whole world.

"Being a German isn't his only vice," the redheaded steward said. "He's also a little crazy."

Heinz laughed boyishly. "We're all crazy, all us fellers what goes to sea."

He preceded me to my cabin, began to unpack my bags and monologued about himself. He grew up in Hamburg, but had spent two years in the States. He knew English before that, learned it in the Hochschule. He was going to study, but the damned war spoiled it all. His father was killed in the Battle of Jutland. And what was the use? The war didn't make things better for Germany.

"You think the republic is better than the Kaiser? Like hell!" Heinz arranged my books on a little shelf above the bunk. "Maybe the French and English workers is worse off, I don't know. But in the States it's better. Here a worker can get a job if he wants one. Even in Germany it's better now. Not like in twenty-one. What a crazy time that was!"

We were scheduled to sail at one o'clock in the afternoon. It was now three, and the hatches were not closed down yet. Men hung around the railing and knocked the ship.

"She's a one-stacked oil burner—not much speed in that."

"Imagine, only 1586 tons net and 265 feet long."

"Hell, Cunard freighters run from 12,000 to 16,000 tons."

"Yeah, but that's dead weight."

"Maybe we'll never get to Russia."

"I don't think so. This s—y ferryboat has never been to sea before."

"Is that so?"

"Yeah, she was built as a laker, then they used her for coastwise traffic, and now they got the nerve to send her across the western ocean to the Black Sea."

"The Black Sea? That's worse than the Bay of Biscay. I nearly died crossing that damned bay."

"Lucky this is spring. If it was winter I wouldn't go on this box for a million."

"I wouldn't risk it even now, but I want to see Red Russia."

"Same here. It's worth the risk. All the fellers came for the same reason."

At sunset the pilot boarded the ship. The whistle blew and we got under way. I went down to supper in the officers' mess. It was small and comfortable, with three portholes and a red-checkered cloth on the long table. At one end sat the captain, silent, looking like a little, dry, old, mathematics professor. At the other sat the chief engineer who looked 250 pounds if he looked an ounce. Only the captain was in uniform; the other officers sat in their shirt sleeves, banged the plates and kidded each other.

"I could kill you easy," the chief mate said to the chief engineer. They both laughed heartily at this. The mate was a slim, hard-boned Yankee with a long face, tight and tanned, and narrow gray eyes.

"Kill hell," said the chief engineer in his broad Georgian accent. "That piece of dung thinks because he killed a couple of Germans in the war with a gun he can kill a real man with his hands. Try it, Yank. I'll kick the last drop of p—— out of you." Everybody laughed, including the mate.

After supper, we went on deck and watched the last lights of New York stretching behind us like a string of glass beads. The salt spray slapped the boat's side with insistent rhythm. I looked down into the water. I was going to Russia. Twenty-two years ago my father came to America. He escaped darkness to find a new world; I was leaving darkness to see a newer world. Funny I had no desire to see the village where I was born. The old Russia meant nothing to me. I wanted to see Bolshevik Moscow. I wondered if Greta would be there. What was the difference? I was not going to see her anyway.

"Do you want to see the officers' cabins?" Heinz slapped me on the back and grinned. I followed him. These cabins were amidships. Each had a bunk, small desk, mirror, washstand, clothes closet, two portholes, window seat, chair and bookshelf. Every officer had a cabin to himself.

"Now I show you where the sailors live." Heinz led me down the narrow iron stairway to the main deck. We walked in semidarkness, aft, to the sailors' quarters. The low messroom was lit by a single electric bulb whose dim light fell on two narrow wooden tables covered with stained oilcloth. Most of the men were lounging in their bunks. There were nine bunks in each half of the fo'c'sle—dark, crowded, stinking holes. On the wall I noticed an old shriveled pink leaflet with large black type:

JOIN THE UNION!

THE OPEN SHOP IS THE WORKERS' DOOM---
THE CLOSED SHOP HIS SALVATION.

Fraternally Yours,
The International Seamen's Union.
(A. F. of L.)

Someone was watching me read the circular—the pale, slim mess boy cleaning up the dishes.

"My name's Jack," he said. He wiped his hand on his pants and shook mine. "All workers ought to belong to unions." I said nothing, but Jack went on. "Some damned fools think they can get along without it, all they have to do is suck around the boss and they'll get along. Then the boss s—— on them."

Suddenly, apropos of nothing at all, he lectured me on trade unionism. I did not know him and he did not know me, and he talked about unionism right off the bat as if it were the weather. In the studios of the intellectuals you had to work up to trade unionism; it was an abstraction like the theory of relativity. In the studios you talked naturally, right off the bat, without introduction about Joyce and Lawrence, and the sexual difficulties of your friends.

Jack and I went on deck and found Heinz looking over the railing into the water.

"Hello, Dutch," Jack said. "Do you think we'll ever get to Batum alive on this tin can? I wonder if the Reds will let us go ashore."

"Why should they, after all the trouble they've had," Heinz said. "It's like war. There's still plenty of bad feeling. Look at this country. It's eight years after the war, and they still hate Germans over here."

The war was a long way off, but they still talked about it.

"Probably the Russian sailors will be glad to meet American sailors," I said.

"If I speak German," Heinz said, "I bet they let me go ashore. Germans and Russians are best friends now. If they always been friends, nobody touch Europe."

We were surrounded by night, sky and water, cut off from the world, which seemed far away, farther than the war.

"Let's go on the hatches," Heinz said.

Men were stretched out on the hatches in the semidarkness; some lay on their backs, some squatted on their haunches, or on inverted buckets.

"Can you get some good vodka in Batum?" a voice said.

"Sure," someone said authoritatively.

"How about a little jane?" I recognized the redheaded steward's lisp. "I'm going to get all the tail I can before the old machine wears out."

The chief mate laughed hard. "I'm going to get that bastard Russian oiler to teach me the lingo. I'm gonna learn enough Russian aboard this ship to tell some baby out there that Frank Williams, Esq., of Boston, Mass., wants a good Russian ppfff!"

"Hey, did you ever work on a British ship?" another voice said.

"Hell, no," somebody replied. "I wouldn't take the job if I was dying. They feed you garbage and lime juice and don't pay you."

"The States is the place to make the money," Heinz said.

Several of us went up to the radio shack. It was warmer there and you could hear the world. I turned the dial to catch something about the British general strike. There came only the baseball scores and the balloon races.

§ 2

The little freighter crawled nine to ten knots. Sea gulls swooped across the poop, resting on the iron-gray back of the sea.

Caught between sea and sky: you can't get off. The world has two billion people in it. We are twenty-nine: American, Greek, Russian, English, Scotch, Welsh, Dutch, German, Finnish, Norwegian, Swedish, Jugoslav, Syrian, Puerto Rican, Canadian—and even one Virgin Islander. Black and white, native and foreign born American workers.

Nothing but work, eat, sleep and talk. They all talked about the mines, ships and factories where they worked, about the war in which nearly all of them had fought while I was dreaming on the campus. They never forgot the war for a minute. When they got tired of talking about it, they talked about the saloons and whorehouses they had been to this year, last year, ten years ago.

Heinz talked the most. He served goulash at the officers' mess in a white barber's coat and talked to us in a rapid hysterical way about Germany after the war, starvation, street battles, revolution. At night he stood in the radio shack stripped to the waist, wiping the day's sweat off with a dish towel and talked about himself.

"The war spoiled me," he said. "I don't care for nothing now but girls. When I get near them I go crazy. The ship hits port and I make a beeline for the c——."

Late at night, I read pamphlets in my bunk, and copied into my notebook a sentence from Lenin: *the endless disintegration, oppression and stupefaction which, under capitalism, inevitably weighs upon exceedingly wide sections of the "untaught," unskilled workers* . . .

The first Sunday out we had wonderful weather, cold and clear. The sunlight lay yellow along the iron deck. The sailors shaved and dressed up in their best ship clothes. They loafed at the rails and on the hatches. When they worked you could not talk to them; when they were off you couldn't stop them from talking.

"Sailor's life is worst in the world," said the short blond Dutchman with the walrus mustache. "All you get is forty-seven lousy dollars a month, and you don't work all year round neither. A guy can't have a home. You can't support a wife on that dirty wage, not if she wants to stay straight. They treat a sailor worse than a dog. You're a slave, that's all. Maybe if we had a decent labor movement things might be better. But look at the damned thing we got that's called a labor movement!" He chuckled derisively, and spat into the sea.

Pete Vosick agreed. Pete was a short, squat Jugoslav with a scar on his face, a dark, round, hard and thoughtful face that made me think of Bill Dunne.

"I wouldn't take this damned job here if I didn't want to see Russia," Pete said. "I've worked all over America, in thirty-six states, had all kinds of rotten jobs, but a sailor's is the worst. Tell a man you're a sailor and he treats you worse than a dog. Fine labor movement we got too; full of grafters. Look at the coal strike. This fellow Lewis sell out sure as hell. The government don't give the workers no chance. Talk about Russia in Czar's time; we gets it worse here. I was working in a mine in Bisbee, Arizona. A bunch of us got deported—you remember Bisbee, Joe, you read about it?"

"Yes," I said, "I read about it as a kid."

"Well, let me tell you something maybe you didn't read. They put us all on a train and sends us out in the desert. They brought cowboys to break the strike. I worked in Butte too. Bloody Butte, and in Seattle. And I was in Centralia when they shot at workers' hall, and frame up the workers who defend their own lives. Look at the hundred I.W.W. in California jails. A free country—like hell."

A blond stocky sailor crawled up on the hatches. His face was young and round, but his head was half bald. He stuck his hand into his pocket, pulled out an apple and began to chew it.

"Hello, Joe," he said. "Join the party. I got two more apples." I jumped on the hatches, said, "hello, Sam," and sat down beside him.

"Look at the food we get here," Sam said. "No fruit, no salad, no vegetables. Look at this apple, half rotten. It's the first I've had since I come aboard. They don't give it to us till it's ready for Davy Jones' locker. We have no decent homes, no decent food, no decent sex, especially in America. This is the most hypocritical country in the world."

We were a thousand miles away from home, but the ship was still America. The Stars and Stripes flew overhead.

"I've met lots of sailors," he went on, "who had the dough and begged me, for Christ's sake, Sam, where can I get a girl? I'm willing to pay for it. But in America you have to be a millionaire for that."

The man with the walrus mustache and Pete the Jugoslav joined us on the hatch. "Last winter," Walrus said, "I had no job. I slept on the goddam dirty floor of the seamen's home. Winter too. Nothing but newspapers and dirt, no bed at all for two months."

"We gotta have a good union," said Pete. "Capital stands over the workers with a whip. We can't fight the bastards if we have grafters for leaders. We gotta have decent sensible leaders."

At night, in my bunk, I recorded the talk verbatim in the notes I made of life aboard ship. If I published a conversation of intellectuals in a Greenwich Village speakeasy, it would be art; if I published the talks on board this ship, it would be propaganda.

The following morning, at breakfast, the fat chief engineer said in his Georgian accent:

"I was working as assistant engineer on the S.S. —— when she went to Yokohama. I was getting $235 a month that time. When we gets there, I find the exchange is two yen something per dollar. We go to the captain to collect our pay. The fat bastard wants to give us one yen something per dollar. I says: Captain, what in hell are you trying to put over on us? Why, he says, that's the exchange. I says: like hell it is; the exchange is two yen something; we're supposed to get paid in American money or its equivalent. One guy was gonna take what the captain offered, but I says: if you let that whoremaster clip twenty-three cents off every dollar we get, I'll bust your goddam ass for you. The captain had to go ashore to get American money to pay us with. You should have heard what he said about me! I was a bolshevik, he said, and a wobbly. When we gets back to the States, the superintendent of the line says to me: Tom, I hear you're a bolshevik and a wobbly. I says: I am if you mean I tried to stop that whoremaster from cheating the crew out of twenty-three cents on every dollar."

"Every time you stand up for your rights," the Greek third assistant said, "they call you a bolshevik."

Later in the radio shack, the redheaded English steward told a group of us why the Allied troops hated the Americans during the war.

"The first bunch of Americans that came over meets us in the café," he said. "We're getting two bob a day, they get a dollar a day. That's a lot of money over there. They comes into the café and throws their bloody money over the counter. Well, boys, they says, you've been messing around with this war long enough. Now we're going to win it.—And you know how women are. They always go where the money is. We get two bob a day, they get a dollar a day. The doughboy steps out with two women. Tommy has none. Tommy is walking along the street alone and drunk. He sees a doughboy with two women and punches him in the eye."

"You call that trouble?" Heinz said, grinning. He was wiping his bare, hairless chest with a dirty dish towel. "After the war, there was nothing to eat in Germany. You couldn't get no work and no food. My brother looked for a job and couldn't get a one. So he join the Schutzpolizei. Then he went with Hitler, he became a what you call it Hackenkreuzler. Crazy. But what could he do? Those Nazis at least give him to eat. I couldn't get no job myself. And even if you had money, the farmers wouldn't sell you nothing. Once my mother was sick. I went to a farmer to buy milk. He wouldn't sell it. I says by myself: O.K. you sonofabitch, I fix you. Four friends and me take bicycles. One of us had a gun in his pocket. If we get stopped we shoot, we don't give a damn no more, we killed in the war, and for nothing too. We creep on our bellies to the farmer's field, just like the war, and fill up the bag with potatoes and beat it. We did that lots of times, believe me. Then I got a job cleaning up mines in the North Sea. We sure thought those mines gonna explode and we never come back alive. We went to church and they make prayers over us." Heinz doubled up with laughter. "Just the same we come back alive. I ain't no fool no more. No more war for me."

If Heinz had the education and the literary talent, he would be like a dozen novelists I knew whose stock in trade was fictioning their sexual adventures. He had the morals of a bohemian without the bohemian's rationalizations. He had never heard of repressions, complexes, Oedipus, sublimation, or the frank and free life. But he was the product of the unhappy hypocrisy of our civilization and occasionally his conscience bothered him. He attributed his "craziness" about sex sometimes to the war, sometimes to the fact that the one girl he really loved—the one who had a baby by him—had married his best friend while Heinz was sailing the seas.

Long ago, I read a poem by Carl Sandburg in the *Masses*. It was about a marine who said: when I was young my uncle used to tell me there were three great words in the world—liberty, equality, fraternity. But tell me how to say the following three phrases in any language and I'll get around the world—ham and eggs, how much, do you love me, kid. Heinz reminded me of that poem. He caught me studying Russian, rushed into his bunk and came out with a notebook.

"I need a few Russian words for Batum and Odessa," he said. "Write them out so I can pronounce them and put down the meaning: *bed, drink, between, mouth, how much, dance, tea, vodka, bread, thanks, naked, all night, ride, eat, walk, yes, no, pretty, two, long time, girl, more, again, finish.*"

§ 3

Sam, the young, bald-headed sailor, saw me reading on the hatch and looked over my shoulder.

"Lenin, eh?" he said. "So you are interested in Russia? Do you know something about that place? What are wages and working conditions? Do you think I could get away with it if I skipped ship in Odessa? I'd like to get a job in Russia and stay there. Conditions can't be perfect, but what in hell has a worker like me to look forward to in the States? At least the workers are free in Russia. I wouldn't mind staying there for the rest of my life."

"Most workers don't talk that way," I said.

"I used to be a wobbly. But I got discouraged with the I.W.W. and disgusted with the corrupt leadership of the A. F. of L."

"What about the Communist party?"

"To tell you the truth, I don't know much about it. Maybe the Walrus knows. He's the most respected seaman aboard because he used to sail in the old sailing ships. He's the oldest and most regular seaman among us. But I guess Pete the Jugoslav is the guy who knows politics."

We went into the radio shack. Sparks, the radio operator, was singing a solo:

> Why the hell don't you work like other men do,
> How the hell can I work when there's no work to do?

Joe Hill's song, far out at sea, thousands of miles from Utah where he lies. I began to sing:

> Long-haired preachers come out every night,
> Try to tell us what's wrong and what's right
> When you ask them for something to eat,
> They will tell you in voices so sweet:

To everyone's surprise, Walrus raised his squeaky voice in the chorus:

> You will eat by and by,
> In the glorious land above the sky,
> Way up high,
> Work and pray, live on hay,
> You'll eat pie, in the sky.

Several voices shouted the final phrase in unison: THAT'S A LIE! I said to Walrus:

"How come?"

"I used to be a wobbly, but the organization is no good any more. Too many fools and grafters now. We need a real union. Nothing is too radical for me, but today the I.W.W. is a waste of time."

"I joined the wobblies a couple of times," Pete the Jugoslav said. "Every time I see those bluffers and crappers I quit. What's the use? Capital stands over the workers with a hammer. We can't fight it with leaders who are grafters. Look at the Russian Communist party. You must hand in an application and wait years before they take you. They investigate you. Even the Young Communist party of America don't take in every Tom, Dick and Harry. They want only serious people who will do work. In Germany they got a good Communist party with millions of votes. In America we got nothing yet, not much anyway. Here capital got the workers by the nuts. If you don't want to be a slave, you can go out in the desert and die."

If the wireless room had had a stove and cuspidor it would have been like a village general store. We met there every night. The mate and the chief engineer did not need a cuspidor. They spat out the open door right out on the deck.

"Did I ever tell you fellers about the time I was hit with shrapnel in France?" the mate said. He did not wait for an answer. "They took me to the hospital. There was a big nigger in our ward. He was shell-shocked, real bugs. He used to tear the bed sheets to pieces. In the middle of the night he'd get behind his bed and holler at the top of his voice: *shoot, you sons of bitches, shoot.* But the thing he used to yell all the time was, *I can't understand it! I can't understand it!* I asked the nurse. Pinkie, I says, what in hell is it this crazy nigger can't understand? She said, why don't you ask him? So when we were walking in the yard I says to him, Big boy, what can't you understand? He looked at me funny and said: Boss, I can't understand why they take me over here to fight guys I never had no argument with."

Everybody laughed. "We got them shell-shocked nuts in Germany, too," Heinz said. "They walk in the street and suddenly they get down on their knees and make believe they got a gun in their hand, they're fighting in the trenches. But if you give them a toy, they are quiet and forget everything."

Sam's never been to the war. His complaints are about our own ship.

"Look," he said, "nobody can be skipper, pilot, mate or engineer unless he passes an exam and gets a license. But any fool can cook aboard ship, even though he never held a ladle in his hand before. The steward and the cook hold the health of the crew in their power. Our cook was never examined. The steward is allowed fifty cents a day for each man on board. He is encouraged to economize at our expense. Anything he saves out of the food allowance he keeps for himself. That redheaded Limey feeds us on twenty-five cents a day each, and pockets the balance. Our meals are overloaded with starch. The meats are coarse and heavy. Nobody can touch that lousy soggy bread. Every goddam day we get the same crap: hamburger, goulash and hash. But do we get an equal division even of this crap? Oh, no, dearie! The officers eat out of stone dishes; we eat out of tin dishes. At night, when we come off watch, we're allowed to come into pantry for coffee. But the bastards don't leave any spoons for us! The officers get *cabin* coffee and tea, we get lousy *crew* coffee and tea. They get Blue Ribbon butter; we get oleomargarine. They get fruit and vegetables. Do we get it? Yes, when it's ready for the garbage can and stinks to heaven."

"I'm feeling sick already," Walrus said, "and I'm an old salt with a cast-iron stomach."

"Why don't you raise hell?" I said.

"With whom?" Sam said. "Do you think those bastards give a damn?"

"Send up a committee of seamen to the captain," I said, "and see what happens."

We went into the sailors' quarters at the other end of the ship. An old phonograph was scratching a last year's record. We turned it off, and held a brief meeting. The sailors elected a committee of three: Sam, Pete the Jugoslav and the Walrus. They went up to the captain.

The next morning I went down to the sailors' quarters. The men smiled and waved orange peels in the air.

"It worked O.K.," Sam said. "We talked to the skipper, the skipper talked to the steward, and the steward talked to the cook—and here we are."

"What did you say?"

"We said," Pete replied, "either give us decent food or run this goddam ship yourself."

Later I went into the pantry. The redheaded steward was boiling.

"Can you imagine!" he growled. "A *committee,* if you please. A committee of *sailors,* the sons of bitches."

"If you had any sense, you'd stick with them," I said.

"And if you had any sense," the steward yelled, "you'd mind your own goddam business! The mate said the next time he sees you he's gonna knock your teeth out."

"Yeah?" We turned around at the new voice. Pete the Jugoslav was grinning in the doorway. "You tell this mate if he lay one finger on Joe we all throw him in the ocean."

At night, in the quiet of the bunk, I jotted down impressions in my notebook. The phrases were one day to become clichés for the American intelligentsia; at this time they were already commonplaces to thousands of American workers conscious of their class, its history, aspirations, literature. For me they were still fresh. My mind knew they were platitudinous phrases; my feelings embraced them warmly because they seemed to be inexorable axioms. It was like discovering for yourself the elemental truths you had too casually taken for granted in school. You wandered for miles through mistaken streets to a friend's house and it suddenly dawned on you: a straight line really was the shortest distance between two points, and what a marvelous moment in history it must have been when men first discovered it. It was in this spirit that I wrote in my notebook, with an enthusiasm which might have struck a more mature mind as amusing, truisms of whose veracity I had never been so sure as on this freighter plowing its way through darkness toward the remote Mediterranean:

One fact looms over our ship all the time. Capitalist civilization is a slave civilization. The exclusive, semicultured society on top rests on a vast herd of wage serfs. All that the sailors do, say, feel, suffer, laugh about is colored by the grim fact that they and their fathers before them have been worked to the bone in return for an insecure existence. When the men talk about the past, it is a past of unemployment, hard work, small pay, hasty and diseased pleasures, war, famine, strikes, sellouts. The labor of sailors enables stockholders of the I.M.M., Cunard, White Star, Panama Line to clip coupons, live in grand style, send sons to Oxford and Princeton, endow operas, sail private luxurious yachts, read Marcel Proust, patronize the sciences after a fashion— in general to have access to such culture and happiness as human society has been able to achieve so far. These are platitudes: but in the wide blue hemisphere of sea and sky with twenty-eight workers fighting to keep alive, these platitudes suddenly assume flesh and blood; they become a flaming prophetic reality.

§ 4

Twelve days at sea, no land in sight, and the ship will crawl on until we hit Constantinople. It was eight o'clock in the morning, our second Sunday out. I went aft to the crew's quarters with some literature in my pocket. The men were all washed, shaved and dressed in their best ship clothes. Orange peels on the table commemorated the victorious strike threat. Jack, the crew mess boy, an Erie, Pennsylvania, guy, waved to me.

"Hello, son of the soil!"

"How are you, fellow worker?" I said.

"What's that blue book in your pocket?"

"It's a present for your library."

"It's about time," Sam said. "Nothing but lousy old detective stories."

I pulled out the British trade-union report on Soviet Russia, and everybody gathered around to look at the pictures. Sam read passages aloud—about wages, rent, education and politics. The oiler from Odessa, who has lived in the U. S. A. for twenty years, said:

"There was a British skipper who landed in Odessa. He wouldn't let the Soviet customs officials come aboard, said they weren't dressed right. He was damned sorry for it afterward. They kept him paying wharfage till he begged them to come aboard even in their night-shirts."

"That's the fifth time you've told that story," Sam said. "It's crap."

"It's true, honest to God," the oiler said.

"Are there any good labor papers in the States?" Jack asked, looking up from the trade-union report on the Soviet press.

"The *Daily Worker* is the best paper we got in the country now," Pete the Jugoslav said. "The best for the workers anyway."

"Say, you're a newspaperman," Sam said to me. "What do you think of Upton Sinclair's *Brass Check?*"

"Where did you hear about that?"

"A guy on my last trip gave it to me to read."

"If you don't take Sinclair's sentimentality too seriously you can learn a lot about the capitalist press from it."

"I wish more sailors would read books like that," Sam said. "Many sailors travel all over the world and see nothing but saloons and whore-houses. They slave like hell for a couple of dollars, and throw all their dough away drinking and whoring. The whore takes your money first, then she says: hurry up, you son a bitch, I can't wait for you all day. It's just like that. There's nothing in it."

After lunch, Sam came up with the British labor report in his hand.

"Thanks for giving this to us," he said. "It's the best book on Russia I've read. In fact, it's the only book on Russia I've read. It's good. It should be in every worker's hands." The last sentence sounded like a review in one of our papers; but I could see how a former wobbly would think agitationally.

"What did the other guys say about it?" I asked.

"Most of them aren't interested in anything except immediate things. They're all pretty friendly to Russia, but they think mostly about food and women. Something a little further away, something like ideas, or, what do you call them—ideals—they can't see at all. That Jugoslav and the oiler from Odessa are about the most intelligent guys in the crew."

"What parts of the report did the fellows like best?"

"You'll laugh when I tell you," Sam said. "They liked the part where the delegates came to a Russian village where nobody had ever used water for anything except drinking, and they washed them, and one guy died of fright."

Sam was interested in politics, but he also had a flair for physical culture and diet, and read the Macfadden papers religiously for the secrets of good health. He specialized in "psychology" too, that is, in bizarre sex theories. Like the other sailors, he recounted his sexual adventures in great detail. With most of them it was pure narration, the hero boasting of his conquests; but Sam always philosophized a little and asked a lot of questions about normal and abnormal sex psychology. In this respect, he reminded me in a way of the Village intellectuals, from whom he differed in education rather than in cast of mind. Days of isolation from women increased sex talk aboard ship. More and more the radio shack became the center of a kind of American *Arabian Nights*.

"I was down in Norfolk one time," the lean-faced mate said, "and a guy named Dick Bacardi and I hired a car and went out to see life. We were driving along fine, till we come to a square and there was an awful jam. In the crowd next to us was a car with two good-looking women in it. I says to one of them:

" 'The congestion is pretty bad, ain't it?'

" 'Sure is,' she says.

" 'Ain't it a shame?' I says. 'Here's two cars, and one's got two men in it and one two women.'

" 'All right,' she says. 'I dare you come over in this car.'

" 'You watch me,' I says and went over.

" 'What am I gonna do?' the other girl says, so Dick says, 'I dare you come over in *this* car,' so she went over.

"The woman and I drove around and had supper and all, and at night she invites me to her house.

" 'I'm married,' she says.

" 'Oh, no,' I said, 'I won't come, I don't want no trouble with your husband.'

" 'It's all right,' she says, 'my husband will be there.'

"So I went to the house and she introduced me to her husband, and we talked a while and we had a few drinks and I left. Before I left she gives me her address and phone number on a piece of paper and says:

" 'Next time you're in Norfolk, call me up.'

"Well, the next time our ship docks in Norfolk I did call her up. I found her husband went to work every night at midnight, and didn't come back till nine o'clock next morning. I took her out and we had one swell time. We got up about seven in the morning and at breakfast she told me all about it. I really felt sorry for the poor bugger. You see, her husband used to work on the docks. One day he fell down and caught himself in the crotch and ruined himself for life; he was no good at all after that, not to her anyway. She was just right, pretty and twenty-eight. I stayed with her every night I was in Norfolk, every time the ship docked there."

I thought: an American version of Ernst Toller's play *Der Deutsche Hinkemann*. Pete the Jugoslav nudged me and said, as if he were talking to me alone but loud enough for everybody else to hear:

"For a worker love is a bunch of crap. I know what it is makes the connection, money. If you have the money, women like you. If you ain't got it, they don't give a f—— for you. I will marry only a class-conscious girl. She got to know where the money come from, how the boss drive you all day, that you don't make dollars from looking on the sky.

"Maybe there are two hundred class-conscious girls in the States altogether. Most of them are money mad. I was working in the Butte copper mines. We used to get four dollar a day, about twenty-five a week. The fellers that was married, their wives go to the movies in the afternoon, then at the end of the day they come to the mines and wait for their husbands. What for they wait? To cook for them? Like hell. They go to restaurant. You work like horse, they make you spend your money in restaurant, wouldn't even cook for you.

"Once an Eyetalian come to the captain of our mine and says:

" 'Captain,' he says, 'give me a job.'

" 'All right,' captain says. 'Can I come to see your wife?'

" 'Sure,' the poor sucker he says, and he got the job.

"Then my partner come and says:

" 'How about a job for me and Pete, captain?'

"The captain knew him and me was single.

" 'I ain't got no job,' he says.

" 'Why not?' my partner says. 'You can come see my wife too.'

"The captain, the son of a bitch, chase us half mile with a broom. I know when a woman kiss me, it's for the money. Once I was living with nice family, boarding, mother and daughter. They got broke.

The old lady borrow ten dollar, then she got off me ten dollar again. She bought some booze and we all got drunk. I go to bed with mother and daughter."

Love has its secrets joy has its revealings love I am sick for thee sick with an absolute grief love love what wilt thou with this heart of mine love seeketh not itself to please love the great master of true eloquence O love my love and perfect bliss.

"Is that respection?" Pete's voice rose in anger. "I know they didn't do it for me, for the money. They got to eat same as me. Maybe she need the money for shoes. But if I didn't have the money, they wouldn't look at me, they wouldn't spit on me, they wouldn't give me to drink a glass of ———."

The radio shack was full of cigarette smoke, crowded with men, silent and uneasy. The redheaded steward coughed, the lean mate spit out the open door onto the deck. *I grow old I grow old I shall wear the bottom of my trousers rolled we have lingered in the chambers of the sea by sea-girls wreathed with seaweed red and brown.*

"Now tell me, go on, how can worker love?" Pete said belligerently. "I *know* the girl got to eat next day same as me. I don't want it for nothing, I pay. I am honest, smart, nice fellah, but I have no money, I can get no girl. And what kind of girl a worker get? Hurry up, you son of a bitch, finish, finish. She got to get the two buck off the next guy. That's what I call getting it on the fly, like Michigan Central take water on the fly. Pssst—all off! Imagine how I feel. Now I am with girl. I am in heaven. In two minutes I am walking down in the street. I beat and beat my head. O you goddam fool. O Pete, you damn, damn fool, what kind of life!

"And once I work in Ford factory. I was good worker; I had job on giant crane and in six months I broke only one man's leg. I make pretty good money too. Now there was good-looking girl and I love her. Every sailor says his girl is best looking in the world, each one, but this one was nineteen and very nice really. I was crazy for her and maybe she was crazy for me. I think so anyway. One day she says:

" 'Pete, buy me a Dodge car.'

"That's what you get in Detroit, buy me a Dodge car. I already bought her a diamond ring and two dresses, but now a Dodge car for a workingman's girl. Where to hell I get the money? But I was crazy for her, so I says O.K. When I says O.K. she smell the money.

" 'How much money you got in the bank, Pete?' she says.

"I get the trick. Just like the rest. Not me she loves, my bankbook.

I take back my diamond ring from her and give it to my sister, the two dresses to my landlady. Good-by, lady! But I get some satisfaction before we quits. Just before the fight I get from her one lay. It's good I'm single. Should a guy like me have kids? You gotta do what boss and ship captain tells you. What I do if I have six little bastards pushing behind me? If you ain't got no kids you sometimes say to captain eff you and you jump ship."

Everybody laughed. The mate stood up and slapped the Jugoslav on the back.

"Hell, Pete," he said, "you're too effing serious."

§ 5

Next morning I painted the fire hydrants on the upper deck. I finished about noon. Water and sky were sunlit and calm. We were passing Cape St. Vincent, and you could see the coast of Portugal. I went to my cabin, got the *Oxford Book of Verse* and walked over to the hatches, where some of the sailors were killing time till lunch. I stretched out on my back and began to read.

"What've you got there?" Sam said.

I read aloud: *"When, in disgrace with fortune and men's eyes, I all alone beweep my outcast state and trouble deaf heaven with my bootless cries . . ."*

They listened in silence until I reached the end of the sonnet.

"Now that's what I call good stuff," Sam said. "Read that again." I read the sonnet again.

"Who said that?" Pete asked.

"Shakespeare."

"You got a typewriter," Sam said. "Why don't you make me a copy of that poem?"

"Me too," Pete said.

Several of the others also wanted copies. I went to my cabin, slipped six flimsies and five carbons into my Corona and typed:

THE LOG
Crew Newspaper of the S.S. *Rushville.*
No. 1

I handed five copies to Sam, Pete and the others, and tacked one up on the wall of the crew's quarters on the fo'c'sle deck. That was how our wall newspaper got started. The next day I tacked up the second issue with doggerel verses which I wrote about the whorehouse adventures which some of the sailors had told. For the third issue I wrote an antiwar jingle:

> Heinie fought in Flanders field,
> Thyssen bought and sold:
> Heinie got his leg shot off,
> Thyssen got the gold.

> Tommy at Gallipoli
> Lies beneath the soil:
> Cowdray stayed in London town,
> Cowdray got the oil.

> Doughboy went to Vimy Ridge,
> Morgan never went:
> Doughboy got the poison gas,
> Morgan ten per cent.

> Thyssen, Cowdray and J. P.
> Had a lovely war:
> Soldiers tramp the streets for jobs,
> Ask themselves: what for?

Word reached the officers that I was "agitating" the crew. The mate came aft, read the wall newspaper, spat on the floor and walked out. At supper he said to me:

"Cut out that poetry."

"O.K.," I said. "I'll try prose."

At night, on the hatches, Sam became philosophical.

"How do you like a sailor's life?" he said.

"It can be improved."

"Which do you think is the most monotonous trade in the world? Which is the most interesting?"

"It depends who you are."

"A traveling salesman's life," Sam said, "must be interesting as hell. You go all over and see lots of people."

"Would you like to be land-sailor?"

"Tell me, if somebody left you a million dollars, would you give most of it to the Communist party?"

"A great deal of it."

"I knew a guy who was a wobbly for many years," Sam said. "But he finally got sick of the fight. He said to himself, why should I waste my life for a bunch of stupid workers when the jackasses don't care for their own interests? He went into the fruit-growing business in California and cleaned up a lot of dough, and kept it all. I told this to an Italian communist once. Do you know what he said? He said that may be true of some lice, but in Italy they had several dukes and counts who became communists and gave their fortunes to the Party and were now poor men."

The next day was our sixteenth at sea. We were passing the Rock of Gibraltar. The coast of Spain lay to port, the coast of Africa to starboard. The men looked out over the rails.

"The two coasts," someone said, "are about as far apart as Manhattan and Hoboken across the river."

"Further," another argued.

"Hey, Red!" one of the American sailors called to the redheaded English steward. "There's you're goddam Rock!"

"Is that all this pebble is?" the mate said. "Why, look, see what it says, Prudential Life Insurance Company."

"Don't worry." The steward was sore. "There's some guns hidden in that Rock."

"BB guns," the mate said.

"Aw, balls," the steward said, "you Americans are so goddam small-minded you make me sick. That Rock is impregnable."

Heinz laughed: "Just the same in the war we got lots of submarines through. Plenty German boats went through and you couldn't stop 'em."

Two days later, we were following the Algerian coast, the nearest we had got to land since leaving New York. The shore was four or five miles away, but you could see the hills and houses, and even the grass stood out clear in the sunlight. The Mediterranean was light green on the starboard side and dark blue on the port side.

At night there was a squall. A vast black cloud, covering almost the whole sky, lowered over the little freighter. The wind howled like an insane cat. Rain, heavy and warm, slapped the deck violently. A lighthouse on the Algerian coast opened and shut its eye. A ship, sliding past us in the opposite direction, hugged the shore, its mastlight rising and falling as bow and stern seesawed from wave to wave.

Next morning the sun was out and the sea quiet. We watched the low hills of Tunis, barren, sandy little mounds, naked rocks, here and there a bright patch of green cultivated grass, now a lighthouse, a small coast town, a rowboat—dots on the blue sea.

Near the shores of Sicily, the Mediterranean was warm and translucent, the sun strong. We stripped to the waist and stood in the sun watching the sea turn from dark blue to light green. A fleet of six fishing vessels followed Sicily's shoreline with bright-colored sails full blown.

Soon we lost sight of land, and were out in the solitary sea again. We had been afloat for twenty days, not touching a single port or seeing a human being except each other. We had been over every inch of the ship working and loafing.

After twenty days at sea, the men talked most of the time about sex. Memory and fantasy ran wild. When they got bored with stories about women, they talked about punks, jockers, wolves, gazonees, gazoks, dingbats, gaycats.

Sam escaped from this kind of talk to the library now scattered around my cabin. He borrowed books and came back with them full of excitement. Louis Fischer's *Oil Imperialism* overwhelmed him.

"That's one of the most wonderful books I ever read. Can all that be true? It must be true!"

"It is true."

"Where could I get an easy explanation of Marx?" he said. "Imagine, I'm a worker and I never even read Marx." I told him where he could find simple things to read in New York, and he said: "Tell me this, will you, how can educated people read so many books and yet be blind to the labor movement? Workers understand, why can't educated people understand these problems?"

"Why, do you think?"

"I suppose it's because workers experience these things, and educated people don't."

Another time, Sam returned my copy of James Dolsen's *The Awakening of China.*

"Listen," he shouted, "everything this guy Dolsen says is true: I was in China a couple of years ago, on a Standard Oil tanker. The people live in huts of mud and straw. One place I saw about four hundred Chinks working on the dock. I asked the British bastard in charge what they got. He said twenty coppers a day. Get it? TEN CENTS A DAY! My God, they keep them people in such a condition you ought to see what happens to their kids. Our bosun, a big guy, brought a girl of ten years. She was so small, he held her up on his hand like a doll. Here, Sam, he says, here's a kid for you. What in hell do you mean, I says; do you want me to ravage that baby? Baby me eye, the bosun says, she wants two dollars."

The Russian oiler sometimes joined our talks. He was in Odessa during the 1905 revolution, fled, became a sailor and subsequently worked in almost every European port. During the war he fought in the Australian army. Afterward he worked in the South Sea Islands, Hawaii, South America, Mexico and the west coast of the United States.

"I'm a real sailor," he used to boast, "not a hobo like them guys, today a seaman, tomorrow a lumberjack, next day a miner." Another thing he was proud of was his observation that Americans were the most cruel race in the world and American women the most hypocritical about sex. Often he talked in slogans: "I know only one thing. There are two classes, capitalists and workers, and I am a worker. In the next revolution, I'll be there."

The Odessa oiler had his share of whorehouse memoirs. Of all the crew the man who was most hurt, ashamed and angry at the sexual life forced on the poorest workers by the present social system was Pete the Jugoslav, ex-wobbly of Bisbee, Seattle and Butte. He talked to me bitterly about it.

One night the crew was eating goulash and discussing the gland theory.

"Did you read about this millionaire who bought a pair of new glands?" Sam asked.

"How can you buy them?"

"This millionaire," Sam explained, "paid a young guy a million bucks, and the young guy gave him his glands. This millionaire was over sixty, but when he got those glands in him, boy, did he get full of pep! He even married a young woman, a beautiful singer."

The sailors laughed skeptically.

"You're full of manure," someone said.

"Honest, Bill, it was in the papers."

"The tissue papers, ha-ha-ha!"

"O.K., Bill, but suppose it could be true, let me ask you a question," Sam said. "If a millionaire offered you a hundred thousand dollars for yours, would you do it?"

"A hundred thousand!" Bill said. "I wouldn't take a million. I wouldn't take all the money in the world."

"But look," Sam argued, "you're poor, you're nothing but a slave, if you had a million you'd be a free man."

"I'd rather be a slave with them than a free man without them."
The crew roared with laughter, and Bill went on: "My glands are
more important to me than all the other things in the world put
together."

"Now there's a smart guy for you," Sam said to the whole table.
"He's had every venereal disease in the world, he's spent half his life
in hospitals, and yet he gets off a line like that!"

"What would I do without them?" Bill said.

"Did you ever hear of mental pleasures?"

"Mental pleasures bull! There's nothing to beat a woman."

"I like 'em myself," Sam conceded. "It's one of the greatest
pleasures in the world, but after you've had it once, twice, three times
you get sick of it for the time being. But when you read a good book
on philosophy or history or the labor movement, it grows on you, you
have something to think about, it makes you feel bigger, you can do
something in the world." Several voices laughed derisively. Sam stood
up and walked to the door. "You dumbbells don't understand things
like that," he said, and walked out.

At midnight it was Sam's watch, and I joined him in the bow
of the ship. A vast silence surrounded us, except for the water's
rhythmic hiss. Against the rules, we lit cigarettes and looked at the
white foam swirling in the blackness.

"Imagine," Sam said, "someone told me this earth is as small in
the world as a drop of water in the ocean. Can that be possible?"

"It's true."

"They say some of those stars are bigger than the earth."

"Yeah."

"Isn't that remarkable? There's so much to know and we don't
know it."

"That's part of the system."

"What did you think about the argument at supper?" Sam said.
"Did you ever see such numskulls?"

"They're not numskulls. They know their jobs. Who teaches them
more than that? Don't be discouraged and don't blame the victim
for his misfortune."

"I'll tell you the truth," Sam said. "I was discouraged for a long
time. I knocked around with the wobblies and it looked hopeless. I
said to myself, why waste time on those fools, if the workers don't
want to be free, the hell with them. I have only one little life to live,

why should I throw it away for something that may or may not happen a hundred years from now?"

Sam was saying what my father had said, and dozens of my middle-class friends, and he was a worker, a former rebel, like Louis Smith, who had also gone off. This, then, was not entirely a matter of class; in every class there would be a mass of the indifferent for every militant, but the mass of workers could not, in the long run, remain indifferent if the system drove them to the wall as it was bound to do.

"Do you still feel discouraged?" I asked.

"Not any more," Sam said. "Those books on Russia you gave me make me feel different. Thanks a lot. I've got hope again. I see we're slaves and the only way out is organization and struggle. Now I want to do something for my own people, because I see it can be done."

When dawn broke, we left the ship's bow. We were now gliding along the Aegean, cutting our way among the islands of the Greek archipelago, small stony little islands washed green by the sea. On the upper deck, I ran into Karatos, the first assistant engineer, an elderly Greek with a gray mustache.

"See that," he said, pointing to the islands. "That's England's door to the East, to us. Where are you going at this hour?"

"To get some sleep. I've been on watch."

"Don't sleep long. We are going soon to pass Lésbos where the lady poet Sappho lived, then Tenedos where Achilles was born, and the plains of Troy."

"O.K. Wake me."

§ 6

It was high dawn when knuckles rapped on my cabin porthole. The sallow, elderly face of the engineer Karatos looked in.

"Come quick and see Tenedos," he said.

I jumped into my clothes and ran out on deck. Close to starboard lay Achilles' cradle, and close to port the legendary plains of Troy. I looked across the blue-green waters and thought: how immense this tiny world seemed to the ancient Greeks with their crude vessels and their limited knowledge which placed the world's end at the Pillars of Hercules; how great their imagination and intellect which have colored the whole culture of the West with bright Hellenic views. Yet as a boy I was taught to despise Hellenic sensuousness, eternal foe of Hebrew spirituality. Those were the rabbis, living imaginatively in the pre-Christian era. Heine and Marx thought otherwise.

Karatos stood by my side and spoke his thoughts aloud. He, too, lived in the past, like the pious Jews of my childhood. The war between Agamemnon's men and Hector's was for him a real, immediate event. He cited passages from Homer not like Irwin Edman on the campus, who loved the great poetry of every age and place, but as my rabbi cited the Bible, piously, as a sacred work voicing the genius of a race loved in direct ratio to its persecution. But, as with the Zionists of my childhood, the imagined golden past was but a mirror for the bitter present consoling itself with a beautiful future. The elderly engineer Karatos stroked his gray mustache and talked about Greece and that part of Turkey which was once Greek like a nationalist Jew talking about Jerusalem and that part of the Moslem empire which was once Solomon's. The Acropolis was for Heine the symbol of intellectual freedom, for Edman the image of eternal loveliness. For Karatos it was the Greek wailing wall.

As we moved slowly past the naked precipices of Gallipoli, a more recent epic agitated the younger sailors. Fortunate the worker for whom poetry was poetry, who shed no futile tears over archaic heroes whose bones had become footnotes to Western literature. From a dredge leaning out of the waters hung the rusty and battered carcass of a sunken cruiser. The fortress was dismantled and deserted; the light gray stone was smashed in places and a jagged shell hole gaped in the center of the wall. High on the hill behind the fort stood the white monument for the Allied soldiers killed in the fantastic attempt to seize the point. The sailors crowded at the rail and looked in silence for a time, then Heinz, the German mess boy, said quietly:

"Two hundred thousand Limeys buried here."

"Five hundred thousand," the Odessa oiler corrected him. "I ought to know. I fought in that place with the Anzacs." He stuck his hand into the breast pocket of his blue denim shirt and pulled out a dirty piece of paper ragged at the edges. "Look, here is my discharge from the Australian army. See that picture? I was young and good-looking then, but no more. I got shot in the stomach."

Karatos bit his gray mustache and sighed.

"Those damn Turkish got this place," he said.

From this place, the shores of the Dardanelles, called by the poets of diplomacy the International Zone of the Straits, stretched rich with green pastures, gray date trees, little red-roofed towns and old fortresses, all apparently dismantled. At the quarantine station of Sankali, a fort sloped down to the point of the peninsula. Between two mounds of earth, an old cannon jutted out. The sea was quiet and the sun poured a golden light over the bitterly contested strip of water. Farther on we saw bright grassy hills, a herd of cattle.

"We have lost all this," Karatos said. "The Byzantine empire. It's all really ours, it belongs to the Greeks." He took out of his pocket a small atlas and a chipped pencil stub and traced on the map the borders of the ancient Greek empire, in which he included Constantinople and Tiflis.

"Tiflis is Russian," the Odessa oiler argued.

"No, no, no," said Karatos. "It used to be Colchis. It was the place Jason got the Golden Fleece."

Karatos' map showed, above Greece and Turkey, the outlines of Palestine and Mesopotamia. I remembered that map well, and the old Jews who talked about it the way the engineer talked about the ancient Greek empire; this is ours, the Holy Land, there is Jerusalem where Solomon's temple stood, and here Haifa: all, all really ours. And now Karatos stood beside me at the rail and pointed to village after village along the shore gliding by us.

"That town has a Greek name," he said. "Only Greeks live there. But the Turks have expelled thousands of our people."

The years had changed me; the national saga seemed remote and unreal. The world was my country, the workers of all lands my race, America my home.

The following morning we were all on deck at five-thirty. The ship was lying in port at Constantinople. The harbor, curved wide in a semicircle, edged like a frame the mosques and minarets rising on all sides. From the rail's edge we watched Skutari, Galata, Stambul, the long low white building that was once the Sultan's palace and harem, the red-roofed houses of stone built in the past century, and the black wooden houses dusty with age—rising in tiers along the hill that sloped up from the shore. See the poplars, the rolling hills with hotels and apartment houses on their backs, see the ships in port flying flags of all colors, Belgian, Greek, Italian, Turkish.

The Turkish Control came aboard. They ignored the sailors, saluted the mate, and went straight to the captain's cabin.

"Them bastards always do that," Sam explained.

"A common sailor ain't good enough to talk to," Pete added. We followed one Turkish official to the wireless room and watched him seal the door with wire and lead.

The Turkish Control brought us news. For the first time since we left New York we heard about the general strike in England. The news passed from the officers' quarters to the fo'c'sle, and the sailors discussed it. Then something happened which made us forget the general strike. The captain issued a strange order: every man must prepare photos and a complete list of personal belongings for the Soviet authorities who would board the ship at Batum in three days. All the hysteria gathered in twenty-five days of isolation at sea concentrated on this order. Most hysterical of all was Paul, the first assistant engineer, the Greek I had met at the rail when I came aboard in New York.

"What in hell do those goddam Russians want our pictures for?" he asked.

The mate explained: "Them Turkish officials say we can't land in Russia unless every man hands in his photo. You can have them made on board. The skipper has ordered a photographer from Constantinople."

"If they want our pictures in Russia," Paul said hotly, "I'll take them in Batum. Why the hell didn't they tell us about this in New York? Why did they wait until Constantinople? It's a Turkish scheme for catching the Greeks in our crew."

Until now, Paul talked like a liberal. His bunk was full of Haldeman-Julius bluebooks. In political arguments at mess, he wanted to see the British Empire smashed and the Soviet Union prosper. Now he became suspicious of the Soviet censorship. He buttonholed sailors on deck all day long and wanted to know why them damned bolsheviks wanted our pictures. It didn't look right. The argument continued at night on the hatches.

"Use a couple of brains, Paul," the ex-wobbly Sam told him. "Russia has been attacked by capitalists from the outside and White guards from the inside. I read there are about a million White guards outside of Russia. You think some of them wouldn't like to get into Russia to start some trouble? Russia's got to protect herself. They want your photo just to know who you are. Didn't you have to take a photo for your American passport? And how about England and France and Argentina? They want your photo too."

"This photo business," Paul said, "only proves that Russia is just as imperialistic as the other countries."

"Nuts," said Pete the Jugoslav. "You used to favor the Soviet Republic because you said it benefited the majority of the people. Now you are against it because of a little pissy thing like a photo which don't hurt you or anybody else."

"It's a matter of principle," the young Greek engineer insisted.

Sam roared with laughter and said: "Paul, if you changed your underwear as often as you change your principles, they'd have to turn every United cigar store into a B.V.D. factory for you."

"Paul swallows the capitalist papers with his ham and eggs," Pete the Jugoslav said. "That's where he gets those wise ideas about Russia."

The mate banged his fist down on the hatch and the tarpaulin trembled. "Cut out this goddam stuff about Russia!" he shouted. "We've been talking Russia for twenty days. That's enough. Let's talk women for a change."

"Yah, let's," Sam grinned. "At least women is something you can understand."

We sailed out of Constantinople at night; for the next three days we bobbed up and down the Black Sea, and for those three days we talked about the order to hand in your photo and a list of your belongings to the Soviet authorities. Russia was seen through the haze of nine years of propaganda as a mysterious dangerous land which had abandoned every civilized practice. The first mate, who disliked my visits to crew's quarters and complained about our wall newspaper, now stopped talking to me altogether. When he had to address Sam or Pete the Jugoslav in the course of duty, he would shout:

"Hey, you, Trotsky, take this mop and clean up that deck."

The captain called us together and explained his order:

"You know about the photos. Now about the list of personal belongings. Write down everything you've got—shirts, socks, collars, ties, cigarettes—yes, the exact number of cigarettes, not how many packages but how many individual Camels or Luckies."

The captain's instructions disturbed the men. Why did the Soviet officials want such a precise list? Obviously in order to confiscate your personal property. On bridge and deck the officers kidded the men.

"Don't forget, Sam," the first assistant engineer, Paul the Greek, said to the ex-wobbly. "Put down everything in your list, put down even your fingernails."

"Whose regulations are these?" Sam said. "The skipper's or Russia's?"

"What in hell is the difference?"

"Because if it's Russian regulations, it's O.K. with me," Sam said. "If Russia wants my two shirts, it can have them."

I typed and distributed six copies of our wall newspaper with the following editorial:

"Military attempts to smash working-class Russia have failed. But capitalist attacks on the first workers' republic have not stopped because the class struggle has not stopped. Everywhere capital and labor are opposed to each other. Everywhere Soviet Russia is an example for all workers as to how they may achieve their freedom. Soviet Russia must protect itself in every way. If these regulations about photos and baggage are as stringent as we are told, we must remember they are aimed not against us, but against the enemies of the working-class republic—against spies and smugglers. We must go through the formalities only because the law must be applied to all." Another editorial gave a brief history of the October Revolution and its significance for workers everywhere.

The typewritten newspaper was passed from hand to hand. The mate got hold of a copy and came tearing down the deck to where I was tacking the original on the wall.

"You can poison them sailors back here," the mate yelled at me, "but you can't poison me. Thank God, I'm an American from head to foot. It's against the constitution to criticize the American government."

"That shows how much you know about the constitution," Sam told the mate.

"You're wrong there, Sam," said Pete the Jugoslav. "It's the capitalists' constitution, and they can twist it any way they like."

"Anyway," Sam said, "we don't say anything about the government. Here, look!" He pulled the mate over to the wall newspaper. "All it says is that Standard Oil and Sinclair Oil tried to grab Russian oil fields. It says here the Russian workers have a right to protect their oil. It's not owned by capitalists but by the Russian workers. We ain't attacking the American government. We're attacking the American capitalists."

"I'm afraid the mate is right this time," Pete the Jugoslav said. "Our bosses and our government are Siamese twins."

The hysteria of the officers only increased the popularity of the wall newspaper. Our last day on the Black Sea, I tacked up some doggerel I had written:

> For seven years I've roamed the seas,
> I've scrubbed the deck upon my knees;

I've greased the stays, I've passed the coal,
And sweated in my glory hole.

> And though I did my duty well,
> Many a skipper gave me hell;
> Many a mate has kicked my can—
> The privilege of a gentleman.

I've oiled the winches, steered the course,
The food I ate would kill a horse;
And when the month was done, they gave
Me fifty bucks for being a slave.

> The gents who own the ships and me,
> They clip their coupons steadily;
> They scrub no deck, they haul no line,
> And yet their income's more than mine.

On the ship's bow I took my stand,
For weeks and weeks I saw no land;
And sick of men, and sick of beef,
My bones were crazy for relief.

> Owners of ships with stocks and bonds,
> They have their dark girls and their blondes;
> They can't think, when they drink their Scotch,
> Like sailors think upon the watch.

The skipper gave us all our pay,
The crew we diddled our dough away;
We spent a little in the stores,
But most of it on booze and whores.

> Grocers and bankers have their wives,
> And college boys lead merry lives;
> Oh, some men love, and some seduce,
> But sailors buy the girls they use.

Rolling from port to port, I see
Other workers, slaves like me;
And as the years they roll along,
It seems to me there's something wrong.

> O gentlemen with tall silk hats,
> And diamond rings and pearl-gray spats
> You won't be bosses very long,
> When workers think there's something wrong.

§ 7

I slipped a copy of this jingle into the collection of my verses I had been making since my fifteenth year. I took the typewritten sheets wherever I went. They were my diary, a record of moods.

Here among the sheets I was reading on the freighter plowing the Black Sea were early poems about the Brooklyn ghetto, poems of love and friendship written at school. The world seemed then infinitely sad, kind, cruel, beautiful, my friends the finest people in it.

Often these poems had started without idea or language. Through my blood there beat the rhythm of an old Ukrainian ballad I had heard in childhood, the ritual chants of the synagogue, wordless iambics from Shelley, Shakespeare and Rupert Brooke, the quatrains of Byron, the anapests of Swinburne. Rhythms insisted relentlessly before any idea came. When sound finally emerged as thought, it was the thought of "love, beauty and justice."

War had shattered this dream-world. *This I beheld and faith within me died.* Yet the idea of love continued to offer consolation, a love full of pain and obdurate riddles. The world around us appeared intolerable; it must be changed. *Let us wrest heaven from the hands of hell.* Let us abandon the prison of the old life. *Let us flee these walls. Man is more than dreamless dust, and life a glorious incongruity of things.* But who shall change this world? The slaves, they who

> . . . will waken with a cry
> Of wrath, like booming waves upon the sand;
> Gather in mighty hordes to sweep the land
> Free of their masters, those who sell and buy
> The souls of men, and send them off to die
> That colored rags may mark some far-off strand.

That was an echo of Louis Smith, socialism, the antiwar agitation of the People's Council. This dream wavered in 1919. Versailles loosed darkness upon the world: *the kings and the councilors have bound us again,* and love once more remained the sole refuge. *O love me in the lyric night of darkness, danger and desire!* But Time was on our side; Time would vindicate us:

> The little kings will clamor for a day,
> The little priests present their masquerade,
> The little merchants count their eager pay,
> And the little foolish soldiers will parade.

> The crowd will stare, and murmur and applaud,
> Confuse the air with violence and cheers;
> But Time, above the tumult and the fraud,
> Will lead the swift invasion of the years.

Time, not man; man, not class. Vague aspirations agitated the heart while the mind underlined paragraphs in the *Communist Manifesto*. Then college days were over, and you went to work, and reality shook you violently by the scruff of the neck, and you looked back, for the last time, you thought.

> When shall we know such peace again, or hold
> The world so dear, or feel the sudden birth
> Of love in beauty that we knew of old?

In this civilization of ours, the world of youth as of adolescence was a prison from which one could escape only through the imagination. All of it was hemmed in:

> Earth, sea and sky; the proud and patient stars,
> The gradual rainbow with its flags unfurled;
> These are but golden unrelenting bars
> Upon the secret edges of the world.
> We move in beauty and are touched to tears,
> Wakened to wonder, and made clean with peace;
> But guarded by a thousand unseen spears
> Like royal captives. There is no release.
> The moments mutiny, the days rebel,
> The passions clamor; better to be still;
> Seek open spaces for a magic spell,
> Kiss lips across a tender book, until
> The last rains falling on the final leaves
> Beat down the darkness on the broken sheaves.

Irwin Edman, for whom I had written this sonnet, said it was a defense of naturalism, and read it to his classes at Columbia. Being no philosopher, I considered it an expression of despair, albeit a literary despair, since the lips kissed across a tender book were remembered out of Dante's story of Francesca and Paolo. From the inferno of the contemporary world flight was possible in the imagination alone, in love, beauty, art. This alone could save us, if only beauty were not so ephemeral:

> O aching loveliness of earth, stand still!
> Do not fade as a dream fades in the night,

Or as a bird, dipping behind a hill,
Drops the immediate splendor of its flight:
Loiter forever in the tender ground,
The deep cool grass, and the warm sunlit places;
Tall trees and idle waters and the sound
Of winds at dawn, the light of happy faces:
Stay, shining benediction, lest we be
Like dark ships crying on a sinking sea.

My verses shared with better poems of my time a horror of the contemporary wasteland, disbelief in the future, nostalgia for a past that was neither American nor twentieth century, but woven out of books and dreams about books, archaic echoes of a dead world. Such moods, however, represented only one of my selves. While that part of me which was molded by the dominant culture faced the past, another part, molded by the workers among whom I had lived, faced the future:

There will be torches and a trail of fire,
And free hearts singing of a new desire.

In Paris the poems of love became alternately melancholy and ironical, two sides of the same shield with which the sensitive and uncertain guard themselves. But now, rereading the verses on the freighter, I thought I understood something which had been obscure when I had written them. When you are transformed by a changing world and your own will, those parts of you which must die struggle furiously against annihilation. That is why, I now supposed, contact with the real world in Europe had raised the problem of "hardness." The intellectual, as a rule, knew only from books about the farm that fed him, the factory that clothed him, the war which he condemned, the revolution which he hoped for or feared. Here was the Paris sonnet in which I had discovered that moral strength was compulsory in every walk of life, a fact which every worker knew at fifteen:

If one would leave a trail of gold, a name
Familiar through the ages, wear a crown:
There are cardinal hearts to trample down,
Bodies to grind, cities to set aflame.
And if one wills a dream of perfect lands,
Where gold and crown are evil memories,
And friends are just, and there are no enemies:
One must shatter and mold with iron hands.

And if one, wounded by the general pain,
Of primitive or philosophic power,
Recoils to work in dolor or disdain
On songs and colors in an ivory tower:
One must twist the senses not to hear
The world crying in agony and fear.

Art was no escape; whatever disguise it assumed it dealt with experience; it had its own hardness, as did love. Rebellion alone seemed to be the way out, though it was still a romantic rebellion since its protagonists were poets:

Lovers of light and freedom, what have we
To do with lords, whatever lords they be,
Crowned or uncrowned, when we have still to lift
On high the golden banners of romance,
And wake the world to freedom with our chants!

Strange how even the worst poems, if only they are written out of genuine feeling (Fool, look in thy heart and write!), mirror changes in experience. Just as in the ghetto I had written about its streets, at college about philosophy and literature, in Paris about the Seine and the Tuileries and Napoleon, in London about Trafalgar Square and Nelson and Kew Gardens, so in Greenwich Village I wrote about the psyche struck silent by the universal traumatism of the postwar period:

For him the days grow grim; his mind congeals
As waters tighten in a savage frost;
There is a caution in each mood he feels;
Fraction by fraction, he computes the cost
Of every word he spends, of every note
That finds its way into his speech or laughter;
He asks of every gesture, as by rote:
What shall I have to pay for it hereafter?
Earth rocks with beauty which he cannot trust;
Voices cry out with power he cannot hear;
Bound to the memory of some fear or lust,
He curses bitterly names that once were dear;
His dreams tear out the guts of those whose folly
Drove through his palms the nails of melancholy.

When I wrote this sonnet, I was already in the Party, yet burdened with archaic ideas and feelings which the mind repudiated and the heart retained. This was a severe split between bourgeois and bolshevik ideology; the mind was fighting to integrate itself in the latter, to "reboil" itself:

> How did we come with our own hands to chain
> Body and soul to the chariot wheel of crazy
> Conquerors and priests? Now that the vain
> Empires fade out, and the mad creeds grow hazy,
> There is good silence to question our belief:
> All things—what 'we've held right and what wrong,
> What folly gave us joy, what beauty grief,
> What idols overpowered us so long:
> We shall go over thoughts from the beginning,
> Follow the surest axioms to the edges
> Of worlds greater than the one we see spinning:
> And better to repudiate all pledges,
> That we may give, if we must give, our blood
> For gods whose faces shine with verihood.

Curious, too, that these verses of agnostic doubt should appear in 1924 in the official organ of the Party. Subsequently active work in the movement, contact with workers, drew me out of the morass. The objective world, however, did not appear in verse. To the movement belonged teaching, oratory, journalism; poetry was reserved for secret states of mind. I got into the habit of writing verses on the principle of free association picked up from psychoanalysis; I thought this would bring up important hidden feelings. What came up out of the "depths of the unconscious" were often remembered rhythms and ideas from other times and lands:

> Rise to nature, know her, bow
> Your proud head to here and now;
> Learn to see the future, look
> On your past as on a book;
> Scan the present deeply, read
> Everywhere the power of deed;
> Fear, as deadly poisons, dreams,
> All that merely shams or seems;
> Let your goal forever be
> Naked, bright reality.

These platitudes recorded a resolution whose basic reference point was the Party which made demands upon reason rather than fantasy, will rather than wish.

One attempt to grapple with naked bright reality was *Dollar*

Diplomacy. In a copy of that book which I presented to KD, I inscribed a sonnet which was "propaganda"; yet it merely said in rhyme what I had already said in prose; the idea had become part of my daily thinking:

> Now look beyond the figures and the charts
> Of this brief chronicle of tyrants' deeds,
> And see how bankers haggle in the marts
> While the world cries in agony and bleeds,
> And glimpse the looming clouds of a new war,
> And workers rising with a mighty roar.

By the time I wrote this in 1925, I no longer took my verses seriously. Mike Gold, who went through a similar experience, attributed the death of lyricism to psychoanalysis and the harshness of New York; but Nearing said to me bluntly:

"I'll tell you why you can't write any more poetry. Your mind is communist, your emotions are bourgeois. Until you bridge that gap, you had better stick to prose, preferably news dispatches."

There was the real key to the dilemma. If certain members of our Party ridiculed poetry it was because most of the verse written by radical intellectuals echoed the uncertainties of the lesser middle class, resentful of big business, fearful of labor, forever vacillating between the two. Marx had defined the petit bourgeoisie as "a transitional class in which the interests of two classes are simultaneously blunted." The contradiction between my Party work and my verses reflected the contradictions of the lower middle-class intelligentsia which surrounded and molded me. No wonder Greta had sneered at my sonnets and called them *Kitch,* and said that distributing leaflets on the street corner was more useful to the revolution. I was through with poetry; yet here, aboard the freighter, I had written jingles for the sailors, crude rhymes compounded of their experiences and phrases.

I slipped the last of these crude rhymes into the batch of three hundred poems I had written over a decade in a language once strange and difficult, now part of my flesh and blood. I placed the poems in the trunk. Through the porthole I saw the vast night and heard the spray hissing against the sides of the ship. The lyric years were done. Here, in the trunk, lay Lenin's *Imperialism.* What tremendous poetry surged through this man's luminous and mighty prose. You must learn to understand science, industrial production, agriculture, politics, war —from a viewpoint, with a purpose. Beyond the night lay the new world.

§ 8

Early one morning at the end of May, 1926, a month after leaving New York, we pulled into the harbor of Batum. The sun yellowed the green waters, and poured its light on the white roofs of the town and the high green mountains looming in the distance.

From the masthead of our ship flew the American flag. Now Sam and Pete the Jugoslav were running up the red flag with the yellow hammer and sickle. I had seen the red flag in Union Square demonstrations, in the workers' halls of Paris and London, the symbol of international working-class solidarity. Then it represented a hope; now it was fluttering over our ship, tribute to power, to the reality of a dream.

A strange sensation overwhelmed me. This was home. It was not Russia, or the vanished village, but the first socialist republic. In America, the communist was looked upon as queer, abnormal. Here he was the norm. The twisted self-consciousness which isolation breeds fell out of my bones. My blood relaxed. Here I would not be a member of a persecuted sect, but one of millions thinking, willing, fighting toward the new world.

A holiday spirit pervaded the ship. Everyone was scrubbed clean and shaved, except for the new mustaches which the younger sailors were growing in the belief that Russia required you to wear at least half a beard.

From the shore a rowboat came toward us. It swished against our starboard and several young men climbed up the rope ladder to the deck. They were freshly shaved and neatly dressed in semimilitary khaki uniforms with red decorations on the collar. One of them smiled and said in accented English:

"Soviet Control. Where is the captain's cabin, please?"

Sam escorted the Soviet officials to the bridge. In a few minutes he came back with the man who had talked English.

"May I see your quarters?" the man said politely.

We walked in a body to the fo'c'sle. The sailors opened their bags and laid out their photos and written lists of personal belongings on the table.

"What is this?" the man said.

"The captain told us you wanted our pictures," Pete explained.

"And a list of all we've got," Sam added.

The man laughed. "No, no! It must be a joke. We don't want anything like that. Have you an American cigarette, please?"

He sat down at the table, and several of the men offered him their cigarette packs. He picked a Lucky, lit it, puffed contentedly for a few seconds, and said:

"Did you have a good trip?"

We exchanged glances. This had not happened at Constantinople. It did not happen in any other port. Control officials never came to the fo'c'sle to chat with the seamen. This one, to our surprise, asked us about our health, our voyage, our wages, hours, working conditions, food, about the general situation in our country, the American labor movement. Our men relaxed, sat down on the bunks, and asked questions about Soviet Russia. Then Sam said:

"What are them four British ships in the harbor?"

"They are being held up on account of the British strike," the Soviet man said. "Have you heard about the general strike?"

"We heard a little in Constantinople."

"The reformist leaders have called it off. They sold out. But the coal miners are still on strike. Our workers will not fail them. Batum will not load British ships with oil till the strike is settled."

Jack, the Erie mess boy, the only member of the crew who belonged to the A. F. of L., grinned and stood up.

"I've heard a lot about class solidarity," he said, "but this is the first time I've ever really seen it."

The Soviet man smiled, shot his head back and blew out a smoke ring. Sam leaned earnestly across the table and looked into the Russian's face.

"Tell me," he said, "are you a communist?"

"Of course."

"How is this thing of yours going?"

"Oh, we are not so rich as America. But when we get technique, we will be all right. We are all right now too. The workers control Russia. We know the future is ours."

The ship docked, the hatches were opened and the Soviet stevedores came aboard. Our seamen changed into their city clothes. We went ashore and walked to the town. Batum was a semitropical seaport with cobblestoned streets lined with palm trees. Swarthy men, either very fat or very thin, sat around café tables drinking and playing chess. Many of them wore white linen or cotton suits. Nepmen, no doubt, yet compared with them our sailors looked like millionaires in their neat blue or gray suits, straw hats, bright brown shoes and smoothly shaved faces. American technique.

Pete the Jugoslav found a group of us in a café and said we were all invited to the sailors' club. We walked down to the long, clean white building on the shore, facing the green sunlit harbor. A small wooden sign said in Russian and Latin letters: Club Marty, a tribute to the communist sailor in the French fleet who led a revolt of those who refused to fight against the Soviet Republic. We entered a large room filled with chairs like a meeting hall. On the walls were red streamers with slogans in Russian, English, French, Italian and German:

Workers of all countries, unite!
Workers, knowledge is power!

Beneath the streamers were large portraits of Lenin, Stalin, Trotsky, Tomsky and Bukharin. The hall led to a library whose tables were piled with newspapers and pamphlets in all languages. Here, six thousand miles from home, were copies of the *Daily Worker* with Bill Gropper's cartoons, an article by Mike Gold on the current mysticism of the American theater, the subject of our last talk before I sailed. Our men, who had not seen a paper for a month, sat down around the long table and read copies of the *Daily Worker*.

"Is this your junk?" Pete said, pointing to an article I had written shortly before leaving New York.

"Guilty."

"So you are not so dumb as you look." He smiled as if I had done him a personal favor. A clean-shaven young man with eyeglasses came in from a side room. He bowed to us politely and said:

"I am the secretary of this club."

We invited him to sit down with us, and he began firing the same questions as had the Control. What wages do you get? What do clothes cost in America? How do you live? What unions do American sailors have? We answered as best we could, and asked in turn: how about you fellows?

"We do not count wages only in money," the secretary said. "Take, for example, a fireman on a Soviet ship. He gets ninety-seven rubles a month in money wages. But in addition he gets thirty-five rubles for food, and four suits of clothes every year free. He also gets free of charge complete bed furnishings, laundry, insurance for himself and family and medical care. He works six hours a day, the sailors eight. Every year he gets a month's vacation with full pay. When the ship saves money on coal or oil, it is divided equally among the crew and officers, and the captain gets no more than the sailors. Officers and men get the same food."

"What!" Sam exclaimed with mock gravity. "No crew tea and cabin tea?"

We all laughed except the secretary, who looked blankly at us for a moment and went on:

"When our sailors are sick, they continue to get full wages. At fifty the sailor retires with a pension. Every ship has a committee of three which is a kind of local government on board. One member represents the crew, another the owner—that is, the government—and the third the seamen's union."

From the sailors' club we went into the town again. After New York, Batum looked like a little village. One must not judge the externals of Russia by those of America. I remembered, also, Nearing's warning: Transcaucasia is not the Soviet Union. The cobblestoned streets of the semitropical seaport were crowded with little shops. Russians, Georgians, Armenians and eight other races swarmed in the streets, cafés and stores. The low, white, red-roofed houses broiled in the Asiatic sun. Dark Kurds in ragged turbans drove their mountain asses through the narrow lanes of the city. Vain Georgians, lounging in the cafés, looked down admiringly on their own soft kid boots tight from toe to thigh.

I wandered through the streets all afternoon, and at night put up at a dingy hotel facing the sea. The room was small and badly lighted. Through the cracked door came the loud rattle of voices and the clink of glasses. The day's impressions were vivid and contradictory. I could not sleep.

In the morning I went down to the seamen's club and asked for the Agitprop committee. I was introduced to a group of three men. Small, dark Comrade Donadio, a political refugee from Fascist Italy, spoke Italian and French. Comrade Vacelko, once an officer in the Austrian army, later in the Red army, spoke German. Comrade Charchakoff, a Russian of twenty-nine whom the war had made prematurely gray and toothless, spoke German and French, so we got along.

"The *Kursk* has just come in from London," Charchakoff said. "I'm going aboard with literature. Would you like to come?"

The *Kursk* was a Soviet ship, but on deck we found a number of British sailors who had signed up with her. We went to the cabin where the crew was holding a meeting in English.

"Comrade chairman," a voice was saying in a cockney accent, "I move we request the captain to dock any man unable to do his work because of drunkenness."

"All those in favor?"

"Aye!"

"It is so ordered."

Charchakoff grinned toothlessly and whispered ιn my ear:

"Self-discipline."

When we reached shore, he said:

"Tomorrow night there will be a general meeting at the Club Marty. The Agitprop committee wants you to speak."

"On what?"

"America, of course."

These people were insatiable about America, especially about American technique and labor conditions. I had never realized how profoundly ignorant I was of my own country. I could recite *fat black bucks in a wine barrel room* from beginning to end without a hitch, but I did not know offhand the price of bread, the number of A. F. of L. members or the wheat area under cultivation in the United States. It was startling to hear such questions popped at you in the sailors' club, in the hotel, at cafés, by the kind of people who at home argued hotly the relative merits of Giants and White Sox. Something had transformed them, given them new eyes with which to see the world, and that something now made me acutely self-conscious. I was politically semiliterate. At home, the intelligentsia considered it bad taste to discuss politics except in moral, literary and Freudian terms. It was all right to talk about Coolidge's "silence" as the expression of a "complex"; it was dull and social-workerish to discuss his agrarian policy. Better retail apocryphal stories about D. H. Lawrence's private life. Here the workers were politically conscious and serious; America's economic situation was more important and exciting than Apeneck Sweeney's epigrams. Thanks to Nearing's advice, I had brought with me the *World Almanac* and the *American Labor Year Book,* which I read every night as one prepares for an examination.

"The meeting will be at eight o'clock tomorrow night," Charchakoff continued. "That gives us plenty of time to see Batum."

For the next two days we tramped the streets of Batum, rode in droshkies and autos to its outskirts, visited factories, schools, plantations. We went to a paint factory, an oilcan factory, a leather factory; then we drove twelve miles past almond trees and fruit trees, fields of tobacco and medicinal herbs to the state tea plantation at Chakva;

then back again to an iron foundry, a railway repair shop, a petroleum station. We visited a tobacco factory operated by 150 workers; the place was well lighted and well ventilated, with a co-operative restaurant, a workers' club, a school, a library. Near by was the apartment house in which the workers of the tobacco factory lived, one of the best buildings in Batum. This was typical of the city: every trade union and workers' club we visited had its library and school. The clubs were themselves educational centers with special courses in politics and economics, and groups devoted to aviation, drama, the film, radio, sports. In addition to the factory clubs, there was a large central club for the whole of Batum, a club for Turkish women, most of whom had dropped the veil, and a peasants' club.

On one beach we saw a group of Comsomols playing soccer, a healthy, sunburned, powerful lot, utterly different from the pale, nervous, introspective people of Chekhov and Dostoevsky whom the West regarded as typically Russian.

We heard complaints too. Living costs had gone up twenty per cent of late. The barber near the seamen's club, who kept pictures of Karl Marx and Lenin on his wall and poked fun at the local commissars, blamed the rising living costs on the arrival of American sailors.

"We have a long way to go yet," he said, clipping my hair with dull scissors, "but we have made the most important start. Industry and agriculture and the state are run by and for the people who work. With such a start, everything is possible."

This idea, so strange and "subversive" at home, sounded commonplace in Batum. Nearly everyone around you seemed to share it. Faith in collective effort, hope for the future, enthusiasm for socialism was not restricted to a handful of militant workers and scattered intellectuals; it was the daily spiritual bread of a people. And this idea, natural and universal here, emanated from material, visible facts. The worker was the center of life; the Nepman was despised and tolerated as a necessary and temporary evil; the big capitalist did not exist; profit was a collective concern for collective purposes. The hysterical pursuit of money which I had seen among the middle classes at home, the fear of unemployment and poverty in Passaic and on our freighter, seemed like a remote nightmare, like the pogroms of my childhood. People here pursued not personal aggrandizement at the expense of others, but a common social goal, the achievement of which was the individual's gain.

In the bourgeois world which I had just left the glorification of the individual led to his sterility and isolation. Here, where the individual was supposed to subordinate himself to the general interests of society as a whole, he actually expanded by virtue of being part of something greater than himself. Except for remnants of the former privileged classes, unable to reconcile themselves to the new world, everyone acted as though the general good was his personal good, as though his personal difficulties could be solved by conquering the common difficulties.

At home, in America, the "average" man—the worker, the farmer, the office employee, the unprivileged members of the various professions—was despised and rejected; he had no real voice in the management of national economy or public affairs; his eyes and ears were bound with lies; he moved blindly through illusion toward catastrophe —toward unemployment, crisis, war. Here the "average" man felt himself master of everything; he was concerned and proud about *our* paint factory, *our* leather factory, *our* tea plantation, *our* oil pipe from Batum to Baku, *our* workers' clubs.

This sense of communion of man with machine, man with man, man with society—a communion based not upon phrases, symbols or metaphysics but upon the simplest material acts of daily life, upon the making and distribution of food, shelter, clothing and knowledge— infected me so strongly that I, too, felt part of this vast section of mankind, 160,000,000 strong, building co-operatively toward a world without tyranny and without privilege. It was as though these factories and fields and schools and theaters and clubs belonged not to the Soviet workers and peasants alone, but to all of us the world over who were engaged in the same struggle for the classless society. The sense of isolation which haunted the declassed intellectual in the Western world, the exploitation which darkened the worker's days, the persecution which hounded the militant proletarian and the revolutionary were like a frightful chimera rapidly dissolving in the dawn. The wreckage of the old world was still here—poverty, ignorance, prejudice, slovenliness—but for the first time I saw the greatest of human dreams assuming the shape of reality. Men, women and children were uniting their efforts into a gigantic stream of energy directed toward destroying the evils of life, toward creating what was healthy and good for all.

Seeing this, how could one despair of the future? Struggle, anguish, error, failure awaited us in the years to come, but what good had man ever accomplished without these? This alone, this new world

at whose rough preliminary gates I now stood, was worth our effort
and our suffering, since it subsumed and integrated all the best hopes
of man, all his greatest possibilities, since history assured its victory
if only we ourselves strained our highest powers of will and intelligence toward it.

"I have been warned," I said to a worker bending over his bench
in the tobacco factory, "that Transcaucasia is not Russia."

"That is true," he replied. "We are a backward section of the
Soviet Union. Yet look what we have already accomplished even here.
Before the revolution, our region, now the republic of Ajaristan, had
only thirty-two schools; today we have a hundred and thirty-seven.
We also have now a daily newspaper for the workers in the Georgian
language, and a weekly in Russian. We have repaired the quays destroyed by the counterrevolution. We are beginning to lay sewers, and
to build a streetcar line, and to put up a forty-five hundred kilowatt
hydroelectric station which will furnish light and power for Ajaristan.
Come back in ten years, and you will not recognize our country."

He rolled off his statistics like a baseball fan rolling off the year's
batting averages. He made cigarettes for a living, but his life was
bound up with the Soviet Union as a whole. *Our* newspaper, *our* electric station, *our* schools.

Some people were out of this. Like Eugene O'Neill's Hairy Ape,
they didn't belong. Occasionally, their thoughts were echoed on the
stage. Communists took me to a theater where two clowns sang satirical songs against the Soviet regime. My communist friends laughed
and applauded with the rest: self-criticism. In a factory office, I was
introduced to a handsome, young, olive-skinned Georgian, once a
prince, now a bookkeeper for a communist enterprise. Looking sharply
at the communists who accompanied me, the ex-prince said:

"I don't like bolshevism."

He went back to his work unmolested. Outside, the comrades
explained:

"He is harmless, politically inactive. He doesn't understand what
is going on, but is not engaged in counterrevolutionary activities. Let
him prattle."

Later the secretary of the seamen's club took me to a charming
little house in one of the best sections of Batum. An old man with a
white mustache and a white linen suit came out and greeted the secretary warmly.

"Here is one of our real bourgeois," the secretary said, laughing.

At home businessmen laughed that way when they introduced their "pet" communist to friends. "He's an adventurer to boot. Imagine: born in France, a cowboy in America, and now he spends his declining years poking fun at us in Batum."

"A cowboy?" I asked in surprise.

"That was centuries ago," the old man said. "You have heard of Buffalo Bill?"

"Who hasn't?"

"I worked with him, and with Texas Jack too, long, long ago. How America must have changed!"

"You have seen changes here too."

"This is all nonsense." The old man laughed. "Crazy dreamers grasping for the moon."

"You talk like my father," I said.

"We like our dear old bourgeois anyway," the secretary said. "If he lives long enough, he will agree with us. He's no fool."

"I have lived too long to be taken in by words," the old man said. "How many times has mankind been fooled by big phrases? Look at Christianity and the French Revolution. First let me see you people achieve something substantial. I may change my mind then. But don't expect me to get excited over slogans."

"Slogans help us to achieve substantial things," the secretary said. "They are drums of the revolution. They set people marching toward the goal."

When we left, the secretary said:

"He's not a bad sort. It's some of these young bourgeois Georgians that give us the most trouble, even when they come over to us. They are lazy, vain and light-minded, carry pistols or poniards, are easily insulted, shoot from the hip at the slightest provocation and think the world owes them a living."

"Like Mexican landowners," I said.

"They are incapable of steady work or technical interests—a bunch of children who love wine, women and song and hate administration."

"Born bohemians. Are you discouraged?"

"Not at all. Our hope lies in other people altogether."

He took me to a meeting of the local soviet. The hall was dim, hot and crowded, like dozens of workers' meeting halls I had known at home. But here power sustained aspiration. Delegates from shop and farm, men and women, young and old, their dark faces furrowed by work and thought, sat forward in their seats listening to reports in Russian and Georgian.

"We use both languages," the secretary whispered. "That is Stalin's policy of national cultural autonomy."

The delegates sent up questions on slips of paper. When the answers from the platform were unsatisfactory, they stood up on the floor and raised hell. The commissar reporting sweated and wiped his forehead with the back of his hand. It must have been a great ordeal for him to face the workers. Standing there in the hot, stuffy, crowded hall, surrounded by workers and peasants in a dozen different native costumes, I could not doubt for a moment as to who ran Batum. I noticed, too, that the proletarian revolution had begun to create an international language. Listening to a Georgian orator I caught many familiar words—*industrializatsia, capitalisti, revolutsia.*

"It's these people we count on," the secretary said as we left the hall.

In the evening we had our meeting at the seamen's club. The hall was jammed with sailors from the German, Russian, British and Italian ships in the harbor. Nearly the entire crew of our own freighter was there; it was their last night in Batum; early the next morning they were shoving off for Odessa. Many workers from the local factories crowded the rear of the hall. I spoke about half an hour in English. A sailor from the *Kursk* translated my talk into Russian. There were questions from the floor in four or five languages about American economic conditions, politics, the labor movement, the Communist party.

At the end of the meeting, a movie screen was put up. The lights went out, and we watched a Soviet film based on the fight against Kolchak. Technically, the film was below American standards, but the story was well built and the acting superb. This was the first film I had ever seen with the social revolution as its theme and workers as its heroes. It was a silent film, but the hall was not silent. We heard the voice of a boy rattling on incessantly, and recognized in the dimness the blond, freckle-faced, five-year-old son of the *Kursk's* English bosun.

"Are those workers, daddy? Those fellers are rich people, ain't they? They got new clothes. Oh, oh, daddy! The rich people are killing the workers! An' now the workers are winning, ain't they, daddy?"

In the morning I took a train for Tiflis. My impressions of Batum were vivid and contradictory; they must be ordered. I fished my note-book out of my handbag and jotted down rapidly:

What is evil in Batum bears the fingerprints of the past; what is good shows the robust hand of the workers' revolution. Centuries of oppression, tribal war, technical ignorance have left their mark on the city's face, on the faces and habits of its people.

Crooked cobblestone streets, moldy houses, who made you? You were built long before Lenin's picture hung in every barbershop, grocery store and factory. The street boys who kiss our American shoes for bakshish are the souvenir of capitalist wars and blockades. Their father was the British occupation, their mother the menshevik counter-revolution.

The petty speculators who try to buy your Arrow shirt, the miserable little shopkeepers crying their wares in the rain, the exchange acrobats juggling dollars and rubles behind the G. P. U.'s back, the incorrigible smugglers and syphilitic whores are the swan-song of a dying class unable to give up its bad habits even on its deathbed.

History scrawled across the streets of Batum: Here czar and sultan ruled; here Asia's savage passions have boiled; here the Tower of Babel was built. Listen to the confusion of tongues! Here through the sweet perfume of the green Caucasian mountains, the long aristocratic noses of the British and American oil magnates caught the smell of petrol. Observe the shell holes left by their excessively civilized generals. This is the city which Jordania's traveling salesmen offered to the silk hats of the Paris bourse.

To this epitaph History wrote finis and added: Listen to the strong feet of the Comsomols marching into the future. Their clear young voices have learned to say in fifteen dialects: Workers of the world, unite! The past will be buried under an avalanche of pamphlets; the future will dance to the vast music of machines. Young mountaineers will discard the poniard for the slide-rule. The ships of the world will marvel at this gateway to a workers' republic.

CHAPTER II

TIFLIS

Comrades, enough! Cast your glance wider!
—ILYA SELVINSKY.

§ 1

SLOPING immense on either side of the Kura, the Caucasus mountains raised their green backs to the sky. The river flowed muddy, loaded deep with avalanches of dust and rock. It twisted abruptly at a hundred points, narrow from bank to bank, angular from town to town, till it reached a plain in the heart of the mountains where it divided into two parts the ancient city of Tiflis.

Where Jason sought the Golden Fleece, where the poet Rustavelli's voice rounded out the resonant periods of his rhymed epigrams, where Turkish scimitars flashed and the spurs of Romanov's officers tinkled, the cobbled streets now rumbled under the soviet-starred tramways. The streets wound and sloped like the back alleys of Paris. The main avenue, wide and fresh with full-blown trees, glided majestically from name to name, starting as the Prospect Rustavelli and ending as Lenin Street—tribute to old and new welded by the flames of the revolution.

The strange eyes of a dozen races passed each other in the Asiatic sunlight. The velvet-eyed Georgian, his handsome face slashed by a thin black mustache, marched vaingloriously along the asphalt in his dark belted blouse and soft high boots; the dark Armenian, wise and melancholy, carried his battered brief case to the commissariat where he served the working class as head bookkeeper. Russians with naked heads, shaved for the summer, and white, high-collared blouses, read *Rabotchaya Pravda* on the benches in front of the Workers' Co-operative Restaurant. Soldiers of the Red army, in light khaki uniforms with little red stars on their caps, rubbed shoulders with Georgian women, wonderfully beautiful in their youth, with mountaineers in rags driving small donkeys, with old beggars.

The sun shone lazily on the stained white walls of the houses; the air was languid with summer perfume. British leather army puttees twinkled on the legs of Soviet journalists, proud of this European

466

touch. The secretary of the Typographical Union parked the organization's new Dodge in front of the Sovnarkom. German and American salesmen carried their fedora hats in their hands, swinging along to the State Bank to cash their travelers' checks.

"I hope to Christ we get a little action," the man from Michigan said to me at the cashier's window. "Why in hell don't they get a move on!"

Lenin's face looks down from every wall. The shop windows are full of lithographs—Stalin, Zinoviev, Narimanov.

"Yes, comrade, things are much better now. The counterrevolution has been liquidated. We are building a hydroelectric station of thirty-two thousand horsepower. There is plenty of food. Ach, if we only had enough machinery. Is it true, comrade, that in America many workers have automobiles?"

Past, present and future descended on me at the Workers' Cooperative Restaurant. One of the waitresses was tall, slim, large eyed; her black hair was combed down tight on her head; her thin nostrils and small curved mouth were naturally red; her overbred thin legs were covered with gray lisle stockings, her feet with gray suède shoes, worn and a little too big. Another waitress was short, well formed, sensuous limbed; her face shone white under her black hair; a dimple lit up her left cheek when she smiled. The third waitress was ungainly; her body was heavy, her ankles thick; she waddled when she walked; yet her face showed breeding, and under her curved nose her mouth tightened, proud and melancholy. She came to my table and asked for my order in Russian. A group of young workers with close-cropped heads sitting at the next table said to her:

"Govori po frantzuski—speak French!"

"Et quesque vous voulez, monsieur?"

"Je veus du pain, du beurre, et du jambon."

"Ah, you want a sandwich!" she broke into English. "You are American, aren't you?"

"I am. But where did you pick up such good English? You speak like an Oxford student. Are you English?"

"I am Georgian. I have never been out of Tiflis in my life. I learned English at home from my governess." She brought me two thick pieces of black buttered bread with a piece of very salt ham on each, the European "sandwich," the Butterbrot. Then she sat down at a nearby table where a little old woman in black, holding a closed umbrella tight in one hand, was drinking tea. I ate my sandwich, drank beer and read the British Trade Union Report on Georgia. Suddenly the man at the next table attracted my attention; he was whispering to my waitress. I noticed his gray hair, his eyeglasses, his youngish face, round and effeminate. The waitress smiled, nodded, came to my table.

"That gentleman," she said, "asks whether you speak German. He would like to talk with you." I said I spoke German, the waitress whispered to the man with the gray hair, and he came to my table carrying his bottle of beer and his glass.

"I beg your pardon," he said, "but you are an American journalist, aren't you?"

"How did you know?"

"I read an interview with you in this morning's paper. I am a journalist too. I work, or rather I used to work, at the *Zara Vostok* until my health broke down. You don't mind if I sit here and talk?"

"No, do sit down, please," I said. The waitress, standing a little distance from our table, motioned to me. I went over to her and she whispered in my ear:

"I wouldn't advise you to talk much with our people. You may say something innocent, and they will report you and twist your words."

"Report me?"

"To the Cheka!"

"I'll be glad to tell the Cheka myself what I think." I went back to my table thinking, the girl must be a dispossessed aristocrat taking the workers' regime rather hard and trying to frighten foreign visitors. As I sat down, the gray-haired journalist smiled sadly, like a woman disappointed in love trying to put on a brave front.

"You have never been in Tiflis before?" he said. "Ah, an interesting city. Have you seen the museums? Georgia has a rich culture. The Georgians were cultured before the Russians. Life has been difficult here of late, but now it is better. You must see the museums. I will introduce you to some Georgian artists. I am not interested in politics, ah, no, not at all. I am a dilettante. I draw a little and write a little. I am interested only in art. I assure you the Georgians are a very cultured race. Won't you let me show you the museums?"

"I'll see later."

"How is life in America?" he asked eagerly. "The Americans are an energetic race, aren't they?"

"Very energetic."

"I thought so. The Americans are a masculine race. We Russians are a feminine race. I am a Don Cossack, that is, my family were Cossacks. I myself studied at a university in Berlin; that's how I learned to speak German so well. How old are you?"

"How old do you think?"

"Twenty-two."

"I'm older than that."

"Ah, but you look so young. Americans all look young. It's the life there, I suppose. You are in good health, aren't you?" He passed his hand over his gray hair, and leaned weakly across his beer glass.

"Yes, I am in good health."

"So I thought. I am in very bad health. Not physically, you understand. It's more of a nervous disorder. The doctor has forbidden me to work on newspapers. It's been a great shock. When I pass the offices of *Zara Vostok* I fall into a terribly nervous state. So you are in good health. Ah, that's splendid! You are never nervous, are you? No, I can see you are never nervous. You Americans have nerves of iron. Can we meet some time tomorrow? I'd like to show you our art gallery."

A casual encounter, yet here was a type of aesthete I knew at home, "nervous" and self-centered, eaten up with trifles. Outside it began to rain hard. It was now almost midnight. The man with the gray hair looked sadly out the window. A droshky rattled over the wet cobblestones; the trees whistled quietly.

"Yes, the bolshevik regime is better than the old regime," the man suddenly said apropos of nothing at all. "I am not a worker; I am what you would call an intellectual, one who is not at all interested in politics. Ah, if I only had good nerves."

Loud footfalls broke into the steady rhythm of the rain. A clear tenor voice began to sing in the street, in the dimness of the wet night, clear above the one-two, one-two of marching boots. I walked to the open doorway and looked out. A detachment of Red soldiers was marching through the rain. The clear tenor voice was engulfed in the chorus, strong and masculine:

> Damned fascisti, we don't fear you!
> When we meet, we'll shoot you down!

The soldiers' steady tramp died down; they disappeared in the fog. I went back to my table and found the waitress standing there.

"Would you like to walk home with me?" she said in English.

"With me and my mother? She is sitting over there. She speaks French."

The little old woman joined us, smiling in a most ingratiating way.

"Let's go," she whispered in French. "We'll wait for my daughter outside. They don't allow you to wait for waitresses here. I suppose it's the same in America."

"Hardly," I said. We walked out into the rain together. The little old lady handed me her umbrella, I opened it and held it over her head, and we marched up and down in the rain in front of the Workers' Co-operative Restaurant.

"Things are terrible here," the little old lady said. "You must be very careful what you say. Don't let them hear you talking in a foreign language. It's dangerous. They will think we are plotting something."

"What are you afraid of, madame? I have been here several days, moved about freely, said and done whatever I wanted and nobody has bothered me."

"That's different," she said. "You are a foreigner, an American at that. But I am the Princess Q. Have you ever heard of the name? We are the oldest Georgian family. We are of the royal household. Our family gave Georgia its kings when our country was independent. Have you ever heard of the great Georgian poet Rustavelli? He was loved by Queen Tamara—in the twelfth century. He was a great poet, and she was a beautiful queen. But Rustavelli loved the first lady-in-waiting, so the queen took poison. Queen Tamara was my ancestor. Our family is four hundred years older than the Russian aristocracy."

The little old lady in black, with a little wrinkled hat on her head and a little umbrella over her, lamented dead glories in the rain.

"We have lost everything," she said. "My daughter must work as a waitress. She is not used to that sort of thing. She is very cultured. Don't you think she speaks English well? As a child, she was taught English, French and German by a governess. How old do you think she is? Only nineteen! How old are you? Twenty? Twenty-six? Oh, you are young and I can see you are well brought up. When I first saw you I said to my daughter, now there is a well-brought-up young man."

"Thank you, madame."

"You are not like most Americans I have met. I have a bone to pick with Americans. There was a certain Mr. Tompkins here. Perhaps you know him?"

"I know a newspaperman by that name. He represents an American paper in Moscow."

"I mean his brother. Mr. Tompkins was here for Harriman and Company. You know that Harriman and Company have a manganese concession in Georgia? Mr. Tompkins promised to get my daughter a good position in the Harriman offices at Chiatouri. Alas, he disappointed us! He was only going to get her a job as a waitress in Chiatouri. That is scarcely an improvement over being a waitress in Tiflis."

The rain fell in long drops on the Prospect Rustavelli. We started back for the Workers' Co-operative.

"Mr. Tompkins was very bad in another way too," the little old lady said. "All Americans think that foreign women are loose women. That's because Americans have money, I suppose. You don't think that way, I hope. This Mr. Tompkins knew my daughter a short time yet he asked her to dine with him."

"Mr. Tompkins meant no harm," I said. "In America a girl of the very best family can dine alone with a man."

"We never allow that," the little old lady said. "Our girls cannot go out unaccompanied."

Several workers passed us, their blouses clinging to their bodies, soaked with rain. The princess seized my arm.

"Sh-sh-sh!" she whispered. "Don't let them hear us talking French. They will think we are plotting something." She waited until the workers were out of earshot. "I have friends in America," she whispered. "Perhaps you know them. There is . . ." She looked around slowly, cautiously. "I can't say his name in anybody's hearing . . . wait till those people get on . . . he was our Czar's ambassador to America . . . Mr. Bachmeteff."

"I've heard the name," I said.

"It's very, very bad for us here. Cultivated people have a hard time. Look at this fellow Stalin, for example. You know he is a Georgian? But he has no culture at all. Yet he is our ruler. Can you imagine such a thing? Oh, I wish we could go to America! But we cannot get a passport. If my daughter married an American—we could get out."

The daughter came out of the Workers' Co-operative and together we walked toward their house. The mother bombarded me with questions. What was my profession? Was I a college graduate? How large was my family? Did I live with them? What was my religion?

I said I was an atheist.

"But that is a meaningless word!" the little old lady exclaimed. "Don't you believe in God?"

"No, I believe in science."

"Religion is also a science!" The rain fell silently between us. When the princess had regained her composure, she said: "Have you seen Mzche? That was the original capital of Georgia. It was built by my ancestors. My family ruled there. You must see the beautiful old church which is there. It is very, very old. You know we Georgians became Christians in the fourth century, long, long before the Russians."

In front of their house we parted; I declined their invitation to come up for a glass of tea.

"Come to see us," the old princess said. "You won't forget the place? We used to have the whole apartment but now they have left us only one room. I hope you will be nice to my daughter—a gentleman."

Was the old lady an impostor? I inquired and found she had told the truth; she was the former Princess Q. I never went to see them.

§2

Stalin came to Tiflis. I tried to interview him for the American press, but Party headquarters was obdurate.

"Very sorry, comrade," a young secretary said; "he can't be seen. He refuses all interviews, statements and speeches. One of our leading Party journalists who tried to get an interview has just been turned away. Comrade Stalin is here only for a rest. He may speak at the Plenum today, or maybe at the Opera tonight. I'll get you a ticket for the Opera."

I went to the Opera that night with Andro, a Georgian journalist, not a communist, one of the numerous non-Party workers in the Soviet press. On the way I noticed that every shop window had a lithograph of Stalin dressed in white blouse, his legs encased in Caucasian boots, a cigarette in his right hand, his eyes half-closed with Oriental watchfulness. He is a Georgian, the "favorite son."

The Opera was jammed with workers. Orchestra, boxes and balconies were dark with Georgian and Armenian faces. Under the bright lights voices rattled in small talk. Suddenly people scrambled to their feet and looked toward a box in which a group of men were taking seats.

"Stalin! Stalin! Stalin!"

The audience was on its feet, hands thundered applause, voices shouted.

"Speech! Speech! *Prosim!*"

Stalin did not move. He sat half hidden behind local Tiflis officials who smiled into their beards. The audience rushed down the aisles to get a better look.

"Stalin! Stalin! Stalin!"

Stalin stood up. His cheeks were ruddy, his body stocky; a black mustache hung over his robust smile; his eyes were half-closed. He bowed slowly, full of reserve, dignity and power. He bowed slowly, said nothing, sat down. The audience shouted louder and louder. *Prosim!* The applause rose and fell like a storm, but Stalin refused to speak. The applause went on for another ten minutes. Finally Stalin stood up a second time. Everyone strained toward him. He slowly took out a watch from the breast pocket of his white blouse; he pointed to the watch in silence, then to the stage. Without saying a word he sat down. The crowd yelled, applauded, whistled. Suddenly a young man in the orchestra with a strong, clean-shaven head held up his hand and shouted to the balconies:

"*Davolno!* Enough!"

The applause stopped abruptly; the audience sat down; silence settled over the hall; the lights went out, the curtain rose. On the stage, a large chorus of men and women in bright-colored costumes burst into the *International*.

The tribute to Stalin evoked a strange feeling in me. Time and experience had altered the size of those beings who, in the flesh or as myths, had played an important part in your life. Jehovah, once everywhere, had faded from the world into the realm of legend along with Zeus, Thor and the Great Spirit. The Czar, who in childhood seemed omnipotent, emerged during the war as a helpless little obscene man, stupid, illiterate, without brain or backbone, a pitiful worm crushed by the immediate wrath of the people's revolution. That pompous, arrogant man who rattled his sword in shining armor and raised his upturned mustache toward the mirage of omnipotence was a powerless old man chopping wood in Doorn like any Spiessbürger, drab and commonplace now that his titles and decorations were gone. History had reduced the stature of these men, destroyed the mists of illusory grandeur which surrounded them.

When the period of hero worship was over, you became acutely conscious of your own ego. You were the free, unhampered individual, "neither bully nor sheep." Nobody was better than yourself, and nobody worse. But time and experience exploded that pleasant fiction. The free, unhampered ego, the world of absolute equals was as much an illusion as the world of gods, czars and heroes. One illusion was a thoughtless, violent reaction against the other. In the kingdom of necessity there was an unequal development of individuals which no democratic dogma could conceal. Men were not born and created equal; men were unequal; hence, even in the socialist society, from each according to his abilities, to each according to his labor. This pointed in the direction of a freedom which could be achieved only through the recognition and mastery of necessity.

Experience destroyed your cult of the ego and taught you that some men have greater intelligence and will power than others; their understanding is deeper, their sight farther, their physical, intellectual and moral energy more sustained and intense. The very years which had reduced the stature of the conventional heroes had lifted to the heights other men whom we had been brought up to consider small and of no consequence. We had studied Macaulay, Wells, Thoreau; the scribes solemnly weighed every word which T. S. Eliot uttered. These were the giants. Somewhere on the shelves of radical libraries were the works of the negligible cranks, Karl Marx and Friedrich Engels. There was also a "despot" named Lenin whose works even now, almost nine years after the Bolshevik Revolution, no respectable professor in America thought worth studying or translating. Yet contemporary history had raised these men to the highest eminence. Their words and deeds molded the lives of 160,000,000 people in a country covering one-sixth of the globe, and of millions of people in every other country of the globe. They were altering the world—in so far as individuals can alter it—more profoundly than Newton or Napoleon. The unequal development of individuals had raised a Stalin, Djerdjinsky, Chicherin, Bukharin, Tomsky, or Vorovsky to that leadership which every social group requires whenever such men showed a greater capacity than the average for understanding and manipulating the mechanics of history. But now it was no longer hero worship; for no man was personally so brilliant and strong that he could not be dispensed with the moment he ceased to serve the revolutionary cause. Lenin had taught us that past revolutionary services could not outweigh present errors when he broke with and castigated socialist veterans like Kautsky and Plekhanov. The measure of a man in revolutionary politics was his present usefulness. To facilitate the work, superior usefulness was given superior place. The revolution at this stage sought to establish a form of economy higher than capitalism, to abolish exploitation and poverty, to abrogate classes and class distinctions. The achievement of that goal would create equal opportunity for all to develop their powers to the utmost. It could not make the foolish wise or the dull brilliant. What men would develop into after the classless society was established, no one could foretell. Every age could solve only those problems which history set it; and the problem of individual equality could not be solved so long as classes and class antagonisms existed. Our problem was the abolition of classes.

On the stage the actors were playing the opera *Tamara*. It was the first opera ever written in the Georgian language—a product of the bolshevik policy of national cultural autonomy. My companion, the Georgian reporter Andro, gave vent to his nationalist feelings in lyrical French.

"The Georgian language is the most beautiful in the world," he explained. "Our great poet Rustavelli is among the world's sweetest singers. This opera is about the love of Queen Tamara for the poet Rustavelli."

The curtain fell. There was sparse applause.

"Let's go out for a smoke," Andro said. "Do you know why there was so little applause? The audience is full of Armenians. There is no love lost between us and them. Do you know why? Georgia is an agricultural country. We have had little industry and hardly any proletariat. Until the revolution there was only a peasantry and a landed aristocracy. You have no idea how many Georgian princes there were. If you owned a couple of sheep, you were a prince. Now a lot of them are in the Communist party. Our princes were gallant fellows: good fighters, marvelous hosts, dancers, singers, bons vivants. But they had no talent for business or administration. The Armenians, on the other hand, were no gentlemen at all. They were businessmen. Most of the stores in Tiflis are run by Armenians; they know how to make money. When the Czar or a great Russian prince came to Georgia, our nobles entertained him. They had grace, beautiful songs, manners, dances—but they had no money. They had to borrow it from the Armenians. Our princes were in debt, and could not pay. Everything was mortgaged to their Armenian creditors; our princes felt they were owned body and soul by these vulgar foreigners. What could they do? If you can't pay your creditor, you can kill him. That's what our princes did—and I don't blame them."

We went back to the theater. The curtain rose on a Georgian chorus, splendid in red and black costumes, and high soft boots. The voices were very deep and very high; the music flowed on a level plain, then rose slowly by quarter notes in the pentatonic scale into war chants full of pride and power.

"What beautiful music we have." Andro sighed in ecstasy. "Georgians always sing—when they eat, when they march, when they go to war. The Georgian peasant sings when he drives his bullock cart to town, or trudges with a pack on his back."

On the way home from the Opera, Andro recited verses from Rustavelli in Georgian and translated them into French.

The little old princess who wanted me to see Georgia's ancient capital was a fragment of the dying past; Andro the last convulsion of a dying present. I met the future in the headquarters of the Communist party. Comrade Z, who spoke German, introduced himself:

"I am in charge of the section for national minorities. We have had a hell of a job, but national animosities are dying down as economic conditions change."

He seemed very young. His face was thin and deadly pale, his head clean shaven for the summer. His deep-set eyes burned with a terrible fire; he looked ill; his lips were very white. For Comrade Z, Tiflis contained no ancient royal capitals or wonderful dances. He was a bolshevik intent upon the tasks of the hour. He said at once:

"Have you seen our workers' homes and clubs? Have you seen our factories? Our hydroelectric station?"

Z took me to the newspaper on which he worked and introduced me to the editor, an Armenian. They telephoned for a car, and soon we were racing down the Prospect Rustavelli in the new Dodge driven by a Ukrainian comrade who was accompanied by a Russian mechanic. Editor, reporter, chauffeur and mechanic talked to each other in terms of complete equality.

At a crossing, a large touring car rushed toward us. The traffic militiaman raised his club, stopped the car, and let us pass first. Our chauffeur grinned at the policeman.

"*Vot molodietz!*—Atta boy!"

"That was the commissar of police he stopped." Z laughed.

We came to the hydroelectric station, built by German and Georgian engineers with Soviet funds. Gigantically it straddled the muddy, twisted Kura. Stronger than all of the old Tiflis rose the new concrete dam.

"See those big pieces of iron lying around?" Z said. "They are our own. Look at the markings: Putilov iron works, Leningrad. And look at those immense turbines sloping up the bank."

We visited the club of the electric station workers; it had a library and reading room, but Z kept looking out the window toward the dam.

"That station," he said, "is going to be thirty-two thousand horsepower. It will supply the whole of Georgia with light and power. We'll be able to run more factories. In ten years this will be a new city."

Opposite the hydroelectric station was a little peninsula on the river Kura. It was so close that I could see how old the houses were that sloped up the hill. A little white church, stained blue and green with age, lifted its delicate spire above the surrounding wooden roofs.

"That's Mzche," Z said, "the original capital of Georgia, where the first kings ruled." This, then, was the place the princess wanted me to see. The old royalist wanted to show me the ancient seat of aristocratic power; the aesthete wanted me to see the museums of the Georgian bourgeoisie; the communist took me to the hydroelectric station built by the proletarian state, towering over the crumbling houses of Mzche, over the moldy little church.

At the close of the day we motored to Zachar Zacharowitch's restaurant in Mzche for dinner. The walls were covered with photographs of Georgian warriors and dancers, standing, sitting, astride horses, the breast pockets of their long Circassian coats full of cartridges, their belts crossed by poniards, their mustaches long and black. From this melange of photographs there stood out one face utterly different from all the others, a young face without a mustache, full of energy and intelligence—Lenin as a student.

We supped in the garden under a tree. The Armenian editor, round faced, with a goatee and a little paunch, ordered Georgian cheese, salad, *shashleek*, wine and lemonade. We drank to the Soviet Union; we drank to the American working class; we drank each other's health.

"Tell me, comrade," the Armenian editor asked, "is there a good communist press in America? How much did you pay for your coat? Are there many unemployed in your country? Why don't you recognize the Soviet Union?"

Zachar's big, black dog came and squatted on the grass beside our table; the Armenian editor fed him soft Georgian bread and fired questions at me about American skyscrapers, machines, immigrant life, labor organizations. The high mountains covered the sky behind him; it was getting dark. Silently he mixed his wine with lemonade, then looked at me in a queer way and said:

"Do you know, comrade, a communist ought not to marry; it interferes with his work."

"That's what I think," Z said, his terribly pale face breaking into a smile. "I've been married for three months, and I've had about enough."

"Are you married?" I asked the elderly editor.

"Yes, and I have three children, and I love them very much. That's the difficulty; it interferes with your work."

He paid the bill and we drove back to Tiflis, to the Central Workers' Club. We sat in for a while at a workers' meeting, then the club secretary took us to the library.

"Do you know how many books we have now?" he said proudly. "Think of it—fourteen thousand!" Several girls were working on a card catalogue. "They do this in their off hours, for the cause, without pay," the secretary explained, "and they are non-Party at that."

The door to the Lenin corner was closed. Through the glass we could see Lenin's bust on a stand. A group of young workers was reading quietly at a table on which stood a large bronze bust of Stalin. The Ukrainian chauffeur pointed to the bust and grinned.

"Do you know what Stalin said to us about last night's opera on Rustavelli and Tamara? He said the music wasn't very original; it was lifted from *Faust* and Tchaikovsky."

In another room there was a movie show, an old American Western. No charge, the comrade at the door explained, movies are free for the workers four nights a week.

Later we went to the industrial exposition. We walked from booth to booth, looking at Diesel engines and oil lamps. We stopped before a group of American tractors; I had seen these before, on our freighter which brought them to Batum. Z was looking at a small printing press, caressing it as he would a pet horse.

"Too slow," he said. "This is the kind of press we use on our paper. What we need is one of those American multiple presses. They have them in Moscow; we ought to have them in Tiflis. But all these things will come. Wait till we begin developing our oil resources!"

The next morning, speeding along the mountain road from Tiflis, we saw dozens of bullock carts carrying logs to town. The peasants used to float them down the Kura, but now the hydroelectric station blocked the river. The logs were hauled by land down to the station and floated from there. Long, thin logs lay across the small cart drawn by two Indian oxen, small, shaggy, with narrow heads. Peasants in purple or green blouses sprawled across the logs on their bellies, often sleeping under the strong sun as the bullocks ambled slowly along the dirt road.

"That's the kind of transportation we still have," Z said tartly. "Bullock carts. How is it in America?"

"Motor trucks."

"Yes, you have the technique; and we have a workers' government. When we get the technique and you have a workers' government, it will be the beginning of a beautiful world."

§ 3

From Tiflis to Baku I traveled "hard"—third class. Our carriage was crowded with workers bound for the oil fields. The top benches in each compartment were loaded with baggage; the two lower benches were occupied by men, women and children sprawling under the broiling Caucasian sun that poured in through the narrow windows.

Inside the carriage all the windows were closed, although it was the middle of June. The heat was oppressive. Two small windows on the platform were open, each filled with the body of a man leaning out to breathe the wind that swept by the rushing train.

Early in the morning the passengers began to undo their straw baskets and paper bundles. They laid out huge slabs of black bread, long sticks of sausage, and bottles of wine, beer and soda, and began to eat and drink. Every time I looked up, someone was eating black bread and sausage and drinking. Usually the beverage was tea. People might have much baggage or little baggage, but they always carried a teakettle. Almost every railway station in Russia serves boiling water free of charge; whenever the train stopped there was a rush for the *kipitok*. The passengers came back with their kettles steaming, arms full of cheese, fruit, roasted chicken, and radishes bought at the buffet or from peasants lined along the tracks.

Many passengers had their own bedding, rolled up in circular wooden boxes. After breakfast they spread out thin blankets and lay down to sleep. Faces and hands grew red under the heat. Several peasants in heavy black boots, crinkled at the ankles, tossed on the hard benches. A young worker, with his shirt open at the neck, read a newspaper and fought off the flies with his blue handkerchief. He was sitting next to me, and opened a conversation:

"Excuse me, you are a foreigner?"

"How did you know?"

"Your shoes. Are you German?"

"American."

He fired the usual barrage of questions: How do people live in America? What wages do workers get? Are they organized in trade unions? In what kind of houses do they live? How much does bread cost? And milk? And meat? Is there a Communist party in America?

A little blond girl about thirteen, sitting on the opposite bench at the feet of her sleeping mother, looked up from her book and listened to our talk. She shook her mother.

"Mama, are you asleep?"

"What is it, Shura?"

"What do you think, mama, bread costs eight cents a pound in America, and they are having a textile strike."

Mama sat up, smiled, nodded politely.

"My father is an oil worker," Shura said to me. "Of course he is a member of the trade union, but he is not a Party member. Mama is a peasant. She is illiterate, but she is going to learn to read when we get to Baku, aren't you, mama?"

"I can't read and write yet," mama said shyly, "but Shura goes to school and is learning all about the world."

Near us sat two Georgians. One was tall, heavy, red faced; his drooping mustache was streaked with gray. The other was young and frail.

"Nowadays life is hell," the older man said.

"It's hell," said the young man.

"They don't let you work, they don't let you serve in public posts."

"No work, no posts," said the young man.

"There's no land."

"There's nothing. What do we get out of life?"

"No work, no posts, no land, no wages," the older man said.

"You get only thirty rubles a month."

"One might as well lie down and die."

"And if you have children they go hungry."

"You can't even study."

"That's only for Party members," the young man said. "It's hell to be non-Party."

"There are some people who make a thousand rubles a month."

"Nepmen," the young man said. "We can't even trade. For the big fellows it's all right, for the people it's hell."

"It's always been hell."

"Maybe in a thousand years from now we'll all be equal," said the young man. "Now life is hell for the people."

"What can you do?"

"There's vodka," said the young man.

"Yes, thank God for vodka."

The young worker next to me flicked his blue handkerchief at the flies and glared at the two Georgians.

"A hell of a lot they care about the people," he said to me. "Kulaks, filthy kulaks, that's what they are. They're putting on a show for your benefit; they can see you are a foreigner. But if you stay in our country long enough you will see they are lying kulaks."

When I arrived in Baku, everything was closed. It was Friday, the Mohammedan day of rest, and as such officially recognized. The tropic town was broiling. I registered at a hotel, took off my shirt and typed four poems for the *New Masses*.

a.

Here from the distant shores of Greece,
Jason sought the Golden Fleece;
These hills heard Rustavelli's voice,
And saw Tamara's love-lit eyes;
The Persian elephant-riders came
And left their mark in blood and flame;
Turkish scimitars were gory
For rich lands, horses, Allah's glory;
Here Russian duke and princess met
And drank the Georgian peasant's sweat;
Sniffing petrol in the air
Britons turned machine-guns here;
This town Jordania's salesmen sold
Upon the Paris bourse for gold;
Till workers, roaring like the sea,
Struck down the head of tyranny.
Now creeps the tramway from afar
Shining with the Soviet star;
The peasant leads his mountain ass

Where commissars and comrades pass;
Red soldiers, singing in the rain,
Swear to defend the workers' gain;
And from the walls look Lenin's eyes,
Impatient, resolute and wise.

b.

Prince Jernikidze wears his boots
Above his knees: his black mustache
Curls like the Kaiser's: when he shoots
Friend and foe turn white as ash;

The movements of his hands are svelt,
Ivory bullets grace his chest,
The studded poniard at his belt
Dangles down his thigh: the best

Dancers in Tiflis envy his
Light lezghinka's steady whirl,
He bends his close-cropped head to kiss
The fingertips of every girl.

Over the shashleek and the wine
His deep and passionate baritone
Directs the singing down the line
And none may drain his glass alone.

When morning breaks into his room,
He dons his long Circassian coat,
Marches to the Sovnarkom,
Knocks at the door, and clears his throat,

Opens the ledger with his hand,
Bows to the commissars who pass,
Calls the janitor comrade, and
Keeps accounts for the working class.

c.

Soldiers marching in the rain,
Send their voices through the night,
Rolling out the loud refrain:
Workers of the world, unite!

The street rings with their steady tread,
Their pointed bayonets shine bright,

Proud and young the soldier's head:
Workers of the world, unite!

d.

Lenin in a marble suit,
Standing in a workers' club,
Hears Tchaikovsky on the flute,
Sees a patient worker rub

His hand across his shaven head,
Watches soldiers drinking beer,
Hears the union minutes read,
Smiles in his marble beard to hear

An engineer in belted blouse
Talking where there once walked queens,
Discourse before a crowded house,
Planning fifty new machines.

Casual encounters, thoughtless episodes measured by the vague rods of outworn symbols; yet so deeply had the proletarian revolution penetrated everywhere that Tiflis would never be the same, nor Russia, nor the world. October had put socialism on the order of the day; like it or not, fight for it or against it, it was 'here remolding the life of men. The organic energy of millions was now directed not toward the pursuit or worship of private gain, but toward a world of co-operative creation. At home the password was "money," here "socialism."

Old and new were in conflict here, but the old was crumbling, the new growing stronger. You walked through the streets of Baku, along the shore of the Caspian, and the bourgeois journalist, his mind moldy with dying myths, points to the tower from which the legendary virgin hurled herself, looks across the bright blue sea and sighs nostalgically, "Persia is twelve hours away." But the youth thinks of others things—even in the most casual encounters.

I walked into the soda shop facing the boulevard along the Caspian Sea and the park, artificially created by the Soviet on arid soil. I sat down at one of the small white tables and ordered a lemonade. The pretty Jewish blonde who brought it wore a large wedding ring on the middle finger of her right hand.

"The proprietor would like to speak to you," she said.

The old Turk was sitting on a little bench at the back of the store, mending a pair of pants. His face was like crumpled brown leather, and the gray mustache straggled down to his unshaven chin. He looked fifty.

"Is it true," he asked, "that everybody in American has lots of money?"

"Only the capitalists have lots of money," I said.

"Is it true that every American worker has an automobile?"

"In America there are people who think every Russian wears a beard."

The young man behind the counter laughed gaily. He was tall, thin, curly-haired; his eyes were dark and merry. He was making ice cream and listening to the conversation.

"These old people," he said in German, "have the most childish fantasies."

"Do you work for the old Turk regularly?" I asked.

"No, only in the summer. The rest of the year I am a student. I'm specializing in chemistry at the University of Azerbaijan, and in the summer I make ice cream to earn a little extra money. They say it's the best ice cream in Baku."

People in Russia are free with their autobiographies. He went on:

"My family comes from Kiev. We've been in Baku only a year. When I've finished my chemistry course, I'm going in for engineering. Student life is not at all bad. We get free tuition, free books, reduced rates for food, and pocket money from the state."

"Are you a Party member?"

"No, but I am a communist at heart."

He offered me some ice cream and said earnestly:

"Don't judge things by Baku. It's all new here. Bolshevism has been here only a couple of years. When you get into Russia proper you will see even more progress. Talk to the people in the streets here; you will see they are all in favor of the Soviet regime. All we need now is technique, machinery."

I started to go. When I was passing through the doorway, he called after me:

"Come back here five years from now. You won't recognize the country!"

Comrade Selimzakee, director of the Soviet news agency in Baku, and the engineer Vannikov, representing Azneft, took me to the oil fields on the outskirts of the city. On the way they poured out facts and statistics.

We stopped to look the station over—a large, spacious, comfortable building covering about two square blocks. The engineer explained proudly that all the material for the railway, except one complicated part which came from Germany, was made in the Soviet Union.

Going on the fields, we passed the new workers' homes, being built for the oil workers by Azneft; white, brick houses, gabled and solid.

"We are building," the engineer said, "not for one year and not for two, but for the longest period during which houses can endure. We mean business; the workers' society is here to stay."

The engineer proudly pointed to pumps, driven six to nine at a time by electric sixty-horsepower wheels.

"Technique," he said. "Under capitalism, increased exploitation; under socialism, increased freedom."

From the Ramanee oil field we went to the workers' club. There was the usual Lenin corner, isolated almost like a shrine. I pointed to it and said to the engineer:

"In America it is said that Leninism is a religion."

The engineer laughed. "It's not true. But if you like to play with words, all right. Religion once represented man's utmost knowledge and hope about the world in which he lived. At present religion is an anachronism. In so far as the doctrines of Marx and Lenin serve to transfer the religious emotions of the masses they are abreast of modern science. If your imagination is so backward that the Lenin corner appears like a church, you must at least admit that it represents the aspirations of man on this earth, aspirations which can be achieved in concrete, material, controllable forms by the efforts of humanity itself. Call that religion if you like; I call it science. Faith, hope, aspiration once centered around religion; but they are not in themselves religious; they are human. Dostoevsky's aspirations clustered around God, Mayakovsky's around the social revolution. The intensity of the aspiration, its beauty and loftiness, may be the same; its object is different—as different as science is from religion."

I said I wanted to visit a worker's home unannounced. We entered one at random. No one expected us. The two women and two children inside were surprised by our visit in their ordinary morning routine of washing and drinking tea. Politely they asked us to come in. The new house had two rooms, was full of sunlight, solid, comfortable. Through the window we could see the shrubs and trees transplanted into the arid soil of Baku. The Soviet regime, I was told, had installed an irrigation system; wherever it built houses for workers it also planted trees. The beauties of nature, so much celebrated by bourgeois poets but so seldom seen in working-class neighborhoods, were here at the disposal of the Soviet workers.

"In addition to free housing," the engineer explained, "the worker gets free medical treatment and free social insurance. This summer three thousand workers are being sent to sanatoria for rest periods ranging from four to six weeks. These sanatoria are free, and the worker continues to get full pay during his vacation."

"All these things are free?"

"No, not really free," the engineer said. "Our oil trust does not give away something of its own to the workers as a favor. Ours is a workers' state, our industry is controlled by the workers. The free houses, schools, sanatoria, workers' clubs, cinemas, medical care and so on come out of the profits which the workers themselves produce. In your country that profit goes to a few private capitalists; here it becomes a social wage which supplements the money wage."

We drove on past the old barracks built for the oil workers by the Swedish magnate Nobel, who owned the oil fields before the revolution. This kindly philanthropist had invented dynamite, and founded the Nobel prizes for peace, literature and science. His goodness of heart, however, did not extend to the workers who drilled his profits from the oil wells. The barracks were long and dingy, like solid, identical, filthy tenements in the slums of New York or Passaic.

From there we rode on to the garden city which the Soviet regime was building for the oil workers—the city called Stenka Razin, after the famous peasant revolutionary of the seventeenth century. From the high hill behind the city rose Stenka's monument.

In the offices of the project we found the construction director at his desk in the customary white belted blouse. He was working on a diagram, his shaved head bowed under a lithograph of Lenin which carried the slogan:

EVERY KOPECK SAVED MEANS MILLIONS FOR OUR ECONOMY!

This was a building project: at home the construction director would be a "realtor," like my father. There would be salesmen pouring out carefully memorized paragraphs designed to sell bricks, shingles, toilet seats, plumbing and fire insurance to the builders.

There would be bargaining, speculating, lying, cheating, exaggeration —the pursuit of profit. There would be "agents" seeking to sell you a house, whether you could afford it or not. Here was clean-cut constructive work for a social end; there was no struggle or intrigue for personal gain. You could not buy a house in Stenka Razin if you wanted to; these houses were being built by the workers for themselves out of the profits of their oil industry. Lucky director, who was no realtor but a creator. Proudly he showed us the plan of the town.

"There will be ten thousand homes for workers, and two thousand for doctors, officials and other functionaries. We shall have three sections, each with its own central labor palace, theater and workers' club. There will be schools and hospitals, built by the oil trust, by Azneft, but distributed to the workers by their trade union according to each family's needs."

We inspected the completed section of the garden city. It reminded me of those sections of Flatbush where only the middle classes could afford to live. The houses, all white for the semitropical climate, ran from two to eight rooms, and some to sixteen. There were bathrooms with showers, American folding beds, parquet floors, green hedges outside. I remembered the dark holes of the Passaic textile workers.

On the way home, the engineer said casually that he and two colleagues had invented an improved method of drilling which would increase oil production three times.

"What do you personally get out of it?" I asked.

"What do you mean?" His eyes were blank, uncomprehending.

"In America such an invention might bring you millions."

"We gave it to the government, of course."

"And your incentive, your reward?"

"I see what you mean." He laughed heartily. "You think a man cannot work unless he thinks he is going to become a Rockefeller. Yes, we shall get a prize, perhaps two thousand rubles. But that is not what you call our incentive. Our job pays us good wages; we are economically secure. But our incentive is something else. We—my two colleagues and I—are part owners of the oil industry, just as the workers are. We are, all of us in this country, part owners of the whole national economy. When it gains as a whole, we gain as individuals. Our incomes rise, our standards of living improve, our culture becomes higher, we move nearer to socialism. Can there be a greater incentive in life?"

§ 4

Strange fragment, magically transmuting past into present, fore-shadowing the future. At Techeretz I had to wait all afternoon for a Stalingrad train. Here was the twin of my vanished village, redolent with old things. The streets were unpaved mud or crudely cobble-stoned. A happy, fragrant stillness, warm with sunlight, lay over the little town. There was the church, and the bells were pealing nostalgi-cally as they did when I lay in the garden of our old house wondering about God. Geese waddled down the gutter, cackling dead memories to life. When you walk through strange towns touching only surfaces they are always beautiful, for you touch only dreams, you are out-side of everything. But look farther: the pigs in that courtyard foul the doorway; against the wooden sidewalk the peasant lies in rags, filthy, brutal, disintegrated, fragment of the old, vicious world. Who speaks romantically of the old village life? Metropolitan poets in far-off Gramercy Park, fleeing imaginatively from the machine to fantasy villages. Much wiser is Maxim Gorky who knew the poverty and cruelty of the old Russian village, and wiser still he who, surveying the world as a whole, poked his finger through the gaudy metaphor, say-ing: *the idiocy of the village.*

I need not go to my own village; I have seen here the trees, the skies, the gardens that will be retained, and the flies, the dirt, the alcoholism, the ignorance that will be abolished. But, see, there is the village park, like the one where my sister and I once watched a circus and wandered off to find the point on the horizon where you could enter the sky. There is a workers' club whose doorway carries a sign: Red October. Farther on, a team of boys is playing basketball against a team of girls, a fast, brisk game, and the girls are giving the boys a run for their money. In my day, Russia had no sports, at least not for the people. Gifts of the new life: ideas, machinery, sports. This game might be played in Michigan, Texas or California. The sixteen-year-old faces are radiant with health and high animal spirits.

"Hey, Shura, Shura, throw the ball here!"

"Quick, Maruska, shoot!"

At the edge of the park stood a high platform, on it a table covered with a red cloth and pitchers of water. The workers rapidly filled the rows of benches. The chairman tightened his blouse:

"Comrades, we shall now elect a presidium. Any nominations?"

The young man next to me whispered:

"So you are an American journalist? Interesting. I used to be a peasant, now I am a worker. Too bad, I am still illiterate; but I am taking courses, I am learning. But Alyosha over there has learned to read. Hey, Alyosha, meet my American comrade. Two years ago Alyosha couldn't read a word, now he reads and writes well, and we are all proud of him."

"Any more nominations?" the chairman said.

"Alyosha Goncharov!" my neighbor boomed.

"All in favor? Unanimous."

Alyosha grinned, shook my hand, and went up to the platform.

When I went for my train, I found the floor of the railway station crowded with peasants in rags asleep across their bags and baskets. Their faces were red from the sun and weary with travel. The train was due in two hours; if we did not get seats on this one, we would have to wait for the next train. Squatting on benches or bundles, mothers opened their blouses, took out huge breasts, fed their babies. The station zoomed with talk. People crowded at the ticket window yelling and quarreling for first place. A militiaman with a rifle strapped across his shoulder tried to keep order. A young peasant woman suckling her baby stopped a pale young man with eyeglasses and a cane.

"Please, citizen, I can't interrupt my baby, will you please buy my ticket for me?"

"Gladly, citizen. Hey, there, let me through this line; the ticket is for a nursing mother, citizens!"

The line at the ticket window—the *ocherid*—sagged. A Red army man inadvertently pushed a peasant out of his place.

"*Yop tvoyoo mat!*" the peasant shouted.

"I beg your pardon," the soldier said. "Here, take my place. You seem to be in a hurry."

When my turn at the ticket window came, I found that my study of the Russian language had not gone far. I could read better than I could speak. A German colonist from the Volga came to my rescue, supported by a Russian worker who knew some German. We got our tickets, went to the buffet, drank vodka and talked.

"These people on the floor," the German colonist explained, "are peasants leaving the village for jobs in the city. That's our industrial revolution."

"How do American workers live?" the young Russian said. "Why doesn't America give us credit? Why do you give credit to sons of bitches like Mussolini and Pilsudski and not to us who are building socialism? What we need now is machinery; as soon as we have machinery, we'll be all right."

On the train I jotted down in my notebook: *Seeing what life is like in a country without machinery, I think of our bright young literati at home who satirize American mechanization and standardization. They think what's wrong with America is machinery; what's really wrong is capitalism. The literary revolt against the machine is the revolt of unimaginative middle-class minds demanding that society supply them with literary themes like those which they had studied at college.*

The Soviet citizen was different; he was not an isolated fragment, he was part of an organic whole. When he said Russia needed machinery, he repeated what the Soviet press was saying, but he repeated the truth. At home, the world was divided into ideals and realities. The ideals obscured the realities; they rationalized the privileges of the ruling class. Here ideal and reality were part of the same process; the ideal was based on reality, reality was transformed in the light of the ideal. And again there hammered through my head: this is not Russian; Marx was not Russian; Lenin was not Russian; Debs was not Russian. The reality-ideal of socialism was world-wide.

By the time I took the eight-day trip by boat up the Volga from Stalingrad to Nizhnii Novgorod, the fragments easily assumed their meaning. You realized after two minutes' conversation that the passengers on vacation were not, as a rule, bolsheviks or workers or peasants, but Nepmen and old-fashioned intellectuals, and their complaints and enthusiasms were no surprise.

"So you are an American, a writer. Do you personally know the famous American author David Freedman?"

"David Freedman?"

"Yes, he writes those charming sketches about Mendel Marantz."

"I've read one or two in the *Saturday Evening Post*. How do you come to know them?"

"Our State Publishing House has translated them in four small pamphlets; they sell in the hundreds of thousands."

"And in America it is said that the Soviet regime has killed all literature and permits the people to read only bolshevik propaganda."

"Ha! ha! ha! And Pushkin and Dostoevsky and Tolstoy? Why,

all the old classics have ten times as many readers as in the old days. Remember, millions who were illiterate have learned to read."

Even the Nepman was proud of that. He was a plump, jolly man with a thick, black beard and glasses, and he enjoyed the light sketches of David Freedman, and our highbrows at home knew nothing of Babel, Seifulina, Vsevolod Ivanov, Mayakovsky, Leonov, Furmanov, and lamented the death of art in the Soviet Union. The Nepman liked to sit at the piano, surrounded by fat ladies, and sing sadly Lenski's aria from *Eugene Onegin,* or artificial gypsy music remembered from the old inns:

> Driver, O lash not your steed,
> I've no place to which I must speed,
> I've no love whose call I must heed,
> Driver, O lash not your steed!

Below decks, in steerage, the peasants, crowded in rags around the freight, sang in chorus, as always, the melancholy songs of the village. One of the passengers, a Jew of about forty-five, boasted to me:

"I am now the head of an artel, I work with my own hands, I am a member of a trade union. Before the revolution I was rich, I had land, a big business, an eight-room house, two servants. And do you know—my wife and I like it better now. Strange, isn't it? First of all, a Jew can breathe freely; we are all equals; no more pogroms, no more ghettos. When I was a young man I studied engineering in Germany, but I never practiced the profession, I went into business instead. But I learned good habits from the Germans. Do you see this little notebook? That's where I jot down the names and addresses of new acquaintances, the names of books and newspapers to be read, everything I want to remember. That's my German training."

"You are not dissatisfied with the present regime?"

"Personally, I am not badly off. The thing I don't like is that the bolsheviks are trying to do in ten years what must take at least a hundred. Communism is a fine idea—but where does the illiterate peasant come to practice it? You must always take the muzhik into consideration."

"Then you would like to see the Soviet regime fall?"

"God in heaven, no! If the Soviet government falls, Russia will be ruined, the Jews will be massacred." He thought a moment and added: "Still, I wish I could go to America, not for myself, you understand, but for my daughter."

He sighed, and went on:

"She's nineteen, you understand, a good girl, but she has one trouble. She's talented. Perhaps you think that's no trouble, but I'll tell you: medicine she doesn't want to study; she wants to play the piano and to paint. Where can that lead to? It takes years to develop painting and musical talents, then who can be sure of making a living at it?"

Remembering my own childhood, I could not help laughing; philistinism was international.

"Just now she works in a factory. She is, you understand, a Comsomol, a young communist. I don't agree with her, but naturally I must follow a diplomatic course. You know how modern children are; if you tell them something is bad, they insist on doing it. So I go easy. Fortunately, she is not a hothead; she thinks a little for herself. But what good is this Comsomol stuff? My opinion is that the younger generation is not as interesting as the old one. Maybe the third generation, the Pioneers, will amount to something; but the second generation is spoiled. In the old days, you understand, a revolutionist fought his way through everything. When he had an idea, it was because he had mastered it himself; he had nothing to gain by parroting other people's ideas. But these young people lazily read pamphlets and refuse to use their heads. They know very little; all they know is abortions. Now if my daughter were in America—"

"She would go to Greenwich Village?"

"To what?"

"To bohemia. She would leave your house and set up a so-called studio and play the piano and paint and have abortions anyway. But she probably would not be a Comsomol, so you ought to be thankful and keep her here."

"I think this is all the result of the new Russian literature," the old man complained. "Today it's terribly free, you understand. They write things now that no one would have dared mention before the revolution. Here's one writer, for example, who says: His wife was the kind of woman who would lift up her skirts to her hips in public. A fine way to write!"

"Why blame the revolution?" I said. "We have a writer named James Joyce who is even freer than that." How, I thought, could one explain similar social and literary phenomena in capitalist America and Bolshevik Russia? The younger generation, abortions, outspoken novels. The explanation must have a Marxian base, but what was it?

Obviously nothing so childish and simple as the mechanical explanation so far given by certain writers at home.

One night, as our boat was heading up the Volga for Kazan, I got into conversation with a handsome woman of about thirty, a lawyer's daughter. Holding her white fingers tight on the ship's railing, she lamented the fate of Russia's intelligentsia:

"I am desperate. The future is a dark iron wall. Here on the ship or the bottom of the Volga—it's all the same to me. I can't read their propaganda, Lenin's brochures and Stalin's. Mayakovsky is a megalomaniac. An idiot could improve *Mandat*. What have I to look forward to? I'm only thirty, yet I feel I'd be better off dead."

She sighed and walked off to her cabin. A young sailor standing near by at the railing came over and said to me:

"Excuse me, it was impolite, but I could not help overhearing. You feel sorry for the lady? So do I. But what can one do? They are chained to the past. The past is dead, and they want to die with it. I fought in the Baltic fleet. How many workers died in the exploiters' wars who did not want to die? Let them perish on yesterday's scaffold; we have a new world to live for. Look, have you seen our club?"

We went through the ship. Officers and men had the same quarters, the same food. If only Pete and Sam were here. . . . The sailors were not outcasts or pariahs; they were part of the ruling class. The club had a good library, a phonograph, a wall newspaper. I noticed a clipping headed: "Excerpt from Comrade Stalin's speech in Tiflis."

"I saw Comrade Stalin in the Tiflis opera," I said. "He didn't speak."

"Why should he?" The young sailor laughed. "Is he an actor? He spoke the same night at the Railway Workers' Club: that's where you should have been if you wanted to hear him."

The clipping read: "The Polish state, Comrade Stalin said, has entered on a phase of complete disintegration. The financial system is breaking down. The Zloty is falling. Industry is crippled. The non-Polish nationalities are being suppressed; and above, in the circles of the ruling classes, there prevails a perfect orgy of fraud and embezzlement, as is quite openly admitted by representatives of all factions in the Seim. These contradictions are connected with three main questions: the labor question, the peasant question and the national question. Can Pilsudski, can the motley Pilsudski crowd solve these contradictions? Can this petit-bourgeois group solve the labor question? No. After defeating the bourgeoisie militarily, the Pilsudski group will cling to its coattails politically, and become the representative of chauvinism and fascism."

"Why does he speak of Poland at this time?" I asked.

"There is talk," the sailor said, "that Poland may attack us."

"But they won't get away with it," another sailor said. The room had filled with seamen, neatly dressed and shaved. We were introduced all around, and the usual exchange of questions and answers followed—about Russia, about America. These men were by natural endowment no more intelligent, and no less, than the men on our freighter; yet they had a keen sense for economics and politics; they were conscious of the essential forces of contemporary life; they felt themselves masters of the ship, of their country. The wall newspaper, containing their articles, poems and stories, hung openly in their clubroom and the officers were as proud of it as the men. I noticed some drawings on it.

"Who is the artist?"

Someone stuck his head out the door, and yelled in a deep bass voice:

"Vaska!"

A sixteen-year-old, blond and blue-eyed boy came into the room panting as if he had run down a flight of stairs.

"Yes, comrades?"

"This is our artist," one of the sailors said. Vaska blushed.

"Those things are very bad. I have better ones in my portfolio." He opened a desk drawer and brought out a large envelope and laid out a series of water colors.

"These are very fine," I said. "Where did you learn to paint?"

"By myself. Six months in the year I'm a cabin boy and six months I work on a farm. In my spare time I draw."

"But he is leaving the Volga," one of the sailors said. "Our trade union is sending him to Moscow to study in an art school. We'll pay for his studies and give him his living expenses, and he'll become a great artist, won't you, Vaska?"

"I'll try to be a good one," Vaska said, blushing.

It was not necessary, then, for talent to perish in frustration because your parents were too poor to let you study art, or because they were rich and wanted you to be a lawyer or a businessman. Lucky Vaska, who lived in the proletarian state. But did the sincere artist have to wait until October to unfold his gifts? Did not Bill Gropper, a genius among cartoonists, find fulfillment in the revolutionary movement of a capitalist country? Here on this Volga boat I thought of him, returning from a bread and butter chore for a bourgeois newspaper, frustrated and disgruntled, to sit down at his drawing board and turn out with a happy smile a profusion of drawings for the working-class press of America.

BOOK FIVE

CHAPTER I

NEW FOUND LAND

> . . . the seed
> springing to flower, flinging its color, its breath,
> into the long-patient channels of our need—
> silent no longer!
>
> —EDWIN ROLFE.

§ 1

MOSCOW was quiet the Sunday morning I arrived; people were walking along the streets with relative ease. Civil war was a memory; the struggle of the classes had shifted its form. Externally, the conflict was now less dramatic; there were no military charges and counter-charges. At home the newspapers had told us Russia was still an armed camp; yet on the surface everything here appeared tranquil. Where were the grim, unsmiling faces you had read about? People were poorly dressed, but were not ashamed of it. Even on Sunday morning they moved in the streets with energy and purpose. The air was electric with a common thought beating through all minds.

Here was the Kremlin, facing Red Square; the Asiatic palace, church and fortress; the high wall under which John Reed slept. And here, starkly dominating the square, was Lenin's tomb.

What a sensitive, thoughtful face Lenin had. His hair was reddish, and his beard too. The hands were small and fine. A long queue of workers and peasants moved slowly and reverently past the embalmed figure.

Outside the vault a peasant buttonholed a Red army soldier.

"You know, comrade, I always thought Ilytch was a big man, and here he's such a little fellow."

"Ilytch was not big, citizen. He was only great."

"The body is a miracle. It's almost alive. A real miracle."

"No, citizen. There are no miracles. This is science."

The soldier explained the Egyptian art of embalming, its loss, its rediscovery in modern times on another level. A crowd gathered. The Red soldier, his shoulders squared, talked like a schoolteacher to a kindergarten, with a curious mixture of pride and humility. An old peasant with long white hair pushed himself forward.

"You seem to know a lot, comrade. Tell me, then, why do we have to pay such high taxes? Why does the government support the poor peasant? Do you know why the fool is poor? Because he is lazy! They call me kulak. Why am I a kulak? Because I work hard."

"You are a kulak because you have land and horses," the soldier said. "The poor peasant has no land and horses."

"It's his own fault! I work hard, and he is a lazy good-for-nothing."

"That's too simple, citizen. Take a kulak. His father has good land and horses. From the day he is born, good health is his. His mother's milk is excellent."

Beads of sweat stood out on the soldier's face. He wiped them off with his sleeve and went on:

"At the age of eight the young kulak goes to school. At fourteen his father teaches him farming and handicrafts. By eighteen he is an able man. Now take the other peasant. He is born in poverty. His mother can't take care of him. At eight, while you are at school, he has to herd swine. He gets no education, learns no trade. What is the result, citizen? He grows up to be an ignorant, filthy son of a bitch. This inequality is unjust. We are going to abolish it."

"Don't let these kulaks boast of their wonderful energy," a high-pitched voice broke in. A peasant with rags around his legs made his way through the crowd, amidst growls of "where to, citizen?" He bent his head under the kulak's chin and shouted: "We know what your energy is for. It's to exploit us! I have a farm outside of Moscow. What does it bring me? Nothing. The kulak who loans out his horses takes it all!"

"Where is your farm, comrade?" the soldier said gravely.

The peasant named his village, and the Red army man jotted it down in a notebook.

"I'll report this to the Party," he said. "The matter will be investigated."

"Great thanks," said the peasant with the *lapti*. "And as long as you are reporting things, there's something else you can report. In our village the young communists stand outside the church and shout bad names at us as we go in and out. Is that right, comrade, or is it wrong?"

"Wrong." The soldier wrote rapidly in his notebook. "We are against superstition. We want to educate all the people in science. But anyone who wants to go to church can do so. The young comrades in your village will be disciplined. I'll see to that."

If communism was a new religion, it was certainly different from the immaculate conception, from the wafer that was the body of a man-god and the wine that was his blood; from the saints, long dead, who performed miracles from the grave; from the priests who betrayed the people, covering poverty and war with the mantle of sanctity. You felt that the man whose body lay in the wooden tomb facing Red Square was a prophet only metaphorically. He was a man who had aroused a class, an entire country to the meaning of scientific knowledge.

He had profoundly affected your own life too; yet how little you knew about him. Six years ago, standing under the vault of Napoleon's tomb in Paris, you had been filled with bitter and cynical thoughts. The imperialist war which you had hated seemed to be the incarnation of the Napoleonic spirit, of the propertied classes who idolized Bonaparte. You had set down your reflections in verse: kill, plunder, rape for empire and for glory; posterity is mightier than heaven; if you are vanquished all shall be forgotten; and if you conquer all shall be forgiven.

Lenin had filled you with hope, had given you a purpose in life by pointing the way to universal freedom. Yet think what the bourgeoisie had said about him, and was still saying at that very moment. And not the unscrupulous propagandists alone who knew they were lying; but the mensheviks too; and the social democrats; and the liberals and the men of letters who fancied themselves above the battle, divinely impartial. They had called Soviet Russia a one-man dictatorship; they had compared Lenin to Genghis Khan and Peter the Great. He was said to have been a barbarous, Asiatic slave who had risen to absolute personal power, thanks to the accidents of history and the dark ignorance of the Russian masses. We in the West, thank heaven, could never have such an overlord. And how had he seized power? As a paid agent of the German general staff! He was a man driven by a fixed idea; a ruthless utopian, ready to exterminate half of mankind for a private futile dream.

This was the view of Lenin with which the mensheviks and liberals had filled the press of the West. Those of us who accepted communism did not believe a word of that black legend. John Reed and Albert Rhys Williams and Robert Minor and Lincoln Steffens and even that good bourgeois, Colonel Raymond Robbins, had given us quite a different picture of Lenin. He was the opposite of everything our enemies said. He was no crazy fanatic, but the greatest political genius which the world had seen in centuries. An inflexible will combined with a flexible mind made him a powerful thinker, organizer and fighter; yet he was utterly selfless, interested in all things human, full of a great love of men.

Now you saw and felt the boundless admiration and love which the Russian people, bolshevik and nonbolshevik alike, had for this proletarian leader. Lenin's work was everywhere. He had thought with irresistible clarity on economics and politics, the trade unions and the army, art and literature, agriculture and child training; and all his mighty thinking had been directed toward the great objective of the proletariat, the classless communist society. Lenin had repudiated bourgeois democracy because it was a fraud, but he was no Genghis Khan or Mussolini. Was it not he who had told the Russian communists: We can govern only if we understand how to express truly what the people think and feel; only he who believes in the people, who again and again dives into the pulsating tide of its activities will keep power? The power he had in mind was not personal.

In Tiflis a communist had told me this story:

In the spring of 1921, Lenin spoke at a transport workers' congress held in Moscow.

"Just now, as I came into your hall," Lenin said, "I saw a poster with the inscription: 'there will be no end to the kingdom of the workers and the peasants.' And when I read that strange poster, which, to tell the truth, was not hanging in the usual place, but somewhere in a corner, as though someone had guessed that the poster was not quite right and had put it out of the way—when I read this strange poster, I thought: 'well, and even about such relatively elementary and fundamental things as this, there exist among us misunderstanding and incorrect ideas.' For, indeed, if there were to be no end to the kingdom of the workers and the peasants, that would mean that there would never be socialism; since socialism means the abolition of classes. So long as there are workers and peasants there will be different classes, and consequently there cannot be complete socialism."

The Tiflis communist had proudly showed me a copy of this speech. Every worker in the Soviet Union was equally proud of Lenin's simplicity and directness in speaking out the truth, in fighting against communist smugness, in persistently pointing to the goal of the revolution as well as to every necessary immediate detail. Workers would explain Lenin to you by saying: Lenin, that's us.

Yet "impartial" scribes had distorted this great leader's character. And if it was possible to falsify the character of a dominant individual, whom you could know more or less through his public utterances and actions, how much easier it was to distort the life of an entire country.

Furious against French feudalism, Voltaire had studied and applauded the parliamentary England of the bourgeoisie, urged it as a model for his own countrymen. Later the European middle classes looked on the France of Danton as the sublime symbol of liberty; the poets of England and France sang odes to it. In the nineteenth century democratic America became the model of freedom and equality. And now that the word freedom had come to mean something new, many men throughout the world looked to Russia as the Pharos that illumined the way in the surrounding darkness.

But Revolutionary France had had its Edmund Burke, and Revolutionary Russia had a thousand Edmund Burkes who distorted and maligned and cursed that which was bound to triumph.

It was necessary for us to understand the new Russia; here socialism was being created for the first time in the history of man. But how do you get to know a vast country covering one-sixth of the earth, half in Europe, half in Asia, with multitudes of races and tongues, and various, contrasting levels of culture ranging from the nomads of the north to the Putilov works in Leningrad?

I decided to live and work in the Soviet Union for a year, to study the language, to visit factories and farms, to participate in the organizational life of the country. Because I did not write Russian well enough, I could not get a job on a Soviet newspaper, and instead earned my living as a translator. I saw the country first from a routine job, as an "intellectual worker," through meetings and reports, through conversations and hearsay; later I took an extensive trip through various regions.

I had come to the Soviet Union entirely prepossessed in its favor. However impartial I might try to be, I could not help seeing Soviet life from the communist viewpoint. That did not mean that you ignored difficulties. It only meant that your attitude toward difficulties differed from the anti-Soviet observer's. The banker, the bourgeois politico, the liberal scribe exclaimed:

"Aha, I told you so; they make mistakes; they are incompetent; socialism is a crazy dream; it is bound to fail."

The communist, seeing the same difficulties, said:

"This is a hardship to be overcome; this is a mistake that is being corrected and will be avoided in the future."

But if I had been animated only by the communist viewpoint, there would be nothing to tell here in this story, which is not about Russia but about the education of one man. The fact is that in Moscow I once more realized how deeply rooted I was in the bourgeois world. Alongside of communist thought and belief, there existed in me the various illusions I had absorbed in the schools, the streets, the books of capitalist civilization. It was one thing to believe in an idea abstractly, quite another to come up against it in the flesh. Reality had a way of shaking dreams and reviving prejudices: logically you may justify war; in the trenches you will perhaps throw down your gun and run in terror.

Had I been a worker, accustomed to factory life, I might have thought about the Soviet scene differently; but I had been trained in letters; I still saw the world through the art of Western Europe and America, the art of the bourgeoisie. Intellectually I was fighting against it. Deep in my heart its values were still alive and potent. Consequently my year in Soviet Russia was not only one of the most exciting and instructive of my whole life, but also one of the most confusing and painful.

§ 2

Looking for work as a translator, I went to the offices of the Communist International. The representative of the American party to the Comintern was Comrade Duncan, a huge, bass-voiced native of North Dakota.

"Have you a letter of recommendation from our Party?" he asked.

"No."

"That's funny. Have you been misbehaving?"

"Not that I know of."

"Maybe it's just an oversight. Write home for one."

I wrote at once to New York, and received a reply from Fred. It was formally favorable, but written in such negative phrases that when you read it through to the end it seemed more like an indictment than a recommendation. Duncan studied the letter for a moment and his face flushed red.

"Personal jealousy," he said, his deep voice agitated with contempt. In those days you did not conceal your private affairs; everybody knew about Greta, Fred and myself. I was terribly upset. Fred was using his position to exercise Party "discipline" over me. In spite of my background, I did not mind genuine discipline. In goal and form, Party discipline differed from other disciplines which had been imposed upon me, or which I had voluntarily accepted. Party members participated in the shaping of policy. Abstractly, discipline could be criticized, but only as against a purely fanciful freedom. I had known the dark discipline of religion, the heartless discipline of the army, the discipline of schools and colleges. Did not the newspaper impose discipline upon its workers? And was there no discipline of a kind among the aesthetes, those grotesque beings who imagined themselves most free of it, who talked most airily against it? First came the market, and the men who controlled the market. America was a free country, but if you wanted to succeed as a writer you had to play the literary game. That was discipline. In the Party you also had the freedom to walk out; you could retire from revolutionary activity as easily as from letters, but if you wanted to follow either, you had to accept its discipline. Even among the anarchists at Stelton there had been authority. As for the world at large, did we not all live in the kingdom of necessity, whose discipline was merciless? Were the Passaic strikers free? the sailors on the freighter? It was not discipline that disturbed me; without it the people could not destroy oppression and build a new world. But there was the abuse of discipline. That disturbed the faith which Scott Nearing had expressed so passionately, the dream that even now, before the ideal of the classless society was fully realized, we should conduct ourselves in the light of that ideal. A communist should be wiser and better than a bourgeois; he should be more honest, more just. It was this dream which Fred's letter had jarred. I must have betrayed my feelings, for Duncan suddenly pulled his cap down over his eyes and said with unexpected sharpness:

"Pay no attention to this. I'll recommend you for a translator's job." He tore the letter to pieces and flung them vigorously into his wastebasket. Suddenly he looked straight into my eyes and said quietly: "Why are you so blue?"

"If a . . . bureaucrat like Fred . . ." I stammered, "if he can use his political position to take personal vengeance, how are we better than the bourgeoisie?" Duncan stood up and said slowly in his deep voice:

"I'm ashamed of you, simply ashamed. You talk like a Greenwich Village poet. How can you expect a political party to be composed exclusively of saints? The predatory system under which men have been living for thousands of years doesn't produce many saints. If you expect socialism to come from noble people alone, you are nothing but a liberal, a damned liberal. We must work with such people as actually exist. It's not the individual but the Party that counts. The Party is different from the bourgeoisie. You see that Fred, vindictive as he is, hasn't the last word. If you are a good bolshevik, no man, however highly placed, can hurt you for merely personal reasons. Don't you think that's something of an advance in the barbarous history of mankind?"

Thanks to Duncan, the Comintern became one of the places where I translated. I was assigned to the bureau which turned into English various documents, appeals, speeches and articles originally written in Russian, French and German. We had an office of two well-lighted rooms in the Comintern Building on the Mokhovaya. You came at nine o'clock in the morning and punched a time clock. This innovation was a result of the current campaign for efficiency. You worked two hours and at eleven went to the restaurant downstairs for "second breakfast." Here the Comintern workers came in shifts, young and old, men and women of every nationality in the world, leaders like Piatnitzky and Kuusinin and Duncan and Roy and Sen Katayama, and typists like Esther and Milly. You got your food as in an American cafeteria by filling a tray from the long table at the end of the room, and you ate sandwiches German style—the open Butterbrot. The food was mediocre, the conversation excellent and always in three or four languages and mostly about the political events of the day in Russia, Germany, England, America, China, Japan, Italy, Mexico.

Outside, in the capitalist world, the Comintern was painted as a den of monsters seeking to "destroy civilization." We knew it for what it was: the heir of the First International, which Marx had founded, with headquarters in New York; and of the revolutionary epoch of the Second International which had its headquarters in Western Europe. The Comintern did not run the Soviet government; it was not a branch of the Soviet government; it had no official connection with it. It was the international center of the communist parties of all countries in the same way that the Second International was the center of the socialist parties of all countries. The capitalist governments did not demand that Holland should expel the Second International from its territory; they did demand that Russia should expel the Comintern from its territory. The reason appeared obvious to us: the Dutch government was capitalist; the Second International was indirectly aiding capitalism. Russia, on the other hand, was building toward communism, and the Comintern was headed in the same direction. The very governments which had since 1917 carried on a persistent campaign against the Soviet regime, which had lied about it and slandered it, which had forged documents against it, the very governments which had invaded and blockaded Russia, now drew up intricate legal documents asserting that the U.S.S.R. was interfering in their domestic affairs through the Comintern. Bourgeois spies and agents provocateurs raided Soviet commercial agencies abroad to establish some connection between the Soviet government and the Comintern. They were never able to do so. Nevertheless the foreign office of every bourgeois state kept shouting: deliver this man unto us, throw out the communists from Moscow, where they are safe, and force them to work among us where we may imprison and kill them and crush their movement. It seemed to us that what the bourgeois states wanted were the heads not of Soviet officials allegedly interfering in their domestic affairs—that was out of the question; they wanted the heads of their "own" nationals. Most of the Comintern leaders had been opponents of capitalism before 1917; it was not Moscow but Japan that had made a communist of Sen Katayama; Finland converted Kuusinin; America, Browder; Germany, Clara Zetkin; France, Marcel Cachin. These had turned to Russia because the proletariat had first come to power there. Had the socialist revolution taken place in Germany, the Comintern would have chosen Berlin as its safest center, and the Czar would have protested against German interference in Russian affairs. In stressing the alleged relations between the Soviet government and the Comintern, the bourgeois states were seeking not only to harm the U.S.S.R. diplomatically, but to conceal a fact most embarrassing to them, namely, that the Comintern represented the rebellion of their "own" slaves, a revolt seven decades older than the Soviet regime, a revolt which did not proceed from but caused the Soviet regime itself.

If you knew anything about communism, you knew this; so you were not surprised, when you saw Manuilsky or Remmelle in the lunchroom, to find that they had no horns, or cloven hoofs, or tails. Surprise came from another quarter. In our bureau, handling the most confidential Comintern documents, were non-Party members. The fastest, most prolific, most efficient translator was a little old lady with white hair. She had been a Russian menshevik who had lived for many years in London. Now she was politically a skeptic who, under the Comintern roof, did not hesitate to mock the bolsheviks. She would come in quietly in the morning, put her umbrella and rubbers in the corner, wrap a black lace shawl around her bent shoulders and dictate to one of the girls—who were also non-Party. This was the period of the great inner Party struggle between the Central Committee and the Opposition. At home, gossips had published hysterical complaints that the Opposition was suppressed and its utterances kept from the Party: in our translation bureau we worked over speeches by the Opposition as well as by members of the majority of the Central Committee. Day in and day out we labored over words and phrases, rendering them into English, and in this way we got to know by heart the arguments pro and con in the debate over whether or not socialism could be built in one country. Whatever thoughts the rest of us may have had, our little old menshevik only laughed.

"Stalin thinks he is a theoretician," she would cackle. "He can't put two and two together. Did you ever see an arrogant ass like Trotsky? Zinoviev is an old woman." The last judgment was one of her favorites, ironical on the lips of an old woman, and showing the immense power of the cliché. Zinoviev was still chairman of the Comintern, hence our little menshevik's boss, so to speak. "In my time," she would say, "schoolboys could argue better than these people. And they are fighting for the honor of building socialism in our country. A plague on both their houses!"

Such remarks infuriated the head of our bureau, an Irishwoman in her middle forties whom, from her initials, we called O. B. She, too, was non-Party. For years she had moved in the radical literary and political circles of Dublin and London. Liam O'Flaherty was one of her friends, and her favorite "genius."

"Oh, he's a wild one!" O. B. would tell me. "Drunk as a lord and crazy for the women but, mark my word, he'll be the pride of English literature."

O. B. had spent a number of years in the suffrage fight under the Pankhursts, then followed them into labor journalism. When I met her as my boss in the translation bureau, she had been in the Soviet Union five years, a devoted friend and bitter critic of the new regime. When I became what she considered too enthusiastic, she would say: "Say that in your sonnets, but don't mix poetry with facts." But when our little menshevik lady got too critical, she would say: "Now what in hell is she kicking about? She ought to be glad she's not in jail. She gets paid three times as much as the rest of us. You've got to take Party pay, I get more because I'm non-Party, but that old growler gets paid by piecework, and what an apartment she has! Like a princess. And she's kicking about Stalin and Trotsky. I suppose her idea of a good socialist is that cheap ham actor Ramsay MacDonald."

O. B.'s best friend in Moscow was an American girl named Ruth, the ex-wife of a Methodist minister from the Middle West, and now the Comintern librarian, although she, too, was not a Party member. Both women vacillated between romantic adoration and bitter despair over the Soviet system. If the water stopped running in their rooms, or they couldn't get a bath for a week, or they found gravel in a sandwich, they would bitterly attack bolshevism from the day Lenin learned to say *mama* to the particular episode which galled them; if they saw a stirring parade in Red Square, or a play in the trade-union theater, or a new Soviet film, or a demonstration of Pioneers, they would bubble over with joy and praise.

§ 3

All Comintern workers lived in either the Lux or the Bristol. Both hotels were on the Tverskaya. The Lux was an old building occupying half a block. One lower corner was occupied by a NEP restaurant run by the Czar's baker. The Lux hallway was dim, and the lift usually out of order. A clerk at the desk challenged every visitor. Who are you? whom do you want to see? You had to show your "documents," to prove your identity. You understand, comrade, we cannot permit everyone to come in. Many of our people are refugees from the fascist governments of the capitalist countries; it is said that a bourgeois spy killed one of our comrades right in this hallway. Here is your *propusk*.

The *propusk* was a permit to enter the building; it showed the time you came, the person you visited, the time you left.

For the room you got you paid a small rental in proportion to your income. My own was a fairly large one, with two windows and two beds. I shared it with an English comrade, a tall, dreamy Oxford graduate who specialized in British labor problems. He was an omnivorous reader, devouring documents, speeches, statistical reports. Now and then he would catch himself reading Stendhal or Tolstoy. He would throw the book on the floor, and exclaim:

"To hell with that stuff!"

"What's wrong with it?"

"It's fine, it's great," he would say. "But I'm not a literary man. I have only twenty-four hours a day and must read for profit, not for pleasure."

I recognized the guilt-sense of the penitent nobleman. Workers the world over were reading Tolstoy without the slightest qualm of conscience. My Oxford roommate had, in addition to his exaggerated intellectual puritanism, a boundless adoration of M. N. Roy, at that time a leader of the Communist party of India, and living in the Lux as representative to the Comintern. Roy was a handsome and clever fellow, but my roommate was kidded about his adulation. The German comrades especially were merciless.

"Don't think you can make up for British imperialism by falling in love with a Hindu," they would say. "Why don't you get a sweetheart, so that you can treat Roy like a comrade instead of a god?"

Although this was an extreme case, it opened my eyes to the obvious fact that in the communist movement, as everywhere else, our ideas and attitudes are influenced not only by theses and slogans, policies and reports, but also by warm human relationships. This was certainly true in my own case. It was through no formal organization that I first met various Soviet writers, but through my friendship with O. B. From these writers I learned much, and what they taught me was given as friend to friend. They were for me in Moscow what Irwin Edman, Floyd Dell and Michael Gold had been in New York.

In O. B.'s room I first met Sergei Dinamov, a proletarian critic who specialized in English and American literature; Ossip Beskin, a novelist then at the head of the foreign department of the State Publishing House; the film critic Ivan Anissimov; the futurist poet Asseyev, connected with Mayakovsky's group; and the young, redheaded professor of literature Ivan Kashkin. It was the most natural and normal induction into Soviet letters, for one of the most obvious factors which determined that these men, and not others, should be my daily companions was that they spoke English and were interested in American literature. If they told me about Plekhanov and Yessenin and Voronsky and Furmanov and Gladkov and Libidinsky, I told them about Hemingway and Dell and Anderson and Ben Hecht and H. L. Mencken; I was "propagandizing" them as much as they were "propagandizing" me.

Kashkin would knock at my door, pale in his neat gray overcoat and black muffler. He had never been outside of Russia in his life, but dressed in what he thought was the English fashion.

"Joe, my dear comrade," he would begin in the lyrical style of the old Russia, "you must do me a favor. I must lecture on Carl Sandboorg at the university tonight, and here are words I can't find in any

English dictionary. What to hell means this? and this? and this?" He pointed to a poem by Sandburg in which he had underlined such words as *cahoots, bulls, dicks, fifty-fifty, petemen, dips, boosters, stick-ups, gazump, slant-head.* I explained as best I could. Kashkin borrowed *The Sun Also Rises.*

"For my class," he said.

I knew damned well he would never return the book, and I borrowed his copy of Plekhanov on art, and he knew I would never return it. That's how literati feel about books even in the Soviet Union; it's like "borrowing" a cigarette. But see, Soviet classes are studying our newest American writers; they are interested in everything, they who have "crushed" culture. But I have to ask Kashkin the simplest, most elementary, most childish questions about Soviet thought and art; for in our free democracy, where thought is unfettered, a colossal ignorance prevails about Soviet literature, and nine years after the October Revolution not a single bourgeois publisher has ventured to bring out a single volume by Lenin, if only as an intellectual curiosity.

There were literary evenings in O. B.'s room. Asseyev read his poetry; Dinamov delivered a long discourse on proletarian art; Beskin reminisced about his childhood in the bosom of a bourgeois Russian family, and threatened to write a novel about it. I felt most at home with Dinamov, who introduced me to the staff of his magazine, *Na Literaturnom Postu (At the Literary Post)*. This was the organ of the proletarian writers group—the much talked of RAPP. At that time it was one of several literary groups competing for "hegemony." The fellow travelers were the main show; they had been sustained by a Party resolution which urged free competition in the arts on a socialist basis. Dinamov generously took me to various groups; he introduced me to the famous critic Polonsky, editor of the *Novy Mir,* spokesman for the fellow travelers; and to a "salon" where the fellow travelers met, including the handsome, dark-skinned Leonov. If I gravitated toward the RAPP group it was as a result of those factors which, earlier, had drawn me to the *Masses* and *Liberator* crowd. They, on a higher level, combined that "justice and beauty" which I imagined was my goal, only now we no longer talked about justice and beauty, but of the communist society where alone they could prevail in some pure form. Of all the literary groups in America, that of the *Masses* and *Liberator* had stood nearest to socialism; in Russia I had the same feeling about the RAPP group. I did not formally affiliate with any literary organization; my relations in this field were those of personal friendship, and perhaps at that stage it was the easiest way for me to learn anything.

My most intimate friends, however, were those in Greta's circle. When I had sailed for Batum I was certain I never wanted to see Greta again. I should have known better. The first thing I did on arriving in Moscow was to call on her. She worked as secretary in the German section of the Comintern, and lived in the Lux. Greta received me as if nothing had happened, as if we had never quarreled. We resumed where we had left off. She had a gift for concealing her real feelings, but I thought she was genuinely fond of me, and that made me very happy.

Four weeks on the freighter among sailors accustomed to a ruthless life, and six weeks in the Caucasus where the class struggle appeared sharp and merciless, had hardened me a little. I began to wonder whether I had not misjudged Greta in New York by standards which were inapplicable to her. The bourgeois and bohemian girls I had known had led sheltered lives based on economic and social security. Barricaded behind their middle-class homes or studios, protected by parents who gave them everything except understanding, they thought of the world as a gentle place whose greatest tragedy was not to have the man you loved or to fail to get on the stage. Such women had all the good qualities which come from security; to the people of their own world, to the equally secure and privileged, they were gentle and considerate. Greta, on the other hand, had been pitched by the breakup of postwar Germany into the maelstrom of social war. At an early age she had to learn to shift for herself, to outwit rivals and enemies and even friends. Upon the sweet and attractive personality which had been hers to start with, war and civil war had superimposed a harder personality, intent upon self-preservation amidst constant danger. Had she been a worker, she would have had the discipline of the proletariat in the rapidly shifting conflict of our times. But she was a bohemian, and her revenge upon the bourgeois world from which she had come and which had repudiated her was to abandon its virtues along with its vices. Like Ivan Karamazoff, prototype of the vacillating intellectual, Greta and her circle thought everything was permitted. You knew that bolshevism taught something quite different, but since I myself at this time had to break with fundamental bourgeois values, I wondered whether Greta was not largely right. Her moral nihilism seemed to have a strength which my paralyzing dualism could only envy. Greta's circle of friends had all lived in many countries, and had fought outside and against the conventional world. They were in many respects, I thought even at this time, like the characters of Hemingway's *The Sun Also Rises*. They were the lost generation of the revolutionary movement, corrupted by the war and by their bohemian heritage; yet sympathetic because of their serious attempts to transform themselves into real communists, to transcend their past in the aggressive present and luminous future. This confused basis of being both drew me irresistibly to Greta and repelled me from her; it was the essential cause of our continued conflict in Moscow.

But perhaps I was only rationalizing. I had the ridiculous habit of surrounding the most commonplace episodes with a mist of "noble" nonsense in which I believed most of the time. This may have been the result of an idealistic training which rendered every object a mere example of some vague and vast generalization. The idea preceded the fact, in this distorted view of the world; and instead of saying simply that Greta and I differed temperamentally, that we weren't suited to each other, I felt impelled to understand all the complex and subtle psychological and social laws which I imagined underlay each of us separately and both of us together. I must have been a great trial to her, intent as she was upon the simple conquest of the obvious goods of life, food, love, power, as she certainly was to me with her unrestrained exercise of a rude will that made concessions to no feelings but her own. At times I was fully aware that the intrusion of our bohemian conflict into the mature political air of Moscow was comic, and I might have abandoned the whole affair sooner but for the fact that almost the whole of Greta's circle seemed for a long time to sustain her mode of being.

First in Greta's circle was her immediate family. Her sister Mimi, who by profession was also a secretary, was ten times as clever as Greta and ten times as decadent. Compared with her, Greta seemed like a healthy prolet. Mimi was full of obscene wit and adroit gossip; her very appearance gave the impression of sly malice. She looked partly like a "modernistic" cover on *Vanity Fair*—pale, gaunt, deathlike; and partly like a laughing marionette, a Billiken. In her presence Greta, who in New York had talked to workers' audiences with moving earnestness, became a reckless competitor in telling dirty jokes or poking fun at the private life of this or that comrade. Among bourgeois girls this was no longer anything new; the war had broken down taboos everywhere, and a lot of nice, clever girls in the Village could recite pages from Mrs. Bloom's soliloquy. In Greta I thought it was shocking. Ought a communist to act like that? Perhaps I was only a puritan who resented in his sweetheart what he was ready to accept in women with whom his relations were less personal.

An ally against Greta's decadence, as we called it, was her fifteen-year-old niece Mathilda, a strikingly handsome girl with a thoughtful, almost ascetic face. Mathilda's father was dead; her mother was a maid on some rich Long Island estate. Her two aunts, Greta and Mimi, could not live in Germany because prison sentences were hanging over them for revolutionary activity. Mathilda went to a Moscow school, spoke excellent Russian, and was a member of the Pioneers. She often went with Greta and me to the movies, or to meetings, or to the Aviators' Home to visit Mimi, whose husband was a Russian flyer. Sunday mornings we would have air-rifle contests here, a serious business for a poor shot like myself; but no business was too serious for Greta and Mimi. The obscene jokes rolled on.

"Don't listen to those two White Guards," Mathilda would say sternly. But she did not talk when the rifle was in her hands; she was a crack shot.

One thing which puzzled me was that Greta was on excellent terms with her former husband, although they had only recently been divorced. Kurt was the most brilliant member of her circle. At twenty-five he had a leading position in the German party, known in advanced working-class circles throughout the world as a clever theoretician, orator, writer and organizer. Kurt also lived in the Lux, and we saw a great deal of him. Sometimes Greta would say peevishly:

"I wish he wouldn't come any more. He stops my development."

"That's ridiculous," I said. "He encourages you to study and to grow."

"It's not what he says that stops me; it's what he is."

Kurt was in fact a man of boundless energy who dominated every circle he entered; when he talked you had to submit or leave the room. His large head with the laughing dark eyes, the sensual mouth, the tall, gangly body were in continual motion. He was silent only when he slept, and for all I knew he talked even then. Still in the prime of youth, he was exuberant, lyrical and bohemian. His professed contempt for art concealed the frustrated artist, or perhaps there was no frustration, perhaps in the downfall of the German empire and the rise of the proletariat he had made a deliberate choice in which he had given up what he considered the lesser for the greater good.

As was to be expected, Kurt read every available political document; less expected was his voracious reading of belles-lettres. Often, when he returned to his room from a meeting of the Comintern executive tired and exhausted, he would stretch out on his bed and read—aloud, if anyone else was in the room—passages from Goethe, Stendhal, Baudelaire, Shakespeare. Like many clever orators, he was something of an actor. Of him it could be said, as Byron said of Curran, that he had fifty faces and twice as many voices. On the platform he mimicked our enemies, and threw audiences into fits of laughter with his imitations of Hindenburg, MacDonald, Poincaré and Churchill.

At parties, Kurt's gift for caricature was directed nearer home. When he drank a little more than was good for anybody, he would imitate the oratorical style of various bolshevik leaders. He was himself a partisan of the majority, a "Stalinite," but he spared neither friend nor foe. He liked to stand on a chair or table, or climb like a monkey to the open transom of the door, perch himself on it, swing his legs and mimic Zinoviev's falsetto, Trotsky's Ciceronian pomp, Stalin's brusque, Georgian accent.

The power of Kurt's imitations lay partly in his striking mimicry of voice, pose, gesture and pronunciation; but the most effective part of it was in the take-off on idea and style.

"Comrades," he would say, his dark eyes tense with mock earnestness, "does caviar make better breakfast than sausage, or shall we break once and for all with the reformist in charge of the degenerate, petit-bourgeois, ultra-left shower bath?"

This lofty theme he would discuss with Clara Zetkin's voice, gestures, mode of thought and expressions, weaving in the frequent references to humanity, justice and truth which marked her speeches. In this respect, Kurt's style was like that chapter in *Ulysses* in which a baby's birth is described in all the styles of English literature from *Beowulf* to our own day. At first it seemed to me there was no sting in Kurt's satire, but later I wondered whether a man in so responsible a position was not playing with fire, whether a mind could not become so agile that at the most critical moment it might slip out of its own grasp.

Perhaps I was only jealous on account of Greta. But there was something else, something outside myself, which stirred my misgivings. Kurt's incurable playfulness, that prolongation of youth which was not unnatural in one who had thrown himself into politics at a time when he was just learning to wipe his own nose, had other, more dubious aspects. Kurt drank, kept irregular hours, lapsed into irresponsible amours. Soon he fell ill and was laid up for several weeks. When I visited him, he showed me a letter from Stalin. I forget the exact wording, but it ran something like this: Kurt, you are a clever boy and a useful comrade. But your mode of life is childish, undignified, injurious to your health and work. Come to your senses; act as befits a responsible bolshevik. As soon as you are able, go to a doctor and get well. You must give up drinking entirely. Fond as your friends are of you, no personal considerations can be permitted to interfere with the work. If you do not grow up to your grave responsibilities, they will be transferred to someone who is better able to bear them.

As he read this letter over and over again, tears came into Kurt's eyes. When he became well enough to leave his room, he wrote out and signed a pledge to stay on the water wagon for three years. He handed copies of this pledge to his nearest German friends. He pretended, of course, that the whole matter was "purely political," but I suspected that he was glad to have a kind of paternal care at a period in his life when the break with his own father was still fresh and painful. Once he said to me proudly:

"Do you know what a German comrade said to me today? I was reporting on some political question, and he said: Kurt, why don't you become a cook? I'm sure you understand cooking better than politics."

"What's there to be proud of?"

"I've been taking myself too damned seriously," Kurt said with unexpected gravity. "I am responsible to the German proletariat; I have everything to learn, and I have been acting as though I knew everything. A fellow like me needs a good kick in the slats once in a while to wake him up."

Greta admired Kurt tremendously, but so did most of the German comrades. When I asked her about her continued friendship with him, she asked sharply:

"Jealous?"

"No."

"All right, I will tell you. Kurt needs me. In politics you seldom have personal friends. There are few people you can trust. But every person needs some friend. Kurt can trust me. We grew up together; we understand each other. He needs only to look the wrong way, and I know what is the matter with him. He knows I will never betray

him if he does something he shouldn't; I won't take advantage of it
to advance my own political fortunes."

In time I had definite proof that Greta was telling the truth, and
then I wondered whether her attachment to me, such as it was, might
not spring from the same need for someone she could trust. One day
we stood on the roof of a new "skyscraper," a six-story building, and
looked across Moscow, a wide sprawling village, with low houses,
awkward squares, streets cobblestoned like Batum. Far down was the
river, and beyond it the new workers' apartment houses.

"The peasant," I said, "has left his mark on the capital; the proletariat will rebuild it in its own image."

"That's a nice speech," Greta said. Her irony came out of a clear
sky. "Why don't you telegraph it to the *New Masses?*" Her face became very white; she looked suddenly drawn and ascetic, like her
Pioneer niece, or herself as an adolescent in a photograph she had
once shown me.

"Greta, wass ist los mit dir, Kind!"

She replied in English, tartly: "Nothing at all." Then she suddenly
cried out: "Oh, take me out of this damned place! Take me back
to New York."

For the third time since I had known her, Greta wept.

§ 4

Greta never referred to this episode, and it was some time before
I discovered what troubled her. We followed the usual routine, went
to work in the Mokhovaya in the morning, had second breakfast at
eleven, dinner at three, when all the Soviet offices closed. Then the
real day began: meetings, unit work, committees, trips to factories,
study. We all took Russian lessons from the same teacher, a buxom
old lady, with two chins, the bosom of a pouting pigeon, and clever
eyes. It was the irony of fate that the foreign communists in the Lux—
the Bill Haywoods and Ernst Thaelmanns—should be taught Russian
by a former princess. She had a permanent *propusk* to the building,
and we all were very fond of her despite her outspoken criticism of
the Soviet regime.

She came to my room late in the afternoon, gave an hour to my
Oxford bunky, an hour to me, then stayed another hour for gossip so
that she could be late for her next pupil, in the best traditions of the
old regime.

"Your friends tell me you are a poet," she said to me one day.

"Shame on you! Why do you waste your time on communism? A poet should write about love and beauty! You know perfectly well that communism is an empty fantasy. Not that I don't appreciate the bolsheviks. I'll say this for them: they are practical, energetic men, while our men were lazy, good-for-nothing spendthrifts who knew how to chase petticoats better than to govern. I knew them very well, to my sorrow. I was married three times, my son, and to generals at that. If we had had one Lenin or one Trotsky we would never have come to this."

In the evening there were informal gatherings, in Greta's room, in mine or elsewhere. Greta picked her friends politically; no bourgeois could enter the Lux, and you didn't associate with them. Within the Party she picked people useful to Kurt's group, of which she was herself a member. In those days, Trotsky's adherents were still in the Party; they were comrades; but to have them in the same room with passionate supporters of the Central Committee was sometimes painful. There were scenes, even when the disputants were bound by ties of blood. Once Alfred came to visit me. He was then in the Agitprop Department of the Comintern—a tall, saturnine German, very capable, earnest and devoted; a gifted linguist and writer. They said he had been a fine orator, but during the war, in which he was a German officer, a bullet cut his palate and caused him to stammer.

We were talking about the events of the day, when the door opened and Alfred's brother came in. Hans was ten years younger, blond and pale, with a touch of T.B. Hans stopped at the doorway, and hesitated. The brothers looked at each other in silence; we all knew they had been quarreling over the inner Party situation. Hans was with the Opposition.

"Come in, Hans," Alfred said. "Take a chair and join us."

"No, I won't. I don't want to be in the same room with a bureaucrat like you!" He banged the door as he went out. Otherwise, Hans was a frequent visitor in our room, and I heard the case of the Opposition day and night.

Another frequent visitor was Sergei Filipov, an official of one of the cultural organizations. He had fought in the Red army during the civil war, but not a trace of its hardships was visible on his round, bland, clean-shaven face, a little pasty with irregular living. He had been abroad with commercial missions, and spoke excellent German, and English with a London accent. He scorned the cap, boots and leather jacket which many bolsheviks wore, and sported an English tweed suit, a waxed French mustache, American tortoise-shell glasses, and occasionally even spats—all in the name of culture. Filipov's visits had nothing political about them; they were on the lofty plane of romance. In his passion for European culture, he had fallen in love with Mimi, Greta's sister, who had many of the qualities of a Berlin singer in a Nachtlokal. As a rule, Filipov sat sternly aloof from our political discussions. But he, too, needed a friend, and one night he unburdened himself to Mimi; of necessity Greta and I had to share his troubles.

"A terrible thing happened in my unit tonight," he said. "An old Party member was expelled for an extremely serious infraction of the rules. He was ordered to leave the meeting. He said: Comrades, I have been a Party member for twenty years; I never dreamed the day would come when I would be thrown out of my own Party. I deserve it, all right. I'll go home. But let me at least stay until the end of the meeting. The chairman insisted that he leave at once, since he was no longer a Party member and therefore could not attend a unit meeting."

"The revolution devours its own children," Greta said, quoting Büchner with bombastic irony.

"I got boiling mad," Filipov continued. "I jumped out of my seat and gave the chairman hell. He could at least let the old man go home in peace."

"Sergei!" exclaimed Mimi in horror. Her pale face became even paler.

"I'm surprised a fat bureaucrat like you had that much feeling," Greta said bitingly.

"Sergei!" Mimi cried. "How could you be such a fool! What do you care about an old man? You should think of your own career."

A curious nausea came over me. This was the kind of opportunism which had repelled me in Greta when she was in New York, and in Fred, who was becoming prominent in our own Party. You expected that kind of thing from a bourgeois, who at least had the frankness to admit he was out for his own gain, and didn't pretend to be fighting for the emancipation of mankind.

That was one thing which disturbed me about Greta. There were other things. She had a reputation which was not pleasant for me to hear about. O. B. was positively savage on the subject. She threw back her graying, bobbed hair, tightened her thin, lined face and said grimly:

"Stick around with Greta long enough, and you'll learn all you want to know about the so-called new life. Mary Pickford may be the sweetheart of a nation, but your little friend is the sweetheart of all nations."

"Nevertheless, there's something remarkable about her," I said. "The best people in the German party seem to take her seriously."

"She is remarkable," O. B. snapped. "What is most remarkable about her is her perfect shamelessness. It's amazing. She doesn't care about anything or anybody. One man is as good as another. Some are ugly, some are handsome, it's all the same to her. She seems to have no emotion whatsoever. Still, I admit I admire her. If I were a man, I'd fall head over heels in love with her. The trouble with most women is that when they fall in love with a man, they *feel* about him just because they sleep with him. To Greta, men mean nothing. Some women loathe her, but I like her. She's charming, and she is the new woman in the sense that she is really free. Of course, there is something essential lacking in her. I've been watching her and Mimi since they came to Moscow in nineteen-twenty-one, the year NEP was started. When she came the German comrades said, O Greta! The most famous courtesan in Berlin. She must be clever, I guess. I can't make out what her power over people is, especially over men, and yet over women too. But I have noticed there are two kinds of men: those who take her as she takes them, as someone to play with without feeling; and the damned fools like you who fall in love with her. These get broken."

O. B. was unmarried and, so far as I knew, celibate; I therefore discounted much of what she said. Yet I could not conceal from myself that there was truth in her indictment. In New York Greta's charm lay partly in her dual nature. Among political radicals she was the pretty bohemian, relatively cultured because of her European background. For her Goethe was not a laborious acquisition in college classrooms, but a national hero, like Babe Ruth. Among bohemians she became the stern bolshevik, whose sternness was tempered with charm, so that one could say: "Goodness gracious, I didn't know communists could be so lovely!" Furthermore, she was in the center of things, close to the leadership in Germany and America, from which I kept more or less aloof so long as my desire to be a sympathizer was greater than my desire to act.

In Moscow, Greta's stature shrank. Here the communist was not, as he was in capitalist countries, a unique creature, assumed by the philistines to be half monster and half saint, and therefore (if he was undeveloped) very important in his own eyes. Here he was one of millions, most of them simple, healthy workers, striving for an epochal goal. Greta was now, like myself, a member of the rank and file. This riled Greta. She had no illusions about herself rising to a position of eminence; she knew she was no Clara Zetkin or Kolontay or Clarissa Ware or Mother Bloor or Larissa Reisner. But she hoped to make the grade through some man. It was painful to be demoted from being the wife of Kurt to being the sweetheart of an obscure scribbler who did not seem to care whether or not he remained obscure. Resenting my lack of aggressive characteristics, she continually expressed disappointment.

"We are not famous," she would complain.

"But, Greta, do you think a communist ought to worry about fame?"

"You may as well know," she said, flushing, "that my heroes are Napoleon and Caesar." Her favorite German proverb was "Mut verloren, alles verloren"—lose courage and you lose everything; but the *Mut* she had in mind was not the courage indispensable for social action, but the nerve to get things for yourself. Her favorite book at this time, one that she knew far better than the *Communist Manifesto,* was *Gentlemen Prefer Blondes,* which she read over and over again, taking delight in the adroitness of the great American gold digger. Her favorite verse was:

> Ruhm muss man gewinnen,
> Dann werden sie sich schon anders besinnen.

"Become famous," she would translate, "and people will think quite otherwise about you. You are proud; you won't lick anybody's boots. But you can't get along in this world without licking boots. Only that way can you get where others will lick your boots."

"Thanks. I don't care to lick or to be licked."

"O.K., my saint. Be good, be noble. See where that will get you."

Greta was, at any rate, consistent. There was a Soviet journalist who used to visit us, the young blue-eyed Fedya, who had abandoned art criticism for newspaper work, and was planning to abandon that for diplomacy—a living testimonial to the fact that under the iron discipline of bolshevism the individual had many choices. Fedya's paper was sending him to Rome, and we gave him a farewell party. Greta put *I'm Sitting on Top of the World* on the phonograph she had brought from New York and danced with him. Fedya patted her fanny.

"You have a steel behind, Greta, absolute steel."

That was the way men talked to her. The following day she wrote Fedya a note in English which he showed me:

"Dear Fedya, I love you from the bottom of my heart. I wish I could go with you to Italien."

"Don't take it seriously, old man." Fedya consoled me. "What she loves is not me but the trip to Italy. Why don't you take her to Shanghai? She will love you to death—or anyway until someone else takes her to Bombay."

It was no doubt idiotic of me to be upset by this trivial episode.

Had Greta been an ordinary bourgeois girl, I would not have been disturbed. I knew girls like her among the disciples of art and psychoanalysis in the Village. She was, in some ways, quite boyish, and suffered from what the Freudians called overcompensation. Like most of the Village Don Juans, male and female, her exaggerated interest in sex was an attempt to conceal her deficiencies in that respect. She was, as a matter of fact, little interested in sensual pleasures. What she wanted most in the world was personal power. That, too, you could understand among bourgeois women, Mabel Dodge, for instance, who had once exercised so strong an influence over John Reed. But Greta was supposed to be a communist—and there was the rub.

Until now I had been able to evade certain things by calling them bourgeois. That was a common evasion among the young left-wing writers in the Village. If you were too lazy to shave you said that daily shaving was bourgeois. I now began to realize that Greta had been my dame aux Camélias. The average bourgeois college boy, on vacation in Paris, creates a romantic figure out of every midinette; he sees in her not what she really is, but an embodiment of his bookish dreams. I had done this myself in Paris six years earlier. In the same way Greta was now for me not a Munich bohemian who had through historic circumstances wandered into the Party, but an imaginary communist heroine. I had read into her things which existed only in my own mind, and in that sense had been unjust both to her and to myself. But Greta was extremely intelligent and a strong character. She insisted on being her own self; she did not know or did not care about the role which my fantasy had assigned to her. The disparity between expectation and reality caused me great pain; and since I could not dismiss her as.bourgeois, I was compelled to face my own defects. One of these was obviously the tendency to see the world through romantic mists. I also had to ask myself, but was Greta a real communist after all? And then that other question, more difficult, more painful still: how much of the old, the confused, the barbarous was still left over even in those of us who were most advanced?

CHAPTER II

No, not in vain the hammer-and-sickle
Blazons its emblem over the earth.
—BRYUSSOV.

§ 1

EVERYTHING appeared different the moment you got out of Greta's hothouse circle, and mingled with people in Moscow. Minds and wills were strained toward the objective world, and not, like your own, sucked into the whirlpool of murky subjective puzzles. Even death in Moscow had more life than your echoes of literary emotions, or real emotions made unreal by literary poisons.

Kurt came in one afternoon from a meeting of the Russian party Plenum.

"You know Djerdjinsky died this afternoon," he said gravely. "I heard him speak at the Plenum. He usually spoke calmly. This time he was frightfully wrought up; he was lacing it into the Opposition, and spoke with a terrible passion. As he sat down, he placed his hand on his heart. We all went out, and later I heard he was dead."

The Lux whispered the news from room to room. To the bourgeois world Djerdjinsky was the "monster" who had organized the Cheka; to the revolutionary workers and intellectuals everywhere he was a hero and a saint.

At ten o'clock that night I walked along the dimly lit Tverskaya. The shop windows already carried Djerdjinsky's portrait draped in red and black. Bookshops, street bulletins, offices had tacked up wall newspapers giving his life history: one of the outstanding workers of the Bolshevik party; for many years a member of the Central Committee of the Social Democratic party of Poland and Lithuania; served five years in czarist prisons, and was released in 1917 by the March Revolution; one of the leaders of the October uprising; then chairman of the Cheka and the G.P.U.; later People's Commissar of Home Affairs, then Commissar of Transport, then chairman of the Supreme Economic Council. What could these dry facts tell about such a man?

524

His extraordinary moral integrity, his devotion to the proletarian cause were legend among the workers.

The following day, everybody in our translation bureau at the Comintern was asked to report at five o'clock in the lunchroom. That was where Party members and office workers held their meetings. Similar meetings were being held all over the country, in factories, shops, state institutions, villages, Red army barracks, all over Russia, along the Volga, in the Caucasus, Siberia, the Ukraine, Crimea, the white north.

At our own meeting the crowd was unusually quiet. Here were representatives of the communist parties of the whole world. There was the gnarled brown face of Martinov, once a leading menshevik and the butt of Lenin's satire, now active in the Comintern; and here is Max Levine, leader of the unsuccessful German uprising of 1923. A Polish comrade is on the platform speaking. He talks Russian slowly, simply, without show of any kind. He worked with Djerdjinsky in the Polish Socialist party—at the time when Pilsudski was one of its leading members; he recounts how the Cheka, under Djerdjinsky's direction, saved the October Revolution. This is the only speech. We rise, sing the *International* and march out into the street toward the Dom Soyuz—the trade-union house—where Djerdjinsky's body lies in state. The streets leading to the Dom Soyuz are jammed with delegations from factories and offices, each holding aloft its red banner. Only twenty-four hours have passed since Djerdjinsky died, but workers all over the city have stayed up all night sewing special red banners draped with black, carrying special inscriptions with Djerdjinsky's name, and special political slogans appropriate for the occasion.

The large hall of the Dom Soyuz, where the late Commissar of War Fiunze had lain in death a while ago, is being repaired; Djerdjinsky's body lies in a small hall. The workers file in slowly. Outside, where we are awaiting our turn, the mass is tremendous. You are supposed to stay with your own delegation, but curiosity impels you to leave the Comintern group and to mingle with the delegates from shop and factory. The July sun is hot; everybody sweats and pushes. There has been no time to organize the procession. A German comrade steps out of the Comintern line and shouts in Russian:

"Comrades, get rid of this Russian slovenliness. Keep your lines in order!"

Nobody pays attention to him. He slinks back to the Comintern line and says in German:

"They just don't know what organization means."

Finally we file into the Dom Soyuz, and pass by Djerdjinsky's body. The face is white in death, noble and strong. Involuntarily I think of Whitman's lines:

> This dust was once the man,
> Gentle, plain, just and resolute, under whose cautious hand,
> Against the foulest crime in history known in any land or age,
> Was saved the Union of these States.

The great American poet had said this of Lincoln, leader in a merciless civil war whose ruthlessness prompted one of its generals to observe that war is hell.

Next day Djerdjinsky's funeral was held in Red Square. This time the organization was excellent. The streets from the Dom Soyuz to the Kremlin were lined with soldiers on foot and horseback. Every street for several miles around was filled with workers' delegations carrying red banners. There, facing Red Square, was Lenin's mausoleum, rising in a series of brown wooden steps, and behind it the graves of bolshevik heroes, the grave of John Reed of Harvard and Greenwich Village. There was a tall post on each side of the mausoleum, and each carried a loud speaker. The ceremony would begin at six; it was now four, and the rain was falling hard, and nobody minded. The brown-faced soldiers munched bread and cake. By five o'clock every inch of Red Square was crowded with workers, and the red velvet banners covered the sky. This time, too, I joined a delegation from a factory; everybody in it had come in working clothes straight from the bench, men and women alike, and the young workers had Comsomol buttons in their lapels or headkerchiefs.

Suddenly, from the distance came the strains of the revolutionary funeral march. Leading members of the Russian party marched slowly up the mausoleum steps. The pallbearers came slowly carrying the red coffin. Behind us, following our line as we moved up to the mausoleum, came the G.P.U. cavalry, with their blue caps and red trousers, and the long lances tipped with pennants red and blue. They were young, tanned, healthy, like Whitman's ideal men, but they had no beards.

By this time our delegation was close to the mausoleum. On the top step to the right, which is the speakers' stand, I could make out Stalin, Rykov, Kalinin, Yenukidze, Bukharin, Voroshilov, and Tomsky. On the step below were three solitary figures: Kamenev, in a white Russian blouse, fat, red-bearded; Zinoviev, fat, with a mop of black hair, short, nervous, the picture of a nineteenth century French révolutionnaire; finally Trotsky, also in a white *rubashka,* very pale, stiff, immobile, his leonine head proudly thrown back, straight as a soldier. For long minutes at a time he did not move a muscle; he was so white of face, so rigid that you were not sure whether that was the man himself or a bust by Clare Sheridan. The crowd around was interested in him.

"Do you think he will speak? A great orator."

Rykov spoke; Bukharin spoke; a German comrade spoke for the workers outside of Russia; Voroshilov spoke. Stalin stood in the background, his arms folded, his energetic brown head lowered on his breast. He did not speak, watching the crowded square in attentive silence.

The last speech over, they lowered the coffin into its grave under the Kremlin wall, near John Reed's grave. Suddenly the world trembled with the booming of cannon. The bands played the funeral march; the crowd dissolved in the rain.

I went home, numb for a long time. It seemed I had no heart. Then a great wave of feeling came over me, and words came, and a pounding rhythm. I started to write a poem on the death of Djerdjinsky. It was a long time since I had written poetry out of deep feeling, and as always under these circumstances I was not writing for anybody in particular. The room was still; it was getting very late, and Oxford was asleep in his clothes with a copy of a pamphlet by Lenin in his hand. Moscow was very quiet; you could hear your own thoughts:

> Time shall forget the monstrous nightmare
> of czars, landlords, bankers, priests,
> Time shall remember our time of heroes
> scouring tyranny's rubbish off the earth;
>
> not one, not ten—millions struck for freedom,
> the world heaved with masses breaking free,
> resolute the advance guard marched before them,
> the iron-hearted leaders showed the way;
>
> these, seeing mankind going mad, cried out,
> blew the sirens, knocked on the factory doors
> (Earth, take this comrade dearly to your bosom
> he was of those who saw, labo-red, fought)

workers' strict battalions, marching,
beat the streets of cities like deep drums;
the dark-faced peasants' roar rocked the meadows,
saluting the sunrise of the new-born day;

nine years loom like nine black tombstones
over the tyrants' graves;
nine years gleam like nine steel gateways,
swinging open to the workers' world;

this was not done with white gloves, this
was not done with prayers and invitations;
(Earth, take this comrade dearly to your bosom,
he was of those who saw, labo-red, fought)

workers and soldiers hold heads high at his grave,
watching the outlines of the world he dreamed of;
he died with the battle raging: bury him slowly:
keep rifles clean: the last shots must be fired.

The next day I attempted to make a rough translation of this for my Russian lesson. The princess read my *urok* smiling.

"There you are, typical, typical!" The Widow of Three Generals puffed out her wide bosom. "That's what these bolsheviks do to a poet. How can you waste your time on such themes? Who is Djerdjinsky, anyway? One more administrator, here today and gone tomorrow. But love is eternal; it is everywhere, always, forever and forever. A poet—especially a young poet—should write about love. Mind you, I'm not saying anything against the bolsheviks; they are building up our country. Share their political views if you like, but keep them out of your poetry. Poetry and politics have nothing to do with each other."

"And Pushkin?"

"Who reads Pushkin's political poems? But everybody in Russia sings that wonderful ballad of his: O sing not, lovely one, for me the melancholy songs of Georgia; they recall to me another life and far off mountains."

As she crooned Pushkin's ballad, the princess's wrinkled face seemed younger, her lips filled with color, and her clever eyes were sad.

"The workers sing Pushkin's political poems, the one about the imprisoned eagle, for instance," I argued.

"Naturally, of course! What can you expect from illiterate workers? Love is the outcome of culture, the true theme of poetry. You smile; you think I am too old and ugly to talk of love. But look!" She waddled her plump old body across the room and picked up her handbag; out of it she fished a photograph which she slapped on my study table. "Now what do you think of this girl?" The portrait was that of a very beautiful and sensual woman in the fashionable décolleté of the nineties, St. Petersburg version. "That's me at thirty—and though I may look like an angel there, rest assured I wasn't. Generals were at my feet, and ministers, and grand dukes, and poets." She sat down and sighed. "Ah, well; it's all gone, no more gay balls or court receptions, no more love, only dry reports on the building of socialism in one country. In my day youth meant joy; nowadays it means stupidity. Look at my daughter: nineteen, beautiful, clever. She could marry a commissar if she wanted to, like some of her friends. And what does the silly goose do? She's in love! With a Jew who is nothing but a fiddler! That's what the new generation understands by love. . . ."

Later in the day, I typed the poem about Djerdjinsky and mailed it to the *New Masses*. That's what you always did these past six years. Incurably lazy, you wrote poetry, like everything else, only when you absolutely had to; you showed it to a few friends and then mailed it to the *Liberator* or the *New Masses*. But now I found that among communists the artist was not "free"; the proletariat gave him "orders." I received "orders" about the Djerdjinsky poem, and the comrade who brought them was Hedda.

§ 2

Whenever I was upset by the opportunism of Greta and her immediate circle, I went to Hedda for consolation. Hedda was Greta's friend and admirer, yet no two women could possibly be more dissimilar. My sweetheart's father was a petty official in Munich, Hedda's a factory worker in some German province near the Polish border.

Hedda was nearly ten years older than Greta. At first I paid no attention to her. She had a small, compact, angular figure, with a narrow waist and broad shoulders, and her clothes were the boyish clothes of the typical Comsomol: woolen stockings, a dark cotton dress, a white shirt, often a man's shirt which Kurt or I gave her, short bobbed hair with one or two gray streaks. She wore the traditional leather jacket, and when she wore a hat at all it was as likely as not a worker's cloth cap. In the beginning, too, you noticed only the negative aspects of her face, its sallow skin, heavy black eyebrows and long tight mouth. But when she talked, her entire appearance changed. You suddenly realized what a strong, thoughtful face she had; you noticed the wide, high forehead, the clever pointed nose, the sharp chin; you heard, too, the decision and certainty in her voice. She had no high opinion of herself as a woman.

"I'm no beauty," she would say, "and I suppose that's why Greta likes me so much; I'll never be her rival. Men like me not as a woman but as a comrade."

It was true that where Greta excited romantic feelings Hedda roused respect. But after a while respect was joined by a kind of love— the nonsensual, nonromantic love which bolsheviks had for a good *tovarish*. Of Greta you heard one erotic adventure after another; of Hedda the stories were nearly always political. Her husband was, like Kurt, a member of the Central Committee of the German party, a factory worker by origin who had fought his way to knowledge and political skill. But one never thought of Hedda: "this is Gustav's wife," as one said of Greta: "she was Kurt's wife." Her political standing was the result not of attachment to a man, but of her own solid efforts and achievements. She was often separated from her husband for a year at a time, owing to the exigencies of revolutionary activity; yet not once during any of these separations did Hedda have any love affairs, and there was a general conviction among the German comrades who knew her best that she had remained faithful to Gustav throughout the fifteen years of their marriage.

This was all the more remarkable since Hedda, like most modern women, bourgeois and communist alike, had liberal theories on love; intellectually she approved of Greta's attempts to caricature Kollontay; but that in her nature which made her a loyal, unswerving bolshevik also made her a loyal, unswerving wife.

As with so many of my first acquaintances in the Lux, my first bond with Hedda was her friendship for Greta, her command of English, and her interest in America. She and Gustav had lived in Canada for six years, and had helped to found the Canadian Communist party. Later they had lived for a year in Detroit. Her knowledge of American industrial life was astonishing for a foreigner; it exceeded that of the average liberal economist at home, and certainly my own which was buried, such as it was, under literary preoccupations. Hedda had been active in Canadian strikes and in the German Revolution of 1923; she had been imprisoned in both countries. Yet, in spite of a heroic life in the class struggle, she did not pose, like so many communists of bourgeois origin, as above art and literature. She knew by heart many passages from Goethe, Shakespeare, Schiller, Hebbel, and Heine, and read every novel and poem and play she could lay her hands on in English, Russian or German.

Nothing human was alien to Hedda; you could talk to her about revolutionary politics, Lenin's electrification plan, the latest Soviet play, or psychoanalysis. On the last she was something of an expert, like most of the German comrades. Ruth Fischer, once a leader of the German party, now head of the ultra-left faction in it, had been a practicing psychoanalyst in Vienna before she entered politics. Besides, the proletariat must take over the best in the old culture, and while Freud was an exotic fad in America he was actually part of contemporary European culture. Bolsheviks, however, did not accept most of Freud; he was not a materialist, but a fuzzy idealist dealing in abstractions like the unconscious, the id, and the libido. That year Trotsky had published an essay on this problem in which he said that both Pavlov and Freud consider that the bottom of the "soul" is physiology; but Pavlov, like a diver, goes to the bottom and minutely investigates the well from below to above; while Freud stands over the well, and with a penetrating look tries through the density of an ever-vacillating cloudy water to perceive or guess at the outlines of the bottom. Hedda, like most of us in this period, employed the Freudian jargon only metaphorically, as one uses literary images; for scientific explanation we used Marxian formulas, even on occasions when they did not fit if only because no Marxian scientist had established them. But in this case, as in most others, the interest in psychological theory did not spring exclusively from a passion for abstract knowledge. Hedda seldom talked about her past; we knew little about her childhood or her family; she did not even use her own name, Hedda being her Party pseudonym without a surname. Nevertheless, her face, especially her dark brown eyes, sometimes betrayed the acute suffering through which she must have passed, and the feeling she would put into the tragic lines she recited from Sophocles or Dostoevsky indicated that privation was something she knew outside classic literature.

But if Hedda's private life was a closed book, this could not be said about Greta. Like all romantics, she aired her amours in public, although she was skillful enough in concealing political ideas. Our personal relations were not secret, and the Lux knew them as fully as the Village had known the private affairs of the older radical writers. Some of the younger and more naïve comrades envied and admired us; we symbolized traditional romance in a new setting—the unhappy, pursuing lover and the beautiful lady who at once gave and withheld herself, always adroitly returning to the chase at the precise moment when the lover was on the point of abandoning it. What intrigued the young and the naïve most were the psychological aspects of the romance; the physical surrender, indicated by the movie fadeout, here began instead of ending the affair, and persisted through the conflict of temperament and will. We were considered a fortunate and happy couple at the very time when my anguish was most acute, and Greta, perhaps, suffered too, from the frustration of worldly ambitions which neither the body nor the heart could assuage.

But this romantic image of us was so remote from the complex truth that I had to ask myself: if these people consider me a careless gay Lothario, utterly ignorant of my sufferings, was it not possible that I had been similarly mistaken about the literary Don Juans of the Village, about some of the *Masses* crowd, let us say? Perhaps they, too, had been less gay and careless than we had imagined; perhaps there was something wrong with the whole pseudo-romantic tradition of our times sustained by prophets of Priapus like D. H. Lawrence.

From West European novels about the aristocracy, now coming into vogue, it was obvious that the hectic and unscrupulous pursuit of pleasure was the chief occupation of the parasitic classes. Their cultural formula read: money—leisure—sex. With the decline of bourgeois society, the final integer in the equation became vice. The endless parties of the idle rich, the flirtations and intrigues, the art and literature centered around the pursuit of women by men, of men by women, of men by men, of women by women. Instead of being the by-product of a healthy, productive, creative life, pleasure had become for the parasitic classes the beginning and end of life, its essence and whole meaning.

On the freighter to Batum, I had learned that workers thought and talked a great deal about pleasure, but it was of necessity a rare parenthesis to labor. Without that labor, which consumed most of their time, neither they nor the parasitic classes could exist.

Love was a sublime joy only so long as it was one aspect of a creative life. When it became the center of all activity it was sickening. That culture was barren, that heaven hell in which Priapus was the chief of the gods.

Now it began to appear as though the bohemian, poor in material goods, insignificant in politics, made a fetish of sex partly out of a desire to absorb the culture of the "best" people. The ruling class of each society determines that society's culture, and the intellectual was voicing the decaying values of the Western bourgeoisie. In the Village I had observed that to imitate Mrs. Bloom's free and easy conduct was not merely a pleasure, but a mark of intellectual distinction; it showed a woman was "advanced," superior to the timid little girls who clung to their mothers' aprons in Flatbush or Iowa. It was disturbing to find the same type occasionally in the Party. Of course, one could reflect that the socialist movement—as the alert Bernard Shaw had long ago observed—attracts not only those who are too good for the old order, but those who are not good enough. The proletariat, motive power and leader of the social revolution, is impelled by its economic position to destroy the old world and create the new; it has no choice but to do so or perish. This makes for objectivity, integration, health. In its name Lenin could say that Don Juan and Tartuffe are equally repulsive, equally philistine, and to point out that while full freedom in the relations of the sexes was desirable, nobody liked to drink water from a glass which had passed a thousand lips.

The successful bourgeois was also integrated; he was disciplined within the prevailing system by the need of safeguarding and increasing the profits wrung from the toilers by violence and fraud. It is the rare bourgeois idealist who is dissatisfied by the monstrosities of capitalist civilization, and he is nearly always an intellectual of middle class origin. By trade and temperament a specialist in moral and aesthetic values, he is—if he remains uncorrupted by success—shocked by the contradictions between the humanistic phrases of bourgeois ideals and the horrors of bourgeois realities. Such a man may be driven to abandon the bourgeois camp, as the war drove Barbusse. At first this type of idealist, at once bound to the humanism of the past and attracted by the socialist society of the future, may attempt to circumvent the tasks of the present by an intellectual tour de force. He may seek—as Clarté first sought—a rapprochement between "bourgeois idealism and Marxism." But the harshness of the class struggle, the intransigeance of the contending parties, soon explodes this illusion. The logic of events leads the sincere idealist, once he understands the proletarian revolution, to abandon an impossible rapprochement; he marches, like Barbusse, openly and proudly in the ranks of the bolsheviks. Here, too, there is complete integration. Bourgeois idealists of this kind may be profoundly transformed by the impact of reality upon minds able to face it, as was the case with John Reed, who did succeed in fusing the highest dreams of past human culture with the revolution which inherits, transforms, transcends and realizes them.

But in addition to such intellectuals, the movement also attracts unskilled intellectuals, a certain type of bohemian who seeks in the revolution precisely those things which he failed to attain in the bourgeois world—personal aggrandizement, power over men, like Greta who sought it in love or Fred who sought it in office.

Hedda's chief attraction for me, at the beginning at least, was that I could speak to her of such things. And I had to speak. I was living in Soviet Russia at a time when very few Americans knew anything about its new society. Even many American Party members had only the vaguest notions as to what it was really like; and the country itself was passing through a political crisis involving the abandonment of NEP and the initiation of socialist construction. These circumstances had the same effect upon me as the World War had had; I discovered that I was still fluid, unformed; my creeds were tentative, easily dislocated by violent contact with reality, anxious at once for a peaceful retreat to the ivory tower and for a daring plunge into the objective world.

And Hedda did not laugh, or scold, or clout you over the head with quotations from the latest *Rote Fahne* editorial. She did not consider it a "deviation" to ponder over anything except the latest political slogan; she looked upon the whole of human life as the legitimate and necessary province of human thought. Nor did she consider this a personal merit. When I complained about what I imagined were the limitations of the Party at home at that time, she said:

"The German party is ahead of the American Party. But it isn't that we are cleverer or nobler than you. We are simply older and more experienced. Our labor movement is older than yours; our social democracy was once in the vanguard of the world revolutionary movement. Millions of German workers, and intellectuals for that matter, have been brought up on socialist doctrine. Many of the American comrades are the first in their family to be revolutionists; but among us there are thousands and thousands whose fathers and mothers and grandfathers and grandmothers were socialists. Neither the Communist party, nor the socialists nor the I.W.W. have played a compelling role in the politics of your country; both the social democrats and the communists must be reckoned with in Germany. We are a real political party; you are still a sect—and you read plenty of Comintern documents to that effect. Naturally we have a more normal outlook on life; we are not political neurotics cut off from the masses. We are and must be interested first and foremost in economics and politics; but we are also interested in art and literature and sports and psychology. All these things go together: for the same reason that we have a bigger, stronger, more influential Party than you, our proletarian culture is on a higher level. We have revolutionary theaters, magazines, novels, poems and even a revolutionary tabloid with a mass circulation. The reason is simple: remember, our proletariat is more mature; it has fought on the barricades in nineteen-eighteen and 'twenty-three. It no longer dreams and talks, but acts."

When I told her that I had stopped writing verse, Hedda was indignant.

"I suppose some of those college boys in your American Party told you a communist mustn't write poetry. To hell with them! Every bolshevik must do what he can do best. You have no common sense, so you will never be a practical politician. But look at Johannes Becher and Bertolt Brecht in Germany, or Mayakovsky and Biedny here! They are loved and respected for doing nothing but writing verse. You just let a good Russian bolshevik discover that you've quit writing. You'll get a bawling out for neglecting your job—and you'll deserve it too."

After I had finished the Djerdjinsky poem, I showed it to her. Her face was motionless as she read it.

"Good!" she said. "I'm glad you are thinking about something else besides Greta. I was afraid you would begin writing poems about her, but I see you understand that a poet today must sing the revolution or die inside like a sick mouse."

Late that evening she knocked at my door, nodded curtly to Oxford, and said to me:

"I have a job with you. I told the German workers' club that you wrote a poem on Djerdjinsky, and they want a translation for their bulletin board."

"Nonsense," I said. "It's a lousy poem. I wouldn't like to show it to workers."

"Don't be a prima donna." Then she added, laughing, "It's a Party order."

"I'll disregard it."

Hedda picked up the telephone on my desk.

"Klub Nemetzky Rabotchi? Da, *pajhaluista* . . . *ist* unser Sekretär dabei? Ja . . . Ja . . . Hier spricht die Hedda . . . Listen, Glaubov, the comrade poet here is a damned fool, a petit bourgeois, and a White Guard. He is sabotaging our memorial wall newspaper. He wants to be begged like a girl, so you beg him. I am tired of these bohemian souls."

The German secretary was less indignant.

"Look, comrade, we don't want to force you, but don't you think you are unfair? We are putting up a wall newspaper to commemorate Comrade Djerdjinsky. Everyone has done his share. Some comrades worked late at night after coming from the factory. You have nothing to do except to let Hedda translate it; maybe you can help her with a few phrases that she doesn't exactly understand. . . . What? . . . Don't worry; even if it isn't as good as Goethe, I assure you nobody will mind."

Hedda translated the poem. It appeared on the bulletin board of the German workers' club in Moscow; later it appeared in the *Rote Fahne* in Berlin; and this was the only literary "order" I received during my year in the Soviet Union.

§ 3

From that day when she stood beside me on the roof of a Moscow skyscraper weeping and begged me to take her back to America, Greta was not herself. She was melancholy, tossed in her sleep, got up out of bed to look through the window at silent, deserted Tverskaya Street. Once or twice I caught her crying softly.

She was most melancholy when we visited her sister Mimi, who lived at the aviators' club in a suburb of Moscow. Mimi's husband was a flyer in the Soviet service between Moscow and Berlin. I never saw Kostya. He always seemed to be in Berlin; I never had the luck to come to the flyers' home when he was on leave. But the aviators and their wives, whom I met in this collective community, agreed that he was a splendid fellow—a Russian noble who had joined the Party at the outbreak of the revolution. This was considered a great merit in an aristocrat, since in 1917 who could be sure that the bolsheviks would actually triumph?

Among the aviators' wives one was especially close to Greta and Mimi, a beautiful Russian woman in her early thirties whom they called Lida Ivanovna. She was a painter active in a group that was experimenting with murals but might herself have served as a model for a revolutionary heroine of the nineties with her large black eyes, dark curly hair, and extremely sensitive full mouth. Her husband also seemed to spend all his time in Berlin. I never saw him on those mornings when the aviators and Greta, Mimi, Hedda and Mathilda came out on the lawn for target practice with air rifles.

Whenever we came home from these visits to the flyers' home,

Greta's face was white and drawn, and she did not talk to me for hours. Finally I said:

"Greta, I think we had better quit."

"Why?"

"You don't seem to care about me any more. It's weeks since I've had a civil word from you."

"Do you think I have nothing to worry about except you? I have other troubles too."

"If you loved me you would tell me about them."

"Some troubles you can't tell."

"If you love you can."

"You're a petit-bourgeois sentimentalist," Greta said. I walked out of the room, but stopped in the hallway. She called my name. When I got back to her she was crying.

"You are a dirty bastard for making me tell you," she said. "All right, then: Kostya has been arrested."

"What for?"

"We don't know. Mimi is crazy with grief. She has been to the G.P.U. a thousand times, but they tell her nothing. Lida Ivanovna, too, has tried. Nothing, nothing, nothing."

"Is her husband under arrest, too?"

"Six flyers. The most we could find out is that they are supposed to have sold military secrets to the Germans. Mimi says she knows the real criminal, some bureaucrat who has saved himself by blaming these six innocent fools."

"How do you know they are innocent?" I asked.

"I swear it!" Greta was now calm. "He is a fine Russian boy, too damned good for Mimi, if you ask me. Of course he comes from the nobility, but his Party record is clean—absolutely clean—and he's been a Party member for ten years. Why should he sell military secrets to the Germans? He never cared for money; he gave every penny he earned to Mimi. He never drank, he didn't chase women; he cared only for the Party and his work. There wasn't a reason in the world why he should do a terrible thing like that."

"Then why did they arrest him?"

"Bureaucracy. Red tape. Mistakes are bound to happen. But it's awful, awful. They will shoot him."

"Have you tried to do anything for him? Is there anything I can do?"

"Nothing, nothing at all. There is no open trial in a case like this, only an administrative one. We have gone to all our Russian friends, some of them in the government. They can't do a thing."

This news depressed me. I could not sleep nights, and would stay up with Greta talking about the six imprisoned flyers, especially Kostya. It was difficult to discuss the case with Mimi; she always got hysterical protesting her husband's innocence. Hedda was not quite sure about his innocence. First she grimly said that some bureaucrats were responsible for this outrage. Then she added quietly:

"But we must also remember that where there is smoke there must be fire. In every great conflict there are spies and traitors, and nowhere more than in the class struggle. That is a dreadful thing, but it can't be helped. An innocent man may be suspected on circumstantial evidence, and the real agent provocateur may get away with it for years. Do you know the story of Malinowski? He was an agent of the czarist secret police. Yet for fifteen years he was in the highest councils of the Bolshevik party. Lenin trusted him, and would not listen to suggestions that he might be a spy. Malinowski was even permitted to edit the official Party newspaper. And all this went on right up to the revolution. When the archives of the old government were opened, Malinowski was exposed. He escaped punishment by fleeing to Germany—but his case is a warning that we cannot be too sure in matters like this, and it is better to take no chances. I'm sure Kostya is guilty."

One day Mimi came with the dreadful news. She and Lida Ivanovna had received permission to bring the prisoners food, but when they got there one of the guards told them the six flyers had been shot. Mimi cried a great deal and Greta was silent all day long. The curious thing was: that day, as on all other days, they went to work in the Comintern, and seemed not to have lost the least interest in the movement.

Several days later the phone rang in Greta's room and I answered it. It was Lida Ivanovna.

"Good news!" she said breathlessly. "They haven't been shot. I have it on official authority. They are being exiled to the north, and we can see them off on the train tonight."

Hastily, Greta and Mimi and Mathilda and Hedda and I packed bundles of clothes and food, chocolate and books for the prisoners. We pooled our money as a gift to them. About eight o'clock at night we all went down to the railway station from which trains left for Leningrad. Lida Ivanovna, heavily veiled, was there ahead of us, and with her the relatives of the other imprisoned flyers. The stationmaster said the prisoners would be taken on a special train which left on the last freight track, a quarter of a mile down the dark yards. Here we all waited in silence. Mathilda, the fifteen-year-old niece of Greta and Mimi, was nervous, and she alone talked.

"I am taking English lessons now," she said. "Now I can tell you what I really think of you, so you'll know it."

Presently there was a hush. A Black Maria came to the tracks and the brakes squeaked as it stopped abruptly. It was so dark we could only make out the huddled figures in the truck, but could see no faces distinctly. Armed G.P.U. men surrounded the truck, and one of them said to us:

"Step back, citizens. You can see the prisoners on the train."

The motor began chugging, the gears creaked, and the truck disappeared into the railway yard.

"How dirty their wagons are!" Mathilda said. "Just like the Russians. They can't keep anything clean. When we have the communist revolution in Germany we'll manage things better."

I had heard the same thing at the Djerdjinsky funeral. The German comrades shouted: "What lines! Russian slovenliness. We know how to organize lines—here, you, straighten out there!"

Soon a G.P.U. guard came out of the darkness and told us we could say good-by to the prisoners. We took our bundles and went to the train. Mimi leaped to the rear platform and hysterically embraced a thin, blond boy.

"Kostya, you can't go."

"I must, darling. It's so good of you to come."

Kostya was pale and haggard, his skin yellow, his chin dirty with a stubble a week old, and his eyes red from lack of sleep, anxiety and tears.

"Mimi, listen," he said quietly, but loud enough for all of us to hear. "I am innocent, absolutely innocent." He took both her hands in his. "I swear it, God is my witness." He fell back into the phrases of his childhood. "When I get out, I'll prove my innocence." He kissed Mimi, and she stepped off the platform quickly. We all shook hands with the prisoners, and piled the bundles we had brought on the platform. We started to go, when suddenly Kostya leaned over the railing and spoke with terrific intensity: he said something so unexpected, so startling that I did not grasp its meaning at the moment. It was only later in the evening that I felt the full impact of his words. He said:

"Mimi, I will serve my ten years in the north; I will get out, and then I will clear up the only thing that matters. I must get back into the Party."

The train whistled and went off. We started to leave the yards. I had an appointment with Mayakovsky, and now, more than ever, I wanted to see him. I needed to talk to him, even if I could not talk about Kostya. But Mathilda was the first to break from the group.

"Good night," she said, shaking my hand. "I must go to my meeting."

"What meeting?"

"The Pioneers."

"Can you go to a Pioneer meeting after this?"

"Of course, idiot! What has this got to do with the revolution? Do you think we can't build socialism because there are some damned bureaucrats around who make mistakes?"

She turned sharply on her heel and walked rapidly down the street. I said good night to the aviators and the girls and promised to meet them later at Lida Ivanovna's.

The poet Mayakovsky lived an hour's ride by tram from the center of the city. You entered a typical Russian courtyard surrounded by small houses. From one of these a huge dog leaped up in the darkness and began to bark at me in a deep bass. A light went up in the hallway, and the equally deep bass of the poet said:

"It's you. Come in."

The poet looked different. In New York I had seen him in the early summer with his head shaved; now that autumn was not far away his hair was heavy. And his face, too, looked different; it was thin and infinitely sad.

Mayakovsky lived in two little rooms with his friend and literary mentor Ossip Brick, and the latter's wife Lili, a retired actress, red-haired, buxom and quite attractive. The poet had recently published a volume of lyrics about her; and it was no secret in Moscow that there was a ménage à trois here in the style of the Herzens and Ogarev, the Hamiltons and Lord Nelson, the Guicciolis and Byron. Only it was said that Mayakovsky was the platonic base of this triangle which caused him untold anguish. It was an old arrangement, dating from prerevolutionary days, the poet's bohemian period. What was typical of this period of the revolution were the cramped quarters —the curse of Moscow's housing shortage, thanks to the influx of a million people from the provinces. One room served as living and dining room, and in it stood the poet's "studio," an old roll-top desk, such as my father had in his Brooklyn office. Here books and manuscripts lay in mountainous disorder.

The poet was now famous and rich; he got a ruble a line for his verses, and the Moscow wits said this accounted for his peculiar style which consisted of breaking up quatrains into lines of one or two words. The housing shortage reduced him to quarters such as he must have had in his poor bohemian days; and as I looked at these two little rooms I began to think I had not been very intelligent in regarding bohemia as a center of "vice." For the most part its inhabitants were penniless, hard-working artists who had fled from the horrors of middle-class philistinism. They had no money, did not especially care for it, and did not as a rule know how to make it. The whole insane pursuit of profit was alien to them. They wanted leisure and peace for creative work, love, thought—and this leisure and peace capitalism denied them. If they were utopian in their methods, they were innocent in their desires. Maturity divided them into those who went back to the bourgeoisie, and those who went forward to the proletariat; but so long as capitalism existed, the narrow little streets of the world's bohemias in Paris, London, New York and Munich would always contain people whose passion for a noble life and art would drive them into the only camp where they could find it—the camp of the working class. But so slowly and painfully do men change their souls even under the impact of a great social revolution that Mayakovsky, who in New York seemed infinitely more of a bolshevik than anyone else I knew merely because he came from the Soviet Union, appeared in Moscow to be a bohemian, unorganized, divided, unhappy.

Brick was a dapper man of about forty, cultured and elegant in the best Western European style. I had known him through his writings as a keen literary critic, founder of the LEF group which developed not only Mayakovsky but the movie director Sergei Eisenstein. Now I was to see him as a charming host. Lili brought tea, the poet found some vodka, and Brick from somewhere produced caviar and sausage and black bread—the indispensable settings of a Russian conversation. Although the two men were writers, they talked chiefly about the film—"the art of the future," the "art of the machine age." As Futurists, they tended to repudiate the old culture, an attitude which the bolsheviks did not share.

"I will give you the whole of the broad Russian soul," Mayakovsky said in his booming voice, "for a couple of good American tractors."

"He means," Brick explained, "that the industrialization of Russian industry and the collectivization of our agriculture is going to be the foundation not only of our new life, but of our new art."

I had by now become accustomed to the Soviet habit of seeing life as a whole of contradictory elements in conflict, moving like a spiral upward, the last visible coil of which was the classless society. But the poet's business is not with the abstract; Mayakovsky read me parts of a long poem on which he was working. NEP had closed a period forever and had thus given it literary unity; it could now be described from prologue to climax, and always described differently. The insurrection and the civil war were now, seen with some perspective, what the myths were to the Greek poets and the histories to the Elizabethan. And now, too, that vigorous, rhetorical style which in New York had seemed to us "bolshevik," appeared to be somewhat dated, to bear the mark of a special period which was closed for the time being. Mayakovsky's verse had the qualities which we associate with oratory, rather than those which we had been taught to associate with poetry. Probably the bolshevik orator, with his sustained, dramatic flow of imagery and invective, did more than any other literary force to shape the poetry of the civil war. Roman actors went to hear the orator Hortensius, in order to learn the art of rhetoric from him; the Soviet poet could not escape the orator, who came to him in meeting hall, factory, theater, and battlefield to explain the aims of the revolution, to stir all to action and combat. As Mayakovsky now stood against his roll-top desk booming out his poem about October, he conveyed to me, more forcefully than abstract theses could, the feeling that the revolution had entered another stage, one in which the economist had replaced the military chieftain, and in which the novel was more fecund than verse. Mayakovsky felt this change too, and was not sure he could adapt himself to it. His soul had already made two tremendous leaps—one in 1917, when he had to re-educate himself from bohemianism to bolshevism; another in 1921, when he had to abandon the drama of the civil war for the hard, prosaic facts of the New Economic Policy. And now they talked of halting the "retreat" of NEP, of rushing forward to the building of socialism in one country. The strain was enormous; you could see it in the deep blue rings under Mayakovsky's eyes. Lili may have been painful, but here the poetry of the ages sustained you, from Propertius to Pushkin to Proust. Ever since men knew love they knew unhappy love, sang about it, analyzed it, and comforted each other in it; but on the sharp turns of the revolution there were no precedents. Here every poet was his own ancestor, his own pioneer.

Perhaps this was why Mayakovsky was so deeply interested in Yessenin's suicide. He had pondered a great deal about it, and had written an article about it. He presented me with a copy of the magazine which had published it, and said:

"Do you think Yessenin was sincere?"

I said I didn't know; but in the streetcar, on my way to Lida Ivanovna's I thought a lot about Mayakovsky's question as I read his piece on the death of Yessenin. I had an uncomfortable feeling that Mayakovsky's preoccupation with the peasant-poet's suicide was not purely literary. I thought, too, about the matter of sincerity. At home, the literati assumed that all politicians were insincere and most artists sincere. Nevertheless, the average artist was blind to everything that lay outside the middle-class gospel. This gave him the advantage of integration. He had what is called "sincerity"; he meant what he said and said what he meant. The meaning and the saying need not necessarily correspond to the facts of the contemporary world; enough that the writer thought they did. To utter an untruth believing it to be true was a form of sincerity; to utter a truth about which you still retained doubts, but for which you were willing to give your life because it was the most plausible value you know, was a form of insincerity: the integration was incomplete.

The bourgeois supporting capitalist society was sincere; the artist ignorant of or silent about its horrors was assumed to be sincere. The worker in revolt against exploitation was considered sincere because "he didn't know any better"; he was misled by "agitators." But woe to the intellectual in transition: he might be compared with one who from childhood had been taking drugs. Some fine day he wakes up in horror; he realizes he has been taking poison. He wants to free himself, to start a new life of healthy labor and love. But it is not easy to break the old habit. There follows a period of intense internal struggle. The man no longer takes drugs, but the craving is there.

From the viewpoint of the aesthetes—to whom intellect, will and action are secondary, and desire is primary—this constitutes a kind of hypocrisy. It is not important that will has triumphed over desire; what is important for them is that desire still shadows will.

The poet, nurtured in bourgeois culture, wills to shake off the old intellectual and moral prejudices; he accepts the ideas and ideals of the proletariat; he fights in its ranks as journalist, orator, editor and organizer. But there comes a day when he returns to the novel, the poem or the play; and the old integrity is no longer there. Mind, will and action move in one direction; but part of his desire is for the old fleshpots. The man is caught between two worlds. The conflict which his abstract, intellectual writings concealed now stands forth naked in his creative writing. Maybe that was why Mayakovsky's work was so full of audible effort, the creaking and groaning of a big machine trying to accomplish a miracle; he was trying so hard to transcend and transform himself that he roared with pain.

The bourgeois is content with pointing out that the hidden craving for opium cancels its surrender in action. The integrated communist goes further; he says: you are a poet whose specialty is to convey the intensity of perception and desire; your job is to refashion the souls of men. How can you do this when you are yourself poisoned by impure longings for what is old and rotten? You still echo your romantic love of opium; you are not free of it. Get it out of your system!

This is not always easy. It is most difficult when the poet's own conscience pricks him. There is a stalemate; conflicting tendencies are deadlocked in the secret chambers of the heart, and Yessenin opens his veins.

Then the gentlemen of the bourgeois press change their tune. Hitherto they had thought of Yessenin as a communist spokesman, hence "insincere." But it turns out that he was not at all a communist; he had strong mental reservations, doubts, disagreements. He was an old-fashioned peasant, the lyric voice of the dying village. He understood the landlord and hated him; he was puzzled by the bolshevik and fled from him. Ah, he is a martyr! Who killed John Keats? The *Soviet Quarterly* so savage and tatarly killed Sergei Yessenin.

Mayakovsky, who for reasons of his own pondered so much over Yessenin's death, made another accusation. He said in effect: You, gentlemen of the bourgeoisie, your poison, the opium of your culture which we all inherit, against which we all must struggle, you killed Sergei Yessenin.

This was the literary equivalent of an idea I had already encountered in politics; for instance, in Lenin's letter to American workingmen. What was bad in the revolutionary world was a leftover of bourgeois life, what was good came from socialism. I had remembered this when I had argued with Anton across six thousand miles, when I had first touched Soviet soil in Batum, when I grappled with the problem of evil which Greta and her circle raised on a new plane. Mayakovsky understood all this far better than I; he, who was perhaps Russia's greatest poet since Pushkin, and certainly the greatest poet of the Soviet epoch; he, the transition singer paramount in the most important of all transition eras. When I left him, I knew he was tormented by the limits which history would set to his gigantic development; he thought only of the future. But when you considered his past, you knew, too, that this revolutionary writer had already achieved immortality because more powerfully than any other poet of his time he had grasped the meaning of the proletariat's creative transformation of the world.

§ 4

On the way to Lida Ivanovna's I did not think about the exiled flyers; it was too painful. I hesitated to ring Lida Ivanovna's bell; they would be talking about it inside. I knocked tentatively and Greta opened the door. The room was warm and friendly; several flyers in uniform and their wives were drinking tea, and when I sat down the conversation was resumed. They were talking about art; that is, Lida Ivanovna, pale and calm, was lecturing Mathilda about art. She talked, like the women in J. Alfred Prufrock, about Michelangelo, but in quite a different way. She held him up to Mathilda as an ideal for Soviet artists to follow, because he represented the healthy and the monumental. We shall have a new Soviet art, she said, that will be greater than that of the Renaissance, because we shall have superior men and women who will be equals. I suddenly realized what Lida Ivanovna was doing. Had her grandfather been exiled to the north, her grandmother would have sought consolation in the church; Lida Ivanovna was seeking it in the secular religion of our times—that blend of sensuous image and ideal aspiration which we call art and which alone in a scientific age can voice the secret dreams of the heart. Lida Ivanovna brought out some reproductions of Michelangelo's frescoes and showed them to Mathilda; she talked to the Pioneer as if no one else were present in the room, as if she were totally disappointed in the older generation and could speak only to the youth.

"Do you know why these faces are so beautiful?" she said. "It's because the people are beautiful. So if we are to have a great art we must have a great life. The greatest artists are the bolsheviks; they are creating new men and women; we painters can only hope to copy them down on canvas."

I was astonished, as I had been at the railway station, that Lida Ivanovna, like Mathilda and Mimi and Greta and the other women affected by the exile, should so calmly and without a shadow of doubt accept communism despite their personal tragedy. It was then that the full force of Kostya's last words struck me: *I must get back into the Party.*

The victim of an injustice wished more than anything else in the world to rejoin the ranks of the "unjust." The scion of the old nobility turned bolshevik understood better than any liberal aesthete or philosopher the difference between the great goal of the proletariat and the mistakes of individual bureaucrats.

I suddenly remembered the story of Nuorteva, the remarkable Finn whom I had met at a meeting in New York when I was still a student. Nuorteva had lived in the United States for many years, was active in the Socialist party and in the Finnish co-operatives, and was one of the founders of the American Communist party. In 1919 he went to Soviet Russia. There an American communist, accused of being a dupe of the Department of Justice, saved himself by implicating Nuorteva. The civil war was at its height, and there was little time to investigate charges of this kind. Trials were of necessity abrupt, in essence courts-martial. Nuorteva was sentenced to prison knowing he was absolutely innocent; and his judges knew that up to that point he had had a clean, heroic revolutionary record. Yet not for a single moment did Nuorteva dissociate himself from the Party which had erroneously imprisoned him; he knew that in time of civil conflict, with the odds against you, with the whole vast land afire, mistakes were bound to happen; the revolution would triumph in spite of them. Thrown into a concentration camp with a bunch of White Guards, Nuorteva unearthed and exposed a counterrevolutionary plot. In spite of this, he was for some reason thrown into solitary confinement. At the end of a year the civil war was over, and Lenin personally investigated the case. Nuorteva was released. He walked out of his prison cell, and the first place he went to was Party headquarters. He called on the secretary, and his first words were:

"How much dues do I owe the Party?"

Nuorteva was reinstated, and subsequently became president of the Karelian soviet republic.

Kostya's attitude, like Nuorteva's, threw a new light on the liberal pretensions about impartial justice and free speech; they explained many things which appeared obscure at the time of Roger Baldwin's meeting on behalf of Soviet political prisoners when the *International* drowned out Charney Vladeck. Here were two bolsheviks who accepted wholeheartedly a social system in which they were personally victims of a miscarriage of justice. They regretted and resented the miscarriage; but they considered it precisely that—a miscarriage of justice. The system of justice itself remained valid for them. This seemed to be a sign of the health and integrity of the proletarian state.

In all societies which are healthy and moving forward, the prevailing justice is accepted by the accused as well as the accuser. It was only to us, who had outgrown feudalism, that the church's persecution of heretics seemed absurd; to Galileo it seemed just, albeit he was himself a victim of the system. He believed in what the church stood for essentially, hence approved its methods of defending the faith. If today we laugh at those methods it is because we laugh at the faith; for he who wills the end wills the means.

One sign of the decay of capitalism was that neither its defenders nor its victims believed in it. Those who ordered the imprisonment of Mooney or Sacco and Vanzetti, knew it was not justice; they were perfectly well aware that it was a frame-up. They were merely cynical; the beliefs of the bourgeois system were dying with the system itself. Even when a rebel against that system was "justly" condemned, even when there was no frame-up, even when the letter and spirit of the law were scrupulously observed, honest and progressive minds condemned the trials. They grasped, however dimly, that the main object was to perpetuate private property, poverty and war. That law was therefore most wrong when it was most "right."

But even when there was a miscarriage of proletarian justice, you regretted the mistake without condemning the system of justice as such; for *its* objective, as distinguished from bourgeois justice, was to destroy the exploitation of man by man, and to establish the classless co-operative society.

Some liberals, like Roger Baldwin, demanded free speech for the Ku-Klux Klan as well as for the communists; Baldwin protested against the imprisonment of politicals in Moscow as well as in San Francisco. He was—or so it seemed—absolutely consistent and impartial in his demand for "fair play" and "free speech." It was we, who demanded the release of Tom Mooney and approved the imprisonment of counterrevolutionaries, who seemed to be inconsistent. We were apparently hypocritical adherents of a double standard of political morals.

You could say, of course, that the whole capitalist world lived on a double standard of morals, with one law for the rich, another for the poor. In the very year I am describing, the bourgeois authorities kept the innocent Sacco and Vanzetti waiting for the electric chair, while President Coolidge pardoned three crooks whom the courts had found guilty and sentenced to prison in the notorious glass casket racket.

But was it enough to say that the proletarian state was no better than capitalist society? If that was all, why the revolution at all? Why fight for something which was simply no worse than the old? No, the proletarian regime must be more just than the world of profiteer and exploiter.

But what was justice—that beautiful dream I had been following since I first heard it from my uncle Moishe in revolutionary terms, from my grandfather in religious terms, and from the *Masses* group in aesthetic terms? Socrates asked what was justice, and the replies, long and circuitous, resulted in a big book on the nature of the ideal state based on chattel slavery. In our epoch, the answers would lead to reflections on the nature of the state in a society based on wage slavery, and in that society in which the wage slaves had created a state of their own intent upon abolishing slavery of every kind by transforming men's economic relations.

Why did Greta in New York denounce the imprisonment of Tom Mooney whom she believed to be innocent, and why did she not openly denounce in Moscow the imprisonment of Kostya whom she believed to be equally innocent? Granted, for the sake of argument only, that it was "dangerous" to agitate like that in Moscow, why did she not go back to Berlin, quit the Communist party, and denounce it as an instrument of tyranny, as various renegades had done, including some of my own guides, philosophers and friends? In a bitter moment of anguish, she had asked me to take her back to New York, as Kostya had called on God to be the witness of his innocence. But that was a slip into old emotional patterns; Kostya did not believe in God now, and Greta, who had every opportunity for going back to New York or Berlin, remained in Moscow and did her work with unabated enthusiasm. This devotion to the cause in spite of a personal injustice ennobled Greta, so that her private foibles seemed as unimportant as flies crawling over da Vinci's "Last Supper."

Her attitude impressed upon me that capitalists and communists alike operated on a single standard of political morals. Lenin said: whatever promotes communism is good, whatever hinders it is bad. The bourgeois said: whatever promotes capitalism is good, whatever hinders it is bad. The difference was that Lenin said it openly, frankly, in so many unmistakable words. The capitalists said it in deeds; their words sang hosannas to an abstract liberty and justice that never was on land or sea.

But what was good for capitalism was good for a handful of exploiters and bad for the mass of mankind; what was good for communism was good for the mass of mankind and bad for a handful of exploiters. The bourgeois ideologues denied that the end justifies the means, but the bourgeois politicians lived by that formula; the interests of the capitalist mode of production and the society based upon it justified in their eyes murder, falsehood, intrigue, theft, everything and anything for which the private citizen would be condemned. The bolsheviks realized that their end justified only those means which could possibly further that particular end; and the end was such that certain means were precluded even on grounds of expediency. The gentlemen of the British cabinet could forge the Zinoviev letter because this could give them the elections; the Soviet regime could forge nothing, because no such subterfuge could hasten the revolution by one day; only the self-consciousness of the workers as a class, only real knowledge, only the truth could hasten it. Even the crudest utilitarian morality would compel the bolsheviks to tell the social truth, for that alone made the classless society possible.

Greta to some extent accepted Kostya's arrest because she knew that he might possibly be guilty of the crime with which he was charged; and more important still, she knew that his judges would not have condemned him unless they felt assured of his guilt. There might be a mistake; there could be no railroading. In principle, she accepted the necessity of rendering harmless those who damaged the building of socialism. She approved the arrest of counterrevolutionaries not despite her agitation for Mooney's release, but because of it. The two actions, which to some appeared so contradictory, proceeded from an identical motive—the desire to abolish the prevailing system of exploitation and create a classless society.

The capitalists arrested Tom Mooney because his agitation injured capitalism; the soviet regime arrested a counterrevolutionary or a saboteur or a traitor because his activity injured socialism. You could not measure the two acts by abstract and undefined and sleight-of-hand terms like "justice"; the real question you had to answer first was: what is better for mankind, capitalism or socialism?

If you thought capitalism, with its wars and poverty and exploitation and ignorance and brutality, was better, you would rationalize the whole business; you would either ignore its evils or fancy they were accidental and remediable, and you would approve of Mooney's imprisonment as the just punishment of one who menaced "civilization." But if you thought it was better for mankind to scrap the remains of the patriarchal system and the accumulated horrors of the bourgeois system of private property and to create in its stead a classless co-operative society, then you would of necessity approve any measure that would break the power of the exploiters—just as in 1776 you would have supported Washington, in 1793 Robespierre, in 1861 Lincoln. To say, as some liberals said, that the conspiracy to electrocute Sacco and Vanzetti and the execution of a counterrevolutionary were identical was to say that the crucifixion of Christ and of the two thieves was identical.

It was not the identity of the punishment that was important, but the difference in the objective of that punishment and in its results. In either case, individuals were bound to suffer, as in all war; but in the long run, it made all the difference in the world whether tyranny or freedom prevailed. In every country, the conscious workers understood this out of their own experience; the exploiters who sent police and soldiers to shoot down strikers, who dragged workers into the trenches to kill their fellow workers of other countries, who imprisoned and tortured the standard-bearers of socialism were the last people in the world to talk about "justice" or "fair play." In every strike, the ethical problem reduced itself to the simple and illuminating question: Are you for the strikers or for the scabs?

In so far as Kostya was near and dear to her, Greta was pained. In so far as he might have been innocent, she was bitter over a possible miscarriage of justice in an individual case. But in so far as he might have been guilty, she accepted the general principle that those who harm the revolution must be rendered harmless. To that extent she approved Kostya's arrest for precisely the same reason that she demanded Mooney's release: she wanted, more than anything else in the world, that socialism should triumph.

§5

The moment Gustav arrived in Moscow, Hedda phoned me, saying:

"Gustav is here, I want you to meet him."

They had been married for fifteen years, but she never called him "my husband"; that was a vulgar petit-bourgeois phrase smelling of private property.

Gustav turned out to be a tall, fat German, with a round, red face like the man smoking a cigar in the old Regensburg advertisements I used to see in the I.R.T. trains. Like all the German comrades I met at this time, he was pure Nordic, blue-eyed and sandy-haired. His tight mouth always smiled, except when he talked politics, then it became soberly straight and thin. Gustav came of a proletarian family, and began to work in a factory at fifteen, but years in the movement had given him a considerable range of knowledge. This, however, was chiefly in politics and economics; he had no literary pretensions, and admired what he considered the superior culture of Kurt and Hedda. But Kurt disturbed him.

"A brilliant boy," he said to me, "but without character." He said it as you might say about a man: poor fellow, he has no legs and arms, only eyes. "Someday," Gustav continued sadly, "he will be in charge of some important action, and his mere cleverness will get the better of him, and we'll lose. A bolshevik needs character just as he needs to breathe." Gustav spoke English with a Canadian-British accent, left over from his days in Toronto and London.

Like Scott Nearing, he was single-minded, completely intent on his work, twin brother to the American puritan at his best without any philistinism about private matters like drinking and love. He never gossiped about other people's affairs, sharply rebuked Hedda when she did, and was reticent about himself. When you asked, How are you? he talked about Party work. You could see that he and Hedda were deeply attached to each other, but there was a beautiful reserve in their attitude.

"How are things, Gustav?"

"Na, Hedda, I think we have entered on a new stage. Hindenburg's election confronted us with the danger of being isolated from the masses. I'm afraid the Party has underestimated the monarchist danger. As usual, the social democrats interfere with our struggle against this danger. Do you know what they had the nerve to say? They said Hindenburg was elected on Thaelmann's shoulders! Swine!"

"Our American liberals talk that way too," I said. "They claim that communism leads to fascism, and point to Mussolini as an example. Communism and fascism are supposed to be more or less the same thing, since neither is democratic in form."

"I know," Gustav said grimly. "We hear the same junk in Germany. Water and poison are the same thing because you drink them both out of a glass. So you might as well support the lesser evil—the poison. But we make plenty of mistakes ourselves. We increase our isolation from the masses by concentrating on purely parliamentary maneuvers; I know because I'm a member of the Reichstag."

"And a good thing too," Hedda laughed, "or you would be in jail."

"Sometimes I wish to be rid of this damned parliamentary life, with its immunity, and talk, talk, talk. I'd like to work in the trade unions. But of course you meet the social democrats here too, the Bonzes, the bureaucrats who hold the stirrup for the Junkers so that they can hurry up and ride over us."

"Aren't you a little harsh on the social democratic leaders?" I asked.

"Harsh? All right, listen. Last year we sent their executive a letter suggesting a united front to disarm the monarchists. We suggested the following program: Immediately disband the monarchist Reichswehr; immediately cease the militarization of the police; confiscate the nobles' estates; clean out all monarchist officials from the government; release all proletarian political prisoners; establish a strict eight-hour day in industry; abolish all taxes burdening the masses. And what do you think the bureaucrats replied? Nothing! Not a word! We propose purely republican demands, and the social democrats, a leading party in the republic, will not co-operate."

Whatever doubts a man like Fred raised in my mind, Gustav resolved by his very existence. In his presence I recalled men like Ruthenberg and Foster, and realized that they were the normal communists, while Fred was a deviation from the norm, an accident which might develop toward bolshevism or away from it. In the same way Hedda was the norm, and Greta the sport; that was precisely the reason why the comrades took Hedda for granted, while Greta was treated like a spoiled, unique child. What was there to notice about Hedda? There were millions of women like her in the revolutionary movement of the various countries: serious, intelligent, strong, spiritually integrated, passionately devoted and hard at work for the common cause; while Greta was a melange of old and new, a communist who retained some of the mercenary, antisocial ethics and habits inherited from a civilization based on private property, theft, fraud and violence. In the movement you took Hedda for granted the way you took the sky, or the earth, or the unit meeting, anything that was to be expected, that surrounded you every day. Greta was something different—an Albino, a bearded lady, a poet with green hair. She set out to épater les bolchevistes the way Gautier wanted to épater la bourgeoisie. But just as bourgeois society accepts and pets its playful, romantic children so long as they support its essence, which is private property, so the movement accepted and petted Greta because she supported its essence, which is the struggle for a classless society. And Fred, with his lust for personal domination, was accepted the same way and for the same reason by the Gustavs and Heddas who were the head and heart of the movement.

Gustav laughed when Hedda told him about Greta and myself. He rolled back his tall, barrel body and laughed until tears filled his bright blue eyes. Under the pretext of explaining the whole business to her husband, Hedda gave me a little sermon. Her face was serious, except for a faint smile, and she did not look at me once during her lecture.

"The joke of it is, Gustav, that Greta is absolutely faithful to him. If she were not it wouldn't be tragic either, but she happens to be. She chatters about sex, she flirts; she may go off with somebody tomorrow to China or India for the sake of the trip, for the curiosity of it, or even for love, her kind of love. But her bark is worse than her bite. And this poor boy here can't sleep; he wonders how the Party can tolerate Greta. You see, Gustav, while we are thinking whether socialism can be built in one country, he is thinking whether Greta is typical among us or exceptional. Oh, and he even writes poems about us, very deep ones. Wait, I have one here."

Hedda opened a book on the table, and drew out a typewritten sheet I had given her.

"Listen to this, Gustav," she said, and began to intone in a mock heroic tone the sestette of my sonnet:

> If we have prophets callings for revolts,
> Who shake the skies until the old worlds crack,
> For every hero there are twenty dolts,
> And Tartuffes skulk behind Ilych's back;
> And Madame Pompadour and you, my dear,
> Differ only in name and class and year.

"Petit-bourgeois novels stink with that kind of stuff," Gustav said dryly. "Everything comes down to love, the Thirty Years' War, the French Revolution, everything." He lit a Russian cigarette, and bit

into its cardboard end. "Consider this, comrade. There is more equality between men and women in the Soviet Union than in the France
of Louis Fourteenth or the capitalist countries today. And this very
equality makes Pompadours impossible among us. Pompadours are
possible only where there are despots in power and women in subjection. The Soviet Union has women administrators, ambassadors,
judges, journalists, authors, engineers, doctors, and even army commanders. But name me one women—one!—that plays the role of
Pompadour. Litvinov's wife is one of the cleverest and most attractive
women in Moscow, but she plays no role in politics whatever. She's
not even a Party member. Do you know what she does for a living?
She is a translator, like you. And Krupskaya is Lenin's widow. We
all love and respect her, even when we disagree with her. But never,
never, even when Lenin was alive, did she play any special role because
she was his wife. At the fourteenth congress of the Russian party, last
December, Stalin criticized Krupskaya. Some comrades were shocked,
and Stalin asked: What is the difference between Comrade Krupskaya's
position and that of any other responsible comrade? Do you think
that the interests of any individual comrade take precedence over the
interests and the unity of the Party? The congress applauded Stalin's
words. The authority which Krupskaya, Kollontai and our own Clara
Zetkin enjoy they enjoy not as females but as people."

Through Gustav and Hedda I got to know other people in the
Lux, and was compelled to revise the picture of it that I had received
from Greta and her circle. Most of the Lux residents were serious,
hard-working revolutionists, little interested in the psychological puzzles which people like Greta created. Such puzzles they would dismiss
by saying either, "that's bohemianism, the old psychology," or by saying, "that's a problem that will have to be liquidated."

One of these people was Jack Murphy, who then represented the
British Communist party in the Comintern. Murphy was about forty,
short, slight and spectacled, with a thin, ascetic face like a priest's. Actually, he was a worker who had spent his youth in Vickers', and the
British trade-union movement. He lived in two small rooms in the
Lux with his wife and a lively son of six. His wife was a red-cheeked,
high-nosed London cockney, a nice and proper English girl who did
not belong to the Party. Greta, as was to be expected, called her "Mrs."
Murphy and poked fun at her "pure, spotless, petit-bourgeois soul."
When a communist wanted to heap the ultimate insult on anyone in
or near the movement, he damned that person as Mr. or Mrs.

Jack Murphy used to come into my room, sometimes to explain a new political development to me, sometimes to ask for advice about the style of some article he was writing.

"Come on, Jack," Greta would tease him, "take a drink; it's wonderful Georgian wine, from Stalin's home town."

"I don't drink," Jack said solemnly.

"Have a cigarette, go on, I won't tell Mrs. Murphy."

"Thanks. I don't smoke."

"Surely you kiss, Jack. How would you like me to kiss you."

"I wouldn't like it at all."

"O my English saint! All right, then I will tell you a good story, and you can tell it to Mrs. Murphy in bed. Or don't you ever go to bed either? Now, there was a Russian officer who came to Catherine the Great—"

Murphy stood up, and said to me with suppressed indignation: "Come up after supper; we'll finish our work in my room."

Once he complained to me that he hadn't had a bath in a week. The Lux was an old building with one shower and one bath. The men and women took showers in alternate groups; the bath cost a ruble and had to be ordered in advance. There was always a mob ahead of you, and you usually lost half a day. I went, instead, to a Russian steam bath, and advised Murphy to do the same. He had never been to one in his life, and was interested to hear that it was a national custom of the country. Through the thick steam, we could see bearded men soaping themselves, beating each other with laurel leaves, dreaming stretched out on wooden benches. Murphy stretched out, and for a long time was silent. Then he said:

"Some of our young people get into trouble because we have destroyed the old morality, and have not yet created a new one. The old morality was bad, vicious, hypocritical; I'm not sure the transition one is much better. We'll have to find something better."

He shifted his thin body and was again silent for a long time; then he said, apropos of nothing at all:

"I've been thinking: Lenin was a wonderful man. When I first came to Russia with a group of British trade unionists, I went to see Trotsky. A brilliant man, but cold and aloof. You couldn't warm up to him, you could only admire him. Lenin was warm, human, simple; there was nothing Olympian about him. You immediately thought of him not as a leader but as a comrade and a friend. He said to us:

"'And how are things going in Britain, comrades?'

" 'Very well,' I said. 'The Welsh coal miners are on strike. They are daily becoming more revolutionary.'

" 'Really!' Lenin said.

" 'Indeed,' I said, 'there is every likelihood that they will come out for the Party.'

" 'Does your Communist party publish a paper?' Lenin asked.

" 'Oh, yes; the *Worker.*'

" 'What percentage of the Welsh miners are literate?'

" 'Almost a hundred per cent.'

" 'What is the price of your paper?'

" 'Tuppence.'

" 'How many miners are on strike?' Lenin said.

" 'Thousands of them; they're out almost a hundred per cent.'

" 'And what is the circulation of your paper among them?' Lenin said.

" 'Oh, several hundred copies.'

" 'They can all read, and only a handful of them read our paper?'

" 'Unfortunately.'

"Then Lenin leaned back and laughed. 'Don't you see, comrades,' he said, 'that you are deluding yourselves? Do you think that men who will not give two pennies for our paper will give their lives for our cause?' That was the way Lenin's mind worked. He didn't mean that our prospect was hopeless in England; he meant: don't ever kid yourself, and don't neglect any detail, however small."

On the way home, Murphy was too preoccupied to talk. We parted at his door.

He walked into his room, saying half aloud:

"What a wonderful man, Lenin. . . ."

Everybody now said this in Russia, even the old princess who taught us the language and liked to compare Lenin with Peter the Great. And when you tried to find out which of Lenin's qualities most endeared him to people it always came down to his extraordinary ability to perceive the truth and his extraordinary simplicity in stating it.

Robert Minor, who visited Moscow that summer, was fond of recalling his talks with Lenin, especially those which helped him to overcome his own anarchist-liberal past. Minor had by this time completely repressed his artistic gifts, and turned his back on all appeals from the revolutionary press for cartoons. His whole being was immersed in politics, and he had the habit of slowly enunciating a political idea out of a clear sky, apropos of nothing at all. You would be walking down the Tverskaya with him and talking about some trifle. Then silence, and out of that silence would come the huge Texan's deep bass voice continuing aloud some thought he had been pursuing secretly, a thought which had nothing to do with the conversation, and everything to do with the central motif of our lives.

"On the question of class justice Lenin once said to me: it all boils down to this—*kto-kavo, who-whom*. Either we crush the counter-revolution, or it crushes us. The point is precisely *whose ox is gored*. And that is the point the liberals miss. They want the same civil rights for progress and for reaction. It's all the same to them whether the scab or the picket gets hurt."

I tried to imagine what set Minor's mind going along these lines, and thought it was perhaps our discussions with members of the Opposition. For of all the lies which the bourgeois ideologues had spread in America about the inner-Party situation in Russia, the biggest was that we were permitted to hear only one side. The fact was that you couldn't turn around without hearing the case of the Opposition; and Minor had just had a session with a Russian whom he had known in America as a fellow anarchist, and who now sought to revive dead anarchist sentiments on behalf of the Opposition.

§ 6

Mimi visited the detention island far up north, and spent a week with Kostya, and mingled with the other prisoners. She came back to us with encouraging reports. They were in good health, well fed, and generally well treated. Kostya had gained weight, was cheerful, and convinced that when he was released he would be taken back into the Party.

This good news relieved Greta's anxiety; she was her old self again, bubbling with energy and humor, once more stern in her political judgments. Ernst Toller, the playwright, an old friend of hers from Munich days, came to Moscow. The Soviet writers made a fuss over him; the German communists boycotted him; they would not forgive his blunders during the short-lived "Red republic" in Bavaria. In the lobby of a Moscow theater, a group of German communists turned their backs ostentatiously on Toller. Greta was impersonal.

"Poor Ernst," she said. "A sweet boy, but he should stay out of practical politics; he doesn't understand such things; he should stick to poetry for he's really a wonderful poet."

But this sensible advice for revolutionary writers did not apply to me. Greta wanted her man to be a political leader, and now that Kostya's exile was off her mind, she returned to her old refrain:

> Ruhm muss man gewinnen,
> Dann werden sie sich schon anders besinnen.

She was delighted when I was appointed to the Comintern commission on imperialism along with Duncan and Roy; she could now say that her comrade did something more useful than scribble verses and translate documents. In general, however, I failed to fulfill Greta's hopes. I continued to write verses, influenced by Greta's contradictory nature, Hedda's purity of purpose, and the new outlook on life which surrounded me in this new world of creative labor.

In the *New Masses* I published *Notes for a Love Poem,* based on what I considered valid in Greta's attitude.

a.

> Troubadours, sonnet-spinners
> cobblers of roundelays
> have kidded the world
> believing their own jingles.
> Out of regard for expert testimony
> I grant beauty has made men crazy
> O red mouths of all time
> setting poets' tongues aflame!

> "The fragrance of her hair
> pursues me through the night
> like a rich dream; the light
> of her quiet eyes fills the star
> of evening with glory
> for the resemblance;
> there lingers the remembrance
> of her body's song; the story
> of her white breasts like fruit
> from a far exotic land,
> the slender fingers of her hand,
> her voice like a lyric on a flute:
> Keep crown and throne,
> the crowd's applause, the splendor of arms,
> I shall walk with her alone,
> the world well bartered for her charms."

b.

I charge you
suspect even the captains
of the poetry industry:
believe Helen's beauty—
doubt her face was the incendiary
that burned the topless towers.

When bows twang and cannons boom
official excuses smile like salesmen:
Iliad's profound roll is flavored
with Foreign Office propaganda;
Paris' girl friend was sister
to the duke of Sarajevo.

c.

The baron's daughter beamed
because her boy friend
knocked two knights for a goal;
bumped them off their chargers
shield and all;
the bleachers' applause
is music to her ears;
the court's smile
approves her secret kisses:

The lovely Heloise
fluttered in a net of theses;
was eventually deflowered
by a theologian's dogmas.

Mary Martin of Leland Stanford
intrigues against two sororities
for the all-American quarterback:
bed was sweet
after licking Harvard 15-3.

"Dear Jenny," wrote Karl Marx,
"you are a legend in your home town,
damned pleasant for a man
to have a wife liked by everybody."

d.

If you would have my love, dear boy,
go build a bridge, run a factory,
lead a strike,
outwit the police,
write theses without deviations:
the times are out of joint,
go fix them:
only the brave
only the brave
only the brave
deserve the fair.

e.

Dearest, not for your eyes alone
nor your mouth envied by roses
nor the electric secret of your thighs—
but for your more essential beauty:
your hand touched life, your lips uttered thought,
being the world's darling, you are mine.

f.

The professors say the world is old;
yesterday—as Time goes—
we crawled on our bellies, ate our foes,
blood dripped from our speechless mouths:

We have groped through a million black aeons,
blind children of blind chance:
the trumpets blow for the advance
over the crumbling walls of history.

Man's true wisdom, joy, power,
true love of woman, child, friend,
shall first begin when false things end,
when yesterday's monsters are safely dead.

We have learned to walk on our hind legs,
exchange ideas across the seas;
smoke stacks loom above the trees:
China beholds the banners of Moscow.

This much seemed true, then, that in every age woman, as a rule,
gives her love to him who succeeds by the standards of his community.

This was the constant among the variables of time; but Greta appeared to be more interested in the success than in the standards. Hedda, it seemed to me, had best transcended the old type of woman, and it was about her that I wrote the *Portrait of a German Comrade,* which also appeared in the *New Masses,* one of the first American poems, I think, about a communist woman.

Moscow's midnight
painting the window blue
exhibits the Independents Show
of gilded academic domes outside
piercing the sky with spires
looming behind
Picasso's beer hall
yellow and green across the street

the waiter shoves the bank clerk
into the droszhky

she serves us tea at home
around the table
with the shaded lamp
shining in the darkness of her room
as shines a good deed etcetera
this delicate touch
expropriated from the world's bohemia.

Lenin's wise face
smiles on the wall behind her head
wonderful clever eyes:
eight inches from his beard
a postcard Stalin
covers Rykov's nose:
hydroelectric stations
slaughtered midnight's magic:
no one remembers nightingales;
buy roses at the corner.

The English comrade
from Hampstead Heath
having once read this fellow Keats
tells how the boys
walloped during the General Strike
the cops in Sheffield.

She lays out ham and sausage
cuts bread like a man
with thumb and penknife
pours tea quickly
statistically damning Ultra-Lefts:
Brunhilde playing housewife.

"Men do not take to me as men."
She lights a cigarette
scorning to explain;
digresses to the year
she learned to read Marx in English
in a Canadian jail,
the time in Dresden
the Party saw the eyes of victory:
"We should have fired;
we had no iron leaders."

O the years, the years,
the hundred miles an hour years!

At twenty, when the war was young,
she wrote three chapters of a novel,
took courses in aesthetics:
"Now is no time for fooling:
next year
back to Germany:
dieses Mal müssen wir gewinnen."

"You are young," she says, pouring tea.
"I do not measure you by calendars:
learn to be critical,
conserve, hit hard."

Behind her wisdom
lurks a deeper wisdom:
how should she say
be strong like me
choose
eliminate
march straight as heroes do.

She—never kneeling at his shrine—
sees what is great in Lenin and in man:
measures this age

with the vast gauges of her nature,
pouring tea quickly
in Moscow's midnight blue
quoting Faust
kidding the English comrade
from Hampstead Heath.

When I showed this poem in print to Sergei Dinamov, he shook his head sadly.

"You are an impressionist," he said, as if he had guessed my own disturbance about the inadequacy of impressions unorganized by the dialectic. "You should not spend so much time with comrades from the old world; you should meet more Russian comrades who have had new experiences."

O. B., my ironic Irish boss, said the same thing. "If you are interested," she said, "in the so-called New Woman, why in hell do you fiddle around with shadows? I'll introduce you to the real thing: Shura."

I had heard of Shura. She was famous all over Russia as a Red general. After the civil war was over, they had dismissed all women from the Red army except two or three women commanders, and Shura was among these. She was now on the general staff of the Red army, a dramatic example of that equality of men and women which socialism was beginning to realize. At home, they talked about "equal rights" too. It meant the right to vote, to hold a job, to smoke, drink and have love affairs. This was for women of the upper and middle classes; the workingwoman got lower wages in the factory than the man and was thus compelled to scab on her father, her brothers, her husband, to cut the living standards of her own family, her own class. In the Soviet Union it was equal pay for equal work—and from this economic equality everything else followed for all women. All rights were open to you on the basis of merit, regardless of race or sex. I had met women engineers, women judges, women administrators, and I never forgot the little old peasant woman from Siberia who traveled thousands of miles alone to attend a meeting of the Central Executive Committee of the U.S.S.R., of which she was a proud member. But Shura was an extreme example of this equality: she was a living refutation of the old argument that women are unfit for military service, apparently the highest point of human ability.

When I finally met her at O. B.'s house, Shura was a sharp surprise. She didn't look like a general at all. She was of medium height, slim and young, about twenty-five. Her hair was cropped close like a man's, but her face was what is called "feminine"—with soft features, large dark eyes, a full tender mouth. Only her small strong chin indicated the remarkable character that was hers. Her neat military uniform with the Sam Browne belt and enormous revolver did not entirely conceal a graceful body, at once vigorous and voluptuous in its movements.

Shura greeted me in English; then it turned out she spoke French and German too, as well as her native Russian. After five minutes of small talk, O. B. induced her to tell her life-story, though Russians as a rule are not reticent on that point.

She was born in Moscow. Her father was a Russian businessman who owned three factories; her mother was English. Until she was four she spoke both languages with equal fluency; then for some reason she dropped English and spoke only Russian. At six she began to have fantasies of being a soldier, especially a cavalryman. She would lie awake in the dark and imagine herself riding on a black horse, faster and faster, with the wind whistling in her ears.

Actually, she was a terrible coward. Loud noises frightened her. She was afraid to walk alone at night in the streets of Moscow. Fear of death haunted her day and night. She would imagine herself falling fatally ill, or being killed by a runaway horse, or a robber, or just going to sleep and never waking up again.

When she was thirteen the World War broke out. Her soldier fantasies became stronger than ever. Awake, she dreamed of running away from home and joining the army. But first you must overcome the fear of death. Every night she walked the dark streets of Moscow alone with her teeth chattering; she sought out-of-the-way places where people said hooligans might attack you any minute. At the end of a week she quit; the strain on her courage was too great.

When she was sixteen she was considered a pretty girl; rather boyish, people said, slim and hard-boned, with a tilted nose; yet there was feminine charm in her soft eyes and clear voice. Her family had not even begun to think of her future.

The February Revolution came, then October, and she began to attend meetings. At one of these she heard a Hungarian orator, a young student. They met afterwards, fell in love. Only then did she discover he was a communist. It took him a week to convert, and another week to marry her in secret. Her family was furious, so the couple went to Budapest. There Shura joined the Party, lived poor and worked hard.

She was on the streets of Budapest when the June uprising started. Bullets were flying all around; the fear of death was unbearable. It lasted a few minutes in the most intense form in which she had ever experienced it. Suddenly she thought: not every bullet hits you; you have as much chance of escaping alive as of getting killed. She became very calm and went to Party headquarters to attend to her duties.

During the brief Soviet regime under Bela Kun she occupied a minor government post; her husband did more responsible work. One night they received a telephone call. The counterrevolution had triumphed; leaders of the revolution had fled, but everything would be all right. They had been compelled to turn the government over to the reactionaries, but there would be no White terror. The new government had made the most solemn promise to that effect.

The following night she and her husband and a number of other comrades were arrested.

In her prison cell she heard that comrades were being tortured. She thought she had lost her fear of death; now she realized that what she had feared most was not death, but pain. If she could only be hit by a bullet and die at once: a swift, clean death. She could never stand torture.

They brought her before a court-martial to be questioned. The White officers asked the most confusing things, and she hesitated in her answers. She determined to incriminate nobody, no matter what it cost; she would be a good communist even if it meant pain. She hesitated too long in answering one question, and the soldier on guard behind her kicked his heavy boot into her back, and she fainted.

Alone again in her cell, she decided to kill herself. She broke the windowpane, picked up a jagged piece of glass and began to cut the veins in her wrist. The prison guard saw her through the spy hole, rushed in and beat her senseless.

In the prison days that followed, she developed T.B. She was sure she was going to die soon; the death fantasies of childhood came back stronger than ever. If she could only be back in Russia, if she could only give her life for the revolution! But to die here in jail like a dog. . . .

They released her and she learned that her husband had been shot. Now she had only one, persistent thought: I must get back to Russia;

I must fight for the revolution with my hands. I have not long to live; let me die on the battlefield.

She fled across the border, made her way to the Ukraine and there joined the Red army as a private. They gave her a man's uniform, boots and a rifle. She shaved her head, the way the Russians do in the summertime, and bandaged her breasts so they would not be noticed. Most people took her for a young boy, and those soldiers who knew she was a woman did not bother her; nobody thought of such things on the battlefield.

One day a White Guard chased her into an empty house with a revolver. They struggled, she got his gun away and emptied it into him. His death grimaces revolted her. This was the first man she had ever killed. After that she was always calm on the battlefield. She was an excellent rider. They assigned her to reconnaissance and to political classes among the soldiers.

Once her regiment captured a village from the Whites. They remained there for weeks, and the soldiers found sweethearts among the village girls. One girl fell in love with Shura. To keep up appearances, Shura went out with her, danced with her, kissed her. When the girl began to demand the logical consequences, Shura broke off the "affair." This happened several times; Shura became known as the regimental Lothario. But her chief reputation in the army was that of a brave soldier. She was the coolest "man" in every crisis, and often rallied her wavering companions to victory. The high command praised her military talents and sent her to an officers' school to specialize in cavalry work and in reconnoitering. Here she began to study Marx seriously.

At the end of the civil war, all women were discharged from the Red army with the exception of Shura and two or three others. She continued her military studies, but suddenly a strange desire came over her. She wanted to have a baby. She did not want a lover or a husband; she just wanted a baby. But not everyone was fit to be the father of a Red commander's child; he must give the baby a good start in life. Such a father must have good health, intelligence and will power, and, of course, he must be of proletarian origin. There was just this kind of ideal father in her regiment; he worked with her in the political courses. Shura came to this man and said:

"I don't love you, I don't want to marry you, but I would like you to be the father of my child. After that we shall have nothing to do with each other."

The comrade obliged her. She took part in cavalry maneuvers

until the sixth month, then she had to give up riding. But she still took part in the infantry maneuvers. Toward the ninth month she was sprawling in a meadow directing troop movements through a field telephone. Suddenly she cut her orders short and called the field hospital. The doctors came and said:

"We have no facilities for this kind of thing in the army, comrade. You had better take a leave of absence and have your baby in Moscow."

For the first time in five years, Shura dressed in women's clothes. This had a curious effect on her. In army uniform she had always felt like a man; now in a skirt she felt like a woman. During the civil war she lay in the mud of the trenches and did not mind the lice and the blood; now, waiting for her baby in Moscow, she wanted to live in a clean room and sleep in white linen.

The baby was born, and Shura wrote her mother in Paris about it. She had often written to her family in Paris, but her mother, an embittered émigrée, had never answered. A baby was different, though. Her mother was overjoyed to become a grandmother.

"I now feel bound to the new Russia by a living bond," she wrote to Shura. "If what is going on in our country meets with the approval of your conscience, my darling, I am satisfied. All I want in this world is to see you happy, even if it's bolshevism that makes you happy."

As soon as she was able, Shura went back to her military studies, this time in the Moscow school. One day she came home to find the baby's nurse crying bitterly. The old peasant woman had left the baby lying face down on the pillow. She had gone out to get some water; when she returned she found the baby had choked to death.

Shura cried for the first time since her husband had been killed by the White Guards in Budapest. But there was no help for it; she concentrated on her military studies, and was known as one of the best students at the academy. Off duty she sometimes wore women's clothes. Men found her attractive; she had a clear, smooth skin; a firm, lithe body; and hands at once graceful and strong.

In a year she decided to have another baby. But this time it was going to be different. In telling me the story, Shura explained:

"We are building the future, but we cannot live in it. Under present conditions a child needs a father, a home, a family."

Perhaps these ideas came to Shura because this time she was in love with a student in the military academy. They were married, took an apartment in Moscow, and went to school together. She continued her military work until the day before the baby was born. She was writing an order during maneuvers when she felt the moment had come; her commanding officer telephoned for a car at once and she was taken to the hospital. The day before she had marched fifteen miles. The baby was very beautiful and Shura and her husband were happy, she said.

"I'd like to meet him," I said.

"All right," Shura said. "But he is hard to see; always busy; no time for social engagements. We have so much work—military studies, languages, Marxism; and then we teach political classes for the Comsomols."

"Then how is it you manage to see friends?"

"I am more experienced than my husband," Shura laughed. "I have finished my homework and put the baby to bed and now I am free."

The telephone rang, and Shura answered it. It was her husband. "Yes, darling," she said. "Oh, no, no . . . the *left* flank . . . that's where the cavalry is. Wait, I'll be home in fifteen minutes and will help you finish the problem. Is the baby sleeping all right?"

The Russians were proud of Shura, but even prouder of the advances made by the ordinary workingwoman; for Shura was the exception, and every class and age has its exceptions; but the test of socialism is the opportunities it gives to the unexceptional person. There was Dunya, for instance, who cleaned our rooms in the hotel. She had only recently come from the village, but she had already learned to read and write, was a member of the houseworkers' trade union and of the Party. She borrowed political pamphlets from us and lent us hers. This plump freckle-faced girl once left my razor on my pillow with the following note:

"Comrade: we are trying to teach our workers and peasants culture, how to build machines and how to wipe their noses. You are an American; you come from an advanced country; you should set us an example in cleanliness and culture. Is this dirty unwashed razor of yours a good example?"

I laughed, remembering an incident Mike Gold had told me on his return from the Soviet Union the previous year. He was walking with a girl in Moscow and spit into the street.

"Do you spit on the streets of New York too?" the girl said indignantly.

"Sure," Mike said.

"All right, but they are capitalist streets. These streets belong to us, to the proletariat, and we want them clean."

These were trifles. Dunya brought a more serious matter to our attention. The wife of a Comintern leader went to the theater and ordered Dunya to stay at home and mind the children. It was Dunya's trade-union night, and she was compelled to miss her meeting. She took up the matter with the Comintern and the foreign communist and his wife got a public bawling out. The comrades considered this example of proletarian social equality more important than an instance of individual genius among women; they thought that equality affected all and underlay the whole of the new life.

CHAPTER III

The idea, of course, is not to restrict individual creation, but to furnish it with the widest means of continued powerful development.

—MAXIM GORKY.

§ I

YOU could travel over the new Russia, as many liberals had done, and write volumes on the backwardness and hardships you saw. You could describe only cruelty, plunder, slaughter, and the bourgeois press at home would hail you as an impartial observer. But you would be lying. Even though every instance you recorded were by itself true, your picture of the Soviet Union as a whole would be false. If you said that Karl Marx suffered from boils, that Cromwell had a big wart on his nose, that Bonaparte was a victim of epilepsy, that Lenin was bald, that Bill Haywood was one-eyed, you would be saying true things; but if that was *all* you said about these men, you would be telling a monstrous lie. To stress the minor infirmity of a man and to ignore his genius, to ignore that very thing for which mankind remembers and cherishes him, would be a criminal lie. When people saw only the negative side of the October Revolution, only what was left over from the past, only what was backward and bad, only what was of necessity destructive, and at the same time ignored the great changes, the construction, the immense movement forward—they lied, monstrously.

I saw backwardness too, and dirt and ignorance and stupidity and error and cruelty. This was the indispensable parenthesis. The bolsheviks were not handed paradise in which to build socialism; nor can you in any environment, however favorable, make a great historical advance without paying for it, without resistance from the old which seeks to destroy the new and which therefore must itself be destroyed.

But who were these gentlemen lamenting the cost of the October Revolution in human suffering? Once you saw the world from the working-class viewpoint, you could not take seriously the bourgeois critics of Socialist Russia when they talked ethics. The British gentlemen who forged the Zinoviev letter and printed a fake issue of *Pravda* for election purposes were hardly in a position to lecture the working class on Soviet propaganda or bolshevik "jesuitism"; the bankers and manufacturers and editors and preachers and college professors who whooped it up for the war were the last people in the world to talk about Soviet "atrocities." The men and women who were silent about the imprisonment of American and European workers for economic and political reasons had disqualified themselves as critics of Soviet justice.

It was not these who disturbed us. The doubt and mistrust which now rankled in the minds of many rank-and-filers in the movement came from other sources. Next to Lenin, Trotsky had been for us the most glamorous figure of the October Revolution. You could not question his great intellectual powers, his character, his integrity, his devotion to the cause, nor his brilliant services to it. Now he was warning us against the degeneration of the Soviet state and the Communist party. Now the bourgeois press, which only yesterday refused to print Trotsky's writing, was citing him with joy. One of Trotsky's American disciples hastened to sell the so-called "testament" of Lenin to the New York *Times*. He was Max Eastman, who had once attacked Robert Minor for daring to criticize the bolsheviks in the New York *World,* a capitalist paper! Where capitalist propaganda could not budge you, these people could sow doubt in your mind. The bourgeois press played up the personal elements in the struggle between the Party and the Opposition: it was all supposed to be a fight for personal power, for Lenin's toga, mantle, throne, crown, and all the other stale metaphors.

Were we being tricked again? Was the revolution going to be another hoax, like Christianity or democracy? Was October to be merely the triumph of a group of intellectuals who would e: .it the workers and peasants for their own purposes? Was this gigantic struggle, this anguish of 160,000,000 people, was the faith and hope of millions in the bourgeois countries, to result in a transfer of power from one group of overlords to another?

A frightful question that knocked all your neat formulas to pieces. For the first time in years your faith in the proletarian revolution faltered. With that gone, what would there be left? Cynicism, despair, decay? What was there left in the face of Thermidor?

The whole trouble lay in approaching the crisis within the Party with aesthetic-ethical criteria, like those former Greenwich Village heroes who were now repudiating their pro-Soviet past and indicting the Soviet Union as degenerate and bureaucratic, despotic and cruel. The arguments of these gentlemen were primarily *ad hominem*. Trotsky was a genius and Stalin a coarse, illiterate lout; Trotsky was a gentleman and Stalin was "rude." Didn't Lenin himself say so? And when the Lotharios turned statesmen tried to rise above the *ad hominem* level they could get no further than the stale ethics of the bourgeoisie.

In Moscow you ran across Oppositionists who were more consistent—and more romantic. One of them, a gifted young Red professor, said to me bitterly:

"If our program is dangerous to the revolution, why doesn't the Party shoot us?"

"Don't be an idiot."

"Why not?" he cried hysterically, thrusting his hands under my eyes. "Do you see these hands? They signed hundreds of orders to execute mensheviks and social revolutionists and anarchists and liberals when I was head of the Cheka in X——. Many of those men were more intelligent, more cultured, more honest, finer in every way than I am. Yet I decreed their death because they were wrong and we were right. Their policy in the long run meant capitalism, ours socialism. If the Opposition is wrong as they were wrong, if we are reverting to menshevism why should we be treated any better?"

But the Party had no intention of shooting Oppositionists. Those bourgeois ideologues were wrong who saw in the October Revolution a repetition of 1793. This revolution was not going to devour its own children; it was strong enough to settle political differences without blood. But the bourgeoisie at home knew better. The *New Masses* sent me clippings from the New York papers saying the Soviet leaders had been murdered. I saw these leaders walking the streets of Moscow unguarded and unharmed; I heard them at public meetings and saw them at a concert listening to Prokofiev, home for the first time since 1917. In the lobby of the Jewish Art Theater I talked with Adolphe Joffe, an Opposition leader who bore a striking resemblance to one of my uncles—small, delicate, with a sallow face, wide nostrils, a black beard and glasses. This was the man whom Benny Ginzburg had interviewed in Riga in 1920, much to the annoyance of Floyd Gibbons. Joffe was already very ill; he was bitter about the political situation, but said he was getting medical attention and was enthusiastic about the theater. I wrote back to the *New Masses* that the reports in the bourgeois press about the murder of the entire Soviet government was propaganda emanating from Poland which was now East European messenger boy for Britain.

The inner-Party crisis could have meaning only if you dissociated it from hysteria, melodrama, ethical fainting spells, and invidious personal comparisons. Lenin said he who makes up his mind on political questions by hearsay, without reading the documents, was a fool. It was when you read the documents on both sides dealing with fundamental *economic* questions that the dispute assumed clarity. The Russian people had passed through four years of war and three years of civil war; they had endured famine and disease. Military conflict had destroyed factories and farms, and the people were even more ragged and hungry than they had been under the Czar. Five years of reconstruction under the New Economic Policy—a reconstruction carried on amidst a hostile world—could scarcely remedy the havoc wrought by czarist exploitation and indifference. Industry and agriculture were restored to prewar levels, but the revolution had increased the appetite of the people. What was significant about the new society was not that it had raised obscure individuals to great heights of power, but that an entire nation was now demanding more bread, more shoes, more clothes, more houses, more schools, more books, more theaters. To meet this demand, a drastic change in Russia's economic life was imperative. Expressing the will of the majority of the Communist party, Stalin formulated the outlines of that change. Salvation, he insisted, lay only in the immediate and rapid mechanization of the country, in large-scale industry and agriculture, in an economy precisely planned and rigorously administered. The Opposition ridiculed this daring and inevitable program; others in the Party, formally supporting the majority, trembled at the boldness of the steps proposed. Yet there lay the solution, and there lay the key to the inner-Party conflict. When you discussed these matters with genuine bolsheviks you heard little invidious psychologic comparison of one leader as against another; what you heard were the pros and cons of mechanization, collectivization, industrialization, the precise form which planned socialist economy was to take at that moment.

§ 2

The proletarian critic Sergei Dinamov liked to organize literary conversations. Sometimes he invited me to his little apartment crowded with Russian and English books. On the mantelpiece was a photograph of himself in Red army uniform. This was nothing unusual. Most of the younger Soviet writers had such photographs of themselves; they were the civil war generation, the thirty-year-old veterans of the armed struggle for socialism, and they were prouder of their uniforms than of their novels. Those uniforms symbolized their identification with the working class which furnished them the inspiration, the theme and the audience for their creative work as it furnished the direction of their lives. But there was no sense of "service" or noblesse oblige here, none of that Christian spirit of self-sacrifice which you found in some Western intellectuals sympathetic to socialism. These were not writers doing the proletariat the "favor" of supporting it; they were often workers themselves in whom the revolution first awakened the creative literary instinct. They resembled such literary heroes of my boyhood as Sir Philip Sidney and Dante in combining action with poetry.

But this was not a special characteristic of unique individuals. When Marxism became the dominant philosophy, the whole country accustomed itself to thinking of everything in relation to everything else, and of all things in relation to socialism. The men of action emphasized the importance of theory; the poets emphasized the importance of action. And just as there was no theoretical division between poetry and action, so there was no caste system which segregated men of letters from politicians. You saw both types in the same houses, meeting on terms of personal intimacy; and you heard the poets discussing industrialization and the politicians reciting verses by Nekrasov or Mayakovsky.

Once Dinamov took me to an "evening" given by the R's. The husband, tall and immensely fat, was a high official in the Soviet banking system; his wife was a thin, athletic blonde with a gentle smile. David was a Jew; Tanya, a Cossack. They had both been through the civil war, he as a soldier, she as a nurse; they were both active Party members, and both passionately fond of literature. The evening I first visited them, their house was crowded with Moscow writers. Every chair was filled, and on the floor sat the dark, handsome, wistful Leonov surrounded by a group of younger admirers. The young poetess Vera Inber was there and the old gray-bearded Mandelstamm. But here, too, was Lozovsky, head of the Red Trade Union International, with a shock of stiff curly hair and a broad black beard. He sat silent and dignified in his old frock coat and white shirt, did not share in the drinking, and closed his eyes reverently when a poet recited his verses. Later he sang several revolutionary songs of the 1905 period, and during the general conversation questioned me in great detail about the American trade-union movement.

It was at this house that I met Tamara, a young Georgian girl, tall, with a handsome dark face that had the hawklike quality so typical of the Caucasian warrior's, and yet was flushed with feminine charm. I saw a great deal of her afterward. Our relations were throughout what the old intelligentsia would have called "platonic" and the communists called "comradely." Such friendships were common in Russia. When the social and economic and patriarchal and religious barriers to love are broken down, when men and women are really equal, it is very easy to have friendships with people in which sex plays as little role as race. In the communist parties of the capitalist countries such friendships were also common; you had your wife or sweetheart, and you also had comrades of both sexes with whom your relations were of another order. Like so many of the younger Russians, Tamara had been through the civil war. She was fifteen when it broke out in the Caucasus. Her family, which had some property and considerable standing in the old society of Georgia, fled before the Red armies. Tamara was lost in the tumult and was picked up by a division of partisan guerilla fighters who made her their mascot. She lived for several years on the battlefield, in the midst of fighting. At the end of the civil war, she entered the women's department of the Party and was active in Tiflis and Baku. For organizing campaigns to unveil the Mohammedan women and to draw them into political life, she was nearly killed by the mullahs. When her position became untenable, she was transferred to Moscow, and subsequently sent with commercial missions abroad. That was how she learned to speak English and German.

Our conversations were chiefly about literature and politics, and in both fields Tamara had her own tastes. Although she was a bolshevik, she had an extreme admiration for Michael Arlen, whose *Green Hat* she read again and again, as Greta read and reread *Gentlemen Prefer Blondes*. In politics, Tamara was an Oppositionist with an acute hostility to Stalin, Thermidor and the "betrayal" of the revolution. While anti-Soviet scribes in New York were lamenting the silencing of the Opposition, Tamara was handing me the literature of her faction. She was not alone in this; in the Lux several American and German comrades active in the Opposition propagated its views freely. There could be no "secret" as to what the inner-Party discussion was about; you heard both sides day in and day out. The Americans and Germans, however, drew the line at certain Oppositional activities. When the Opposition met secretly in the woods and set up a secret printing press and in general acted as if the Party were an "enemy," they quit its ranks.

Tamara's bitterness about the inner-Party situation deflected her mind from the present to the past, which she saw fondly through the haze of selective memory. Over and over again, she told me stories of the civil war days, of the partisan detachment whose virgin mascot she had been. Her favorite story revealed both her own generous character and the ethic which animated the bolsheviks.

She told me that shortly after the civil war she was demobilized and joined the Georgian Communist party. Once, when she got a four weeks' vacation, she took the train from Tiflis for her native village to visit her parents; she had not seen them since the outbreak of the revolution.

The train was crowded, and she could not find a seat; but she did not mind riding on the platform. En route, she got into an argument with the conductor about her ticket. She asserted she had boarded the train at Tiflis; the conductor swore *yeah bogu* that he saw her get on long before Tiflis.

Out of the crowd on the platform emerged a startling figure. The man was dressed in filthy rags, his head was covered by a high sheepskin hat thick with mud, his legs were wrapped in stinking rags; his bare feet, his hands and his beard were caked with earth. But what struck Tamara was the refined delicacy of the man's features, his large and thoughtful eyes, and his long thin fingers. In a rich deep voice, and in an unexpectedly cultured Russian, the man said to the conductor:

"I saw this citizen board the train at Tiflis."

He said this with such authority that the conductor retreated at once. Tamara thanked her benefactor and watched him closely. At every station passengers got off, and soon Tamara and the man were alone on the platform.

"Who are you?" she said.

"I'm a shepherd."

"You are dressed like one," Tamara persisted, "but you don't look like one, and certainly you don't speak like one. The mark of aristocracy is on your face. Where are you bound for?"

"Baku. And you?"

"The village of Q—— at the next station."

"I have friends there," the man said. "Do you know the lawyer Gurgaslan?"

"Slightly," Tamara said. "He is my father."

"Gurgaslan! Your father! Think of it." The man seemed at ease for the first time. As the train pulled into the station, he said courteously: "Do you mind if I get off with you? We can talk until the train goes on."

He helped Tamara with her bags and they went into the buffet.

"Gurgaslan is one of my dearest friends," the shepherd said. "Since I've had the honor of meeting his daughter under these strange circumstances, I will tell you who I am. I am Prince X, the sole surviving son of the Emir of Baku. The civil war has finished us; the bolsheviks have killed off my entire family. Now the civil war is over, but they are still looking for me. They needn't. I am not a fool. I know when I am licked. Bolshevism has come to stay and there isn't anything I can do to stop it. I am completely out of politics but I love my country and I don't want to go off to Paris to rot in exile. I have been living quietly in Tiflis, hoping that the bolsheviks will recognize that I am harmless, and will let me become a useful Soviet citizen."

"Why are you going to Baku?" Tamara said.

"Only to see old friends. Now don't you think you ought to tell me about yourself? Where do you live and what are you doing?"

"I live in Tiflis," Tamara said, "and I am a member of the Communist party."

The prince's face became as yellow as wax, then furiously crimson.

"Impossible," he cried. "Gurgaslan's daughter a bolshevik! Poor, poor Gurgaslan."

Tamara said nothing. Suddenly the prince straightened his body and squared his shoulders.

"Very well," he said, "do your duty. Turn me over to the Cheka. Arrest me."

"If you were still politically active," Tamara said, "I would have you arrested. But you told me your story when you thought of me only as Gurgaslan's daughter. I'm convinced you told me the truth. You are politically harmless, and that is all we bolsheviks are interested in. We don't want revenge; we only want to guarantee the victory of socialism; and you cannot hamper that victory. So good-by and good luck."

Swiftly the prince bowed his head and kissed Tamara's hand. The locomotive whistled, the wheels slowly turned; the prince leaped to the platform and disappeared into the train.

Tamara enjoyed Michael Arlen but she did not approve of him. She shared Trotsky's views that proletarian literature was impossible, but had the old Russian attachment to the social novel, and the Soviet feeling for the novel reflecting the revolution. Her favorite Soviet writer was Boris Pilnyak. My Moscow friends described Pilnyak as a master stylist who created new Russian words and phrases. His innovations in language were not abstract, architectural labors like Mayakovsky's but rather developments of folk speech. He was especially gifted, they said, in creating those oaths for which the old Russia was famous, oaths in which incest is lifted ten stories high in an imagination at once voluptuous, ascetic and guilty. Tamara wanted me to meet Pilnyak, but for the moment that was impossible. Pilnyak was on vacation; he was touring Japan.

Five years later, when I was to meet him in New York, Pilnyak was to be more mature, more profoundly changed by the socialist revolution. Later still, idle American aesthetes, ignorant of Soviet life, attacked left-wing literature by pointing to the alleged humiliation of Boris Pilnyak.

Had some Moscow gypsy read my palm in 1926 and predicted this state of affairs, I would have laughed incredulously. For at that time Pilnyak was considered a writer saturated with the ancient Russian tradition of self-exposure and self-castigation. He had once said to Tamara:

"There are two kinds of Russian writers, those who descend from the sun, and those who descend from the moon. Pushkin, Tolstoy, Mayakovsky descend from the sun; Gogol, Dostoyevsky, and I descend from the moon. We are the children of night, almost of darkness."

Another time he had explained to Tamara—or so she claimed, anyway—that his difficulties in adjusting himself to the socialist revolution sprang from his identification with the old Russian village.

"Everything that was wonderful in the old Russian culture," Tamara quoted Pilnyak as saying, "was rooted in the old village. Our folk-songs came from the village, and without our folk-songs we would have had no Glinka, no Rimsky-Korsakov. Our ballads came from the village, and without them—no Pushkin, no Nekrasoff, no Yessenin even. Our folk-dances came from the village, and without those dances no Ballet Russe, no Nijinsky. And now that old village is dying. It should die. Something better, greater, more inspiring will take its place. But before that new something comes, there is a vacuum. And I am living in that vacuum, in that no man's land between that which is dying and that which is just being born. You have no idea how painful that is for a writer who creates out of nostalgic memory, out of love for his earliest experiences, for a son of the moon."

It was strange to hear such stories from the lips of Tamara. You knew she was exceedingly fond of Pilnyak, and was describing him to me because she was fond of him, and wanted me to understand him. What was curious about the whole affair was the different shapes men assumed according to whether you heard of them in America or Russia. Pilnyak's *The Naked Year,* a powerful work of observation and imagery, had already appeared in New York. There the critics, misinformed by distance and ignorance of the actual course of events in the Soviet Union, assumed that every Russian who wrote after 1917 was of necessity a bolshevik. In Moscow it was different. Pilnyak was not a bolshevik; he was a fellow traveler. He was not yet of the vanguard; he was still part of the past, though anxious to follow the future.

But those very bonds with the past which made Pilnyak a fellow traveler in literature made him a muddle-head in politics. The dying village of the kulak which haunted his writing also pursued his political notions. As Tamara described him, I had a strange feeling of caution. Just as in Paris, six years earlier, John O'Brien's fate had warned me against certain dangers in American journalism, so now I said to myself that every intellectual steeped in the old world ran the risk of misunderstanding the new.

From Tokyo, Pilnyak sent his Japanese diary to one of the leading Moscow newspapers which published it without changes. One day this diary revealed that Pilnyak had gone to a geisha house with a Soviet official who had been sent to Japan to purchase dairy products for the butter-and-egg trust. Shortly after this section of the diary appeared, the Communist party published a two-column statement in the press announcing the expulsion of the butter-and-egg man. It is all right—the statement said—for an irresponsible writer to visit any place he likes and to write anything he pleases about it, but other standards must be applied to an official sent on a responsible mission.

I felt that under the circumstances Pilnyak had been treated like a favorite spoiled child; Tamara was bitter; she thought he was being "persecuted" for his political notions. Dinamov, himself a "Stalinite," was more objective. He explained that Pilnyak suffered from the difficulty of so many fellow travelers: he understood the old better than the new. His roots were deeper in the dying than in the rising world. Consequently, his most vivid characters were decadent left-overs of the old regime; his "new" people were often abstractions. Furthermore, his preoccupation with the old led to an overemphasis of all that was evil and rotten in Soviet Russia—all that remained from the czarist days—and to a distortion, a blindness to the new and healthy forces. This one-sided description of Soviet reality, especially by so gifted and dramatic a writer as Pilnyak, created a false picture. It was as though a writer devoted a whole book to describing Beethoven's deafness without mentioning that he was one of the world's greatest composers; it was like that American critic who, at the height of the Freudian craze and the reaction against the democratic dogma under Coolidge, disposed of the whole of Whitman's poetry by saying he was a homosexual. But was I not guilty of the same error in exaggerating the importance of Greta's circle? Was I not describing Cromwell by the wart on his nose? The past weighs upon us like an alp.

Pilnyak's writing gave me the impression of an impulsive genius who created not from observation but from hearsay; and it was not difficult to imagine where he heard the gossip which influenced him at this period. Political discussions were not always on the lofty level of dialectic materialism. Tamara said to me one day:

"I did not tell you this before, but I will tell you now: I am no longer in the women's department of the Party. For the past few weeks I have been assigned to work in a factory."

By this time I was accustomed to such belated confidences. Tamara was as good a friend as I ever had, but like most people in politics she sharply separated her subjective from her political emotions. So long as our conversation was personal—whether directly so, in the form of reminiscence and confession, or obliquely, in the form of literary discussions—she was ardently frank. But when we touched on political questions she became another person. Knowing that I was partial to the Party rather than to the Opposition she tried to convert me to her viewpoint, but always in the most cautious manner. Every direct statement was preceded by hints and allusions as an army is preceded by scouts. So that when she told me she was now working in a factory, I knew this was only a prelude to a political sermon.

"And today," Tamara continued, "as we were walking home from work a terrible thing happened. One of the women workers took me aside and said, 'Tamara Grigorovna, I must apologize to you.

You may have thought we were all cool toward you because we did not like you personally, but it was only this morning we discovered you are Georgian.' I said: 'Why should you have been cool before?' 'You see,' she said, 'you are dark and all along we thought you were Jewish.'"

"All right, Tamara, and now let's have the moral."

She laughed: "Must there be a moral?"

"Are you telling me stories for art's sake?"

Her face became dark and earnest. "Trotsky is a Jew," she said, "and Kamenev and Zinoviev and Radek."

That was all she said, but I understood: she wanted to give me an instance out of her own experience to sustain the charge I heard in some Opposition circles that the Central Committee was stirring anti-Semitic feelings against the Opposition. But most supporters of the Opposition were not Jews, and many Jews supported the Central Committee; and since I had never encountered any anti-Semitism during my stay in the Soviet Union, I dismissed Tamara's story as an erroneous connection between an actual personal episode and her growing political bitterness which blinded her to the vast realities about her.

§ 3

Placards on the streets of Moscow announced a poet's Olympiad. The public was invited to come to the Second State Circus to see and hear representatives of every poetic school, from the half-dead imagists to the brand-new, hitherto unheard-of Con-Fun.

The Second State Circus was next to Meyerhold's Theater. I had seen some pretty good jugglers and clowns there. At the present time they were running an Oriental show with nine elephants and an Indian sword swallower; but they suspended the circus for one night to accommodate the poets who were to appear under the auspices of the writers' trade union. The doors were opened early; people sweated and pushed at the box office. The citizens actually paid to hear poets recite their verses.

Every seat under the vast tented dome was filled, all the way up to the last gallery. The presidium was seated on the stage at a long table, and the poets were seated in three rows behind them. There seemed to be a lot of poets in Moscow, and most of them were young and clean-shaven and they even wore their hair short.

Professor Kagan of the Moscow University opened the Olympiad with a *daklad,* as indispensable in the U.S.S.R. as a presidium. A *daklad* was a report or general review of the situation in any given field or in all fields. Meetings of the Party, of the trade unions, the Young Communist League, the Pioneers opened with a general review of the world situation. Art reflected Soviet life even in this particular. Professor Kagan, an old Marxist literary critic, reviewed Russian poetry since the revolution. He defined, discussed, dissected and criticized Symbolists, Constructivists, Futurists, Peasant Poets, Proletarian Poets—their work before NEP and after NEP, their aims, shortcomings and achievements. He did not forget to take a crack at the late Sergei Yessenin. That was a necessary contribution to the current campaign against "yesseninism." Now there was a great poet for you, "just as Bonaparte was a great general;" but unfortunately he agitated in favor of decadence and hooliganism. He misused his splendid gifts.

During this speech, the audience was restless. You could hear the sunflower seeds explode like bombs. This preliminary bout was old stuff; they had heard it before. There were few members of the old classes in the audience; they were mostly Party workers, new proletarian intellectuals, teachers, office workers. In one box I noticed a movie director, an actor and the fat conférencier of the circus. One row was filled with Chinese students of the Eastern University. Red army men were scattered throughout the house, the most attentive members of the audience.

Professor Kagan finished his *daklad*. Four buglers blew a salute, and Deev Kamekovsky, young peasant poet, rose to read his verses. I closed my eyes and tried to imagine Madison Square Garden crowded to the doors with people listening to a farmer poet describing the effect of the revolution on his village in Wisconsin. But then so many things were different here. In the presidium on the stage sat the presidents of the All-Russian Union of Writers, the All-Russian Union of Peasant Poets, the All-Russian Union of Poets. Here poets and writers were organized; they faced their readers in public, like orators, actors, politicians or prizefighters.

Tremendous applause greeted the poet Alexander Kruchenikh, member of the futurist LEF group whose poetic leader was Mayakovsky. Kruchenikh was interested in form, particularly in sound. He was small, dark and young; his voice was soft, yet he got some remarkable effects out of the language. He chanted his verses, he acted them, he almost danced them. He was followed by several peasant and proletarian poets, who recited verses about the new life in the factories, the cities and the villages. A member of the defunct Acmeist group tried to handle the same subjects in an academic style. One poet forgot his lines. The vast throng waited in polite silence for a moment, then applauded to encourage him. He smiled and went on with his poem. The stuff was poor, but the audience applauded. The Russians are a generous people.

The sensation of the evening was the Con-Fun school, of which nobody had ever heard. The entire school consisted of one unknown poet who stood up to explain its principles. He understood the value of advertising; he wore an orange scarf and a coarse sack shirt and had various slogans painted in bright colors. He started to read a manifesto. Voices from the gallery shouted:

"Cut out the speech! Read your poems!"

Voices appealed to the presidium to stop the manifesto. The man with the orange scarf was granted ten minutes in which to state the principles of his school and to recite his verses. Con-Fun, it was finally revealed, stood for Construction and Function. Like little children, poetry should be seen, not heard. It was a waste of time for poets to recite their verses when poetry was written for the printed page. Needless to say, even the prophet of Con-Fun made the usual references to the world situation and the construction of socialism. After explaining so earnestly that poetry was meant for the eye and not for the ear, the poet proceeded in a rich baritone to *sing* a long plaintive ballad.

Dinamov, sitting next to me, whispered:

"He is quite mad. A leftover of the old life. The village fool, Ivanka Doorachok. What a wide range we have."

The man with the orange scarf was the equivalent of my childhood friend, the idiot Avromtsie, and of all those idiots, madmen and eternal infants whom the bourgeois romantics had always worshiped in art, down to our own day with its cult of Dada. He seemed remote and unreal. The Soviet writers were wise to let village idiocy die on its feet by exposing it to the public, by letting it sing itself to death.

When the man with the orange scarf reached the sixth stanza, the audience laughed mercilessly; at the eighth stanza it clapped in rhythm; at the fifteenth the chairman asked the poet to sit down.

Several proletarian and peasant poets restored the audience to the real world of factories and farms, streets and machines, workers, peasants, Young Communists. Very little of the poetry read that evening dealt with personal emotion. The one exception was a tall, powerfully built imagist poet, who struck a Byronic pose, proclaimed his unhappiness in tetrameter quatrains, and in the most resounding rhythms announced that he would kill himself.

"Don't believe a word of that poetry," Dinamov whispered in my ear. "He tries to write like Verlaine, but he is as healthy as a horse. He is tennis champion of Moscow and will probably live to be a hundred."

A group of girl students in the gallery began to shout:

"Mayakovsky! Mayakovsky!"

The entire audience, thousands and thousands of voices, joined the cry for Mayakovsky. The poet was out of town. Nevertheless, the audience got its thrill. The hit of the evening was Ivan Pribloodny, a peasant poet of nineteen who looked like a college athlete. He was, in fact, a boxer as well as poet and university student. One poem he recited told about a Russian who went abroad, and people asked him: Do you come from that wonderful Russia that has such immense fields, gold, oil, factories, whose workers and peasants are building a new world? Another poem said: I don't want to marry; I have no money; I don't work in Gosbank or Selkotrest; but when I marry, I want a girl who is healthy and clever, who doesn't paint and powder, but understands what we are trying to do in Russia; she must be not only my sweetheart and wife, but the mother of future generations.

Not one of the twenty poets who recited verses that evening used free verse; nearly all employed the classic meters of Pushkin. One young man who was announced as a peasant poet stirred Dinamov to whisper:

"He lies. His father is a university professor and his mother is a banker's daughter. He is a student. He is ashamed of his social origin. A very silly pose, and quite unnecessary."

The Olympiad was a holiday. Elsewhere the relations between poet and audience were more serious and businesslike. The factories, for instance, had literary circles of workers. At their meetings leading Soviet writers read from their works. The author gave an account of his work; the audience then gave an account of its reactions to that work. The basic criterion in these factory discussions of literature was truth to life from the socialist viewpoint. But this criterion left room for an astonishing variety of creative work! At meetings of literary circles, or in the workers' libraries, or even in casual conversations with workers in their homes, the park, the factory restaurant, you realized how rich and individual life and art could be within the general socialist framework.

Unless we are little critics whose "judgments" of works of art are conditioned by the fads of the moment, by our desire to be important, and by the consequent need for playing literary politics, praising those writers, however stupid, who can help us in our practical ambitions, and damning those who cannot help us or even stand in our way—unless we are such myopic wirepullers, we cannot fail to recognize that revolutionary art, like the art of previous classes in society, has many facets, indeed more facets than all the previous arts. The developed bourgeois reader enjoyed and gained something from writers as diverse as Milton and Joyce, Voltaire and Proust, Dante and Anatole France; the developed worker enjoyed not only these classics, but also revolutionary writers as diverse as Mayakovsky and Upton Sinclair, Jack London and Boris Pasternak, Johannes Becher and Henri Barbusse, Nexö and Serafimovich, Gorky and Leonov. But through the diversity of Soviet art there ran the unity of the socialist idea, as the Christian idea ran through Western art, or the democratic idea through nineteenth century art.

What was true of literature was equally true of the film, the most popular of the arts in Russia as everywhere else. I often went to the meeting place of the Friends of the Soviet Cinema, across the street from my hotel. Here I saw previews of new films and heard them criticized by the audience and defended by the director.

The Friends of the Soviet Cinema clubrooms had an outer lobby where the members and their guests lounged and talked before the performance. From the Western middle-class viewpoint, they were a curious audience. There were, of course, actors and actresses of screen and stage, handsome and better dressed than the average citizen; there were directors, electricians, cameramen, journalists, critics and professors who specialized in the film and in the drama. There were also those pretty and febrile hetairai, themselves without any creative talent except perhaps in love, whom you find at artistic gatherings the world over in the company of those who enjoy the fame of the moment. All this was "normal"; you could see such people, or their equivalent, at any first night in Berlin, Paris or New York. What was different here was that at least half the audience were workers in caps, leather jackets and boots. The aesthetes and intellectuals looked upon them with special regard.

Inside the meeting hall the air was full of gay chatter. The odor of leather boots mingled with the fragrance of cheap perfume as workers and actors, electricians and actresses rustled in their chairs.

We were going to see Dziga Vertov's *One-Sixth of the Earth,* an example of the new style of film known as the Cinema-Eye, a creative newsreel in which shots from actual life were co-ordinated around a central theme. Vertov walked up to the stage and made a speech: My new film proposes to show the building of socialism in the U.S.S.R. and the decay of capitalism in the other countries. My method is montage, the method of symbolic shots and striking contrasts. We create factories, develop farms, open schools, invent machines; they go to pieces in alcohol and sex. After the film, the floor will be open for discussion to all.

The director tiptoed to a seat. The lights went out; a screen came down slowly and the title flickered in the darkness. Here was the new Russia—north, east, south, west—harvesting, drilling oil, manufacturing. Huge workers welded steel, enormous peasants tilled fields, women tended their babies in the factory nurseries, a life of vigorous, co-ordinated creation, of joy in labor. Interspersed among these were shots of European capitals—cafés, dance halls, drinking orgies.

One shot, presumably taken in a foreign capital, showed a crowd of fat men and women celebrating New Year's Eve. A phonograph played American jazz; the fat, greasy couples waddled obscenely along the floor, their behinds grotesquely bobbing up and down like vast watermelons. The chimes rang midnight, and the fat behinds stopped. Swinish faces looked up, drunk and reverent. The party began to disperse. The guests, soggy with alcohol, helped each other out the door and across the snow into waiting limousines. An elderly Falstaff, smirking into the face of a plump woman, bowed gallantly, slipped and sat on his rear.

The audience laughed loudly.

"Do you know where this scene was taken?" a woman behind me whispered to her companion. "Right here in Moscow, at the home of H, the American concessionaire who has a factory in this city. The director flattered him; he said: Everyone in Moscow admires your beautiful home and your gay parties and won't you let us film one of them. The concessionaire was delighted. When he sees himself and his friends as the decaying bourgeoisie in this film he'll drop dead."

She leaned back with a little malicious smile, and watched the screen on which a state farm unrolled with its well-kept cattle and new tractors. When the film was over—the fadeout being a flag fluttering high in the air, bearing hammer and sickle—members of the audience sent up their names to the presidium. Everybody wanted to talk, and everybody did—actors and actresses, journalists and cameramen, critics and workers. They discussed the photography, the ideas, the co-ordination. The reaction to the film was, on the whole, favorable; but there were important reservations.

"The director," said one young worker in a cap, "makes the world appear much too simple. His intention is to tell us the truth; actually he deceives the backward workers. If the bourgeoisie does nothing but drink and dance and gamble, if it is only vicious and self-indulgent, then the class struggle would be easy. The proletariat would have no trouble winning power in every country. But outside of the Soviet Union the proletariat has not yet won power. So it seems this film has omitted something. No doubt a section of the bourgeoisie is vicious. They get drunk and gamble and whip each other in perverse sex play, and that's a very interesting theme for a bourgeois novelist, who thinks he is quite revolutionary when he enjoys himself vicariously with the vices of the decadents. But who builds the battleships, who commands the armies, who runs the factories, who maneuvers diplomatically in London, Paris and Berlin? Obviously the people who count most in the bourgeois world are sober, hard-working people. Otherwise they would not be in the saddle now. It is not they who are decadent but their social system—which is another matter. The bourgeoisie is still strong, it is well armed, it is prepared to attack us. In order to defend ourselves we must not underestimate their strength, we must not indulge in childish fantasies about their orgies. That would be the worst kind of self-indulgence on our part. We must face the truth; we must recognize the strength of the enemy in order to overcome it. The director would have done better had he shown us the battleships and cabinets of the capitalists rather than their orgies."

The audience applauded loudly. Another young worker stood up and said:

"I disagree with the previous speaker. What he said is absolutely true, but a film need not be a political tract. Enough that the director has shown us the vices of the ruling classes abroad; from these we can presuppose their political blindness. I, for example, am agitprop director in my factory, and after the film is shown I can explain the problems which the previous speaker has raised."

"That is all very well," said an actress behind me, without rising. "But it's a pretty poor film that needs an agitprop director to make a speech after it. This film will be shown in every cinema house of the country. There won't always be a bright agitator like you around to explain to the workers what the film has omitted. No, a film, a play, a novel, any work of art must speak for itself. It must contain the truth within itself—and this film certainly gives a lopsided picture of the bourgeoisie abroad."

The director spoke last. He admitted that he had overemphasized vice and underestimated political and military power. This would be remedied in the final version of the film—which would thus become the joint product of a director, cameramen and other technicians, and the audience.

As I walked home, thinking of the factory workers who had just discussed the art of the film, and the actors who talked about the class struggle, I remembered our old campus dream of the universal man, now taking on the faint outlines of a probable reality.

§ 4

What made you feel most at home in Moscow was the integration and continuity of life. From New York, for example, I received clippings praising Sergei Eisenstein's film *Potemkin,* the first Soviet movie to make any impression in America. But every critic who praised the picture added that it was "propaganda." In Moscow the picture appeared as "pure" art; it represented life as a socialist normally saw it.

That was the way Eisenstein himself saw life, and that was the way he talked about it in the most casual conversations. I used to visit him in his studio on the Chisti Prudi, toward the outskirts of Moscow. He lived in one large room, furnished simply. There was a cot behind a screen, a working table littered with movie stills and clippings and notes; a small writing desk and several bookcases crowded with magazines, pamphlets and books. The ceiling was decorated with concentric circles, red and blue. This bizarre target was painted by Eisenstein himself in his early, futurist days.

It was strange to think of "early" in connection with Eisenstein. He was only twenty-nine. Yet, like most art workers in Soviet Russia, he had gone through decades of experience in nine years. Starting as an architect, he had been attracted to the theater even before the revolution. When October swept away the old stage along with the old regime, he was at the head of the Proletcult Theater and a member of the LEF group together with Meyerhold, Tretyakov and Mayakovsky.

Proletcult had been the extreme left wing of Soviet art; yet its theater had been directed by a young man in his earliest twenties who frankly described himself not as a proletarian but as an intellectual. So thoroughly, however, did Eisenstein identify himself with the proletariat, that when I met him he was already entrusted by the workers' and peasants' state with the direction of its most important films. This was no easy task and no small honor; the Soviet Union believed with Lenin that "of all forms of art, the film is for us the most important."

In the opinion of cinema specialists, *Potemkin* had placed Eisenstein among the greatest movie directors in the world. That summer Douglas Fairbanks and Mary Pickford had arrived in Moscow; the Russians smothered them with compliments; they paid homage to the Soviet film and invited Eisenstein to Hollywood. He told me he would probably go there someday. Like most Russians, he had a profound admiration for American technique and was curious to see the results of combining it with Soviet ideas.

For the present, however, he was engaged on a new film to be shown during the celebration of the tenth anniversary of the October Revolution. When I went to see him about it, I found him talking over the phone, his pale face intent, ascetic and ironical, his curly hair standing high like a shako. He was saying the most curious things in the tone of a man declaiming from the rostrum:

"Had it not been for Leonardo da Vinci, Marx, Lenin, Freud and the movies, I would in all probability have been another Oscar Wilde."

He excused himself over the phone, hung up the receiver and greeted me with a whimsical smile.

"You are puzzled by my strange words, eh?" he said. "I was just talking to the author of *Roar China*. Tretyakov is writing a biography of me and I am telling him a few truths about myself. I have urged him to include a chapter on Freud whose influence on me has been enormous. Without Freud, no sublimation; without sublimation, a mere aesthete like Oscar Wilde. Freud discovered the laws of individual conduct, as Marx discovered the laws of social development. I have consciously used my knowledge of Marx and Freud in the plays and movies I have directed in the past ten years. I look at American films— and I know to what extent the director has sublimated. Von Stroheim, for example. Very badly sublimated."

Eisenstein grinned politely and showed me his library. He spoke and read fluently Russian, German, English and French. His library was full of books in all four languages on politics, sociology, literature, biology, mechanics, anatomy, psychology, the plastic arts, the theater, the film and phrenology.

Eisenstein neither smoked nor drank, and, as in Hamlet's case, man delighted him not nor woman either. In other respects, he was no ascetic; he dressed neatly in English or American clothes, and took an almost sensual delight in logic and humor.

Essentially he thought of himself not as the traditional "artist," intuitive, emotional, stirred by the spontaneous and unpredictable forces of "inspiration," but as a scientific engineer whose field happened to be cinema. He studied the film from every angle, related it to the life about him, and built his pictures rationally and deliberately with the conscious aim of producing specific, premeditated effects.

Even before the revolution had made the Russian artist mass conscious, Eisenstein had developed the theory of the "play without a hero." He experimented with this kind of play in the Proletcult Theater; here, even in the classics of Ostrovsky, he was able to transfer attention away from the individual and to focus it on the entire group involved in the action. There were scenes where the satire was deliberately heightened through burlesque, as in a celebrated nineteenth century comedy where Eisenstein converted a ballroom scene into a circus.

Eisenstein manipulated his knowledge of Freud not to dissect the difficulties of the disturbed individual soul, but to evoke certain feelings in his audience. He directed no psychological plays or movies; his productions had no stars, and many of the players were not professional actors at all, but men and women filmed in real life. All but one of the players in *Potemkin* were amateurs, most of whom had never appeared on the screen before. The *Potemkin* sailors were played by sailors in the Soviet fleet; other players were picked up in Odessa from various walks of life. For every new film, Eisenstein personally selected the types he wanted from factories, farms and state institutions.

As Eisenstein explained the Soviet attitude toward art, I involuntarily thought of a passage in Joyce's *Portrait of the Artist as a Young Man,* that passage in which Stephen Dedalus says:

"Art is the human disposition of sensible or intelligible matter for an esthetic end. . . . It means certainly a stasis and not a kinesis. . . . The instant wherein that supreme quality of beauty, the clear radiance of the esthetic image, is apprehended luminously by the mind which has been arrested by its wholeness and fascinated by its harmony is the luminous silent stasis of esthetic pleasure, a spiritual state very like to that cardiac condition which the Italian physiologist Luigi Galvani, using a phrase almost as beautiful as Shelley's, called the enchantment of the heart."

To many Soviet artists this aesthetic was idealistic superstition.

"Who is writing the scenario for your new film?" I asked Eisenstein.

"The Communist party."

"What? No freedom for the artist at all?"

"No, no, no! Let me explain. I myself am writing the scenario. What I meant was that the Communist party creates the life which gives me the material, and develops the ideas which illuminate that life, which give it meaning. Without the Communist party there would be no socialist construction, and I would not have these new monumental themes. Take my proposed film, for example. When I finished *Potemkin,* the Russian cinema faced two burning questions: events in China and the development of the Soviet village. The Chinese workers and peasants are going through a life-and-death struggle for freedom. There is a profound need for the fighting film. Concrete agitational material is needed in China itself. Perhaps for the first time in history, the film has become as terrible a weapon as the hand grenade. There, on the battlefield where the fight is carried on, is the place of that art which stands in the front ranks of battle—the art of the film. Art is only a means, an instrument, a method of struggle."

Eisenstein went on to explain how he planned a gigantic Chinese film in three parts, but had to give it up for technical reasons. There remained the theme of the Soviet village. For more than a month he and his assistants studied the problems of the village. They visited farms of all kinds; they went to the editorial offices of the peasant newspapers, to the Commissariat of Agriculture, to the trade union of agricultural workers, to the peasant co-operatives, to the poor villages, to the government model farms. Then they read newspapers, magazines, Party theses, reports, statistics.

Eisenstein planned to turn out a film which would give the spectator more than scenes of country life or a story connected with the village. Far from merely enchanting the spectator's heart, the film was intended to grip him and bring him face to face with the most important problems of the village. It was to make him conscious of the work of the communist youth in the villages, the cultural activities among the peasants, the new Soviet family, the peasant correspondents' movement, the struggle against religion, the women's movement, the fight against the rich peasants, the industrialization and reorganization of the village. Eisenstein wanted his art to be not static but kinetic; the new film was to stir the spectator to *participate* in the solution of agricultural problems.

"The movies of the bourgeois West," Eisenstein said to me, "carry on propaganda for patriotism, for God, for the honest traveling salesman; they erect monuments to the unknown soldier. We must make our vast audiences fall in love with the peasant's daily work. We must acquaint him with cattle, hens and tractors. Even when it is drawn by two skinny horses, the tractor is vital in building socialism; the tractor is a heroic theme for the film."

But a work of art needs unity. For a principle to integrate the unlimited material afforded by the changing Russian village, Eisenstein went to the theses of the Fourteenth Congress of the Communist Party of the Soviet Union, which formulated the general line of economic progress. That line was the collectivization of national economy and the industrialization of the village. This was the theme of Eisenstein's new film, *The General Line.* (This film was later shown in the United States under the title *Old and New.*) It was the first major film based on peasant material, dealing in images and in dramatic terms with problems of profound social import.

"The official terminology of theses, resolutions and decisions," Eisenstein told me, "comes to life on the screen in herds of fat cattle, in the rustle of harvesters and tractors, in warm stables, in the opening of the earth under the spring snow, in the thick layer of manure on a field which is collectively cultivated."

Then he asked me: "Does America know about the extraordinary struggle on our 'peace front'? About the heroism of the first attacks of the pioneers of the agricultural revolution? Many Soviet movie houses are now running Buster Keaton's film *Three Epochs.* My new film involves Lenin's analysis of the 'five epochs.' It will show the five stages of economic development which exist side by side today in Soviet Russia. We still have patriarchal economy, domestic economy and private capitalism alongside of state capitalism and socialism. The Stone Age lives side by side with the latest achievements of science and social organization, and, what is more remarkable, we are building in all five epochs at once."

If Eisenstein differed from bourgeois artists in his preoccupation with socialist problems, he differed no less from many radical artists

I had known at home in his intense preoccupation with form. He defined "sublimation" for the artist as "matter finding its most adequate form." Certainly to find the most adequate artistic form for the economic theses of the Fourteenth Congress was a theme worthy of the greatest artists.

Eisenstein showed me stills of his new film. The action of *The General Line* was a thread on which the director had strung a thousand effects. The story moved simply through the various problems which confronted the Soviet village. It opened with a group of poor peasants organizing an artel—a small co-operative—to manage their affairs in common. They obtain credit from the government on easy terms and buy a milk separator.

"The milk separator," Eisenstein said, fingering several stills, "plays the same role in my film as the Holy Grail plays in *Parsifal*. The poetry of the milk separator! Think of it, from milk separator to first-class bull, from the bull to the tractor, from one tractor to ten tractors, a thousand tractors, to the industrialization of the village, to raising the economic, political and social level of the entire Russian people. Compared with such a colossal social transformation, what is the poetry of *Parsifal*? Why do the hearts of the spectators beat when, under Wagner's thundering melodies, the Holy Grail appears? What on earth can we do with that mystic dish? Of what use is it to anybody? How much better if eyes become bright and hearts beat faster at the sight of a copper milk separator owned by a peasants' co-operative!"

Eisenstein continued the story of his new film: With the profits obtained from the milk separator, the peasants purchase a young bull at a government model farm. Enter the bureaucrat, one of the villains of Soviet life. He ties up the peasants' activities with red tape. For this part of the film, Eisenstein secured the co-operation of a member of the Central Committee of the Communist party prominently identified with the war against bureaucracy.

The kulaks of the district take advantage of the delay due to bureaucracy; they offer to advance the artel money for the tractor in return for a mortgage on it. The poor peasants reject the offer and complain to the Workers' and Peasants' Inspection which fights bureaucracy, graft and maladministration. Representatives of the Inspection may descend without warning at any time on any office, factory or government farm and investigate it; that visit is judgment day for the inefficient, the corrupt and the counterrevolutionary.

In revenge for being reported to the Workers' and Peasants' Inspection, the kulaks kill the young bull of the peasants' co-operative. Among the rushes which Eisenstein showed me, this was one of the most moving sections. It was, the director proudly pointed out, an absolutely new situation in the movies, the "first collective economic tragedy in the film." The killing of the bull affects the life of every man, woman and child in the co-operative. The peasants recover from this blow, however, and manage to obtain a tractor from the city. Joyfully, the village arranges a festival with red flags and brass bands. The village street is crowded with old peasants and their wives, young communists and their sweethearts. The young people start the tractor, but after crawling along for a few feet it breaks down. Near by horses bolt through the crowd in terror; old and superstitious peasants run away shouting that the devil is in the machine. But the young communists mend the tractor and start it going again. As it rolls across the horizon, the old peasants, intent on stopping it, hop on their horses and give chase. Eisenstein said this part of the film was a deliberate parody on the Hollywood Wild West movie in which mounted cowboys race trains. But here a new social content filled the old form; the chase symbolized the struggle of the machine to replace the beast of burden. The young communists on the tractor come to a narrow bridge, blocked by a huge wagon loaded with hay. The wagon is stuck in a rut, and cannot let the tractor pass. While the tractor is trying to pull the wagon out of the mud, the peasants on horseback come up. The wagon is finally freed by the combined efforts of tractor and horses.

"This," Eisenstein explained, "is in accord with the Party policy of encouraging the use of horses as well as tractors until the tractor is available to all our farmers."

From this climax, the film went on to show the development of Soviet agriculture that year. There were shots of model farms, the breeding of cattle, the latest methods of sowing and reaping, even the Baku oil fields, all connected with the story of which the hero was no single individual but the Soviet village.

"Among other things," Eisenstein said, "this film shows that we already have enough developed resources to build socialism in our country."

As Eisenstein showed me parts of his film and talked about it, he appeared to be not only a striking individual, but the precursor of a new type of man. He was in many respects the traditional genius of the old culture, self-centered and conscious of it; a narcist who knew the fact and the name for it, its causes and consequences; a man physically ascetic and spiritually alone in all personal relationships. This was Pico della Mirandola and Michelangelo and Thomas Chatterton. Yet other aspects of Eisenstein's character made it clear that the more one was identified with the revolutionary movement, the more one's ego became socialized. Personal episodes and tastes which loomed so large in private lives, and seemed so significant in the traditional autobiographical novel, were of little consequence in the revolutionary struggle, except when they interfered with your usefulness to it. In that sense, history was more important than autobiography, and autobiography itself only a historical footnote. *We* replaced *I*, and to speak of your own life in certain periods was to speak of the life of mankind in whose development you found your whole undivided being. When Eisenstein compared the milk separator with the Holy Grail, he indicated the difference between his own soul and Wagner's, the contrast between the bourgeois and the socialist artist. But he also clarified for me the main problems which were then agitating his country. And because that country had, by historical circumstances, become the pioneer in the progress of mankind during our epoch, he clarified for me the class struggle the world over, consequently my own life whose integration was possible only around that struggle in which the *I* transcends and fulfills itself by becoming the *we*.

§ 5

I spent a great deal of time in the Comintern library reading. Once I found an old copy of the minutes of the Second Congress. The people whose words were recorded there appeared in a new light. I thought of them as great men and courageous idealists, but anyone who said that communism abolished the individual personality was crazy. Some of the men who spoke at that famous congress reminded you, in their proud self-regard, of warrior chieftains, of Chapayev, let us say, about whom the bolshevik Furmanov had written such a beautiful novel. Personal pride was evident in the speeches of the irrepressible Zinoviev, the satirical Radek, the passionate John Reed, the aloof, self-centered Trotsky, the bombastic Bombacci, the bright unhappy Fraina. Even Gallacher, proletarian from the Clyde docks, was touched with a just pride. Some of these men tried to solve complicated political problems by citing themselves as authorities, almost infallible: I am an old trade-union man; I understand the trade-union question thoroughly; my personal experience has taught me this and that. Debates sometimes became acrimoniously personal. John Reed complained in an offended tone of the treatment he had received in the trade-union commission, and Radek brushed the complaint aside with somewhat malicious wit.

When Lenin spoke, something strange happened. He appeared to be wholly impersonal, and under the spell of his sublime detachment every ego subsided and became part of an impersonal mind. But that was a stupid way of putting it; that was the way mystics used to talk about God. How strong the old images were! All I meant was that Lenin possessed the secret of sublimating his ego completely. Surely no man is without an ego, but here was one whose ego was so great that it became identical with the world. You could not see where the individual ended and the idea began; they were one. That seemed to be the mystery of great leadership.

Greta's circle, which was interested in psychology, discussed these notions at length. The question of class power was theoretically clear; the difficulties were practical ones. But even in theory the question of personal power was dark and disturbing. The establishment of a socialist regime in one country did not abolish individual differences. No man had the legal right or the social sanction to exploit another economically, but there were individual differences in talent and position; there was rank and title; there was a hierarchy with superiors and inferiors. Some communists suffered from pride, arrogance and even snobbishness. On first coming to Moscow, for example, I found P an important official. He was a clever and affable fellow, full of information and wit. Whenever he entered a room, the atmosphere became charged with warm affection, admiration, respect. Here and there you even heard the invisible sound of tongues against his boots. He had what was known as prestige; he could also recommend you for a better job, get you tickets for the theater, introduce you to important people. Through him—if he took a fancy to you—you could move in the "higher circles" of the Party and the country. But six months later a great change came over P. He was removed from his post for some reason, and with that post went his prestige—that mysterious aura which bathed his personality in a subdued glory. No doubt P remained at bottom the clever and affable fellow he had always been. But on the surface he was no longer so. Not only was there a change in the attitude of other people toward him, but his attitude toward himself altered. In America you saw a similar alteration in the man who lost his million dollars in stock speculation. Loss of position meant loss of power, loss of prestige, loss of self-assurance. It was almost as if P had lost his legs, or his nose. Those who had fawned on him, and laughed at his jokes, now pitied him or despised him. Some even dropped him socially. This change emphasized the gradations in the new society. Of course Marxism never promised anything so utopian as universal individual equality; but Lenin did thunder against communist conceit. If you were a person who could never hope to hold important posts, you were disturbed by hierarchical tendencies.

Hedda agreed that someday this problem would have to be solved; but just now she insisted the victory of socialism in all lands was the most important thing. To this all other things had to be subordinated for the time being.

"Do we need good men, or strong men?" she said. "The hardness and pride which shocks you now is invaluable against our ruthless enemies. Where would the working class be under the leadership of a sweet man like Martov?" Then she added gently: "You still have something of the utopian, the dreamer about you. You want a better system of society, you apprehend its coming emotionally, but you do not see clearly enough the road that leads to the new world. Your wishes are very nice, but if you want to be of real use to the proletariat you must supplement your dreaming with knowledge. You must master the science of the proletariat—the ideas of Marx, Engels, Lenin and Stalin. You must substitute science for fantasy, action for wish."

"I must become the slave of new abstractions."

"You are wrong there. You have been disappointed in the ideas of the bourgeoisie, so you fear all ideas. Don't you think that's a little bohemian? Dialectic materialism is no abstraction. It teaches us that nothing is final, absolute or sacred. Dialectic materialism reveals the transitory character of everything. Nothing endures except the uninterrupted process of becoming and passing away, of endless ascendancy from the lower to the higher. The world is not a complex of ready-made *things,* but a complex of *processes.* Things which are apparently stable go through an uninterrupted change of coming into and passing out of being. The workers dreamed of freedom for centuries before Marx and Engels, but these giants taught the working class to know itself, to become class conscious, and they substituted science for dreaming."

"Why must we bother with metaphysics?"

Hedda laughed gaily as if I had told a joke.

"Every man," she said, "proceeds on certain assumptions, conscious or unconscious. Every action has its theoretical justification, every theory its effect on action. Do you think skepticism is not a class philosophy? Look at your skeptics. Who are they? People whose position in society is equivocal and uncertain; they justify their insecurity in metaphysical terms. But the science of Marxism alone explains their position as well as the ideas which spring from that position. It's a pity that people are not all equal. But won't we advance further by facing and reducing that inequality than by lying? The Declaration of Independence says all men are created free and equal, and everybody in America knows it's a damned lie and acts accordingly. Marx said: from each according to his abilities, to each according to his needs—and we proceed to do the only thing possible at this stage of human development—to abolish classes and class privileges."

"A curious, heretical thought occurs to me," I said. "Now the Soviet writers are dealing with the struggle of the proletariat as a class against its class enemies; but when its victory is unequivocal, when socialism is established beyond question, they will no doubt write about individual conflicts *within* the proletariat itself. A Soviet Gogol may someday satirize P while P is still in his glory, just as I would like to satirize Fred while he is still a member of our Central Committee. I feel that Fred's position does not alter the fact that he is a louse. Everybody will say that Fred is a louse the moment he loses his post, or is expelled from the Party. I wish I knew how to say it now while he still basks in a glory to which he is hardly entitled. If I wrote that about him, it would be the truth—and the truth is good art and good revolution, I think."

"You are not clever enough to do that," Hedda said. "You would write it so artlessly that you would do more harm than good, and you would get a well-deserved crack on the head. Telling people the truth is the most difficult art in the world. One must know how to do it, just as one must know how to lead an army. Good intentions alone will get you nowhere. Your truth, awkwardly stated, may turn out in effect to be a lie."

Hedda harped on this idea whenever we went together to the theater, where she could point to specific examples of her thesis. At this time the problems of Soviet art (that is, of Soviet life) were quite different from what the literati of New York imagined. It was not true that bolshevism had killed art. Even the old art was alive, thanks to government subsidies. At the opera I used to see *Boris Godunov,* the

Hunchback of Notre Dame, the *Czar Feodor,* and all the operas of Rimsky-Korsakov, including some very religious ones. So far as I was concerned, the opera could die. I liked music and I liked drama, but I had no high regard for a bastard form in which music and drama mutually crippled each other. But there were people in Moscow, chiefly members of the old intelligentsia, who liked opera and the Bolshoi Theater was always filled to capacity. The workers preferred the trade-union theaters and the Theater of the Revolution, where the class war in Russia and abroad was drama's central theme. The lines were clearly drawn; the proletariat as a class was the hero, the bourgeoisie as a class was the villain.

This basic theme now appeared normal to me. You judged Soviet plays as works of art, not as propaganda. All plays, novels, poems and films in the U.S.S.R. had the same relation to the building of socialism that bourgeois literature had to the cult of the ego, or medieval art to the Christian *mythos,* or ancient art to the legends of Mount Olympus and the House of Atreus. There were specific depth and variety in works of art, but always there was the general outlook upon life, the Weltanschauung, the central source and reference point.

The Soviet author had this advantage: his works had the directness and simplicity which are possible when the artist can take for granted the whole substratum of knowledge and belief, the whole system of values, by reference to which the story achieves its meaning.

Ibsen, Shaw, D. H. Lawrence, Dreiser, Joyce fought their audience. The Soviet writers were en rapport with their audience. Yet the Western liberals considered the first artists, the second propagandists. Might it not be said, rather, that the liberal writers of the West, seeking to *convert* their audience, were propagandists, while the Soviet writers, sharing with their audience a basic philosophy of life, were artists who unfolded a tale on the basis of that common viewpoint?

In capitalist countries, the revolutionary artist occupied another position. Culture was a bourgeois monopoly; the reader of books, the spectator in the theater, came as a rule from the upper and middle classes. Hence a Toller, a Piscator, a John Howard Lawson could tell a story whose significance was clear only *after* the author had succeeded in revolutionizing the moral and intellectual attitude of the audience. Here the sermon overshadowed the image; the story became a fable, and the person who had to be revolutionized was the spectator, the reader, the auditor.

In the Soviet Union the dominant audience was proletarian. Consequently, in presenting a socialist story the author did not have to alter the reader's viewpoint, but to understand it, absorb it, make it his own. The Soviet play, novel, poem or film did not—in its own social setting—have the qualities of the sermon. Its presuppositions were taken for granted; they were "natural." Even when a character in a play, or the author of a novel, exclaimed baldly, "Capitalism is bad; it must be destroyed, communism must take its place," it did not sound like propaganda. In the U.S.S.R. it sounded like an axiom; it was like saying two and two are four, the sky is blue, I love you. It was like the mid-Victorian poet saying God's in his heaven—all's right with the world. Such ideas are, each in its time and place, held to be self-evident until life shows them to be false. When you stated the axioms of communism to an audience of Soviet workers, you were not propagandizing them. At the worst, you might be accused of banality.

But since the Soviet author was often by social origin a middle-class intellectual, the substratum of ideas, emotions and images to be taken for granted were at first alien to him. His difficulty lay not in converting his audience to his own ideas, but in grasping and assimilating the ideas of his audience. Here the emphasis shifted: the author did not revolutionize the audience; the audience revolutionized the author.

This state of affairs became strikingly clear when you compared the reactions to a Soviet film in Moscow and in New York. The middle-class audience in the bourgeois metropolis complained: The Soviet director is a propagandist; he is violating our will; he is cramming his revolutionary message down our throats. In the proletarian capital it was the director who complained: My proletarian audience is too critical; they do not see how hard it is for a bourgeois intellectual to become a bolshevik; they are pushing us fellow travelers too fast.

In Western Europe and America, the liberal was accustomed to the artist fighting his audience, revolutionizing it in a limited way. Who were our literary heroes? Whom did the campus and Greenwich Village teach us to revere? Byron and Shelley, Whitman and Poe, Shaw and France, Baudelaire and Eliot, Ibsen and Dreiser and O'Neill —the "men against the mob," the so-called pioneers and rebels. But at bottom did not these artists preach bourgeois ideals? They wanted to reform middle-class conduct in the light of middle-class utopias. This the enlightened Babbitt—the editor, critic, professor or preacher—could understand and applaud. This was *art*—especially since the ideal upheld had the sanction of time and the official culture, since the foundations of capitalist society were taken for granted. What the enlightened Babbitt hated was proletarian art—Jack London, Michael Gold, Sergei Eisenstein. He hated it for two reasons chiefly: The new art was based on the working-class revolution which aims to change the social-economic base of the world, and in this art it was not the capitalist market, but the proletarian audience which disciplined the poet.

To the enlightened Babbitt, the spectacle of the individual genius lecturing his bourgeois audience for its own good on the "new" sex, the new biology, or reformist politics was not unpleasant. What was unbearable was the spectacle of the proletarian audience lecturing the individual genius for the good of all, for the sake of that classless society whose foundations were being firmly laid. That was awful; that was described in the bourgeois press as humiliating and persecuting the artist. In the first case, the artist lectured his audience without altering society; in the second, a changed society changed the poet, transformed him into a revolutionary force. This was what horrified the enlightened Babbitt, who shuddered over his cocktail at the New York literary teas, and said piously: there but for the grace of capitalist democracy go I.

In the proletarian republic it was no longer a question of theme. As Eisenstein said, the Communist party, the working class, "wrote" the artists' scenarios across the whole of the land. It was now another question, the one Hedda touched on, the art of telling the truth so that your reader or spectator would see it as truth. Sometimes this was relatively easy. I went with several friends to see Tretyakov's *Roar China* at the Meyerhold Theater. Here was the class struggle in the Far East, and the struggle of the Chinese people against British imperials—all based on an actual episode. Meyerhold was still using that style of production which obliterated the gap between stage and audience. The drama was acted almost in the aisles of the theater; and you felt you were part of the cast. At the end the barrier between stage and life was completely shattered; a screen came down over the final curtain and flashed the slogan: Comrades, support the Chinese Revolution! Every time I saw the play, the audience was stirred tremendously, and it was stirred in the direction of deeds. The play roused not only imagination, but will.

I went to see Meyerhold afterward. He was about fifty then, thin faced, thoughtful and ascetic, with a long nose, a narrow chin, a full sensitive mouth, altogether a very gentle and courteous man. He had been responsible for three or four revolutions in the theater, and was ready for several more. He had joined the Communist party before the revolution. But this was unknown on the Continent whose capitals applauded his daring and colorful innovations in the theater. Meyerhold's art was in the service of socialism, but he was neither ashamed nor proud of that. He took it for granted as you take your face for granted. I asked permission to have *Roar China* translated for production in New York, and he granted it.

"But," he said, smiling shyly, "do you really think America is ready to see a play about the Chinese Revolution in which the workers are the heroes?"

I thought it was. If Broadway would not take it, perhaps it could be shown in the new theater which Mike Gold, John Howard Lawson, John Dos Passos and others were beginning to organize in the Village. Meyerhold's smile broadened. He gave me a copy of the play, and O. B., my Irish mentor, made a translation of it. We spent several days behind the scenes of the Meyerhold Theater, making production notes, drawing sketches of the sets, studying the revolving stage. I did not imagine then that the American theater would be afraid to touch *Roar China* for three years. Perhaps I was too hopeful because of the young American I saw night after night at the play taking careful technical notes. He told me he was a poet interested in the theater, and his name was Denby, and his father had been Secretary of War. In those days I thought one swallow did make a summer.

In Moscow a play like *Roar China* presented few difficulties. It showed class against class pitted on obvious issues. Under these circumstances, telling the truth was a simple art. It was at the Moscow Art Theater that I saw how hard it was to convey the more complex truths. They were playing *The Days of the Turbines,* a civil war drama like most Soviet plays of that period. In one essential respect, however, this play was strikingly different. Hitherto the bolsheviks and their allies had been presented on the stage as animated solely by the loftiest motives. The Whites, on the other hand, were shown to be nothing but scoundrels, drunkards and cowards. But *The Days of the Turbines* showed the Whites, too, as human beings. They were presented as men and women who sincerely believed in their false cause; they were genuinely devoted to the old regime; they loved it and suffered for it as the workers loved and suffered for the triumph of socialism.

This play had been approved by the censor. The authorities felt that the old regime had been thoroughly defeated; now the civil war could be presented with some perspective. The extreme left of the

Soviet literary world thought otherwise. This play, they said, was counterrevolution; it idealized the Whites.

The authorities prevailed, and the play was produced. I saw it the opening night, and realized at once that the civil war period was by no means dead in the hearts of the spectators. When the curtain went up on a Christmas celebration in the home of the Whites, the bourgeois ladies and gentlemen in the audience began to sniffle. The Whites on the stage stood up, raised their glasses and solemnly sang *God Save the Czar,* and the ladies and gentlemen in the audience wept softly. O the good, dear, sweet, dead old days! The workers in the audience sat grimly silent.

The following day the left-wing writers were furious. Was it not obvious that the play was reviving old conflicts? The Whites may have been nice people personally, but when attractive actors rose to sing the czarist hymn solemnly, they roused emotions which the empire had cultivated for generations. Thereby the truth became a lie. The true idea that the Whites were human was transformed into the false idea that czarism was noble.

This left-wing viewpoint was generally acknowledged to be correct. A technical device was employed to break down the monarchical and religious sentiments which the singing of the czarist hymn had evoked in the hearts of the bourgeois spectators. In all the subsequent performances of the play, the actors who sang that hymn pretended to be drunk; they sang in cracked, whining, repulsive voices. What had been noble became grotesque; and this was essentially the truth. For the czarist hymn could appear noble only to the beneficiaries of the old regime, not to its victims, not to the millions of the people who, through blood and anguish, had emancipated themselves from it.

§6

American newspapers which arrived in Moscow ballyhooed the paradise at home. From Berlin you heard that European capitalism, too, had recovered. There was life in the old system still. The future of capitalism seemed rosy to all except the Marxists. Eugene Varga, the Hungarian professor who had served in Bela Kun's government during the Commune, dissented sharply from the Western prophets of hope. He was now chief economist of the Comintern, and I saw him frequently both in the office and in the Lux. He was a slight, wizened little man with eyeglasses and a mordant sense of humor. If he dropped in to spend an evening with us, you could not get him to talk economics.

"I've come to relax," he would say, "by contemplating the magnificent ruins of Mimi's beauty, and you want to make me work."

"Du Schweinehund!" Mimi would say. "What do you mean, the ruins of my beauty?"

"Do you object to being compared with a work of art like the Acropolis?" Varga would say. But he answered your questions eventually if you read him in the *Inprecor*. Here in the fall of 1926 he made his own prophecy:

"The idea of a fresh uplift of European capitalism built up on the aid of America is an illusion. Not only is American capitalism unable to carry European capitalism with it on an upward path, but American capitalism is itself already showing signs of decline, of slower progress. It will be drawn into the crisis of European capitalism."

What happened in the Soviet Union was of the utmost importance to the rest of the world; similarly, the progress of the October Revolution was conditioned by the international situation. At the Fourteenth Congress of the Communist party, held in December, 1925, the majority of the bolsheviks had announced boldly: From the NEP we go directly to the building of socialism in Russia. Doubters asked: What, socialism? in one country? and our backward country at that? Look at the texts! Marx said, Engels said, Lenin said, Stalin said. You are mistaken, comrades of the Opposition. They said something quite different. The mensheviks used to cite Marx and Engels to prove that a backward country like Russia could not have a proletarian revolution. Lenin proved in deeds that it could. Now we are going to prove that we have the resources, the strength, the will to build the economic and social foundations for socialism in one country, yes, and our backward country too.

In his report to the Fourteenth Congress, Stalin had not minimized the difficulties. Soviet Russia's constructive work, he had said, must of necessity be carried on in a world which outside of Russia was still capitalist. The development of Soviet economic life and of socialist construction took place amidst the antagonisms, the clashes between the Soviet economic system and the capitalist system. These antagonisms could not possibly be avoided. That was the framework within which the struggle between the two systems had to go on. This meant that socialist economy in Russia had to be built not only in opposition to the capitalist economy of the outside world, but also in opposition to certain elements in Russia itself. It had to be built under the strain of the conflict between the socialist elements and the capitalist elements within the Soviet Union itself.

Stalin therefore urged that Soviet economy be built up in such a way that Russia should not be transformed into an appendage of the capitalist system. The Soviet Union must not be a subordinate power enrolled in the general system of capitalist development; Soviet economy must not develop as a subsidiary part of world capitalism, but as an independent economic entity, relying mainly on the home market, on the interrelations between the Soviet manufacturing industry and Soviet agriculture.

On this problem, there were within the Communist party several different outlooks. Some comrades thought that Soviet Russia would, for a long time, remain an agrarian country; it would have to export agricultural products and import industrial machinery for many, many years to come. But Stalin and the majority of the bolsheviks thought that so long as Soviet Russia was surrounded by capitalist states, it would have to devote all its energies to remaining an independent country based upon the home market. The Party emphatically rejected the policy of transforming Soviet Russia into an appendage of the capitalist world system. It advocated the path of socialist construction within Russia. Naturally, Stalin had pointed out, this situation would be altered as soon as the revolution had taken place in Germany or in France or in both these countries, as soon as socialist construction had begun there upon a higher technical foundation than existed in Russia. Then Russia's policy of becoming an independent economic entity would be changed; Russia would be incorporated in the general system of socialist development. But meantime, pending the revolution in Germany or France, the Soviet Union would maintain that minimum of independent economic life which was essential as a safeguard against the economic subordination of the country to the system of world capitalism.

When you considered the problem economically rather than emotionally, the issue between the Party and the Opposition appeared clear enough. You understood the indignation of the bolsheviks against the fractional activities of the Opposition. At the end of September, the Opposition started a campaign throughout Russia at meetings of the Party units with the purpose of forcing a discussion regarding fundamental questions of policy which had been decided by the Fourteenth Congress. Trotsky and Zinoviev themselves took the initiative in this campaign by appearing at the Party unit meeting in the Aviopribor factory in Moscow. The rank and file realized that this sort of conduct by members of the Central Committee was a violation of Party discipline and repudiated the Opposition accordingly. Such rebuffs, received throughout the country, compelled the leaders of the Opposition to submit a statement to the Political Bureau promising to discontinue their factional struggle. Three days later they opened the fight in Leningrad, again meeting with defeat.

These activities retarded constructive work, and compelled the Party to talk and talk about policies already decided upon. I was at the German workers' club when Stassova, representing the Central Committee, explained the Party line. Contrary to reports I had heard in New York, discussion from the floor was unhampered. The Opposition had its full say on the impossibility of building socialism in one country, on the "degeneration" of the Party, on the necessity of breaking relations with the British trade unions, on the "Stalinite bureaucracy." One girl in a wide-brimmed feathered bonnet and emerald earrings as big as hazelnuts attacked the Party policy on wages. From the beginning of the October Revolution there had been a division of opinion on this question. Various opposition groups had urged crushing the peasantry by economic means; the majority of the Party had always felt that wage increases should not break the alliance of peasants and workers. Emerald earrings began in a high voice lamenting the miserable lot of the Soviet workers. Hedda, sitting in back of the hall, sharply interrupted her:

"Take those earrings off, then your crocodile tears might have some effect."

A German worker from a shoe factory said:

"Comrades, the economics of the Opposition are silly. But I want to point out—here they are, shouting that the Party suppresses them, doesn't give them a chance to state their views. Yet right in our club you can see how tolerant we have been to their stupid and dangerous notions. I am convinced the Opposition will come to a very bad end. Meantime, listen to them. They are damning themselves out of their own mouths, and are sliding to total perdition."

On October 16th, the *Pravda* published a declaration by six members of the Central Committee who had adhered to the Opposition bloc, including Zinoviev, Kamenev and Trotsky. This declaration said:

"At the Fourteenth Party Congress of the Communist Party and afterwards, we disagreed with the majority of the Party and the Central Committee on a number of questions of principle. Our views are laid down in official documents as well as in speeches delivered by us at the Party conference, in the Plenum of the Central Committee and in the Political Bureau. We also stand at present on the basis of these views. We decidedly reject, however, the theory and practice of 'freedom of factions and groupings,' and recognize that such a theory and practice are contrary to Leninism and the decisions of the Party. We consider it our duty to carry out the decisions of the Party regarding the impermissibility of factional activity. At the same time, we consider it our duty to admit openly before the Party that we and our supporters, in putting forward our views on a number of occasions after the Fourteenth Party conference, have committed acts which violated Party discipline, and that we have followed a factional course which goes beyond the limits of ideological struggle within the Party as laid down by the Party. In recognizing these acts as wrong, we declare that we emphatically renounce the factional methods of propagating our views, as these methods endanger the unity of the Party; and we call upon all comrades who share our views to do the same. We call for the immediate dissolution of all factional groupings which have been formed around the views of the Opposition. At the same time we admit that by our appearance in Moscow and in Leningrad in October we violated the decision of the Central Committee on the impermissibility of a discussion, in that we opened such a discussion against the decisions of the Central Committee. . . . We consider the decisions of the Fourteenth Party Congress, of the Central Committee and the Central Control Commission as absolutely binding for us, and we shall unconditionally submit to them and carry them out. We call upon all comrades who share our views to do the same."

In thus condemning their own factional activities, the leaders of the Opposition condemned their future ones. When it became clear that the declaration of October 16th was only a "maneuver," a meaningless promise to be violated at the first favorable opportunity, the rank and file lost whatever sympathy it may have had for the Opposition. It therefore approved the Central Control Commission's actions in removing Trotsky from the Political Bureau and Zinoviev from the Comintern.

What disturbed me most at this time was the reaction of the opportunists in the Party. They did not seem to care about the objective merits of the controversy, or its effects upon the revolutionary movement as a whole. They were chiefly interested in saving their own hides. Greta and I ran into one of these fellows in the corridor of the Lux. He was part of the Zinoviev group in the Comintern and fell with his chief. Now he wanted to switch to the majority, but the Party properly suspected his sincerity.

"Ah, my tongue, my tongue," he said to us. "It has ruined me."

"What have you said?" Greta asked him.

"Nothing, but for nine months my tongue has been licking the wrong boots."

Greta laughed. She, too, considered politics mainly from the viewpoint of licking, and was herself an expert in this art. It was depressing to think there were such people in the Party at all. You had to talk with Gustav and Hedda to feel cleaner.

"The matter comes down to this," Gustav said to me. "The Opposition acts as if the Party were a bourgeois government. If they were right in their charges of degeneration and Thermidor, if the Party were actually betraying the revolution, then the Opposition would be justified in whatever it did. Against a degenerated Party which is sliding down the path of counterrevolution everything is permitted. If I thought the Opposition was right, I'd join it. But it's wrong. We are not degenerating. Quite the contrary. We are now ready to begin building socialism in earnest. This makes the Opposition wrong in its tactics and policies, its secret meetings, illegal printings, inflammatory leaflets. They confuse and mislead people. Their declaration of October sixteenth admits as much, but even that declaration was dishonest. They continue to defame and sabotage and dishearten. If they go on like that, there will be no room for them in the Party. Many of us have urged their expulsion. Stalin is against it. He says we cannot spare talented people; they are too precious to be wasted. But mark my word, they will have to go. They are bitter, blind, intransigeant; they have refused every offer of peace; they will play first fiddle or nothing. They believe that unless they run the Party it will degenerate. Louis Fourteenth said: the state, that's me. The Opposition says: the revolution, that's us. But you know Louis the Fourteenth was not the state; the feudal nobility was the state. And the Opposition is not the revolution. The proletariat is the revolution. And there you have the parting of the ways."

§ 7

That fall I got a month's vacation. Like every employee in the Soviet Union, I received a free medical examination. The doctor said I was in excellent shape and could go anywhere I liked. This came as a surprise. I had always had a tendency to frequent illness; yet here in "starving" Russia I was healthier than at any other time of my life.

A group of Americans were taking a tour through the Ukraine and the Caucasus, and Greta and I joined them. It was typical of Greta that she wangled her expenses for this trip out of one of the American women in the party.

Greta was proud of her new conquest, so useful from the practical viewpoint. In discussing it with me, she managed to combine a boast with a sermon:

"I always get what I want by being clever. If you are clever, you get all you want. The trouble is you are too naïve, too open. You take your skin off in the frost and walk around in your bones and complain that you are colder than anybody else."

In winning Grace over, Greta had more in mind than the trip through the Ukraine and the Caucasus.

"Maybe," she mused one afternoon to me, "maybe Gracie will send me to college in America. I never had a chance to study, never had the money, so I am only a stenographer in the Comintern. I want to be more; but European women don't get a chance to do anything real. Only American women get that chance."

"And Soviet women?" I said. "And Shura? And Clara Zetkin in Germany?"

Greta's campaign was persistent. It was Gracie this and Gracie that, and, O Gracie, you are so beautiful today, and so clever and so kind. And because Grace was a serious social worker and something of a puritan, Greta suddenly gave up drinking and swearing and telling dirty stories, and acted like a saint, reprimanding me for any deviations from decorum. Fortunately, I had known Grace in New York, where we worked together in a labor organization. She was a middle-aged woman with snow-white hair, tall and aristocratic. The widow of a Midwestern businessman, she had given up society for the labor movement. Her father was a well-known professor in one of the largest American universities, and she herself had gone through an art school. But she seldom talked of these things. She was prouder of her deserved reputation as a competent labor organizer. Against the Russian landscape she was a startling and appealing figure in her riding breeches, leather boots, orange shirts and blue silk ties. The peasant women would study her long, lanky figure and call me aside to ask why the American comrade wore trousers. Feminism in male attire had not yet reached the backward regions of the Caucasus.

Our party traveled by train, automobile and haywagon through the five economic epochs which Lenin had described and Eisenstein had photographed. It was good to get out of the hothouses—the offices and hotel rooms where talk and introspection smothered you. I would always hate the four walls of an office; they imprisoned your mind as well as your body. When you saw factories and fields, meeting halls and villages, when you talked to workers and peasants, everything seemed clearer.

Here was Kharkov, about which my father used to tell me when I was a boy. He would not recognize it. It was a lively industrial town, white and clean in the morning sunlight, with wide asphalt streets and big new buildings. A trade-union delegation came to meet us, accompanied by an interpreter. Greta and I both spoke Russian, so she said undiplomatically to hell with the interpreter. But he stuck to us like a leech; he got paid for the job and he would not let it go. He had lived in New York and talked English rapidly.

"How do you do, everybody, glad to meet you all. I have been the interpreter for all the American and British delegations which have come here. I don't know everybody, but everybody knows me. How is my friend Scott Nearing? He was here last year. A great guy. Does he still wash his own underwear? Ha! ha! ha! We had a wonderful time with him. We are teaching the people the division of labor, and he insists on washing his own socks and dishes. A Tolstoyan, you understand."

We managed to ditch the interpreter, and went to the Kharkov branch of the state electrical trust. Grace took notes for the delegation, always and everywhere the organizer, American, efficient. Look at the rise in production. Wages have gone up from 12.50 rubles to 17 rubles in the first category alone. The workers are 100 per cent organized in the metal workers' union. There are thirty-one nationalities in this factory—Russians, Ukrainians, Czechs, Germans, Poles, Austrians, and even one Yank from Detroit who has no desire to go home. There are 450 boys and girls, apprentices, who work four hours a day and go to school in the factory four hours. Fine-looking kids, crowding around us, bombarding us with questions about America. Here is the crèche for the children of the women workers in the factory, clean, well run by efficient nurses. Outside is a new building, the workers' club with a theater and a gymnasium, a library and a labor bank. Seven hundred of the workers are Party members, 1400 are Comsomols, over half the apprentices are Pioneers. "The factory," Grace jotted down in her notebook, "corresponds to the American type of construction and equipment; fairly good ventilation and cleanliness." But there was something different here; it was the workers' factory; they owned it and ran it and improved it for their own benefit.

We want to see Dimitri Yefimov, health commissar for the whole of the Ukraine, a self-taught worker, an exceptionally strong personality, busy day and night in the All-Ukrainian Ispolkom, the Supreme Council of Physical Culture, the municipal Soviet of Kharkov, the Sovnarkom. In his spare time he was studying medicine.

"How does health work in the United States differ from ours?" he asked, not unexpectedly. "What are the wages of health workers? hours? organization? What care do you take of mothers and children?"

He was interested in sports and wanted to know if America would send a soccer team to play the Ukrainians.

"We beat the Finns," he said proudly.

Organized sport was a new thing in Russia, and it belonged to the people, not to commercial rings. Machinery was new too. Here was *The Unexpected Guest,* a vast building under construction. It would cover eight acres and would be the municipal center, housing trusts, administrative bodies, the soviet, a restaurant which would seat 1000 people at a time, a theater, a gymnasium. The workers showed us around the place, proud of their electrified stone crushers and cranes and steam shovels. Every week, the workers and the managers met to discuss the progress of the building. We attended one such meeting and heard director Paul Rotert report to the workers on the technical problems confronting the entire construction staff, which included 1800 workers.

In the mining center of Gorlovka, in the Don Basin, we went to see the almost completed palace of labor, to be opened on the tenth anniversary of the revolution. Everywhere in the Soviet Union the most important buildings are for the people. One of the construction engineers and Comrade Gonta of the Cultural Commission took us over the scaffolding by moonlight. Again, an auditorium, clubrooms, a library, a school. Next morning we visited some of the 900 new houses built for the workers in the five coal mines of Gorlovka. They were stucco houses in the English style, with trees around them, yards and fences. The cottages were scrupulously clean, well furnished. Bookcases and flowers lined the walls. The workers received the houses, the furniture, electric light and coal free of charge. At the workers' club, the home of the mine manager under the old regime, we saw the anthropological exhibit showing the evolution of tools, of animals, of man himself; and the exhibit showing the evolution of religion from primitive idols to the Russian Orthodox Church; and the physiological exhibit showing the evolution and structure of the human body. At home, in New York, this education of the Soviet workers in modern science was called propaganda, because its logical conclusion was communism. The library of this workers' club had translations of Upton Sinclair's *100%—The Story of a Patriot* and John Reed's *Ten Days that Shook the World:* at home even the educated classes knew next to nothing about the new Russian literature. We visited the dramatic circle and saw the Blue Blouse put on a "living newspaper," dramatizing the events of the day in the Soviet Union and abroad, satirizing bureaucracy and inefficiency, poking fun at British imperialism. Another group rehearsed a play to be given for the benefit of the homeless children in Gorlovka. The radio group got Berlin for us on short wave; and in another room a workers' band played for us on condition that we address a meeting of the workers.

Next day we went to Mine Number One, showered in the new baths, put on miners' clothes and boots, hats and lamps, and went down 500 meters in the elevator. We walked along a dark alley lined with pine timber, and saw the coal being taken out by mules. At the end of the alley we were shown the place where 32 miners were killed in the fire of 1917; there was no mining at this level now. We started down the horizontal shaft to the lower level. You could not walk, but had to climb down like a monkey holding on to the pine timbering with your hands and feet, sliding from post to post. Clouds of coal dust enveloped you. The alleys were divided by burlap curtains which relieved the terrific draft. It took us an hour and a half to make this zigzag descent. The miners had to do this every day when they came to work; they said it took them five minutes, but we did not believe them. There was no light except from the lamps on our caps. The passages were narrow and without footing. Our hands, clothes, faces and eyes were completely covered with coal dust, which we also coughed out of our lungs. At the end of the alley we saw miners chipping coal with picks. There were borings to let water and gas escape, and holes for dynamite charges. We walked back through water up to our ankles to the elevator at the lower level, and ran into the night shift coming to work. Upstairs we joined the day shift in the showers. We were all knocked out when we got back to our hotel and fell asleep at once.

At midnight there was a loud knocking at my door. I opened it and faced three young workers, wide awake and smiling.

"You are leaving Gorlovka tomorrow," one of them said, "and you haven't even seen our new safety station."

"We are very tired."

"You can always sleep, but you may never be in Gorlovka again."

I roused the party and we all got dressed and went down to the safety station, and Grace jotted down in the American delegation's notebook the precise number of wagons, trucks, and oxygen bags, new style and old; the number of active workers and the number of volunteers, the number of mines served and their distance in kilometers from the safety station; the number of doctors and internes attached to the station; a description of the chemical laboratory and how many minutes and seconds it took from the ringing of the alarm until the safety station workers reached the mine.

The three young workers who had roused us were delighted with our visit. They gave us their photographs with warm comradely inscriptions and asked us to come back in five years to see the incredible improvements which were being planned.

Thanks to this pride in their work, we missed our train next morning, took a later one, and arrived in Artiomovsk in the dead of night. There wasn't a vacant hotel room in that town of half a million inhabitants, but the workers at the railway station put us up in their homes. In the daytime we visited the salt mine named after the Ukrainian poet Schebshenko. It was like a crystal cave. The worker-manager shouted up to the worker-dynamiters that an American delegation was here to greet them, and the worker-dynamiters came down, and stood around in a group on a hill of salt. Candles and lanterns lit up the mine. Grisha, an old worker with a drooping gray mustache, who had been in that mine for twenty-eight years, asked the permission of his comrades to address us. Certainly, Grisha.

"Comrades from America! Thank you for coming to see us. We are happy to greet you in the name of the Soviet Union, our workers' republic. I am an old man. I have worked much in my life, and I remember the days of the Czar. Well, better forget them. They are gone forever. We are a free people now. We are building socialism. Have you seen the fine houses we have built? They are for us, not for the exploiters. We don't pay rent. We get light and heat free. We have our own clubs, our theaters, our movies, our gardens. What a lucky man I am to live to see this new life. And it will get better, every year. Please send our comradely greetings to the workers in your country. Someday they will also build a new life for themselves."

Greta had tears in her eyes. She could be sentimental at the most unexpected times. Yet that very morning she had sent off a number of letters to Moscow and Berlin for some political intrigue of which she would tell me nothing.

From the salt mine, we went to the Dom Ugol, the Coal House, where they gave us rooms. Several of us dropped in on Grace to say good night. She lay across her bed in a purple silk dressing gown, obviously tired.

"Sit down," she said. "Let's forget for a while. Let's read *Faust* or something."

"Let's read *Gentlemen Prefer Blondes*," Greta said.

"I've never read the book," said Grace.

"Greta always wants to read it," I said. "She sees herself in Lorelei."

"Who is Lorelei?" Grace asked.

"The great American heroine," I said. "The gold digger who gets something for nothing."

"Let's not read," Greta said. "Let's talk."

"All right," I said. "May I ask you a question?"

"Go ahead," Greta said.

"How in hell did you ever become a communist?"

"I'll tell you," she said. "I was eighteen years old and a secretary to the foreign minister of Bavaria. I had a girl friend who was a socialist. At that time I knew nothing about socialism. My father was a petty Bavarian official. My family considered socialism low, dirty and dangerous. But I liked my socialist girl friend. I let her take me to a socialist meeting where Kurt Eisner spoke. Eisner's talk impressed me very much. I discovered that socialist ideas appealed to me. I began to attend lectures and meetings. Then the war broke out and I had to take a stand. I joined the Social Democratic party. When the split came, I went with Luxemburg and Liebknecht. . . ."

I wasn't listening any more. I had heard Greta's story before, and now I felt it had no meaning. Her heart was not really in the movement. Or perhaps I did not really know her. Perhaps she was for me only an abstract symbol which I had mixed up with the movement, and now that I was beginning to catch a glimpse of her as a woman I felt we had little in common personally.

"What are you thinking about?" I heard Greta say.

"I am thinking that in another age you would have been a Pompadour," I said.

"And you would have been a father confessor," she said bitterly. "You worm out the soul from women."

But you are not a father confessor, I said to myself. You worm out the soul from everyone in order to understand yourself and others, to convert the unknown into the known, the irrational into the rational. Or maybe you are kidding yourself. That is not important. What Grisha said on the hill of salt is important. Nothing is more important.

From Artiomovsk we went on to the Caucasus. Everywhere there was energy, creation and hope. Even in the little unpaved villages, where the children ate the soup we gave them thinking it was candy, the people talked of socialism. Everything was considered in relation to socialism—the new railway, the new hospital, the new school; the newspaper in the native language, the first in that region; the state model farm which showed the peasants modern ways of farming; the workers' clubs and theaters and gymnasiums.

By the time we reached Tiflis and Baku, I saw things which I had missed on my first visit to those cities. Every corner of the former empire, however remote or backward, was concentrating its energies on the creation of the new world, proud and happy to participate in the colossal, planned effort.

Seeing these things detached me from Greta and from the conflict between us which appeared obscure to me. But this detachment made me see Greta more truly than I had seen her when my spirit was so entangled with hers that I could hardly tell the two apart.

At the very moment when I realized that the bond between us was dissolving, I was closer to her than I had ever been. It was the night our American party of travelers came to a tiny Cossack village high in the Caucasus Mountains. Our guide, a journalist from Kislovodsk, could locate no place to sleep except the lime floor of a peasant's house. The men in the party stretched out on one side of the room, the women on the other. There was no bedding and we huddled fully dressed on the cold lime. In the darkness I lay awake thinking of my grandfather's lime floor, and the musty books along the shelf, and the long clock with the two weights that slowly ticked eternity. I tried to sleep but couldn't. For covering we had *burkas,* uncured sheepskins, which stank, and were alive with fleas. I could hear in the darkness the restless tossing of my companions, and across the black room Greta laughing softly in whispered conversation with Grace.

"Three days," she was saying, "and nothing but fleas. In Germany you won't find a flea from Schleswig-Holstein to Breman."

I heard her moving, and when I looked up I could see her compact body swiftly sliding out of the door. I got up and followed her. She stopped when she heard my steps.

"The fleas are killing me," she said. "You know—Russische Wirtschaft. I am going to take a swim."

The little white house behind us stood on a high hill, dark green and silver under the full moon. In that bright nocturnal light you could see the stream at the foot of the hill. We walked down in silence. How fragrant the earth was, and how beautiful the fragrance of Greta near you:

We reached the stream; without saying a word, Greta quickly took off her clothes and stood naked in the moonlight. She plunged into the stream, shivering with cold and laughing. After a minute she came out, white and trembling. Her body was firm and beautiful, her small breasts taut like a young girl's, her hips full and strong.

"Greta," I said, "you are very beautiful."

"Love can't live on beauty alone," she said, "and people need more than love."

I wrapped my overcoat around her and she sat down on a knoll. Taking a comb out of the pocket of her sweater lying on the grass, she began to caress her yellow hair like the Lorelei. Again she resembled the photograph of herself at seventeen which she had once given me, with its thin, tense, dreamy face, tight-lipped and questioning. I thought, too, of the night I had taken her to a film of *La Bohème* in Union Square, and she had cried at Mimi's death.

"What are you thinking of?" I heard her voice saying. Her eyes were a startling blue in the Caucasian moonlight.

"Nothing," I said.

"When will you start thinking about your future?" she said, and it sounded almost like my father talking.

"I know, I know." My own voice sounded remote and impatient, as if it were someone else's. "Ruhm muss man gewinnen, and so on and so forth. Let's go in."

We climbed the hill in silence. At the door of the little white house she kissed me warmly on the lips.

On the way back to Moscow, our train, cutting through the Ukrainian steppes, passed within fifty miles of the village in which I was born. There was nobody there I knew. Grandfather was dead, Uncle Moishe was running a bookstore in Riga, another uncle was in Paris, others were scattered over Soviet Russia, one of them a bolshevik commissar in an industrial center. I did not stop to see the village. The past was going from me; there was only the future.

CHAPTER IV

The debate which ensued was in its scope and progress an epitome of the course of life. Neither place nor council was lacking in dignity. The debaters were the keenest in the land, the theme they were engaged on the loftiest and most vital.

—JAMES JOYCE.

§ 1

ON the fringes of the movement earlier, in 1921, you had found stragglers from the world of D. H. Lawrence and Aldous Huxley; you took to them because that world had not yet entirely died within you.

Now, in 1926, the Comintern itself was another world, lucid, energetic, purposeful. Here was Kusinin, of the presidium, a Finn of forty-six, with years of struggle and suffering behind him, pure in his devotion to the cause; a quiet, deliberate, slow-speaking man, cautiously sifting facts. Mistakes were dangerous; too much was at stake. He turned your mind inside out, asking a thousand questions about your country, your Party, your labor movement. He carefully probed everything you knew, and everything everybody else knew, before coming to any conclusion of his own. He reminded you of Professor Woodworth on the campus, with his lined sallow face, his scientific meticulousness; but here science was wholly in the service of the classless society to be achieved by millions in co-operation.

Manuilsky, also of the presidium, had the same thoroughness; he, too, examined and cross-examined men and documents before arriving at decisions, but his method was different. He drew you out by humor; he rocked your memory loose by anecdote and laughter.

"What do you think of the possibilities of working in the A. F. of L.?" he would say.

You told him what you thought, and his eyes twinkled.

"Well," he would say, laughing, "Foster would hardly agree with that, would he?"

You had to tell him what every group thought. He kidded you into remembering what you had forgotten: the factional struggle, which antedated the Party, was no plaything for cliques; it was a con-

flict of views for the purpose of arriving at a bolshevik line valid for
all.

The methods were different, the results the same. In the leadership
of the Comintern were men of varied temperaments and varied experiences. They came from all the leading countries of the world to the
one place where they were safe from the merciless persecution of the
exploiters. Armed with the science of Marx and Lenin, they gathered
and collated the experiences of the working class in all lands day in
and day out; they exchanged opinions with all the parties; they outlined policies, democratically arrived at, for the direction of the struggle for a new world.

In the offices of the Comintern, the library, the council rooms you
found representatives of every Communist party, from New York to
Tokyo, from Budapest to Buenos Aires. Here were not only formal
delegates, but specialists in various fields, economists, sociologists, journalists, gathering and interpreting the details of the daily struggle the
world over. Here was the American Bosse, who had left a well-paid
teaching job to devote his talents for research to the revolution; and
the English comrade Eric, so passionately preoccupied with his economic studies that he had given up every vestige of personal life.
Wherever they came from, whatever their social origin, the paths of
these men had all led to the same goal.

When you met Americans this evolution toward a common viewpoint seemed most clear. There was Clarence Hathaway, for instance,
whom I first saw catching in a baseball game which the American
workers in the Comintern played against the Koreans. The Americans
won. Later Hathaway and I went out for dinner together.

"The Korean tovarishi are O.K.," Hathaway said. "They're swell
fielders, but light in the poop. They can't bat."

The speaker was tall, well built, with loose blond hair combed
back, cool gray eyes, a deep voice. He spoke slowly and deliberately,
weighing even the most trivial words as though everything depended
on them. He gesticulated vigorously with his right hand, from which
the two middle fingers were missing.

"You put up a good game," I said.

"I used to be a semipro, before I became a socialist."

I was interested in how people became socialists; the transition
from the old culture to the new was bound to be the most universal
spiritual change of our times. At the beginning of the century the
Comrade, a literary magazine published by American socialists, used

to run brief autobiographies on that theme. Now, in the Soviet Union, you could hardly pick up a novel or a collection of poems without finding an autobiographical sketch in which the author explained how he came to communism. This was natural in a period of profound social transmutation. In his day St. Augustine had explained how a Roman gentleman became a Christian. Dante's *New Life* was the testament of a man caught between the Middle Ages and the Renaissance. Rousseau bared his heart to the world at the moment when bourgeois society was preparing to overwhelm and exterminate feudalism. And in our own country, Henry Adams, moving from an agrarian culture to the machine age, had summed up his long education by saying that he should have been a Marxist. These were all stories of spiritual transformation at historical moments when civilization itself was being transformed. For me the external event was accidental, the psychological change paramount. Not every Roman who embraced Christianity had had an illegitimate child in Carthage, nevertheless St. Augustine's feelings were his; just as we who had read the *Education* on the campus had shared Adams' intellectual experiences although our ancestors had never been presidents of the United States.

In my own epoch, in which mankind was again making a basic turn in its development, those who abandoned the bourgeois world for communism went through various external experiences, but the fundamental psychological pattern had a common outline. Had John Reed written his personal story, it would have been one of vivid objective adventure among strikes and battles; Nearing, in a similar enterprise, would probably have stressed more the evolution of his economic thought, Floyd Dell his states of mind. Had not Lenin already told us that various people came to communism for various reasons? I was interested in those reasons more than in the specific events. Probably I was anxious to discover those points at which the experiences of the intellectual touched the experiences of the worker; I was seeking the lowest common factors and the highest common denominators of my age in its forced march from Eternity to Time, from Time to the class struggle, thence to the classless society.

Hathaway admitted that he had started as a bitter opponent of socialism. That admission immediately won my confidence; I was skeptical of people whose memory falsified the past to suit the interests of the present. Hathaway was a Nordic, native-born American; a Midwesterner, a factory worker, one of those whom the chauvinists described in their demagogic speeches as the hope of America. His boyhood was marked by sharp conflict with his father, but the usual pattern was reversed. The elder Hathaway was a socialist; the son was devoutly religious and headed the young men's club in a St. Paul church. In 1913 the presiding elder of that church was running for governor of Minnesota on the socialist ticket. Clarence was then working as a machinist's apprentice; he was a member of the trade union; yet he fought his father's proposal to permit the socialist candidate for governor to speak in the church. Such was the power of Eternity over Time, of illusion over reality.

Shortly afterward Hathaway worked in a Canadian factory, still antisocialist, religious, active in the church. One day the machine lopped off two of his fingers. He went to the minister of his church for advice. The minister suggested a lawyer to handle the compensation claim. The case was settled out of court. The lawyer took $150 for himself in fees, and gave Hathaway $100 as compensation. Then the young machinist learned that his lawyer was also the company's lawyer. The company's machine had cut off your fingers; the company's lawyer had cheated you. Did the minister of the gospel know this? Hathaway spoke to God's representative on earth and received the cold shoulder. He thought: the priest is for the company, just like the lawyer. From that moment he stopped going to church. But he continued to believe in religion. God was O.K.; his ministers were corrupt bureaucrats; and nobody could restore your two fingers. The inner conflict was acute. He worked his way through the western parts of Canada and the United States, and came in contact with I.W.W. agitators. Other workers were cheated like himself. Class consciousness. Class struggle.

In 1915 he went abroad and worked in the machine shops of England and Scotland. He caught the war fever. His own country was betraying the world in its fight for democracy; the world was fighting Kaiserism, it was fighting a war to end war, and our President, Mr. Wilson, was staying out of the holy struggle, he was letting mankind down. The young machinist shared the illusion common among the intellectuals of that period.

But here were workers returning from the front; here was the British antiwar movement, and the shop stewards' movement. The war was a bosses' war; the ministers in the churches, the lawyers in the cabinets were cheating again, on an immense scale, with workers' fingers and hands and heads piling high on Flanders fields.

He came back to America, joined the left wing of the Socialist party in 1917, the Communist party when it was formed two years later. Subsequently he was elected vice-president of the Minnesota State Federation of Labor. A class-conscious fighter, a communist.

Now, in the year 1926, he was in Moscow, studying Soviet life, working in the Comintern, sure of the future. But here, too, the road had been neither straight nor easy. In his slow, deliberate way, he told me of his first reactions.

"When I first came to Moscow early this year, I was depressed. I saw all around me the damages of the civil war. Homeless waifs, broken streets, dilapidated buildings, poor food and clothing. My God, were things so bad under socialism? Unconsciously, I was comparing conditions in Soviet Russia with conditions at home, in America, and the comparison was not at all favorable to the U.S.S.R. That was an emotional, a thoughtless reaction. Then I began to reason: This is Russia today. What was it yesterday? Has the revolution made conditions worse than they were under the old regime? Or has it opened the way for a decisive change, for tremendous improvement? This summer I found my answer. I worked at my trade in the textile mills of Orekhovo-Zuovo, sixty miles from Moscow. I found five separate plants. All the equipment was old, English machinery dating back to eighteen-seventy, and even this old equipment was in an abnormal state as a result of the civil war. This was the junk which the Russian workers had inherited from the old world. Russia is now passing through the reconstruction period; it is rapidly catching up with pre-war production, and it takes a little vision to foresee where communist methods will lead to. But I saw a sample at Orekhovo-Zuovo. I found them combining the five old plants into one. All the scattered dyeing equipment was concentrated into one dye department; ditto for the weaving and the spinning equipment. During the six months I worked there I saw the reconstruction process completed, the prewar production level surpassed. In the absence of private ownership, the workers were able to rationalize the production process to the highest degree. When I saw this plan carried out, I had faith in the plans for the future. Once the creative energies of the masses are released from the private profit system, there are no limits to its achievements. You won't know this country in ten years; its new social system will raise it to the highest levels of world production."

Hathaway absent-mindedly tried to light the wrong end of a Russian cigarette.

"I'll tell you what else impressed me," he went on in his deep, deliberate voice. "When I worked in factories at home, I was under the foreman's orders from the moment I came until I went home. You have no voice in the management of the factory, no matter what you know, what you think. You are chained to the machine. In the Soviet factory where I worked, every single change in production or administration was the subject of the widest and most heated discussion among the workers. The workers felt that what was being altered was their property. A change is proposed, and at once the workers ask: is it really better? will it increase production? will it improve the quality of the goods? At lunch there was no idle chatter; the workers argued back and forth about factory problems. There were formal discussion meetings too. The manager reported, the trade-union representative reported, the Party representative reported, and every report was discussed by the workers in the minutest detail. From the floor came not only criticism but constructive proposals. The rank and file contributed enormously to the reorganization of the factory. If this isn't democracy, I don't know what the word means."

This time Hathaway succeeded in lighting the right end of his cigarette. He smoked in silence. He was not steeped in nineteenth century literature, which inflated the importance of the complicated, petit-bourgeois heart. He talked of factories, production, rationalization; yet see how these, once altered, could change the hearts of workers, unleashing tongues silent for centuries, animating minds imprisoned by oppression, releasing a flood of creative power such as the world had never witnessed before. No wonder he was sure of the communist future. I was now sure too, although I had arrived at this certainty by another road. I had found in Soviet arts and letters that assurance which Hathaway had found in a Soviet factory; that Marxian method, older than the Russian Revolution, and as international as the working class itself which enabled mankind consciously to advance itself.

§ 2

In the corridors of the Lux, the Comintern building on the Mokhovaya; on tramways and buses, you ran across intent men and women with black brief cases, in groups and singly, hurrying to and from conferences. They were Chinese, Italian and French, Mexican and English, German and Japanese—representatives from all parts of the world to the enlarged plenum of the Executive Committee of the Communist International which met toward the close of 1926.

Here was the American delegation, and in it friends I had known in New York. The delegation was divided into two factions, one headed by Jay Lovestone, the other by Bill Foster and Earl Browder. The two groups boycotted each other, so fierce was the factional dispute in our party then. Lovestone ran from room to room in the Lux, blond and breathless, lining up supporters. If Browder was trying to do the same, you would never guess it; he talked to you about literature intelligently and asked you in a quiet voice what you were writing.

The American delegates brought news from home, some of it amusing. Bohemian gossipmongers were explaining the political crisis in Russia to the readers of the bourgeois press. It was all very simple, like a ten-twenty-thirty melodrama in the old days. The great, good and wise Lenin was dead; now the two "elder sons" of the bolshevik family, Stalin and Trotsky, were fighting for the heritage, for the mantle of the dead leader. The rude and ruthless Stalin had tricked and browbeaten his brilliant rival.

In Moscow the facts appeared less melodramatic and vastly more important. The political crisis was the result of an economic crisis in which the collision of personalities represented the collision of principles and social classes. Aesthete-politicians and confused liberals ready to glow over Soviet difficulties without understanding them, noted a molehill and called it a mountain. They observed that the new opposition within the Party had crystallized in 1923, when Lenin had been ill and inactive. This purely subjective version of events was as unjust to the Party as to the Opposition, which was politically far superior to its foreign claque of scribblers. The claque ignored the truly mountainous fact which the Opposition itself understood; 1923 was the year of the "scissors" crisis in national economy. The new Opposition, like previous blocs of its kind within the Party, had been formed on the basis of differences of opinion on fundamental economic questions —socialist accumulation, the building of socialism in one country, relations with the peasantry, the world revolution. When you talked with Russian bolsheviks at this time, whether they supported the Central Committee or the Opposition, they did not overemphasize the personal qualities of the various leaders, though recognizing the importance of subjective factors. They talked about more basic issues, about the two prevailing and contradictory views of the New Economic Policy, and of the entire transition period from capitalism to socialism. Was the Soviet Union ready to begin socialist construction? Did it have the necessary resources and organization to leap forward to socialist industrialization and the collectivization of agriculture? That was the essential problem to which all other factors, however important or interesting, were subordinate. The majority of the Party, headed by Stalin, had the foresight and the courage at this time to answer those questions in the affirmative, to propose the abandonment of NEP and the commencement of socialist construction. That would be a daring step, but if successful, it would mark the most important turning point in contemporary history since October, 1917. It would mean the first concrete proof that socialist economy was actually superior to capitalism. This was how the matter appeared in Moscow at this time even to rank-and-filers like myself, not too well developed politically.

No wonder the delegates from every part of the world to the Comintern plenum were stirred. The Soviet Union could never be considered apart from the world labor movement, less than ever now, when the first test of planned socialist economics was about to be made.

When the sessions of the plenum opened in December, the translation department in which I worked was transferred to the meeting place, St. Andrew's Hall in the Kremlin. At the high gates, you presented the inevitable Soviet *propusk,* the document without which you could not get into certain places, no matter who you were. Once Bukharin stood in front of me in the long line seeking admission. He fumbled in his pocket and smiled charmingly at the Red soldier.

"Terribly sorry," he said. "I have forgotten my *propusk.* I must get in at once, I am Bukharin."

"And I am Lenin," said the young soldier without smiling.

Bukharin had to go home for his pass. The rest of us went into the Kremlin, walked down the old little streets to the building where the plenum was meeting. You walked up the broad marble staircase to the vestibule whose main wall was covered with Brodsky's academic painting of the Second Congress of the Comintern, with Lenin speaking in the center and John Reed among the delegates. Down the long corridor was St. Andrew's Hall, the former throne room of the Czar, with its high, vaulted ceiling, its almost ecclesiastical architecture. The throne had been replaced by a dais reserved for the presidium of the plenum. The long table stretching across the platform was covered with red cloth.

Translators and newspapermen had a special room near by where they did their typing and mimeographing. Here O. B. had her own English department in which our little old menshevik lady dourly dictated translations for the British and American delegates. On the floor of our large workroom, I saw crawling after a big rubber ball the six-year-old son of Joe Feinberg, translator of Lenin's works into English. His mother, a typist in the Comintern, did not want to leave the pale, redheaded kid at home, and we all liked him anyway. Nine years earlier neither the boy nor his parents would have been allowed in Moscow, much less the Kremlin. But that was long ago. When the kid would grow up, he would hear about those queer days and would hardly believe they could have existed. I imagined that for him socialism would be a matter of course, like the sky or the wind.

As one of the translators for the American delegation, I sat at a long table under the platform, close to the speakers. The sessions were solemn and tense; much was at stake. In the corridors, or at lunch in the dining room below, once a royal suite whose Byzantine murals in blue and gold still glittered at us, the delegates laughed, told stories, wisecracked.

"Did you hear that fellow attack Stalin?" Kurt asked me. "He reminds me of the sparrow and the mare. What, you never heard that story?" He told it to me. I had heard the story before, but in the American version it was about the monkey and the elephant. "That fellow also attacked the old giant," Kurt laughed. Kurt felt that his own attack on Trotsky was on a much higher intellectual level, almost as good as that of Heinz Neumann, a leader of the German party whom Kurt admired tremendously.

Inside St. Andrew's Hall, the delegates sat hushed and attentive as speaker after speaker rose to defend his position. Here was Stalin, robust in his semimilitary khaki tunic and leather boots, his strong face tanned, his hair cropped short. Silence settled on the hall, and Stalin increased the tension by saying nothing for a few seconds. Again his silence had the effect I had noticed in Tiflis; the audience became more attentive. Then he began in a voice so quiet that only the translators, sitting right under the platform, could hear him. The delegates strained forward, many cupping their ears. Stalin cleared his throat, took a glass of water.

"You must excuse me, comrades," he said. "I ate herring for lunch."

The hall rocked with laughter. The tension was broken. Stalin went on in a reserved voice, but you could hear every word all over the hall. He was no orator or actor; his Russian had a marked Georgian accent and his rhetoric was void of flourishes or periods. It was muscular like Caesar's narrative of the Gallic wars. His one gesture was to cleave the air with the open palm of his hand, like a workman chopping wood. But that was his power precisely, to talk like a worker saying simply how to build something. You knew exactly how things stood, where you were going. Through his words you felt an indomitable will—you felt that this iron determination would overcome the tremendous obstacles on the road to socialism. And there was another quality there too, hard to define, intangible and all-pervading. Stalin was a powerful personality, yet somehow the person vanished behind the idea. He was not talking about himself at all, only about socialism and how to build it. Toward that objective every force must be strained.

Nor must we be bound by rigid formulas. The Opposition claims socialism cannot be built in one country, Stalin said. It cites Engels in support of its thesis. True, Engels did say something like that. When? In eighteen-fifty. The world has changed a great deal since then. We have resources and knowledge today undreamed of seventy-five years ago. That was why Lenin said socialism *is* possible in one country. If Engels lived today, he would himself consider the historic context of his first statement.

These were the people whom western ideologues called religious fanatics. In St. Andrew's Hall they sounded more like scientists. Nowhere else in the world could you find the best minds of a social class concentrated upon the problem of reconstructing society for the benefit of the people as a whole. This was the scientific temper in the reorganization of society which the socialist teachers of my youth had praised, only to forget it when Lenin's death gave them the excuse to return to the bourgeois world. But the science and the class that now embodied it were going on. You were sure of that when you heard Stalin's quiet and assured voice, dramatic in its understatement of the most vital issues of our epoch.

Curiously enough, Stalin was the one man of all the outstanding bolshevik leaders of whom we had heard least in America. Lenin, Trotsky, Chicherin, Zorin were names familiar to us, in our limited knowledge. Of Stalin we heard once from the American journalist Ernestine Evans, who had written about him in one of the respectable family magazines. Scott Nearing, too, returning from Russia to New York in 1925, had talked of Stalin with that peculiar reverence which he reserved for revolutionaries who worked unusually hard and lived with unusual frugality and had no thought but socialism. When I had seen Stalin in Tiflis and felt his greatness through his reticence and tried to communicate it to the readers of the *New Masses,* I did not know much about the internal history of the Russian party. Now the background was a little clearer, and against it the man's extraordinary will, his applied logic, his boundless daring loomed up to encourage and inspire us.

Toward the close of Stalin's speech, I noticed Radek, then an Oppositionist, sitting on the steps leading to the platform. His clever clean-shaven face was framed in whiskers that ran under the chin like the lighthouse keeper's in the Uneeda Biscuit advertisements. His face grew longer as Stalin calmly analyzed the social democratic deviation in the Russian party. At lunch, tension relieved itself in wisecracks. Kurt, his blue eyes twinkling, described his real or imaginary conversation with Radek:

"I said to him, you sit there so calmly while your colleagues of the Opposition are tearing their hair in desperation. He said, and what do you think I'm doing? You understand, he had his hands in his pockets. What a wit!"

"Kurt, you're an idiot," Hedda said, looking up from her plate. To me she added aside: "Don't believe a word of this. In Germany you attribute every moral maxim to Schiller, in Russia every joke to Radek."

But wisecracks in lobby and dining hall did not obscure the solemnity of the occasion, a solemnity which percolated to the bourgeois world. There the press was trying to sense what was going on. Those papers which saw in the Opposition an indictment of the Soviet regime applauded Trotsky, who only yesterday was their bête noir, a bolshevik whose articles they would not publish free of charge. And those who saw in the Central Committee a new "moderate" tendency away from the mad fantasy of world revolution applauded Stalin, yesterday scarcely known in the bourgeois West, yet hated as part of the communist movement. Both groups within the Party flashed bourgeois newspaper clippings from the dais in St. Andrew's Hall. To be praised by the capitalist press was nothing for a bolshevik to boast of. You could damn an opponent by showing that the exploiters thought well of him. This had its logic. At that time the bourgeois press praised you for "coming to your senses," for abandoning the dream of world socialism. It had not yet discovered the subtler trick of attacking the Party for "betraying" the revolution, so dear to the capitalist heart, and praising renegades as the exponents of pure, unadulterated communism, whose chief objective was to discredit the Soviet Union.

As the plenum went on, leaders of the Opposition took the floor to defend their views before the delegates. Zinoviev, short, stocky, with a crown of high curly hair, criticized the Party line in his famous falsetto. How different some of our old heroes now looked from their early photographs which I had seen year after year in the left-wing American press. Thin, ascetic, long-faced revolutionaries had become heavy, plump, stolid. Was it age, power? To be sure, there was the biologic factor. The weak baby bull, barely able to stand on its legs, becomes year after year fatter, heavier, stronger. But the bull had a simple physical cycle of birth, reproduction and death. Civilized man lives by more. Here among the delegates in the auditorium were men of fifty, gaunt, with flaming hungry eyes; and here on the dais was Zinoviev plump with self-assurance, well fed on authority. I expounded this theory to Lydia Gibson in the corridor outside the throne room, and she laughed.

"Glands," she said.

Kamenev, following Zinoviev, looked like a mild little professor lecturing on paleontology. But he was a subtle debater who made serious accusations. The pretension of building socialism in one country, he said, rendered the Party guilty of national reformism.

The delegates sat back listlessly; they were waiting for Trotsky. For him there remained that old interest which is retained for a father or brother with whom one has irrevocably quarreled. Most of the delegates, steeped in the discussions of the past three years, looked upon him as a theatrical and stubborn man, a literary genius with no understanding of practical politics. For the good of the cause, they would vote against him, but it would always be a pleasure to listen to him talk. No one could talk better. Now the chairman called on him, and he came from the side of the hall, solid and erect, his pink face set grimly, his eyeglasses glistening in the afternoon light, his pointed beard aggressively forward. Behind me the wife of a "Stalinite" whispered to Lydia Gibson:

"Isn't he handsome!"

"As handsome as a blue Persian cat," Comrade Gibson said tartly.

Trotsky walked slowly to the dais, like a Moscow Art Theater actor into the finale of *Czar Feodor*, all his movements deliberate and elegant. Our eyes watched his body, compact and graceful. You felt at once how intensely personal he was. The revolution disappeared before the man; his whole being demanded personal attention. Now he stood at the reading desk and spread his papers on it. He was directly above the translation table where I sat, and I could see his lips tighten as he made sure of his composure before asking the chairman in meticulous German, the chief language of the plenum:

"How much time am I allowed?"

"One hour," the chairman said.

"That is out of the question." Trotsky measured every syllable in his beautiful baritone. "It will take at least two hours to deliver my report."

"I'm very sorry," the chairman said, "we cannot give you any more time than the other delegates. One hour has been the maximum for all. Kamenev had only an hour, and Zinoviev too."

Without saying a word, Trotsky slowly folded his papers, deliberately placed them in a folder, and wheeled left like a soldier on parade. Slowly, silently he walked down the steps from the dais. The delegates stirred uncomfortably. A *Pravda* reporter near me whispered:

"He always dramatizes himself."

The chairman turned to the delegates.

"Comrades, no one has received more than an hour. Perhaps we had better put this to a vote?"

Discussion followed. An English delegate argued for giving Trotsky two hours, others said no exceptions must be made. A vote was called, and the chairman announced the result:

"Comrade Trotsky will be granted the same time as Comrade Zinoviev—one hour."

Slowly Trotsky ascended the steps to the dais a second time; slowly he laid out his papers on the reading stand; slowly he said in his beautiful baritone:

"I shall take—the same time—as Comrade Zinoviev—which was precisely—one hour—and thirty-five minutes."

The hall echoed with laughter. This was what everyone had waited for, a brilliant drama with an attractive hero, a hero politically wrong, doomed to defeat, but greatly gifted and still regarded with the remains of a once boundless affection. The baritone poured out glamorous polemic. The ax of metaphor and invective fell mercilessly upon the heads of foes.

"Only too well do we remember the three gospels of Comrade Pe-pper."

The name Pepper was pronounced syllable by syllable so that it sounded like a humiliating insult. The house roared; even Mrs. Pepper, in the row behind me, smiled. On the dais, Pepper himself, sitting in the presidium, leaped to his feet, scarlet of face. His lips moved rapidly and violently, but amidst the merciless gale of laughter no one could hear what he was saying. Such was Trotsky's power of personal assault. In that power lay his weakness; you felt the objective meaning of the revolution shrivel in the fire of his individual talent. It was all magnificent rhetoric, and moral force, and intellectual brilliance, and all personal, as if the whole dispute were really nothing more than one over the relative merits of Trotsky and everyone else. Little good came out of the conviction that everyone was a fool and an ignoramus except the amazing rhetorician before us. Such an unequal development of wisdom among men did not sound plausible; even if true, it was irrelevant to the issues at stake. If the rest of mankind consisted of idiots, except for those fortunate few who supported the Opposition, it was those idiots who would have to build the socialist society. The delegates laughed, many of them applauded Trotsky's performance, to the consternation of someone, who stood up and asked, in German, Who applauded? When Trotsky concluded his speech, the translators started back for their respective delegations. We thought the show was over. But Trotsky's personality did not easily dissolve into the mass; it was not his destiny to say his say and retire; at every moment that flashing, isolated ego had to challenge attention and stimulate discussion about itself. Some of the French delegates requested that he be allowed to translate his own speech to them. Through the hall ran the memory, familiar to all of us if only through hearsay, of that Comintern congress at which Trotsky had spoken tirelessly for two hours in Russian, then repeated the speech for another two hours in German, and said it again for two hours in French. Seemingly, the French delegation wanted that amazing tour de force repeated; or perhaps the Oppositionists among them wanted to give Trotsky an opportunity to finish a speech for which "Zinoviev's hour" was too short. The majority of the delegates voted Trotsky the privilege of translating himself to the French delegates in a special room adjoining St. Andrew's Hall. This was at once a tribute to his remarkable rhetorical talent and an indication of his tragic guilt. He had a way of obscuring political discussions with arguments about the privileges of one man. This was perhaps the chief psychological limitation of the magnificent narcissist which frustrated his unusual talents and forced him politically into a blind alley dank with counterrevolutionary spleen.

The majority of the delegates did not forget that humanity's fate was bound up with programs rather than personalities, and that the workmanlike project presented by Stalin had been nearest the truth.

They voted, toward the close of the plenum, that the Opposition in the Russian party represented in its ideological content a right danger screened by left phrases. Kamenev's charge of national narrow-mindedness was condemned as a slander against the Russian party, which by all its work, past and present, had proved its internationalism not in words but in deeds. The program of socialism in the Soviet Union was endorsed, its significance for the international working class emphasized. The road for building was cleared.

§ 3

Greta and I hardly talked to each other now. Our relations had reached the breaking point, and each of us tried to forget the other in work. We saw each other daily in the secretarial room outside St. Andrew's Hall, in the lobbies, in the Byzantine dining room but scarcely exchanged civil greetings. Yet Greta seemed to be very gay. She was in her element at last, playing the game she loved most, the game of factional politics. When Fred arrived with the American delegation she was delighted, though it was obvious that by this time the bond between them was factional rather than personal. Fred embraced Greta enthusiastically in public, but said to me in private:

"Don't take her seriously; don't take any women seriously. Play with them, dance with them, but don't let them get their clutches into you. Give them an inch and they want a mile. They want to own you—and that's bad in politics."

This sounded remote from the communist tenet of the equality of men and women. But I did not take Fred too seriously on any subject even when he was a leader of our Party, a devoted lieutenant of Lovestone's and his fanatical admirer. Besides, a daydreaming romantic like myself would not be changed overnight by fiat or counsel. I realized that Greta and I had to part because I could never be the kind of successful practical politician which her craving for power and notoriety demanded. I was incurably interested in art. For every social class art would necessarily be of secondary importance to economics and politics, and secondary importance was precisely what Greta could not tolerate in anybody intimately connected with her.

What she really wanted became abundantly clear at a farewell party given to the plenum delegates. The lion of the evening was Thaelmann, husky, red-faced and smiling in the uniform presented to him that day by a Red army regiment which he had addressed. A phonograph played American jazz; the rooms were crowded with comrades laughing and dancing. In one corner, Fred was busy at his old trick of getting a member of his own faction drunk in order to steal his correspondence. Kurt was perched on the chandelier imitating Zinoviev, in a high falsetto. Greta was all over the suite, in corners, behind curtains, in side rooms, casting out lines for a new roommate.

I watched the various candidates gloomily, and before the party broke up thought I detected my successor. Whether he was aware of it at the moment or not, the Egyptian, Osman Digna, was the man. And a good choice too, considering Greta's needs. Osman was tall, well proportioned, athletic; his dark face had something of the strength and glamour evident in the photographs of the cracked granite figure of Amenophis III. He came of an aristocratic family, was an Oxford graduate, and had all the culture and manners of those upper-class Englishmen whom he detested as the oppressors of his people. But even the years he had spent in London, Mexico, Berlin and New York could not entirely obliterate his exotic qualities. For a Continental bohemienne like Greta, the synthesis of Egypt and Europe must have been irresistible at any time, but most of all at a moment of emotional void. Yet all these were perhaps minor matters, decorations for a more essential structure. Osman was something of a national hero in his own country, to which he could not return because of the prevailing political terror. In the Comintern he was a figure—a well-known writer, orator and organizer, a spokesman for the oppressed Orient in the revolutionary councils of the world. Such political eminence combined with personal charm made the catch perfect.

At first Greta appeared to be interested in Osman only "politically." She arranged conferences for him with German and American delegates, took notes for him, helped him with his book on the Egyptian question. Shortly afterward, they opened a ménage together.

A wonderful peace now settled upon Greta. Her restlessness disappeared. The same people who used to speak of her in amazement as a hetaira now sang her praises as a housewife. If I may anticipate my story, I will add that after I left Moscow in the spring of 1927, I never saw either Greta or Osman again, and never heard from them directly. But from mutual friends I learned that Greta became a model, old-fashioned wife, domestic, respectable and loyal. She darned her husband's socks, cooked his dinners and typed his reports, content to bask in the glory of his political achievements. Eventually, both of them were expelled from the Party for deviations to the right, but this did not alter Greta's devotion. Osman returned to his native country, was arrested and given a twelve-year prison sentence for nationalist activities. At once Greta dropped her commercial job in Berlin and went to Egypt to work for her husband's liberation. All this, however, was several years away. Early in 1927, Osman and Greta lived somewhere in Moscow, and moved in circles which I did not frequent.

I threw myself into feverish literary activity. For one thing, I was homesick. I wanted to be back in New York, busy in the *New Masses,* possibly also on a newspaper job; occupied, too, with Marxist literary criticism.

The desire to go home was not mitigated by news of difficulties. A fight had developed in the *New Masses* staff. I first heard of it vaguely from Mike Gold, who cabled me to send him my proxy vote in order to restore him to the editorial board from which he had been removed. A subsequent letter explained that, with Nearing, myself and several others absent from New York, the liberals on the staff had mustered enough votes to fire Mike on the alleged ground of "inefficiency."

Mike Gold was not exactly the most conscientious and precise of editors, but I felt that this was a side issue. The real issue was between those who, like Mike Gold, had enlisted in the revolutionary movement for life and those who jumped on and off the band wagon as it offered or deprived them of convenient opportunities for "self-expression." Among writers as among politicians, there were those who wanted to give themselves to socialism and those who wanted to get something out of it. Mike, it seemed to me, was a protagonist of that revolutionary literature which would reveal America to us in new terms. But he was something else too. Like most artistic people, like myself, for that matter, he appeared from the practical viewpoint to be preoccupied, irresponsible. His lack of a time sense and of order, his tendency to disappear for weeks to commune with his imagination, made him a difficult colleague in any organized venture. But he had that which many reliable writers lacked; he really cared about social-ism more than he cared about his personal career. This was the secret of his passionate literary style, his poverty in the lodging houses of the East Side, ridden with bedbugs, his irritable polemics against aesthetes who supported the status quo. The men who had arbitrarily removed him from the editorial board of the *New Masses* were more interested in their literary careers than in socialism. I thought one had the right to conclude that much from the facts. They had remained outside the left-wing literary movement until the *New Masses* had raised $27,000 and furnished them with jobs, an audience and new literary themes which they did not fully grasp but whose vitality they could not help feeling.

"I do not know the actual details which led to your removal," I wrote Mike at the opening of 1927, "but I know enough about the profound and irreconcilable differences between the group represented by you and the group represented by them, to realize that essentially your suspension is part of an attempt to make the magazine another *Playboy* or *Vanity Fair*. Our magazine is by no means what you or I would like to see it become, but considering all the difficulties—including the difficulty of working with so-called intellectuals who do not understand the purposes of the labor movement or the problems of a literature that tries to reflect that movement—the magazine is pretty good and of late has been getting better. Certainly it is the only literary magazine in the United States working in the right direction. To turn it over to people with dead or frivolous ideas in art and a bohemian attitude toward politics is disastrous. X is personally a nice fellow, but he is the last man in the world to edit a left-wing literary magazine. The action of the board in substituting him for you is objectively a vote for playboyism in literature and politics; it is a blow against the avowed policy of the *New Masses*. I am absolutely opposed to this change. I am opposed to turning over the magazine to art-for-art's-sakers, single taxers, national-liberals, etc. I want to see it firmly in the hands of people who are closer to the labor movement and to the revolutionary age in which we live."

Michael Gold belonged to the third generation of revolutionary American writers, and was recapitulating an old experience. The first generation, which had given us Upton Sinclair and Jack London, came out of the muckraking period, when discontented middle-class intellectuals sought refuge in the Socialist party against the oppressive growth of big business. The second generation, which produced Floyd Dell and John Reed, arose in the Lyric Year 1912, when the search for new values in life and art seemed to lead logically to the socialist society. Michael Gold, like myself, Bill Gropper, Hugo Gellert, John Dos Passos and others, was propelled toward socialism by the World War. Each generation had its givers and takers, its sincere revolutionary artists who stuck it through thick and thin, and its opportunists who abandoned the movement at the first risk or the first temptation. And in every generation the opportunists utilized their brief affiliation with the proletariat to attack, hamper and even remove where they could the "dogmatists, fanatics and sectarians." Perhaps in my naïveté, I exaggerated the matter, but since this volume does not go beyond the spring of 1927, I may add that before long my forebodings were justified. The peak of prosperity which America reached in 1928-1929, at once reduced the circle of *New Masses* readers and shrank its income to zero. Neither editors nor contributors were paid for their work. At the same time, the boom in production and consumption opened lucrative posts everywhere for young men and women of talent. The careerist then had a still larger audience and still bigger income and still more important prestige than revolutionary arts and letters could offer him at this time. At once the very same men who had removed Mike Gold from the *New Masses* early in 1927 abandoned the left-wing movement and secured themselves good jobs in the advertising and publishing world. Mike Gold stuck to his guns, as he always did. However irresponsible he may have been toward any specific job, his basic responsibility toward the revolutionary movement was unshakable. He always served it in his own erratic way, but he served it loyally and consistently.

At the time covered by this part of my narrative, Mike's removal appeared to me as a struggle between national-liberal ideas and proletarian literature. We solved the problem the best way we could. By obtaining proxies from various left-wing members of the staff absent from New York, we obtained the majority necessary to restore Mike to his editorial post.

But while we were struggling with the opportunists, we had another problem on our hands. There were among us actual sectarians whose illiterate and fanatic attitude hampered the development of revolutionary culture. Their attitude was so extreme that they looked upon the reading of Shakespeare or James Joyce as in itself a counter-revolutionary act.

This was by no means the attitude of the leading Russian bolsheviks. Pushkin and Shakespeare were their favorite poets; the State Publishing House issued editions unprecedented in size of Tolstoy's and Dostoevsky's works, and published manuscripts by these men which had been suppressed by the czarist censor. Foreign authors like W. E. Woodward and Eugene O'Neill were published in Russian. And when Meyerhold took liberties with the text of Gogol's *Inspector-General* for a production in which an elaborate set and tricks of acting overshadowed the author's ideas, the Soviet press published indignant protests by Radek, Litvinov, Bukharin, and other prominent bolsheviks against this desecration of a classic. Marxism taught us that proletarian culture absorbs all that is best in the old culture, that it does not "throw out the baby with the bathtub." I tried to say as much in articles which I sent to the *New Masses,* obliquely criticizing our American sectarians and presenting, as best I could, the communist idea of the dialectic continuity of culture. On this subject I conducted a lengthy correspondence with Mike Gold. My letter supporting him against the opportunists on the editorial board of the magazine added:

"I meet American comrades in Moscow who think it a crime to read Shakespeare at all on the ground that in some subtle manner he dilutes your revolutionary ardor. My reference to Marx's addiction to Shakespeare was directed against these Red Puritans. You say to me: read Shakespeare, but read him critically. I say to them, read him critically but *read* him. Engels says that Hegel and Goethe, though both philistines, were among the giant intellects of history. I say to my ultra-left friends, no man has the right to assume half of Engels' position without the other half. Only he can justly call Hegel and Goethe philistines who also realizes their greatness. This seems obvious to me. One of our extremely kosher fellows was lecturing me the other day about *Ulysses.* He said it was a decadent book, full of *smut.* I asked him whether he had read the book, and he said 'a little of it'—which means not at all. I consider *Ulysses* a marvelous mirror of the decay of capitalist civilization. It also raises the question: what is the future of the novel, if any. But the book is a great book, and the man who wrote it a genius. It seems to me that when these fellows attack it *without reading it* they are really attacking *all* literature indiscriminately, whether left or right, healthy or decadent. They are the Shliapniakovs and Medvedyevs of literature who, under left phrases, advocate liquidation. This *wholesale* attack is an attack on seeing any aspects of life to which they want to close their eyes. It is another form of Cotton Matherism. I doubt whether you and I have any quarrel on this score."

In later years it was to seem absurd to question Shakespeare's genius or his continued value for mankind as one of its very greatest poets. But often sectarianism results from misunderstanding of and lack of experience in the revolutionary movement. The drowning man clutches at a straw and the neophyte at a formula. The most seasoned communists, whether German or Russian, American or Chinese, had a profound respect for the old culture, critically interpreted, and often a mastery of it. They were seeking neither the equivalent of the her-mit's self-abnegation nor his sterile "purity" of soul, but a life more abundant for the whole of mankind in the spiritual goods of the world as in its material. For this, all knowledge and all insight to which men had attained everywhere at any time was essential. In the revolutionary pantheon we retained Plato as well as Engels, Shelley as well as Maya-kovsky, Spinoza as well as Lenin. In that wasteland of theft and blood which the bourgeoisie was leaving behind it, socialism alone could preserve the cultural heritage of the past, while creating new spiritual values upon its foundations. Such was the position of the Party on culture from Marx's day to our own.

The sectarian, however, was something of a nihilist in this realm, anxious to dynamite the past out of existence and memory, a fantastic desire that could have no practical results of any value. His motives varied, but nearly always the sectarian had no real interest in culture and was as ignorant of the Party's attitude as of Europe's and Amer-ica's. His only interest was the immediate political task, which he also saw out of its general context, thereby falsifying its real import. Aggra-vating as this attitude might be in discussion, it did not eventually hinder the development of revolutionary culture. Any simple test would show you the difference between sectarianism and real Marx-ism. I had brought with me to Moscow a copy of Ernest Hemingway's *In Our Time.* Some of the American sectarians in the Lux, people utterly disinterested in literature, yet convinced that they were called upon to express the Party "line" about it, sneered at the book as "bourgeois" without reading it. But it did not take me five minutes to induce *Our Path,* a magazine published in Moscow for students of English, to reprint sections of that book—the first time Hemingway ever appeared in Soviet Russia.

Out of the literary discussions in the Lux, but perhaps more out of my longing to go home, to participate in the development of left-wing literature in America, grew an essay in which I attempted to orient myself in relation to the country which was mine wherever I might travel. The essay, called *The Wilsonian Era in American Litera-ture,* appeared first in translation in a Soviet literary magazine, later in the original in V. F. Calverton's *Modern Quarterly.* I did not quite realize when I wrote it that, for all its objective façade, it was an at-tempt at intellectual autobiography. As Floyd Dell had summed up his spiritual pilgrimage from the Lyric Year to the Coolidge era in his *Intellectual Vagabondage,* so I felt the need to settle accounts with the past in order to proceed more clearly in the future. In doing so, I imagined that I was speaking not only for myself but for my "genera-tion." This, I thought, included not only the *New Masses* group, but unknown young men and women throughout the country whom the development of American capitalism would eventually awaken to socialist ideas.

The essay attempted to trace the economic, political and social background of American literature in the twenties, the literature which had most affected my "generation." It sought to analyze leading writers like Theodore Dreiser, Sinclair Lewis, Sherwood Anderson, H. L. Mencken, Upton Sinclair, Floyd Dell, James Branch Cabell, W. E. Woodward, and Waldo Frank. The literature of the twenties was marked by a conscious and semiconscious national and regional pride in the might and machinery of America, and the confused, ironic, bitter revolt of the intelligentsia against some of the implications of this highly standardized, trustified world. Much of this literature was subjective. The autobiographic novel was one of the commonest ways to begin a literary career. Here the sensitive declassed mind tried to adjust itself through literature to a world which it could not fit into otherwise. A best seller often marked the difference between failure, humiliation, spiritual exile, poverty—and success, a good income, ac-ceptance by the world. A gifted young man or woman, pitched out of bourgeois society for inefficiency, or escaping it out of discomfort, returned riding Pegasus in triumph. Nine times out of ten the quarrel of such writers with bourgeois society was personal; most of them essentially accepted that society.

But their work had great social value; it revealed an important truth; it expressed the utter helplessness of the intelligentsia in the face of modern industrial civilization controlled by industrial and financial capital. Most of the novelists stemming out of the Wilson era expressed the attitude of the middle-class intelligentsia of the period when the United States emerged as the leader of the world's imperialist forces. The Wilsonian writers were pained, ironical and even "theoretical" in the face of universal industrialization, the rule of Wall Street and the machine, the prevailing lust for profits, the pressure of respectability, the commercialization of art, the collapse of the individual under a cartel civilization with its consequent changes in American life. Most of them had been trapped by the illusions of the war for "democracy and civilization," and much of their satire was directed against those who had misled them. But this satire lost some of its edge because the authors saw no way out of the dilemma;

they were sadder but not always wiser men. The friction between the harassed petit bourgeoisie and the smug, prosperous, buccaneering big bourgeoisie stamped the literature of the twenties with its social characteristics, evoking Dreiser's melancholy reporting, Lewis' satirical documents, Woodward's smiles and Anderson's tears.

But the tendencies of the Wilsonian era had already run their course, I thought, at the opening of 1927. New tendencies in American literature were already manifesting themselves on the ground prepared by the older group, which had severed once and for all the umbilical cord which had bound American letters to British tradition. The most significant contribution of the older group, it seemed to me then, was its break with the self-satisfied attitude of the Howells period, and even with the sentimentalism and rhetoric of well-meaning, useful journalists like Upton Sinclair, who occupied a unique place in American letters as a pioneer in describing proletarian life. On the whole, Wilsonian literature was essentially without roots. In so far as this literature had exploded a number of middle-class illusions it was progressive; in so far as it was preoccupied with and dominated by such illusions, it had definitely exhausted itself. The end of that liberal tradition in American literature seemed to have been reached; but it seemed too early yet to speak of a revolutionary literature in our country. There was not even a well-developed revolutionary theory of the relation of art to society.

So far only three serious attempts had been made to discuss literature and revolution in America. One was Upton Sinclair's *Mammonart*, which, after a year in Moscow, appeared in a different light than when I first saw it in New York. Although it was presented as a socialist analysis of literature, it was extremely subjective. It made, as was often the case with Sinclair, entertaining reading, but it shed little light on the problems with which it grappled. Flippantly it dismissed Goethe because he took his hat off to the Duke of Weimar. It snubbed Dostoevsky's genius because the Sage of Pasadena could not finish *Crime and Punishment*. Jack London was given more attention as an alcoholic than as the man who wrote *The Iron Heel*.

The second attempt was Floyd Dell's *Intellectual Vagabondage,* useful because it was frankly an autobiography of ideas. This failed to indicate the laws which governed the development of American literature, but it gave a brilliant analysis of the prewar radical intelligentsia of letters in the United States.

Leaning heavily on these two books, and on translations from

Plekhanov, was V. F. Calverton's *The New World*. Under this cosmic title the young Baltimore schoolteacher, molded by Socialist Labor party influences, wrote a mechanical sociological analysis of English literature. The analysis was not Marxian, not dialectical; but it had the merits of collating some material of value.

These critical books by Sinclair, Dell and Calverton seemed to me symptomatic of a literary movement which was beginning to crystallize in the United States. Under the impetus of the October Revolution, a number of American writers were already attempting "consciously to stimulate a proletarian literature." There was a proletarian writers' association in New York formed in 1926, most of whose members were connected with the *New Masses,* one of the few publications in America seeking to inspire a literature rooted in the socialist revolution.

Time to go home.

§ 4

The train that was taking me to the Polish border retained the atmosphere of Soviet life. The second-class carriage was dingy, the dining service slow, people were friendly to each other, the train officials comradely rather than pretentious or servile, and caste lines wholly absent.

Opposite me in the compartment sat a small woman with a large round head. Her hair was jet black, bobbed in rigid lines down to her almost-Mongolian cheekbones. The face was dark and oval, the eyes round like saucers, and the whole effect was that of an Indian or Eskimo. I felt the sensation, which people so often have who live in books, of seeing in reality someone I had known in imagination. I took the liberty of introducing myself. The lady at once became frank and charming as only Russians can be. She was indeed someone I had known in the imagination, Lydia Seifulina, one of the best-known of the new Soviet novelists.

"So there are Americans who have heard of me," she smiled, "and they even read my books. I can hardly believe it."

Seifulina was on the way to Berlin, where she was scheduled to lecture on Soviet literature, but her thoughts were at the moment on Russia. In spite of material difficulties, it was surprising how all Russians not directly hostile to the new regime hated to leave their country for the mythical paradise of the West. Seifulina was already homesick. Yet it was less than an hour since the train had left Moscow.

Sergei Dinamov and Ivan Anissimov and Ossip Beskin and Tamara had kissed me good-by at the station in the warm Russian fashion. None of my German comrades had come. They had already left for Berlin, and it was of them I was thinking as Seifulina talked of the land she was leaving regretfully. The petite novelist, looking like a Chinese doll and talking gravely like a Chinese sage, was no romantic. She loved her Soviet land, she wanted to see it achieve communism, but she felt that it would be no easy matter.

"If you do not know our peasants," she said, "you cannot understand our greatest problem. Do you know how Gorky described the peasant? Cruel, cunning and infinitely cruel."

"Oppression makes people cruel."

"So it does. No one is as cruel as our peasant, because no one has been so oppressed. Have you any idea how stubborn and cruel he is? For twelve years I worked in a little Siberian village as librarian, and I know. Steal a peasant's horse and he will not have you arrested, he will beat you to death. Our peasant is the chief obstacle to socialism."

She turned her face away and looked sadly out the window at the flat landscape rushing by. I knew where her fear of the peasant was politically expressed, and I fancied I knew why the intellectual feared the peasant, for I feared him myself. He was a force we did not understand, whether we knew him through personal contact or through books. The Party understood and was not afraid. I realized that when I had heard Stalin talking to the plenum about socialism in one country as quietly as if he were describing how to put a house together.

At the Polish border, Seifulina and I came out of our conversation with a start. How strange the world outside Russia seemed. Had I been out of it only a year? It felt more like a century. The place was full of soldiers and officers in natty white uniforms. There were plenty of officers in Moscow too, but they were not arrogant, they did not dominate the atmosphere, they tried to act like workers. Here the bayonet itself was authority.

The customs officials went through everything carefully. I remembered how the men on the freighter had been worried at Batum and how the Soviet customs had taken nothing from them. The Polish officials emptied my trunks, took away books, pamphlets, manuscripts and letters. I never again saw notes and essays on which I had worked for months. Poland was the outpost of bourgeois culture.

Several Polish officers entered the train. One of them, a tall, lithe aviator in white uniform with tight boots and a blond mustache, was assigned to our compartment. He sat down gingerly, and listened to our talk for a while. Then he looked arrogantly at Seifulina, and called the conductor.

"How dare you," he shouted to the cringing Pole, "how dare you put me in the same compartment with people like that! They are talking Russian. They are Reds!"

"I'm awfully, awfully sorry, captain, your excellency." The conductor shriveled and rubbed his hands nervously. "I'll get you another compartment."

That was the last we saw of the chocolate soldier except in the dining room. When Seifulina and I came in for dinner with an American businessman we had met on the train, the officer ostentatiously stood up like a wooden marionette and changed his seat so that his back was toward us. In the bourgeois press they were saying that communism destroyed all the finer things of life, including good manners.

In Berlin, Seifulina and I shook hands at the station, she grave as usual. Outside, my head began to swim. Most of my life I had lived in the great cities of the Western world, New York, Paris and London. Now, after only a year in Russia, a Western metropolis like Berlin appeared fantastic. How clean the streets were; wide and orderly and clean. Had I ever seen so many taxis and limousines before? Somewhere, long ago. The streets were full of shops and restaurants too, and their windows glistened with food of all kinds. People were dressed queerly; they had no boots and their shirts did not hang over their trousers, and only workers wore caps. Strange workers. Why didn't their faces have that air of authority and assurance which you had seen in Moscow? Here workers' faces were pinched or puffed, rebellious or submissive. Slaves. And here was the avenue of victors, generals and admirals and kings in granite, statues celebrating greed and blood. I was back in the old nightmare.

My English comrade Jack Murphy had given me the address of a lodging house in Berlin. The landlady was a sympathizer, an old widow who put up Genossen when they passed through Germany. The house was beyond the Reichstag building, over a little bridge that crossed the Spree. From the beer joint down the street you could hear students at night singing *Gaudeamus Igitur*. It reminded you of your own student days which no longer seemed to have anything to do with you.

I went to see Frederick Kuh, head of an American news bureau in Berlin. He had an office on Unter den Linden, not far from the Adlon. I had known him in the days when I edited the *Liberator* and he sent it clever correspondence from Vienna. Later I had known something of him in New York. It was he who had sent his news agency that article by Trotsky which my colleagues on the *New Masses* had refused to publish for fear of branding the magazine as communist. How the world had changed. Those very colleagues were now Trotsky's verbal partisans. He had given them the excuse they needed to abandon and attack the movement. They could be "communists" without being communists. Kuh, originally from Chicago, was now suave and good-looking with his little black mustache, very much a European man of the world. He took me to the Adlon and introduced me to other American reporters. Then he was kind enough to put me up at his house for several weeks. He did everything to make me feel at home, and still I did not feel at home. But it was not Kuh's fault, and he knew it; he had himself lived in Moscow. It was hard to forget the Soviet land where everyone thought and talked and worked for socialism. I was back in a world where socialism was treated as something queer, remote, monstrous.

"Ah, you've just come from Russia? How are *things* over there?" That was what they asked you casually at the cultural center known as the Adlon bar. Ordering some drinks, Kuh greeted a small dapper man with a high forehead and a clever mischievous smile.

"Hello," Kuh said. He spoke in that reserved lower register which the cultured American had begun to develop in the boom period when sophistication forbade emotion. "When did you leave Moscow?"

"Oh, about a month ago." The other man spoke in the same casual way, but his English accent made the casualness sound natural, as it did when I had first heard it in London.

"Are you here on business?" Kuh said.

"No," the other man said, "I am here for pleasure, so to speak." He leaned over heavily on a rubber-tipped cane and his full mouth parted in a refined grin. "As you probably know, the second best thing I enjoy in life is good conversation. I like to talk—especially to women. Now Russian girls are all right in their way. I like them very much. They're temperamental, intellectual and serious—too damned serious at times. But they lack that peculiar Anglo-Saxon humor which our women have. I can talk to a Russian girl about Lenin's funeral, the collectivization of agriculture, Eisenstein's system of montage. But I can't jolly her apropos of nothing at all. As you Americans would say, you can't kid a Russian girl. She wouldn't understand you. And what is conversation without humor? That is why I take my annual conversational holiday. Once every year I must get out of Moscow to Paris or Berlin where I can look up English and American girls and have some good Anglo-Yankee fun talking." The speaker turned to me and with a courteous bow of his head asked: "Don't you agree with me?"

"I'm sorry," Kuh said. "I thought you knew each other. This," he added, pointing to the man with the charming smile, "is Walter Duranty."

Later in the day, Kuh took me to an interview with Chancellor Stresemann, attended by journalists from every country. The room was large, with many tall windows; the bright afternoon light fell on the long table with the snow-white cloth, the cognac, the coffee and the sandwiches. I was introduced to the plump, handsome, shrewd correspondent of the New York *Evening Post*, Dorothy Thompson, to other reporters, finally to the chancellor, who entered briskly, despite his weight. He had the reserve of most highly placed bourgeois statesmen; it lent dignity to his bull neck, heavy jaw and mustache which looked like the teeth of a comb.

The interview was brief. The reporters respectfully rose from their half-finished drinks and asked many questions; the chancellor answered only the most innocuous. Without committing himself to anything specific, he managed to convey the impression that Germany was in a tough spot.

At the Party headquarters on the Alexanderplatz, there was no formality, although the place was run with unusual efficiency. This was the Ordnung of which German comrades had boasted in Moscow. Everything was properly arranged and departmentalized. Flamboyant Soviet and German placards on the walls, huge agitational cartoons, communist slogans suddenly reminded you that the class struggle was not confined to Russia. Now at last you felt at home.

Here were Wilhelm Pieck and Ernst Thaelmann and Gustav and Hedda and Kurt and a lot of other people whom you had known in Moscow, all busy, rushing to meetings, to the Polbureau, to the *Rote Fahne*. Everyone now looked different. Hedda seemed aloof, she was so busy; Gustav's face was grim instead of smiling. Even the irresponsible Kurt managed to look severe. In Moscow these people had been happy expatriates; they were essentially on a holiday, however hard they may have worked. Now they were in their own land, face to face with the oppressor whose ruthlessness and power made them as alert as soldiers surrounded by the foe. Yet despite danger and tension, they felt more at home. This was their country, their language, their people; they understood the Nazis better than they did the kulaks.

The world was topsy-turvy. Why did you have to go to the Wedding district to see the revolutionary movement clearly? They took you there as if it were Chinatown, a "sight." The workers' homes were spotlessly clean; the windowpanes were washed even where there was no furniture, no food and no jobs.

In the evening, Gustav and Hedda took me to a meeting. The workers sat in a large square hall that was chilly because March was no time to burn coal. Portraits of Marx, Engels, Lenin, Stalin, Liebknecht and Luxemburg hung around the walls. You felt the power of the working class heaving to throw off a huge intolerable burden. There were the speeches familiar in New York, London and Paris and Moscow, but in Moscow you heard them from the seats of political power, from the universities, the factories, the villages. When I had first left Russia as a boy I went from the prison of the peoples to the free West; now, on my second journey, it was the other way round. Clean, orderly Berlin was a clean, orderly prison of the people; I had left a free nation behind when I had crossed the Polish border. Now you saw the green-clad police patrolling Berlin's streets, and you knew they were protecting profit and exploitation against the discontented masses. No wonder people walked in and out of Party meetings carefully; the exploiters held the town.

How strangely beautiful Beethoven sounded in these surroundings, as poignant as a strip of blue sky seen through prison bars. Hedda and Gustav took me to a concert one afternoon, and their faces, grim with the day's struggle, relaxed and softened, suffused with secret love and ecstasy. Gustav was constantly being watched by the police; there was a warrant out for his arrest dating from the Hamburg uprising. For the time being he was protected by parliamentary immunity; he was a communist member of the Reichstag. But if he failed to win his seat in the coming elections, they would pick him up at once and clap him into prison. He closed his eyes as Beethoven's *Seventh* filled the auditorium with grandeur and aspiration. The last time we had heard it was when the Persimphans played it for a factory outside Moscow, and the workers sat awed and silent before the beauty floating up to the machines at which they labored during the day. I thought again, in that childish kind of daydream which music often inspires in us, that if by some miracle I could choose to be any man in history I would rather be Beethoven than Bonaparte, and best of all a Beethoven in a socialist society. But great music stirs more than dreams; the will itself becomes uneasy, longs for action, wishes to bring the ugly world nearer to that luminous realm of being which the loftiest symphonies suggest. Once the dreams which music stirred were retroactive. Listening to Tchaikovsky's *Fourth* in the City College Stadium, I used to remember the gypsy melody on which his counterpoint was based, and the wooden corridor with the water barrels where I first heard it, and my mother, agitated beyond words, ripping my shirt open at the throat to ward off the Evil Eye. Now even the most secret dreams concerned the future, and not ours alone. Strange that you felt this unmistakably in the most hackneyed small talk.

"Beethoven is wonderful," Hedda said as we went out of the concert hall. She looked different dressed in conventional Berlin style. Instead of a leather jacket, she now wore a long cloth coat that hugged her sturdy form. Her face was as always intense. "He is so beautiful you want to cry and you want to do things, to fight."

"Did you see the smug fat faces in the audience?" Gustav said. "What does that music mean to them? They will go to a café and get drunk with their mistresses. Some day every worker in Germany will hear that wonderful music. We will have even better orchestras for them than the Persimphans. Every factory will have music."

I was thinking how good it would be if language could stir people as music did. Shakespeare did it, and Shelley. But this was an arid time. There were so many harsh, important things to say that you could not stop to model melodies around the imperative idea. Maybe that would come too, and soon; somebody would do it when communism was at last universally taken for granted as was once the Holy Virgin. Social science would give birth to its own art. Now ideas clashed nakedly, though in the bourgeois world the old ideas came out in the old rags. Hedda and I went to hear Franz Werfel. The middle-class audience fluttered in its evening clothes. The author of the *Goat Song,* who was perhaps even then dreaming of the *Forty Days of Musa Dagh,* also appeared in full dress. His round face crowned with a circle of thick curly hair sat heavily on the winged collar, like an erudite pumpkin, Hedda said. The swallowtail coat fell down to the back of his knees. He talked for a few minutes about literature in the abstract, read from his *The Man Who Conquered Death.* A somnolent sterility spread over the hall. The distinguished author's voice died down, the ladies and gentlemen politely tapped their palms together, and helped each other on with their coats. There were no questions from the floor. What was there to ask? What had been said? You would never think that hunger was spreading through German homes, that the reaction, subsidized by Stinnes and Krupp and the bankers and the Junkers, was arming to assault the few liberties won in the anguish of civil war. This was "literature"; it had nothing to do with the political struggle of the mass of mankind. To hear that you had to go elsewhere, you had to hear those "renegades" who had abandoned art for propaganda.

Every afternoon at four you would find Johannes Becher in his dark, ill-furnished studio. He worked standing at a high bookkeeper's desk. I don't want to get fat, he explained. That was why he boxed too. Instead of presenting me with a copy of his poetry, he gave me a photograph of himself in trunks and boxing gloves posing like Benny Leonard. Becher had once been a popular bourgeois poet, the darling of Munich society. Why not? His father was a Bavarian supreme court judge, and Johannes himself wrote sizzling erotic verses. And then, the personal scandals, indispensable to the bourgeois poet! But those damned communists had ruined Johannes. He stopped writing "real" poetry about hips and lips, and was writing rhymed propaganda, stupid stuff—you know, those factories and demonstrations and red flags and Lenin. The German workers thought otherwise; they read Becher's verses about the proletarian revolution in the *Rote Fahne* and recited them at meetings or in beer halls.

Johannes Becher took me to a meeting of the literary faction of the German party. A week hence there was going to be a general discussion with fellow travelers and liberals on literature and revolution, and the Party comrades wanted to agree on a "line." The poets themselves went into a two hours' discussion of the political and economic situation in Germany, the struggle within the Russian party, socialism in one country, the possibilities of fascism in Western Europe. Toward the end Becher raised the question of form and content, but here, too, the class struggle was omnipresent. It all sounded a little too desiccated until the following week, when the fellow travelers and liberals came. We met in a cheap hotel in the working-class district at a long table, drank beer and argued. Here was Fritz von Sternberg, the left social democrat, an economist dabbling in aesthetic theory, fat, red faced, witty, fluent. And here was Bertolt Brecht, slight and pale, with the dead-pan of a Buster Keaton, only merciless in its composure. He was the poet who had celebrated Rosa Luxemburg:

Red Rosa has also vanished now;
Where she lies, nobody knows;
Because she told the truth to the poor,
The rich have driven her out of the world.

There was also Alfred Döblin, a well-known poet, middle-aged and well-dressed, whom the left-wing writers attacked for spinning out an epic about ancient Asia at a time when the German people, indeed the whole of humanity, had come to a crossroads in its destiny. The poet said art must not be journalism; it must lift us out of the everyday world, so that we can transcend it in the imagination. But that is opium, Genosse! How does that differ from religion? You might as well give us incense and orisons! We will transcend the present in action; we will change the world in deed, and art is one of the instruments for that transformation. The arguments were the same in Berlin as in Moscow and New York, no doubt because fundamentally the class struggle was everywhere the same.

Later I met the communist director Piscator, an admirer of Meyerhold. He was putting on a new play at the Volksbühne, a trade-union theater, and invited me to the opening. Outside of Russia, you felt the impact of revolutionary art more forcefully in the theater than anywhere else. Piscator was a cunning régisseur. The play was about the struggle of the Hanseatic League against princely aggression some time in the fifteenth century. The actors, in Renaissance armor, made up their faces to look like Lenin, Trotsky, Liebknecht. At the end of the play a movie screen came down, in Meyerhold's *Roar China* manner, and flashed:

1418
1649
1793
1917
1921
?

Everyone knew the meaning of those revolutionary dates. Social democrats and liberals whistled, stamped their feet, hissed; the workers applauded. In Moscow the theater was re-creating the civil war just ended; in Berlin it was projecting the civil war to come.

Class feeling was running high in Germany. Nazi and Stahlhelm youths, clean cut and well dressed, bobbed up in cafés and restaurants to sing nationalist songs and taunt socialists of their acquaintance.

We ran into some of them in a wine cellar one night. Kurt was with us. A responsible leader of the German party, one of its theoreticians, orators and strategists, Kurt was being sought by the police under a warrant issued in the days of the Munich uprising. He had no parliamentary immunity. He was in his native land illegally at this moment. His friends begged and the Party ordered him to be extremely circumspect. But Kurt was young, careless, romantic and sensual. He could not restrain himself from attending parties in public places. Even there he did not have the sense to sit quiet in a corner, to make himself obscure. This time we could not induce him to stay at home, but we did manage to get a side table and to place Kurt with his back to the large room crowded with boisterous guests. A group of young Nazis came in, full of beer and song. They banged the table with their mugs, damned the French and praised the Führer. Kurt, full of beer and high spirits, leaped up on our table.

"Hunde!" he shouted.

"Kurt, sit down!" Hedda warned.

Kurt burst into the Buddeny march. The young Nazis watched him in puzzled silence; the song meant nothing to them. But Hedda knew Kurt would not stop until he had made his meaning unmistakable.

"Kurt, I am leaving," she said. "You are an irresponsible idiot. The Polbureau will hear of this." To me she whispered: "You stay here and see that nothing serious happens. Come to our house later. See that this fool gets home as soon as possible."

Kurt was swinging his mug to the Buddeny march, spilling the beer over the table and on his clothes. He finished, looked at the crowded room with a pleased smile, and took a swig. The young Nazis began to sing *Die Wacht am Rhein*. They had hardly finished the first verse when Kurt broke in:

> Völker hört die Signale,
> Auf zum letzten Gefaecht,
> Die Internazionale
> Erkaempft das Menschenrecht.

A sick feeling came over me. The *International* in this place. Kurt's beer hall putsch. The Nazis knew the song only too well. From their table mugs came flying through the air. One of these cracked the mug in Kurt's hand, cutting his wrist. He jumped off the table. We both lifted glasses, chairs, plates, anything that came to hand, and fired them across the room at the Nazis. When our ammunition gave out, I seized Kurt by the arm and dragged him out the door.

The air sobered him. Tears filled his large blue eyes.

"I am a damned fool, no?" he said.

"Don't become remorseful on street corners," I said. "You've had enough for one evening."

"In my position a man should not do this," he said.

I took him home, and went to see Hedda and Gustav. The latter was furious. He walked up and down his study, incessantly puffing at his curved pipe, his huge body shaking with rage.

"This is the end," he roared. "Enough of such Schweinerei. The German working class is facing the greatest crisis in its history and that's the time he picks out to play the buffoon. Out of the Central Committee he goes, out of Berlin. Let him edit a literary paper in the provinces. There are lots of cafés there and plenty of girls. They can use him, we can't."

Hedda lay on the couch with her hands behind her head. Her face was sallow and lined; she looked older than in Moscow.

"I am terribly afraid," she said. "I am afraid Kurt will some day be entrusted with a serious task—on account of his brilliance—and he will get drunk or fall in love with a slut, and the enemy will walk off with the victory."

The next day I had an unexpected visitor. Roger Baldwin was in town. He had just returned from Paris, and was arranging to go to Russia to study political prisoners there. He hadn't changed a bit in three years—the same smooth, intense, smiling face, the same boundless energy. Even in Berlin he pointed out the birds on the trees, called them by their American and Latin names, and described their habits and songs—an Audubon with his foot caught in the constitution. A millionaire friend of his, whose mother was a leading civil-libertarian in her state, had lent Roger his limousine and chauffeur. The car took us through the city, to suburbs. Everywhere we saw soldiers and policemen armed as soldiers; everywhere the Wandervogel, whose walking tours were not purely sport; everywhere young Nazis with swastikas on their clothes. I thought of Thaelmann and Gustav and Hedda and wondered whether they would stop the fascists; I thought of Kurt and my heart sank.

Pointing to a group of young Nazis in a suburban restaurant where we were lunching, I said to Roger they might someday run Germany.

"Why?"

"Because they are subsidized by big business; because the coalition government gives them a free hand; because the social democrats will not unite with us."

That March, the Party announced its preparations for a big May Day parade. The fascists announced a counter-demonstration for May 8. From all parts of the Reich, the black hordes of reaction would march into the capital. The subsidized Nazi hooligans openly proclaimed their intention of terrorizing the workers. But they were impatient. They wanted violence at once.

One Sunday the workers of Jüterborg, on the outskirts of Berlin, celebrated the anniversary of the Paris Commune. A brass band of twenty-five men came down from Berlin to play for them. They represented the Rot Frontkämpferbund, the communist veterans' organization. On the same day, four hundred Nazis held their maneuvers in Trebbin, not far from Jüterborg. Both groups returned to Berlin on the same train. The four hundred Nazis attacked the twenty-five communists. They beat them with heavy stones; they fired revolvers into the small group of unarmed workers. This assault took place when the train stopped at Lichterfelder-Ost. The police at the railway station looked on and did not move. Twenty of the communists were wounded; six had to be taken to the hospital. From Lichterfelder-Ost the Nazis went to Berlin shouting, "Kill the Jews!" In the capital, they marched down Kurfürstendamm beating up people.

The Party protested to the police, headed by the social democratic politician, Zoergibble. An investigation was promised; nothing was done.

On March 22nd, the Rot Frontkämpferbund called on the workers of Berlin to demonstrate against the fascist terror. Nearly a hundred thousand workers gathered at the end of the Tiergarten in the evening. I came there with Hedda from a Party unit meeting. Thaelmann was standing in the first row of marchers, and invited us to join him.

"We are going to the Friedrich-Karl-Platz," he said.

Thaelmann was cheerful and proud of the multitude which the Party was able to muster at such short notice. The members of the R.F.B. and of its women's auxiliary wore gray-green uniforms and carried huge red banners. There were several detachments of nurses in white uniforms, bearing stretchers. The sidewalks and the gutter were lined with workers young and old, men, women and children, talking loudly about Sunday's assault. We started to march eight abreast. Just ahead of us, as a guard of honor, marched half a dozen victims of the Nazi attack with their heads swathed in bandages. They were preceded by a line of Green Police on horseback, armed with swords, pistols and carbines. The streets were full of police in uniform and in plain clothes.

Behind us we could hear the thunder of thousands of feet marching in unison. From the side streets which we passed on the way to the Kurfürstendamm came pouring new contingents, R.F.B. workers in uniform, on foot and in motor trucks, carrying red banners. Placards rose high in the air:

"Down with the fascist terror!"

"Workers, defend yourselves on May 8!"

"Down with fascism and reaction!"

"Prepare against the danger of international war!"

"Our blood shall not flow in vain!"

Behind each contingent of R.F.B. workers came a truckload of Green Police. Brass bands scattered through our lines struck up the *International,* and thousands of voices took up the refrain solemnly:

> Völker hört die Signale,
> Auf zum letzten Gefaecht . . .

Out of the lines, an excited young man came running toward the head of the demonstration.

"Faster! faster!" he shouted. "We are losing time. Don't let those green swine on horseback hold up the march."

"Be careful!" Thaelmann said quietly to Hedda, who was next to him. "He's obviously a provocateur."

Hedda wheeled around like an officer facing troops, and shouted to the marchers in a loud, clear voice:

"Ge-no-ssen! Lassen sie sich nicht provozieren.—Don't let them provoke you!"

She wheeled into position again; we continued marching in solid formation. The hoofs under the Green Police rapped the rhythm steadily like hollow shells, and our feet kept pace. The excited provocateur disappeared into the crowd on the sidewalks.

We came to a streetcar crossing. The horses in front of us reared on their haunches as the police backed them up against our line. I could smell horseflesh and cops' sweat. We tried to go on, and the horses gave way a little. The mass stood still a moment and raised its voice in song.

"Down with the fascists!" someone shouted from the line of march.

"Down! Down! Down!"

The police wheeled their horses and faced us. Sabers flashed in the air. Thaelmann's forehead began to bleed profusely. He turned quietly to the young man on his left and said:

"Get me a nurse in the first contingent."

"Dogs! Fascists!" voices behind us roared at the police.

"Murderers!"

The cops drew their pistols and began firing at us.

Bullets really do whiz past your ear, they whistle like a gale at sea, like that storm on the Black Sea.

People around me were scattering in all directions; the front line was broken; the shots kept whistling; I could feel the wind against my cheek.

"Idiot, get out of their way!" Hedda was yelling into my ear and pulling my sleeve.

She pushed me violently and I stumbled into the crowd on the sidewalk. Christ, what a tremendous demonstration! I had not realized how big. Pinnng! Pinnng! Pinnng! Hedda was back at the head of the line. Thaelmann was back too, with a bandage around his head. I stepped into the line behind him. Thousands of voices around us were shouting:

"Weiter! Weiter!"

"Keep together, comrades! March on!"

Hedda wheeled: "Order, comrades! Forward, march!"

The firing had stopped. We were marching along Bismarckstrasse. I looked down into the gutter and saw a line of blood which continued for a block. Some wounded worker was marching in front of me. Behind the deep-voiced mass was singing again:

> Die Internazionale,
> Erkaempft das Menschenrecht . . .

We turned into Kantstrasse. Kant, a German philosopher. Irwin Edman used to talk about him on the campus. In Königsberg Kant took a walk every day at four o'clock precisely. He wrote *The Critique of Pure Reason.*

Look down, look down, there is blood on the street of pure reason.

"Forward, comrades! Forward!"

At the Friedrich-Karl-Platz we were met by three trucks filled with Green Police. At the corner stood a tall police officer in a long green coat, glittering patent leather boots. He surveyed the demonstration with the exaggerated hauteur of a Simplicissimus cartoon. Behind us the R.F.B. fife and drum corps struck up *Wir sind die junge Garde,* and the mass moved forward again with fists raised in the communist salute.

"Red front! Red front! Red front!"

Here was our meeting place, a square surrounded by trees. Thaelmann, bandaged heavily around his head, stood up and spoke. He reported the casualties: three workers wounded by revolver shots, twenty by saber cuts.

"Comrades, they will try to kill us, but they cannot kill the proletariat! We shall win! We shall have a Soviet Germany!"

I was thinking of the demonstration I had seen in Moscow just two weeks ago. They were celebrating the elections. Soviet Square was filled with groups of workers, Comsomols, and Red army men from early morning till late at night. From the balcony of the House of the Soviet, speakers addressed us on the significance of the elections, the British note, the world situation. A few "miltons," constables in light khaki uniforms, quietly directed *izvozchiks* to go down a side street so as not, please, to disturb the comrades in the square.

I realized Hedda was talking to me.

"We've had no food since breakfast," she said. "Aren't you hungry?"

"No."

"You'd better come with me anyway. We'll pick up Gustav at Party headquarters. A little food will do you more good than you imagine. Have you any idea how near you were to death?"

§5

On the line of march, surrounded by thousands and thousands of workers, with Thaelmann and Hedda near, everything seemed simple. Of course, the Freudians would say: papa and mama. I was unconscious of danger, intent upon similes, until Hedda pushed me out of the firing zone. Later, at a frugal midnight supper in a working-class restaurant to which Gustav took us, I listened to his analysis of the demonstration and the political significance of police violence under a social democratic chief. I felt calm. I walked the two miles to my lodging house, whistling *Wir sind die junge Garde, Mi molodoya gwardia,* we are the young guard of workers and peasants. The old widow, the sympathizer, in a funny long nightgown, opened the door.

"How was it?" she said.

"Fine. A hundred thousand. The Schupos fired, but no one was killed. A saber cut Teddy."

"They hurt Thaelmann?"

"He's all right. He's probably still speaking at the Karl-Friedrich-Platz. They hurt twenty-three workers, but they are alive and cheerful. Good night, comrade."

"Gute Nacht, Genosse. Schlafen sie wohl."

I flopped into bed like a log of wood. My whole body began to shake with extraordinary violence, and I could not control the trembling of hands and feet. The letdown, the fear I had repressed while the mass was singing *Völker hört die Signale,* and Thaelmann cried, Weiter, weiter.

You had been near death, and you wanted to live, and you were no hero. The workers had boundless courage, they had kept marching while the bullets wheenged through their ranks. A coward dies many times before his death, and you had thus died before, in the military hospital with the flu, and you were sorry then because you didn't believe in the war, and now it was all right because you believed in the socialist society, and one life didn't matter even if it happened to be yours. You had lived too many lives anyway, and it was time to do something with the one you had left, which good luck had granted you or Hedda's violent thoughtfulness. Time to live in the twentieth century, to erase all traces of the vanished village, the Middle Ages, the church bells and grandfather. There was pain in the shadows of the pogrom, in the isolation of an immigrant boy, but life had been good to you and you owed it something. Your friends had invested love in you and were entitled to a fair return, Louis Smith who had taught you socialism, and Irwin Edman who had reminded you that poets had obligations, and Floyd Dell who had healed the breach between poetry and politics, and Mike Gold who saw the glory of the proletariat amidst bedbugs and fire escapes, and Ruthenberg who had lent nobility even to political maneuvers, and Scott Nearing who infused socialist economics with lofty aspiration, and Sergei Dinamov who broke the chains of sectarianism, and the shrewd Eisenstein and Gustav and Hedda, and the workers you had known in meetings and units and shops and classrooms and strikes and demonstrations, they, the inexhaustible mass to whom we all owed our deepest responsibilities. In a few days you would be going home to America, whose people would someday convert it into the golden realm of which you had once heard. Twice before ships had borne you from Europe's shores to New York, once to a dream, then to a half-dream. Now you must see your vast country with clear eyes that know the mechanics of making dreams come true.

I slept quietly. At breakfast, the old widow said, how well you look this morning, and handed me my mail. A letter from Floyd Dell in Croton:

"I will have my publishers send my books to your Moscow friend for translation into the Russian. His remarks had a very soothing effect upon my exacerbated spirit, rubbed the wrong way this long time by radical criticism in America. I have felt about it very much the way various people I know feel about parental criticism. When they talked about how unreasonable the old folks were, I used to laugh and say, 'Well, let them talk; you just go ahead and do things your own way; what do you care?' It seemed to me unreasonable that they should care. I am now in a better position to understand how they felt, since socialism is my father and my mother. Any God-damned fool who chose to say something asinine in print in a socialist paper about my books upset me as nobody else could do. I convicted myself of sin, and all that, but to no avail. I had to go on writing what was in me to write. If I could have told them to go to hell, as I inwardly can my bourgeois critics, I should have been serene, doubtless. But I could not do that. They had the right to chastise me, and doubtless it was for my own good, since I was a child of the movement. I can foresee trouble for you, too, and I only hope that your stay at the fountainhead of wisdom has fortified you to meet criticism. Because—did I say this before?—you write from the Freudian point of view, and you don't see everything in terms of the class struggle! In your last excellent story, *The Gentleman from Arkansas,* there is one brief passage in which you reflect the outward existence of a large social situation, and then—I am not blaming you, but there are them as will!—you settle down to a contemplation of the delightful idiocies of human nature, and, not at all unnaturally from my point of view, those in particular which center about the w.k. fact of sex."

I put the letter in my pocket, lit my pipe and walked out into the city. It was still early, but the stores were open, and people were breakfasting in the open-air cafés. The short story to which Floyd had referred told about an American colonel who had served with the A.R.A. in Moscow and had had a love affair with a Russian girl.

It had appeared in the *New Masses,* and later in the *Rote Fahne,* translated by a German comrade. True, Gustav and Hedda and Kurt had said the story was too "Freudian," nevertheless they printed it. But the dualism of my mind was only too evident. When I wrote economic or political articles, when I tried my hand at Marxist literary criticism, when my *mind* got busy, I was a communist. When I wrote poems and stories, when my emotions went into action, all the old feelings cropped up; the vanished village, the Brooklyn ghetto, the campus, the Renaissance, idealistic philosophy and romantic art crept out of their holes and spoke in my name. Fusion of intellect, emotion and will around the communist idea had not yet been achieved. Wouldn't I have to quit poetry for a while and concentrate on ideas, on work in the movement, so that these might permanently alter emotion?

On the Friedrichstrasse a woman stopped me.

"Hey, you American! Ten marks."

This was Berlin's whore street. The town was full of them, an index of the state of bourgeois society. The newsstands carried magazines especially devoted to homosexuals and Lesbians.

"What, so early in the morning?" I said.

"We work in shifts. There are night women and day women. I am a day woman."

"No, thanks, I have just left my seraglio."

Further down the street I stopped to look into the window of a bookstore. A photograph of Michelangelo's Moses caught my eye. It was pasted to the cover of a slight gray book, which bore the title: SIGM. FREUD Psychoanalytische Studien an Werken der Dichtung und Kunst.

I went into the store and bought a copy of the book and sat down at a table in a nearby café. Last night had shaken me up considerably; wine was the best thing. The bottle was half empty when I reached the essay on *The Moses of Michelangelo.* People swam by along the street in which I was sitting at the little wooden table, as in the days of the Rotonde. The sun made Unter den Linden seem cleaner than ever; it was good to live. Michelangelo had quarreled with the Pope for whose sarcophagus he was making the statue, and he obliquely immortalized that quarrel in marble by changing the prophet's character. The man Moses, according to tradition, was subject to fits of anger and waves of passion. In one outburst he had killed an Egyptian and was compelled to flee the country; in another he had broken the tablets of the law. Now observe this, saith the Freud: on the tomb of his patron and enemy the Pope, Michelangelo hewed out quite another Moses. He gave the motif of the broken tablets of the law another meaning. They are not broken by the prophet's anger. On the contrary, the warning that the tablets may be broken halts the anger, prevents its conversion into action. Thereby the artist put something new into the figure of Moses; the mighty mass of body and the forceful muscles of the figure became the corporeal expression for *the highest spiritual achievement of which man is capable, for the subordination of one's own passions in the interest of a goal which one has chosen.*

Those were Freud's words, and I underlined them and read them over several times. Then vividly there leaped to mind, like a precisely remembered dream, the story my mother had told me long ago, when she rebuked me for losing my temper. That story, too, was about Moses. When that prophet and captain led the Jews across the wilderness, a king of a bordering country wanted to find out what sort of man he was. Court painters visited Moses and brought the king his portraits; court seers read the face. This man, they said, is violent and deceitful. The king was angry. Fools, he said, you are reading the face of Moses. Either the painters had brought back a false portrait or the seers could not read faces. The king decided to settle the matter by visiting the prophet himself. When he saw Moses face to face, he realized that the painters had done an accurate portrait. He explained the dilemma to Moses, and the prophet said: Your seers are also right. By nature I am violent and deceitful, but I have a mission in life. I am leading my people to freedom. This places obligations upon me; all the evil sides of my nature must be submerged to my task.

Funny I should remember that story after so many years, and funnier still that the modern science of psychology should agree with an old legend. I wondered what my mother looked like now; she had written me that things were going marvelously well in America and my father was now unusually rich. But that had nothing to do with me. I had my own life to lead and it was going somewhere else. I phoned Hedda and made an appointment for lunch.

"You have been drinking," she said reproachfully.

"No, no," I said, "I have been making a discovery."

I went back to Freud's little gray book, and reread the passage about the highest spiritual achievement of which man was capable, the subordination of his passions to a goal of his own choosing. And again, as vividly as a dream precisely remembered, there leaped to mind the book I had read over and over again in Mr. Neumann's school, the one where the hero seeks to win his beloved's hand by fulfilling her father's demand for true goodness, wisdom and nobility. The hero tried everything—money, military glory, politics, learning, charity—but he was always wrong. And the last page was missing. For a long time I could not get over being deprived of that secret. Perhaps, unconsciously, I had been seeking that lost page; and at this moment I felt that I had found it. The hero's mistake was to subordinate all goals to his private passions, and the girl's father wanted him to learn that man's highest spiritual achievement et cetera.

Oh, I knew damned well what Floyd and Freud would say about this; I was scared to death last night when the Schupos fired at us, and the death instinct tends to "reinstate in us an earlier level of personality development." Blah.

I started to walk down the avenue. It was time to meet Hedda. The air cleared my brain. I lit my pipe and began to march steadily, left, right, left, right. It was good to live. For what? I had known it for a long time, but hadn't done it, I mean to subordinate and so on. Subordinate everything personal and trivial and important, to transcend yourself in a great goal.

Hedda was waiting in front of the restaurant. She looked at me queerly and said:

"I have never seen you look so happy since I know you."

We went into the restaurant and ordered lunch.

"What great discovery have you made?" Hedda said.

I was embarrassed. The whole thing was only a childish fantasy, an emotional reaction to the events of the night before, to blood on Kantstrasse. Communism would be proved by logic and action; I had only found out something about my own feelings, which had so long been separated from my ideas. I had discovered that I felt at home in the demonstration, among the workers. It had never occurred to me to ask what I was doing there. And that discovery was of no importance to anyone but myself.

I evaded Hedda's question, and asked her instead if any mail had come for me at Party headquarters. She handed me one letter which I began to read at once. It was from Scott Nearing.

"I remember very particularly," he said, "the talk that we had just before you left for Russia. At that time you said that the movement was a very vital force and important factor in your life, and that you proposed to devote your major attention to it from then on.

Devoting your attention to the movement means, of course, finding some place in the movement where you can work to advantage, becoming a specialist in it, sticking to it through thick and thin. The movement in the United States is weak enough. It needs every atom of strength to its support. I think that you should have a definite piece of large-scale work cut out for you. This work may be either in the realm of literature, of science or of administration. I am inclined to think that you will get along better in the first and second fields. *Then everything should be subordinated to that main task."*

I began to laugh loudly, and Hedda looked at me in alarm.

"What on earth is the matter with you?" she said.

"I am thinking of all kinds of strange people," I said. "A man named Louis Smith, and a man named Scott Nearing, and Freud, and my mother, and Moses, and Michelangelo, and a book whose last page was missing, and Lenin."

"That doesn't make sense."

I gave her Nearing's letter. She read it through in silence, and said: "Have you made up your mind?"

"Yes."

"I hope you will not try administration," she said. "I don't know a worse executive than you. Stick to literature; the movement needs that."

"I will stick to it, but I'm afraid I won't be able to write proletarian literature myself."

"Then teach others what you know," she said, "just as you have been taught by those who came before you."

"We have a magazine that is trying to do that. I'll work with it."

"I've been reading the *New Masses,"* Hedda said, "and I don't know what to think of it. It contains more stuff than it used to, catering to working-class interest. But I think it deals too much with the worker's life and leaves out too much of the worker's fight. It is not enough to show up the misery of the poor. We have to show something of the eternal light—a class rising in society destined to become the ruling class. I miss that thought in your magazine. It must be expressed artistically, but it must shine through the pages, not as propaganda but as the leading thought."

"That is what I would like to do," I said. "I want to go home and work in the Party, and discipline myself in revolutionary journalism and in literary criticism, to clean out of my heart all that remains of the old world. Then perhaps I may be fit someday for creative writing in the spirit of our movement."

"Journalism will be easy," Hedda said, looking at me with a strange intensity. "It deals with externals, with historic events in which the features of the individual are lost. But what of the secret life of the individual? We all have it, even when we are most identified with the movement. Our experiences are different from those of the bourgeois, but our experiences are personal too. We laugh and suffer for different reasons, and that is what must be shown."

"You will be surprised someday: America will have a great revolutionary art. But you are right, *Leiden* can be discussed only in that deep disguise known as *Kunst*."

Hedda watched me in silence for a moment, then said quietly:

"There are two meanings to that. Do you mean that only artists can really feel that deep mystery of pain and intensity which Leiden is? Or that they alone can express it? When Goethe made Tasso say that, he gave him some realistic background. The poet Tasso was thwarted in love, in ambition. He was full of hatred and jealousy. He was physically weak, and envied his friend's friend, who was a military commander, physically strong, admired by women, useful to the Duke of Este. And then Tasso found consolation for his supposed wrongs. He might be weak, he might not be recognized for his greatness by the military commanders and the dukes, but God gave him the power of sublimating his pain in works of art. Do you mean all that?"

"I don't know yet."

"I think pain that can be transmuted into a work of art is the only creative pain. But pity those poor creatures who feel pain unmitigated by creative power, for they are the poor animals who succumb to pain, and all for nothing. The revolutionary worker is fortunate, the movement converts his pain into something sublime, into the conscious struggle for a new society. That is the spirit that should animate revolutionary art: the pain should be there, but the struggle too, the consciousness, the planning, the organization, the great vision and the collective will. Is that what you had in mind?"

"I hardly know how to explain it. I've thought a lot about myself, and written poems about my feelings, and now I've suddenly lost interest in the subject. My heart says *we* instead of *I*. That's a silly way to put it, perhaps. What I mean is that I've grown up in several contradictory worlds, and have had contradictory feelings and ideas which I could not reconcile. For a long time I've been a communist because the bourgeois world seemed barbarous, cruel and sterile. It is built on the anguish of humanity. Oh, I know the theory of the class struggle, and it's true, but men do not act out of abstract theory alone. Behind the revolution of the proletariat is not only knowledge and analysis, but passion, the will to wipe out poverty and suffering and ignorance and humiliation. The worker revolts when he can no longer endure. And many times I was foolish enough to think that I was 'giving' something to the movement. The intellectual's noblesse oblige. But that's a lie. You can't do the proletariat any favors. We all have a personal ax to grind. Bourgeois society makes me personally unhappy, and from that came the passion which made the revolution legible for me. Then Russia taught me that the revolution gives you infinitely more than any individual, however gifted, can give it. Floyd Dell wrote me today that socialism is his father and mother. It's that and more, it's a world, vast and variegated. But I don't mean a new religion, either. I don't mean communism is a panacea, though I used to think that. The movement doesn't pretend to solve all your personal problems. I was shocked when I first learned that, but I realize now what an infantile expectation that was. A class has arisen that will transform society, but it is not the savior arisen. You don't get on your knees and say I believe, and all is well. Each one of us, whether born in the proletariat or coming to it from other classes, has to exert his mind and will. That is the way the movement grows, and the individual too."

"But that is so obvious," Hedda said.

"Yes, to you and to millions of workers like you, and it was obvious to me intellectually too. But I've been to a university, and lived in European capitals, and in bohemia, and I could not quite relate the two most important things in my life. I could not see where poetry touched politics. I could understand it, but I could not quite feel it. Part of me remained an outsider to the movement; it was bound by an umbilical cord to the past—to the village in which I was born, to the ghetto, the campus, Paris and Greenwich Village, to the art of the past loved uncritically and sentimentally. Of course, I could explain it all, but explanation and emotion are two different things. I could follow the right road intellectually only by violently shutting my heart. But last night, I don't know why, what happened on the Kantstrasse opened my heart; my feelings flowed freely. I was at home in the world, the movement. I was no longer alien to myself. I had the wonderful feeling of being like others, like those hundred thousand marching with us, and the millions like them in all countries. Perhaps it is because I am not accustomed to actions, especially violent actions. Perhaps I needed just that kind of detonation, that shooting on the street of pure reason, which the worker finds so commonplace. But there it was, and a painful breach in me was healed. I'm afraid I haven't made myself clear."

"I think I know what you mean," Hedda said. "You want to be a revolutionary writer, and it has taken you a lot of time and many wanderings to realize your duties and your problems."

"Something like that. There are other things too, things I knew in my head, and suddenly accepted with my heart last night. Ever since I can remember I have rebelled against authority of every kind; then I learned up in my head that you can't build socialism without organization, and you can't build organization without leadership and you can't have leadership without authority."

"Wonderful, wonderful," Hedda said, but not impatiently, "That is your great discovery, then. You found out at last that grass is green and skies are blue."

"Don't laugh, Hedda. You have simply forgotten the time when you had to discover that for yourself, as every rebel must before he becomes a revolutionist."

"Oh, I am not that old." She laughed.

"I'm sorry. I mean that I have known this truth for a long time, but last night I felt it with my whole being. I was glad Thaelmann was there to say weiter, weiter, when a hundred thousand people behind us could not know what the Schupos were doing up front, and were in danger of being confused, and breaking up. And I was glad you pushed me out of the hail of bullets. And I was glad the workers have such strength and courage, for they alone are in a position to save society from destruction."

"Any comrade in my place would have done the same," she said.

"That's it. That's the whole point. Any comrade who has the capacity might be at the head of the line saying weiter, weiter and pushing the confused when necessary. Individual rebellion has somehow passed out of me, and now I would more than anything else like to be a disciplined worker in the movement."

"Will you write up last night's demonstration for the *Daily Worker?*"

"Of course. I have been thinking about it, and that's where the new problems come in. In my story for the *Daily* there will be the situation in Germany, the fascist assault, the demonstration, the hundred thousand workers, the shootings, the social democratic police chief, the comparison with the Soviet Union—but you won't be there, and I won't either. That I shall leave for something in which the truth will have three dimensions."

"If you will study Marx and Lenin, as I've urged you a hundred times, you will have the fourth dimension too."

"Yes, they are the core of the whole thing, the unifying element I have been seeking. I've been a romantic looking for the golden realm in a dozen places and a dozen circles, and now I am going to look for the principle of reality. Do you know what my mother, and Louis Smith, and Freud, and Nearing, and Lenin have said to me? To the great goal everything must be subordinated."

"That's what the fascists say too." Hedda smiled slyly.

"The abstract formula holds for them too, but the goal makes all the difference in the world. It changes the nature of the subordination, and of the means, and of the people. In every great turning point of human history there have been great fundamental choices to which men subordinate everything: paganism or Christianity, feudalism or democracy, King George or Thomas Jefferson, chattel slavery or Lincoln. And now fascism or communism, decay or life for mankind. There is no other choice in our times, and our choice is the living one.

"But America will be hard for you these coming years," she said. "Everywhere it is the proletariat which steadies and guides the revolutionary artist, and the movement in your country is weak. In Russia the whole country breathes and feels socialism; in Germany we have millions organized and conscious. But you are only beginning; you will know what isolation means." She lit a cigarette and laughed softly. "Do you know," she went on, "I have a peculiar horror when I think of America. For some reason I see it in the shape of a devouring beast, when I think of the skyscrapers, those monoliths with the romantic palaces on top of thirty stories of steel and cement. That is America—the steel and cement is real, and the romantic palaces are *kitch*."

"No, no, Hedda. You are a bolshevik but you are also a European, and the European thinks the skyscrapers of New York are the whole of America. There is something else there too. We have a revolutionary tradition—seventeen-seventy-six and eighteen-sixty-one. Our working class is the largest and economically the most important class in American society, and it has a revolutionary heritage too, with gigantic strikes from Homestead to Passaic. And we have our revolutionary literature, from Jack London and Upton Sinclair and John Reed to the younger people whom they have influenced. You must not be too impressed by the present mad march of the plutocracy. Varga says America will be drawn into a world economic crisis. Then you will see the American working class in action, and thousands of young men and women will spring up all over the country, ready to fight and write for the proletarian revolution. Revolutionary America will catch up with revolutionary Europe. All the resources are there for contributing to the world movement, organizational, intellectual and spiritual forces of the first order. Our country has youth and boundless energy and the tradition of fearlessness, and Gene Debs and Bill Haywood and John Reed are no exceptions, but the logical products of 'seventy-six and the forerunners of millions of Americans like them."

"So you can be optimistic on a long perspective when the short one is pessimistic," Hedda said, smiling. "That is good."

"Today is not the last day of history," I said. "You will yet see other things happening in America."

Hedda stood up and looked at her watch.

"I have a meeting," she said abruptly. "I'll go to the bus by myself."

As she leaned over and gently kissed my forehead, I noticed she looked younger than she did in Moscow, and that I felt older.

"Good-by," she said. "I shall not see you before you go to America. I have been assigned to Essen for a while."

"Shall we ever see each other again?" I said.

"No doubt," she laughed. "In Mexico, China, India, maybe even in New York, who knows? The world is my country."

"And mankind my religion. Tom Paine said that, an American revolutionary."

She laughed again, shook my hand affectionately, and walked briskly away.

§ 6

I went home that week, sailing for New York on the *George Washington*. Often in the nine years that followed, during which I lived and worked in my own country, except for a six months' sojourn in Mexico on a newspaper assignment, I thought of that spring in Berlin, of the workers' blood on the street of pure reason.

I remembered the fascist assault at Jüterborg and the communist protest meeting at the Friedrich-Karl-Platz especially that August night when my editor sent me to Union Square to report the reactions of the crowd in front of Party headquarters watching the screen that described, step by step, the march of two men in Boston to the electric chair.

Thousands of working men and women crowded Fourth Avenue, their heads raised in awed silence as the news bulletins flashed the processional of death.

Sacco and Vanzetti were dead.

A great sob convulsed the crowd; workers shook their fists.

That was the year when my former politics professor announced the dawn of the capitalist gods in America.

I thought often of Boston, where those gods had murdered two working-class idealists; and of the workers' blood on the streets of Berlin; and of Passaic, and Herrin, and Youngstown, and Ludlow.

I thought often of my year in Moscow, and the workers I had met, assured, determined, full of plans and proud in achievement, victorious in factory and soviet; and that memory, strengthened by the news of persistence and progress, sustained my belief that only in socialism could modern man find the solution for the basic, inexorable problems of life. The doubts which had tormented me were now faintly remembered nightmares. Distance in time restored them to their true proportions; they were drops in the sea of mankind. I had exaggerated their importance because as an individual I had been immersed in them. I had confused little personal difficulties with great social problems because the romantic literary tradition in which I had been nurtured had placed the ego in the center of the universe.

The march of mankind toward the socialist society was not in the slightest affected by such private complications. On the contrary, history altered our most intimate thoughts, feelings and acts. Yet personal conduct counted; will and choice counted; character counted; and if I were to write a companion volume to this one, describing the decade from 1927 to 1937, I would have to tell how the coming of a great economic crisis, and the growth of fascism, and the astonishing successes of the Soviet Union in well-being and freedom, and the development of the People's Front in the capitalist countries so profoundly changed the personalities of the people I knew that every man's life was, so to speak, cleaved into two sections scarcely resembling each other.

But that would be another story, a narrative of the triumph of reality over romantic faiths. Here I have tried to tell the story of that no-man's land which lay, during the postwar period, between the myths of an old culture and the realities of the new, and how one man, typical of thousands, made the crossing.

In the spring of 1927 I returned to my home in America with new eyes, with many illusions about the old world irrevocably dead, with some misconceptions about the new one still to be unlearned. But already life in the Communist movement appeared to be something more simple, more normal, more meaningful than I had realized earlier under the spell of certain middle-class assumptions. For one thing, it was becoming clear to me that there was a deep continuity between the great aspirations of the Renaissance, the French Revolution, the American Revolution, and the modern aspirations of socialism, rendered all the more sublime because we now lived in a historic epoch where liberty, justice, beauty, all which the best of men in every age had held most dear, could now be realistically achieved for the millions of mankind.

This made even personal choices simpler. You no longer sought a way of life. The Communist movement had given that to you as to millions of others. What you had to find was your own place in the struggle, your own adaptation to the needs of a world-wide movement whose aims and requirements transcended those of any individual, however great or small. The internal struggle allayed, you could turn your energies to thought and action in the real world. Much remained to be done. The Party's emergence as an inspiring national force in American life lay in the future, how near it was few of us guessed. And in the confusions and clarifications which lay ahead, it was good to have comrades with whom you could speak freely, like Hedda in far-off Berlin. I was not ashamed to tell her about moments of transition which, to most people more mature than I, must have appeared rather comic. Perhaps she, too, smiled when she received, in the summer of 1927, my letter saying:

"Dear Hedda, you have been writing me so much from Berlin, and I've hardly had a moment to answer. I've thrown myself wholly and unreservedly into the work; this leaves me little time to write and practically nothing personal to write about. Now it's all the newspaper desk, the *New Masses,* the literature courses in the Party school, the anti-imperialist committee, lectures, reviews, organizations. I make practically no personal visits, have no 'emotional life,' go to the theater and movies rarely, and have stopped writing letters; no doubt a violent reaction against the lyricism and romanticism of my past life."

It was good, too, to teach at the Workers' School, where men and women came straight from the shop, pale, tired, without supper, and asked for knowledge and corrected my mistakes. Then they went to unit meetings, and handed out leaflets in the streets, and made plans for teaching their fellow workers at the bench the road to the new world. This was the rank and file of the Party, selfless, incorruptible. From them the organizer drew his strength, organizing today in Pittsburgh, tomorrow in Detroit, next week in San Francisco. So in Berlin, Shanghai, Paris, Bombay.

To abolish poverty, ignorance, war, the exploitation of class by class, the oppression of man by man.

On the other side of the chasm were profit and privilege, force and fraud. I had known this a long time, and the choice had been made long ago between two irreconcilable worlds.

To choose is not enough. Learn and work.

You are a writer and are trying to find your way to the new literature which speaks for the new world. In 1928 you write about literature and the great choice of our epoch; you state your creed:

"No age has been so rich in 'ideals' as this one. It is possible to define an 'ideal' as the projection of class aims into the future. The most secret personal 'ideals' would come under this definition too, for private ambitions and aspirations have their roots in the standards of the class in which a man has his being. In this sense we may say that our age is marked by two colossal social 'ideals': fascism, or the utmost imaginable power for the imperialist bourgeoisie; and socialism, or the utmost imaginable freedom for the mass of humanity."

And that was the year of the presidential campaign in which a Great Engineer promised the American people a chicken in every pot and a car in every garage; and a man in a Brown Derby promised them real beer; and the liberal intelligentsia applauded "recent gains in American civilization"; and the communists predicted "a new, profound, and most acute crisis of world capitalism fraught with wars."

INDEX